FOUNDATIONS OF
PHYSICAL EDUCATION
AND SPORT

FOUNDATIONS OF
PHYSICAL EDUCATION AND SPORT

DEBORAH A. WUEST, Ed.D.

Associate Professor, School of Health Sciences
and Human Performance
Ithaca College, Ithaca, New York

CHARLES A. BUCHER, Ed.D.

Professor, School of Health,
Physical Education, Recreation, and Dance,
University of Nevada, Las Vegas, Las Vegas, Nevada;
Consultant to the President's Council on
Physical Fitness and Sports;
President, National Fitness Leaders Association

ELEVENTH EDITION

With 228 illustrations

Mosby
Year Book

St Louis Baltimore Boston Chicago London Philadelphia Sydney Toronto

Mosby
Year Book
Dedicated to Publishing Excellence

Editor: Donna Sokolowski
Editorial assistant: Loren Stevenson
Project manager: Linda J. Daly
Book design: Laura Steube
Part opener illustrations: David Madison Photography

ELEVENTH EDITION

Mosby–Year Book, Inc.
11830 Westline Industrial Drive, St. Louis, Missouri 63146

Previous editions copyrighted 1952, 1956, 1960, 1964, 1968, 1972, 1975, 1979, 1983, 1987

Printed in the United States of America

Library of Congress Cataloging in Publication Data

Wuest, Deborah A.
    Foundations of physical education and sport   /   Deborah A. Wuest,
Charles A. Bucher.—11th ed., with illustrations.
      p.   cm.
    Rev. ed. of: Foundations of physical education and sport   /   Charles
A. Bucher, Deborah A. Wuest. 1987.
    Includes bibliographical references and index.
    1.   Physical education and training. 2.   Sports. 3. Physical
education and training—Vocational guidance.   4.   Sports—Vocational
guidance.   I.   Bucher, Charles Augustus, 1912-   Foundations of
physical education and sport.   II.   Title.
GV341.B86   1991
796 .07—dc20
ISBN 0-8016-6297-4

90-19929
CIP

GW/DC/DC 9 8 7 6 5 4 3 2 1

In Memoriam

Charles A. Bucher, Ed.D., was a well respected author affiliated with Mosby–Year Book for more than 35 years. He was an active member of the American Alliance for Health, Physical Education, Recreation, and Dance, and was also internationally respected as an authority on health and fitness.

As professor of physical education at the University of Nevada at Las Vegas, Dr. Bucher helped form the School of Health, Physical Education, and Recreation in the College of Education and served as its director for 5 years. Prior to his 10 years there, he taught at New York University. For more than 40 years, Dr. Bucher devoted himself to administering programs in physical education, sports, physical fitness, health, and recreation at universities across the nation.

A pioneer in the health, physical education, and recreation field, Dr. Bucher was one of the first ten recipients of the Healthy American Fitness Leaders Award. This award, presented by the President of the United States, was given to those who have made outstanding contributions to the nation's health and fitness. He also led the fitness community as president of the National Fitness Leaders Council and was a consultant to the President's Council on Physical Fitness and Sports.

Dr. Bucher was a prolific author; he wrote numerous textbooks, professional articles, and a syndicated news column on health and fitness. He was author or coauthor of three successful Mosby–Year Book texts: *Foundations of Physical Education and Sport, Management of Physical Education and Athletic Programs*, and *Fitness for College and Life.*

Mosby–Year Book mourns the passing of Charles A. Bucher, whose career achievements helped shape the development of worldwide health and fitness.

Preface

The eleventh edition of *Foundations of Physical Education and Sport* is designed to provide a comprehensive, contemporary text for introductory and foundations courses in physical education. During the past 10 years the knowledge base of physical education has increased tremendously, both in depth and breadth. The dedication of scholars and increasingly sophisticated research techniques have contributed to this expansion. The growth of this knowledge base is reflected in further development of the specialized areas of study, the subdisciplines of physical education and sport.

Career opportunities have grown dramatically as well. Increased opportunities are available for individuals desiring to teach and coach in nonschool settings, such as community-based programs, senior citizen centers, and corporations. Teachers and coaches increasingly work with people of all abilities and ages. Nonteaching and noncoaching careers have grown in availability, and many prospective physical educators aspire to careers in fitness, exercise science, sport management, athletic training, and sports communication.

CHANGES IN THE ELEVENTH EDITION

This eleventh edition has been revised to reflect current changes and new developments in physical education and sport. This edition has retained its strong emphasis on the foundations of physical education and sport as well as the expanded information on career preparation and opportunities that was new to the tenth edition.

The knowledge base of the subdisciplines of physical education and sport has grown substantially in the past 10 years. To ensure that the information presented in these areas is up-to-date and timely, specialty reviewers were used as part of the revision process. The reviewers and the chapters that they analyzed are noted:

Dr. Judith E. Rink
Chapter 3—Role of Physical Education and Sport in Society and Education
Chapter 11—Teaching and Coaching Careers in Physical Education and Sport
Dr. Jay Coakley
Chapter 8—Sociological Foundations of Physical Education and Sport
Dr. Susan Hall
Chapter 9—Biomechanical Foundations of Physical Education and Sport
Dr. Robert V. Hockey
Chapter 12—Fitness and Health-Related Careers in Physical Education and Sport

These reviewers, because of their expertise in the particular subdisciplines, were able to offer many thoughtful comments and practical suggestions that were most helpful in revising and reorganizing the chapters.

This edition of *Foundations of Physical Education and Sport* follows the pattern of the previous editions but has been revised to reflect current thinking and research. This text represents the latest thinking and research that form the foundations for this dynamic field.

Organization

The 16 chapters that comprise the text have been grouped into four parts. Part One provides the student with an orientation to physical education and sport. Chapter One introduces the student to the discipline of physical education and sport, defines physical education and sport, clarifies terminology that will be used throughout the text, discusses various philosophies, and provides information on how to develop a personal philosophy of physical education and sport. In Chapter 2, the objectives of physical education and sport programs are identified, the priority for various objectives is discussed, and the assessment of objectives is presented. Chapter 3 examines the role of physical education and sport in society and in education as well as the educational reform, fitness, and wellness movements. Part One concludes with Chapter 4, which presents information about the nature of human movement—the keystone of physical education and sport.

In Part Two, the historical and scientific foundations of physical education and sport are presented in five chapters. The historical foundations of physical education and sport are covered in Chapter 5. The development of physical education and sport from early cultures to today is traced. The physiological, psychological, sociological, and biomechanical foundations are reviewed in Chapters 6, 7, 8, and 9, respectively. These chapters present students with information about the development of the subdiscipline, questions that are typically addressed by researchers within the field, key concepts, and current areas of study.

Part Three, which consists of five chapters, addresses professional considerations, such as career opportunities within the field, preparation for a career in physical education and sport, and professional responsibilities. Chapter 10 identifies numerous career opportunities, assists students in the process of self-assessing their abilities and interests, provides a general overview of professional preparation curricula, and suggests strategies that students can employ to enhance their professional marketability. Chapters 11, 12, and 13 offer more in-depth information about specific career opportunities in physical education and sport, including the responsibilities associated with each career, advantages and disadvantages of specific career choices, and specific strategies to enhance professional marketability relative to these chosen careers. Chapter 11 describes teaching and coaching careers and how opportunities for these careers have broadened from the school setting and school-aged population to nonschool settings and to include persons of all abilities and ages. In Chapter 12, the many new employment opportunities in fitness and health-related careers are examined. Careers in sport management, sport communication, performance, and

other sport-related careers such as officiating are described as well as information on the growing field of sport entrepreneurship in Chapter 13. Professional responsibilities and the development of leadership is the focus of Chapter 14. Various professional organizations are identified and advantages of belonging to such organizations are also described within this chapter.

Part Four explores issues and challenges confronting professionals today and looks at the future of physical education and sport. Chapter 15 addresses timely issues in physical education and sport. Five issues are examined: the role of the physical educator in the consumer education movement, the promotion of values, the role of physical educators in youth sports, the growing discipline and the debate over its name, and the gap between research and practice. Four of the challenges facing professionals are making quality daily physical education in the schools a reality, conducting effective public relations programs, attaining the health objectives for the year 2000, and promoting lifespan involvement in physical education and sport for all people. The final chapter, Chapter 16, examines the future of physical education and sport. Societal trends are analyzed in light of current developments. To prepare for the future, professionals must be willing to assume the responsibility for the leadership of our field and work to improve the manner in which we provide services to people of all ages.

PEDAGOGICAL FEATURES

To facilitate use by instructors and students, several pedagogical aids have been incorporated into this textbook. These aids include:

Instructional Objectives. At the beginning of each chapter the instructional objectives and competencies to be achieved by the student are listed. This identifies for the student the points that will be highlighted in the chapter. Attainment of the objectives indicates the fulfillment of the chapter's intent.

Introductory Paragraphs. A short introduction is provided for each chapter. This serves to provide students with a transition from previously presented material to the material to be presented within the chapter.

Summaries. Each chapter ends with a brief review of the material covered, assisting the student in understanding and retaining the most salient points.

Self-Assessment Tests. Self-assessment tests and activities are presented at the end of each chapter to enable students to check their comprehension of the chapter material.

References. Each chapter provides up-to-date references to allow students to gain further information about the subjects discussed within the chapter.

Suggested Readings. Additional and easily accessible resources from current literature that relate to the chapter topic have been selected and **annotated**. These readings offer students the opportunity to further broaden their knowledge and understanding of various subjects.

Photographs. Numerous photographs, many new, have been used throughout the text to enhance the presentation of material and to illustrate key points.

INSTRUCTOR'S MANUAL

The *Instructor's Manual* provides the instructor with additional material to facilitate the use of this text. The *Instructor's Manual* includes the following features for each chapter:

Chapter Overview. The chapter overview presents the salient points covered in the chapter.

Test Items. Subjective test questions and a variety of objective test items are given, including multiple choice, true/false, completion, and matching.

Suggested Activities. Suggested in-class student activities as well as outside assignments are presented.

Other features include *case studies* to provide opportunities for practical application of the material presented and *resources* for further information.

Foundations of Physical Education and Sport has been written in a style that students find readable and that provides them with important insights into the foundations and the roles of physical education and sport in the world today. Students will find substantial information about the career and professional opportunities that exist for knowledgeable, dedicated, and well-prepared physical educators.

ACKNOWLEDGMENTS

My thanks are gratefully extended to the publisher's reviewers for their insightful comments and critical suggestions which helped greatly in the revision of this book. They include:

Ralph Ballou
Middle Tennessee State University

C. Jessie Jones
University of New Orleans

Mildred Lemen
Indiana State University

Joe W. Gillespie
Tarleton State University

I would also like to extend my appreciation to the specialty reviewers whose thoughtful advice was of considerable assistance in the planning and writing of this new edition.

A special recognition is extended to the outstanding professionals at Mosby–Year Book, Inc. Their professional expertise and guidance were invaluable in the completion of this revision. In particular, I want to recognize the efforts of Loren Stevenson, editorial assistant. Loren assisted me throughout the revision of this book by offering many useful suggestions, much feedback, and thoughtful advice, as well as enlivening the process with her fine sense of humor. Thanks, Loren!

Special heartfelt thanks are extended to my friends and colleagues who helped in many ways in the revision of this book. From critically reviewing parts of the manuscript to taking photographs under all sorts of conditions to offering encouragement when it was most needed, they were unfailing in their support. Thank you for being there.

Contents

FOUNDATIONS OF
PHYSICAL EDUCATION
AND SPORT

Introduction

The young person choosing a career in today's world is faced with a critical decision. Many changes have occurred in the last few years that make the choice extremely difficult. The nation's economy has been in a state of upheaval, resulting in problems such as budget cutbacks, inflated prices, inner city difficulties, unemployment, and mounting government deficits. Increased technology has resulted in changes in the work place. Concern for the environment has generated the implementation of protective measures against noise, radiation, and the pollution or destruction of land, forests, and waterways. Concern about the quality of education provided for young people has led to calls for educational reform. The growth of knowledge in recent years and projected future developments in the areas of information and technology has led educators to emphasize the need for lifelong learning.

Many changes in the American culture that have taken place in the past few years have implications for physical education and sport. Americans have witnessed the growing interest in sport by all segments of society typified by the fitness boom and the wellness movement. More people are engaging in physical activities of all types, the number of spectators at sport events is growing, and the sale of sport equipment is booming. Sport events receive worldwide coverage. More people of all ages and abilities are aware of more and different kinds of sport and physical activities and have a desire for instruction in skills to participate. New interest has been generated in health and fitness. The wellness movement has increased people's awareness of their responsibility for their own health and has drawn attention to the role of fitness and health in the attainment of optimal well-being. The interest in sport and fitness by people of all ages and abilities has stimulated the growth of nonschool physical education and sport programs for all segments of the population.

Most young persons like sport and other forms of physical activity. They are also concerned with the nation's health and fitness. As a result many young persons are exploring the field of physical education and sport as a possible career. As part of this exploration process they want to know the realm of employment opportunities in physical education

The growth of sport in recent years has created interest among young and old alike.

and sport and if they can contribute to this profession. They also want to know the developing trends in the field, and what the future holds for the profession, and the personal and professional qualities that will help them attain success if they choose physical education and sport as a career. Young persons want information that will give them new insights into the true meaning of physical education and sport; a sound philosophy that will guide them in their future endeavors; knowledge of the history of this field and its influence; and an understanding of the physiological, psychological, sociological, and biomechanical foundations on which this profession rests.

This text is designed to expose students to the answers to these and other pertinent and thought-provoking questions. It also will provide insights into the meaning, objectives, and philosophy of physical education and sport. It traces the history of physical education and the changes that have taken place in the field, including the emphasis on movement as a keystone of physical education. This text investigates the physiological, psychological, sociological, and biomechanical

Aerobic dancing contributes to cardiovascular fitness, muscular fitness, and flexibility.

foundations of physical activity. It explores a variety of careers, both in the school and non-school setting, with people of all ages and abilities, and describes how individuals can prepare themselves for their chosen careers in this exciting and dynamic field. This text examines physical education and sport teaching and coaching careers; fitness- and health-related careers; and careers in media, management, performance, and other related sport areas. Professional responsibilities, such as providing leadership and attaining membership in professional organizations, are described. Finally, this text discusses the issues and challenges confronting physical educators and the future of physical education and sport.

Part

Nature and Scope of Physical Education and Sport

One

Introduction

Part One introduces the reader to the field of physical education and sport. The four chapters in Part One present in a logical manner a definition of physical education and sport and specialized areas within this realm, the influence of various philosophies on physical education and sport programs, the objectives of physical education and sport, the role of physical education and sport in society and in education, and the keystone—movement. Part One provides the foundational information needed to understand the nature and scope of physical education and sport, the role of sport in today's world, and the contribution that persons involved in physical education and sport can make to society. Physical education and sport is a growing and expanding profession. The growth of physical education and sport is reflected in the enlargement of the knowledge base and the development of specialized areas of study. The expansion of physical education and sport has created a diversity of career options for professionals in this field.

Chapter 1

Meaning and Philosophy of Physical Education and Sport

INSTRUCTIONAL OBJECTIVES AND COMPETENCIES TO BE ACHIEVED

After reading this chapter the student should be able to—

- Define the following specialized areas of study within the discipline of physical education: sport sociology, biomechanics, sports medicine, exercise physiology, history, sport pedagogy, sport psychology, motor development, motor learning, sport management, and adapted physical education. Discuss how these areas are interrelated within the discipline of physical education.
- Justify the need for every physical educator to develop a meaningful philosophy of physical education and sport.
- Discuss the key concepts of each of the following philosophies: idealism, realism, pragmatism, naturalism, and existentialism.
- Discuss the characteristics of education and physical education and sport programs guided by traditional and humanistic philosophies.
- Develop their own philosophy of physical education and sport.

The profession of physical education has changed dramatically in the last two decades. Programs have broadened from schools to nonschool settings and from school-aged populations to people of all ages. The breadth and depth of knowledge within the discipline of physical education has grown as well. This expansion has promoted the growth of specialized areas of study within physical education and has led to the development of new employment opportunities.

As a professional it is important to have a philosophy of physical education and sport. One's philosophy serves as a guide for one's actions. Philosophy guides the profession, improves professional practices, and explains the values and contributions of physical education and sport to society and education. Traditional philosophies include idealism, realism, pragmatism, naturalism, and existentialism. In recent years the philosophy of humanism has had a significant impact on education and physical education and sport practices. Development of a philosophy of physical education and sport is an important task for every physical educator.

This chapter introduces the study of physical education and sport. Physical education and its various subdisciplines are defined. The importance of having a philosophy is discussed, traditional and modern philosophies are reviewed, and guidelines for developing one's own philosophy of physical education and sport are presented.

INTRODUCTION TO THE STUDY OF PHYSICAL EDUCATION AND SPORT

The physical education profession is entering one of the most exciting, dynamic eras in its history. Traditionally the physical education profession has been viewed as providing services within the educational field, specifically to the schools and to the school-aged population. However, within the last 20 years the scope of physical education has expanded tremendously. This growth has led not only to substantial increases in knowledge but also to the expansion of programs and the populations served. Employment opportunities have grown from the traditional career of teaching and coaching in the schools to teaching and coaching careers in nonschool settings, health- and fitness-related careers, sport management careers, and sport media careers.

This growth has been influenced by many factors. The fitness movement and the increase in leisure time has created a market for physical education and sport programs to serve individuals of all ages and needs. The emphasis by society on achieving and maintaining optimal health and well-being throughout one's lifespan and on disease prevention and health promotion has also served as the impetus for expansion of professional opportunities. Appropriate physical activity is acknowledged to be an important factor in the attainment of optimal health for people of all ages. This belief was strongly supported by two reports on the health status of Americans—the 1979 report, *Healthy People*,[1] and the 1980 report, *Promoting Health/Preventing Disease: Objectives for the Nation*.[2] *Healthy People* established broad national health goals for the improvement of the health of the American people. Exercise and fitness were identified as one of 15 priority areas in which changes in the habits of people would have a positive influence on their health. *Objectives for the Nation* listed specific objectives for achieving the goals set forth in *Healthy People*. For example, one objective was to increase by 1990 the number of adults ages 18 to 65 participating in appropriate physical activity to 60% of the population; this would be a substantial increase from 1978

Corporate fitness programs are growing rapidly.

Physical activity contributes to health and fitness throughout life. Bicycling is an excellent activity for young and old alike.

when it was estimated that 35% of adults participated in physical activity. Further support is offered by the 1989 report, *Promoting Health/Preventing Disease: Year 2000 Objectives for the Nation.*[3] These objectives are derived from the 1990 objectives for physical fitness and exercise. The objectives for the year 2000 reflect the growing appreciation for the benefits of engaging in moderate physical activity on a regular basis and focus on the development of health-related fitness. Taken together, these national reports substantiate the need for well-trained physical educators to provide

quality programs to serve individuals of all ages and needs.

However, while the profession is experiencing an exciting era of growth, it would be naive to think that the physical education profession is without problems. While most physical education professionals consider physical education to be an integral part of the schools' educational programs, this belief is not universally shared. In this era of accountability, changing school enrollments, and fiscal problems, the status of physical education programs in our schools is often threatened.

Reduction in physical education and sports is often one of the first steps considered by parents and school boards when they are confronted with a budgetary crisis. Furthermore, calls for educational reform abounded in the early 1980s. One report, the 1983 report on American education entitled *A Nation at Risk: The Imperative for Reform*[4] decried the rising tide of mediocrity in our schools. The report stressed the need for greater emphasis on educational basics, specifically math, English, and science. Physical education, unfortunately, was not considered one of the basics. Recent reports[5,6] on the fitness status of school children in the United States has raised concern among parents and educators as to whether physical educators are indeed doing their jobs. Because of these problems, it is particularly important at this time that professionals make a commitment to conducting sound, quality programs of instruction and to actively communicating to the public the many contributions of physical education both to the education of individuals and to their quality of life.

Societal and educational factors have encouraged the broadening of the scope of physical education programs to a variety of settings and to include people of all ages. Researchers and scholars have increased the knowledge base through their activities, and specialized areas of study within the discipline of physical education have emerged. The broadening of our scope and expansion of the field of study have led to the development of new and diverse career opportunities. The traditional teaching career has expanded from the school setting to nonschool settings, such as community and youth-serving agencies and corporate fitness settings. Programs have been developed to reach populations other than school-aged students, such as preschoolers, senior citizens, adults, and individuals with special needs. Nonteaching careers in athletic training, exercise science, sport management, and sport communication, just to name a few, have become popular career choices. Regardless of the career chosen, it is important as a professional to be knowledgeable about the various facets of the discipline, be cognizant of the tremendous worth and substance of physical education, and understand and appreciate the role of physical education and sport in our changing society.

As you start your professional career and as you gain knowledge and solidify your career decision, remember that your future is in your own hands. The writers of *A Nation at Risk* stated that it is the student's responsibility to put forth a "first rate effort." They continue:

> You forfeit your chance for life at the fullest when you withhold your best effort in learning. When you give only the minimum to learning, you receive only the minimum in return . . . In the end it is your work that determines how much and how well you learn.[4]

Make a commitment at the onset of your career to excellence. Go forth and be the best you can be.

WHAT IS PHYSICAL EDUCATION?

Physical education is an educational process that has as its aim the improvement of human performance and enhancement of human development through the medium of physical activities selected to realize this outcome. In this definition, *education* is broadly defined as representing the ongoing process of learning and total development that occurs throughout our lifespan. Physical education includes the acquisition and refinement of motor skills, the development and maintenance of fitness for optimal health and well-being, the attainment of knowledge about physical activities and exercise, and the development of positive attitudes toward physical activity as a means to improve human performance.

Physical education is not only concerned with the physical outcomes that accrue from participation in activities but also the development of knowledge and attitudes conducive to lifelong learning and lifespan participation. For the benefits of physical education activities to be realized, physical educators must conduct sound physical education programs and select activities judiciously so that participants may attain the maximum benefits from participation. Sound physical education programs can be conducted in school as well as in nonschool settings such as corporate fitness centers and commu-

Instructional opportunities have expanded to community centers. Parents guided by an aquatic specialist help their young children develop swimming skills.

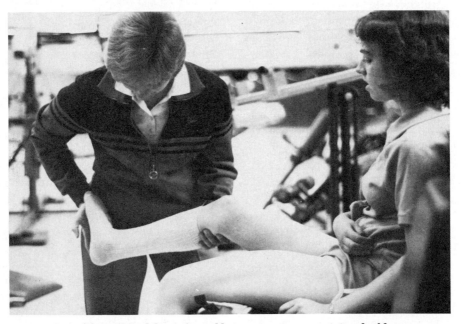

One of the responsibilites of an athletic trainer is to treat injured athletes.

nity agencies. A physical education program under qualified leadership enriches the participants' lives.

A New Name for Physical Education?

In recent years there has been considerable discussion among members of the physical education profession regarding whether physical education is the best name for this field of endeavor. Concern has been raised as to whether the term *physical education* best represents the focus and ever-expanding scope of this broad field. Does the term accurately reflect the practice of professionals within the field, its nature, and its jurisdiction?

Many other names have been proposed to replace

Satisfaction and enjoyment contribute to individuals developing positive attitudes toward physical activity.

the term *physical education*. These names include human movement, movement sciences, kinesiology, sport sciences, exercise science, exercise and sport science, and physical education and sport. Recently the prestigious American Academy of Physical Education endorsed the term *kinesiology*, the study of human movement, as a descriptor for the discipline. Strong support has also been offered for the term *exercise and sport sciences*. Still other professionals are in favor of retaining the term *physical education*. They argue that instead of changing a title, a new image of physical education should be developed to accurately reflect its dynamic nature and expanding scope.

The term *physical education*, often in conjunction with the term *sport*, is used in this text. Physical education has been defined as a process that enhances the development of individuals through physical activity. A vital concern of physical education, sport is defined as physical activites with established rules engaged in by individuals attempting to outperform their competitors. These terms are broadly defined to reflect the contemporary status of this dynamic field and its expanding scope. The term *physical education and sport* encompass-

es a diversity of programs serving school-aged individuals to nontraditional programs in a variety of settings serving people of all ages.

DISCIPLINE OF PHYSICAL EDUCATION

Frequently physical education is discussed with reference to its status as an academic discipline. A discipline is an organized, formal body of knowledge. The discipline of physical education has as its primary focus the study of human movement.

Within the past two decades the knowledge in this field has grown tremendously. As the scope of physical education broadened physical educators became interested in specific areas of study within physical education. Subsequently, subdisciplines or specialized areas of study emerged. One effect of this growth and subsequent specialization is the increase of job opportunitites within the physical education and sport field.

The number of subdisciplines is subject to some disagreement among physical educators. Rather than debate the point, the most common subdisciplines and areas of specialization within physical education are defined below.

Sport sociology is the study of the role of sport in

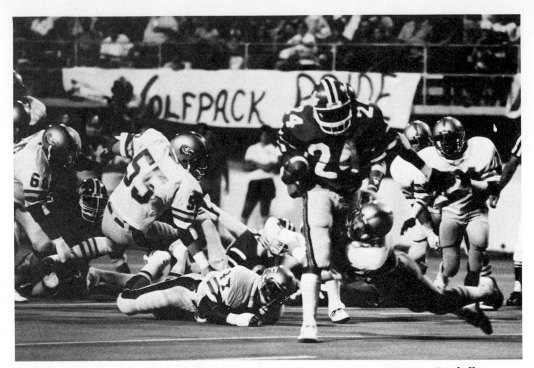

Sport sociology is concerned with the social behaviors of persons in sport situations. Football team in action at the University of Nevada, Las Vegas

society. Sport sociologists are concerned with how sport influences and is influenced by institutions (i.e., educational institutions), politics, religion, economics, and the mass media. (See Chapter 8.)

Biomechanics is the study of the various forces that act on the human body and the effects that such forces produce. Biomechanics is concerned with the scientific study of movement and areas such as the musculoskeletal system, the application of principles of physics to human motion and sport object motion, and the mechanical analysis of activities. In sport, biomechanists may work with athletes to identify specific aspects of their technique that limit performance and make suggestions for improvement. (See Chapter 9.)

Sports medicine is the medical relationship between physical activity and the human body. It is concerned with the scientific study of the effects of physical activity on the human body and also the factors that influence performance. Sports medicine includes the study of the influence of ele-

ments such as the environment, drugs, and growth on human physical activity. Sports medicine is also concerned with prevention of injury as well as therapy and rehabilitation. (See Chapter 12.)

Exercise physiology is applied physiology or the study of the impact that exercise and work conditions have on the human body. The exercise physiologist is concerned with aerobic capacity, fatigue, and the effects of various training programs on participants' physiological responses. (See Chapter 6.)

Sport philosophy focuses on critically analyzing issues as well as examining beliefs and values as they relate to participation in sport and physical education. The philosopher may use logic and problem solving as an aid to decision-making. (See pp. 19 to 27.)

History is the study of the past with a view to describing and explaining events. The sport historian is concerned with analyzing events and explaining their significance in relation to past, concurrent, or future events. (See Chapter 5.)

Biomechanics focus on mechanical aspects of an individual's motion and enhancement of performance.

The sport psychologist can help individuals achieve their optimal level of performance.

Consideration of an individual's level of development is an important factor in planning activities.

Pedagogy is the study of teaching. Sport pedagogy is concerned with the study of curriculum, teaching, teacher education, evaluation, administration, and organization as it applies to the field of physical education and sport.

Sport psychology utilizes various principles, concepts, and facts from the field of psychology to study behavior in sport. Sport psychology concerns itself with motor learning and performance. The sport psychologist studies psychological factors that affect the learning and performance of motor skills. (See Chapter 7.)

Motor learning focuses on factors that influence an individual's acquisition and performance of motor skills. Understanding the stages of learning as well as how to facilitate learning are concerns of the motor learning specialist. (See Chapter 7.)

Motor development examines the factors that influence the development of abilities essential to movement. The motor development specialist uses longitudinal studies, that is, studies that take place over a span of many years, to analyze the interaction of genetic and environmental factors that affect individuals' ability to perform motor skills throughout their lifetime. (See Chapter 7.)

Adapted physical education is concerned with studying the capacities and limitations of persons with special needs or disabilities and designing appropriate physical education programs for these individuals. (See Chapter 11.)

Sport management encompasses the many managerial aspects of sport, including organized sport and sport enterprise or business. Professionals within this area are concerned with facility management, budgeting, programming, and personnel. Career opportunities within this field encompass positions within sport administration, sport market-

An adult with a mental disability learns basic movement concepts with the guidance of his teacher.

ing, sport communication, and facility management. (See Chapter 13.)

The emergence of subdisciplines and specialized areas of study has broadened our knowledge base tremendously. Despite specialization of these fields of study, their focus is still the study of human movement, albeit of a particular facet. The separateness of these specialized fields of study should not be overemphasized; rather, their interrelatedness and their contribution to the discipline of physical education should be stressed.

The growth of specialized areas of study has led to the development of related career opportunities. One consequence of this specialization is that practitioners in these areas may describe their occupation in terms of their specialty, such as exercise physiologist, sport psychologist, or biomechanist. These practitioners may lose sight of the fact that they are physical educators. Additionally, physical education students in an effort to fully prepare themselves for a career in a particular area may become too narrowly focused and fail to learn about the other areas within the discipline.

It is important for professionals to be knowledge-

able about the specialized areas within the discipline and to have an appreciation and an understanding for the interrelatedness of these areas. For example, a professional who is working in the area of corporate fitness certainly needs expertise in exercise physiology to be able to evaluate the fitness levels of program participants and to design exercise prescriptions for them. The professional's philosophy will also guide the manner in which the program is conducted. Additionally, the practitioner may find knowledge from the realm of sport psychology helpful in motivating individuals to adhere to their exercise programs and to work at their fullest potential. Teaching skills (pedagogy) will assist the practitioner in clearly explaining exercises and activities to the program's participants and in educating them about the values to be derived from participation. If as part of a corporate fitness program one teaches participants sports skills, for example, how to play racquetball, one needs to be knowledgeable about the principles of motor learning. Application of motor learning theory enables the practitioner to teach the participants the skills most efficiently and effectively and in such a way that they experience success. Success in performing skills is an important factor in motivating participants to continue to participate in an activity throughout their lifetime. Knowledge gleaned from the area of motor development will help the practitioner design experiences appropriate for the age of the participants. Perhaps one of the program's participants complains of pain while jogging. An understanding of biomechanics will be useful in evaluating the participant's jogging technique, and knowledge from the area of sports medicine helpful in the prevention of injuries. As a future practitioner, it is important to learn about the entire discipline of physical education and the relationship among the specialized areas.

In 1972 professionals seeking to describe the theoretical structure of physical education as an area of scholarly study proposed the term *human movement phenomena*. Human movement phenomena may be defined as the broad category under which the body of knowledge labeled physical education can best be subsumed. Some other areas that comprise the human movement phenomena include human ecology, physical therapy, recreation, and human engineering. A depiction of the discipline–body of knowledge relationship is shown by the model in Figure 1-1. Many other disciplines could be added to form a multifaceted star. While the areas that comprise the human movement phenomena each have a specific focus, they also share a meaningful relationship with other areas.

The second illustration in Figure 1-1 shows that physical education as part of the human movement phenomena is for all people throughout their lifespan—the typical and atypical, the skilled and unskilled, the young and the old. This belief is reflected today in the expansion of physical education programs to nonschool settings and to all segments of the population.

ALLIED FIELDS

Health, recreation, and dance are frequently referred to as *allied fields* of physical education and sport. These fields share many common purposes with physical education and sport, that is, the development of the total individual and concern for qual-

ity of life. However, the content of the subject matter of the allied fields and the methods used to accomplish their goals may vary. The American Alliance for Health, Physical Education, Recreation, and Dance (AAHPERD), the largest national professional organization, reflects the close relationship between these fields.

Health

Health education concerns itself with the total fitness of the individual, encompassing physical, mental, social, emotional, and spiritual health. Three areas within health education are health instruction, the provision of health services, and environmental health.

Teaching the basics of healthful living is the focus of health instruction. Health instruction is targeted to individuals of all ages, ranging from preschoolers to the elderly, and is delivered through a diversity of agencies—including educational institutions at all levels, public health services, and private programs. Health instruction can encompass many areas including disease prevention, mental health, nutrition, physical fitness, stress management, and dealing with abuse of drugs and alcohol.

Delivery of health services is the second area of health education. These services are concerned with developing and maintaining a satisfactory level of health for all people. Health services are provided at educational institutions at all grade levels and are more frequently becoming an integral part of employee health services offered by corporations. Services may include routine eye examinations, cholesterol and blood pressure monitoring, and cancer screening.

Environmental health is the third area included within health education. Its primary concern is the development of healthful and safe environments. Standards have been developed to ensure that individuals within an environment are not needlessly exposed to hazards such as toxic chemicals or infectious materials.

Americans are becoming increasingly conscious of the instrumental role health plays in one's quality of life. Moreover, Americans are being encouraged to take personal responsibility for attaining an opti-

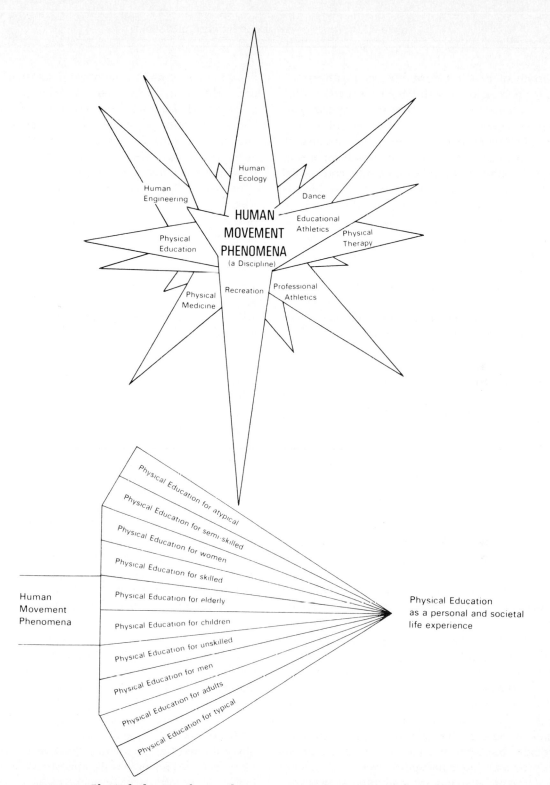

FIGURE 1-1 *Physical education thrusts—human movement phenomena and physical education as a personal and societal life experience.*

mal state of health and well-being. Furthermore, data supporting the health benefits of participation in appropriate physical activity on a regular basis continue to mount. Accrued benefits of regular physical activity include the prevention of coronary heart disease, hypertension, noninsulin–dependent diabetes mellitus, osteoporosis, obesity, and mental health problems. Additional benefits may include the reduction of the incidence of stroke and the maintenance of the functional independence of the elderly. Additionally, it has been found that, on average, individuals who are physically active outlive individuals who are physically inactive. The strong role regular and appropriate physical activity plays in the health and well-being of individuals further confirms the allied nature of health and physical education and sport.

Recreation

Another area allied with physical education and sport is recreation. Recreation is generally thought of as self-chosen activities that provide a means of revitalizing and refreshing one's body and spirit. Recreation is important for individuals of all ages. Through recreation, individuals can learn to use their leisure time constructively.

Recreation is experiencing a period of rapid growth and expansion similar to that of physical education. The number and types of available activities have increased, the settings in which programs are offered have become more diverse, and the number and range of populations served have expanded. Increased leisure time and larger discretionary incomes have contributed to this growth. Concern for the environment has also led to calls for resource management by national and local authorities to preserve the environment while providing for the careful expansion of outdoor recreational facilities.

Recreational opportunities abound. Schools, communities, and businesses offer a diversity of activities to meet the fitness and leisure needs of individuals. Increasingly common are worksite fitness programs, industrial sport leagues, community and commercial recreation and fitness programs, competitive recreational leagues for males and females of all ages in a number of sports, instructional clinics, and open facilities for drop-in recreation. School facilities are used during nonschool hours with increased frequency as community centers with diverse recreational offerings for people of all ages. Many individuals and families pursue recreational activities independently as well.

Recreation, like physical education and sport, can contribute to the quality of an individual's life. It provides opportunities for individuals to engage in freely chosen activities during their leisure time.

Dance

The third allied area is dance. Dance is a popular activity of people of all ages and is both a physical activity and a performing art that provides participants with an opportunity for aesthetic expression through movement.

People dance for a variety of reasons. Dance is used to communicate ideas and feelings and is considered a creative art form. As with all of the arts, dance is an integral part of the educational experience. As a form of recreation, dance provides opportunities for enjoyment, self-expression, and relaxation. Dance also can be used as a form of therapy, providing opportunities for individuals to express their thoughts and feelings. It provides a means to cope with the various stresses placed on individuals. Dance is increasingly used as a means to develop fitness.

There are many forms of dance that are enjoyed by individuals—including ballet, ballroom, folk, clog, modern, square, and tap. Cultural heritage is reflected in and passed on through dance activities.

Within the past two decades, aerobic dance has grown in popularity. Aerobic dance provides participants with an opportunity to develop fitness and experience the fun and enjoyment of working out to music.

• • •

Health, recreation, and dance are allied fields to physical education and sport. The overall focus of these fields of endeavor is the education of the total individual and the enhancement of each person's quality of life. Attainment of these aims involves health promotion, pursuit of worthy leisure-time activities, and creative expression through dance. These experiences, coupled with the movement activities that comprise the realm of physical education and sport, offer the potential to enhance the lives of people of all ages. Fulfillment of this potential will depend on the quality of leadership provided by practitioners of health, recreation and leisure, dance, physical education, and sport.

TERMINOLOGY

Before continuing this chapter, it is appropriate at this time to define several terms that are used frequently throughout the text.

Health-related and Motor-performance–related Fitness

Fitness is comprised of many different components. These components can be classified into two categories: those pertaining to health and those pertaining to motor-skill performance (see the box below).

COMPONENTS OF FITNESS

Health-related Fitness Components	*Motor-performance–related Fitness Components*
Body composition	Agility
Cardiovascular endurance	Balance
Flexibility	Coordination
Muscular endurance	Power
Muscular strength	Reaction time
	Speed

Health-related fitness is concerned with the development and maintenance of the fitness components that can enhance health through prevention and remediation of disease and illness. Health-related fitness enhances one's ability to function efficiently and maintain a healthy lifestyle. Thus, health-related fitness is important for all individuals throughout life.

Motor-performance–related fitness is concerned with the development and maintenance of those fitness components that are conducive to performance of physical activities such as sport. (See Chapter 6 for further discussion of fitness.)

Health and Wellness

Health is comprised of several dimensions: physical health, mental health, social health, spiritual health, and emotional health. Traditionally, the public has viewed good health as the absence of disease. Given this perspective, if an individual was not sick, he or she was, by definition, healthy.

Today, however, this perspective is different; the emphasis is on wellness. It is realized that not being ill is only one aspect of being healthy. Wellness is a state of optimal well-being. Wellness emphasizes each individual's responsibility for making decisions that will lead not only to the prevention of disease but to the promotion of a high level of health. Wellness is multidimensional. Achieving a high degree of wellness requires developing and maintaining a satisfactory level of fitness, expressing emotions effectively, maintaining good relationships with others, maintaining one's mental health, and consideration of ethics, values, and spirituality.

According to wellness philosophy, the achievement of a healthy lifestyle is the responsibility of the individual. Attainment of a healthy lifestyle is achieved through proper nutrition, regular and appropriate exercise, adequate rest and relaxation, effective stress management, adherence to sound safety practices, and elimination of controllable risk factors such as smoking or drug use. Those individuals who adopt a healthy lifestyle may experience an optimal state of well-being, while those who choose to practice an unhealthy lifestyle may be at an increased risk for disease, such as coronary heart disease.

Holistic health is closely related to wellness. Holistic health is based on the premise that an individual's health is affected by virtually all aspects of an individual's life. Physical, psychological, emotional, spiritual, environmental, genetic, and social factors all interact to influence an individual's state of health. Thus, all of these factors must be considered when helping an individual achieve a state of optimal health.

Athletics

Athletics are organized, competitive games or sports engaged in by skilled individuals. Within educational

Athletics include sport engaged in by highly skilled individuals.

institutions, athletics have prospered and grown rapidly. In recent years the interest in athletic participation has expanded to other segments of the population. Competitive youth sport programs have become very popular. The International Senior Games for older adults and the Paralympics for individuals with disabilities are two examples of this expanded interest.

Many lay persons frequently think of athletics and physical education as synonymous. However, athletics is only one aspect of a broad physical education program.

AAHPERD

AAHPERD is the acronym for the American Alliance for Health, Physical Education, Recreation and Dance. AAHPERD is the largest national professional organization that represents professionals in physical education, sport, athletics, health, safety, recreation and leisure, and dance.

PHILOSOPHY

One of the most significant outcomes of undergraduate professional preparation will be the development of a philosophy of physical education and

Reston, Va headquarters of the American Alliance for Health, Physical Education, Recreation, and Dance.

sport. Whatever your career choice—whether you are pursuing a career in education, a teaching career outside of the school setting, or a fitness-related career—as a physical educator it is important that you have a philosophy of physical education and sport.

Philosophy provides direction; it enables use of knowledge and skills learned during your professional preparation in the most effective manner. Philosophy promotes the development and clarification of beliefs and values, which serve as a foundation for one's behavior. Philosophy is a process of critical examination, reasoning, and speculation undertaken in an effort to arrive at truth and reality. Philosophy aids in decision-making; morals and values guide our conduct not only in a professional capacity but also in daily living.

What Is Philosophy?

Just as terminology is essential to the understanding of physical education, so is philosophy. The essence of any discipline can only be appreciated by a thorough consideration of philosophy in general and the philosophies of the particular field being investigated.

Philosophy is a field of inquiry that attempts to help individuals evaluate, in a satisfying and mean-

ingful manner, their relationships to the universe. Philosophy helps people evaluate themselves and their world by giving them a basis to deal with the problems of life and death, good and evil, freedom and restraint, beauty and ugliness.

Aristotle said that philosophy is the grouping of the knowledge of the universals. Dictionary definitions report that it is the love of wisdom and the science that investigates the facts and principles of reality and of human nature and conduct. Philosophy helps individuals answer problems that confront them and the world through critical thinking and reflective appraisal of experiences. Philosophy offers an explanation of life and the principles that guide human lives.

Some of the questions that reflect the concerns of philosophers include the following:

What is the role of human beings on this earth?
What is the origin and nature of the universe?
What constitutes good and evil, right and wrong?
What constitutes truth?
Is there a God?
Do human beings have souls, that is, some essence that exists yet cannot be seen?
What is the function of education in society?
What relationship exists between mind and matter?

To comprehend more clearly the meaning of philosophy, it is important to examine the components of philosophy. The components of philosophy are metaphysics, epistemology, axiology, ethics, logic, and aesthetics.

Metaphysics

Metaphysics is associated with the principles of being. This component attempts to answer a series of related questions: What is the meaning of existence? What is real? How are human actions governed? How and why did the universe evolve? What is the nature of God? The following question is metaphysical in nature: What experiences in the physical education program will better enable students to meet the challenges of the real world? Philosopher Will Durant said that metaphysics investigates the reality of everything concerned with human beings and the universe.

Epistemology

Epistemology is concerned with methods of obtaining knowledge and the kinds of knowledge that can be gained. It is a comprehensive study of knowledge that attempts to define the sources, authority, principles, limitations, and validity of knowledge regarding the role of physical activity and its impact on the physical, mental, emotional, and social development of individuals. Students are seeking the truth about physical activity, and epistemology seeks to answer the question: What is true?

Axiology

Axiology helps to determine to what use truth is to be put. It asks the question: How do we determine what has value, and on what criteria is this judgment based? Axiology is concerned with the aims and values of society and is extremely important in physical education because the aims and values set by society become the basis of curriculum used in schools and colleges. In physical education the following question must be answered: How can the values that society holds be embraced in the physical education program? American society holds dearly the value of "equality for all," which is exemplified by having students from all walks of life playing together and developing tolerance for one another. Students who

learn to respect one another on the playing fields, it is hoped, will be more likely to carry those feelings off the field.

Ethics

Ethics is a more individualized and personalized subdivision of axiology. It helps to define moral character and serves as a basis for an individual code of conduct. Ethics attempts to answer the question: What is the highest standard of behavior each person should strive to attain? The strengthening of moral conduct is an important function of physical education. In physical education the following questions must be answered: How can games and sport be utilized to help the individual learn acceptable conduct? Is character education through physical education possible? Physical education and sport places individuals in situations that reveal their true nature and character. One who plays on a team with an excellent coach may soon realize that using "four-letter" words is not acceptable. The athlete who plays by the rules and acts like a sportsman or sportswoman at all times is more likely to win the respect of teammates. It is hoped that the relationships formed in physical education and sport and the character that is developed from that activity will carry over to behavioral situations occurring outside of that specific setting.

Logic

Logic seeks to provide human beings with a sound and intelligent method of living and thinking. Logic describes the steps that should be taken in thinking and puts ideas into an orderly, structured sequence that leads to accurate thinking; it helps to set up standards by which the accuracy of ideas may be measured. Logic is the orderly connection of one fact or idea with another. It asks the question: What method of reasoning will lead to the truth? Physical educators must use logical thought processes in arriving at the truth. When students ask questions such as, "Why should I play football?" the physical education teacher should not answer by saying, "Because it's in the program." The teacher should clearly explain the benefits and risks associated with

Athletic opportunities for women have increased in recent years. Qualified leadership is important to the realization of desired outcomes.

playing football, since only then will the student really understand its true value.

Aesthetics

Aesthetics is the study and determination of criteria for beauty in nature and the arts, including dance, drama, sculpture, painting, music, and writing. Aesthetics, which is a less scientific branch of axiology, is concerned not only with art but also with the artist and the appreciation of what he or she has created. In an attempt to determine the close relationship of art to nature, aesthetics asks the question: What is beauty? Aesthetic appreciation is involved in watching a gymnast perform on the balance beam, a football player leap high to catch a pass, or a baseball player dive to catch a line drive, just as aesthetic appreciation is gained from viewing great works of art or listening to music played by a symphony orchestra. The physical movements that one can view in athletics are often a source of great pleasure.

• • •

The components known as metaphysics, epistemology, axiology, ethics, logic, and aesthetics represent aspects of philosophy. In developing a philosophy for any particular field, one would seek information in each of these areas. These components would be applied in formulating a philosophy for any particular field within this educational endeavor, such as health, physical education and sport, recreation, or dance. Philosophy yields a comprehensive understanding of reality, which, if applied to education or any other field of interest, gives direction that would likely be lacking otherwise.

Philosophy and Physical Education and Sport—Why Have a Philosophy?

In today's changing society a sound philosophy of life and physical education and sport is necessary for the professional to survive. Physical educators must ask themselves the following important questions:

• What has value in today's society?

- What is relevant to the needs of today's youths and adults?

Physical educators also may find a philosophy helpful in addressing more specific questions confronting them. For example:

- Should youth sport programs mandate playing time for all participants?
- Should physical education credit be granted for participation on interscholastic teams?
- Should intercollegiate athletes be required to maintain a certain grade-point average to participate?
- Should athletic trainers be required to report illegal drug use by an athlete?
- Sould the coach, athletic trainer, or athlete make the final determination if an injured athlete can play?
- Should employees be required to participate in a corporate fitness program?
- Should certification be required of all health/fitness club employees?
- Should physical educators be role models and "practice what they preach?"

A philosophy of physical education and sport can help physical educators resolve these and other questions and concerns confronting them. A philosophy of physical education and sport serves several functions.

A philosophy of physical education and sport articulates the worth of physical education and sport. Philosophy is a process through which people search for truths, reality, and values. Through philosophy, physical educators are able to study the meaning, nature, importance, and source of values in physical education. Philosophy guides the physical educator in determining the aims, objectives, principles, and content of physical education and sport and provides a logical means of determining whether or not physical education and sport is providing worthwhile services in the formal and informal continuing education of human beings.

A philosophy of physical education and sport results in the improvement of professional practices. If professional practices are based on intuition or emotional whim and fancy, they are usually not sound; however, if they are based on a well-defined philosophy, they are more

likely to be correct. This is especially true if physical educators develop their philosophies in a rational, logical, and systematic manner and if they represent the best interest of human beings.

A philosophy of physical education and sport is essential to professional education. Persons who claim to be physical educators should carefully develop their philosophies. Doing so will help them to have a common basis for thinking about their profession, properly articulate the meaning and worth of their field of endeavor to the public at large, become motivated to achieve greater professional accomplishments, and better evaluate physical education and sport programs and practices.

A philosophy of physical education and sport guides the professional. To function as an intelligent being, a philosophy of life is needed to guide one's actions. Knowledge about what is acceptable is needed before any program can be created. A philosophy will help the professional to decide what outcomes should be attained by the program's participants and the manner in which they will be realized.

A philosophy of physical education and sport provides direction for the profession and individual programs. Today many physical education and sport programs lack order and direction. The aims and goals of programs—our objectives—are a reflection of our philosophy. Also, when assumptions are made by a physical educator, for example, that physical education and sport strengthens human relationships because people play together, they should be based on a system of reflective educational thinking that embraces logic and other philosophical tenets. A philosophy of physical education and sport will provide this system.

A philosophy of physical education and sport makes society aware that physical education and sport contributes to its values. In today's changing society people want to know how physical education and sport can contribute to issues such as human performance, quality of life, and productivity. A well-defined philosophy of physical education and sport will assist in interpreting those values important in society so that programs can be established to help meet these needs.

A philosophy of physical education and sport aids in bringing members of the profession closer together. Many members of the physical education and sport profession are dissatisfied with what they see happening in their field today. A philosophy of physical education and sport will enable physical educators to determine how they can best contribute to humanity and to society and will provide members of the profession the opportunity to work together in making such a contribution.

A philosophy of physical education and sport explains the relationship between physical education and sport and general education. A philosophy of physical education and sport will help the professional explain that the objectives of physical education and sport are closely related to the objectives of general education. In the definition of physical education and sport the importance of education "of and through the physical" is stressed. A philosophy of physical education and sport that enunciates basic goals will give evidence that the profession has objectives related to those of general education.

Physical educators must strive to develop their educational philosophies in a rational, logical, and systematic manner and to represent the best interest of all persons. This means that scientific facts must be assembled and workable theories applied that support the worth of physical education and sport as an important and necessary service to humanity.

A philosophy of physical education and sport is essential for all physical educators. Traditionally philosophy as it applies to physical education and sport programs in schools and colleges has been emphasized; however, the implications are clear for programs outside of the schools. A philosophy of physical education and sport also must be applicable to these diverse programs. For example, the importance of physical education and sport is now stressed for all segments of the population, including industrial employees, the elderly, youths, and the public in general. Physical educators who serve as leaders, administrators, and instructors for these groups should also be concerned with developing a sound philosophy of phys-

ical education and sport. Most of the concepts of a philosophy for programs in schools and colleges are applicable to programs that exist outside the educational realm. A philosophy of physical education and sport for both school and nonschool programs should be humanistic in its approach, meet the needs of the participants, have a sound scientific basis, understand the role of physical activity in human performance, and enhance the quality of life for its participants.

As future practitioners, be it in the school or the nonschool setting, it is important to have an understanding of the forces and philosophies that guide the physical education and sport experiences of program participants. This knowledge will facilitate better program planning to meet participants' needs.

The next section discusses the influence of five major philosophies on educational programs. It is likely that as more nonschool physical education and sport programs are established, these philosophies will influence these nonschool programs as well.

General Philosophies[8]

Five general philosophies have prevailed through the years and have influenced educational thinking. They are idealism, realism, pragmatism, naturalism, and existentialism (see the box on p. 26).

Idealism

As a philosophy, idealism emphasizes the mind as central to understanding. Idealism encompasses such general concepts as: The mind is the focus of the person's being. All reality comes from the mind. In the scheme of the universe, people are more important than nature because nature is interpreted by the mind. Values and ideals exist independently of individuals and are universal and absolute; they never change. An individual exercises free will in choosing between right and wrong. Reasoning and intuition help individuals arrive at the truth.

When these general principles of idealism are applied to educational thinking, they result in such concepts as: Education develops the personality and character, particularly the moral and spiritual values, of the individual. Acquisition of knowledge and

---

**CENTRAL BELIEFS UNDERLYING
TRADITIONAL PHILOSOPHIES**

Idealism	The mind interprets events and creates reality; truth and values are absolute and universally shared.
Realism	The physical world is the real world and it is governed by nature; science reveals the truth.
Pragmatism	Reality is determined by an individual's life experiences; the individual learns the truth through experiences.
Naturalism	Reality and life are governed by the laws of nature; the individual is more important than society.
Existentialism	Reality is based on human existence; individual experiences determine what is true.

---

the development of the mind is of primary importance. Education is a process that originates within the self, thus the student is responsible for his or her own motivation and learning. The curriculum is centered around ideals. The student is a creative being who is guided by the teacher.

When the general principles of idealism are applied to the area of physical education and sport, they result in such concepts as: physical education and sport involves more than the "physical." Even though the mind and body are to be developed as one, in reality idealism emphasizes the development of the mind and thought processes. Physical fitness and activities are valued for their contribution to the development of one's personality. Ideals are emphasized in the physical education and sport program. The teacher is a role model for the students, particularly in terms of character and values. Self-development is to be emphasized.

Realism

The physical world is the central focus of the philosophy of realism. Realism deals with such concepts as: The physical world of nature is the real

world. All physical events that occur in the universe are the result of the laws of nature; nature is in control. The truth can best be determined through the scientific method. People's senses and experiences also help people to understand nature. The mind and the body have a close, harmonious relationship.

When the general principles of realism are applied to education, they result in such concepts as: Education develops one's reasoning power and ability to apply the scientific method to interpret the real things in life; this is essential for lifelong learning. The educational process is scientifically based. The teaching process and curriculum should be based on scientific principles and provide for orderly learning. Evaluation should be objective and standardized.

When these general principles are applied to the area of physical education and sport, they result in such concepts as: Education is for life. Physical education and sport should focus on the development of the total person. Physical education and sport is valuable because of its contribution to health. A healthy person can lead a fuller life and be more productive. Programs are based on scientific knowledge and an orderly progression. Drills are used extensively, and learning is evaluated objectively.

Pragmatism

According to the philosophy of pragmatism, experiences—not ideals or realities—are the means to achieving the truth. Pragmatism deals with such concepts as: Truth is based on one's experiences. Because individuals experience different circumstances and situations, reality changes in pragmatism. Success is the only criterion of the value and truth of a theory. Truth is situational; whatever works in a given situation is correct at that time. Values are relative and are derived from one's experiences. Social responsibility is important; individuals are an integral part of a larger society.

When the general principles of pragmatism are applied to education, they result in such concepts as: The individual learns through experience. Problem solving is the primary educational method and is a necessary skill for coping with an ever-

Practitioners who work in corporate fitness programs should have a philosophy of physical education to guide their efforts and programs.

changing world. Individual differences are considered; education is child-centered. Education is for social efficiency, with the emphasis on becoming a productive member of society. Development of the total individual is important.

When the general principles of pragmatism are applied to the area of physical education and sport, they result in such concepts as: The curriculum should be based on the needs and interests of the students. The curriculum should be varied to provide a diversity of experiences for learning. Learning is accomplished through the problem-solving method. Social outcomes from participation in the program are important. The teacher serves as a guide.

Naturalism

A belief that life is governed by the laws of nature is central to the philosophy of naturalism. Naturalism includes such general concepts as: Any reality that exists is found only within the physical realm of nature. Nature itself is the source of value. The individual is more important than society, but society is necessary to prevent chaos.

When the beliefs of naturalism are applied to educational thinking, they result in such concepts as: Education must satisfy the inborn needs of the individual. Education is guided by the individual's physical, cognitive, and affective development. The teacher has an understanding of the laws of nature and serves as a guide in the educational process. Students must be self-directed. Students learn through inductive reasoning. The development of both the mind and the body are important.

When the principles of naturalism are applied to the area of physical education and sport, they result in such concepts as: Physical activity is important for the development of the total person; it provides a medium for the development of physical, mental, social, emotional, and moral skills. Teachers pace instruction according to the individual's needs. Students are self-directed. Individualized learning through self-activity leads to the attainment of individual goals. Highly competitive performance between individuals is discouraged; competition against oneself is encouraged, however. Play is an important part of the educational process. Noncompetitive activities and outdoor pursuits provide beneficial opportunities for individual growth.

Existentialism

Reality is determined by individual experiences according to the existentialistic philosophy. Existentialism deals with such concepts as: Human existence is the only true reality. Individuals must accept responsibility for themselves and the choices they make. An individual's experiences and choices are unique, affecting their perception of reality.

Individuals must determine their own systems of values and follow them, but they also must accept the consequences of their actions. Individuals are more important than society; however, they must acknowledge their societal responsibility.

When the general principles of existentialism are applied to educational thinking, they result in such concepts as: Education is an individual process. The curriculum presents to students a variety of activities from which they choose activities suited to their needs. The teacher serves as a stimulator in the educational process.

When the general principles of existentialism are applied to the area of physical education and sport, they result in such concepts as: Each student is free to choose from a variety of activities within the curriculum. Individual activities provide opportunities for students to develop self-awareness and self-responsibility. The teacher serves as a counselor, promoting reflective thinking while allowing students to make choices and deal responsibly with the consequences of those choices.

Traditional and Modern Educational Philosophies

From past reading it may be apparent that some philosophies tend to be more traditional than others. Many philosophical thoughts are no longer applicable to general or physical education and sport programs. Most schools today follow a modern educational philosophy that is based on much of what John Dewey, a pragmatist, advocated.

Education today emphasizes the individual by recognizing that people have different needs. Individualized learning is advocated for all, including programs for persons who are mentally, emotionally, or physically disabled. Students are often free to choose the subjects they want to study and to receive training in various vocational areas. Educators also are concerned not only about academic excellence but also about improving speech, coordination, values, and social effectiveness.

A Humanistic Philosophy

Humanism may be defined as a revolt against depersonalization and as the emergence of the belief that a human being is an individual and should be treated as such rather than as part of a larger group. The humanist philosophy allows for individual development of talents and total fulfillment. Humanism encourages total involvement and participation in all that is going on around us.

The humanistic teacher must encourage students toward self-actualization and self-fulfillment. Some of the ways that this philosophy can be imparted are as follows:

1. Expressing open, genuine feelings.
2. Placing a value on humanity and the individual.
3. Accepting oneself and accepting others for what they are.
4. Adapting readily to innovative teaching methods.
5. Being creative and independent and encouraging the same in students.
6. Working effectively with others and increasing experiences and person-to-person interaction.

In recent years educational programs have adopted a humanistic orientation, reflecting a concern for the needs of each student. The box below shows a comparison between school programs guided by traditional and modern, humanistic educational philosophies.

MODERN HUMANISTIC VIEW OF PHYSICAL EDUCATION AND SPORT

Physical education and sport programs today, just like modern educational programs, reflect a more humanistic philosophy. Just like traditional education programs, the physical education programs of yesteryear were very teacher-centered and formal in nature. If you were to ask your parents or grandparents about their physical education experiences, they would be markedly different from those that occur today. It would be likely that they would report that their physical education programs emphasized physical fitness attained through formal exercises and calisthenics, focused on a few activities, and oftentimes included marching and other drills. Students moved around in formal lines and were required to strictly follow a large number of rules.

Today our programs reflect a more humanistic

COMPARISON OF SCHOOL PROGRAMS GUIDED BY TRADITIONAL AND MODERN EDUCATIONAL PHILOSOPHIES

Modern	*Traditional*
Child centered	Teacher centered
Permissive classroom atmosphere	Rigid classroom atmosphere
Based on pupil's interests and needs and relating to needs of society	Based on fact, knowledge, and subject matter irrespective of societal changes or needs
Teacher a guide—plans along with child	Teacher as taskmaster
Focus on total development of child—physical, emotional, and social needs complement and supplement the mental needs	Focus on the intellectual development
Self-directed study; opportunities for creative expression, socialization, problem solving, and experimentation	Formal drills, memorization, lectures, questions-answers and examinations
Close school-community relationship and parental cooperation	School isolated from home and community
Self-discipline	Discipline by external authority
Broad curriculum	Limited curriculum
Healthful school environment	Austere school environment
Geared to individual student	Geared to mass of students
Classroom a laboratory for testing new ideas	Classroom impervious to change

A humanistic philosophy encourages the expression of feelings.

approach. Curriculums are more student-centered. Programs are more individualized as teachers realize that one type of physical education program is not suited to all individuals. The feelings, needs, ambitions, goals, capabilities, and limitations of individuals should be considered in designing programs. Teachers, while stressing the need to learn skills and acquire an acceptable level of fitness, also realize the importance of educating students as to the "whys" of the activities. Curriculums in the early years emphasize creativity and exploration while building a skills foundation for later years. Students in the upper grades are exposed to a variety of team and individual sports.

In addition, physical education programs have an important responsibility to students with disabilities. Each disabled student has an individualized education and physical education plan. Some students may be mainstreamed into the regular physical education class while others may require special teachers, facilities, and programs.

Programs of instruction outside of the school also reflect the humanistic approach. For example, corporate fitness programs are primarily designed to meet the needs of the individual participants; in a sense they are "student-" or individual-centered. In addition to improving the physical fitness and skills of the individual, a great deal of emphasis is based on education. Individuals receive information and guidance from exercise leaders and program directors so that they can make wise choices regarding their life-style.

The humanistic philosophy has had a pronounced impact on education and physical education and sport programs. Consideration for individual differences and valuing the dignity of the individual are two hallmarks of humanistic programs.

ECLECTIC APPROACH TO PHILOSOPHY

One fairly common approach to philosophy is the eclectic approach. The major philosophies that have influenced education and physical education and sport practices have been reviewed in previous sections. Many people find it difficult to believe in all the tenets associated with a particular philosophy. Thus in an effort to develop a philosophy that they could believe in, they have combined a variety of concepts and tenets from different philosophical schools into a set of fairly compatible beliefs. The combining of the beliefs from various philosophical schools is called eclecticism. While this combination of beliefs resembles no single philosophical school, these beliefs, when woven thoughtfully together, provide a sound philosophy for the individual.

YOUR PHILOSOPHY OF PHYSICAL EDUCATION AND SPORT

What is your philosophy of physical education and sport? Development of a philosophy is a difficult task but one that is necessary as you proceed toward your goal of becoming a physical educator. Regardless of your career aspirations, it is important that you have a philosophy to guide your actions and efforts. During your undergraduate professional preparation you will be encouraged in your classes to develop your own philosophy, to think logically and analytically about your beliefs. The following guidelines are presented to help you in your endeavors to determine, define, and articulate your philosophy of physical education.

1. **Review your past experiences in physical education and sport.** Examine them critically.

What were some of your most outstanding experiences in this field? What were some of your most disheartening ones? Why? Is there a physical educator that you particularly admire, one perhaps that served as a role model for you and even prompted your entry into this field? If so, what was his or her philosophy?

2. **Read about the different philosophies.** What theories are compatible with your beliefs? What theories are at odds with them?

3. **Review the philosophies of the leaders in physical education and sport.** Determine the philosophies of leaders in the field. Then determine which of their beliefs are compatible with yours and which are not compatible.

4. **Take advantage of opportunities you have during your professional preparation to talk to various professors about their philosophies.** What beliefs are evident in their teaching? How are their beliefs reflected in their grading? Critically examine your experiences during your professional preparation. Ask why things are as they are. Speculate on how things could be changed. Talk with practitioners in the career you are seeking to enter and determine the beliefs that guide their actions.

5. **Express your philosophy.** Undoubtedly during your preparations you will be asked to write and discuss your philosophy several times. Take advantage of these opportunities for expression to clarify your thinking and more closely examine your beliefs. You may wish to save your papers so that you can look back and see how your philosophy has evolved during your education.

Developing a personal philosophy is a difficult task and some would say a never-ending process. Your philosophy will likely change as you learn more, come in contact with different professionals, and have the opportunity to actively practice your career. Try to be open to the various experiences in your life, reflect upon them and learn from them, and view your life as an ongoing process of change and growth.

SUMMARY

Physical education can be defined as an educational process that has as its aim the improvement of human performance and enhancement of development through the medium of physical activities selected to realize this outcome. Physical education is concerned with the acquisition of motor skills and the maintenance of fitness for optimal health as well as attainment of knowledge and the development of positive attitudes toward physical activity.

The growth of knowledge in physical education has led to specialized areas of study, such as sport psychology, sport pedagogy, sport sociology, exercise physiology, and motor learning. Each practitioner should be knowledgeable about these specialized areas of study as well as appreciate their interrelatedness and their contribution to the discipline as a whole.

Philosophy is critical to our endeavors. The major components of philosophy include metaphysics, epistemology, axiology, ethics, aesthetics, and logic. Philosophy can aid practitioners by guiding their efforts and assisting them in resolving problems that may confront them. Philosophies such as idealism, realism, pragmatism, naturalism, and existentialism have influenced the nature and practice of education and physical education and sport programs. Within the last 20 years a shift from the traditional philosophy of education and physical education and sport to a more modern, humanistic philosophy has been seen.

Each professional should develop his or her own philosophy. One's philosophy influences the objectives or outcomes sought from one's programs and the methods by which these objectives are attained. The objectives of physical education and sport are discussed in the next chapter.

SELF-ASSESSMENT TESTS

These tests are designed to assist students in determining if the materials and competencies presented in this chapter have been mastered.

1. Without consulting your text, describe 10 specialized areas of study within the discipline of physical education. Discuss how these areas are interrelated. Use examples to illustrate why it is important to be knowledgeable about the various specialized areas within the discipline.

2. You are an employer interviewing candidates for a physical education and sport position. If given two physical educators—one who has a well-defined philosophy of physical education and sport and one who cannot convincingly articulate a

philosophy of physical education and sport—which person would you hire? Defend your position.

3. Compare the characteristics of physical education and sport programs, be they in a school or a nonschool setting, guided by each of the following philosophies: idealism, realism, pragmatism, naturalism, and existentialism.

4. Write an essay describing the changes that have taken place in school education and physical education programs in the last 50 years. Your essay should reflect the differences in the characteristics of programs guided by a traditional and a modern, humanistic philosophy.

5. Attempt to write your philosophy of physical education and sport. Try to follow the suggestions given in the text for the development of a philosophy. Reflect on your past experiences, review various philosophies, and take time to talk with some of your professors about their philosophies. Discuss your philosophy with a classmate.

REFERENCES

1. US Department of Health, Education, and Welfare: Healthy people: the surgeon general's report on health promotion and disease prevention, Washington, DC, 1979, US Government Printing Office.

2. US Department of Health and Human Services: Promoting health/preventing disease: objectives for the nation, Washington, DC, 1980, US Government Printing Office.

3. American Alliance for Health, Physical Education, Recreation, and Dance: The national children and youth fitness study II, Journal of Physical Education, Recreation, and Dance 58(9): 50-96,1987.

4. National Commission on Excellence in Education: A nation at risk: the imperative for reform. A report to the nation and the Secretary of Education, US Department of Education, Washington, DC, 1983, US Government Printing Office.

5. American Alliance for Health, Physical Education, Recreation, and Dance: Special report: national children and youth fitness study, Journal of Physical Education, Recreation, and Dance 56(1):44-93,1985.

6. US Department of Health and Human Services: Promoting health/preventing disease: Year 2000 objectives for the nation, Washington, DC, 1989, US Government Printing Office (draft).

7. American Alliance for Health, Physical Education, Recreation, and Dance: Tones of theory, Reston, Va, American Alliance for Health, Physical Education, Recreation, and Dance, 1972.

8. Bucher CA and Koenig CR: Methods and materials for secondary school physical education, St Louis, 1983, Times Mirror/Mosby College Publishing.

SUGGESTED READING

American Alliance for Health, Physical Education, Recreation, and Dance: Four on one—should we seek reunification of health and physical education? Journal of Physical Education, Recreation, and Dance 59(3):18-20, 1988.

A series of four essays that explore the question of whether health and physical education should be unified as a discipline.

American Alliance for Health, Physical Education, Recreation, and Dance: The national children and youth fitness study II, Journal of Physical Education, Recreation, and Dance 58(9):50-96, 1987.

This series of articles reviews the procedures and findings of the youth fitness study, examines the activity of children in elementary school physical education programs, discusses the role of the community and home in children's exercise habits, and reviews factors associated with health-related fitness.

American Alliance for Health, Physical Education, Recreation, and Dance: the naming debate, Journal of Physical Education, Recreation, and Dance 60(8):66-72, 1989.

This series of articles examines arguments for alternative names for physical education, including movement science, kinesiology, and exercise and sport science.

Burke-Walker D and Grebner F: Professional status within AAHPERD— our newest challenge, Journal of Physical Education, Recreation, and Dance 60(9):12-14, 1989.

A profession is defined, the professionalization process reviewed, the occupation/discipline dichotomy in AAHPERD explored, the barriers to professionalism presented, and points to consider are listed in this second report of AAHPERD's President's Committee on Credentialing.

Carter MJ, Grebner F, and Seaman, JA, editors. Professionalization of the Alliance, Journal of Physical Education, Recreation, and Dance 60(5):19-22, 1989.

The process of becoming a profession, characteristics of a profession, role of AAHPERD, and cautions pertaining to credentialing are discussed. This is the first report of AAHPERD's President's Committee on Credentialing.

Carter MJ and others: Occupation to profession continuum: Status and future of HPERD, Journal of Physical Education, Recreation, and Dance 61(3):106-10,. 1990.

This third report of the AAHPERD's President's Committee on Credentialing further discusses the steps in the development of a profession, HPERD's current status, and challenges for the 1990's.

Hennessy JT: A successful philosophy of coaching, Physical Educator 46(2):58-61, 1989.

Development of a sound philosophy and practical suggestions for its application in terms of achieving success, enhancing rapport, and improving skill execution are provided.

Klienman S: The reunification of health and physical education, Journal of Physical Education, Recreation, and Dance 53(4)19-21, 1982.

The author suggests that the currently distinct fields of health, physical education, recreation, and athletics be reunified. Reunification would be consistent with the holistic view of the individual, which emphasizes the integration of the mind and body rather than their separateness. Reunification would lead to career opportunities as "wellness or somatic educators" who would deal with the total needs of the individual.

Miller DM: Philosophy, whose business? Quest 36:26-36, 1984.

This article expresses concern that increased specialization in physical education may lead to narrowness and abandonment of the humanities. Philosophy is important for all professionals. Philosophy helps in the development of critical thinking, interpretation of the values in our field, and resolution of professional issues. Philosophy can help professionals better understand human existence as well as the discipline of physical education.

Morgan WJ and Mier KV: Philosophic inquiry in sport, Champaign, Ill, 1988, Human Kinetics.

Composed of 56 classic and contemporary essays, this book explores a diversity of philosophical topics, ranging from the relationship of body and soul to sportsmanship to women's participation in sport.

Palaestra: The forum of sport, physical education, and recreation for the disabled 5(4), 1989.

This entire issue is devoted to the Paralympics, including its history, a report on the 1988 games in Seoul, and perspectives on the 1992 games in Barcelona.

Schwartz V, editor: Dance dynamics—a dance for all people, Journal of Physical Education, Recreation, and Dance 60(9): 49-64, 1989.

This series of articles describes the use of dance for individuals with special needs (e.g. autistic, deaf) and emphasizes that dance enriches the lives of individuals of all abilities.

Thomas CE, editor: Talking a good game, Journal of Physical Education, Recreation, and Dance 53(1):31, 1982.

"Talking a Good Game" serves as an introduction to a series of articles that reflects the various aspects of sport philosophy. Questions about the meaning and value of the sport experience are examined. The authors, titles, and page numbers of these articles are listed below:

Ermler KL: Two expressions of failure in sport, pp 37-38.

Fraliegh WP: Why the good foul is not good, pp 41-42.

Harper W: The philosopher in us, pp 32-34.

Hellison D: Philosophy: back to the drawing board, pp 43-44.

Kretchmar RS: At the heart of athletics, pp 35-36.

Thomas CE: The sport contest as drama, pp 39-40.

Chapter 2

Objectives for Physical Education and Sport

INSTRUCTIONAL OBJECTIVES AND COMPETENCIES TO BE ACHIEVED

After reading this chapter the student should be able to—

- Justify why physical educators should clearly state professional objectives for what they wish to achieve.
- Show clearly why physical development, neuromuscular development, cognitive development, and affective development are important objectives for physical education and sport.
- Determine what constitutes a priority for the objectives of physical education and sport.
- Identify the characteristics of a physically educated person.
- Discuss how the conceptual approach to learning, as exemplified by the Basic Stuff Series, promotes lifelong learning.
- Describe the purposes and the importance of measurement and evaluation in physical education and sport.

Professional objectives are essential in physical education and sport so that practitioners may know the goals toward which they are directing their programs' participants. Simply stated, objectives are goals or desired outcomes that can be realized through participation in a sound physical education and sport program. As described in Chapter One, one of the functions of philosophy is to serve as a guide for one's actions. Philosophy influences the physical educator's selection of goals, subject matter to be taught, and methods of teaching.

The broadening of the scope of physical education and sport to reach all segments of the population and the expansion of programs from school to a variety of nonschool settings was discussed previously. Our professional objectives have been traditionally defined for school physical education programs. However, they must now be redefined in light of the expansion of our scope and setting. Thus as professionals physical educators need to develop objectives for nonschool-based programs, for example, those conducted in a community or corporate fitness center, and for people of all ages—preschoolers, adults, and the elderly.

WHAT DO WE MEAN BY THE TERM OBJECTIVE?

In this chapter the term *objective* is used in a general sense to include aims, purposes, goals, and desired outcomes to be derived from participating in a physical education and sport program. Regardless of the setting in which it is conducted, a quality program has a clearly defined mission. Objectives are relevant to participants' needs, experiences, and interests. They define the intent and direction of the program, and are communicated in a timely fashion to all participants. Objectives can be long-term in nature; these are often expressed as goals or general statements of intent. Objectives can also be short-term in nature; these are typically stated in specific terms. Short-term objectives can be used as stepping stones to the attainment of long-range goals, providing a means for both leaders and participants to assess their progress toward the desired outcomes.

Children, youth, and adults are involved with movement—getting their bodies into action. Movement is the medium through which physical education and sport achieves its objectives. Movement offers people an avenue for fun, recreation, physical fitness, sociability, emotional release, communication, and healthy growth. Movement is the medium for educating people in regard to their physical, mental, emotional, and social development. (See Chapter 4 for a more complete discussion of movement.)

WHY ARE OBJECTIVES NEEDED IN PHYSICAL EDUCATION AND SPORT?

Physical educators must have clearly defined objectives and must communicate these objectives to program participants. Whether a physical educator is working as an elementary school teacher, an intercollegiate coach, an athletic trainer in a sports medicine clinic, an exercise leader in a corporate or cardiac fitness program, a program director in a health club, or as a practitioner in a diversity of settings, relevant and defensible objectives are needed. Some of the reasons for objectives are as follows:

1. **Objectives will help physical educators to understand better what they are trying to achieve.** Physical education and sport has purpose. This purpose must be clearly imprinted on the teacher's mind when instructing students in physical skills and on the leader's mind when instructing

an activity class in a YMCA (Young Men's Christian Association) or corporate fitness program. If the objectives are clearly understood, this will have an impact on what activities are taught and how they are taught. The objectives will serve as guidelines for the physical educator in steering a course that is meaningful, worthwhile, and in the interest of human welfare.

2. **Objectives will help physical educators to better understand the worth of their field.** The objectives of physical education and sport must be compatible with the objectives and goals of our society. Physical education school programs must have objectives that are compatible with general education objectives. Also, by understanding the relationship between the objectives of physical education and sport and our society we can better understand and appreciate the contribution of physical education and sport to our society.

3. **Objectives will help physical educators make more meaningful decisions when issues and problems arise.** Physical educators will face problems daily as they carry out their responsibilities and administer their various programs. Parents, civic clubs, booster clubs, general administrators, youth sport coaches, corporate executives, health spa managers, professional sports promoters, big league players, and others who do not understand the objectives of physical education and sport may try to influence programs in the direction they think is important. An understanding of the objectives of physical education and sport will help practitioners to make wise decisions when such pressures and issues arise.

4. **Objectives will help physical educators better interpret their endeavors to the public.** Physical education and sport is often misunderstood. One reason for this misunderstanding is that many professionals are not cognizant of the objectives of physical education and sport. Another problem is that we, as a profession, have often failed to communicate our objectives to the public. Physical educators must know the objectives of their field and their worth and be able to effectively communicate them to the public in a meaningful manner. This ability will help to correct misunderstandings and misconceptions and

Objectives help physical educators to understand what they are trying to achieve.

assist the public in formulating an accurate understanding of physical education and sport.

5. **Objectives will help physical educators to know and appreciate the outcomes participants will achieve through participation in a sound program under their direction.** Because accountability is being stressed more and more, physical educators are held responsible for behavioral changes in the persons whom they are instructing. Knowing the desired outcomes of the program, practitioners can carefully design experiences and programs to help their participants attain the sought-after goals. Evidence of participants' achievement can be used to document the success of the program and may be helpful in securing additional financial support, personnel, facilities, and supplies.

WHAT ARE THE OBJECTIVES OF PHYSICAL EDUCATION AND SPORT?

Objectives are desired learning outcomes that can be realized from participation in a sound physical education and sport program. The four traditional objectives of physical education are physical or organic development, neuromuscular or motor development, cognitive development, and affective development. Traditionally the objectives of physical education have been defined in terms of school programs and school-aged populations. The broadening and expansion of the scope of physical education and sport has made it necessary to develop objectives for people of all ages and all types of programs. This is imperative. As Zeigler[1] stated:

The profession has a responsibility to function and serve through the entire lives of people, not just when they are children and young people in schools and colleges. This means we should serve both boys and girls and men and women of all ages who are "special," "normal," and "accelerated."

This can be carried out throughout the lifespan by both public and private agencies, as well as by families and individuals in their own ways. To assume lifetime responsibility would permit us to enlarge the

Objectives are important for both school- and nonschool-based programs.

scope — the breadth and the depth — of our profession's outlook.

The implications for practitioners are clear. Objectives must be relevant to the population served and the type of program in which the participant is involved; they must be responsive to the needs of the individual. For example, one objective for an elementary school child in a physical education class may be to develop fundamental motor skills, such as running, skipping, and hopping. One objective for an adult participant in a corporate fitness program may be to improve health through participation in a regular program of exercise, adoption of sound nutritional practices, elimination of bad habits (e.g., smoking), and use of stress management techniques. Finally, an elderly individual, participating in a community fitness program for senior citizens, may receive help from the practitioner in reaching his or her objective of increased flexibility necessary for daily living, through participation in an exercise program.

The four objectives of physical education and sport contribute to the growth of well-rounded individuals who will become worthy members of society. While statements as to the objectives of physical education and sport differ in wording, they typically can be incorporated into four groups: physical, neuromuscular, cognitive, and affective. All physical educators, regardless of the setting in which they work, should be concerned with fostering the development of these objectives within their program so that participants can successfully realize the desired outcomes (see box on p. 39).

OBJECTIVES OF PHYSICAL EDUCATION AND SPORT
Physical Development Objective

The objective of physical development (see also Chapter 6) deals with the program of activities that build physical power in an individual by developing the various organic systems of the body. It results in the ability to sustain adaptive effort, the ability to

Development of motor skills is one objective of elementary physical education programs.

recover, and the ability to resist fatigue. The value of this objective is based on the fact that an individual will be more active, have better performance, and be healthier if the organic systems of the body are adequately developed and functioning properly.

Muscular activity plays a role in the development and maintenance of the organic systems of the body. The term *organic* refers to the digestive, circulatory, excretory, heat regulatory, respiratory, and other systems of the human body. Activities such as hanging, climbing, running, throwing, leaping, carrying, and jumping help these systems to function efficiently. Health is also related to muscular activity; therefore activities that bring into play all the fundamental "big-muscle" groups in the body should be engaged in regularly. Furthermore, the activity should be of a vigorous nature so that the various organic systems are sufficiently stimulated.

With vigorous muscular activity several beneficial results take place. The trained heart provides better nourishment to the entire body. The trained heart beats slower than the untrained heart and pumps more blood per stroke, with the result that more food is delivered to the cells and waste products are removed more efficiently. During exercise the trained heart's speed increases less and has a longer rest period between beats, and after exercise it returns to normal much more rapidly. The end results of this state is that the trained individual can perform work for a longer period of time, with less expenditure of energy, and much more efficiently than the untrained individual. This trained condition is necessary to a vigorous and abundant life. From the time of rising in the morning to retiring at night, an individual is continually in need of vitality, strength, endurance, and stamina to perform routine tasks and to be prepared for emergencies and lead a vigorous life. Therefore physical education should aid in the development of the trained individual so that he or she will be better able to perform routine tasks and live a healthful and happy existence.

The components of health-related fitness — cardiovascular endurance, muscular strength and endurance, flexibility, and body composition — are essential to proper physiological functioning. Research and clinical practice support the fact that these components can improve the quality of life for those individuals who develop them to optimum levels.

Neuromuscular Development Objective

The neuromuscular development objective is concerned with developing body awareness, making physical movement useful with as little expenditure of energy as possible, and being proficient, graceful, and aesthetic in this movement. This has implications for work, play, and other activities that require physical movement.

Effective motor behavior results in aesthetic qualities of movement and in the development of a movement sense, which in essence is the development of motor skill together with an appropriate

knowledge about the skill and an appropriate attitude toward its development and use. In other words, proper control of skill in movement during all life's patterns and routines takes place in the movement-educated person.

Effective movement depends on a harmonious working together of the muscular and nervous systems. It results in greater distance between fatigue and peak performance. It is found in activities such as running, hanging, jumping, dodging, leaping, kicking, bending, twisting, carrying, and throwing. It will many times enable a person to perform daily work much more efficiently and without reaching the point of being "worn out" so quickly.

In physical education and sport activities the function of efficient body movement, or *neuromuscular skill* as it is often called, is to provide the individual with the ability to perform with a degree of proficiency. This will result in greater enjoyment of participation. Most individuals enjoy doing those particular things in which they have acquired some degree of mastery or skill. For example, if a person has mastered the ability to throw a ball consistently at a designated spot and has developed batting and fielding power, he or she will be more likely to play baseball or softball. If the person can kick and trap a ball with some degree of accuracy, then it will be soccer. Few individuals enjoy participating in activities in which they have little skill. Therefore it is the objective of physical education and sport to develop in all individuals as many skills as possible so that their interests will be wide and varied. This will not only result in more enjoyment for the participant, but at the same time it will allow for a better adjustment to the group situation.

Other values of skill are that it reduces expenditure of energy, contributes to confidence, brings recognition, enhances physical and mental health, makes participation safer, and contributes to the aesthetic sense.

The neuromuscular objective also has implications for the health and recreational outcomes of the program. The skills that persons acquire will help to determine how their leisure time will be spent. If a person excels in swimming, much leisure time may be spent in a pool, a lake, or another body

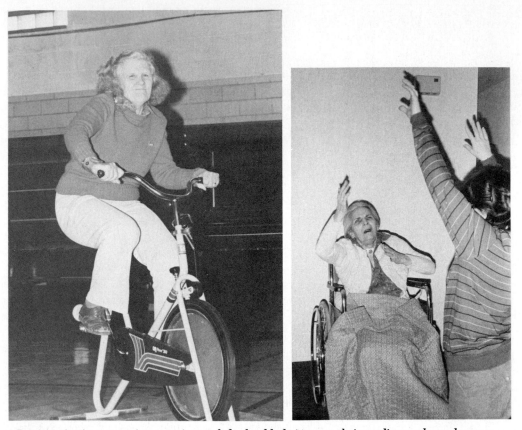

Participation in appropriate exercise can help the elderly increase their cardiovascular endurance and flexibility.

of water. If the person excels in tennis, he or she may be found frequently on the courts. Physical educators should develop in all individuals an understanding and appreciation of human movement and their unique movement potentialities.

When considering the value to young people who are in school of having in their possession fundamental skills that will afford them much satisfaction and happiness throughout life, it is important to consider the balance that should exist in any physical education program between team sports and dual and individual, or lifetime, sports. Team sports such as football, basketball, and softball perform a great service in providing an opportunity for students to develop physical power and enjoy exhilarating competition. However, in many school programs of physical education they dominate the cur-

riculum at the expense of various individual and dual sports, such as tennis, swimming, badminton, handball, and golf. In such cases the students are being deprived of the opportunity for developing skills in activities that they can participate in throughout their adult lives. It has been estimated that only one out of every 1,000 students who play football, for example, ever play the game again after they leave school. On the other hand, if they have the skill, many students will swim or play tennis, badminton, handball, or golf. Only through a well-balanced program of team, dual, and individual sports will it be possible to develop the well-rounded individual.

Physical educators can and should be proud of the contribution they make to humanity. It is within their power to help many persons learn physical

Physical fitness is one objective of physical education and sport. Men jogging at the Dow Health and Physical Education Center, Hope College, Holland, Mich.

Neuromuscular development objective is concerned with the development of efficient, skilled movement.

Promoting the understanding of the background, rules, techniques, and strategies involved in a sport contributes to the cognitive development objective of physical education and sport.

skills and thus help them to lead healthier, happier, and more worthwhile and productive lives.

Cognitive Development Objective

The cognitive development objective deals with the accumulation of a body of knowledge and the ability to think and to interpret this knowledge.

Physical education and sport is concerned with movement. A body of knowledge comes from the sciences, humanities, and other sources, which interprets the nature of human movement and the impact of movement on the growth and development of the individual and on his or her culture. Scientific principles regarding movement, including those that relate to such factors as time, space, and flow, should be considered. This subject matter should be part of the education of each person who comes in contact with a physical education and sport program.

Physical activities must be learned; hence think-

ing on the part of the intellectual mechanism is needed. The coordinations involved in various movements must be mastered and adapted to the environment in which the individual lives, whether it be in walking, running, or wielding a tennis racquet. In all these movements the participant must think and coordinate the muscular and nervous systems. Furthermore, this type of knowledge is acquired through trial and error, and then as a result of this experience meaning in the situation changes.

The individual not only should learn coordination but also should acquire a knowledge of rules, techniques, and strategies involved in physical activities. Basketball can be used as an example. In this sport a person should know the rules, the strategy in offense and defense, the various types of passes, the difference between screening and blocking, and finally, the values that are derived from playing this sport. Techniques learned through experience result in knowledge that should also be acquired. A ball travels faster and more accurately if one steps with a pass, and time is saved when the pass is made from the same position in which it is received. Furthermore, a knowledge of followership, leadership, courage, self-reliance, assistance to others, safety, and adaptation to group patterns is important.

Knowledge concerning health should be an integral part of the program. All individuals should know about their bodies, the importance of cleanliness, factors in disease prevention, importance of exercise, need for a well-balanced diet, values of good health attitudes and habits, and the community and school agencies that provide health services. With the accumulation of a knowledge of these facts, activities will take on a new meaning, and health practices will be associated with definite purposes.

Physical educators can intellectualize their activities more. Physical activities are not performed in a vacuum. Physical educators should continually provide appropriate knowledge and information for participants and encourage them to ask, "Why?" *Why* is it important to play this activity? *Why* should an hour a day be devoted to physical education? *Why* is exercise important? *Why* is it important to play according to the rules? Physical educators should also give participants more opportunities to think, that is, allow them to make choices, plan strategies, and call plays and not usurp all of this responsibility themselves. *The more thinking that takes place on the part of the participant, the more educational the activity becomes.*

Affective Development Objective

The affective development objective is broadly defined to encompass social, emotional, and affective development. The social development objective is concerned with helping an individual in making personal adjustments, group adjustments, and adjustments as a member of society. Activities in the physical education and sport program may offer one of the best opportunities for making these adjustments if proper leadership is provided.

Physical educators should find as many ways as possible to influence human behavior for the good. The rules of the game are the rules of the democratic way of life. In games one sees democracy in action and appreciates an individual on the basis of ability and performance. Economic status, background, race, or other discriminatory characteristics do not play a role. Performance is the sole criterion of success.

Another aspect of the social objective of physical education that is being recognized is the need for each person to develop an appropriate self-concept. Participants need to develop wholesome attitudes toward themselves as maturing persons. During the various stages of physical growth through which young people go, they are often accepted or rejected by their classmates because of their physical characteristics. It is therefore important for individuals to develop themselves physically, not only for reasons of their own self-awareness, but also because of the implications that their physique and physical skills have for their social image.

Each individual has certain basic social needs that must be met. These include a feeling of belonging, recognition, self-respect, and love. When these needs are met, the individual becomes well adjusted socially. When they are not met, antisocial characteristics may develop. For example, the aggressive bully may be seeking recognition, and the member of the gang may be seeking a feeling of belonging. The "needs" theory has implications for the manner in which physical education and sport programs are conducted. The desire to win, for example, should be subordinated to meeting the needs of the participants.

All human beings should experience success. This factor can be realized in play. Through successful experience in play activities, persons develop self-confidence and find happiness in their achievements. Physical education and sport can provide for this successful experience by offering a variety of activities and developing the necessary skills for success in these activities.

In a democratic society it is necessary for all individuals to develop a sense of group consciousness and cooperative living. This should be one of the most important objectives of the program.

Fostering the growth of concern about others is one example of the affective development objective of physical education and sport.

Therefore in various play activities the following factors should be stressed: aid for the less skilled and weaker players, respect for the rights of others, subordination of one's desires to the will of the group, and realization of cooperative living as essential to the success of society. Individuals should be made to feel that they belong to the group and have the responsibility of directing their actions in its behalf. The rules of sportsmanship should be developed and practiced in all activities offered in the program. Qualities such as courtesy, sympathy, truthfulness, fairness, honesty, respect for authority, and abiding by the rules will help considerably in the promotion of social efficiency. The necessity of good leadership and followership should also be stressed as important to the interests of society.

Another factor that should not be overlooked is the "plus factor," or affective development. Physical educators cannot be content once they have developed the physical body, laid down the skills in the nervous system, and developed the amenities of social behavior. Something else still remains, affective development, and this represents one of the greatest challenges to the field in which so many young people have a drive to engage.

Affective development is involved with attitudes, appreciations, and values. Therefore physical education and sport should be concerned with such things as helping individuals to develop a healthy response to physical activity and to recognize the contribution that physical activity can make to health, to performance, and to the worthy and interesting use of leisure. The individual should develop a positive attitude toward physical education and sport, a respect for other persons and leadership, and cooperation in group work and play.

Members of the physical education and sport

As officials, students have the opportunity to apply their knowledge of the rules as well as promote fair play and sportsmanship among their peers.

profession should be concerned with helping young people to clarify and think through their value judgments, appreciations, and attitudes. Although physical educators should not indoctrinate students with their own value systems, much can be done to motivate boys and girls to analyze and assess their own values and attitudes.

IS THERE A PRIORITY FOR OBJECTIVES OF PHYSICAL EDUCATION AND SPORT?

Leaders of physical education and sport often ask questions such as the following: Is one objective of physical education and sport more important than the others? Where should the emphasis in physical education and sport programs be placed? Physical educators cannot do everything, but what

comes first? Does physical education and sport have a master purpose? Do the objectives have a hierarchy?

Historically, physical education in its early days was primarily concerned with organic development. (See Chapter 5.) However, at the turn of the century other objectives more closely identified with general education such as social development were included. Today viewpoints vary in regard to the question of priority of objectives.

A survey of selected leaders in the field of physical education and sport asking for their views about a priority of objectives resulted in some interesting information. Most professionals contacted believed that physical development and neuromuscular and movement development are the objectives of highest priority. These leaders listed reasons such as the following: These objectives are uniquely tied in with physical education, they are essential for fitness throughout life, they provide the impetus for the program, and they represent the objectives that can more readily be achieved. After physical and neuromuscular development, the leaders surveyed indicated that the most widely accepted objective in terms of importance is mental or interpretive development. The reasons listed for the importance of this objective included the fact that it is important to develop a favorable attitude toward physical education and sport if any objective is to be achieved at all. Also included was the fact that education is primarily involved with developing a thinking, rational human being in respect to all matters, whether it be concerned with one's physical development or other aspects of living. Social development ranked lowest in the survey. Reasons given to support this place on the priority listing were that all areas of education are interested in the social objectives and that it was not the unique responsibility of one field, such as physical education and sport. Therefore the other objectives should receive a higher priority rating.

The survey of national leaders in physical education and sport brought out another important consideration. Many professional leaders stressed that, with the national curriculum reform movement taking place today and with increased emphasis on educational priorities, physical educators should rethink their positions in regard to their place in the educational system. They should reexamine how they can contribute their best effort and make their greatest contribution in today's changing world.

Within the last 15 years the United States Surgeon General released three health policy reports that hold tremendous implications for our profession and will help to shape the objectives of our programs, both school and nonschool, for many years to come. The first report, released in 1979, *Healthy People*[2] chronicled the gains in the health of the American population over the previous 100 years. The report identified preventable threats to health and listed those chronic diseases that with modification of life-style could be alleviated if not prevented. Specific health goals and subgoals for five major life stages—infancy, childhood, adolescence and young adulthood, adulthood, and older adulthood—were delineated. Fifteen priority areas for action were identified: physical fitness and exercise was selected as one of the priority areas.

The second report, *Promoting Health/Preventing Disease: Objectives for the Nation,*[3] released in 1980, described the specific objectives necessary to achieve the broad health goals set forth in *Healthy People*. This report acknowledged that substantial physical and emotional benefits and subsequent health benefits may be realized through participation in appropriate physical activity. Unfortunately, most Americans do not participate in the vigorous physical activity necessary to achieve these benefits. While delineating specific objectives to be achieved by 1990, the report challenges physical educators to teach all Americans the necessary skills and knowledge to maintain a physically active life throughout their lifespan.

The third report, *Promoting Health/Preventing Disease: Year 2000 Objectives for the Nation,*[4] further expanded upon and revised the objectives set in 1980. A total of 226 specific objectives are contained within the report that address improvements in preventive services, health protection, and health promotion. An increased emphasis has been placed on prevention. Furthermore, additional attention has been focused on specific population groups and goals, such as the vitality and independence of the elderly. Specific objectives relative to physical activity and fitness reflect the growing support for the health benefits of regular physical activity and an appreciation for the value of maintaining a satisfactory level of health-related fitness. Perhaps it will help the reader to clarify his or her own priority system by answering the following questions:

1. *Does the nature of education give us a clue to a priority arrangement of physical education and sport objectives?* According to many educational leaders today, the business of education is concerned primarily with the development of the intellect, the power of good reasoning, and the application of logic. The "life adjustment" type of education is being sidetracked, and more and more

emphasis is being given to the development of mental skills, the acquisition of knowledge, and cognitive development. Does this mean that physical education and sport, since it is a part of education and since we use the term *physical education*, should also give more emphasis in this direction? Such emphasis would not be for the purpose of being labeled *academic* but instead to help human beings become more fully aware of the values of physical activity in their physical, social, and mental development.

2. *Does history give us a clue?* A historical analysis of objectives of physical education indicates that in addition to organic development and the teaching of physical skills, it is also important to consider the interpretive-mental and social development objectives. History seems to have recorded that physical educators should not limit themselves merely to muscular grace but should also be concerned with these objectives, which can be accomplished through the physical. The emphasis on human relations—for example, the fact that this nation is a democracy and the belief that the individual has worth—should permeate programs of physical education.

3. *Do the outcomes that we more readily achieve give us a clue?* Physical educators proudly demonstrate with measurement and evaluation instruments the amount of strength and other qualities of physical fitness they develop in their students. The headlines of newspapers and other communication media proclaim the success that is theirs in developing skills. However, data are not readily available to show the degree to which physical educators develop mental skills and qualities such as sportsmanship, respect for opponents, and courage. It is not difficult for physical education and sport to show its accomplishments in the physical and skill objectives, but less evidence exists for the other objectives. Part of the reason for this lies in the lack of objective instruments for measurement purposes, such as being able to measure qualities of sportsmanship. However, at the same time it may also indicate the lack of interest on the part of many physical educators to gear their programs in these directions, their failure to recognize the importance

of these objectives, the difficulties encountered in trying to achieve these goals, or a belief that such responsibilities belong with the academic subjects or the home.

4. *Do the nature and needs of society and the individual give us a clue?* Will the study of social problems, including poverty, juvenile delinquency, crime, and health, provide a clue as to what we should be concerned with in physical education and sport? If so, does this mean that objectives become more important in some segments of society than in others? Also, what about the needs of the individual? What represents the needs of human beings for

Employees of Kimberly-Clark Corporation engage in a variety of activities to enhance their well-being.

the "good life"? Are they physical, mental, neuro-muscular, or social? What needs are the most important for physical education and sport to consider? What needs should be met by the home, church, and school? Which ones should be met by academic subjects, by physical education and sport, and by agencies outside the school? If a boy or girl is subpar physically, does this mean that the physical development objective should get priority? If he or she is a delinquent, should the social objective get priority? What does it mean?

5. *Does the term "physical education" give us a clue?* If physical education is concerned with education of and through the physical, does this indicate a priority? All the objectives of physical education are implied in the term as defined. Physical educators are concerned with the *physical* and also with *education.* This means that all objectives should be involved, but does it provide a priority rating?

6. *Do the fitness and wellness movements give us a clue?* As a result of the national concern for physical fitness and the acknowledgment of the role of regular, appropriate exercise in promoting health, should fitness be our primary objective? Should the components of health-related physical fitness be the physical educator's main consideration, namely, cardiovascular function, body composition, muscular strength and endurance, and flexibility? In some institutions of learning and in other agencies priority has been given to organic development or the physical development objective. Has this been good or harmful?

The three national health policy reports, *Healthy People, Objectives for the Nation,* and *Year 2000 Objectives,* offer strong support for physical fitness as the primary objective for the forthcoming decade. However, it is important to note that the emphasis is not only on the attainment of a healthy level of physical fitness but also on acquisition of neuromuscular skills to participate in a wide variety of activities, knowledge, and appreciation of the value of physical education and sport.

Should all objectives receive equal emphasis? Is this the answer? How do physical educators resolve this important problem? Professional associations should give considerable thought and effort to finding the answer. Leadership must be given because many practitioners are concerned about this issue.

Regardless of the outcome, in the last analysis the individual physical educator will make the decision. What will be emphasized in the program day to day will reflect the physical educator's answer. This will depend on the instructor's philosophy and understanding of the worth of physical education and sport and what physical education and sport can and should be trying to contribute to human beings and to society.

Physically Educated Students: the Ultimate Objective for School Programs of Physical Education

When a boy or girl becomes mathematically educated, he or she has taken fundamental courses in arithmetic, algebra, geometry, trigonometry, and calculus. When he or she becomes science educated, experiences have been provided in general science, biology, physics, chemistry, and the other sciences.

What does it mean to be *physically educated?* An important challenge facing the profession of physical education is to establish standards in regard to skills, knowledge, attitudes, and social attitudes for the various educational levels, the mastery of which will result in a student being physically educated.

To address this issue the Physical Education Outcomes Committee of the National Association of Physical Education and Sport (NASPE), an association of AAHPERD, was given a twofold task in 1986. First, the committee was to describe the characteristics of a physically educated person. Second, the committee was to develop competencies for youth from kindergarten to twelfth grade to serve as a means of determining progress toward the stated outcome of becoming physically educated.[5]

The characteristics of a physically educated person as defined by the Outcomes Committee are shown in Table 2-1. According to the committee, this is a broad, generic statement applicable to everyone. Leaders must interpret this definition

TABLE 2-1   The Physically Educated Person

A Physically Educated Person
• **Has** sufficient skills to perform a variety of physical activities • **Participates** regularly in physical activity • **Is** physically fit • **Knows** the benefits, costs, risks, and obligations of physical activity involvement • **Values** the effects of regular physical activity in maintaining a healthy lifestyle

From Franck DM: Physical Education outcomes project making progress, Update, Reston, Va, 1989, AAHPERD.

and the related competencies for specific programs and individual learners.

Marsh[6] has outlined what he believes will be some of the characteristics that tomorrow's student will need to be physically educated for the future. In terms of the futurists he or she should be prepared to learn, to relate, and to choose in each of the cognitive, affective, and psychomotor domains. To do this effectively tomorrow's student will need to have (1) an accurate concept of his or her capabilities and limitations; (2) a broad-based familiarity with the varied activities and resources available within the community; and (3) a scientific knowledge of the special physical, mental, social, and emotional benefits of each of these activities.

With the current educational emphasis on lifelong learning and the objective of active participation in physical education and sport activities throughout the lifespan, it is important that school physical education programs teach their participants not only the skills and concepts of physical education but how to learn as well. As Mancuso[7] aptly states:

No learning content, however strong, lasts a lifetime. Since knowledge doubles every five years, the need for individuals to be self-educative is apparent. Physical educators must recognize that as we enter the information age, the process of physical education may be as important as the content. By emphasizing the process, we can teach students how to learn . . . this is essentially what education is about—providing basic tools to enable consumers to become self-educative throughout their lives.

CONCEPT APPROACH AND PHYSICAL EDUCATION AND SPORT

One approach to helping individuals acquire the necessary skills for lifelong learning is known as the concept approach. According to Webster's Dictionary, a concept is "a mental image of a thing formed by generalizations from particulars." Concepts are generalizations derived from facts expressed in understandable form. The more basic the concept, the broader the situation to which it can be applied. Concepts allow individuals to generalize findings from one situation to another. Concepts allow adults to apply principles learned during their school years to situations that they are confronted with in their adult life.

The real purpose of education is to teach concepts. If students understand a concept, it will free them from remembering many isolated facts. Many areas of education use the concept approach to structure their curriculum. Physical education should consider the use of established concepts as a means of structuring its field so that physical education can be taught in a more meaningful manner, promoting lifelong learning. The basic concepts of physical education are to be found within the stated objectives of the field.

In creating this structure of physical education, an analogy can be drawn between this field and the construction of a house. Just as key pillars and beams give the house form and support, so key unifying elements within physical education give it a strong foundational framework and hold it together as a valuable experience for every individual. These key elements would be identified and would tie together the various parts of the discipline into a meaningful and cohesive learning package. These elements would be the concepts of physical education and, as such, would represent the basic structure of physical education in the school program.

Concepts in physical education would not be memorized by the student. Rather, they would be ideas, analytical generalizations that would emerge and be understood by students as a result of school experiences in physical education. They would also provide students with a reservoir of information

TABLE 2-2   Examples of Content from Basic Stuff Series I

Basic Stuff Book	Focus	Example[*]
Exercise physiology	Effects of physical activity on the body	"Strength training must use the correct muscles."
Kinesiology	Factors that influence the initiation and continuation of human movement	"A follow-through facilitates projection at maximum velocity."
Motor learning	Factors that influence the learning and performance of motor skills	"Feedback directs adjustments in performance."
Psycho-social aspects of physical education	Influence of psychological and social factors on participation in physical activity	"Feelings about one's body image are greatly influenced by social stereotypes."
Humanities in physical education	Understanding of the humanities as they apply to physical education	"Achievements contribute to self-identity."
Motor development	Influence of individual's growth and development on the learning and improvement of motor skills	"Performance quality is influenced by maturity and experience."

[*]Examples from American Alliance for Health, Physical Education, Recreation, and Dance: Basic Stuff Series I and II, Reston, Va, 1981.

that would be of help in meeting new problems and situations throughout their lifespan.

As a result of the conceptual approach students would have greater mastery of the field of physical education, would have an increased understanding and power in dealing with new and unfamiliar problems related to their physical selves, and would be better motivated to want to become physically educated in the true sense of the term. The concept approach would provide a stable system of knowledge and guideposts for thinking intelligently about physical education.

Basic Stuff: A Conceptual Approach to Physical Education

One example of the conceptual approach to physical education is the Basic Stuff Series.[8] The Basic Stuff Series was developed by physical educators working under the auspices of the National Association of Sport and Physical Education of AAHPERD. The purpose underlying this project was the identification of basic knowledge as it applies to physical education programs and to organize it in a manner that can be used easily by practitioners. Basic Stuff stresses basic concepts, which are presented in simple, concise language, involved with the areas of exercise physiology, kinesiology, motor learning, psychosocial aspects of physical education, humanities, and motor development. This project is

applicable to children of elementary and secondary school age, the time when foundations are laid for adult years.

The Basic Stuff Series is comprised of two series, Series I and Series II; nine books comprise the total series, six in Series I and three in Series II. These books were designed for both preservice and inservice teachers. Series I represents the body of knowledge that supports the worth of physical education. The chapters in each book share a similar organizational format relating to questions asked by students. "What do you have to help me?" "How do I get it?" "Why does it happen this way?" A concept is presented and then the student is shown how it can be best applied. The book also explains why the concept is valid. Examples of the Basic Stuff concepts from each of the six areas in Series I are given in Table 2-2.

In Series II examples of instructional activities are provided for the teachers. These activities are provided for early childhood (ages 3 to 8 years), childhood (ages 9 to 12 years), and adolescence (ages 13 to 18 years). The scientific knowledge in the six areas of Series I is related directly to the physical education class and enables physical education practitioners to have at their disposal the basic information and learning activities that will make it possible to physically educate students. Such general concepts as the way to learn a new skill, the way to better one's performance, and the beneficial effects of exercise are identified, and then it is shown how they may be included in activity programs and presented to students by showing them why these concepts are important. This is accomplished by relating the concepts to outcomes that most children and young people desire to achieve. These goals or objectives are health (they want to feel good), appearance (they want to look good), achievement (they want to achieve), social concerns (they want to get along with other people), aesthetic concerns (they want to develop aesthetic and affective qualities), and ability to cope with the environment (they want to survive).

The Basic Stuff Series* makes it easier for physical educators to teach students important concepts in physical education and to explain how and why they are important. An understanding of the concepts underlying physical activity and performance coupled with proficiency in basic skills and a positive attitude toward participation will contribute to lifelong learning.

MEASUREMENT AND EVALUATION IN PHYSICAL EDUCATION AND SPORT

It is important to set the objectives one wishes to accomplish in a physical education and sport program. However, more must be done. It is important to determine whether or not the objectives have been accomplished. This is vital. For example, regardless of whether a program to improve cardiovascular fitness takes place in a school setting, a commercial health club, or in a corporate fitness center it is important that the teacher or the fitness director knows the extent to which the participants have achieved the program's objectives. This is important regardless of whether the objectives are physical development—improvement in the participants' level of fitness, cognitive development—gain in knowledge of how to construct an individualized fitness program, or affective development—appreciation for the role of exercise and fitness in the promotion of health.

*The Basic Stuff Series may be ordered from AAHPERD Publications, P.O. Box 704, Waldorf, MD 20601

To determine whether or not the program's objectives have been met, measurement and evaluation techniques are employed. Simply stated, measurement is the use of tests and techniques to collect information or data about a specific skill (e.g., tennis serve), knowledge (e.g., rules), or ability (e.g., sportsmanship). These data provide specific information about the participant's level of achievement relative to that particular outcome.

Evaluation takes the data obtained from the measurement process and makes a determination from the data as to whether or not the stated objectives have been met. Most students reading this text have taken some type of physical fitness test. More than likely, the test included a measure of cardiovascular endurance; it might have been the time to run a mile or a mile and a half or the distance that you could run in a certain period of time such as 9 or 12 minutes. The score obtained provided data from which the teacher made an evaluation about the level of cardiovascular endurance. One part of the evaluation process probably entailed comparing your score against the scores of students of the same grade level. The scores of a large population with similar characteristics, for example, age and sex, are called norms. By comparing your score to the norms, you can see how your level of fitness compares with others. Your teacher can also use this information to assess the extent to which you have met the objective of improvement of cardiovascular endurance. By looking at scores of all students the teacher can assess the extent to which the program has promoted the attainment of the objective— cardiovascular endurance. The information about individual performance, class performance, and the effectiveness of the program can be used by the teacher to make changes in the program to more readily achieve the sought-after outcomes.

You will undoubtedly take a course in measurement and evaluation during your professional preparation. Additionally, courses within a subdiscipline may expose you to measurement and evaluation techniques appropriate to that specific area. For example, in sport psychology you may receive information about various psychological tests, that is, personality tests, tests of leadership style, and

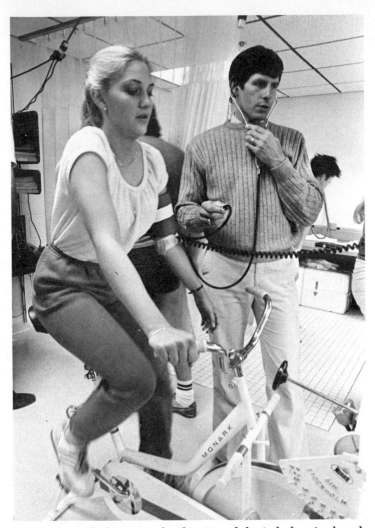

It is important to determine whether or not the objectives of physical education have been accomplished. Testing for one aspect of the physical development objective at the Dow Health and Physical Education Center, Hope College, Mich.

tests of attentional style. In your exercise physiology class you will be exposed to different tests used to measure various physiological functions and how they are affected by exercise.

The ability to use various assessment techniques to determine whether or not the stated program objectives have been attained is essential for physical educators. Without measurement and evaluation it is difficult to accurately determine the extent to which the objectives have been met; measurement and evaluation procedures can help physical educators make necessary program changes to meet the stated objectives.

Measurement and Evaluation for Adapted Physical Education

In developing a measurement and evaluation program for the disabled it is important to determine the developmental status of the individual before preparing an outline of activities that will constitute

Measurement and evaluation of participants' attainment of objectives is important in adapted physical education.

the program. Therefore a step-by-step procedure would be first to determine the individual's physical limitations. Second, the physical limitations that are imposed should be carefully analyzed after which objectives should be established. Third, using the objectives that have been indicated, a program of physical activities can be developed that fits the individual. One should be careful to select activities in which the individual can be successful. Fourth,

after the activities have been engaged in for a period of time, progress that has been made should be determined for each participant. If progress has not been made, this should also be noted. Fifth, the progress made or not made should be evaluated and the activities engaged in studied and then suitable changes made, if necessary. Periodic testing and retesting are utilized throughout the program to assess the physical functioning of the disabled

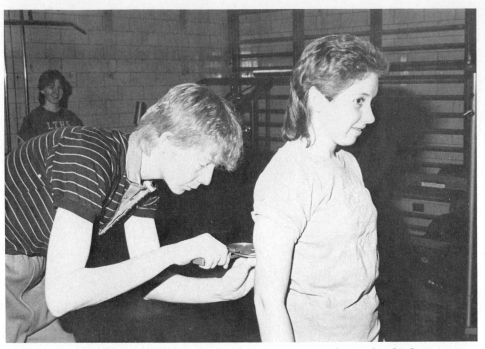

Skinfold test as part of the health-related fitness test at Lyons Township High School in LaGrange, Ill.

person and then to make necessary modifications where needed to ensure educational progress. It should, however, be noted that the rate of improvement is different for each individual. In some cases a regression may be seen and as a result objectives will need to be modified.

Purposes of Measurement and Evaluation

Measurement and evaluation help to determine the progress being made in meeting objectives. They aid in discovering the needs of the participants. They identify strengths and weaknesses of participants and instructors, aid in curriculum planning, and show where emphasis should be placed. They also give direction and help to supply information for guidance purposes.

Measurement helps to determine where instructional emphasis should be placed and which procedures are effective and ineffective. It also is used to help persons to determine their own progress in respect to physical education and sport practices, as a basis for giving grades, and as a means of inter-preting programs to administrators and the public in general.

The information provided by measurement techniques and evaluation can also be used in other ways. Findings can be used for determining a person's exercise tolerance and for grouping individuals according to similar mental, physical, and other traits that will ensure better instruction. Measurement yields information that can be used as an indication of a person's achievement in various skills and activities. It provides information that can be used to predict future performance and development. It affords data on attitudes that determine whether or not the participant has proper motivation, and it focuses attention on future action that should be taken in the program.

Obtaining Information about Objectives

Particular instruments, materials, resources, and methods are available for measuring a person's status in respect to physical, neuromuscular, cognitive, and affective development.

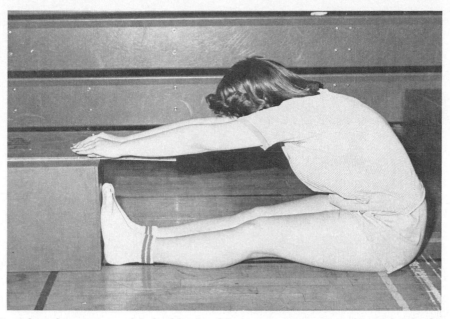

Sit-and-reach test as part of the health-related fitness test at Lyons Township High School in LaGrange, Ill.

Physical Development Objective

A medical examination is a valuable technique for obtaining information about the organic development of an individual. Such an examination should be given at least once each year by a competent physician.

Numerous tests have been developed over the years to measure such qualities as cardiovascular endurance, posture, body mechanics, muscular strength and endurance, power, and flexibility. For example, the AAHPERD Health-Related Fitness Test[9] was developed to measure the health-related fitness components of cardiovascular endurance, flexibility, body composition, and muscular strength and endurance.

One of the most recent tests developed to measure health-related fitness is *Physical Best*.[10] Introduced by AAHPERD in 1988, Physical Best is a comprehensive educational and assessment program designed to help youth incorporate the psychomotor, cognitive, and affective dimensions of fitness into their lives. Youths are helped to achieve a lifetime commitment to fitness through education,

individualized goal-setting, motivation, and participation.

Five test items are used by the Physical Best program to assess the health-related components of fitness. These fitness components and test items used to measure them are listed below:

- Aerobic endurance: one mile walk/run
- Body composition: sum of triceps and calf skinfolds
- Flexibility: sit and reach
- Muscular strength and endurance
  - Abdominal: modified sit-ups
  - Upper body: pull-ups

Test results can be used by teachers and youths to set reasonable, accessible fitness goals based on current fitness levels. Individualized programs are developed to attain these goals, maintain a satisfactory level of fitness, and incorporate appropriate physical activity into each individual's lifestyle.

Neuromuscular Development Objective

Physical skills represent a major part of the physical education program; therefore appropriate valid

Tenneco Health and Fitness Department. The computer as an aid to fitness.

tests of physical skills should be used. Such qualities as motor educability, motor capacity, physical capacity, motor ability, and motor efficiency are terms frequently used in connection with neuromuscular development.

Tests have been developed for skills in such sports as archery, badminton, soccer, basketball, bowling, football, golf, handball, field hockey, and ice hockey. Tests should be studied carefully to determine their suitability or adaptability to a particular situation. Examples of skill tests are the Hyde Archery Test, Miller Wall-volley Test, Achievement Level in Basketball Skills for Woman, Johnson Basketball Ability Test, Lehsten Basketball Test, Borleske Touch Football Test, McDonald Soccer Test, Dyer Tennis Test, and French-Cooper Volleyball Test.

Cognitive Development Objective

In the field of physical education and sport several standardized tests are available for written examinations in various sports. Also, some tests may be found in rule books and source books. An example of some knowledge and understanding tests in physical education and sport that should be explored are the French Tests for Professional Courses in Knowledge and Sports, Hewitt Comprehensive Tennis Knowledge Tests, Scott Badminton Knowledge Test, Scott Swimming Knowledge Test, and Scott Tennis Knowledge Test.

Physical educators may design their own tests appropriate to the subject and age level being taught. When tests are developed, however, such principles as the following should be kept in mind. The items selected should stress the most important aspects of the material. The length of the test should be determined in relation to the time available for testing. The test should be appropriately worded and geared to the age level to be tested. Questions or test items should be worded to avoid ambiguity. Statements should be simple and direct, not tricky and involved.

Affective Development Objective

General tests of social adjustment have been developed, such as the Ball Adjustment Inventory, Science Research Associates Inventory, Minnesota Multiphasic Personality Inventory, and Bernreuter

THE AAHPERD YOUTH FITNESS TEST

Following are the individual fitness tests:

50-Yard Dash
Measures: Speed

Standing Long Jump
Measures: Explosive Power

Sit-Ups
Measures: Abdominal Strength
and Endurance

**Pull-Ups
for Boys**

**Flexed-Arm
Hang
for Girls**
Measures: Upper Body
Strength and Endurance

Shuttle Run
Measures: Speed with Change of Direction

Distance Run
(1 mile or 600 yard, 12 and under, 1.5 miles, 13 and over)
Measures: Cardiovascular Endurance

THE AAHPERD HEALTH RELATED PHYSICAL FITNESS TEST

Sit and Reach
Measures: Flexibility of the Low Back
and Hamstring Muscles

Sit-Ups
Measures: Abdominal Strength
and Endurance

Distance Run
(1 mile or 1.5 miles, 13 and over)
Measures: Cardiovascular
Endurance

Skinfold Test or Body Mass Index
Measures: Body Composition

FIGURE 2-1 A, *Test items for the FitnessGram*   *Continued*

Personality Inventory. The guidance department in almost any school or college is a good source of information for many tests of social adjustment.

Attitudes of students may be measured in different ways, including evaluation (observation of stu-dents with an anecdotal record being kept by the teacher), opinion polls, and rating scales. The physi-cal educator should ask for the assistance of other teachers, particularly the guidance personnel, in this type of testing.

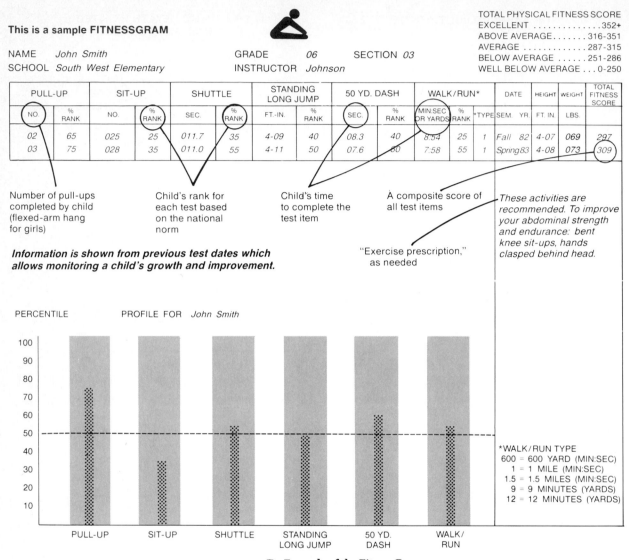

This is a sample **FITNESSGRAM**

NAME   *John Smith*

SCHOOL *South West Elementary*

GRADE   *06*   SECTION *03*

INSTRUCTOR *Johnson*

TOTAL PHYSICAL FITNESS SCORE
EXCELLENT . . . . 352+
ABOVE AVERAGE 316-351
AVERAGE 287-315
BELOW AVERAGE 251-286
WELL BELOW AVERAGE . . . 0-250

PULL-UP		SIT-UP		SHUTTLE		STANDING LONG JUMP		50 YD. DASH		WALK/RUN*		*TYPE	DATE		HEIGHT	WEIGHT	TOTAL FITNESS SCORE
NO.	% RANK	NO.	% RANK	SEC.	% RANK	FT.-IN.	% RANK	SEC.	% RANK	MIN:SEC OR YARDS	% RANK		SEM.	YR.	FT. IN.	LBS.	
02	65	025	25	011.7	35	4-09	40	08.3	40	8:54	25	1	Fall	82	4-07	069	297
03	75	028	35	011.0	55	4-11	50	07.6	60	7:58	55	1	Spring	83	4-08	073	309

Number of pull-ups completed by child (flexed-arm hang for girls)

Child's rank for each test based on the national norm

Child's time to complete the test item

A composite score of all test items

These activities are recommended. To improve your abdominal strength and endurance: bent knee sit-ups, hands clasped behind head.

"Exercise prescription," as needed

Information is shown from previous test dates which allows monitoring a child's growth and improvement.

PERCENTILE   PROFILE FOR *John Smith*

100
90
80
70
60
50
40
30
20
10

PULL-UP   SIT-UP   SHUTTLE   STANDING LONG JUMP   50 YD. DASH   WALK/ RUN

*WALK/RUN TYPE
600 = 600 YARD (MIN:SEC)
1 = 1 MILE (MIN:SEC)
1.5 = 1.5 MILES (MIN:SEC)
9 = 9 MINUTES (YARDS)
12 = 12 MINUTES (YARDS)

FIGURE 2-1 *B, Example of the FitnessGram.*

Sociometrics is being used extensively for measurement of social relationships as determined by use of a sociogram. The sociogram points out the natural leaders in a group and the outsiders trying to become members. When used more than once with the same group, a comparison of the results indicates social growth or change. A sociogram may be taken, for example, by asking all members of a team to list two persons whom they would like to have as their friends, with their choices limited to a given group or team. Results may be pictured with arrows pointing to the names listed.

Other instruments in the affective domain are class behavior check lists such as that developed by Genevieve Dexter, State Department of Education, Sacramento, California, and the Sportsmanship Attitude Scale developed by Marion Johnson. Despite the number of tests available, this objective is frequently evaluated by the teacher observing the students and making comments and written notes about their behaviors.

Using Test Results

For most effective use of test results records should be kept up-to-date. Microcomputers can be helpful in maintaining records of test results or keeping a log of participants' involvement in the program.

One example of computerized recordkeeping is the Fitnessgram program. This program was developed through the cooperation of the President's Council on Physical Fitness and Sports, the Institute for Aerobics Research, AAHPERD and the Campbell Soup Company's Institute for Health and Fitness. The Fitnessgram is a computerized report card, designed to provide parents and students with a comprehensive fitness profile. The Fitnessgram test items and a sample of the Fitnessgram can be seen in Figure 2-1. The fitness profile is constructed from the child's performance on either the AAHPERD Youth Fitness Test or the AAHPERD Health-related Fitness Test. When necessary, an exercise prescription for improvement of fitness levels is also provided. Parents, students, and teachers can use this information to monitor fitness levels from year to year. The Fitnessgram also provides information on the student's rank against the national norm for each test, an overall fitness score and its rank, and the student's height and weight. The Fitnessgram will not only help teachers keep track of their students' performance but also provide parents with feedback about their children's fitness levels. Students will also benefit from this feedback as well as the accompanying exercise prescription.

Corporate fitness centers also use microcomputers in their fitness programs. Employee participation is recorded through a computerized check-in system. This also assists corporate management in charting the use and activity of their employees. After exercising, employees use the computer to record the type of exercise they performed, the duration of the exercise period, and their weight. By using the computer, a record of each employee's progress toward his or her goals can be easily maintained.

The purpose of testing is to help the participant and to improve the conduct of the program. Therefore, after the testing has been accomplished, the results should be used appropriately. The program's participants should have their results explained to them so that they may understand their current status with respect to achievement of the stated objectives. Test results should also be used to evaluate the effectiveness of the program as well so that necessary improvements can be made.

SUMMARY

Objectives are goals or desired outcomes that can be realized from participation in carefully planned physical education and sport programs under qualified leadership. Objectives can assist the physical educator to better understand the goals toward which participants in the program are striving, to understand better the worth of the field, to make decisions, and to better interpret this field of endeavor to the public. The four traditional objectives of physical education and sport are the physical development objective, the neuromuscular development objective, the cognitive development objective, and the affective development objective.

Traditionally, objectives have been defined for schools and the school-aged population. Since physical education has broadened its scope to include people of all ages and expanded its offerings to nonschool settings, its objectives must be defined relative to the population served and the nature of the program. The priority of our objectives and the characteristics of a physically educated student have been discussed. The use of the conceptual approach to physical education has also gained attention in recent years. One example of the conceptual approach to physical education is the Basic Stuff Series.

While it is important to have objectives, it is equally as important to measure and evaluate the extent to which they have been attained. Numerous tests to measure the various physical education and sport objectives have been developed. Evaluation of the test results provides information that can be used to improve the conduct of the program.

The next chapter will discuss the role of physical

education and sport in our society as well as in our educational institutions. The objectives of physical education will be related to the goals of our society.

SELF-ASSESSMENT TESTS

These tests are designed to assist students in determining if the material and competencies presented in this chapter have been mastered.

1. Describe the consequences to a physical education and sport program if no objectives to be achieved by the program's participants were stated.

2. You are in attendance at a budget hearing called to determine whether your program, be it a school program, community agency program, or corporate fitness program, will be allocated much-needed additional funds. You are asked to tell why physical development, neuromuscular development, cognitive development, and affective development objectives are important objectives of physical education and sport. How do you respond to the comment that the only objective of physical education and sport is the development of fitness?

3. Survey the physical education faculty at your institution to determine what priority they would give to the objectives of physical education and sport. When possible, the instructor of your class should assign one or two class members to interview a specific faculty member. The results of this survey of most of the institution's faculty members should be reported to the class.

4. Summarize what you consider to be the characteristics of a physically educated person.

5. Discuss why the conceptual approach to teaching physical education is important in view of the emphasis on lifelong learning. Identify five concepts from the Basic Stuff Series and relate these concepts to physical education objectives for a specific population, that is, preschoolers, adolescents, adults, or elderly.

REFERENCES

1. Zeigler E. The profession's relationship to fitness for people of all ages, Journal of Physical Education, Recreation, and Dance 56(1):15, 1985.

2. US Department of Health, Education, and Welfare: Healthy people: the surgeon general's report on health promotion and disease prevention, Washington, DC, 1979, US Government Printing Office.

3. US Department of Health and Human Services: Promoting health/preventing disease: objectives for the nation, Washington, DC, 1980, US Government Printing Office.

4. US Department of Health and Human Services: Promoting health/preventing disease: year 2000 objectives for the nation (draft for public review and comment), Washington, DC, 1989, US Government Printing Office.

5. Franck DM: Physical education outcomes project making progress, Update, Reston, Va, 1989, AAHPERD.

6. Marsh RL: Physically educated—what it will mean for tomorrow's high school student, Journal of Physical Education, Recreation, and Dance 49(1):49-50, 1978.

7. Mancuso J: A place for public school physical education? Journal of Physical Education, Recreation, and Dance 56(2):17, 1985.

8. American Alliance for Health, Physical Education, Recreation and Dance: Basic Stuff Series I and II, Reston, Va, 1987, AAHPERD.

9. American Alliance for Health, Physical Education, Recreation, and Dance: Health related fitness test, Reston, Va, 1980, AAHPERD.

10. American Alliance for Health, Physical Education, Recreation, and Dance: Physical Best, Reston, Va, 1988, AAHPERD.

SUGGESTED READINGS

American Alliance for Health, Physical Education, Recreation, and Dance: Special Focus: Playing Fair, Strategies 1(3):5-21, 27-29, 1988.

Playing Fair is comprised of four articles dealing with scoring ethically in sport, coaching conduct, coaching the crowd, and the "good" foul.

Bain LL: Socializing into the role of the participant: physical education's ultimate goal, Journal of Physical Education, Recreation, and Dance 51(7):48-50,1980.

The ultimate objective of physical education is to "socialize the student into the role of the participant." Central to the attainment of this objective is providing the student with opportunities to learn skills and gain knowledge relative to specific movement activities that the student finds meaningful. Physical education programs should also educate participants about the relationship of physical activity to health. The implications of this philosophy for various school programs are discussed.

Carlson GP, editor: Physical education is basic, Journal of Physical Education, Recreation, and Dance 53(1):67-69, 1982

This article discusses physical education as an educational basic, stressing the contribution of physical education to learning in the three domains. However, our field's status as a basic is threatened because some professionals have failed to be accountable for their programs and to effectively communicate to the public our contribution to education.

Disch JG, editor: The measurement of Basic Stuff, Journal of Physical Education, Recreation, and Dance 54(8):17-31, 1983.

This series of articles describes the measurement approaches associated with the various content areas in Basic Stuff. Included are the humanities, motor development, motor learning, biomechanics, psychosocial aspects, and exercise physiology.

Lacy AC and Hastad DN: Measurement and evaluation, Strategies, 2(3):21-25, 1989.

Techniques to assess student progress in meeting program goals are presented, including an easy-to-read chart that highlights the learning domains.

Powell KE, Christenson GM, and Kreuter MW: Objectives for the nation: assessing the role physical education must play, Journal of Physical Education, Recreation, and Dance 55(6):18-20, 1984.

Three important aspects of the reports *Healthy People and Objectives for the Nation* are emphasized: (1) the goals delineated are realistic and attainable by 1990, (2) the goals focus on health promotion, and (3) the support of the American people is essential if these goals are to be achieved. Physical educators are challenged to promote lifelong activity for all segments of the population.

Romance TJ: Promoting character development in physical education, Strategies 1(5):16-20, 1988

Specific methods to develop character in physical education are presented.

Wilmore J: Objectives for the nation: physical fitness and exercise, Journal of Physical Education, Recreation, and Dance 53(3):41-43, 1982.

Key points from the physical fitness and exercise section of the report *Objectives for the Nation* are presented. Necessary prevention, promotion, legislative, and economic measures are described relative to the objectives. The specific objectives for 1990 are delineated. Finally, to attain these objectives physical educators must work together within professional organizations as well as make a personal committment to be role models of a healthy, active life-style.

Wood TM, editor: Measurement and evaluation—theory to practice, Journal of Physical Education, Recreation, and Dance 61(1):29-44, 1990.

A series of six articles focusing on current trends and practical approaches to resolution of problems in measurement and evaluation.

Zeigler E: The profession's relationship to fitness for people of all ages, Journal of Physical Education, Recreation, and Dance 56(1):15, 1985.

Zeigler in this editorial states that it is the responsibility of the profession to serve people of all ages, needs, and abilities through schools as well as through both public and private agencies. As a profession, we must change our image to reflect this commitment.

Chapter 3

Role of Physical Education and Sport in Society and in Education

INSTRUCTIONAL OBJECTIVES AND COMPETENCIES TO BE ACHIEVED

After reading this chapter the student should be able to—
- Define education and discuss its role in our society as well as the role of physical education in education.
- Explain what is meant by the cognitive, psychomotor, and affective domains of education and how physical education contributes to development in each domain.
- Discuss the current educational reform movement and the implications for physical education programs.
- Interpret the role of physical education and sport in the promotion of health and the attainment of wellness to colleagues and to the public.
- Discuss the fitness movement and the implications of the movement for physical education and sport.

Contemporary society's needs and trends influence the education of its citizens. The education of the individual may be described as taking place through three learning domains: cognitive, affective, and psychomotor. Physical education contributes in many ways to learning in each of these domains.

The objectives of education and the manner of their attainment are influenced by various forces within society. Societal needs, trends, and forces also affect the role of physical education and sport within society as well as within the educational process. The educational reform movement is a significant trend in our society. Recent years have been marked by calls for educational reform, specifically revitalization and strengthening of the educational process. The nature of the educational reforms that are implemented may have far-reaching consequences on the conduct of physical education programs in our schools.

Two other trends within our society that are of interest to physical educators are the wellness movement and the fitness movement. The wellness movement stresses that the individual is responsible for taking actions leading to attainment of an optimal state of health. The fitness movement reflects the current enthusiasm of citizens of all ages for exercise and physical activity. These two movements have profound implications for physical education and sport.

This chapter discusses the role of education in our society and the contribution of physical education to the educational process. The effects of three societal trends—the educational reform movement, the wellness movement, and the fitness movement—on the conduct of physical education and sport programs are also explored. The term *physical education* will be used to refer specifically to school-based programs, and the term *physical education and sport* will be used to encompass a diversity of programs offered in a variety of settings.

ROLE OF EDUCATION IN TODAY'S SOCIETY

The role of education in general and physical education in particular is constantly undergoing change. At one time education was left to the educators, but this is no longer the case, as characterized by parent committees, student curriculum groups, widespread teacher evaluation procedures, and constant reappraisal of educational policies.

Education contributes to the development, advancement, and perpetuation of the nation's culture. Educational institutions play a primary role in the development of the human resources of society.

Physical education provides a variety of challenges to individuals. This young girl strives to achieve her best effort in the broad jump.

Schools, colleges, and universities are clearly the most powerful and effective institutions that this society has for the achievement of intellectual skill, knowledge, understanding, and appreciation necessary to make wise decisions, good judgments, and logical analyses of problems. Directly or indirectly, these educational institutions are the chief agents of society's progress, whether it is progress concerned with knowledge, arts, technology, social conscience, or other areas essential to a nation's growth. Education must meet the challenges presented in society. In the present decade this means that the nation's schools and colleges should be concerned with the well-being of students in their preparation for a productive and happy life in which their potentialities as individuals are enlarged and fulfilled and in which freedom will be assured.

Physical education, as a phase of the total educational process, helps in achieving these purposes. It is one link in a chain of many influences that help to realize the country's ideals and contribute to the proper functioning of American society. It is continually striving for excellence so that it can become an increasingly dynamic force in education.

MEANING OF THE TERM *EDUCATION*

Before one can evaluate the role of education, one must understand the meaning of the word. The term *education* means different things to different individuals. One individual will define it as a training process that comes about through study and instruction; another person will say that it is a series of experiences that enable a person to better understand new experiences; to others it means growth and adjustment. John Dewey, an educator who has most profoundly influenced education, defined education as the reconstruction of events that compose the lives of individuals so that new happenings and new events become more purposeful and more meaningful. Furthermore, as a result of education individuals will be better able to regulate the direction of ensuing experience. Dewey's interpretation it seems sums up in a few words what is meant by education, namely that a person thinks in terms of previous experiences and, further, that the individual's education consists of everything he or she does

from birth until death. Education is a "doing" phenomenon. One learns through doing. Education takes place in the classroom, in the library, on the playground, in the gymnasium, on trips, and at home. It is not confined to a school or a church but rather takes place wherever individuals congregate.

The question now arises as to what experiences will best result in a productive, happy, and rich life. The solution seems to be in the provision of experiences that will have a practical value in the lives of individuals as they live from day to day. Worthwhile experiences will enable a person to live a more purposeful, more interesting, and more vigorous life.

Today education is looked on as preparing the individual for a meaningful, self-directed existence. For young people to be prepared to accomplish this goal they must have an understanding of (1) the nature of self and others and capacity for continuing self-development and for relating to others, (2) the contemporary social scene and the values and skills necessary for effective participation, (3) their cultural heritage and the ability to evaluate it, (4) the role of communication and skill in communicating, (5) the world of nature and the ability to adapt to it, and (6) the role of aesthetic forms in human living and the capacity for self-expression through them.

EDUCATIONAL DOMAINS

The education of an individual takes place through three learning domains—the cognitive domain, the affective domain, and the psychomotor domain. The **cognitive** domain includes the development of intellectual abilities including the acquisition of knowledge; formulation of ideas and concepts; problem-solving; and the analysis, synthesis, and evaluation of information. The **affective** domain focuses on the development of interests, attitudes, and values. The **psychomotor** domain includes the development of physical fitness and the acquisition of neuromuscular and motor skills. These domains are interrelated. Educators should consider all three domains when planning activities to meet individuals' needs. Figure 3-1 illustrates the interdependence of the affective, cognitive, and psychomotor domains.

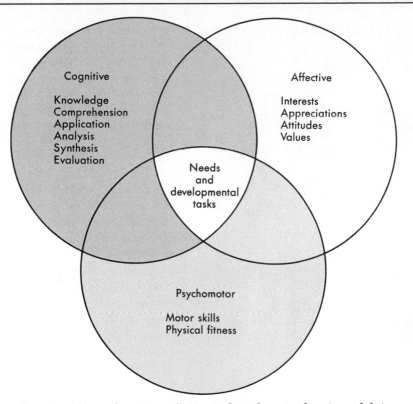

FIGURE 3-1 *Interdependence of cognitive, affective, and psychomotor domains and their relationship to needs and developmental tasks.*

PHYSICAL EDUCATION: ITS RELATIONSHIP TO EDUCATION

Today preparing individuals for a meaningful, self-directed existence is viewed as a primary focus of education. When properly taught, physical education, with its emphasis on building a physically, emotionally, mentally, and socially fit individual, plays an important role in the educational process. A heavy responsibility rests on the shoulders of those who spend a large share of their time with the youth of today. If experiences are provided that are satisfying, successful, and directed toward enriching the student's life, the purposes of education will be accomplished.

To describe more fully the role of physical education in the educational process, the potential of physical education will be discussed in relation to the three educational domains, namely, cognitive, affective, and psychomotor.

Cognitive Domain

The objective of cognitive development is increased knowledge and understanding. Physical education can contribute to cognitive development in such ways as the following:

1. **Physical education contributes to academic achievement.** Research indicates that physical education programs may contribute to academic achievement in a number of ways. The following research findings have implications for physical education: Intellectual, physical, and emotional developments are closely associated. Endocrinology has shown that mentality changes as body chemistry changes. Biology has linked the cell to the learning experience. Psychology points to the fact that the child's earliest learnings are factual and kinesthetic. Just as it is important to teach English so that students can communicate effectively with one another, history so that they have an understanding of

All three learning domains should be considered when planning instruction to meet each child's needs as a thinking, feeling, and moving human being.

A child's earliest learnings are motor in nature and form the foundation for subsequent learning.

their cultural heritage, and mathematics so that they can understand the technology of society, it is also important to educate students regarding their physical selves so that they can function most efficiently as human beings.

2. **Motor activity is related to higher thought processes.** Authorities such as Swiss psychologist Jean Piaget have found that a child's earliest learnings are motor (involving neuromuscular systems and resulting in movements such as running and reaching) in nature and form the foundation of subsequent learnings.

Various research studies indicate that the child's earliest and first learnings accrue from an interaction with the physical and social environment. Physical movement provides the experience to clarify and make meaningful concepts of size, shape, direction, and other characteristics. In addition, through physical activities the child has new feelings and develops new interests as well as satisfies old curiosities.

3. **Physical education contributes to a knowledge of exercise, health, and disease.** The educated person should have an understanding of the facts pertinent to exercise, health, and disease. To a great degree, an individual's success depends on personal health. One's state of health and physical fitness will determine in large measure whether one succeeds in realizing self-potentialities.

Physical education can contribute to this knowledge by instructing individuals about their bodies and movement and the importance of nutrition, physical activity, rest, and sleep; by informing them of the dangers of drugs; by exploring the preventive and control measures that exist to guard against diseases; by providing opportunities for vigorous out-of-doors activities; by motivating the formation of wholesome health attitudes and habits; by stressing safety factors for the prevention of accidents; and by establishing various health services.

The educated person has a knowledge of sound health practices; gets adequate amounts of exercise, rest, and sleep; eats the right kinds of food; engages in activity conducive to mental as well as physical health; and sees that others also have the same opportunities to maintain and improve their health. The educated person should realize that health is a product that increases proportionately as it is shared and that health is everybody's business.

4. **Physical education contributes to the understanding of the human body.** Individuals should know something about their bodies and their biological makeup. Physical education can provide knowledge and understanding relating to the various organ systems and how these systems function and can be best maintained. It is also concerned with knowledge of short- and long-term effects of activity and the relationship of physical activity to body structure and function. Such knowledge and understanding can result in greater intellectual productivity and play an important part in the general education of each individual.

5. **Physical education contributes to an understanding of the role of physical activity and sport in the American and other cultures of the world.** Sport and physical activity constitute a very important part of the American culture as well as the other cultures of the world. They affect the country's politics, government, economy, and educational systems. Sport and physical activity dominate the newspapers, magazines, radio, and television. Over 1,500 books are in print on the subject of physical fitness alone, together with many thousands more books devoted to various sports, thus giving this part of Americana an important place in the literature. Outstanding scholars such as Paul Weiss, former Yale professor of philosophy, and James Michener, outstanding novelist, have contributed books to this field of endeavor. Therefore, since sport and physical activity represent an important part of American culture, they should be understood not only from a biological but also from a sociological and psychological point of view. Of course, a body of sport knowledge also exists concerning such things as rules, safety measures, terminology, and game etiquette.

6. **Physical education contributes to the wise consumption of goods and services.** The educated person should buy goods and services with wisdom, be well informed as to their worth and utility, use standards for guiding expenditures,

An increasing number of schools at all levels are including the conceptual approach to physical education within their programs. Here students enter the Physical/Motor Fitness Laboratory at Rock Springs High School, Rock Springs, Wyo.

Sport is an important part of a country's culture.

and follow appropriate procedures to safeguard personal interests.

Physical interests can help to enlighten children and adults about the relative values of goods and services that influence their health and physical fitness. The field of health is an area in which goods and services of doubtful value find a ready public market. Advertisements in many of the more popular magazines seem to indicate that one must eat certain types of cereal to be an outstanding athlete, visit certain salons and slenderizing parlors to have a well-developed body, and use special types of toothpaste to keep teeth shiny. Literature that offers advice on health matters occupies a prominent place on newsstands, drugstore counters, and various shops throughout the country. Advice is also given via billboards, posters, press, radio, and films. Some of the material is specially prepared and disseminated as a money-making scheme to exploit the public. Human welfare is not always considered in much of the advice being given.

By nature of their position and background in health matters, physical educators can help the student and the adult to take a critical view of such literature and pronouncements.

Affective Domain

The affective domain is primarily concerned with interests, appreciations, attitudes, and values. It stresses the individual's value system and philosophy that are basic to maturity. Following are some of the contributions of physical education to this domain:

1. **Physical education contributes to self-actualization, self-esteem, and a healthy response to physical activity.** A well-planned and conducted physical education program can achieve such outcomes as a recognition of the potential of activity for the relief of tension, an awareness of what one's body is capable of doing, and a better physical self-image.

2. **Physical education contributes to an appreciation of beauty.** The educated person should develop an appreciation of the beautiful. From the time of early childhood the foundation of an appreciation of beautiful things can be developed. Architecture, landscapes, paintings, music, trees, rivers, and animals can ring a note of beauty in the mind of the growing child and the adult.

Physical education has much to offer in the way of beauty. The human body is a thing of beauty if it has been properly developed. The Greeks stressed the "body beautiful" and performed their exercises and athletic events in the nude to display the fine contours of their bodies. Physical activity is one of the keys to a beautiful body. Also, a beauty of movement is developed through physical activity. When a person picks up an object from the floor, it can be done with a great deal of skill and grace or it can be done awkwardly. When a football pass is caught, a basketball goal made, a high jump executed, a two-and-one-half somersault dive performed, or a difficult dance displayed, included in the performance of these acts can be rhythm, grace, poise, and ease of movement that are beauty in action. Anyone who has seen Nancy Lopez drive a golf ball, Steffi Graf stroke a tennis ball, Michael Jordan dunk a shot through the net, or Dave Winfield hit a home run knows what beauty of performance means. Such beauty comes only with practice and perfection.

3. **Physical education contributes to directing one's life toward worthwhile goals.** The educated person should conscientiously attempt to guide his or her life in the proper direction. On the shoulders of each individual rests the responsibility of determining how one will live, what religion one will choose, the moral code one will accept, the standard of values one will follow, and the code of ethics one will believe. This is characteristic of the democratic way of life.

A person should develop a philosophy of life. The way one treats fellow human beings, the manner in which one assumes responsibility, the objectives one sets to attain, and the type of government in which one believes will all be affected by this philosophy. As a result of the philosophy that is established, individuals help to determine their own destiny.

Physical education can help in the formulation of an individual's philosophy of life. Through the medium of physical education activities, guidance is given as to what is right and proper, goals that are

Dance provides an opportunity for expression. University of North Carolina, Greensboro, Dance Company, Save the Waltz Production.

worth competing for, intrinsic and extrinsic values, autocratic and democratic procedures, and standards of conduct. Children and youth are great imitators, and the beliefs, actions, and conduct of the teacher and the coach are frequently reflected in the beliefs, actions, and conduct of the student.

4. **The physical education program stresses humanism.** The human being is the most valuable and important consideration in this life. Therefore human welfare should receive careful consideration in all walks of life. When a new law is passed by Congress, its effect on human welfare should be considered.

The physical education program should stress humanism. When an activity is planned, it takes into consideration the needs and welfare of the participants; when a rule or regulation is made, the player's welfare is considered; when a student is reprimanded, the welfare of the student and that of others are considered. The physical education program takes into consideration unfit, less skilled, and disabled individuals and makes sure that adequate arrangements have been made for such individuals. It is a student-centered program, with the attention focused on the individuals for whom the program exists. Throughout the entire program the thought that the human aspects are the most important con-

sideration is prevalent among students, teachers, and administrators.

5. **The physical education program enables each individual to enjoy a rich social experience through play.** Play experiences offer an opportunity for a rich social experience, which can help greatly in rounding out a child's or youth's personality, in helping the child to adapt to the group situation, in developing proper standards of conduct, in creating a feeling of "belonging" and in developing a sound code of ethics.

Children and youths need the social experience that can be gained by associating with other persons in a play atmosphere. Many children and youths live in cities, in slum areas, and in communities where delinquency runs rampant, where their parents do not know the next-door neighbor, and where the environment is not conducive to a rich social experience. In such neighborhoods the school is one place where children and youths have an opportunity to mingle, and physical education offers an opportunity for them to play together. The potentials are limitless in planning social experiences through physical activities, rhythms, games of low organization, and more highly organized games. Here the child or youth can learn behavior traits characteristic of a democratic society. Because of

In many activities cooperation is the basis for the achievement of individual and group goals.

the drive for play, a child will be more willing to abide by the rules, accept responsibility, contribute to the welfare of the group, and respect the rights of others.

6. **The physical education program helps individuals to play cooperatively with others.** The physical education program should stress cooperation as the basis for achieving the goals an individual or group desires. Each member of the group works as though he or she were a part of a machine. The machine runs smoothly, and every part does its share of the work. Pulling and working together

bring results that never are obtained if everyone goes in different directions.

Physical education should stress leadership and followership traits. Everyone cannot be a captain on a basketball, relay, or soccer team. Everyone does not have leadership ability. Both leaders and followers are needed for the accomplishment of any enterprise.

7. **The physical education program teaches courtesy, fair play, and good sportsmanship.** The amenities of social behavior should be a part of the repertoire of every educated person. Courtesy and politeness are characteristic of good family training, just as fair play and sportsmanship are characteristic of good training in physical education activities. On the one hand, it reflects the character of the parent or guardian and, on the other, the teacher or coach. When a player kicks an opponent in the groin, trips him or her, or does not play according to the rules, this behavior may reflect the spirit of the leader. The main objective of a physical education program should be to provide an experience that will help the members of a group realize values that will help them live enriched lives.

8. **Physical education contributes to humanitarianism.** Physical education can, within reason, emotionalize democratic play experiences to the point at which young people see the importance and the value of cooperative living and contributing to the welfare of all. Here is an ideal setting for developing humanitarian values. Children and youth from all walks of life, creeds, colors, and races are brought together for a social experience. Interest and a natural drive for activity provide a laboratory for actual practice in developing these values.

Psychomotor Domain

In physical education the psychomotor domain is largely concerned with motor skills. In the schools a planned program of physical activity is offered as an essential to optimum body functioning of young persons during this developmental period of their lives. Physical education can contribute to psychomotor development in the following ways:

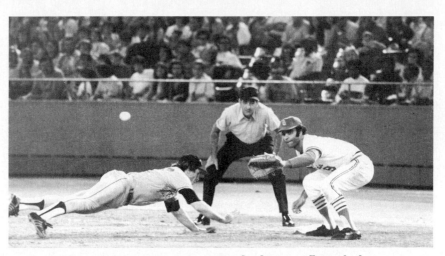

Spectator interest in sport at every level is at an all-time high.

1. **Physical education contributes to movement skills as a participant and spectator in sports and other physical activities.** The development of physical skills in all persons rather than in just a select few individuals is an educationally sound objective. The so-called recreational sports receive greater emphasis because these activities may be engaged in during an entire lifetime. Swimming, golf, tennis, badminton, and similar activities occupy a prominent place in many physical education programs.

Physical education not only develops skill in the participant but at the same time develops an interest and knowledge of other activities that at times may be engaged in by individuals as spectators. Although the benefits from participation outweigh the benefits of being a spectator with regard to physical activity, many leisure hours may be spent in a wholesome manner by observing a ball game or some other sports activity. Physical education can help by supplying a knowledge of various sports so that the role of the spectator may be more meaningful and interesting.

2. **Physical education contributes skills to utilize leisure hours in mental and cultural pursuits.** A whole gamut of activities offer entertainment and relaxation after working hours for a great many people. A sport such as fishing moti-

vates the development of a skill and a hobby such as tying flies. Many other examples could be listed.

3. **Physical education contributes skills essential to the preservation of the natural environment.** Part of the great wealth that belongs to the United States is represented in terms of wildlife, fish, forests, water, soil, and scenic beauty. These resources contribute to the living standard, appreciation of beauty, recreation, and pride that characterize this country. Physical education is concerned with ecology and especially with preserving national resources such as wildlife, fish, water, and forests. These represent the medium through which many enjoyable moments are spent by sportspersons, campers, and seekers of recreation and relaxation. Many physical educators teach skills such as the right method and procedure for making a camp fire, the right way to preserve wildlife and fish, and how to prevent forest fires.

• • •

Physical education can contribute to the education of each individual in many ways. Physical education contributes to learning in all three domains: cognitive, affective, and psychomotor. However, the role of physical education in the educational process must be considered in light of the educational reform movement in society today.

Individuals can learn lifetime sports as a result of participation in physical education programs. Students at Conard High School, Conn receive instruction in golf.

EDUCATIONAL REFORM MOVEMENT

In recent years public concern about the status of education within our nation's schools has become more pronounced and calls for educational reform more frequent. This concern was prompted by several factors, including the public's emphasis on accountability, the poor reading and writing performance of students, and the questionable quality of teachers. Less rigorous academic curriculums, reduction of the standards for high school graduation, and relaxation of the standards for college entrance have contributed to this concern. This concern is expressed in several reports issued in the early 1980s on the status of American education; these reports include *A Nation at Risk: The Imperative for Educational Reform*,[1] *The Paideia Proposal: An Educational Manifesto*,[2] and *High School: A Report on Secondary Education in America*.[3]

The report *A Nation at Risk* decried the "rising tide of mediocrity" that pervades American education. America's very future as a free, democratic nation and as a people were at risk because the youth of the country were failing to develop the skills to compete with the world in this era of technology. Academic performance and subsequent standards have declined. In an effort to remedy this downslide, the report calls for sweeping changes and a commitment on the part of the students, parents, teachers, and the public to excellence. The report suggested that each student attain competency in the five "new basics" as a requirement for a high school diploma. The "new basics" are English, math, science, social studies, and computer science. Unfortunately, the "new basics" did not include health and physical education; these courses were relegated to the status of personal service courses. The report advocated a commitment to lifelong learning with the view that education provides the necessary foundation.

Then Secretary of Education Terrell Bell[4] echoed the findings and the recommendations of the *Nation at Risk* report and called for high school students in all 50 states to complete the "new basics" as a requirement for graduation in 1989. However, he also acknowledged that "there must be room in the curriculum for physical education and athletics . . . ."

The Carnegie Commission report, *High School,* criticized American education as lacking a "clear and vital mission," a common purpose, and widely shared educational priorities. The report stated that high schools should help all students think clearly, communicate effectively, understand themselves and their heritage, prepare for work and further education, and fulfill their social and civic responsibilities. The proposed common core curriculum included English, history, science, math, technology, and health and called for a required senior project focusing on a significant social issue. Unlike the *Nation at Risk* report, health was viewed as an essential course of study. The *High School* report stated "clearly no knowledge is more crucial than knowledge about health. Without it, no other life goal can be successfully achieved." It was also recommended that the common core of learning include a course in lifetime fitness.

The *Paideia Proposal* stressed attainment of quality education for all citizens. The *Proposal* cited three common educational objectives: personal growth and development, preparation for responsible citizenship, and preparation for living. Attainment of skills for lifelong learning was emphasized. The common core curriculum focused on the acquisition of knowledge, development of intellectual skills, and understanding of ideas and values. The common core also included auxiliary subjects, one of which was physical education. Physical education was required for all 12 years of schooling.

Several common themes are apparent in the three educational reports discussed in this chapter as well as other reports not included in this discus-

sion. First, quite obviously, these reports make a clear, strong case for reform in the nation's schools. Concern about the quality of teachers and their teaching is evident. These reports suggest an urgent need for the enhancement of the professional status of teachers. This may be accomplished by giving teachers more competitive salaries, providing continuing education, requiring more stringent entrance requirements for teacher preparation programs, and changing the content and the format of teacher preparation. The poor quality of students' reading, writing, and performance on standardized achievement tests has prompted a call for a greater emphasis on the basics. While there is agreement about the need to return to the basics, there is disagreement as to which subjects constitute the basics as well as the length of time to be spent on each subject. However, a consensus that achievement of literacy and citizenship are priorities is apparent. The basics are viewed as providing a foundation for lifelong learning, a theme that surfaces repeatedly. Since we live in the information age, individuals must be taught how to seek information, process information, and communicate information in an articulate, accurate, and meaningful manner. To accomplish these educational goals, a longer school day and year is suggested.

Consensus was lacking about the status of physical education and health within the school curriculum. Some reports advocated the inclusion of these subjects, other reports viewed physical education and health as nonessential, and still other reports failed to mention these subjects at all.

Since the cries for educational reform in the early 1980s, all 50 states have, to various degrees, implemented changes. School systems have been significantly revamped in approximately 12 states, and high school graduation requirements have been raised in approximately 40 states. However, while there is a strong belief that significant progress has been made, much more needs to be accomplished to improve American education. The implications of the educational reform movement for physical education are discussed in the next section.

What Are the Implications of the Educational Reform Movement for Physical Education?

The educational reform movement and its emphasis on the "new basics" has important implications for physical education. Many of the reports and advocates of educational reform regard physical education as a frill or a nonessential subject. In some discussions physical education is not even mentioned while in other cases physical education is relegated to the status of a personal service or an ancillary course. In essence, physical education is viewed by some as a subject that cannot be justified for inclusion in the new educational curriculum.

An opposing point of view exists, however. Some advocates of educational reform support physical education as a basic, integral part of the new educational curriculum. These supporters recognize the valuable contribution physical education can make to students' education and lives.

In addition, strong support for the inclusion of physical education in the curriculum is offered by three national health reports: *Healthy People,*[5] *Objectives for the Nation,*[6] and *Year 2000 Objectives.*[7] *Healthy People* listed 15 health priorities for the nation including physical fitness and exercise. *Objectives for the Nation* delineated specific health objectives to be achieved by the year 1990. *Year 2000 Objectives* built further on the 1990 objectives, seeking increased improvement in the health of Americans through disease prevention and health promotion efforts. The specific objectives for physical activity and exercise are shown in Figure 3-2.

The attainment of many of these stated objectives is at risk because of the lack of support for physical education programs in the schools. Obviously, most directly at risk is the objective supporting daily school physical education programs for students in all grades. However, a greater number of objectives are affected than is immediately apparent if school physical education programs are further reduced or, worse, eliminated. Daily physical education programs are essential to attain many of these objectives and to realize the concomitant health goals. School physical education programs should lay the foundation for participation in regular, appropriate physical activity throughout one's life. These programs should teach basic skills and knowledge as well as provide participants with positive and meaningful experiences that will foster a wholesome attitude toward participation.

Is physical education a basic? The best strategy, it seems, for physical educators to follow in promoting physical education as a basic is to set forth clearly and articulately how and why physical education is an integral part of the educational program of every educational institution. In response to the educational reform reports, Osness,[8] past president of AAHPERD, stated that it is essential that the public, legislators, and other decision makers be accurately informed about the contribution of physical education to the educational process.

One positive step in the recognition of the contributions of physical education to education was the passing of a resolution by the U.S. Senate and the House of Representatives in 1987 encouraging state and local governments to provide quality, daily physical education programs for all students in kindergarten through grade 12. The resolution noted that physical education enhanced the following educational objectives:

- academic performance
- mental alertness
- readiness to learn
- enthusiasm for learning
- self-esteem
- interpersonal relationships
- responsible behavior
- independence
- overall health
- skillful movement
- physical fitness
- active lifestyle
- constructive use of leisure time

It was noted in the resolution that the Surgeon General of the United States had recommended increasing the number of school physical education programs focusing on health-related fitness. Furthermore, the resolution cited the Secretary of Education as recognizing the mandate of elementary schools to provide their students with the knowledge, skills, and attitudes that will enable chil-

FIGURE 3-2 Year 2000 Objectives for the Nation

Specific Objective	Goal (Percent)	Base (Percent) [Year]
Risk Reduction		
Increase the proportion of people* who participate in moderate physical activity 3 or more days per week for 20 or more minutes per session	60	50 [1985]
Increase the proportion of people* who participate in vigorous physical activities designed to promote the development and maintenance of cardiovascular endurance 3 or more days per week for 20 or more minutes per session	30	25 [1985]
Increase the proportion of people* who regularly perform physical activities designed to maintain muscular strength, muscular endurance, and flexibility	50	— †
Reduce the proportion of people ages 20 to 74 who are overweight	20	25 [1976-80]
Reduce the proportion of people ages 12 to 17 who are overweight	less than 15	15 [1976-80]
Increase the proportion of overweight people 12 years of age or older who have adopted a program of sound nutritional practices in conjunction with physical activity to achieve weight reduction	75	25 for men 30 for women [1985]
Public Awareness		
Increase the proportion of people* who know that regular physical exercise reduces the risk of heart disease, helps maintain appropriate weight, reduces the symptoms of depression and anxiety, and enhances self-esteem	80	—
Increase the proportion of people* who know that cardiorespiratory fitness, muscular strength and endurance, flexibility, and body composition are important to health	40	—
Increase the proportion of people* who can accurately identify the frequency and duration of exercise thought to be most effective in promoting cardiorespiratory endurance	25	10 [1985]
Professional Education and Awareness		
Increase the proportion of primary care providers who evaluate and counsel their patients regarding the type, frequency, duration, and intensity of their physical activity practices	65	47 [1985]
Services and Protection		
Increase the proportion of children, grades 1-12, who participate in a daily physical education program	45	36 [1985]
Increase the proportion of teachers who teach physical education and who spend at least 30 percent of the class on skills and activities that promote lifetime physical activity participation	30	—
Increase the proportion of companies and institutions that offer employer-sponsored fitness programs		
50-99 employees	25	14 [1985]
100-249 employees	35	23 [1985]
250-749 employees	45	32 [1985]
750 or more employees	65	54 [1985]
Increase the proportion of people who participate in at least one community physical activity program during a year	40	—
Increase the number of community recreational resources		
Swimming pools (per person)	1/25,000	1/53,000 [1986]
Hiking, fitness, and bike trail miles (per person)	1/10,000	1/60,000 [1986]
Park and recreation open and developed spaces (acres per 1000 people)	4/1,000	1.8/1,000 [1986]
Increase the number of life insurers that offer lower premiums to people who exercise regularly and maintain a physically active lifestyle	30	only 1 company

*People refers to individuals age 6 and older
†Indicates no baseline data available.

From Public Health Service, U.S. Department of Health and Human Services, *Promoting Health/Preventative Disease: Year 2000 Objectives for the Nation* (Draft), 1989, U.S. Government Printing Office, Washington, DC.

Daily, quality physical education is an educational basic.

dren to lead a fit and healthy life. The resolution acknowledged that physical education is an essential part of a comprehensive curriculum for all students. Thus, the Congress encouraged state and local governments to provide quality daily physical education programs for all school-age children. However, while this sounds encouraging, the responsibility for education resides with state and local governments and within the past two decades, many states have reduced the amount of time students are required to take physical education in the schools. A strong national effort by professionals is needed to increase the time requirement for physical education in the nation's schools and to make quality, daily physical education a reality for all students.

The educational reform reports hold other implications for physical education. Just as in other educational areas, standards for individuals seeking entry into teacher education programs as well as

nonteaching programs need to be carefully scrutinized and more rigorous standards adopted when necessary. Careful consideration should be given to enhancing the professional status of practitioners and to maintaining and upgrading their education through continuing education. Practitioners must strive to promote excellence in their programs; they must be accountable for program outcomes.

One point that received considerable emphasis by advocates of educational reform is the importance of preparing students to be lifelong learners. Physical educators must also prepare their students to be self-educative. Attainment of proficiency in basic skills and knowledge is important to achieving this aim. Acceptance of the premise of lifelong learning implies that much of an individual's learning will take place outside of the school setting. Thus nonschool programs designed to meet the needs of individuals of all ages are needed. Two other societal trends—the wellness movement and the fitness movement—also support the need for nonschool physical education and sport programs for individuals of all ages.

WELLNESS MOVEMENT

Americans today are expressing a greater interest in being healthy and fit. This interest has been stimulated by the growing realization that one's life-style—the way in which one lives—influences greatly the attainment and the maintenance of personal health.

Traditionally good health has been viewed by the public as freedom from disease; thus if an individual was not sick, he or she was considered to be healthy. However, this perspective is changing. While it is generally agreed that not being sick is one part of being healthy, health can be defined in terms of being well. Thus health may be viewed as an optimal state or sense of well-being. This well-being may be achieved and maintained by an individual properly managing his or her life-style.

This change in attitude has created an interest in the holistic approach to health. Holistic health, philosophically, is based on the premise that health is affected by every aspect of an individual's life. Physical, psychological, emotional, spiritual, genetic, environmental, and social forces all interact to influence one's health. Advocates of the holistic approach consider all these factors when assessing an individual's health status.

Closely related to the holistic health movement is the wellness movement, which emphasizes the individual's responsibility for his or her own well-being. This movement stresses such efforts as health promotion and disease prevention rather than focusing on the treatment of illness. Those who adhere to the wellness doctrine believe that it is the responsibility of the individual to work toward achievement of a healthy life-style to realize an optimal sense of well-being. A healthy life-style should reflect the integration of three components: proper nutrition, regular and appropriate physical activity and exercise, and stress management. Elimination of controllable risk factors (e.g., smoking or drug abuse) that contribute to illness is also essential. Unhealthy

Learning tennis skills allows individuals with disabilities to participate in recreational activities.

life-styles are associated with diseases, particularly stress-related diseases (e.g., hypertension or heart attack) and early mortality for those who do not choose to control their life-style.

Healthy People, Objectives for the Nation, and *Year 2000 Objectives* emphasized that improvements in the health of Americans depended not only on advances in health care and increased health care expenditures but also on a national commitment to disease prevention and health promotion through life-style management.

The latest report, *Year 2000 Objectives,* stated that improvement of health and well-being is the ultimate goal of health promotion and disease prevention. Five broad goals for improving the health of the nation were identified. The goals to be accomplished by the year 2000 include:

- reduce infant mortality to no more than 7 deaths per 1,000 live births
- increase life expectancy to at least 78 years
- reduce disability related to chronic conditions

Exposure to a variety of activities allows individuals to determine which ones are personally satisfying. However, individuals also must have the opportunity to develop competency in their chosen sport.

to a prevalence of 6 percent or less of all people
- increase years of healthy life to at least age 65
- decrease the disparity in life expectancy between white and minority populations to no more than 4 years.

These goals set forth the health agenda for the nation and reflect a commitment to reducing preventable morbidity and disability, reducing health disparities between population groups, and improving the quality as well as the length of life. To realize these outcomes, specific objectives addressing improvements in health status, risk reduction, public awareness, professional education, services, and protection were delineated. These objectives provide a means to measure progress toward attainment of these health goals. These objectives were organized into 21 priority areas focusing on health promotion, health protection, preventive services, and delivery systems. Physical activity and fitness was listed as a priority in the area of health promotion. The 16 objectives for this priority area are shown in Figure 3-2.

The *Year 2000 Objectives* report recognizes the increasing evidence of the health benefits of regular physical activity. In particular, the potential of physical activity to reduce the risk of coronary heart disease, the leading cause of morbidity and mortality in this country was noted. Physically inactive individuals are almost twice as likely to develop coronary heart disease as those who engage in regular physical activity. Furthermore, there are more people at risk for coronary heart disease because of physical inactivity than for any other single risk factor (e.g., cigarette smoking, high blood cholesterol, hypertension).

The escalating costs of health care have increased the awareness of individuals and corporations of the benefits to be accrued from health promotion efforts. In 1989 national health expenditures were $541 billion, about 11% of the gross national product. Costs continue to rise at an alarming rate.

These spiraling health care costs and the realization of the benefits to be gained from participation in health and fitness programs have prompted many corporations to establish programs for employees. Corporations have found that such programs make economic sense. Poor employee health is costly. Illness and premature death cost American industry billions of dollars a year. Poor health and fitness contribute to decreased productivity and increased absenteeism. Premiums for medical insurance continue to rise. Industry has become increasingly cognizant of the short- and long-term benefits of employee health and fitness programs (i.e., greater productivity and decreased medical expenditures); it appears that preventive measures may be cheaper in the long run than curative ones. The number of programs has grown nationwide. Programs vary but may include fitness programs, recreation activities, and health education programs, such as cancer and hypertension screening, nutritional counseling, and smoking cessation. The growth in programs has led to an increase in career opportunities in this sector. (These will be discussed in Chapter 12.)

Individuals are also responding to the wellness movement. Evidence of this is seen in the fitness movement, which will be discussed shortly, and other life-style changes. People are becoming more conscious about their diet and making modifications where necessary, such as decreasing the sodium intake and becoming aware of the cholesterol potential of food. In short, individuals are becoming increasingly aware that the manner in which they live can have a significant impact on the quality of their life.

What Are the Implications of the Wellness Movement for Physical Education and Sport?

The most obvious role of physical education and sport in contributing to the enhancement of well-being is through the instruction of individuals with respect to physical activity and exercise. This can be accomplished through sound school and nonschool physical education and sport programs for people of all ages. Programs should lay the foundation for participation in fitness and physical activities throughout one's lifetime. This foundation is best laid in the early years so that physical activity and exercise become an integral part of each individual's life, a lifelong habit. Physical education programs for young children should focus on the attainment of proficiency in fundamental skills and activities. Adolescent participants need to be exposed to a variety of activities designed for lifetime participation. Exposure to a variety of activities allows individuals to determine which are enjoyable, satisfying, and meaningful to them and desirable for participation in their adult years. Individuals need to become acquainted with the knowledge base of physical education so that they can learn how to

direct their own exercise programs, physical activities, and leisure time experiences. Finally, physical educators must ensure that participants will experience success and satisfaction, thus providing the motivation for continued participation throughout life.

As you review the *Year 2000 Objectives* shown in Figure 3-2, ask yourself:

- How can physical education and sport contribute to the realization of these objectives and the goal of optimal health and well-being for all segments of the population?
- What are the implications of these objectives for the structure and content of physical education and sport programs in all settings and for a diversity of populations?
- What are the implications for the manner in which we deliver services?
- What are the implications for job opportunities in this field?

These are just some of the questions that need to be addressed by the profession.

Physical education and sport can make a contribution to another component of a healthy life-style—stress management. Stress management involves several steps: (1) recognition of the stressor, that is, people and events that cause a person to feel stress, (2) identification and awareness of one's reaction to stress (e.g., bodily tension, tension headache, or sweaty palms), and (3) alleviation of stress either through the elimination of the stressor or the reduction of the effects.

A variety of approaches for alleviating stress are available. These include relaxation training, participation in physical activity, cognitive strategies, time management, and biofeedback. The selection of the approach or approaches depends on several considerations including the stressor, one's reaction to the stressor, and the individual's personality.

Physical activity has long been acknowledged as a means of releasing tension and in terms of stress management may be the primary responsibility of the physical educator. However, physical education and sport can contribute in other ways to stress reduction. Such relaxation techniques as progressive relaxation and yoga can be incorporated into

Yoga may help in the management of stress. College students learn yoga in class at University of Nevada, Las Vegas.

the current physical education and sport program. Individuals can also be taught to become aware of their stress as manifested by bodily tension through a variety of movement experiences.

In summary, it appears that physical education and sport can play a significant role in the enhancement of well-being and the maintenance of health. Even so, physical educators must realize that physical activity and exercise are only a part of the means to achieving optimal health. Nutritionists, health educators, medical personnel, and others have a critical role to play in the wellness movement. It is important that all professionals work cooperatively to achieve the realization of the nation's health objectives and the attainment of optimal well-being for each individual.

FITNESS MOVEMENT

Enthusiasm for exercise and fitness is at an unprecedented level in the United States today, with millions of people spending countless hours and billions of dollars on exercise and sport.[9] Men and women of all ages are participating in fitness

and sport activities to an extent not witnessed before in this country. The fitness movement, initially perceived by some as a fad or a short-lived phenomena, has grown for over a decade, becoming perhaps a historically significant trend. It appears that exercise and fitness for many adults has become ingrained in American life.

However, when data about adult participation in fitness activities are closely examined, neither the widespread extent of the fitness movement nor its pervasiveness in American society is supported. Available data indicate that only 10 to 20% of adults exercise with sufficient frequency, intensity, and duration (e.g., exercise involving large muscles in dynamic movement for a minimum of 20 minutes, 3 or more days per week at an intensity of 60% or greater than cardiorespiratory capacity) to develop and maintain adequate levels of health-related fitness.[7,10,11] Also noteworthy is that even though 80 to 90% of the adult population does not get a sufficient amount of weekly exercise to maintain satisfactory levels of health-related fitness, approximately half of those individuals—40% of the adult popu-

Road races have become an integral part of American life.

lation—do engage in moderate intensity (below the level recommended for cardiorespiratory endurance) physical activities sufficiently often to realize some health-related benefits.[7,10,11]

Research has also indicated that the extent of participation in fitness activities is influenced by such factors as age, sex, race, education, economic level, occupation, community setting, and geographic location.[7,12] The prevalence of physical activity decreases with age, is higher among men than women, and is greater among whites than non-whites. High school and college graduates, middle- and upper-middle income people, and professional persons tend to participate more. Higher participation rates are also noted for individuals who live in suburban settings and those who live in the western part of the United States.

Although the fitness movement is not as pervasive as it seems, the number of participants are growing each year. Adults are becoming more cognizant of the value of regular exercise and are beginning to incorporate it into their lifestyle. It is hoped that the number of adults willing to make a commitment to exercising on a regular basis, with sufficient intensity, duration, and frequency to maintain an adequate level of health-related fitness, will continue to grow in the future. Walking, bicycling, jogging, and swimming are among the most popular activities, although enthusiasm for all forms of exercise continues to grow.

While the fitness movement is not as large as it may appear, active individuals are spending an increased amount of money on sporting goods and equipment. Expenditures for sport and exercise equipment has reached an all-time high. It is estimated that Americans spend $4.8 billion a year on sports clothing and $4.9 billion a year on athletic shoes.[13-15] Sales of home exercise equipment has

Sales of home exercise equipment have grown. Various equipment is available that allows individuals to work out at their own convenience in their home.

skyrocketed, from $723 million in 1982 to over $1.4 billion in recent years.[14] Home exercise equipment has become more expensive and more sophisticated. Stationary bicycles, treadmills, cross country ski machines, stair masters, rowers, and weight systems are popular. More and more equipment incorporates heart-rate monitoring electronics and workout computers to provide users with increasingly sophisticated feedback about their efforts. Sales of diet books and exercise videos continue to rise. It is important to note, however, that buying apparel, shoes, and exercise equipment does not guarantee that they will be used by their owners on a regular basis.

Corporate fitness and commercial health clubs have attracted a record number of participants. The number of participants in athletic and recreational programs in the schools and communities has increased as well during recent years. An increasing number of communities have fitness and bicycling trails, which have proven to be popular with community residents.

The fitness status of the nation's children and youth has caused considerable public concern in recent years. Fitness levels of children and youth were found to be discouragingly low.[16,17] One popular newsmagazine, *Time,* awarded the fitness status of our nation's children a grade of "F for flabby."[18]

Two recently completed comprehensive studies of children's and youth's fitness substantiate the need for concern.[16,17] These studies were conducted by the U.S. Department of Health and Human Services Office for Disease Prevention and Health Promotion in cooperation with other interested agencies, including AAHPERD. These studies emphasized health-related fitness and test items were selected to assess the participant's current health status and potential resistance to disease. The test items included the following:

- Distance runs to provide a general indicator of cardiovascular capacity; maintenance of a high capacity may reduce the individual's susceptibility to cardiovascular disease.
- Determination of percent of body fat by skinfold measures from selected sites. A large percent of body fat indicates vulnerability to a host of degenerative diseases including hypertension, heart disease, and diabetes.
- Assessment of lower back flexibility and abdominal strength, which are important in preventing lower back or other musculoskeletal problems, through the individual's performance on the sit-and-reach test and the sit-up test.
- Chin-ups or modified pull-ups to measure upper body strength. An adequate level of upper body strength is needed to perform various functional tasks associated with daily living without risk of injury.

The National Children and Youth Fitness Study I (NCYFS I),[16] the first nationwide assessment of youth fitness in nearly a decade, was designed to

Community fitness trails are popular with residents.

elicit information about the health and fitness of youths aged 10 to 17 (grades 5 through 12) as well as information about their physical activity habits. A total of 8,800 boys and girls completed the five-item fitness test (bent-knee sit-ups, chin-ups, 1-mile walk/run, sit-and-reach, and skinfold thickness) and a self-report questionnaire on physical activities to assess health-related fitness. The results, released in 1985, revealed much cause for concern: compared to children tested in 1960, there was a significant increase in percent body fat, indicating the nation's youths had become fatter. Another concern was the poor performance of the youths on the cardiorespiratory measure—the 1-mile walk/run. Examination of the average score revealed that many of the children completed the distance at a slow jog, with girls taking more time to complete the distance than boys.

According to NCYFS I, only slightly more than one-third of the students (36.3%) participated in daily school physical education programs, and only about half the youths participated in appropriate physical activity essential for maintenance of an adequate level of cardiorespiratory function. The data revealed that secondary school physical educa-

tion programs tended to focus more on competitive and team sport activities rather than on lifetime and individual skills and activities that can be used by adults for participation throughout life. Furthermore, more than 80% of the physical activity of students was performed outside of the school physical education classes, primarily in community programs.

The NCYFS II[17] examined the fitness levels and physical activity habits of 4,678 6- to 9-year-old children (grades 1 to 4). Fitness levels were measured using five test items [bent-knee sit-ups, modified pull-ups, 1-mile or 1/2-mile walk/run (depending upon the child's age), sit and reach, and skinfold thickness], similar to those utilized in the first study. Parents completed a questionnaire describing their own and the child's activity patterns, and information about the school physical education program was obtained directly from the teachers.

The results, released in 1987, raised concerns similar to those voiced about the findings of the NCYFS I. Compared to results of fitness tests conducted 20 or more years ago, children today have a higher percentage of body fat. The tests also indicated that neither the cardiorespiratory capacity nor

Children's exercise patterns and activity interests are influenced by their parents.

the upper body strength of the typical child is well developed.

NCYFS II revealed that nearly all children were enrolled in a physical education program of some kind and that 36.4% of the children had daily physical education. In the early grades, the physical education program largely focused on movement experiences and development of fundamental skills. However, by grades 3 and 4, a shift toward competitive team sports was noted, an emphasis that persisted throughout the high school years. Nearly all children engaged in at least one physical activity through a community program.

Examination of the data on parents also revealed cause for concern; only 30% participated in vigorous physical activity sufficient to realize maximum health benefits and 50% of the parents reported that they never engage in vigorous exercise. Children who watched a greater amount of television as compared with their peers also tended to have lower physical activity levels and lower levels of participation in organized sports and community activities.

The health and fitness of children was found to be influenced by several factors. In terms of cardiorespiratory capacity, children who performed well on the distance run participated in more community-based activity, watched less television, were rated more physically active by their parents and

their teachers, received more of their physical education instruction from a physical education specialist, and had greater opportunities to participate in periodic fitness testing than their peers who scored lower on this measure. These children were also leaner in terms of body composition. Equally noteworthy, the parents of leaner children were physically active and exercised more frequently with their children.

The findings of the NCYFS I and II provide a wealth of information about the fitness status of our nation's children and youth. Concerns about the poor fitness status of this population appear to be well-founded. Policy makers, teachers, parents, and community members need to collaborate to enhance the fitness status of children and youth. This is particularly important in light of the increased evidence supporting the relationship between childhood health-fitness and adult degenerative diseases. Heart disease does begin in childhood. Children whose percent of body fat is too high and whose patterns of inactivity contribute to low levels of cardiorespiratory function tend to maintain these risk factors as they age, placing them at increased risk for degenerative disease.

What Are the Implications of the Fitness Movement for Physical Education and Sport?

Although the fitness movement is not as pervasive as it appears, interest in fitness is at an all time high. Although many Americans of all ages are not exercising vigorously with sufficient frequency, intensity, and duration to maintain an adequate level of health-related fitness, an increasing number of people are making a commitment to incorporate appropriate exercise into their lifestyle. Furthermore, the increased documentation of the positive relationship between adequate levels of health-related fitness and wellness offers strong support for physical education and sport programs. It also emphasizes the need for fitness programs to reach all ages of our society, regardless of sex, race, educational level, occupation, economic status, and community setting. As professionals, we must capitalize on the interest in fitness and its contribution to health to promote and secure funding for our programs.

Jumping rope is a popular means to develop and maintain cardiorespiratory endurance.

Professionals must also become leaders in the fitness movement and exert a significant influence on its direction. Corbin[19] pointed out that medical doctors, self-appointed experts, and movie stars are at the vanguard of the fitness movement. Many of these people lack the qualifications, training, and expertise to direct this movement. Additionally, the proliferation of products and programs related to exercise and fitness has raised some concern about their validity. Corbin argues that professionals have the necessary knowledge and skill and must take over the leadership responsibilities within the movement. This viewpoint is further supported by the prestigious American Academy of Physical Education. The Academy urged professionals to be "active in the consumer education movement relat-

ed to physical activities."[20] Specifically, professionals should educate the public to be wise consumers of exercise products and programs; they should serve as a resource to which the public can turn for help and guidance. Additionally, professionals should provide the participants in their programs with the knowledge and skills to solve their own exercise and physical activity problems and to evaluate their own fitness needs.

In assuming the burden of leadership, Corbin states that it is important to practice what we preach. Professionals should be role models and should reflect a commitment to a healthy lifestyle, with physical activity as an integral component of that lifestyle. Failure to practice what we preach damages our credibility.

NCYFS I and II indicate an urgent need for the fitness movement to reach the children and youth of our nation. Schools should emphasize lifelong fitness and this education should begin early in life. School-based programs must teach students the skills for lifetime participation and foster an appreciation for the value of fitness and physical activity in maintaining an optimal state of well-being. Fitness education should also be extended to parents. Parents' role in shaping their children's physical activity habits should be recognized and professionals should involve them in creating positive physical activity patterns. Because much of children's and youth's physical activity takes place outside of the school setting, school and community physical activity programs should be closely coordinated so that the maximum benefits are derived from participation.

A concerted effort by professionals must be made to reach all segments of the adult population and to provide them with the necessary skills, knowledge, and attitudes to develop and maintain adequate levels of health-related fitness. We must sustain participation by that small segment of society, the 10 to 20% of individuals who exercise vigorously enough to maintain an adequate level of health-related fitness. We must encourage the 40% of the population that engage in moderate physical activity to upgrade the intensity of their efforts to achieve the full benefits of appropriate vigorous exercise. Finally, we must reach out to the 40% of the population who exercise irregularly, if at all, and help them to begin to incorporate physical activity into their lives. Accomplishment of these goals requires committed, qualified professionals and a diversity of programs conducted in a variety of settings and targeted to all segments of the population.

Interest in fitness has led to the development of a wide range of job opportunities. Tony Mobley, Dean of Health, Physical Education, and Recreation at Indiana University stated, "there has probably never been a time in society with greater opportunities in sport and recreation than there are now."[21] The growth of interest in fitness and exercise has opened up jobs in community physical education and sport programs, corporate fitness centers, health clubs, and the sporting goods industry, to name just a few. Job opportunities are discussed in Part Three of this text.

SUMMARY

The education of a society's citizens is influenced by contemporary societal needs and trends. Today one of the primary purposes of education is to prepare individuals for a meaningful, self-directed existence. The education of the individual can be described as taking place through three learning domains: the cognitive domain, the affective domain, and the psychomotor domain. Carefully planned programs of physical education conducted by qualified professionals can contribute in many ways to learning in each of these domains. Three societal trends that hold considerable implications for the conduct and status of physical education and sport in our society are the educational reform movement, the wellness movement, and the fitness movement.

The educational reform movement received its impetus from a series of reports decrying the status of education in America's schools and identifying specific areas for reform. These reports called for a greater emphasis on the "new basics" of English, science, social studies, math, and computer science. Lifelong learning was stressed as well. These reports disagreed on the status of physical education as an educational basic. Thus it is up to physical educators to make a strong case for physical education as a basic, before physical education is eliminated from the educational curriculum.

The wellness and fitness movements also hold several implications for physical education and sport. The wellness movement emphasized health promotion and disease prevention through life-style modification and individual responsibility for one's own health. Physical activity and exercise are integral parts of a healthy life-style. Within the past decade tremendous interest has been shown in physical activity and exercise. However, it appears that only a small percentage of the population participates in vigorous physical activity of sufficient frequency, intensity, and duration to sustain an adequate level of health-related fitness. Professionals need to increase the number of individuals within all segments of the population who engage in appropriate physical activity on a regular basis.

The wellness and fitness movements offer strong support for the development of nonschool physical education and sport programs. The emphasis on lifelong learning by educational reform leaders supports the need for physical education and sport programs for individuals of all ages.

Regardless of the setting and the population served, movement is the keystone of physical education and sport. The nature of movement is discussed in the next chapter.

SELF-ASSESSMENT TESTS

These tests are designed to assist students in determining if the material and competencies presented in this chapter have been mastered.

1. You are attending a school faculty meeting and one of the members of the faculty states that physical education should not be considered a part of the educational curriculum. You disagree and make a presentation that indicates that you believe that physical education is an important part of education. What points would you emphasize in your presentation?

2. Explain what is meant by the cognitive, psychomotor, and affective domains. Provide specific illustrations of how physical education contributes to learning in each domain.

3. Discuss the educational reform movement and its implications for physical education.

4. You have been invited to speak to a community group on the role of physical activity in the promotion of health and attainment of wellness. Prepare a short speech reflecting the contribution of physical education and sport to a healthy life-style.

5. For each of the *Year 2000 Objectives* shown in Figure 3-2, provide specific examples of how physical education and sport can help in their attainment. Explain the implications of each of these objectives for the structure and content of physical education and sport programs and the manner in which we deliver our services.

6. The fitness movement has been perceived by many as an enduring trend. Discuss the role of the physical educator in providing leadership for this movement. What are the implications of this movement for career opportunities?

REFERENCES

1. Gardner D: A nation at risk: the imperative for educational reform, Washington, DC, 1983, US Government Printing Office.

2. Adler M: The Paideia proposal: an educational manifesto, New York, 1982, Macmillan Inc.

3. Boyer E: High school: a report on secondary education in America, New York, 1983, Harper & Row.

4. Bell T: American education at a crossroads, Phi Delta Kappa 65(8):531-534, 1984.

5. US Department of Health, Education, and Welfare: Healthy people: the surgeon general's report on health promotion and disease prevention, Washington, DC, 1979, US Government Printing Office.

6. US Department of Health and Human Services: Promoting health/preventing disease: objectives for the nation, Washington, DC, 1980, US Government Printing Office.

7. Public Health Service, US Department of Health and Human Services: Promoting health/preventing disease: year 2000 objectives for the nation (draft), Washington, DC, 1989, US Government Printing Office.

8. Osness WH: A response to national reports, NASSP Bulletin 68(470):24-27, 1984.

9. Keeping in shape: everybody's doing it, US News and World Report, pp 24-26, August 13, 1984.

10. Blair S, Kohl H, and Powell K: Physical activity, physical fitness, exercise, and the public's health, The Academy Papers 20:53-69, 1987.

11. Montoye H: How active are modern populations? The Academy Papers 21:34-45, 1988.

12. Lupton CH III, Ostrove NM, and Bozzp RM: Participation in leisure-time activities: a comparison of existing data, Journal of Physical Education, Recreation, and Dance 55(9):19-23, 1984.

13. New products aim to fit the cross-training market, USA Today, p 8D, September 21, 1989.

14. Firms go toe-to-toe on marketing, USA Today, p 2B, September 27, 1989.

15. Samuelson RJ: The american sports mania, Newsweek, p 49, September 4, 1989.

16. Ross JG and Gilbert GG: The national children and youth study: a summary of the findings, Journal of Physical Education, Recreation, and Dance 56(1):45-50, 1985.

17. Ross JG and Pate RR: The national children and youth fitness study II, Journal of Physical Education, Recreation, and Dance 58(9):51-56, 1987.

18. Putting on the Ritz at the Y, Time, p 65, July 21, 1986.

19. Corbin CB: Is the fitness bandwagon passing us by? Journal of Physical Education, Recreation, and Dance 55(9):17, 1984.

20. Park RJ: Three major issues: the academy takes a stand, Journal of Physical Education, Recreation, and Dance 54(1):52-53, 1983.

21. New jobs blossom in leisure field, US News and World Report, p 28, August 13, 1984.

SUGGESTED READINGS

AAHPERD: The national children and youth fitness study II, Journal of Physical Education, Recreation, and Dance 58(9):51-96, 1987

A series of ten articles that detail the procedures, summarize the findings, and discuss the implications of the National Children and Youth Fitness Study II.

Annarino AA: Changing times: keeping abreast professionally, Journal of Physical Education, Recreation, and Dance 55(5):32-34, 52, 1984.

Annarino initially provides an overview of the educational reform reports. The article then continues to discuss the problems and concerns that confront professionals who desire to keep abreast professionally. Various strategies for continuing education programs are discussed. However, commitments from professionals, professional organizations, and institutions are required to improve educational practices.

Aubrey RS: Reform in schooling: four proposals on an educational quest, Journal of Counseling and Development 63:204-213, 1984.

This article provides an excellent overview of four educational reform reports: *A Nation at Risk; High School: A Report on Secondary Education in America; Paideia Proposal;* and *A Place Called School: Prospects for the Future.*

Clark MW, editor: Coping with stress through leisure, Journal of Physical Education, Recreation, and Dance 53(8):32-61, 1982.

Following the introduction, 16 articles are presented dealing with the various aspects of stress and stress management. These articles include stress reduction through leisure, running, challenging activities, and cognitive approaches. Stress management in the leisure services, with teachers, and with special populations is discussed. A curriculum and resources for teaching stress management are also represented.

Hastad DN and Lacy AC: Health-related fitness: an emerging learning domain in physical education, Strategies 2(2):14-17, 1988.

The importance of health-related fitness within the curriculum is discussed.

Oliver B: Educational reform and physical education, Journal of Physical Education, Recreation, and Dance 59(1):68-71, 77, 1988.

    The proposed areas of educational reform are summarized and implications for physical education are presented.

Pollock ML and Blair SN: Exercise prescription, Journal of Physical Education, Recreation, and Dance 52(1):30-35, 81, 1981.

    The authors provide practical guidelines to develop health-related fitness in an easily understood manner. Both the physiological and behavioral components of exercise prescription are discussed.

Public Health Service, US Department of Health and Human Services: Promoting health/preventing disease: year 2000 objectives for the nation (draft), Washington, DC, 1989, US Government Printing Office.

    This document identifies each of the 21 priority areas, the specific objectives within each area, and background information pertaining to each objective.

Ravizza K: An old/new role for physical education: enhancing well-being, Journal of Physical Education, Recreation, and Dance 54(3):30-32, 1983

    The concept of holistic health as an integrated approach to well-being is discussed. Five health concepts that can be incorporated into the physical education curriculum are identified: integration of the whole person, stress management, establishment of a balanced perspective, self-awareness, and individual responsibility.

Chapter 4

Movement: The Keystone of Physical Education and Sport

INSTRUCTIONAL OBJECTIVES AND COMPETENCIES TO BE ACHIEVED

After reading this chapter the student should be able to—
- Explain why movement is the keystone of physical education and sport.
- Discuss and provide examples of the four movement concepts of body awareness, spatial awareness, qualities of movement, and relationships.
- Define and give examples of locomotor, nonlocomotor and manipulative skills.
- Discuss the relationship between locomotor and nonlocomotor skills and manipulative skills in the performance of specialized sport skills.
- Compare the traditional approach to teaching physical education to the movement education approach.
- Identify the key concepts of movement education.

Movement represents the key concern of physical educators. Movement is the central focus of this field of endeavor. Physical educators strive to help human beings to move efficiently, to increase the quality of their performance, to enhance their ability to learn, and to promote their health. Movement may be affected by biomechanical, physiological, sociological, and psychological factors. Since movement represents the keystone of physical education and sport, it is important that professionals in this field understand some of its dimensions.

Understanding of movement concepts such as body awareness, spatial awareness, qualities of movements, and relationships helps physical educators construct meaningful movement experiences to

obtain their stated objectives. Such experiences allow their students to understand the capabilities of the body with respect to movement. It is also important that children receive instruction in fundamental motor skills. Fundamental motor skills include locomotor skills such as running and jumping, nonlocomotor skills such as bending and stretching, and manipulative skills such as throwing and kicking. These fundamental skills serve as a foundation for the development of more complex and specialized skills that are utilized in sports and other physical education activities, work, and life situations in which human beings are involved in movement.

One approach that may be used to help children

develop an understanding of movement concepts and attain proficiency in fundamental motor skills is movement education. Movement education provides children with a variety of problem-solving situations carefully designed to help them explore the body's movement abilities and to develop movement skills.

GENERAL FACTORS THAT AFFECT MOVEMENT

Human movement involves most of the systems of the body, such as the skeletal system (e.g., skeletal levers), the nervous system (e.g., nerve impulses to the muscles), and the muscular system (e.g., muscular contractions for force). Human movement is concerned with mechanical principles or the forces that act on the human body and the effects that these forces produce (e.g., gravity).

All movement is governed by certain mechanical principles. An understanding of the forces that act on the body as it moves is essential if people are to engage in creative and meaningful movement. Understanding of the biomechanical principles of movement is important for physical educators if they are to teach movement skills effectively. (See Chapter 9.)

Physiological factors affect movement as well. Physical fitness and body build are two factors among the many that affect the way humans move. Poor muscular development is a deterring factor in generating force, and the mechanical advantage of levers might be reduced in a person that is small in stature. Furthermore, physical fitness qualities such as flexibility, endurance, and strength are basic to and will greatly influence motor performance. (See Chapter 6.)

Movement is also affected by psychological factors. Phenomena such as fear, anxiety, and self-concept might affect human movement in a positive or negative way. Fear or anxiety, for example, may prevent a performer from relaxing, thus impeding effective performance. (See Chapter 7.)

Sociological factors influence human movement. The persons with whom one is competing or performing, the relationship of the performer to the group, and the desire for social mobility are examples of sociological factors that may leave their impact on the quality of movement. (See Chapter 8.)

The biomechanical, physiological, psychological, and sociological factors that affect human movement are discussed later in this text, in Part Two.

Creative playgrounds provide opportunities for children to explore how the body can move.

MOVEMENT CONCEPTS

Certain concepts relating to movement must be understood by both physical educators and their students (regardless of age) if a meaningful understanding of the basic movement is to be attained.[1] These concepts are aspects of Rudolph Laban's[2] four components of movement: (1) *body awareness* (What can the body do?), (2) *spatial awareness* (Where does the body move?), (3) *qualities of movement* (How does the body move?), and (4) *relationships* (With whom or what does the body move?). Each of these concepts is discussed in this section. Objectives and suggested questions that teachers may pose to students to explore each of these areas are presented.

Body Awareness

The "what" aspect of movement refers to body awareness. The child should be able to identify body parts, be aware of what his or her body can do, and understand the relationship of body parts to the total self. Many body actions are developed by the time the child enters school, but the teacher should provide opportunities for students to continually explore body awareness.

In posing some of the problems that are suggested in this section, the teacher might find that some students will not be able to respond favorably. These students might have what are variously described as learning disabilities, perceptual-motor problems, and poor coordination. Children with perceptual-motor problems have difficulties in receiving information from stimuli of the various senses, processing the information, and responding with the appropriate movement pattern.

This section on body awareness deals mainly with identification of body parts and the ability of the children to engage in basic movement. Inherent in this type of study is an understanding of *laterality* (the awareness of right and left within the body) and *directionality* (the awareness of directions in space; that is, right, left, back, front, up, and down).

The objectives for studying body awareness are:
1. To be able to identify the parts of the body and the whole

2. To establish the relationship of parts to the whole
3. To have students locate body parts
4. To determine if students know what the body can do
5. To determine if students know what body parts can do
6. To provide opportunities for students to explore numerous body movements

Suggested questions for studying body awareness include:

Can you follow your partner, changing your shape as he or she does?

Can you do just what your partner does if you face each other?

Can you put two or three parts of your body together to make a hole that your partner can go through?

Movement of the Body and Its Parts

Basic skills can be divided into three categories: locomotor, nonlocomotor, and manipulative movements. Each can be considered separately for clarification. It is possible for a child to isolate and perform a selected movement or group of movements in a particular category. On the other hand, a move-

Students practice body part identification in this activity.

ment pattern might include a number of skills from different categories. For example, a child make shake his or her body (a nonlocomotor activity) while running across the floor (a locomotor skill).

Objectives for studying movement of the body and its parts are:

1. To develop locomotor movements:
   a. Even rhythm: walk, run, leap, hop, roll, and jump
   b. Uneven rhythm: skip, slide, and gallop
2. To develop nonlocomotor movements:
   a. Bend (curl) and stretch
   b. Twist and turn
   c. Push and pull
   d. Swing and sway
3. To develop manipulative movements:
   a. Bounce   f. Spin
   b. Throw   g. Roll
   c. Catch   h. Tap
   d. Strike   i. Turn
   e. Kick   j. Elevate

Suggested questions for teaching basic movement include:

Jumping:

If you are standing, how can you get both feet off the ground?

Can you land on both feet lightly? Heavily?

Can you jump forward, backward, and sideways?

How can you change the shape of your body as you jump to make your body tall, round, or other different shapes?

Can you do the following combinations of movements: walk and jump; run and jump; and hop and jump?

Pulling (think of something or someone that you can pull):

Can you pull it toward you? From the front? From the sides? From the back or up or down?

Can you show how heavy or light it is by the way you pull?

Can you pull yourself or something away from your partner?

Can you pull yourself up from a low position while hanging on to your partner?

Body Shape

Body shape refers to the position of the body to space. Changing shapes is movement. For example, the body can be extended (long or wide or straight) or flexed (tucked or curled small and round). In addition to shaping the body to move in certain restricted spaces, various activities require the body to assume certain shapes. In performing somersaults from a diving board, for example, a tuck position will enable the performer to turn faster. A tuck position is assumed by bringing the knees close to the chest and the heels close to the buttocks. In performing the front somersault, however, the diver would have to extend the legs to straighten out the body before it reaches the vertical position. The feet would begin the entry into the water when performing a forward somersault.

The objectives of a program to study body shape are:

1. To learn what shapes the body is capable of assuming
2. To be able to control changes from one shape to another with a smooth, flowing action

Suggested questions for studying the concept of body shape include:

Can you make a crooked shape and walk that way?

Can you make yourself tall, then small; wide, then narrow? Can you make yourself both wide and tall; round and tall; round and small?

Can you make a different shape, hold it for 5 seconds then make another shape? Can you develop a smooth flow from one shape to another?

Other Aspects of Body Awareness

Young children are eager to learn about and explore the myriad possibilities of the various parts of the body in movement. In addition to the ability of body parts to engage in basic movement, the body is also capable of absorbing the impact of its weight on different body parts (for example, landing from a jump), or receiving the weight of an outside object (for example, catching a ball). The weight of the body may be supported by many body parts. This is important in many gymnastic and dance movements.

The body parts also can be used to express certain feelings (for example, sadness, happiness, and joy) and to imitate animate and inanimate objects (for example, like a dog wagging its tail, like a bird flapping its wings, or the Statue of Liberty). Many other body actions are possible, and the teacher must be imaginative in posing problems for the students and bringing out some of their creative energies.

Some of the specific objectives of a program to further explore capabilities of body parts are:

1. To be able to use parts to support the body (bear weight), such as performing a headstand
2. To be able to use body parts to transfer weight, such as executing a skipping movement
3. To be able to use body parts to lead an action, such as bending the knees and thrusting the arms upward in a jump
4. To be able to demonstrate that body parts can meet and part, as in performing bending and stretching exercises
5. To be able to express ideas with body parts, such as exhibiting a feeling of happiness by using the arms
6. To be able to perform activities using both symmetrical and asymmetrical movements, such as performing a forward roll (symmetrical) in gymnastics and a buzz step (asymmetrical) in dance.*

Suggested questions for studying selected aspects of body parts include:

Can you balance on a part of your body all curled up?

Can you balance on your back?

Can you balance in an inverted position?

Can you balance on your hands?

Can you use your body parts to imitate an animal?

Can you move on your knees?

---

*Symmetrical movement refers to movement executed by the body when both sides contribute equally to the impetus for the movement. (Symmetrical movement can occur in only four directions: forward, backward, up, and down.) When a body part or body parts on one side dominate a movement, it is an asymetrical movement.

Spatial Awareness

Spatial awareness includes the type of space in which the body moves as well as the direction, level, and pathway that the body takes in movement.

Space

All movement takes place in space. Space is of two kinds—personal and general. Personal space is the largest space available to a person in a stationary position. This includes the space that a person can reach by stretching, bending, and twisting. General space includes the area in which one person or several persons can move. It might be in the gymnasium, the swimming pool, or the hallway.

The amount of space available and the number of persons in a particular space affect movement possibilities. Understanding the concepts of personal space and general space is crucial to the student's future growth in movement. Rarely is this understanding reached in a single lesson; therefore this concept should be reinforced often.

The objectives of a program to teach spatial awareness include:

1. To establish verbal cues to begin and to stop movement in a particular area
2. To establish awareness of personal space and general space
3. To establish safety awareness while moving in personal and general space by encouraging no touching and no collisions

Suggested questions for studying personal space and general space are the following:

Can they explore space around the body by reaching in all directions with different parts of the body?

Can they keep the feet in one position on the floor and reach for something circling around them?

Can they move into general space, bounce a ball, and maintain control without running into anyone or letting the ball hit anyone?

Direction

With an understanding of personal and general space, the student can now apply directional

The teacher poses questions to help students explore their self-space.

changes while moving in space. Direction refers to movements forward, backward, sideways, upward, downward, diagonally, or any combination of these. The ability to move in a variety of directions is vital to success in such areas as sport, dance, and gymnastics.

The objective in teaching the concepts of direction is to have the students understand directional terminology. They should understand all of the directions listed in the preceding paragraph.

Suggested questions for studying direction might include:

In what direction can they walk? Can they walk in another direction?

Can they walk forward? Backward? Sideways?

Can they move a ball around in all directions within their personal space? Can they keep passing the ball from hand to hand?

Level

The body moves on various horizontal planes such as high, medium, and low. Levels exist in personal and general space and in all locomotor and axial (nonlocomotor) movements.

The objectives of teaching the concept of level include:

1. To differentiate among high, medium, and low levels
2. To be able to change levels
3. To combine level changes while using directions and space

Questions for studying level might include:

How low can the body go? How high can the body go?

Can the student move with hands low and toes high?

Can the student change from high to medium to low level while running, skipping, and jumping in a forward direction?

Pathways

A pathway is a line of movement from one place to another in a given space. It might be the movement of the entire body in a general space (e.g., to run from home to first base in a softball game) or the movement of a part of the body in a personal space (e.g., a level [horizontal] swing of the bat with the arms).

All movement takes place in space. Dancer Nelson Neal utilizes space as he makes his turns, leaps, and jumps look effortless.

The objectives for teaching the concept of pathways are:

1. To create student awareness of alternative pathways in which they can move; that is, direct and indirect pathways
2. To develop the ability of the body to move through many pathways
3. To have the students identify and move on specific pathways

Suggested questions for studying pathways might include:

What is the shortest pathway to the wall?

Can the students travel in a zigzag path? Circular path?

In what pathways can the arm move? What other parts of the body can move in different pathways, and what are the pathways?

Qualities of Movement

How the body moves is affected by certain qualities of movement including time, force, and flow. Additional factors such as body shape and the relationship of the body to other people or objects also affect body movement.

Time

Time is related to the speed at which movement takes place. This may vary from very quick movements to extremely slow movements. In many sport activities a change in speed is necessary. For example, a runner in touch football might be required to slow down to let the blockers ward off the opponents and then speed up to outrun them to the goal line. Sudden explosive movements are also necessary in some sport activities such as basketball, in which considerable power is necessary to rebound the ball.

The objectives of a program to study the concept of time are:

1. To differentiate among speeds—slow, moderate, or fast
2. To be able to increase or decrease the speed of movement—accelerate or decelerate
3. To be able to perform evenly or unevenly in time—sudden, jerky, smooth, or even movement; variation in rhythm

Suggested questions for studying the concept of time include:

How slowly can you walk from one end of the gymnasium to the other, keeping your feet moving all the time?

Can you slide to the side of the gymnasium at regular speed and return in slow motion?

Can you walk (run, skip, or hop), changing your speed each time the drum is sounded?

How fast can you make your body go while staying in one place?

Force

Force is the effect that one body has on another. Force generated by the body is produced by the contraction of muscles. In addition to producing force, the body is also capable of applying and absorbing force. Different movements or actions

How the body moves is affected by certain qualities of movement, including time, force, and flow.

require the production of varying degrees of force and proper application of that force to sustain those movements. For example, because of the difference in the weight of the object, it takes more force to throw a softball than it does to throw a wiffleball. However, less force would be required to hit a ball with a long bat than it would to hit the same ball with a shorter bat; the longer lever would create a mechanical advantage.

The extremes of force might be described as strong and weak, heavy and light, hard and soft, and harsh and gentle. The amount used will depend on the movement attempted. In kicking a soccer ball, for instance, it would take a stronger force to kick the ball 25 yards than it would to kick the ball 10 yards. On the other hand, it takes a light force to properly dribble a soccer ball.

Many opportunities exist for the use of force in movement. It might be used to move the body or its parts in space, to resist the natural pull of gravity, or

to maintain a good posture. An important factor in the consideration of force is that it can be controlled.

The objectives of a program to study the concept of force are:

1. To differentiate between light or weak and heavy or strong forces and in between these extremes
2. To be able to control the tension of muscles to the extent that is needed to fulfill the purpose of a task
3. To be able to effectively utilize different degrees of force

Suggested questions for studying the concept of force include:

Can you walk softly?

Can you jump into the air and land very lightly like a feather?

Can you throw the ball softly to a classmate?

How hard can you bounce the ball against the wall? How softly?

Flow

Flow is the continuity or coordination of move-ments. A smooth, flowing movement requires the control of external and internal forces so that there will be proper transition among the various move-ments. Movements may be free flowing or they may be movements of bound flow. Free flow movement describes a movement that is continued to a con-trolled conclusion. On the other hand, bound flow refers to movements that can be momentarily stopped while the balance is maintained at several points in the movement. A good example of bound flow movements is a routine on the mat in free floor exercises. At several points in the routine the per-former is required to hold movements in a balanced position yet create a continuous, well-coordinated routine.

The objectives of a program to study the concept of flow are:

1. To differentiate between free flow and bound flow
2. To be able to perform efficient, graceful movements
3. To perform movements with sudden breaks and holds

Suggested questions for studying the concept of flow include:

Can you make your body quiver?

Can you run and go into any type of roll, come out of it into a run, and keep your flow of movement going?

Can you roll on the floor, stop in a balanced posi-tion, hold for 3 seconds, and continue rolling?

On the horizontal bar, how many times can you swing back and forth without stopping? How can you increase the number of swings? Why?

Relationships

In most games, dance, and apparatus activities chil-dren do not move alone in space. They move with someone, oppose someone, overcome obstacles, or use implements of some type.

Relationships with Objects

Relationships with objects are of two basic forms—manipulative and nonmanipulative. In the

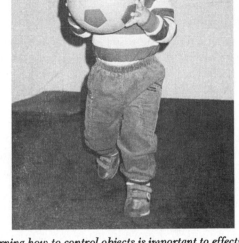

Learning how to control objects is important to effective movement.

first case the performer is concerned with control-ling the movement of the object. In the second case the purpose is to adapt his or her movement to a stationary object. An example of a manipulative form is throwing a ball; an example of a nonmanip-ulative form is the movement of a boy or girl on a tumbling mat.

The basic objectives of a program for studying the relationships of the performer to objects are:

1. To be able to exercise control over an object through isolated or intermittent contact with it (hitting a ball) or through continuous contact (carrying a ball)
2. To be able to adapt one's movements to an obstacle
3. To be able to direct one's movement toward a target, goal, or focal point (shoot a basketball at a goal)

Suggested questions for studying relationships with objects include:

Can you go over (along, under) benches using different movements and body shapes?

How many times can you and your partner hit the volleyball back and forth to each other without stopping?

Can you discover different ways to volley a ball against a wall? Who can volley the ball against the wall in a way that has not been shown?

Relationships with People

Movement may be and often is done in relationship to other people. Several possibilities may develop. The absence of another mover (individual work) provides a situation in which the performer is entirely free and responsible for his or her own movement. When working with a partner one may imitate the other's movement pattern, perform a movement together, or oppose the other's pattern, or each may do his or her own pattern but relate it to that of the other. When working in a group, one may move following a teacher, move with several other people, move in response or opposition to another group, and move in many other situations. All movements with other people must be coordinated.

The overall objective in a program to study relationships of persons to persons is to be able to coordinate the movement patterns in space, with a view toward utilizing the knowledge about qualities of movement, body awareness, and different movement forms.

Many problems are available in games and everyday activities to study relationships. The suggested questions to get teachers started include:

Can you move across the room with a partner? Can you stay close together without touching each other?

Can you face a partner who is the leader and mirror his or her actions? (Change leaders.)

Can you move with a partner, each moving in your own pattern, always adjusting to the movement of your partner?

Acquiring an understanding of movement is an essential part of the early physical education experience. A knowledge of the factors affecting movement is important to future learning. Since effective movement requires the ability to modify one's movements to fit the context of the situation and

An understanding of movement concepts aids in the performance of sport skills. Selected movement concepts applied to soccer are shown in Figure 4-1.

the intended goal, learning to use the body and space efficiently and to modify the quality of one's movement is essential.[1] This understanding is then applied to the performance of fundamental motor skills and later to the development and execution of specialized sport and dance skills.

SELECTED FUNDAMENTAL MOVEMENTS

Fundamental movement actions refer to those locomotor and nonlocomotor skills that are the foundation for successful participation in games of low organization, sports, dance, tumbling, and gymnastics, and aquatic and other physical activities. Locomotor skills are those in which the body moves through space, and nonlocomotor skills are those positions that the body assumes without moving the base of support. Fundamental movement skills must be combined with manipulative skills to create

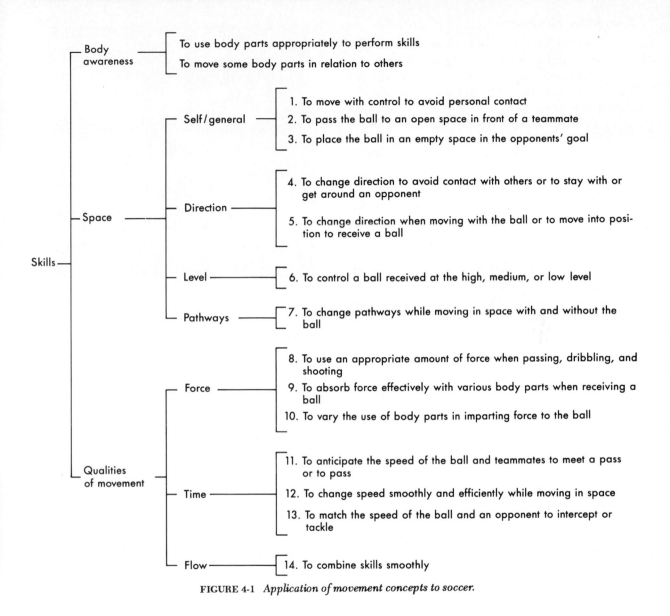

FIGURE 4-1 *Application of movement concepts to soccer.*

the specialized movement necessary in many activities. Manipulative skills are body activities involving objects; throwing and catching, striking, and kicking an object are examples of manipulative skills. One example of a combined skill is the softball throw. The softball throw requires a combination of slide stepping (locomotor skill) and throwing (manipulative skill) as well as nonlocomotor movements such as stretching, swinging, twisting, and turning. Other specialized sport skills require more complex combinations of movements.

This section contains an analysis of eight locomotor and eight nonlocomotor movement skills. Four manipulative skills are also discussed.

Locomotor Movements

The following locomotor movement skills are discussed: walking, running, jumping (for distance and height), hopping, leaping, skipping, sliding, and galloping. These are the skills most commonly used by elementary school children. Provisions for students to explore and use these skills by themselves and in combination with nonlocomotor movements should provide a sufficient foundation for more complex movement skills.

Walking. Walking involves the transfer of weight from one foot to the other while moving. In walking the weight of the body is transferred in a forward direction from the heel to the ball of the foot and then to the toes. The feet should move parallel to each other, with the toes pointing straight ahead. The arm action is coordinated with leg action; the opposite arm and leg move in the same direction. All of these movements should be rhythmical and natural.

Running. Running is actually walking at an increased tempo. In running the body is not supported at all for a momentary period. The body leans forward in running to place the center of gravity above the front foot in the stride.

Jumping. Jumping for distance and jumping for height are commonly the goals involving these skills. The standing broad jump, for example, is performed by bending the knees and lowering the upper body into a stooped position. As the body rocks back on the feet, the arms are brought down and beyond the hips; the upward pull of the arms is coordinated with the push of the feet and legs. The body is propelled forward as if reaching for an object in front of the body. The landing is on the feet with the body falling forward.

Hopping. Hopping involves jumping from one foot to the same foot after a brief suspension in the air. The push off from the floor is made from the toes and the ball of the foot, with the knee of the opposite foot bent and the foot off the ground. The arms are thrust upward to aid in body lift. The landing is on the toes, ball, and heel of the foot in that order. The knee is slightly bent to help absorb the shock of the landing.

Bending movements are frequently used in gymnastic activities.

Leaping. A leap is a jump from one foot to the other foot while moving the body forward. In a sense it is an exaggerated run, with the stride longer and the body projected higher in the air. In the leap the toes of the take-off foot leave the floor last and the landing is on the ball of the opposite foot. Before the execution of the leap a short run should be taken to gain momentum for the leap itself. The arms should be extended upward and forward to give added lift to the body during the leap.

Skipping. A skip is a combination of a step and a hop with alternating feet after each step-hop. A long step is taken on one foot, followed by a hop on the same foot, and then a step with the opposite foot, again followed by a hop. Balance is aided by swinging the arms in opposition to the legs.

Sliding. A slide is a sideways movement in which the weight of the body is shifted in the direction of the slide. In a slide to the right the left foot pushes off the floor and the right foot moves sideways and assumes the weight. The left foot is quickly brought close to the right foot, and the weight is transferred back to the left foot. The same foot continues to lead in sliding movements. The body maintains an upright posture and the arms may be used for balance. The legs should not be crossed.

Galloping. Galloping is a combination of a step and a leap, and it is performed in a forward or backward direction. The gallop is similar to the slide except that the leap is higher and it is not a sideways movement. In a forward gallop the lead foot moves forward and assumes the weight; the rear foot is brought forward and close to the lead foot. In the gallop the step is long and the leap is short. The stepping leg is always the lead leg.

Nonlocomotor Movements

The nonlocomotor movement skills discussed are bending, stretching, twisting, turning, pushing, pulling, lifting, and swinging. Some of these skills have been performed by children since their infancy. However, a conscious effort by physical education teachers to ensure that they are executed correctly is important.

Bending and Stretching

Bending. Bending is a movement occurring at the joints of the body in which body parts are brought closer together. For example, by bending the body at the hips to touch the toes, a person is decreasing the angle between the upper and lower body at the hip joint. This is technically called *flexion*. Bending movements may be in several directions; for example, forward, backward, sideways, or in a circular motion. Also several bending movements can occur at the same time. An example of a skill in which two bending movements are necessary is the arm curl with weights, which requires bending of the elbows and wrists. When using a barbell, the arm curl is executed by holding the barbell in the hands (palms away from the body) with the elbows close to the body. The arms are flexed, first at the elbow and then at the wrist, to bring the weight up to the chest. The upper arms should remain stationary throughout the movement. Contrast this bending with the many body parts that must bend to position for a forward roll.

The range of bending movements is determined by the type of joint at which the movement occurs. Ball-and-socket joints permit the greatest movement. Hip joints and shoulder joints are examples of ball-and-socket joints. Hinge joints permit only backward and forward movements. The knee joint is a hinge joint.

Stretching. A stretch is an extension or hyperextension of the joints of the body. Stretching is the opposite of bending. Most movements require only complete extension where the body parts adjacent to the joints are at a straight angle (180 degrees). However, in movements such as the wrist cock before a throw, hyperextension is needed to give added impetus to the throw. Bending and stretching are necessary to maintain flexibility—the full range of movement about a joint.

Bending and stretching are common to most of the activities of daily life, and they are very important to physical education activities. Teachers should provide daily activities in which these skills can be practiced and refined.

Twisting and Turning

Twisting. Twisting is a rotation of the body or a body part around its axis while maintaining a fixed base of support. As in bending and stretching movements, twisting and turning movements are determined by the structure of the joints involved in the movement. The upper body may be twisted at the waist, or the shoulders may be twisted about the spinal column.

Turning. Turning is a rotation of the body or a body part around in space. When the entire body is turned, the base of support is shifted from one position to another. Turning of a body part is the result of twisting of adjacent body parts. For example, the foot can be turned in or out by rotating the leg. Likewise, when the head is turned, the neck is rotated.

Pushing and Pulling

Pushing. Pushing involves the exertion of the body's force against a resistance force. The purpose of pushing movements is to move objects away from their base of support. The body may also be moved away from its base of support by pushing it against an object.

Pulling. Pulling involves directing an object

Swinging activities utilize the concept of flow.

toward the body. Children usually pull wagons or toys and during play might pull one another. Pulling and pushing are usually done with the hands and arms, although one can use the legs and feet.

Lifting

To lift an object or body part is to raise it from one level to another. In lifting heavy objects, the base of support should be wider than normal and the body should be lowered (by bending at the knees) and close to the object that is to be lifted. Primarily the muscles of the legs are used in lifting heavy objects. The back should be relatively straight. Lifting objects is a skill that is used in many everyday activities and should be executed properly to avoid muscle strain.

Implements such as balls and bats must be lifted and manipulated in games and sports. Spotters in gymnastics and partners in some dance activities are required to lift each other at various times. Care must be taken in performing efficient lifting movements.

Swinging

A swing is a circular or pendular movement of a body part or of the entire body around a stationary center point. The center point may be a joint, such as the shoulder in swinging the arm, or an outside axis, such as the swing on a high bar. When the force necessary to hold a body stationary is released,

the force of gravity will cause that body part to swing. In most body movements the force of muscular contractions is necessary to maintain body swing. Swinging movements should be continuous and free flowing.

Manipulative Skills

Manipulative skills involve the utilization of body parts to generate force to propel an object as well as to absorb force from an object. The manipulative skills discussed are throwing, catching, kicking, and striking.

Throwing

Throwing an object may involve the utilization of an underhand, sidearm, or overhand pattern incorporating the use of one or both hands, depending on the purpose of the throw. Since the overhand throwing pattern is most frequently employed by children and adults, this movement will be described.

When throwing, the ball is held in the fingers of the throwing hand. As the throwing action is initiated, the ball is brought back and the body rotates so the opposite side is towards the target. Weight is transferred back to the foot on the same side as the throwing hand. The arm is bent at the elbow, and the elbow leads slightly as the arm is brought forward for the throw. As the arm accelerates, a step forward onto the opposite foot is taken and the hips rotate forward. The arm quickly extends, the wrist snaps, and the ball is released. The arm follows in the direction of the throw, coming down and across the body.

Catching

Catching involves the use of hands to stop and gain control of an object. As the object approaches, the individual makes a judgement as to where it can be intercepted and moves to a location directly in line with the object, placing the hands in a position for effective reception. The eyes follow the flight of the object, and both hands reach out toward it. The object is grasped by the hands and pulled in by the arms and hands toward the body to absorb the object's force.

Kicking

Kicking is imparting force to an object through the use of the foot and the leg. The kicking of a stationary object is the foundation for the kicking of a moving object and for punting.

In kicking, the supporting foot is placed alongside the object. The kicking leg, knee bent, moving freely from the hip, swings through an arc toward the object. As the foot contacts the object, the knee is extended, and the body leans back for balance. The kicking leg follows through, continuing its movement toward the direction of the flight of the object. The arms, relaxed, move in opposition to the legs. The eyes focus on the object throughout the kick.

Striking

Striking involves using the body part (e.g., hand) or an implement (e.g., paddle or bat) to apply force to a stationary or moving object. The length, size, and weight of the implement as well as characteristics of the object being struck influence the nature of the movement pattern. Kicking, described above, is also considered to be a striking task.

For the striking action typically seen in batting, the body is positioned perpendicular to the line of flight of the oncoming ball. The feet are placed in a forward-backward stride position, approximately shoulder-width apart. The trunk is rotated back, the weight is shifted to the rear foot, and a backswing is taken. The flight of the ball is followed by the eyes until just prior to making contact. Body weight is shifted onto the forward foot in the direction of the intended flight of the ball. With the hips leading, the hips and trunk are rotated in the same direction as the weight shift. Arms move forward into contact, and the follow-through action occurs in the direction of the line of flight.

Fundamental motor skills are the foundation for the development of specialized sport and dance skill. Acquisition of sport and dance skills for lifetime participation begins with the mastery of these fundamental movement skills. Teachers of children must make sure that all students, the skilled and the unskilled, the typical and the atypical, have suffi-

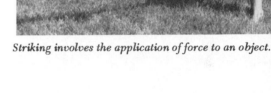

Striking involves the application of force to an object.

cient opportunities and experiences to master these important movement basics.

• • •

Movement is the central focus of physical education. Teachers have an obligation to become familiar with the science of movement if they are to help children learn to execute movement skills in the most efficient manner of which their bodies are capable. Opportunities should be provided for children to explore the various possibilities of human movement and to understand why and how their bodies move as they do in performing movement skills.

NATURE OF MOVEMENT EDUCATION

Movement education is an important aspect of physical education programs, particularly at the elementary school level. Movement education explores the science of movement and consists of an educational program designed to help young people become more aware of their bodies and teach them how to have better and more effective movement.

Physical education in the elementary school is

Fundamental skills are the foundation for the development of specialized sport skills. Can you identify the other fundamental skills used in softball?

FIGURE 4-2 *Relationship of Fundamental Motor Skills to Specialized Sport Skills*

Fundamental Skills ⟶	Specialized Sport Skills
Locomotor Skills	Archery skills
Walking	Baseball skills
Running	Basketball skills
Leaping	Dance skills
Jumping	Football skills
Hopping	Gymnastic skills
Galloping	Hockey skills
Sliding	•
Skipping	•
Climbing	•
	•
Nonlocomotor Skills	•
Bending	•
Stretching	•
Twisting	•
Turning	•
Pushing	•
Pulling	•
Lifting	•
Swinging	•
Starting	•
Stopping	•
Dodging	•
Manipulative Skills	•
Throwing	Racquet skills
Catching	Skiing skills
Kicking	Soccer skills
Striking	Softball skills
Volleying	Swimming skills
Dribbling	Track and field skills
Rolling	Volleyball skills

emerging as the art and science of human movement. It instills in the child the "why" of movement, the "how" of movement, and the physiological, sociological, and psychological results of movement. In addition, concern is shown for movement skills and motor patterns that make up the movement repertoire of human beings.

Through movement children express themselves, are creative, develop a positive self-image, and gain a better understanding of their physical selves. It is through movement experiences that young children explore, develop, and grow in a meaningful manner.

Movement is integral to the human being. Everything that people do, whether they are reacting to the environment or simply expressing themselves, involves movement of some sort. Movement is thus a tool of life; the more efficiently a person moves, the more meaningful life is.

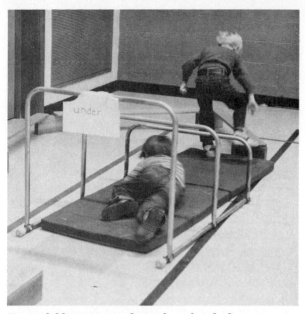

Young children enjoy exploring how their bodies can move.

Movement is a means of communication, often called *preverbal language.* It is with movement that one can express feelings without using spoken language. Dance educators have advocated that it is almost impossible to communicate the emotions of a dance by using language, but the imagery of a dance can be conveyed with the body.

Movement experiences can be extremely beautiful, and a knowledge of movement will contribute to a richer appreciation of such experiences. Being aware of the gracefulness of a skier gliding down the slopes or the well-controlled movements of the gymnast performing on the parallel bars can make these events more enjoyable for the viewer. Of course, the experience derived by the individual performer yields the greatest reward of all.

Movement educators seek not only to have the individual understand and appreciate the movement of which he or she is capable but also to appreciate the varieties of movement of which others are capable.

Programs of movement education are not conducted haphazardly. Rather, they are structured on a problem-solving basis, leaving individuals free to relate to force, time, and space through their particular use of balance, leverage, and technique. Movement educators believe that numerous activities have common elements, all of which are based on a comprehensive knowledge of movement fundamentals. The better the individual is able to perceive movement patterns, they believe, the more ease there will be in developing skills, since these skills will tend to develop as a concomitant of learning to move.

Movement education strives to make the individual aware of the movement of the entire body and to become intellectually as well as physically involved. The challenge set by a problem in movement is first perceived by the intellect and then solved by the body moving through space, reacting to any obstacles within that space and to the limitations and existing restrictions. Learning accrues as the individual accepts and attempts to solve increasingly difficult problems. Inherent in this is the concept of individual differences. Numerous ways to solve a stated problem may exist, and one chooses the method that best suits one's abilities and capacities. Individual development rather than group development is the basic premise of movement education.

Thus movement education may be defined as individual exploration of the ability of the body to relate and react to the physical concepts of the environment and to factors in the environment, be they material or human.

Both the terms *movement education* and *movement exploration* are used in educational circles—sometimes synonymously. However, those who have studied this subject intensively generally think that *movement education* refers to the system, the sum of the educational experiences, or programs that are utilized in teaching children about their bodies and movement and that help them to develop desirable movement responses. On the other hand, *movement exploration* refers more to the methodology, or the process, that is used, such as the problem-solving approach, which helps children to develop body awareness and utilize their bodies in an effective manner unique to their own physical resources.

ORIGINS OF MOVEMENT EDUCATION

The roots of movement education may be traced to the theories of Rudolf Laban,[2,3] a dancer, and to the effect his theories had on physical education in England, where he established the Laban Art of Movement Centre, an institution that has trained many movement educators.

Laban stressed that the body is the instrument through and by which people move and that each individual is endowed with certain natural kinds of movement. Laban believed strongly in exploratory movement and in a spontaneous quality in movement. He was opposed to the rigidity of set series of exercises that restrained creativity and self-expression. Laban was a movement analyst, and as such he believed that people not only could learn to move efficiently and effectively, but also could develop a strong kinesthetic awareness of movement.

During World War II England revised its entire educational structure and restated its philosophy of education. Physical education had once been little more than formal gymnastics, but now freedom of bodily movement, creativity, and expression were emphasized. Laban's principles were freely employed. Through the years they have been expanded and broadened into the concept of movement education as it is known in England today.

In England the classroom teacher is in charge of physical education in the elementary schools. Beginning in the first grade both boys and girls are educated in movement. In the secondary schools the movement education program is continued under the guidance of a trained physical educator. The program is based on problem solving. The teacher sets the problem and then guides, assists, and suggests but in no way dictates a solution. There is no teacher demonstration and thus no imitation, leaving children to establish their own patterns of movement, set their own tempo, and make wise use of space.

Within the last 25 to 30 years a trend toward concentrated movement education has developed in the United States, based on the English programs. Unlike programs in England, however, where

Developing confidence as a mover is important to the young child.

movement education is concentrated in the early school years, U.S. movement education programs first received impetus in the college and university physical education programs for women. These programs have attempted to develop movement patterns as the dancer's vehicle of expression. A working definition of movement education terms was introduced in 1956 by the National Association for Physical Education of College Women so that educators could communicate with each other more effectively.

In recent years movement education has become incorporated into elementary school programs in the U.S. Many nonschool physical education programs for younger children have made an effort to incorporate movement education into their programs. The leaders in the field of movement education agree that this concept should play a vital role in determining the future direction of physical education, particularly in the elementary grades.

TRADITIONAL APPROACH VERSUS MOVEMENT EDUCATION

The traditional approach to physical education needs little explanation. Syllabuses, or course outlines, specify several weeks of one activity followed by several weeks of another, often unrelated, activity. In the elementary schools in the U.S. games of low organization, folk and square dances, tumbling and gymnastics, and lead-up games often make up the major part of the program. Later school years, for both boys and girls, are devoted to the learning of specific sport skills. Rhythmics, or fundamental movement, is sometimes included but as a minor phase of the program.

The movement education approach to physical education is founded on an entirely different premise. Movement education is not a "gap filler" or several lessons but an ongoing method of teaching physical education beginning with the earliest school years. Movement education does not abandon or fully supplant the traditional approach as we know it. Rather, it forms a firmer foundation for more meaningful skill learning, for increased pleasure in the skillful use of the body, and for the development of lifelong physical effectiveness and efficiency.

To understand the full meaning of movement education, it is necessary to identify and compare its various key concepts. In so doing it will be possible to see it as a part of the whole that is physical education. Table 4-1 shows a comparison of movement education concepts and traditional physical education concepts that will prove useful in differentiating between these two approaches to the teaching of physical education.

KEY CONCEPTS OF MOVEMENT EDUCATION

Movement education has been widely accepted by physical educators because certain basic concepts emphasize its importance in educational programs.

Movement education is individual exploration. Through individual exploration students are encouraged to find their own solutions to problems involving physical movement. Although various ways to solve the problem may be available, children choose the method that best suits their abilities. Furthermore, this individual exploration is concerned with the natural movements of childhood. Children enjoy running, jumping, climbing, leaping, and other physical movements, and they tend to perform these movements of their own volition. Movement educators seek to capitalize on these natural movements of childhood as they guide the child through an individual exploration of the many variations of these movements.

Formal physical education programs tend to stress conformity to stylized patterns of movement. Movement educators believe that the child's individualized patterns of movement can be reinforced and retained. Movement education classes provide unlimited opportunities for children to explore the uses of their bodies for movement in ways that are creative and self-expressive.

Many patterns are used for the exploration process, two of which are the locomotion and balance patterns. In the *locomotion pattern* the child moves about from one area to another. For example, a child may be asked to walk around a room without colliding with other children or with walls or apparatus. This is the beginning of learning to use space wisely and controlling the body within the confines of an area. With the various locomotor patterns such as running, jumping, and hopping the child is encouraged to analyze the differences between these movements and the concept known as walking. The child who is given the opportunity to participate in such experiences will soon become aware of how the movements of one part of the body influence the other parts. For example, the child who runs around in a circle will become aware of how the body leans toward the center as this movement pattern is performed. By individual exploration the child is encouraged to discover what the body can and cannot do while walking, running, or jumping.

Through individual exploration the child is also given the opportunity to participate in experiences that will help in understanding the concept known as *balance*. The child will become more fully aware of the mechanisms involved in maintaining the same position in space by participating in the vari-

TABLE 4-1   A Comparison of Movement Education and Traditional Physical Education Concepts

Movement Education	*Traditional Physical Education*
A. The program	
1. The program is activity centered.	1. The program is verbally centered.
2. The program is student centered.	2. The program is teacher centered.
3. The program attempts to develop an intellectual awareness of the body.	3. The program attempts to develop skills often lacking in intellectual comprehension.
4. The program emphasizes the problem solving method, which includes exploration and discovery, based on the individual needs of the student.	4. The teacher serves as a model to be imitated by the students, and the method includes lecture and demonstration based on the needs of the group.
5. Repetition of problems leads to a greater variety of solutions.	5. Repetition of drills leads to improved performance in motor skills.
6. Syllabus develops as each class period uncovers individual needs that must be explored.	6. Syllabus, often unrelated to previous learning experiences, is presented to the students.
B. Role of the teacher	
1. The teacher educates students in the learning process.	1. The teacher trains the students in the learning process.
2. The teacher uses imaginative and creative teaching methods.	2. The teacher utilizes the traditional teaching methods.
3. The teacher guides the students in their activities.	3. The teacher leads the students in their activities.
C. Role of students	
1. Motivation for learning comes from inner self.	1. Motivation for learning comes from the teacher.
2. Students experience the joy of their own natural movements and unique style.	2. Individual body types are not considered.
3. Students demonstrate their ability to reason logically and intelligently.	3. Students demonstrate their ability to take orders and follow directions.
4. Students demonstrate independence.	4. Students often lack independence.
5. Students face each new situation in an enthusiastic and intelligent manner.	5. Students often exhibit difficulty when confronted with new situations.
6. Students evaluate their own progress.	6. The teacher evaluates each student's progress.
7. Students develop at their own rate of progress.	7. Rate of progress depends on the norm of the student development within the class.
8. Success is based on each student's goals.	8. Success is based on the teacher's goals.
9. Students compete with themselves.	9. Students compete with classmates.
D. Class atmosphere	
1. The class atmosphere is informal.	1. The class atmosphere is formal.
2. Varied formations are used.	2. Set formations are used.
3. The teacher exhibits permissive behavior.	3. The teacher exhibits strict behavior.
4. Individual needs of the students determine the allotment of time for any activity.	4. The completion of the subject matter determines the allotment of time for any activity.
E. Facilities and equipment	
1. The facilities are considered secondary to the need for a resourceful and creative teacher.	1. Facilities are of prime importance, although the need for a creative and resourceful teacher is recognized.
2. The equipment is created to meet the needs of the individual.	2. The individual must adjust to the equipment.
3. The equipment is used in many different situations.	3. The equipment is limited in its use.

Movement education encourages children to explore the various positions of their bodies in space.

ous balance patterns. One of the basic balance patterns is the standing position. Through individual exploration the child, by changing the position of the feet or by moving the head, will become aware of the position that must be maintained if proper balance is to result. For example, the child who places all body weight on the toes will soon realize that this is not the proper standing position, and by exploring other foot positions, the child will become aware that weight must be concentrated on the whole foot if one is to experience proper balance.

With individual exploration the child is given the opportunity to be creative. As one participates in various movement patterns, one discovers what movements the body can make, in what directions the body can move, and what parts of the body are involved in executing a specific movement. Individual exploration is an extremely important concept of movement education. Physical education teachers should motivate their students and encourage them to participate in experiences that will aid them in creating various movement patterns. Through individual exploration it is hoped that

students will discover their unique abilities and solutions to their particular problems.

Movement education is student centered. Whereas traditional physical education has been concerned with the role of the teacher in the learning process and has focused much attention on the teacher, movement education looks to the student as the center of the learning process. In movement education the individual needs of each student have priority, and the motivation for learning comes from the student's inner self rather than from the teacher. It is the task of the teacher to guide, observe, and set the tone of each class. In movement education students are given the opportunity to experience the joy of their own natural movements and unique style. The student who participates in movement programs does not merely take orders and follow the teacher's directions but instead demonstrates independence and ability to reason logically and intelligently. Students are challenged to discover their own unique methods and techniques for solving problems in movement or in a skill performance. No one method is assumed to be the only acceptable answer; thus students are free to use their own bodies in an individually suitable manner.

The teacher should be creative and imaginative, thereby guiding students to success by helping them to evaluate and refine their movements and by providing encouragement. For example, if a child is experiencing difficulty in attempting to jump onto a platform, the teacher might ask: "Can you use your arms in any way to jump higher?" After receiving this information from the teacher, the student will still be encouraged to perform the movement and discover by individual exploration whether the arms help in jumping higher. Thus students become resourceful and are better able to face new problems with the confidence that they can solve them.

Any student can participate meaningfully in the movement education program regardless of size or athletic ability. Individual students can work on their own needs and progress at their own pace, compete with themselves rather than with the group as a whole, and look to personal abilities to provide solutions to problems.

In movement education programs it is frequently apparent that while some children are working on a simple movement, others in the class are working on a more complex movement. The answers that children find to their own problems will be different, but all are acceptable because success is measured with respect to the particular movement and abilities of the participants in performing that movement.

Movement education involves problem solving. Movement education begins with simple problems. Learning accrues as the student solves these problems and then seeks to solve increasingly more complex ones. Repetition of various problems is aimed at obtaining a greater variety of solutions. If children are first asked to walk around a room without colliding with each other and perform that task successfully, the movement educator may then ask the children to run or hop or jump around the room without colliding with anyone. By beginning with the simple, natural skills of childhood the movement educator is adhering closely to the known facts of child growth and development; that

is, the large muscles and gross motor skills develop first. The movement educator seeks to enhance this development to pave the way for the later development of the finer motor skills and coordinations.

A child who is becoming educated in movement begins with problems such as walking, running, twisting, and falling. As the child solves the initial problem of walking without colliding, he or she may then be asked to express a mood or feeling, to change direction at will, to change direction at a signal from the teacher, or to walk while using the hands and arms in different ways. Music may be added to lessons. As a specific lesson progresses, games may be played encompassing the problem that has been set. A lesson in hopping or leaping may include a game of modified tag. At the conclusion of a lesson a period of demonstration by the children may be held so that the movements they have created may be evaluated and discussed by the entire class. In this way a depth of understanding is reached concerning the movements.

As an apparatus is added, the problem facing the child may be to move along a horizontal ladder in any way desired. As facility is gained, the problem may be made more complex by specifying that the child move along using hands only or using the outside rails only. With other equipment the same procedure is used. General movement precedes more advanced problems such as mounting, vaulting, and dismounting. This approach allows each child to succeed, since no patterns of movement are required or specified. As children experience success, they are motivated to improve their performance.

The problem-solving method allows students to depend less on the teacher, thus forcing them to use their own thought processes. In this manner children will be developing independence. Students who merely imitate the actions of the teacher will not benefit as much as those students who attempt to discover various solutions to problems by themselves. The educated student is one who has developed the ability to analyze critically each new situation in an intelligent and logical manner. Teachers should not be models for students, since the best education will only result when students discover

Through individual exploration the child is given the opportunity to participate in experiences that will help in understanding the concepts of balance.

the answers to questions by utilizing their own thought processes and resources.

Children learn to perceive the position of each segment of their bodies intellectually before attempting any physical skill performance. By utilizing the problem-solving approach, children begin to think about what their bodies can do and how they can be best utilized. The understandings that result help to give children insight into individual differences in skill performance as well as help them to develop confidence in the capabilities and capacities for movement in their own bodies. Time, space, force, and flow of movement are key words. Children learn to consider these factors intellectually as the core of the movements they execute.

Movement education is less formal than traditional physical education. Class organization in movement education does not follow the formal patterns of traditional physical education. Lines, circles, and set formations are avoided. For the sake of safety, structure may be imposed to avoid collisions or needless use of space or equipment. Interaction is encouraged, and frequently the individual may work with a partner or in small groups, depending on the nature of the problem. Since the determining factor in deciding what problems are to be presented to the class is based on the needs of individuals within the group rather than the group as an entity, most instructions by the teacher are given individually rather than to the class as a whole. For example, the teacher will instruct a student who is working on the balance beam to discover what he or she can do and where he or she can move. Furthermore, in movement education no formal drills or highly organized classes of activities are used. The learning climate is intentionally informal so that children will be free to express themselves as individuals rather than as instruments who move to the command of the teacher.

At the same time movement education is highly organized and structured in the sense that it has definite objectives that must be met, classes follow a logical sequence, and progression exists that leads to the realization of program objectives and goals. In addition, these programs are not lacking in discipline. Much of the discipline in movement education classes comes from the activity and from the inner direction of the children themselves. Movement education classes demand much of the teacher in regard to a concrete philosophy, sound objectives, logical progressions, the understanding of proper techniques and methodology, and liberal amounts of imagination and creativity.

Movement education facilitates the learning of motor skills. The natural movements of childhood form the basis for future motor skill development. These movements will tend to develop haphazardly and future skill performances will be inefficient unless the body is effectively educated in movement.

The ability of the child to perceive the body as an

entity helps to promote physical skill development. The child who is retarded in physical skill development often does not have the insight to consider the body as a whole; this child tends to be concerned first with the individual segments, and thus he or she attempts to correct performance errors by altering the position or action of a single arm or leg and fails to measurably improve performance. Movement educators believe that the experience will be most meaningful if the child learns to consider the interaction of all parts of the body before skill performance is significantly improved. Movement educators recognize the need to learn specific sports skills, such as strokes of swimming, methods of pitching or batting a softball, thrusts and parries of fencing, or ways to trap and kick a soccer ball. The English have found that many of these specific skills, such as trapping and kicking a soccer ball, must be taught by traditional methods, and they allot time in their physical education programs to accomplish these tasks. However, they have found that prior experience in movement problem solving gives the child a vast store of knowledge on which to build so that specific learning skills in the context of their application to a game are made easier. For example, a problem-solving experience in using the feet or legs to stop a rolling ball will help the child in learning the fundamentals of a soccer trap. Solving a problem in propelling the body across a shallow pool will help the child discover how the body reacts in water and give the child confidence in learning swimming strokes.

Movement education seeks to produce a feeling of satisfaction in movement. Movement educators seek to produce a feeling of satisfaction in the movement experiences engaged in by students. By emphasizing individual explorations, it is hoped that students will participate in meaningful and pertinent activities. By making the student the explorer in the educational process, it is hoped that this child will be encouraged to try new activities and to discover new insights in relationships to other persons. By utilizing the problem-solving method, it is hoped that the child will select a solution to the problem based on personal abilities and

therefore one that is personally meaningful. By emphasizing an informal class atmosphere, in which students are given instructions based on their individual needs, it is hoped that students will better understand their own physical movements. By not emphasizing competition, movement educators believe that children will be free from the tensions that can be aroused by participating in highly competitive activities. Movement educators believe that when such a learning environment is established, students will derive meaning from the activities in which they are participating, and a feeling of satisfaction will result.

Movement education encourages an analysis of movement. Traditional physical education gives little instruction to students in the analysis of movement. Movement education provides an opportunity for students to observe and analyze themselves and others in the process of movement. At the conclusion of a lesson a period of student demonstration may be held so that the movements in which students have been involved can be evaluated and discussed by the entire class. Greater understanding of movement is an outcome of this process. For example, demonstrations at the end of the lesson may show that one child vaults higher than another because he or she has learned that using the arms will aid the jump. Discussion of this point by the class will give helpful information to those children whose own vaults are inadequate but who have not been able to discover why. Through an analysis of their own movements and those of other children, they will better understand what needs to be done to achieve the best performance.

Movement education involves equipment. Many pieces of apparatus and equipment found in a traditional physical education class can be used in movement education classes. At times the teacher will have to devise various pieces of equipment to fit the needs of a particular lesson. When apparatus or equipment is used, rules of safety, space, and appropriateness of use need to be stressed. Equipment and apparatus must conform to the age and size of the child. Balls should be easy to grasp, and paddles should fit the hand of the child. Heavy apparatus such as vaulting boxes and climbing lad-

Movement education allows students to discover their own unique answers to movement problems and experience joy and satisfaction.

ders must be scaled to sizes most appropriate to the children using them.

Movement education programs must be constantly evaluated. The need for program modifications and adaptations are frequent in movement education. The need for revision will be noted only if programs are objectively evaluated periodically to see whether the goals that have been set are being achieved.

SUMMARY

Movement is the keystone of physical education and sport. Human movement may be affected by a variety of factors, including biomechanical, physiological, psychological, and sociological factors. Understanding of the basic concepts of movement—body awareness, spatial awareness, qualities of movement, and relationships—is essential for physical educators and their students. Physical educators must also be concerned about individuals' development of fundamental skills (locomotor, nonlocomotor, and manipulative skills) for they form the foundation for participation in a variety of activities throughout life.

Movement education, a system based on the theories of Laban, is an important part of physical education. Movement education explores the science of movement and helps people of all ages move more

effectively. Movement education differs from the traditional approach to physical education in terms of the roles and responsibilities of the teacher and the students as well as the conduct of the program.

SELF-ASSESSMENT TESTS

These tests are designed to assist students in determining if the material and competencies presented in this chapter have been mastered.

1. You have been asked by a local recreational group to give a presentation on the subject "Movement: The Keystone of Physical Education and Sport." Prepare in writing your presentation.

2. Analyze the movement concepts associated with the performance of the following skills:

Hitting a baseball

Playing tackle in a football game

Running 100 meters

Performing a free exercise routine in gymnastics

3. Select five sport skills, each from a different sport (e.g., punting a soccer ball). List the locomotor, nonlocomotor, and manipulative skills necessary for skill performance.

4. Pretend you are a participant in a debate on the following subject: "Resolved that movement education is better than the traditional approach in teaching physical education." Outline pertinent arguments for both the affirmative and negative sides.

5. Programs of movement education are typically perceived to be taught in the schools, primarily at the elementary level. Outline key concepts of movement education and discuss how either movement education can be used at the secondary level to teach sports skills or used in a nonschool program working with preschoolers or the elderly.

REFERENCES

1. Nichols BA: *Moving and learning: the elementary school physical education experience*, St Louis, 1990, Times Mirror/Mosby College Publishing.
2. Laban R: Modern educational dance, London, 1948, MacDonald and Evans.
3. Laban R: The mastery of movement, London, 1960, MacDonald and Evans.

SUGGESTED READINGS

Docherty D: Organizing and developing movement ideas, Journal of Physical Education, Recreation, and Dance 53(3):51-54, 1982.

This article presents a comprehensive model for the development of a foundation of movement skills in elementary children. A summary of movement concepts is provided as well.

Gallahue DL: Understanding motor development: infants, children, adolescents. Indianapolis, 1989, Benchmark Press.

A comprehensive approach to motor development, with excellent diagrams and descriptions of fundamental motor skills, is presented.

Jensen MA: Composing and guiding creative movement, Journal of Physical Education, Recreation, and Dance 54(3):85-87, 1983.

Suggestions to guide in the use of creative movement experiences with elementary school children are presented. Diagrams describing the basic movement actions and their variations and inclusion of a table listing descriptive vocabulary for movement exploration enhance the author's presentation.

Kruger H and Kruger JM: Movement education in physical education: a guide to teaching and planning, Dubuque, Iowa, 1981, WC Brown Co, Publishers (Group).

This text presents a comprehensive overview of movement education as well as providing the reader with specific guidelines for teaching and planning lessons.

National Association of Physical Education for College Women and National College of Physical Education Association for Men: The language of movement, Quest, Monograph 23, Jan 1975.

This entire issue of Quest is devoted to movement. Thematic areas include the meanings of movement, symbols of movement, forms of movement, and expression of movement.

McClenaghan BA and Gallahue DL: Fundamental movement: a developmental and remedial approach, Philadelphia, 1978, WB Saunders Co.

This book presents fundamental movement skills as well as activities to promote their development and improve their performance. Excellent diagrams of the fundamental skills and their stages of development enhance the usefulness of this text.

Nichols BA: Moving and learning: the elementary school physical education experience, St Louis, 1990, Times Mirror/Mosby College Publishing.

Combining the philosophies of movement education and motor skills development, this text serves as an excellent resource for teaching elementary physical education.

Welsh DJ: Power beyond performance, Journal of Physical Education, Recreation, and Dance 58(1): 82-83, 1987.

Defines the concept of grace and discusses the experience of grace as it pertains to all forms of movement and people of all ages.

Part

Foundations of Physical Education and Sport

Two

Introduction

In Part One the term physical education and sport was defined and its philosophy and objectives discussed as was the role of movement. Part Two builds on that knowledge by discussing the foundations of physical education and sport. Trained physical educators should understand the foundations for their field of endeavor. Part Two commences with a discussion of the historical foundations of physical education and sport in Chapter 5. Then the physiological, psychological, sociological, and biomechanical bases from which physical education and sport derives the principles and concepts that guide its endeavors are presented in Chapters 6, 7, 8, and 9. These areas of study are the major sciences or subdisciplines of physical education—namely, exercise physiology, motor learning and sport psychology, sport sociology, and biomechanics. A mastery of the principles and concepts discussed in these chapters will provide the physical educator with insight regarding the knowledge necessary to plan and conduct meaningful programs in physical education and sport.

Chapter 5

Historical Foundations of Physical Education and Sport

INSTRUCTIONAL OBJECTIVES AND COMPETENCIES TO BE ACHIEVED

After reading this chapter the student should be able to—

■ Trace the history of physical education and sport from earliest times to the present.

■ Explain the contributions of the Athenian Greeks to physical education and sport.

■ Explain why asceticism, scholasticism, and puritanism were deterrents to physical education and sport's progress.

■ Identify events that served as catalysts for physical education and sport's growth.

■ Identify some of the outstanding leaders in physical education and sport over the course of history and the contributions each made to this field of endeavor.

■ Discuss recent developments in physical education and sport.

■ Draw implications from the discussion of history of principles that will guide the professional future of physical education and sport. Project future developments for physical education and sport based on recent trends.

The beliefs and experience of physical educators today rest on the history of this field of endeavor. It is the source of physical education's identity. In a sense, little basis exists for this professional field, except its past. The experiences of yesteryear help guide physical educators' endeavors today. The only professional maturity is that which is built on the events of days and years gone by.

The nature of physical education and sport today in the United States has been influenced by the contributions of many different cultures. The influence exerted by leaders in the United States was also profound. By knowing the accomplishments of leaders in the past, today's physical educators can

attempt to build on their achievements. One qualification exists—physical educators must use only that from the past which is true, significant, and applicable to the present and the future. This chapter provides an overview of the history of physical education and sport from ancient times to recent developments. Much can be learned about physical education and sport from a critical analysis of its history.

WHAT LESSONS CAN BE LEARNED FROM HISTORY?

What can be learned about physical education and sport from studying its history? Many of today's activities have their forerunners in history. For example, the first recorded Olympics date back to 776 BC in ancient Greece. Yoga and karate, activities of current interest, date back to ancient Oriental societies. Many more facts that will help the physical educator to understand the present better can be gained by studying the past.

In Chapters 1 and 2 the influence of various philosophies—idealism, realism, naturalism, pragmatism, existentialism, and humanism—on physical education and sport objectives and programs were discussed. The influence of the various philosophical schools of thought on physical education throughout history will be evident. Traditionally the objectives of physical education have been categorized as either promoting **"education of the physical"** or **"education through the physical."** Education of the physical focused on the development of the body as an end in itself, that is, precedence was given to the development of the body and physical skills rather than outcomes that could be accomplished through physical activities.

Education through the physical emphasized the acquisition of physical skills and bodily development as well as attainment of other educational outcomes, such as affective, social, and intellectual objectives, through physical activity. The emphasis on these two approaches may be discerned throughout the history of physical education and sport.

It is interesting to note the various purposes for which physical education and sport has existed in the lives of people of various countries and cultures. From the earliest times until the present, either directly or indirectly, physical activity has played a part in the lives of all people. Sometimes this activity has been motivated by a factor such as the necessity for earning a livelihood, whereas in other instances it has resulted from a desire to live a fuller life. Furthermore, it is clear that the objectives of physical education and sport have changed over the course of history so that at the present time they are directed at the better development of human beings, not only physically but also psychologically and socially. These changing concepts of physical

Women's basketball in 1904 at Smith College, Northampton, Mass.

education and sport have come about as a result of many years of experience and study in regard to the values inherent in participating in physical activity under qualified leadership.

Members of primitive societies did not think of physical education as people do today. No organized physical education program was found in primitive society or in the cultures of the ancient Oriental nations. From the physical point of view primitive people did not need to set aside a period during the day when they could participate in various forms of activity—activity was part of their daily regimen. Well-developed bodies and sound organic systems were commonplace among primitive people. Their physical activity consisted of hunting and searching for food, erecting shelters, and protecting themselves from the hostile environment.

History has shown that certain tendencies in human beings have been responsible for their formal and informal participation in physical activity. Some of the more important of these throughout history have been the search for food to satisfy hunger, the desire for protection against enemies, innate drives for mating and propagation, the urge to manipulate brain and brawn, fear of the strange and unknown, and the need to associate with others. Hunting, fishing, dancing, warfare, and play evolved as a result of these general tendencies, explaining to some extent why primitive people and all persons in general have been likely to engage in motor activities whether they wanted to or not. Whether these activities should be characterized as work or play depends on the motive behind the participation in the activity. Work is characterized by need and necessity and is more or less compulsory. On the other hand, play is spontaneous, internally driven, and utilized for fun and relaxation.

Civilization has brought the need for an organized physical education and sport program. As a result of labor-saving devices, sedentary pursuits, and security, the need has arisen for some type of planned program whereby individuals may realize the physical benefits that were once a part of a person's daily routine, as well as many sociological, psychological, and intellectual benefits. Therefore it is interesting to examine certain ancient cultures to

determine the part that physical education and sport played in the lives of their people. Through an understanding of the history of physical education and sport, a person is better able to understand and interpret the field today.

PHYSICAL EDUCATION AND SPORT IN ANCIENT NATIONS
China

Ancient China followed a policy of isolation. This country did not care to associate with the rest of the world but instead desired to live unto itself. At first the topography of the land provided China with the necessary natural protection against invaders. When the Himalaya Mountains no longer served this purpose, the Great Wall was built; when the Wall became obsolete, laws were passed to keep invaders out of the country.

The fact that the ancient Chinese lived an isolated existence was detrimental in many ways to a belief in physical education. Because China did not fear aggression, it lacked the military motivating factor of being physically strong. Furthermore, the teaching of the people of ancient China was mainly concerned with memorizing the works of Confucius. Ancestor worship was also an important part of their religious life. Individuality was suppressed, and all persons were destined to live a rigid and stereotyped existence. In a country that espoused such beliefs little room was made for organized physical education. Physical activity meant stress on the importance of the body and individual freedom of expression, which were contrary to the teachings of this ancient culture.

Certain evidence exists of participation in physical education and sport activities in China despite the emphasis on intellectual excellence and the influence of Taoism, Confucianism, and Buddhism, which stressed the studious, quiet, and contemplative life. In many Chinese classics discussions abound of how sons of rich families engaged in music, dancing, and archery. Wrestling, jujitsu, boxing, ts' u chu (football), polo, tug-of-war, water games, ch'ui wan (similar to golf), shuttlecock, and flying kites were also popular. Thus play was engaged in by the more favored classes, and it

The Oriental influence can be seen today in the martial arts.

seems the masses had little opportunity for participation in formal physical activities.

It is interesting to note that the Chinese thought that certain diseases were caused by inactivity. As a result history discloses that the Cong Fu gymnastics were developed in 2698 BC. These were medical gymnastics intended to keep the body in good organic condition. It was believed that illnesses were caused by internal stoppages and by malfunctioning of organs. Therefore if certain kneeling, bending, lying, and standing exercises could be performed, together with certain types of respiratory training, the illness could be alleviated.

India

Ancient India in many ways was similar to ancient China. People in this country lived an existence that was very religious in nature. Two of the major religions were Hinduism and Buddhism. Hinduism stressed that the human soul passed through several reincarnations before being united with Brahma, the supreme goal. The quickest and most certain way to attain this goal was to refrain from catering to the body and enjoying worldly things. The person who desired to be holy ignored the physical needs of the body and concentrated solely on spiritual needs. It can readily be seen that physical activity had little place in the culture of these religious people.

Buddhism emphasized that right living and thinking, including self-denial, will help the individual's soul reach Nirvana, a divine state. However, Buddha's prohibitions of games, amusements, and exercises in ancient India did not totally prevent participation in such activities. Evidence is available about pastimes such as dice, throwing balls, plowing contests, tumbling, chariot races, marbles, riding elephants and horses, swordsmanship, races, wrestling, boxing, and dancing. Yoga, an activity common in India and involving exercises in posture and regulated breathing, was popular. This disciplining of mind and body required the instruction of experts, and a person fully trained in this activity followed a routine involving 84 different postures.

Ancient Near East

The civilizations of ancient Egypt, Assyria, Babylonia, Syria, Palestine, and Persia mark a turning point in the history of physical education and sport. Whereas the objectives in China and India had stressed religious and intellectual matters, these countries were not restricted by a static society and religious ritual. On the contrary, they believed in living a full life, and therefore all types of physical activity contributed to this objective. It is in these countries that physical education and sport also received an impetus from the military, who saw in it an opportunity to build stronger and more powerful armies.

Egyptian youths were reared in a manner involving much physical activity. As young boys they were instructed in the use of various weapons of war, such as bow and arrow, battleaxe, mace, lance, and shield. They were required to participate in exercises and activities designed to make the body supple, strong, and capable of great endurance and stamina. These activities included marching, running, jumping, wrestling, pirouetting, and leaping. Before their military training started, they had numerous opportunities to engage in many sports and gymnastic exercises. They also found great enjoyment in hunting and fishing expeditions.

In the countries between the Tigris and Euphrates rivers great stress was placed on physical activities, especially among the upper classes. Whereas the lower social strata of the population found few opportunities for recreation and sport, the upper classes indulged themselves in these pastimes at regular intervals. Horsemanship, use of bow and arrow, water activities, and training in physical exercises were considered as important as instruction that was more intellectual in character.

Persia is a good example of a state that had as its main objective the building of an empire through military aggression. A strong Persian army meant a healthy and physically fit army. Under King Cyrus the Great the imperialistic dreams of Persia were realized. At the end of his rule in 529 BC the Persian Empire encompassed the area that is referred to today as the Near East. The success of King Cyrus' campaigns was largely the result of the moral and physical conditioning of his soldiers. At the age of 6 years the state required all boys to leave their homes for training, which consisted of events such as running, slinging, shooting a bow, throwing a javelin, riding, hunting, and marching. The soldier had to be able to travel without much food and clothing and was compelled to endure all sorts of hardship.

Where the military emphasis existed, physical education and sport was aimed at imperialistic ends. Strength, endurance, stamina, agility, and other physical characteristics were not developed so that the individual could live a full, vigorous, and more interesting life but, instead, so that the state could utilize these physical attributes in achieving its own national militaristic aims.

PHYSICAL EDUCATION AND SPORT IN GREECE

Physical education as well as sport experienced a "golden age" in ancient Greece. The Greeks strove for physical perfection, and this objective affected all phases of their life. It had its influence on the political and educational systems, on sculpturing and painting, and in the thinking and writings of that day. It was a unifying force in Greek life, played a major part in the national festivals, and helped in building strong military establishments. No country in history has held physical education or sport in such high respect as did ancient Greece.

Evidence exists of physical education and sport activities being popular in Cretan culture as early as 2500 BC. Archeological investigations at Mycenae and other centers of Aegean civilization have unearthed buildings, pottery, and other artifacts that point to the important place of physical education and sport in this ancient culture. Literature such as Homer's *Iliad* and *Odyssey* also is a source of this information. Lion hunting, deer hunting, bull grappling, boxing, wrestling, dancing, and swimming are commonly referred to by historians who have written about these ancient civilizations.

Physical education was a vital part of the education of every Greek boy. Gymnastics and music were considered the two most important subjects—music for the spirit, and gymnastics for the body. "Exercise for the body and music for the soul" was a common pronouncement. Gymnastics, it was believed, contributed to courage, discipline, and physical well-being. Furthermore, gymnastics stressed a sense of fair play, development of the individual's aesthetic values, amateurism, and the utilitarian values inherent in the activity. Professionalism was frowned on. Individuals ran, wrestled, jumped, danced, or threw the javelin not for reward but for what it would do for their bodies. Beauty of physique was stressed, and boys and men participated in the nude, which motivated development of the "body beautiful."

Because of the topography of the land and for various political reasons, Greece was composed of several city-states, each exercising its own sovereignty and existing as a separate entity. It waged war and conducted all its affairs separately from the other city-states. This situation had an influence not only on the political aspects of each city-state but also on the objectives of physical education and sport within each state. Sparta and Athens exemplify two such city-states.

East Greek amphor, 550 to 525 BC. Found at Fikellura, Rhodes.

In Sparta, a city-state in the Peloponnesus district of Greece, the main objective of physical education and sport was to contribute to a strong and powerful army. The individual in Sparta existed for the state. Each person was subservient to the state and was required to help defend it against all enemies. Women as well as men were required to be in good physical condition. It was believed that healthy and strong mothers would bear healthy and strong sons. Spartan women may have begun their physical conditioning as early as 7 years of age and continued gymnastics in public until they were married. Newborn infants, if found to be defective or weak, were left on Mount Taygetus to die. Thomas Woody, an educational historian, points out that mothers bathed babies in wine to test their bodies and to temper them for future ordeals. A boy was allowed to stay at home only for the first six years of his life. After this he was required to stay in the public barracks and entered the agoge, a system of public, compulsory training, in which he underwent an extremely vigorous and rigid training schedule.

If he failed in this ordeal, he was deprived of all future honors. A major part of this training consisted of physical activities such as wrestling, jumping, running, throwing the javelin and discus, marching, horseback riding, and hunting. This Spartan conditioning program secured a strong army that was second to none.

Athens, a city-state in eastern Greece, was the antithesis of Sparta. Here the democratic way of life flourished, and consequently it had a great bearing on the objectives of physical education and sport. Athens did not control and regulate the individual's life as rigidly as Sparta. In Athens the people enjoyed the freedom that is characteristic of a truly democratic government. Although the military emphasis was not as strong in Athens as in Sparta, the emphasis on physical education and sport was just as great or greater. Athenians engaged in physical activity to develop their bodies, for aesthetic values, and to live a fuller and more vigorous life. An ideal of Athenian education was to achieve a proper balance in moral, mental, physical, and aesthetic development. To the Hellenes, each person was a whole and was only as strong as his or her weakest part.

Gymnastics for the youth were practiced in the palaestra, a building that provided rooms for various physical activities, for oiling and sanding their bodies, and an open space for activities such as jumping and wrestling.

Some of the more noted palaestras were those of Taureas, Timeas, and Siburtios. The *paidotribe*, or proprietor of the palaestra, was similar to a present-day physical educator. He taught many activities, understood how certain exercises should be adapted to various physical conditions, knew how to develop strength and endurance, and was an individual who could be trusted with children in the important task of making youthful bodies serve their minds. As a boy approached manhood, he left the palaestra and attended the gymnasium.

Gymnasiums became the physical, social, and intellectual centers of Greece. Although the first use was for physical activity, men such as Plato, Aristotle, and Antisthenes were responsible for making gymnasiums such as the Academy, Lyceum, and Kynosarges outstanding intellectual centers as well. Youths usually entered the gymnasium at about 14 to 16 years of age. Here special sports and exercises received the main attention under expert instruction. Although activities that had been engaged in at the palaestra were continued, other sports such as riding, driving, racing, and hunting were added. Instruction in the gymnasium was given by a paidotribe and also a *gymnast*. The paidotribe had charge of the general physical training program, whereas the gymnast was a specialist responsible for training youth in gymnastic contests. The chief official at the gymnasium, in overall charge of the entire program, was called a *gymnasiarch*. In keeping with the close association between physical education and sport and religion, each gymnasium recognized a particular deity. For example, the Academy recognized Athena; the Lyceum, Apollo; and the Kynosarges, Hercules.

The national festivals were events that were most important in the lives of the Greeks and were also important in laying the foundation for the modern Olympic games. These national festivals were in honor of some hero or deity and consisted of feasting, dancing, singing, and events involving physical prowess. Although many of these national festivals were conducted in all parts of Greece, four of them were of special importance and attracted national attention. The first and most famous was the Olympia festival in honor of Zeus, the supreme god, which was held in the western Peloponnesus district. The second was the Pythia festival in honor of Apollo, the god of light and truth, held at Delphi, which was located north of the Corinthian Gulf. The third was the Nemea festival in honor of Zeus held at Argolis near Cleonae. The fourth was the Isthmia festival in honor of Poseidon, the god of the sea, held on the isthmus of Corinth. Athletic events were the main attraction and drawing force at each festival. People came from all over Greece to see the games. The stadium at Olympia provided standing space for approximately 40,000 spectators.

During the time the games were held, a truce was declared by all the city-states in Greece, and it was believed that if this truce were broken, the guilty would be visited by the wrath of the gods. By the middle of the fifth century this truce probably lasted for 3 months.

A rigid set of requirements had to be met before anyone could participate as a contestant in the games. For example, the contestant had to be in training for 10 months; he had to be a free man; he had to have a perfect physique and be of good character; he could not have a criminal record; he had to compete in accordance with the rules. The contestants, as well as their fathers, brothers, and trainers, had to swear to an oath that they would not use illegal tactics to win. Once enrolled for a contest, the athlete had to compete. Physical unfitness was not a good excuse. Events included foot racing, throwing the javelin, throwing the discus, wrestling, broad jumping, weight throwing, boxing, and horse racing. The victor in these events did not receive any material reward for his victory. Instead a wreath of olive branches was presented. However, he was a hero in everyone's eyes and had many receptions given in his honor. Furthermore, he had many privileges bestowed on him by his home city-state. To be crowned a victor in an Olympic event was to receive the highest honor that could be bestowed in Greece. The Olympic games were first held in 776 BC, and continued every fourth year thereafter until abolished by the Romans in AD 394. However, they have since been resumed and today are held every 4 years in a different country.

Physical education and sport in ancient Greece will always be viewed with pride by members of this profession. The high ideals that motivated the various gymnastic events are objectives that all persons should try to emulate.

PHYSICAL EDUCATION AND SPORT IN ROME

While the Hellenes were settling in the Grecian peninsula about 200 BC, another Indo-European people was migrating to Italy and settling in the central and southern parts of this country. One of these wandering tribes, known then as Latins, settled near the Tiber River, a settlement that later became known as Rome. The Romans were to have a decided effect not only on the objectives of physical education and sport in their own state but also on those of the Greek world, which they conquered.

The Romans, through their great leaders and well-disciplined army, extended their influence throughout most of the Mediterranean area and all of Europe. This success on the battlefield brought influences into Roman life that affected Roman ideals. They were not truly interested in the cultural aspects of life, although often some of the finer aspects of Hellenic culture were taken on as a means of show. Particularly during the latter days of the Roman Empire, wealth became the objective of most citizens, and vulgar displays became the essence of wealth. Luxury, corruption, extravagance, and vice became commonplace.

In respect to physical education and sport the average Roman believed that exercise was for health and military purposes. He did not see the value of play as an enjoyable pastime. During the period of conquest, when Rome was following its strong imperialistic policy and before the time of professional troops, citizens between the ages of 17 and 60 years were liable for military service. Consequently, during this period of Roman history army life was important, and physical activity was considered essential to be in good physical shape and ready to serve the state at a moment's notice. Soldiers followed a rigid training schedule that consisted of activities such as marching, running, jumping, swimming, and throwing the javelin and discus. However, during the last century of the Republic mercenary troops were used, with the result that the objectives of physical training were not considered as important for the average Roman.

After the conquest of Greece, Greek gymnastics were introduced to the Romans, but they were never well received. The Romans lacked the drive for clean competition. They did not believe in developing the "body beautiful." They did not like nakedness of performers; they preferred to be spectators rather than participants; they preferred professionalism to amateurism.

Athletic sports were not conducted on the same high level as in ancient Athenian Greece. The Romans wanted something exciting, bloody, ghastly, and sensational. At the chariot races and gladiatorial combats, excitement ran high. Men were pitted against wild animals or against one another and fought until death to satisfy the spectators' cravings for excitement and brutality. Frequently large groups of men fought each other in mortal battle in front of thousands of pleased spectators.

The rewards and incomes of some individuals who engaged in the chariot races were enormous. Diocles of Spain retired at 42 years of age, having won 1462 of 4257 races and rewards totaling approximately \$2 million. Other famous contestants were Thallus, Crescens, and Scorpus.*

The thermae and the Campus Martius in Rome took the place of the gymnasium in Greece. The thermae were the public baths, where provision was also made for exercise, and the Campus Martius was an exercise ground on the outskirts of the city. Most of the exercise was recreational in nature.

PHYSICAL EDUCATION AND SPORT DURING THE DARK AGES

The fall of the Roman Empire in the west about AD 476 resulted in a period of history that is frequently referred to as the Dark Ages. This period, however, was anything but dark in respect to the physical rejuvenation brought about by the Teutonic barbarians overrunning the Roman Empire.

Before considering the Dark Ages it is interesting for the student of physical education and sport to note a cause of the fall of Rome that brought on this new period in history. Historians list many causes for the breakdown of the Roman Empire, but the most outstanding one was the physical and moral

---

*At the site where once the inhabitants of Rome yelled with delight at the skill and daring of their favorite charioteers and gladiators, Romans of today are applauding the exploits of soccer players, who have replaced the chariot drivers and slaves in the public estimation.

The Circus Maximus, the oldest and greatest of the Roman circuses, was situated at the foot of the Palatine Hill and dated back to the last king of Rome, Tarquinius the Younger (534 to 510 BC). It reached its greatest splendor in imperial times and seated as many as 200,000 persons. It reached its final form under Trajan (AD 53 to 117). The Roman Municipal Council decided that this unusual site should be transformed into a sports center.

decay of the Roman people. The type of life the Romans led, characterized by the dissolution of marriage and family through divorce, "blood-sport" games, and suicide, caused a decrease in population. Extravagance, doles, slave labor, and misuse of public funds caused moral depravity and economic ruin; luxurious living, vice, and excesses caused poor health and physical deterioration. The lesson is borne out in Rome, as it has been in many civilizations that have fallen along the way, that for a nation to remain strong and endure, it must be physically as well as morally fit.

As a morally and physically weak Roman Empire crumbled, physically strong Teutonic barbarians overran the lands that once were the pride of the Latins. The Visigoths overran Spain, the Vandals— North Africa, the Franks and Burgundians—Gaul, the Angles and Saxons—Britain, and the Ostrogoths— Italy. These invasions brought about the lowest ebb in literature and learning known to history. The so-called cultural aspects of living were disregarded.

Despite all the backwardness that accompanied the invasions with respect to learning, public works, and government and that resulted in the name "Dark Ages," which accompanied this period of history, the entire world still received physical benefits. The Teutonic barbarians were a nomadic people who lived out-of-doors on simple fare. They were mainly concerned with a life characterized by hunting, caring for their cattle and sheep, and participating in vigorous outdoor sport and warfare. A regimen such as this built strong and physically fit bodies and well-ordered nervous systems. The Teutonic barbarians helped to guarantee a stronger, healthier, and more robust stock of future generations of people.

Asceticism and Scholasticism

Although the Teutonic invasions of the Dark Ages supported the value of physical activity, two other movements during approximately this same period in history worked to its disadvantage—asceticism and scholasticism.

Out of pagan and immoral Rome, Christianity and asceticism grew and thrived. Certain individuals in ancient Rome became incensed with the immorality and worldliness that existed in Roman society. They believed in "rendering unto Caesar the things that are Caesar's and unto God the things that are God's." They would not worship the Roman gods, attend the baths, or visit the games. They did not believe in worldly pleasures and catered to the spirit and not to the body. They believed that this life should be used as a means of preparing for the next world. They thought that physical activities were foolish pursuits because they were designed to improve the body. The body was evil and should be tortured rather than improved. They preached that the mind and body were distinct and separate entities and that one had no bearing on the other. The Christian emperor Theodosius abolished the Olympic games in AD 394 as being pagan.

The spread of Christianity resulted in the rise of asceticism. This was the belief that evil exists in the body, and therefore it should be subordinated to the spirit, which is pure. Worldly pursuits are evil, and individuals should spend their time by being alone and meditating. The body is possessed of the devil and should be tortured. Individuals wore hair shirts, walked on hot coals, sat on thorns, carried chains around their legs, and exposed themselves to the elements so that they might bring their worldly body under better control. Such practices led to poor health and shattered nervous systems on the part of many.

As Christianity spread, monasteries were built where Christians could isolate themselves from the world and its evils. Later schools were attached to these monasteries, but early Christianity would not allow physical education to be a part of the curriculum. The medieval university also frowned on physical education and sport.

Another influence that has had a major impact on the history of physical education and sport is scholasticism—the belief that facts are the most essential items in education. The key to a successful life is knowing the facts and developing one's mental and intellectual powers. Scholasticism deemphasized the physical as being unimportant and unnecessary. This movement developed among the scholars and universities of the Middle Ages.

PHYSICAL EDUCATION AND SPORT DURING THE AGE OF FEUDALISM

As a result of the decentralization of government during the period of the Dark Ages, the period of feudalism came into being between the ninth and fourteenth centuries.

The feudalistic period appeared because people needed protection, and since strong monarchs and governments that could supply this protection were rare, the people turned to noblemen and others who built castles, had large land holdings, and made themselves strong. Feudalism was a system of land tenure based on allegiance and service to the nobleman or lord. The lord who owned the land, called a *fief,* let it out to a subordinate who was called his *vassal.* In return for the use of this land the vassal owed his allegiance and certain obligations to his lord. The large part of the population, however, was made up of serfs, who worked the land but shared little in the profits. They were attached to the land, and as it was transferred from vassal to vassal, they were also transferred.

Two careers were open to sons of noblemen during feudalistic times. They might enter training for the church and become members of the clergy, or they might become knights. If they decided in favor of the church, they pursued an education that was religious and academic in nature; if they decided in favor of chivalry, they pursued an education that was physical, social, and military in nature. To the average boy, chivalry had much more appeal than the church.

The training that a boy experienced in becoming a knight was long and thorough. Physical training played a major role during this period. At the age of 7 years a boy was usually sent to the castle of a nobleman for training and preparation for knighthood. First, he was known as a page, and his instructor and teacher was usually one of the women in the lord's castle. During his tenure as a page, a boy learned court etiquette, waited on tables, ran errands, and helped with household tasks. During the rest of the time he participated in various forms of physical activity that would serve him well as a knight and strengthen him for the arduous years ahead. He practiced for events such as boxing, running, fencing, jumping, and swimming.

At the age of 14 years the boy became a squire and was assigned to a knight. His studies included keeping the knight's weapons in good condition, caring for his horses, helping him with his armor, attending to his injuries, and guarding his prisoners. During the time the boy was a squire, more and more emphasis was placed on physical training. He was continually required to engage in vigorous sport and exercises such as hunting, scaling walls, shooting with bow and arrow, running, climbing, swordsmanship, and horsemanship.

If the squire proved his fitness, he became a knight at 21 years of age. The ceremony was solemn and memorable. The prospective knight took a bath of purification, dressed in white, and spent an entire night in meditation and prayer. In the morning the lord placed his sword on the knight's shoulder, a ceremony known as the accolade; this marked the conferring of knighthood.

Jousts and tournaments were two special events in which all knights engaged several times during their lives and that were tests of their fitness. These special events served both as amusement and as training for battle. In the jousts two knights attempted to unseat one another from their horses with blows from lances and by skill in horsemanship. In tournaments many knights were utilized in a program designed to exhibit the skill and showmanship gained during their long period of training. They were lined up as two teams at each end of the *lists,* as the grounds were called, and on a signal they attempted to unseat the members of the opposing team. This meleé continued until one team was declared the victor. Many knights wore their lady's colors on their armor and attempted with all their strength and skill to uphold her honor. During these tournaments death often resulted for participants. It was during these exhibitions that a knight had the opportunity to display his personal bravery, skill, prowess, strength, and courage.

PHYSICAL EDUCATION AND SPORT DURING THE RENAISSANCE

The transitional period in history between the dark years of the medieval period and the beginning of modern times, the fourteenth to the sixteenth centuries, was known as the period of the Renaissance and was an age of great progress for humankind.

During the medieval period people lacked originality. Individuality was a lost concept, and interest in the hereafter was so prevalent that people did not enjoy the present. The Renaissance caused a change in this way of life. There was a revival or rebirth of learning, a belief in the dignity of human beings, a renewed spirit of nationalism, an increase of trade among countries, and a period of exploration. Scientific research was used to solve problems; books were printed and thus made available to more people; renewed interest was shown in the classics. This period is associated with Petrarch, Boccaccio, Michelangelo, Erasmus, da Vinci, da Gama, Columbus, Galileo, and Harvey.

The Renaissance period also had an impact on physical education and sport. With more attention being placed on enjoyment of the present and the development of the body, asceticism lost its hold on the masses. During the Renaissance the theory that the body and the soul were inseparable, that they were indivisible, and that one was necessary for the optimum functioning of the other became more popular. It was believed that learning could be promoted through good physical health. A person needed rest and recreation from study and work. The body needed to be developed for purposes of health and for preparation for warfare.

Some outstanding leaders during the Renaissance who were responsible for spreading these beliefs concerning physical education and sport are mentioned briefly.

Vittorino da Feltra (1378 to 1446) taught in the court schools of northern Italy and was believed to be one of the first teachers to combine physical and mental training in a school situation. He incorporated daily exercises in the curriculum, which included dancing, riding, fencing, swimming, wrestling, running, jumping, archery, hunting, and fishing. His objectives emphasized that physical education was good for disciplining the body, for preparation for war, and for rest and recreation, and that good physical condition helped children learn other subject matter much better.

Pietro Vergerio (1349 to 1428) of Padua and Florence wrote a treatise entitled *De Ingenius Moribus,* in which the following objectives were emphasized: physical education is necessary for the total education of the individual, as preparation for warfare, to better undergo strain and hardship, as a means of fortifying the mind and body, as an essential for good health, and as a means of recreation to give a lift to the spirit and the body.

Pope Pius II's (1405 to 1464) objectives of physical education were good posture, body health, and aid to learning.

Sir Thomas Elyot (1490 to 1546) of England wrote the treatise on education entitled *The Governor,* which elaborated on such objectives of physical education as recreation and physical benefits to the body.

Martin Luther (1483 to 1546), the leader of the Protestant Reformation, did not preach asceticism as a means of salvation. He saw in physical education a substitute for vice and evil pursuits such as gambling and drinking during leisure hours, a means of obtaining elasticity of the body, and a medium for promoting health.

François Rabelais (1490 to 1553), a French educational theorist, emphasized the objectives of physical welfare and the fact that physical education is an important part of education, aids in mental training, and is good preparation for warfare.

Roger Asham (1515 to 1568), professor at Cambridge in England, proclaimed the value of physical education as a preparation for war and as a means of resting the mind.

John Milton (1608 to 1674), the English poet, expressed his views on physical education in his *Tractate on Education.* In this treatise he discussed how physical education helps in body development, is a means of recreation, and is good preparation for warfare.

John Locke (1632 to 1704), famous English philosopher and a student of medicine, supported physical education in a work entitled *Some Thoughts Concerning Education.* His objectives could be summarized as a means of meeting health emergencies involving hardships and fatigue and as a means of having a vigorous body at one's command.

Michel de Montaigne (1533 to 1592), a French essayist, stressed that physical education was necessary for both body and soul and that it was impossible to divide an individual into two such components, since they are indivisible to the individual being trained.

John Comenius (1592 to 1671), a Bohemian educational reformer, and *Richard Mulcaster* (1530 to 1611), an English schoolmaster, both wrote on the subject of physical education. Both men defined the objectives of physical education as a means to maintain health and physical fitness and obtain rest from study.

Jean Jacques Rousseau (1712 to 1778), a French writer, in his book *Emile* points out that in an ideal education, physical education would contribute to the objectives of health and a vigorous body. He stressed that an individual's mind and body are an indivisible entity and that both are bound together.

The Renaissance period helped to interpret the worth of physical education to the public in general. It also demonstrated how a society that promotes the dignity and freedom of the individual and recognizes the value of human life will also place in high respect the development and maintenance of the human body. The belief became prevalent that physical education is necessary for health, as a preparation for warfare, and as a means of developing the body.

PHYSICAL EDUCATION AND SPORT IN EUROPE

A study of the various individuals and countries that influenced physical education and sport during the modern European period shows what each contributed to the growth and advancement of this field.

Germany

Physical education and sport in Germany during the modern European period is associated with names such as Basedow, Guts Muths, Jahn, and Spiess.

Johann Bernhard Basedow (1723 to 1790) was born in Hamburg and early in life went to Denmark as a teacher, where he witnessed physical education in practice as part of a combined physical and mental training program. After gaining a wealth of experience in Denmark, he went back to Germany and decided to spend all his time reforming educational methods. In 1774 he was able to realize his objective of establishing a school at Dessau that he called the Philanthropinum. In this model school physical education played an important part in the daily program of all students. The activities included dancing, fencing, riding, running, jumping, wrestling, swimming, skating, and marching. This was the first school in modern Europe that admitted children from all classes of society and that offered a program in which physical education was a part of the curriculum. Such an innovation by Basedow greatly influenced the growth of physical education in Germany as well as in the rest of the world.

Johann Christoph Friedrich Guts Muths (1759 to 1839) was influential in the field of physical education through his association with the Schnepfenthal Educational Institute, which had been founded by Christian Gotthilf Salzmann (1744 to 1811). Guts Muths succeeded Christian Carl Andre as the instructor of physical education at this institution and remained on the staff for 50 years. His beliefs and practices in physical education were recorded for history in various books, two of which are of special importance—*Gymnastics for the Young* and *Games*. These books provide illustrations of various exercises and pieces of apparatus, arguments in favor of physical education, and discussions of the relation of physical education to educational institutions. Because of his outstanding contributions, Guts Muths is often referred to as one of the founders of modern physical education in Germany.

Friedrich Ludwig Jahn (1778 to 1852) is a name associated with the Turnverein, an association of gymnasts that has been in evidence ever since its

The turnplatz.

innovation by Jahn. Jahn's incentive for inaugurating the Turnverein movement was love of his country. It was during his lifetime that Napoleon overran Germany and caused it to be divided into several independent German states. Jahn made it his life's work and ambition to help bring about an independent Germany free from foreign control. He believed that he could best help in this movement by molding German youth into strong and hardy citizens who would be capable of throwing off this foreign yoke.

To help in the achievement of his objective, Jahn accepted a teaching position in Plamann's Boys' School. In this position he worked regularly with the boys in various outdoor activities. He set up an exercise ground outside the city called the Hasenheide. Before long Jahn had erected various pieces of apparatus, including equipment for jumping, vaulting, balancing, climbing, and running. The program grew in popularity; soon hundreds of boys were visiting the exercise ground or turnplatz regularly, and more apparatus was added.

Jahn's system of gymnastics was recognized throughout Germany, and in many cities Turnvereins were formed, using as a guide the instructions that Jahn incorporated in his book *Die Deutsche Turnkunst*. When Jahn died, his work continued, and turner societies became more numerous. In 1870 there were 1500 turner societies, in 1880 there were 2200, in 1890 there were

4000, in 1900 there were 7200, and in 1920 there were 10,000. Turnvereins are still in existence in many parts of the world.

Adolph Spiess (1810 to 1858) was the founder of school gymnastics in Germany, and more than any other individual in German history, he helped to make physical education a part of school life. Spiess was proficient in physical education activities himself and was well informed as to the theories of such men as Guts Muths and Jahn. His own theory was that the school should be interested in the total growth of the child—mental, emotional, physical, and social. Physical education should receive the same consideration as the important academic subjects such as mathematics and language. It should be required of all students, with the possible exception of those whom a physician would excuse. An indoor as well as an outdoor program should be provided. Elementary school children should have a minimum of 1 hour of the school day devoted to physical education activities, which should be taught by the regular classroom teacher. The upper grades should have a progressively smaller amount, which should be conducted by specialists who were educators first but who were also experts in the physical education field. The physical education program should be progressive, starting with simple exercises and progressing to the more difficult ones. Girls as well as boys need an adapted program of physical activity. Exercises combined with music offer an opportunity for freer individual expression. Marching exercises aid in class organization, discipline, and posture development. Formalism should not be practiced to the exclusion of games, dancing, and sports.

Other outstanding individuals in modern German history who have influenced physical education include Eiselen, Koch, Hermann, and Von Schenckendorff. However, the names of Basedow, Guts Muths, Jahn, and Spiess stand out as the ones who in large part have influenced physical education the most.

Sweden

The name of *Per Henrik Ling* (1776 to 1839) is symbolic of the rise of physical education to a place

Turnverein societies were still popular in the 1920s. Members of the Durlach Turnverein are shown. A member practices his skills on an apparatus in the turnplatz.

of importance in Sweden. The Lingiad, held at Stockholm, in which representatives of many nations of the world participate, is a tribute to this great man.

Ling's greatest contribution is that he strove to make physical education a science. Formerly physical education had been conducted mainly on the premise that people believed it was good for the human body because it increased the size of musculature; contributed to strength, stamina, endurance, and agility; and left one exhilarated. However, many claims for physical education had never been proved scientifically. Ling approached the field with the mind of a scientist. By applying the sciences of anatomy and physiology, he examined the body to determine what was inherent in physical activity to enable the body to function in a nearly optimum capacity. His aims were directed at determining such things as the effect of exercise on the heart, the musculature, and the various organic systems of the body. He believed that through such a scientific approach he would be able to better understand the human body and its needs and to select and apply physical activity intelligently.

Ling is noted for establishing the Royal Central Institute of Gymnastics at Stockholm, where teachers of physical education received their preparation in one of three categories—educational gymnastics, military gymnastics, or medical gymnastics.

Ling believed that physical education was necessary for weak persons as well as strong persons, that exercise must be prescribed on the basis of individual differences, that the mind and body must function harmoniously together, and that teachers of physical education must have a foundational knowledge of the effects of exercise on the human body.

In 1839 *Lars Gabriel Branting* (1799 to 1881) became the director of the Royal Central Institute of Gymnastics after the death of Ling. Branting spent the major part of his time in the area of medical gymnastics. His teachings were based on the premise that activity causes changes not only in the muscular system of the body but also in the nervous and circulatory systems. Branting's successor was *Gustaf Nyblaeus* (1816 to 1902), who specialized in military gymnastics. An innovation during his tenure was the inclusion of women in the school.

The incorporation of physical education pro-

Participant in Swedish gymnastics program.

grams in the Swedish schools did not materialize as rapidly as many leaders in the field had hoped. As a result of the teachings of Ling and other leaders a law was passed in 1820 requiring a physical education course on the secondary level. More progress was made in education as the values of physical education in relation to the growth and development of children became apparent in Sweden. To *Hjalmar Fredrik Ling* (1820 to 1886), most of the credit is due for the organization of educational gymnastics in Sweden. He was largely responsible for physical education becoming an essential subject for both boys and girls in all schools and on all institutional levels.

Denmark

Denmark has been one of the leading European countries in the promotion of physical education. *Franz Nachtegall* (1777 to 1847) was largely responsible for the early interest in this field. He had a direct influence in introducing physical education into the public schools of Denmark and in preparing teachers of this subject.

Franz Nachtegall had been interested in various forms of physical activity since childhood and had achieved some degree of skill in vaulting and fencing. He began early in life to teach gymnastics, first to students who visited his home and then in 1799 in a private outdoor gymnasium, the first to be devoted entirely to physical training. In 1804 Nachtegall became the first director of a Training School for Teachers of Gymnastics in the Army. The need was great for instructors in public schools and in teachers' colleges, therefore graduates readily found employment. In 1809 the secondary schools and in 1814 the elementary schools were requested to provide a program of physical education with qualified instructors. Shortly thereafter Nachtegall received the appointment of Director of Gymnastics for all Denmark.

The death of Nachtegall in 1847 did not stop the expansion of physical education and sport throughout Denmark. Some of the important advances since his death have been the organization of Danish Rifle Clubs, or gymnastic societies, the introduction of the Ling system of gymnastics, complete civilian supervision and control of programs of physical education as opposed to military supervision and control, greater provision for teacher education, government aid, the incorporation of sport and games into the program, and the work of *Niels Bukh* (1880 to 1950).

One of the innovations in the field of physical education and sport has been the contribution of Niels Bukh with his "primitive gymnastics." Patterned to some extent after the work of Ling, primitive gymnastics attempted to build the perfect physique through a series of exercises performed without cessation of movement. His routine included exercises for arms, legs, abdomen, neck, back, and the various joints. In 1925 he toured the United States with some of his students, demonstrating his primitive gymnastics.

Great Britain

Great Britain is known as the home of outdoor sports, and that country's contribution to this field has influenced physical education and sport throughout the world. When other European countries were using the Ling, Jahn, and Guts Muths systems of gymnastics, England was using a program of organized games and sport.

Athletic sports are a feature of English life. As early as the time of Henry II English youth were wrestling, throwing, riding, fishing, hunting, swimming, rowing, skating, shooting with the bow and arrow, and participating in various other sports. The games of hockey and quoits, for example, were played in England as early as the fifteenth century, tennis as early as 1300, golf as early as 1600, and cricket as early as 1700. Football is one of the oldest of English national sports.

In addition to outdoor sports, England's chief contribution to physical education and sport has been through the work of *Archibald Maclaren* (1820 to 1884). Maclaren enjoyed participating in many kinds of sport at an early age, especially fencing and gymnastics. He also studied medicine and was eager to make physical training a science. In 1858 he opened a private gymnasium where he was able to experiment. In 1860 Maclaren was designated to devise a system of physical education for the British Army. As a result of this appointment he incorporated his recommendations into a treatise entitled *A Military System of Gymnastic Exercises for the Use of Instructors*. This system was adopted by the military.

Maclaren contributed several other books to the physical education field, including *National Systems of Bodily Exercise, A System of Fencing, Training in Theory and Practice,* and *A System of Physical Education*. In his works he points out that the objectives of physical education should take into consideration that health is more important than strength; that the antidote for tension, weariness, nervousness, and hard work is physical action; that recreative exercise as found in games and sport is not enough in itself for growing boys and girls; that physical exercise is essential to optimum growth and development; that physical training and mental training are inseparable; that mind and body represent a "oneness" in human beings and sustain and support each other; that exercises must be progressive in nature; that exercises should be adapted to an individual's fitness; and that physical education should be an essential part of any school curriculum.

Since the time of Maclaren the Swedish system of gymnastics has been introduced into England and has been well received. Many ideas were also imported from Denmark and other countries.

One of the major contributions of England to physical education and sport has been move-

ment education, which is discussed at length in Chapter 4.

• • •

Germany, Sweden, Denmark, and Great Britain led Europe in the promotion of physical education and sport. Other countries of Europe as a rule imported the various systems of Jahn, Guts Muths, and Ling. Persons from other countries also contributed much to the field of physical education and sport and should be mentioned. From Switzerland, Pestalozzi with his educational theories, Dalcroze and his system of eurythmics, and Clias did a great deal to advance the field of physical education and sport. Colonel Amoros from France inaugurated a system of gymnastics, and Baron Pierre de Coubertin was instrumental in reviving the Olympic games in 1896 at Athens. Johann Happel from Belgium was an outstanding physical educator and was director of a normal school of gymnastics. Dr. Tyrs from Czechoslovakia organized the first gymnastic society in his country.

PHYSICAL EDUCATION AND SPORT IN THE UNITED STATES

Physical education and sport in the United States has experienced a period of great expansion from the colonial period. At that time there was little regard for any planned program of activity as contrasted with today, when programs are required in the public schools of most states and when physical education and sport is becoming a respected profession.

Colonial Period (1607 to 1783)

During the colonial period conditions were not conducive to organized physical education and sport programs. The majority of the population lived an agrarian existence and thought that they received enough physical exercise working on the farms. Also, during this period few leisure hours could be devoted to recreational activities. In certain sections of the country such as New England religious beliefs were contrary to participation in play. The Puritans, especially, denounced play as the work of the devil. Participation in games was believed to be just cause for eternal damnation. Pleasures and recreation were banned. Stern discipline, austerity, and frugality were thought to be the secrets to eternal life and blessedness.

People of some sections of the nation, however, brought with them from their native countries the knowledge and desire for various types of sport. The Dutch in New York liked to engage in sports such as skating, coasting, hunting, and fishing. However, the outstanding favorite was bowling. In Virginia many kinds of sports were popular such as running, boxing, wrestling, horse racing, cockfights, fox hunts, and later, cricket and football.

During the colonial period little attention was given to any form of physical activity in the schools. The emphasis was on the three Rs at the elementary level and the classics at the secondary level. The teachers were ill prepared in the methodology of teaching. Furthermore, at the secondary level students were prepared mainly for college, and it was thought that physical activity was a waste of time in such preparation.

National Period (1784 to 1861)

During the national period (the period from the American Revolution to the Civil War) of the history of the United States, physical education and sport began to assume an important place in society.

The academies, as many of the secondary schools were called, provided terminal education for students; instead of preparing for college, they prepared for living. These educational institutions utilized games and sports as after-school activity. However, they had not reached the point at which they thought its value should occupy a place in the daily school schedule. They encouraged participation during after-school hours on the premise that it promotes a healthy change from the mental phases of school life.

The United States Military Academy was founded in 1802, and physical training held an important place in its program of activities. Throughout history this training school has maintained such a program.

It was during the national period that German gymnastics were introduced to the United States. In 1823 Charles Beck introduced Jahn's ideas at the Round Hill School in Northampton, Massachusetts, and Charles Follen introduced them at Harvard University in Boston. Both Beck and Follen were turners and proficient in the execution of German gymnastics. Their attempt to introduce German gymnastics into the United States, however, was not successful at this time. A few years later they were introduced with more success in German settlements located in cities such as Kansas City, Cincinnati, St. Louis, and Davenport. Turnverein associations were organized, and gymnastics were accepted with considerable enthusiasm by the residents of German extraction. As for Americans of other extraction, the majority thought that a formal type of gymnastic program was not suitable for their purposes.

The Turnverein organizations spread, and by 1852, 22 societies were in the North. The oldest Turnverein in the United States, which still flourishes today, is the Cincinnati Turnverein, founded November 21, 1848. The Philadelphia Turnverein, one of the strongest societies today, was founded May 15, 1849. A national organization of Turnvereins, now known as the American Turnerbund, was established in 1850 and held its first national turnfest in Philadelphia in 1851. Societies from New York, Boston, Cincinnati, Brooklyn, Utica, Philadelphia, and Newark were represented. In 1851, 1672 turners were active in the United States. At the outbreak of the Civil War approximately 150 Turnverein societies and 10,000 turners were in the United States. After the Civil War these organizations continued to grow and exercised considerable influence on the expanding physical education profession. The Turnverein organizations were responsible for the establishment of the Normal College of the American Gymnastic Union. Many outstanding physical education leaders graduated from this school.

Notable advances in physical education and sport were made before the Civil War. In 1828 a planned program of physical education, composed mainly of calisthenics performed to music, was incorporated by Catherine E. Beecher in the Hartford Female

Wand drills were an important part of program activities in the 1890s.

Seminary in Connecticut, a famous institution of higher learning for women and girls. The introduction of the Swedish Movement Cure in America, the construction of gymnasiums in many large cities, the formation of gymnastic and athletic clubs by many leading institutions of higher learning, and the invention of baseball were all important events in the progress of physical education and sport in America during this period.

Civil War Period until 1900

Many outstanding leaders and new ideas influenced physical education and sport in the United States in the period from the Civil War to 1900.

After the Civil War the Turnverein societies were established for both boys and girls. The members of these associations gave support to various phases of physical education and sport and especially encouraged the program in the public schools. The objectives of the turners were notable. They disapproved of too much stress being placed on winning games and professionalism. They believed that the main objectives should be to promote physical welfare and to provide social and moral training. They opposed military training as a substitute for physical education in the schools and supported the playground movement.

In 1852 Catherine Beecher founded the American Women's Educational Association.

From 1859 to the early 1870s Dr. George Barker

Winship gained considerable publicity by emphasizing gymnastics as a means of building strength and large muscles.

In 1860 Dr. Dio Lewis devised and introduced a new system of gymnastics in Boston. As opposed to Winship, Lewis was not concerned with building muscles and strength. He was more interested in the weak and feeble persons in society. Instead of developing large muscles he aimed at developing agility, grace of movement, flexibility, and improving general health and posture. He also stressed that teachers should be well prepared, and in 1861 he established a normal school of physical education in Boston for training teachers. Lewis opposed military training in schools. He thought that sports alone would not provide an adequate program and that gymnastics should also be included. Through lectures and written articles Lewis became a leading authority on gymnastics used in the schools and the public in general. He is noted for advancing physical education to a respected position in United States society. Several leading educators, after hearing Lewis, set up planned physical education programs in their school systems.

In the 1880s the Swedish Movement Cure was made popular by Hartvig Nissen, head of the Swedish Health Institute in Washington. This system was based on the Ling or Swedish gymnastics, well known in Europe and recognized in the United States for inherent medical values. Also in the

Staff and first normal class in physical education of the Chautauqua school in New York, 1886.

1880s Mrs. Hemenway and Amy Morris Homans added their contributions to physical education. They stimulated the growth of Swedish gymnastics; founded a normal school for teachers at Framingham, Massachusetts; offered courses of instruction in Swedish gymnastics to schoolteachers; and influenced the establishment of the Boston Normal School of Gymnastics.

In the 1890s the Delsarte System of Physical Culture was introduced by Francois Delsarte. It was based on the belief that by contributing to poise, grace, beauty, and health certain physical exercises were conducive to better dramatics and better singing.

During this period American sport began to achieve some degree of popularity. Tennis was introduced in 1874, and in 1880 the United States Lawn Tennis Association was organized. Golf was played in the United States in the late 1880s, and in 1894 the United States Golfing Association was formed. Bowling had been popular since the time of the early Dutch settlers in New York, but it was not until 1895 that the American Bowling Congress was organized. Basketball, one of the few sports originating in the United States, was invented by James Naismith in 1891. Some other sports that became popular during this period were wrestling,

boxing, volleyball, skating, skiing, lacrosse, handball, archery, track, soccer, squash, football, and swimming. In 1879 the National Association of Amateur Athletics of America was developed, from which the American Athletic Union was formed.

Physical education has played a large part in the Young Men's Christian Association (YMCA), an organization that is worldwide in scope and that is devoted to developing Christian character and better living standards. Robert J. Roberts was an outstanding authority in physical education for the YWCA in the late 1800s. In 1885 an International Training School of the YMCA was founded at Springfield, Massachusetts. Roberts became an instructor there, as did Luther Gulick, who later became Director of Physical Training for the New York City Public Schools. After Gulick left Springfield, Dr. McCurdy became head of the physical education and sport department.

The first Young Women's Christian Association (YWCA) was founded in Boston in 1866 by Mrs. Henry Durant. This organization is similar to the YMCA and has a broad physical education and sport program for its members.

Physical education and sport made major advances in colleges and universities with the construction of gymnasiums and the development of

Dr. Rich's Institute for Physical Education.

departments in this area. Two of the leaders in physical education during the last half of the nineteenth century were Dr. Dudley Allen Sargent, who was in charge of physical education at Harvard University, and Dr. Edward Hitchcock, who was head of the physical education department at Amherst College. Sargent is known for his work in teacher preparation, remedial equipment, exercise devices, college organization and administration, anthropometric measurement, experimentation, physical diagnosis as a basis for activity, and scientific research. Some of the schools that constructed gymnasiums were Harvard, Yale, Princeton, Bowdoion, Oberlin, Wesleyan, Williams, Dartmouth, Mt. Holyoke, Vassar, Beloit, Wisconsin, California, Smith, and Vanderbilt. With the first intercollegiate meet in the form of a crew race between Harvard and Yale in 1852, intercollegiate sport began to play a prominent role on college campuses. Williams and Amherst played the first intercollegiate baseball game in 1859, and Rutgers and Princeton, the first football game in 1869.

Other intercollegiate contests soon followed in tennis, swimming, basketball, squash, and soccer.

Organized physical education programs as part of the curriculum began to appear early in the 1850s in elementary and secondary schools. Boston was one of the first communities to take the step under the direction of Superintendent of Schools, Nathan Bishop; St. Louis and Cincinnati followed soon afterward. During the next two decades physical education was made part of the school program in only a few instances. However, in the 1880s the drive in this direction was renewed, and the result was that physical education directors were appointed in many larger cities, and many more communities recognized the need for planned programs in their educational systems.

In 1885 in Brooklyn the American Association for the Advancement of Physical Education was organized with Edward Hitchcock as the first president and Dudley Sargent, Edward Thwing, and Miss H. C. Putnam as vice-presidents. William G. Anderson was elected secretary and J. D. Andrews, treasurer.

An early physical education program.

This association later became the American Physical Education Association and until recently was known as the American Association for Health, Physical Education, and Recreation (AAHPER). It is now known as the American Alliance for Health, Physical Education, Recreation, and Dance (AAHPERD).

A struggle between the Swedish, German, and other systems of gymnastics developed in the 1890s. Advocates of each system did their best to spread the merits of their particular program and attempted to have them incorporated as part of school systems. In 1890 Baron Nils Posse introduced the Swedish system in the Boston schools, where it proved popular, and it was later adopted throughout the schools of Massachusetts. The Swedish system had more popularity in the East, and the German system was more prevalent in the Middle West. A survey in the 1890s indicates not only the prevalence of the various systems of gymnastics but also the prevalence of physical education programs in general throughout the country. It was reported after a study of 272 cities that 83 had a director of physical education for their school systems; 81 had no director, but teachers were responsible for giving exercises to the students; and in 108 cities the teachers could decide for themselves

whether exercises should be a part of their daily school programs. A report on the dates the physical education programs were established in the schools surveyed showed that 10% were established before 1887, 7% from 1887 to 1888, 29% from 1889 to 1890, and 54% from 1891 to 1892. In respect to the system of gymnastics used, the report showed 41% used the German type of gymnastics, 29% Swedish, 12% Delsartian, and 18% eclectic. Only 11 cities had equipped gymnasiums. It was not long, however, before expansion occurred in gymnasiums, equipment, trained teachers, and interest in physical education. Ohio in 1892 was the first state to pass a law requiring physical education in the public schools. Other states followed, and by 1925 33 states had a physical education law. Today only a few do not provide such legislation.

Early Twentieth Century

A survey by the North American Gymnastic Union of physical education programs in 52 cities showed that gymnastic programs averaged 15 minutes daily in the elementary schools and two periods weekly in the secondary schools. Cities that were surveyed showed 323 gymnasiums in existence and many more under construction.

Extensive interscholastic programs also existed. A

survey of 290 high schools in 1907 showed that 28% of the students engaged in one or more types of sport.

The controversy over interscholastic athletics for girls was pronounced, with people such as *Jessie Bancroft* and *Elizabeth Burchenal* stressing the importance of intramural games rather than interscholastic competition for girls.

A majority of colleges and universities had departments of physical education, and most institutions of higher learning provided some program of gymnastics for their students.

A survey by *Thomas D. Storey* in 1908 gave information concerning leadership in physical education. It showed that of the institutions surveyed, 41% of the directors of physical education possessed medical degrees, 3% of the directors held doctor of philosophy degrees, and the remaining possessed a bachelor's degree.

Intercollegiate athletics were brought under more rigid academic control as abuses mounted. Intramural athletics gained in prominence as the emphasis on athletics for all gained momentum.

Some of the names that should be mentioned in any discussion of the history of physical education and sport during the early part of the twentieth century include the following:

Thomas Dennison Wood made an outstanding contribution to the field of physical education. He attended Oberlin College, was the first director of the physical education department at Stanford University, and later became associated with Teachers College, Columbia University. He believed more emphasis should be placed on games and game skills and introduced his new program under the name "Natural Gymnastics."

Clark Hetherington was influenced by his close association with Thomas D. Wood, who chose Hetherington as his assistant when he was at Stanford. Hetherington's contributions resulted in a clearer understanding of children's play activities in terms of survival and continued participation. This was also true of athletics and athletic skills. Hetherington became head of the physical education department at New York University and, with his successor *Jay B. Nash,* was responsible for its

RECREATION AND STUDY

Chautauqua Affords Opportunity for Instruction Under the Best Instructors, Together with Abundant Outdoor Recreation and an Attractive Program of Concerts, Popular Lectures and the Best Entertainments.

Boating on Lake Chautauqua. The Chautauqua institution, located on Lake Chautauqua in southwestern New York state, was an early showcase for physical education in the late 1800s and early 1900s. William G. Anderson, founder of the American Association for Health, Physical Education, and Recreation was active at this institution.

becoming one of the leading teacher training schools in the nation.

Robert Tait McKenzie, a physical educator, surgeon-scientist, and artist-sculptor, served distinguished periods at McGill University and the University of Pennsylvania. He was known for his contribution to sculpture, for his dedication to helping physically underdeveloped and atypical individuals overcome their deficiencies, and for his writing of books such as *Exercise in Education and Medicine,* published in 1910.

Jessie H. Bancroft, a woman pioneer in the field of physical education, taught at Davenport, Iowa;

Field hockey in 1904 at Smith College, Northampton, Mass.

Hunter College; and Brooklyn and New York City public schools. She greatly influenced the development of physical education as a responsibility of homeroom teachers in elementary schools. She also contributed much to the field of posture and body mechanics and was the first living member of the AAHPER to receive the Gulick Award for distinguished service to the profession. She was well-known for her book *Games for the Playground, Home, School, and Gymnasium.*

Delphine Hanna, an outstanding woman leader of physical education, developed a department of physical education at Oberlin College, which sent outstanding graduates all over the country. She was instrumental in motivating not only many female leaders but also encouraged men such as Thomas Wood, Luther Gulick, and Fred Leonard to follow illustrious careers in physical education.

James H. McCurdy studied at the Training School of Christian Workers at Springfield Medical School of New York University, Harvard Medical School, Springfield College, and Clark University. He was closely associated with Springfield College, where he provided leadership in the field of physical education. He published *The Physiology of Exercise* and was editor of the *American Physical Education Review.*

Luther Gulick, born in Honolulu, was director of physical education at Springfield College, principal of Pratt High School in Brooklyn, Director of Physical Education for Greater New York City public schools, and president of the American Physical Education Association. He taught philosophy of play at New York University, helped found and was the first president of the Playground Association of America (later to become the National Recreation

Association), was associated with the Russell Sage Foundation as director of recreation, and was president of Camp Fire Girls, Inc.

The playground movement had a rapid period of growth after the first sand garden was set up in 1885 in Boston. In 1888 New York passed a law that provided for a study of places where children might play out-of-doors. The name *Jacob A. Riis* symbolized the playground movement in New York. In Chicago a playground was managed by Hull House. In 1906 the Playground and Recreation Association of America was established to promote the development of rural and urban playgrounds, with Dr. Gulick as president.

In the teacher education field of physical education higher standards were established and better trained leaders were produced. The two-year normal school became a thing of the past, with four years of preparation being required. The trend in professional preparation required students to receive a broad general education, a knowledge of child growth and development and the psychology of learning, and specialized training in physical education.

Sports, athletics, and team games became more important in the early twentieth century, with broad and extensive programs being established in schools, recreational organizations, and other agencies. The National Collegiate Athletic Association (NCAA), the National Association of Intercollegiate Athletics (NAIA), and other leagues, organizations, and associations were formed to keep a watchful eye on competitive sport.

During the early twentieth century a new physical education started to evolve. By means of a scientific basis it attempted to discover the physical needs of individuals and the part that a planned physical education program can play in meeting these needs. This new physical education recognized that education is a "doing" process and that the individual learns by doing. It stressed leadership, in which exercises and activities are not a matter of mere physical routine but, instead, are meaningful and significant to the participant. A varied program of activities was stressed that included the fundamental skills of running, jumping, climbing, carrying, throwing, and leaping; camping activities; self-testing activities; organized games; dancing and rhythmical activities; dual and individual sports; and team games. This new physical education stressed the need for more research and investigation into what type of program best serves the needs of children and adults. It stressed the need for a wider use of measurement and evaluation techniques to determine how well objectives are being achieved. Finally, it provided a program that better served to adapt individuals to the democratic way of life.

World War I (1916 to 1919)

World War I started in 1914, and the United States' entry in 1918 had a critical impact on the nation and education. The Selective Service Act of 1917 called to service all men between the ages of 18 and 25 years. Health statistics gleaned from Selective Service examinations aroused considerable interest in the nation's health.

Social forces were also at work during this period. The emancipation of women was furthered by passage of the Nineteenth Amendment. Women also began to show interest in sport and physical education, as well as in other fields formerly considered to be "off limits."

During World War I many physical educators provided leadership for physical conditioning programs for the armed forces and also for the people on the home front. Persons such as Dudley Sargent, Luther Gulick, Thomas Storey, and R. Tait McKenzie contributed their services to the armed forces. The Commission on Training Camp Activities of the War Department was created, and Raymond Fosdick was named the head of this program. Joseph E. Raycroft of Princeton University and Walter Camp, the creator of "All-Americans," were named to head the athletic divisions of the Army and the Navy, respectively. Women physical educators were also active in conditioning programs in communities and industries at home.

When the war ended, the public had an opportunity to study the medical examiner's report for the men who had been called to military duty. One third of the men were found physically unfit for

1851

1866

1910

1920

1927

*yesterday
today
tomorrow...
the right costume
for gymnasium,
pool & dance*

Physical education costumes for American women in early years.

armed service and many more were physically inept. Also, a survey by the National Council on Education in 1918 showed that children in the elementary and secondary schools of the nation were woefully subpar physically. The result was the passing of much legislation in the various states to upgrade physical education programs in the schools. The following states enacted laws between 1917 and 1919: Alabama, California, Delaware, Indiana, Maine, Maryland, Michigan, Nevada, New Jersey, Oregon, Pennsylvania, Rhode Island, Utah, and Washington. To provide supervision and leadership for the expanded programs of physical education, many state departments of public instruction established administrative heads.

Golden Twenties (1920 to 1929)

The period between 1920 and 1929 showed the way for a "new" physical education advocated by such leaders as Hetherington, Wood, Nash, and Williams. The move away from the formal gymnastic systems of Europe was well received. The temperament of the times seemed to emphasize a less formal program. More games, sports, and free play were the order of the day.

The belief that physical education had greater worth than building strength and other physical qualities, as incorporated in the thinking of the new physical education, aroused much discussion. Franklin Bobbit, a University of Chicago educator, commented: "There appears to be a feeling among physical educationists that the physical side of man's nature is lower than the social or mental, and that...they, too, must aim primarily at those more exalted, nonphysical things of mental and social type." William Burnham, of Clark University, thought that physical education could contribute to the whole individual. Clark Hetherington believed that physical education had different functions in a democratic society than in Europe, where some of the gymnastic systems prevailed. Jesse Feiring Williams stressed the importance of physical education in general education.

Thomas D. Wood, Rosalind Cassidy, and Jesse Feiring Williams published their book *The New*

Tennis at the turn of the century at Smith College, Northampton, Mass.

Physical Education in 1927; it stressed the biological, psychological, and sociological foundations of physical education.

Another development during this period included the emphasis on measurement in physical education by such persons as David K. Brace and Frederick Rand Rogers as a means of grouping students, measuring achievement, and motivating performance.

Programs of physical education and sports continued to expand in schools and colleges. The elementary school program of physical education stressed mainly formal activities. The secondary school program also felt the influence of the formalists. In addition, periodic lectures on hygiene were provided. Interscholastic athletics continued to grow in popularity, with the need being felt to institute con-

trols. The National Federation of High School Athletic Associations was established in 1923. At the college level a study by George L. Meylan reported in 1921 that of 230 institutions surveyed, 199 had departments of physical education presided over by administrative heads and an average of four staff members per institution. Many of the staff members had professional rank. More than three fourths of the institutions required physical education for their students, with the most general requirement being for 2 years in length. The 1920's also saw a boom in the area of stadium construction.

Many problems arose in respect to college athletics. As a result, the Carnegie Foundation provided a grant in 1923 for a study of intercollegiate athletics in certain institutions in the South by a Committee

Fifty Years Ago in the Journal

The currently controversial issue of sex instruction in the schools was a topic of concern to members of the American Physical Education Association in March 1919. "Sex Instruction in Connection with Physical Training in High Schools" was the subject of a meeting in Connecticut, at which statements of policy were agreed to by participants, who represented both college and high school physical education programs. The document was published in full in the Journal of fifty years ago, and the quotations below show that while some of the arguments are still pertinent, the developing role of the school health educator has brought about a new perspective on sex education in today's schools.

"The necessity for sex education in high schools is plain and apparent. Since, however, investigations show that knowledge of sexual matters comes to children before high school age the desirability of sex education in grammar and primary grades is established. At the present time, however, it may be more practical to confine sex education to high school pupils. . . .

"Physical training holds a unique position in this respect [as an agency to communicate the facts to all high school students] for all high school pupils no matter what courses they might elect come for physical training. This is the first advantage of the physical training teacher. All teaching is so much more effective if it can be linked up with life itself and if it can be made practicable. In this respect physical training has once more unusual opportunities.

"The practice of physical education in a high school makes necessary certain precautionary measures in regard to both sexes so that no harm may come to the sexual apparatus by exercise. This means for the female to be made acquainted with the facts underlying menstruation and the effect of exercise thereon. This matter must be broached to every female student in a high school and might as well be made then the basis of further sex instruction which will come in as a matter of course. In dealing with the males, advice as to the wearing of protective appliances so as to prevent harm to the testes in physical training practice is likewise necessary and opens the way for general sex instruction. . . .

"Physical work in itself is an antidote against undue manifestations of sexual life in the young. . . . The selection of individuals for games gives occasion to point out that sexual development is closely allied with the development of not only physical properties but also mental and moral ones as evidenced especially in the different physiques and mentalities in domestic animals where unsexing is practiced. The advantage of continence to preserve fitness for certain games, the unfitting influence of premature sexual indulgence, can be readily brought to the attention of especially the male in the high school.

"With all this advantage of physical education one thing must be insisted upon that such knowledge gained by formal and informal instruction will be no help unless character building is coupled with it. The demand then for character building through physical education must be reiterated in this connection."

50 Years Ago in the Journal

The February 1919 issue of the *American Physical Education Review* was the "Western District Convention Number." It contained the two-day program details on one and a half pages of its 6" x 9" format. In contrast with one of today's district meetings, the program consisted of general sessions only, seven in number, plus three demonstrations (swimming, dance, and calisthenics). Both morning and afternoon schedules had "community singing" breaks, evidently a welcome moment of relaxation since the second day's program began with a display of calisthenics by the cadets of the School of Military Aeronautics (University of California, Berkeley) at 6:20 a.m.

The impact of World War I on the theory, philosophy, and curriculum of physical education is evident in the titles of the main articles for the issue—"Physical Education in the Light of the Present National Situation," "American Athletics Versus German Militarism," and "The Influence of the War Upon Physical Education"—and the notes, which included a synopsis of the practical guide used by the French centers of military and physical re-education.

Of special interest is the description of a new game invented by James Naismith. Called Vrille (or Vree) Ball, its underlying principle was "to be simple enough so that it could be played by the novice and yet require such skill as to interest the expert," but it never gained the popularity of the other game Naismith created. Played on a rectangle 24' x 24' by two teams of three men each, the game involved batting a ball back and forth so that on each exchange it bounced off a rectangular wood or cement target on the ground in the middle of the field. The regulation ball was a leather covered rubber bladder 12" in circumference and it was hit with the hands. Like basketball, it was invented by Naismith to fit certain requirements demanded by the physical education instructional program. It was designed to give many of the benefits of handball or tennis, providing exercise, developing skills, and combining recreation with competition. It was economical of expense and space; elastic enough to be played on almost any kind of grounds; and capable of being played when only two could get together but flexible enough to accommodate several. Perhaps in attempting to meet too many special requirements, it failed to meet a basic need of maintaining enthusiasm. We would be interested in knowing if any teacher is still using Vrille Ball in his physical education classes.

Samples of articles taken from journals of 70 years ago.

of the Association of Colleges and Secondary Schools. Later a study was conducted of athletic practices in American colleges and universities. The report of this study was published in 1929 under the title *American College Athletics*. The report denounced athletics as being professional rather than amateur in nature and as a means of public entertainment and commercialization. Problems such as recruiting and subsidizing athletes also were exposed.

During this period the intramural athletic programs increased in colleges and universities. Women's programs experienced an increase in the number of staff, hours required for student participation, activities offered, and physical education buildings in use.

Depression Years (1930 to 1939)

The 1929 stock market crash ushered in the Great Depression, which affected education. Unemployment and poverty reigned. Health and physical education had a difficult time surviving in many communities.

During the period of economic depression in the United States many gains achieved by physical education in the schools of the nation were lost. Budgets were cut back, and programs in many cases were either dropped or downgraded. Between 1932 and 1934 an estimated 40% of the physical education programs were dropped completely. Legislative moves were made in several states such as Illinois and California to do away with the physical education requirement.

Another development during the depression years was that the physical educator became more involved in recreation programs in the agencies and projects concerned with unemployed persons. These later programs were being subsidized with special government assistance. The national association, recognizing the increased interest in recreation, voted to change its title to include the word *recreation*—the American Association for Health, Physical Education, and Recreation.

A new interest captivated many physical educators—that of facilities concerned with programs of physical education, athletics, and recreation.

Several publications appeared before the end of the 1920s on this subject.

The trend in physical education programs was away from the formal-type approach to an informal games-sports approach. Also, what constitutes an acceptable program of physical education at various school and college levels was outlined by William R. LaPorte of the University of Southern California in his publication *The Physical Education Curriculum—a National Program,* published in 1937.

Interscholastic athletic programs continued to grow and in some situations dominated physical education programs and created many educational problems. The collegiate athletic program received a temporary setback from the Carnegie Report but then started to grow again. The National Association of Intercollegiate Basketball was established in 1940 for the purpose of providing an association for the smaller colleges. It later changed its name to National Association of Intercollegiate Athletics in 1952. In 1937 representatives of the Junior Colleges of California met for the purpose of forming the National Junior College Athletic Association.

Intramural athletics continued to grow in colleges and universities. Women's athletic associations also increased in number. The principles that guided such programs were established largely during the early years by the National Section of Women's Athletics.

Mid-twentieth Century (1940 to 1970)

Physical education made progress in the middle of the twentieth century.

Impact of World War II

The country was jolted from depression by World War II. Physical education received an impetus as physical training programs were established under Gene Tunney in the Navy, Hank Greenburg in the Air Force, and sports leaders in other branches of the armed forces. Schools and colleges were urged to help develop physical fitness in the youth of the nation. A return to more formalized conditioning programs resulted.

The need for a national program of physical fitness was evident as a result of Selective Service examinations and other indications that young people were not in sound physical condition. Several steps were taken in this direction. President Roosevelt appointed John B. Kelly of Philadelphia National Director of Physical Training. In 1941 Mayor Fiorello LaGuardia of New York City was appointed by President Roosevelt as Director of Civilian Defense in Charge of Physical Fitness, and a National Advisory Board was established. William L. Hughes of the national association was appointed chairman. In 1942 a Division of Physical Fitness was established in the Office of Defense, Health, and Welfare Services. In 1943 John B. Kelly was appointed chairman of a Committee of Physical Fitness within the Office of the Administrator, Federal Security Agency.

The war years had their impact on programs of physical education in the nation's schools and colleges. In many instances elementary school physical education classes met daily, and secondary and college classes also increased in number. The program of activities took on a more formal nature with the purpose of physically conditioning the children and youth of the United States for the national emergency that existed. Girls and women, as well as boys and men, were exposed to these programs.

The Physical Fitness Movement

In December 1953 an article was published in the *Journal of the American Association for Health, Physical Education, and Recreation* entitled "Muscular Fitness and Health." The article discussed the physical deficiencies of American children in contrast with European children and brought to the attention of the American people the deplorable physical condition of the nation's youth. As a result a series of events followed that may be called the physical fitness movement.

James B. Kelly of Philadelphia and Senator James Duff of Pennsylvania alerted the President of the United States about the information discussed in this article. In July 1955 President Eisenhower gathered a group of prominent sports figures in Washington, D.C., to explore the fitness problem.

Later he called a Youth Fitness Conference at the Naval Academy in Annapolis. At the conclusion of the conference President Eisenhower issued an executive order establishing a President's Council on Youth Fitness and appointed Dr. Shane MacCarthy as executive director. After this a President's Citizens Advisory Committee on Fitness of American Youth was appointed.

As a result of President Eisenhower's decrees fitness became a national topic for consideration. Several states established their own committees on physical fitness. Cities such as Flint and Detroit developed special projects. The YMCA, Amateur Athletic Union (AAU), and other organizations put forth special efforts to promote fitness. Several business concerns became involved. *Sports Illustrated* magazine devoted regular features to fitness. The National Research Council of the AAHPER authorized physical fitness testing of American children. The College Physical Education Association for Men published a special report entitled "Fit for College." Operation Fitness USA was inaugurated by the AAHPER to promote fitness, leadership, public relations, and research. The project established motivational devices such as certificates of recognition, achievement awards, and emblems for students at various levels of achievement.

When John F. Kennedy became President of the United States, he appointed Charles "Bud" Wilkinson to head his council on youth fitness. The name was changed to the President's Council on Physical Fitness. The council introduced its "Blue Book" with suggestions for school-centered programs.

When Lyndon Johnson became President, he appointed Stan Musial to head his Council on Physical Fitness. Later, when Stan Musial resigned this position, the President appointed Captain James A. Lovell, Jr., U.S.N. (retired), to replace Musial. The council's name was again changed to the President's Council on Physical Fitness and Sports.

Professional Preparation

The war and postwar teacher shortage represented a critical problem for the nation. During the war

200,000 teachers left jobs, and 100,000 emergency certificates were issued. Many of those who left did not return, and inadequately trained replacements were hired. The critical shortage forced administrators to discard their standards in selecting teachers.

Professional preparation programs increased in number during this period, with over 600 colleges and universities participating in such programs. Some of the larger institutions developed separate professional programs for health, physical education, and recreation personnel, whereas many smaller institutions were concerned with only physical education.

Athletics

Four significant developments occurred in athletics during the midtwentieth century. Renewed interest was shown in girls' and women's sport, intramurals, lifetime sports, and sport programs for boys and girls below the high school age.

Girls' and women's sports. In 1962 the Division for Girls' and Women's Sports (DGWS) and the Division of Men's Athletics of the AAHPER held their first joint conference so that the views of both men and women in the profession could be expressed. Two years later the first National Institute on Girls' Sports was held to promote sports for girls and women. In 1965 a study conference met to discuss and develop guidelines needed in the areas of competition for girls and women. In addition to these steps taken to promote girls' and women's sports, other moves included the development of a liaison with Olympic Games officials as a part of the Olympic development movement, the publication of guidelines for girls and women in competitive sports by the DGWS, and the exploration of the social changes in society that had implications for sport programs for women. All these steps represented a new departure toward providing greater opportunities for girls and women to engage in competitive sports at both the high school and college levels.

Intramurals. As sport became increasingly popular at various educational levels, interest was renewed in providing sport competition for all students, not just for the skilled elite. A meeting that

helped to spur this movement was held in 1956, when the National Conference on Intramural Sports for College Men and Women met in Washington, D.C. Its purpose was to consider intramural programs for college men and women, to formulate principles, to recommend administrative procedures relating to current and future programs, and to provide greater opportunity for more young men and women to participate in healthful recreational activities. The intramural movement continued to grow, with leadership being provided by the National Intramural Association.

Lifetime sports. An emphasis was placed on sports that can be played during a person's entire lifetime. Giving leadership to this movement was the establishment of the Lifetime Sports Foundation in 1965. Its purpose was to promote fitness and lifetime sports and to give assistance to groups engaged in these areas. This same year the AAHPER approved the Lifetime Sports Education Project, an adjunct of the Lifetime Sports Foundation. School and college physical education programs reflected the influence of such projects, with greater emphasis being given to teaching activities such as bowling, tennis, golf, and badminton.

Sport programs for boys and girls below the high school level. Considerable controversy was generated during this period concerning sports for children below the high school level. In 1953 a National Conference on Program Planning in Games and Sports for Boys and Girls of Elementary School Age was held in Washington, D.C. It was the first time that organizations representing medicine, education, recreation, and other organizations serving the child had ever met with leaders of organizations who promote highly organized competitive activities for children. Two recommendations to come out of this conference were (1) that programs of games and sport should be based on the developmental level of children and that no contact sports should be allowed for children under 12 years of age and (2) that competition is inherent in the growth and development of the child and will be harmful or beneficial depending on a variety of factors.

International Developments

International meetings of leaders of health, physical education, and recreation from various parts of the world were initiated in the midtwentieth century. Furthermore, the Peace Corps recruited many physical educators to work in selected countries of the world.

World seminars in physical education were held, such as the one in Helsinki in 1952. The first International Congress in Physical Education was held in the United States in 1953 and considered such topics as recreation, sport, correctives, dance, and tests and measurements.

In 1958 at the annual meeting of the World Confederation of Organizations of the Teaching Profession (WCOTP), a committee was appointed to make plans for a World Federation of National and International Associations of Health Education, Physical Education, and Recreation. The purpose was to provide a way in which to unite representatives from all associations of these fields in a worldwide organization. The following year the WCOTP established the International Council of Health, Physical Education, and Recreation (ICHPER).

Programs for Individuals with Disabilities

In the mid-twentieth century physical educators realized that their field of specialization could make a contribution to students with disabilities, including the mentally retarded, the physically handicapped, the poorly coordinated, and the culturally disadvantaged. One event that accented this movement was a grant from the Joseph P. Kennedy, Jr., Foundation in 1965, which enabled the AAHPER to establish the Project on Recreation and Fitness for the Mentally Retarded for the purposes of research, program development, and leadership training.

Since its inception in 1968, the Special Olympics has provided competitive sport opportunities for individuals with mental retardation.

Adapted physical education programs received increasing attention, with special programs being included in professional preparation institutions to provide leadership for this area. Furthermore, governmental grants of funds enabled greater emphasis

to be placed on this particular phase of the physical education program.

Research

The need for research in physical education grew to much greater importance in the eyes of physical educators than it had heretofore. The Research Council of the AAHPER was established in 1952 as a section under the General Division. Its functions and purposes included promoting research along strategic lines, developing long-range plans, preparing the disseminating materials to aid research workers in the field, and synthesizing research materials in areas related to the professional fields.

As a result of the increased recognition of the importance of research, studies were conducted in areas such as exercise physiology, motor learning, sociology of sport, and pedagogy.

Facilities and Equipment

With the growth of physical education programs and the construction of new facilities to accommodate these programs, meetings, research, and interest were generated regarding facilities and equipment for physical education.

In 1947 a grant was made by the Athletic Institute to help sponsor a National Facilities Conference at Jackson's Mill, West Virginia. Fifty-four outstanding education, park, and recreation leaders met with architects, engineers, and city planners to prepare a guide for planning facilities for health, physical education, and recreation programs. Facilities conferences have been held periodically in various parts of the United States since 1947.

The Council on Equipment and Supplies of the AAHPER was formed in 1954. Its purpose was to allow manufacturers, distributors, buyers, and consumers of materials used in the areas of health education, physical education, and recreation to work together on problems of mutual concern.

The great amount of monies expended for facilities and equipment in physical education, including sports programs, has been responsible for continued

Special Olympics provide a diversity of sport opportunities for individuals with mental retardation.

interest in this area so that these monies may be expended in the most profitable manner possible.

SIGNIFICANT RECENT DEVELOPMENTS (1970 TO PRESENT)

Physical education and sport today is perhaps in one of its most exciting eras in its history. The body of knowledge comprising the discipline of physical education is growing rapidly. Expanded and rigorous research efforts on the part of dedicated researchers, coupled with improvements in technology, have contributed to the quality and quantity of knowledge. Specialized areas of study or subdisciplines such as exercise physiology, motor learning, and sport psychology have emerged. (See Chapter 1.) In the late 1960s and early 1970s, the proliferation of research and the desire to share findings with colleagues helped stimulate the formation of specialized scholarly organizations. For example, the North American Society for the Psychology of

Sport and Physical Activity was founded in 1967 and the Philosophic Society for the Study of Sport was founded in 1972. Today numerous professional organizations focusing on specialized fields of study within physical education and sport exist, providing an outlet for the dissemination of research findings through presentations at conferences and through professional journals.

The growth of the discipline influenced professional preparation programs at colleges and universities. New courses were developed to embrace the knowledge within the subdisciplines. At the undergraduate level, these courses were initially incorporated into teacher preparation programs. Graduate programs were further developed to offer study within those areas of specialization. Beginning in the late 1970s, an increasing number of undergraduate programs offered their students the opportunity to specialize. To this end, undergraduate programs in specialized areas such as exercise science or sport management were developed. The broadening of professional preparation programs within physical education and sport to encompass specialized areas of study has allowed students to prepare for a diversity of career opportunities within this expanding field.

The scope of physical education and sport widened considerably in the 1970s and it appears that it will continue to do so throughout the 1990s. Physical education and sport programs have expanded from serving school- and college-age populations to serving people of all ages—from preschoolers to the elderly. Expansion of programs from the traditional school setting to nonschool settings such as community centers and corporate fitness centers has occurred at an increasing rate. The increased depth and breadth of knowledge and the widening scope of the field has created a diversity of career opportunities for well-prepared individuals. (Professional preparation programs and career opportunities are discussed in Part Three.)

One milestone in this period was the celebration in 1985 by the American Alliance for Health, Physical Education, Recreation, and Dance (AAH-PERD) of the one hundredth anniversary of its founding as the American Association for the Advancement of Physical Education. Interest in research has grown markedly, and in 1980 the *Research Quarterly* was renamed the *Research Quarterly for Exercise and Sport*.

In the 1970s and 1980s attitudes toward health and physical activity began to change. Preventive medicine and wellness were emphasized. This emphasis led to recognition of the potential of physical education and sport to contribute to health and to impact favorably on the quality of life. (See Chapters 2 and 3.) Three national health reports—*Healthy People*,[1] *Objectives for the Nation*[2] and *Year 2000 Objectives for the Nation*[3]—affirmed the contribution of physical activity to the attainment and maintenance of health. Professionals increased the emphasis on health-related fitness as opposed to motor-skill related fitness in their programs. During this time many Americans became enthusiastic about fitness and people of all ages began to participate in physical activities and exercise to an extent never before seen. However, it appears that the interest in fitness is limited to certain segments of the population; it also appears that many Americans do not exercise with sufficient intensity, duration, and frequency to realize desirable health benefits. (See Chapter 3.)

Federal legislation and court decisions during this time had a significant impact on girls' and women's participation and on the participation of individuals with disabilites in physical education and sport programs and athletics. Changing societal attitudes toward these groups also contributed to their increased participation. Reports on the status of education in our schools and the call for educational reform may, in the years to come, significantly affect the role of physical education programs as an integral part of the school curriculum. (See Chapter 3.)

Technological advances have led to changes in the construction of facilities. Computers have not only facilitated research but have also begun to be used with increased frequency by the practitioner. The use of videotape has also become increasingly common. A few of these significant developments will be discussed in the next section.

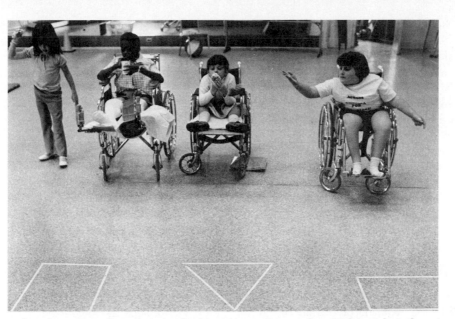

Group of myelomeningocele patients involved in perceptual motor class. Girl on right is throwing bean bag at square in response to command by classmate. The task combines auditory processing and visual motor integration work. It is both therapeutic recreation and adapted physical education.

Preventive Medicine

One of the most significant changes in society during the past decade was the increased emphasis on preventive medicine. Whereas in the past the emphasis was to a great extent on how to treat and cure various diseases and maladies, the emphasis today is on how to prevent these health deterrents. This movement is sometimes referred to as wellness. That is, humans are gradually becoming more concerned with how they can prevent sickness and disease. Research suggests that this goal can be accomplished by such means as engaging in physical activity on a regular basis, eating the right kind of food in the right amount, watching one's weight, practicing stress management, using moderation in the use of alcohol, and not smoking. (See Chapter 3.)

Physical Fitness

The physical fitness movement is another development that is receiving more attention in all segments of society. People are striving to improve their fitness and are engaging in such activities as jogging, racquetball, tennis, cross-country skiing, and aerobic dancing. AAHPERD is now stressing health-related fitness as well as performance-related fitness. Some physical education leaders believe that to date the emphasis has been largely on performance-related fitness. Today they believe that for the majority of the population the emphasis should be on health-related fitness, since this may help to prevent certain diseases, obesity, and musculoskeletal disorders. These physical education leaders indicate the same qualities, namely, cardiovascular function, strength, body composition, and flexibility, should be stressed for both health-related and performance-related physical fitness. Although the qualities are the same, the extent to which each quality is developed will vary with the individual and the goals he or she wishes to achieve.

In 1980 AAHPERD inaugurated the Health-Related Physical Fitness Test[4] (HRPFT). The test was designed to measure the physical fitness components associated with health. The test battery includes a distance run to assess cardiorespiratory endurance, skinfold measurements to determine body composition, one-minute sit-ups to measure neuromuscular function of the lower trunk and abdominal strength and endurance, and the sit-and-reach test to determine lower back and hamstring flexibility. From 1982 through 1984 the United States Department of Health and Human Services Office for Disease Prevention and Health Promotion in cooperation with AAHPERD and other agencies conducted the National Children and Youth Fitness Study[5] (NCYFS), the first nationwide assessment of youth fitness in nearly a decade.

The results, released in 1985, revealed that only one-third of youth aged 10 to 17 participated in appropriate physical activity essential for the maintenance of cardiorespiratory endurance. Moreover, the results revealed that youths in that age group had a higher percentage of body fat than those of the 1960s.

In 1985 a second study was undertaken to assess the health-related fitness and physical activity habits of children aged 5 to 9. The National Children and Youth Fitness Study II[6] results, released in 1987, revealed a low level of cardiorespiratory endurance within this population. As did the older youths, these children had a greater percentage of body fat than their counterparts of the 1960s.

Both of these studies raised the concern that current school physical education programs may be inadequate to promote lifetime fitness. In 1987 AAHPERD released the results of its study of state physical education requirements. Entitled *The Shape of the Nation: A Survey of State Physical Education Requirements,*[7] the study reported that 40% of children aged 5 to 8 exhibit coronary risk factors such as obesity, elevated blood pressure, high levels of cholesterol, and inactivity. As many as half of the children are not exercising sufficiently to develop adequate cardiorespiratory endurance. Furthermore, one-third of school-aged boys and one-half of school-aged girls cannot run a mile in less than 10 minutes. The lack of quality daily physical education programs contributes to the poor fit-

ness status of our country's youths. The survey found that only one state, Illinois, requires all students from kindergarten through grade 12 to take physical education every day; eight states have no physical education requirements for schools.

In 1987 Congress passed a resolution urging individual states to mandate high quality, daily physical education programs for all school-age children. Organizations supporting the resolution included the National Education Association, American Heart Association, American Medical Association, National Association of Elementary School Principals, Association for Supervision and Curriculum Development, American School Health Association, and the American Alliance for Health, Physical Education, Recreation and Dance.

A new fitness test and educational program entitled *Physical Best*[8] was introduced by AAHPERD in 1988 to replace the *Health-related Physical Fitness Test. Physical Best* emphasizes the cognitive, affective, and psychomotor dimensions of fitness. The fitness test battery assesses five components of fitness—cardiovascular endurance, body composition, flexibility, and upper body and abdominal strength and endurance—with the use of a distance run, skinfold measurements, sit-and-reach test, pull-ups, and sit-ups, respectively. The educational program helps teachers assist students in attaining desirable fitness habits through the use of individualized goal-setting, motivation techniques, and encouragement of participation in physical activities outside of the school setting.

The involvement of the federal government in the nation's health and fitness continues. In 1981, President Reagan appointed George Allen to head the President's Council on Physical Fitness and Sports. When George Bush began his term of office as President in 1989, Dick Kazmar chaired the Council. In 1990 President Bush appointed Arnold Schwarzenegger the new chairperson. In an address to the 1990 AAHPERD National Convention, Schwarzenegger emphasized the importance of improving the fitness of the nation, especially that of its youths. Quality daily physical education programs are necessary in the schools if the fitness status of youths is to improve. Furthermore,

Arnold Schwarzenegger, Chairman of the President's Council on Physical Fitness and Sport, addresses the AAHPERD members at the national convention on the need for cooperation to improve the fitness of Americans of all ages.

Schwarzenegger noted that physical activity and dance have the potential to improve the quality of life and health of people of all ages. Finally, Schwarzenegger stated that AAHPERD and the President's Council must work cooperatively to accomplish these goals.

Physical Activity as a Therapeutic Modality

Another development of the past two decades is the increased use of physical activity as a therapeutic modality for individuals who are disabled or who suffer from an affliction requiring therapy. As a result of this development, physical therapy and rehabilitative medicine, corrective therapy, occupational therapy, dance therapy, and recreational therapy have become specialties requiring professionals who have expertise in using movement, exercise, dance, and sport as a therapeutic modality. (See Chapters 4 and 12 for a further discussion of these activities.)

Girls' and Women's Sports

Participation by girls and women in sports has grown rapidly in the 1970s and continued unabated into the 1980s. The changing attitudes toward women in society was one factor that promoted the growth of participation. Participation was also greatly enhanced by the passage of Title IX of the Educational Amendments Act in 1972. In essence, Title IX states, "No person in the United States shall on the basis of sex be excluded from participation in, be denied the benefits of, or be subjected to discrimination under any education program or activity receiving Federal financial assistance." This legislation has had wide-ranging effects on physical education and athletic programs in the United States.

One of the major reasons why Title IX came into existence was to ensure that girls and women receive the same rights as boys and men. Testimony before congressional committees prior to the enactment of this legislation indicated that girls and women were being discriminated against in many educational programs, including physical education and athletics. While Title IX applies to all types of educational programs, probably the most dramatically affected have been sport and physical education programs. Girls' and women's athletic programs, in particular, have grown rapidly in only a few short years. In the early 1970s comparatively few varsity interscholastic and intercollegiate teams were for girls and women. However, as a result of the federal regulation banning sex discrimination, girls' and women's sport teams have come into their own and are in evidence throughout the nation.

Participation in sports by girls and women has risen dramatically since the enactment of Title IX. According to the National Federation of State High School Associations,[9] during 1971, the year before Title IX legislation, 3,366,000 boys and 294,000 girls competed in interscholastic sports in the United States. In 1988-1989 the Federation reported that 3,416,884 boys and 1,839,352 girls took part in interscholastic sports.* Participation by women at the intercollegiate level also showed substantial increases. For example, according to the NCAA, 32,000 women competed in intercollegiate sports in 1972 whereas in 1988-1989 the NCAA reported that 88,413 women and 156,765 men competed.[10] (These figures include only NCAA-sponsored championship sports; thus the number of participants is greater than reported here.)

Title IX mandated certain provisions for physical education and athletic programs. With respect to physical education, no discrimination could occur in program offerings, quality of teachers, and availability and quality of facilities and equipment. Physical education classes must be organized on a coeducational basis. However, classes may be separated by sex for contact sports such as wrestling, basketball, and football. Also, within classes students may be grouped by ability or another basis, except sex, although such groupings may result in single-sex or predominately single-sex groupings.

Title IX also resulted in changes in the conduct of athletic programs. Separate teams for men and women or a coeducational team must be provided in schools and colleges. For example, if only one team is organized in a particular school for a sport such as swimming, then students of both sexes must be permitted to try out for this team. Both sexes in educational institutions must be provided with equal opportunities for the following: equipment and supplies, use of facilities for practice and games, medical and training services, coaching and academic tutoring, travel allowances, housing and dining facilities, compensation of coaches, financial assistance, and publicity. Equal aggregate expenditures are not required; however, equal opportunities for men and women are mandated.

Equal opportunities are to be figured on a proportional basis relative to the number of women and men participating. For example, Title IX requires that colleges and universities provide reasonable opportunities for men and women students to receive athletic scholarships and grants-in-aid in proportion to the number of men and women participating athletes. Thus, if the total scholarship fund is $200,000 in a school with 70 men and 30 women athletes, the men athletes are entitled to $140,000 while the women athletes are entitled to $60,000.

The implementation of Title IX and the rapid growth of girls' and women's sports did lead to some problems, both in the physical education and athletic realms. Teachers in many cases were unprepared to teach many activities on a coeducational basis. Students also encountered problems such as feeling uncomfortable performing some activities, particularly those in which they had little skill, in front of the opposite sex. In athletics the effort to achieve and maintain high-quality athletic programs requires a tremendous commitment of funds and strained some institutions' resources. Many women teachers found themselves unprepared to coach highly skilled women athletes. As athletics grew the girls' and women's athletic programs were confronted with the same pressures that boys' and men's programs have faced over the years such as the emphasis on winning, recruiting, and maintaining academic eligibility. Governance also was in question. The Association of Intercollegiate Athletics for Women (AIAW), founded in 1972, initially was the governing body for women's intercollegiate sports. The AIAW established policies and procedures governing competition and conducted national championships for women's intercollegiate sports. In 1980-81 960

---

*A person who plays two sports could be counted twice.

Title IX has expanded sport opportunities for girls and women at all levels of competition.

institutions were members and 99,000 women participated in AIAW events; the AIAW conducted 39 national championships encompassing 17 sports. In 1982 the NCAA and the NAIA (National Association of Intercollegiate Athletics) assumed the governance of intercollegiate sports for women at all NCAA and NAIA institutions.

Throughout its history many challenges to Title IX have been heard by the courts. In 1984 the United States Supreme Court in a six to three decision ruled in the *Grove City College v. Bell* case that Title IX should be regarded as program specific. In essence, this narrow interpretation of Title IX held that only programs directly receiving federal aid were required to comply with Title IX, not the institution as a whole. Prior to this ruling Title IX was interpreted broadly, that is, institutions receiving any federal funds were required to comply with Title IX in all institution activities. Since athletic programs typically receive little, if any, direct federal funding, the threat of losing funding for noncom-

pliance and nonsupport of women's athletics is without substance. While some institutions remained deeply committed to women's athletics the fear existed that some institutions, with the threat of noncompliance removed from over their heads, allowed women's athletics to stagnate or even to become victims of budgetary cutbacks.

In 1988 the Civil Rights Restoration Act superceded the 1984 United States Supreme Court ruling. Once again, Title IX was interpreted broadly and its applicability to athletics was reinstated.

Title IX has led to dramatic changes regarding the conduct of physical education and athletic programs and to significant increases in participation by girls and women within these programs. However, the impact of Title IX has been limited by several factors including gender biases, limited budgets, inadequate facilities, lack of qualified leadership (i.e., coaches), and resistance to change. Although equal opportunity is mandated by law and great strides have occurred within the last decade, much still needs to be accomplished within both physical education and athletic programs to achieve equity.

Programs for Individuals with Disabilities

In recent years many court decisions have been made and laws passed supporting the right of students with disabilities to have the same educational opportunities as other students. These mandates have resulted in significant changes in the conduct of physical education programs as well as athletic programs for individuals with disabilities. The rights of the disabled in programs for which schools and other sponsoring organizations receive federal funds was guaranteed by Section 504 of the Rehabilitation Act of 1973 (P.L. 93-122). This law provided for access to all school programs, including physical education and athletics.

The Education Amendment Act of 1974 (P.L. 93-380) ensured that individuals with disabilities were placed in the least restrictive alternative environment for educational purposes. The law stipulates that whenever appropriate children with disabilites should be educated with children without disabilities. Removal from the regular educational environment should occur only when the nature or the severity of the disability prohibits education achievement despite the use of supplementary aides and services.

One of the most widely known laws is P.L. 94-142, or the Education of All Handicapped Children Act of 1975. This law provided for mainstreaming of some children with disabilities into the schools. Section 121a.307 of the regulations stated that physical education services, specially designed if necessary, were to be made available to every disabled child. All educational services are to be provided for disabled students in the least restrictive environment. In essence, this means that a disabled child is placed in a special class or a regular class or moved between the two environments as dictated by his or her abilities and capabilities. Furthermore, the school assumes the responsibility of providing the necessary adjunct services to ensure that students with disabilities perform to their optimum

capacity, whether they are integrated into a regular program or left in a special class.

P.L. 94-142 also stipulated that after identification and eligibility have been determined for disabled students, an individualized educational program, often referred to as an IEP, must be developed for each student. The IEP is to include a statement of the present levels of educational performance, annual goals as well as short-term instructional objectives, specific educational services to be provided, and evaluation procedures. The IEP is developed by using a team approach; input is solicited from the classroom teacher, special education and physical education teachers, representatives of special services such as guidance, and the parents.

In 1986 the Education for All Handicapped Children Amendments of 1986 (P.L. 99-457) was passed and implementation began in 1990. This law mandated educational services to individuals with special needs from 0 to 2 years of age be provided and that services for 3 to 5 year olds be expanded. Special educational services, including physical education, are required. Preschool physical education programs will need to be expanded to accommodate the diverse needs of these individuals and to fulfill the mandate of the law.

The aftermath of the federal legislation directed toward improving conditions of persons with disabilities and meeting their educational needs has brought about many changes. Schools are now required to provide physical education, intramurals, recreational programs, and athletic programs for students with disabilities. Adapted physical education programs have expanded. Teachers had to learn different strategies to enhance the learning opportunities for students with disabilities mainstreamed into regular physical education classes. Facilities had to be altered and modified to meet the needs of the disabled. It is hoped that the commitment to improve the educational opportunities and to meet the educational needs of individuals with disabilities will continue in the years ahead.

In the 1970s and 1980s the number of individuals with disabilities participating in competitive sports has increased. The Amateur Sports Act of 1978 (P.L. 95-606) charged the United States Olympic Committee to encourage provisions for sporting opportunities for the disabled, specifically to expand participation by individuals with disabilities in programs of athletic competition for able-bodied individuals. This charge served as the impetus for the formation of the Committee of Sports for the Disabled in 1983. The committee is to promote participation in sport by handicapped or disabled individuals and to support amateur sports programs for athletes with disabilities. Participation in national and international competitions and games by athletes with specific disabilities continues to rise. Competitions include the Paralympics, the Special Olympics, World Games for the Deaf, and the World Wheelchair Games, to name just a few. Competition at the state and local level, such as Connecticut's Nutmeg Games for the Disabled, continues to grow. It is likely that this trend will continue as all segments of our society find participation in sport to be a meaningful and satisfying experience.

Facilities and Equipment

Scientific and technological advances had a tremendous impact on the design and construction of facilities during this time. Many types of artificial playing surfaces have been manufactured since the inception of artificial grass surfaces. Synthetic surfaces are replacing wooden gymnasium floors, cinder tracks, and various types of surfaces on tennis courts. Enclosed facilities and stadiums have become increasingly common, and many of these buildings feature dome-shaped and air-supported structures. Solar collection devices are starting to be used in buildings to reduce heating costs. Legislation has prompted changes in facilities as well. Federal legislation mandated that existing facilities had to be modified to provide access for individuals with disabling conditions and new construction must be "barrier-free" or accessible to individuals with disabilities.

Scientific advances in computer technology have helped researchers, but practitioners have also found that computers can facilitate their work. Practitioners are using personal computers for record keeping as well as, in some cases, to display models of ideal performance. Students have used these computers to learn material as well as keep track of their own fitness performances. Technology has modified videotape recorders to make them easier to use and increasing sophistication has led to greater utility. Practitioners can provide their students with videotape displays of their own performance as well as the performance of experts. The ease of use encourages practitioners to employ this equipment more often.

SUMMARY

History provides the foundation for the discipline of physical education. Many of today's activities have their forerunners in the past. Many of our physical education and sport programs and activities today have been shaped by the heritage from our past. Studying history also provides one with an appreciation for other cultures and the role of physical education and sport in these societies.

An adage states that "history tends to repeat itself." Recurring themes are apparent throughout the history of physical education and sport. For example, wars frequently served as the impetus for societies to intensify their physical education program or to justify its existence. Physical fitness was promoted among the populace to prepare for these war efforts.

However, obviously not all history repeats itself. Changes are apparent too. The impact of different philosophies on the content and structure of physical education and sport programs and changes in the nature and the importance of objectives can be discerned throughout the years. It is important that one be aware of the events that served as catalysts and deterrents to the growth of physical education and sport.

Physical education and sport today is entering one of the most exciting eras in its history. The fitness movement, the emphasis on preventive medicine, the increased specialization of the field, and the broadening of physical education and sport programs to reach all segments of the population are some of the significant developments in physical education and sport today. By understanding the history of physical education and sport a professional can better understand the nature of the profession, appreciate the significant developments of today, and project trends for the future.

SELF-ASSESSMENT TESTS

These tests are designed to assist students in determining if the materials and competencies presented in this chapter have been mastered.

1. Reflect on the history of physical education and sport and then prepare a graph that traces its history from ancient times to recent times. Identify the high and low points of physical education and sport in the graph, and supply a rationale for your analysis.

2. Conduct an evaluation of Athenian Greek physical education and sport. As a result of this evaluation identify the contributions that can be directly traced to the Athenian Greeks. Be specific in your answers.

3. Discuss the influence of the various philosophical schools of thought on the growth of physical education and sport. Additionally, describe events and philosophies that served as catalysts for the growth of physical education and sport and events and philosophies that served as deterrents to the growth of physical education and sport.

4. After each of the following names write a sentence that will identify the person and his or her historical contribution to physical education:

Rousseau	Sargent	McKenzie
Jahn	Hitchcock	Hanna
Ling	Wood	Gulick
Maclaren	Anderson	Hetherington

5. Your professor has requested that you supply evidence to show substantial interest in sport, health, and fitness can be found among various segments of the population. Cite evidence of this interest and the implications of such interest for individuals seeking careers in physical education and sport.

6. Project future developments for physical education and sport based on historical events, including both events from early as well as recent times.

REFERENCES

1. US Department of Health, Education, and Welfare: Healthy people: the surgeon general's report on health promotion and disease prevention, Washington, DC, 1979, US Government Printing Office.

2. US Department of Health and Human Services: Promoting health/preventing disease: objectives for the nation, Washington, DC, 1980, US Government Printing Office.

3. Public Health Service, US Department of Health and Human Services: Promoting health/preventing disease: year 2000 objectives for the nation (draft), Washington, DC, 1989, US Government Printing Office.

4. American Alliance for Health, Physical Education, Recreation, and Dance: Health related fitness test, Reston, Va, 1980, AAHPERD.

5. Ross JG and Gilbert GG: The national children and youth study: a summary of the findings, Journal of Physical Education, Recreation, and Dance 56(1):45-50, 1985.

6. Ross JG and Pate RR: The national children and youth fitness study II, Journal of Physical Education, Recreation, and Dance 58(9):51-56, 1987.

7. AAHPERD: The shape of the nation: a survey of state physical education requirements, Reston, Va, 1987, AAHPERD.

8. AAHPERD: Physical best, Reston, Va, 1988, AAHPERD.

9. National Federation of State High School Associations, March 1990.

10. National Collegiate Athletic Association, March 1990.

SUGGESTED READINGS

American Alliance for Health, Physical Education, Recreation, and Dance: Centennial issue 1885-1985, Journal of Physical Education, Recreation, and Dance 56(4), entire issue, 1985.

    This Alliance centennial issue documents the growth of AAHPERD and analyzes the progress of this organization over 100 years.

Baker WJ: Sports in the Western world, Totowa, NJ, 1989, Rowan and Littlefield.

    This text examines the origins and the role of sports in western societies and the foundations of American sport.

Cordts H, editor: Physical education, recreation and dance—an international view, Journal of Physical Education, Recreation, and Dance 58(9):18-49, 1987.

    These 14 articles provide an overview of physical education programs in other nations, specifically Nigeria, USSR, New Guinea, China, Denmark, Federal Republic of Germany and Bahrain, as well as offering cross-cultural perspectives.

DePauw KP: Committment and challenges: sport opportunities for athletes with disabilities, Journal of Physical Education, Recreation, and Dance 55(2)34-43, 1984.

    Sports opportunities for athletes with disabilities are described and a list of 25 organizations sponsoring competitions is included, providing an excellent resource. Specific information is given about the National Association of Sports for Cerebral Palsy, American Athletic Association for the Deaf, National Handicapped Sports and Recreation Association, National Wheelchair Athletic Association, United States Amputee Athletic Association, United States Association for Blind Athletes, and the Special Olympics.

Gerber EW: Innovators and institutions in physical education, Philadelphia, 1972, Lea & Febiger.

    The contributions of outstanding leaders and institutions in American and European physical education are described in this comprehensive text.

Gerber EW and others: The American women in sport, Reading, Mass, 1974, Addison-Wesley.

A multidisciplinary analysis of the involvement of women in sport in the United States is the focus of this text. The analysis includes a historical overview of women's participation in sport, analysis of the institutional nature of sport, the relationship of the feminist movement to sports involvement, and psychological and physical performance profiles of women athletes.

Lee M: A history of physical education and sports in the USA, New York, 1983, John Wiley & Sons, Inc.

The author traces the history of physical education and sport from the heritage of the ancient world to the latter part of the twentieth century.

Nixon HL, editor: Sport and disability, Arena Review 8(1), entire issue, 1984.

This issue focuses on sport for the disabled. Topics include sport and the disabled, sport involvement for the disabled, sport and the elderly, the Special Olympics, and sport and recreational skills for the disabled.

Oxedine JB: American Indian Sports Heritage, Champaign, Ill, 1988, Human Kinetics.

The role of sport in Indian societies, the emergence of American Indians into sport, and current developments are examined.

Rees CR: The Olympic dilemma: applying the contract theory and beyond, Quest 37(1):50-59, 1985.

From the perspective of social psychology the interaction of spectators, athletes, and organizers at the Olympic Games is discussed. Suggestions are offered to increase the positive feelings of the Olympic participants.

Rintala J, editor: Women and the Olympics, Journal of Physical Education, Recreation, and Dance 59(3):34-64, 1988.

These 10 articles discuss the experience of women in the Olympics, women's leadership role, and psychological aspects of the female Olympic athlete.

Seagrave JO and Chu D: The Olympic Games in transition, Champaign, Ill, 1988, Human Kinetics.

A critical examination of the philosophy and past and future issues and problems of the Olympics Games are presented.

van Dalen DB and Bennett BL: A world history of physical education, Englewood-Cliffs NJ, 1971, Prentice-Hall, Inc.

A comprehensive history of physical education throughout the world is presented.

Welch PD and Lerch HA: History of American physical education and sport, Springfield, Ill, 1981, Charles C Thomas, Publisher.

The recreational, educational, and professional activities of the American people are presented in this text. The history of today's sport, games, and programs is traced.

Chapter 6

Exercise Physiology

INSTRUCTIONAL OBJECTIVES AND COMPETENCIES TO BE ACHIEVED

After reading this chapter the student should be able to—
- Define exercise physiology and understand the importance of exercise physiology to the practitioner.
- Describe what is meant by fitness and physical fitness and the extent of interest among the general public about this subject today.
- Understand concepts of health and motor-performance fitness.
- Understand and appreciate the role of exercise in achieving physical fitness.
- Explain the principles and guidelines for designing exercise programs.
- Identify and discuss contributors and deterrents to fitness.

One of the most rapidly growing fields of specialization in physical education is that of exercise physiology. Exercise physiology is the study of the effects of exercise on the body. Specifically, exercise physiology is concerned with the body's responses and adaptations to exercise ranging from the system to the subcellular levels. These modifications can be short-term, that is, lasting only for the duration of the activity, or long-term, present as long as the activity is continued on a regular basis. Knowledge of exercise physiology is essential to the practitioner. It is critical that the practitioner understand the effects of exercise on the individual's body to plan programs to achieve the desired outcomes and to monitor the effects of such programs on the individual.

The field of exercise physiology provides the practitioner with a wealth of information to guide his or her endeavors. Practitioners, whether they are teachers in a school or nonschool setting, coaches, or fitness leaders or exercise physiologists employed in a commercial or corporate fitness center, must understand the responses of the body to exercise. The knowledge of principles governing the different types of training programs and cognizance of the guidelines to be followed in constructing an exercise prescription will enable the practitioner to design exercise programs to meet the individual's needs and goals.

The field of exercise physiology has become increasingly sophisticated. New research procedures and measurement techniques coupled with advances in equipment, computer technology, and other related disciplines such as biochemistry have contributed to the rapid advancement of the knowledge base. Fitness is a major area of study for the exercise physiologist. While fitness and the elite performer long have been a key concern of the exercise physiologist, interest in recent years has encompassed virtually all aspects of human performance and people of all skill abilities and of all ages, from the very young to the elderly, including individuals with disabilities.

EXERCISE PHYSIOLOGY: AN OVERVIEW

Exercise physiology is the study of the body's responses and its adaptation to the stress of exercise. Exercise physiologists are physical education specialists who are concerned with investigating both the immediate and the long-term effects of exercise on all aspects of body functioning. These effects include the responses of the muscular system, the action of the nervous system during physical activity, the adjustments of the respiratory system, and the dynamics of the cardiovascular system.

Improving the response of the body to exercise also is an important area of study. The effects of exercise are examined at different levels, ranging from the subcellular level to the systemic level. Describing and explaining the myriad of functional changes brought about by exercise sessions of variable duration and intensity are the functions of exercise physiology.

As a subdiscipline, exercise physiology is one of the largest and most popular areas of study within the realm of physical education and sport. It has one of the richest traditions; interest in the effects of exercise on the body can be traced to ancient times. Today the depth and breadth of knowledge in exercise physiology is growing rapidly because of the proliferation of research, which is facilitated by increasingly sophisticated technology and by the widespread interest of professionals in this field.

Scope and Status of Exercise Physiology

Exercise physiology encompasses a broad range of topics. Examples of some typical areas of study are listed on the next page.

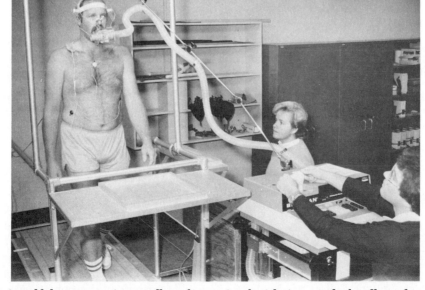

Sophisticated laboratory equipment allows the exercise physiologist to study the effects of exercise on various body systems.

- Effects of various exercise programs on the systems of the body, including circulatory, respiratory, nervous, skeletal, muscle, and endocrine systems.
- Relationship of energy metabolism to performance.
- Effectiveness of various training programs in promoting gains in specific components of fitness (e.g., effects of Nautilus training on strength).
- Effects of various environmental factors such as temperature, humidity, altitude, pollutants, and different environments (i.e., space or underseas) on physiological responses to exercise and performance.
- Effects of individual differences such as age, sex, initial level of fitness, or disability on fitness development and performance.
- Identification of factors that limit performance.
- Effectiveness of various rehabilitation programs on the recovery of injured athletes, on healthy and diseased individuals, and on individuals with disabilities.
- Effects of ergogenic aids such as drugs or music on performance.
- Health and therapeutic benefits to be accrued from engaging in appropriate levels of physical activity.
- Effects of nutrition on performance.

Historically, fitness and performance are the two areas of research that have dominated exercise physiology. Much attention has been directed by researchers in the area of cardiovascular exercise physiology, which examines how oxygen is used by the cardiovascular system during exercise. Researchers have also focused a great deal of effort on the study of exercise metabolism, investigating the metabolic responses to exercise and training conducted under a variety of conditions.

In recent years, cardiac rehabilitation and exercise biochemistry are two areas that have become increasingly popular as major fields of study. Cardiac rehabilitation focuses on the assessment of cardiovascular functioning as well as on the determination of the effectiveness of various exercise programs in preventing cardiovascular disease and rehabilitating individuals suffering from the disease. Exercise biochemistry involves examination of the effects of exercise at the cellular level, specifically within the muscle cell.

Although the field of exercise physiology is becoming increasingly specialized, many professionals in this field recognize that to fully investigate and understand human performance, an interdisciplinary approach is necessary. Physiological, psychological, biomechanical, neurological, and biochemical factors must be considered.

The application of knowledge from the realm of exercise physiology appears to focus predominately on preparing the body for physical activity. Two primary areas of application can be discerned: first, the enhancement of fitness, promotion of health, and prevention of disease and, second, the improvement and refinement of motor performance, especially in the area of sport. The principles of exercise physiology can be used to improve and maintain both health-related fitness and motor-skill related fitness.

There is a widespread interest in health and fitness among the American public. Many Americans are aware of the principles of exercise and can successfully apply these principles to the design and conduct of personal exercise programs. More and more Americans are becoming familiar with the frequency, intensity, and duration of exercise necessary to realize concomitant health benefits. Worksite, hospital, community, and commercial fitness programs continue to grow both in number and in the magnitude of services they offer to their clients. Home-based fitness programs also are increasing in popularity as many individuals prefer the convenience of working out at home rather than at a club. Sales of athletic shoes, fitness equipment, and exercise clothing are at an all-time high. Videocassettes, television programs, magazine articles, and books all help the public to be informed of the latest information in this field. However, despite the growing number of people exercising regularly, there is concern among professionals that many segments of the population are sedentary or are not exercising sufficiently to realize health benefits (see Chapter 3 for further discussion). Moreover, even though the public is better informed about exercise and fitness than ever before, a greater educational effort is needed. Many people employ improper exercise habits and hold erroneous beliefs. Qualified professionals are needed to help inactive people to incorporate appropriate physical activity into their lives and to dispel erroneous beliefs.

The current tremendous interest in health and fitness by the public and the expansion of the knowledge base of this field also have enhanced professional opportunities. An increasing number of young people are undertaking undergraduate and graduate study in exercise physiology and preparing to pursue careers in adult fitness, cardiac rehabilitation, strength development, and athletic training (career opportunities within these areas are discussed in Chapter 12).

Sports Medicine

Sports medicine is an area of study closely associated with exercise physiology. A growing area, sports medicine encompasses both the medical and the scientific aspects of exercise and sport performance. The primary concern of the sports medicine specialist is the prevention and treatment of sport injuries. This includes planning activities to prevent injuries, using various treatment approaches to rehabilitate injuries, and designing equipment to assist athletes in staying healthy. Nutrition, drugs, ergogenic aids, and ethical matters pertaining to the training, exercise, and treatment of athletes also are concerns of the sports medicine specialist.

In addition to medical training, sports medicine specialists must have a thorough understanding of the principles of exercise physiology. Because exercise is an essential component of sports conditioning as well as important for injury prevention and rehabilitation, adherence to the principles of exercise physiology in designing programs to accomplish these goals is critical.

Physical Fitness and Exercise Physiology

Contemporary professionals view physical fitness as a quality comprised of several different compo-

nents, each with specific requirements for its development and maintenance. AAHPERD and many other professionals classify the fitness components into two categories: those pertaining to health and those pertaining to motor-skill performance. The terms health fitness and motor-performance fitness[1] are currently used when discussing these two areas. Table 6-1 identifies and defines the health and motor-performance components.

Health fitness is important for all individuals throughout their lifespan. The achievement and maintenance of those qualities necessary for an individual to function efficiently and to enhance his or her health through the prevention and remediation of disease and illness is the central focus of health fitness. An increasing body of research supports the contribution of regular, appropriate physical activity to health and to one's quality of life.

Motor-performance fitness emphasizes the development of those qualities that enhance the performance of physical activities such as sport. Whereas health fitness was concerned with living better, motor-performance fitness is concerned with performing skills better and more efficiently.[1] Moreover, motor-performance fitness is specific to the sport or activity in which the individual engages. Different combinations of motor-performance fitness components are needed, depending on the specific motor activity. For example, the degree of power, agility, and speed needed by a football player is different from that required by a tennis player, even though both individuals need all of those qualities to perform at an optimal level.

Fitness, be it health-related or motor-skill related, must be viewed in relation to individual characteristics (e.g., age), needs, goals, and tasks that must be performed. All individuals possess certain levels of each of the health and motor-performance fitness components. The extent to which each quality is developed depends on the individual. A weekend tennis player needs a different level of physical fitness than a competitive wheelchair marathoner, a 70-year-old grandparent requires a different level of fitness than the 10-year-old grandchild. Professionals charged with the responsibility of designing and implementing fitness programs

TABLE 6-1   Physical Fitness Components Defined

Fitness Component	Definition
Health Fitness Components	
Body composition	Amount of body fat expressed as a percentage
Cardiovascular endurance	Maximum functional capacity of the cardiorespiratory system to sustain work or physical activity involving large muscle groups over an extended period
Flexibility	Range of movement possible at a joint or joints
Muscular endurance	Ability of a muscle or muscle group to repeat muscular contractions against a force or to sustain a contraction over time
Muscular strength	Maximum amount of force that can be exerted by a muscle or muscle group against a resistance during a single contraction
Motor-performance Fitness Components	
Agility	Ability to change direction rapidly with control
Balance	Ability to maintain equilibrium while stationary or moving
Coordination	Ability to execute movements smoothly and efficiently
Power	Ability to produce force at a fast speed; a combination of strength and speed usually applied during a short period
Reaction time	Time elapsed between the administration of a stimulus and the body's response to the stimulus
Speed	Ability to move the body quickly

should ask the program participants, "fitness for what?" Does the participant desire physical fitness that will contribute to general health or to outstanding performance in a particular sport? All people should seek to achieve and maintain an optimal level of physical fitness with respect to their individual needs.

Physical activity is essential to the achievement of physical fitness. Proper development and maintenance of physical fitness requires the application of knowledge from the realm of exercise physiology. Because exercise physiology is concerned with both the body's immediate and long-term responses to exercise, the design and conduct of fitness programs to meet an individual's specific fitness needs should be guided by knowledge from this field. Elite athletes preparing for competition, healthy adults desiring to work out on a regular basis, adults recovering from heart disease, youth sport athletes rehabilitating from injury, elderly citizens aspiring to live independent lives, and individuals with a disability who are striving to fully meet the challenges of life can all benefit from participation in a well-designed physical fitness program based on the principles of exercise physiology.

PHYSICAL FITNESS: HEALTH FITNESS DIMENSIONS

Concern about the quality of life and health is at an unprecedented level in the United States. Health promotion and disease prevention efforts are an important national priority. There is increased recognition not only by the medical and scientific communities but by the general public as well that the manner in which one lives one's life can have a profound effect on individual well-being and quality of life. Proper nutrition, regular and appropriate exercise, effective stress management, and freedom from destructive health habits such as smoking can lead to the attainment of a high level of health.

The importance of physical activity as an integral part of a healthy life-style is becoming more widely recognized. Moreover, scientific evidence of the health benefits of exercise continues to grow. Studies show that significant benefits can be realized by individuals who regularly engage in physical activity of appropriate frequency, intensity, and duration. Maintenance of an adequate level of the health-related components of physical fitness— cardiovascular endurance, muscular strength and endurance, body composition, and flexibility— can

Employees of the Kimberly-Clark Corporation participate in aerobic dance class.

help reduce the risk of heart disease, hypertension, noninsulin-dependent diabetes, osteoporosis, obesity, and certain mental health problems such as depression. Reduction of the incidence of stroke and maintenance of functional independence of the elderly are also benefits that may be realized through participation in regular physical activity. Furthermore, individuals who are physically active typically outlive those who are not.

An increasingly large number of people of all ages are engaging in physical activity on a regular basis to improve fitness. Enrollment in fitness clubs and health spas continues to increase each year. Approximately 50,000 corporations in the United States spend an estimated $2 billion each year on fitness and recreation programs for their employees. Billions of dollars are being spent on exercise apparel, shoes, equipment, facilities, and programs. Community programs have long waiting lists for fitness classes. Thousands of books on fitness are in print; some of them have sold millions of copies in a single year.

Although it appears that most of the nation's people are exercising, when the fitness phenomenon is examined more closely, it is not as widespread or as pervasive as it seems (see Chapter 3 for further discussion). It is estimated that only 10 to 20 percent of adults engage in physical activity to the extent necessary to realize the concomitant health benefits associated with health fitness.[2-4] Moreover, two recently completed national studies of youth fitness, the *National Children and Youth Fitness Study I* and *Study II*, indicated that the typical young person possesses inadequate levels of cardiovascular endurance and is significantly fatter than youths tested in the 1960s.[5,6] Based on this information, it appears that the fitness status of our nation still needs improvement.

The less-than-desirable fitness status of the nation's people offers a challenge to dedicated and qualified fitness educators. Physical educators need to use the increased documentation on the relationship of health fitness to well-being and the great interest in fitness by the public to engender support for fitness programs and to reach all segments of the population. Our professional resources must be used for improving the nation's fitness. Furthermore, it remains to be seen if physical educators will be recognized by the public as those specialists who possess expertise in this area and will be sought out by the public desiring to improve their level of fitness.

The Need for Fitness Education

More people in the United States are interested in becoming physically fit than ever before. Unfortunately, even though enthusiasm for fitness is great, a close examination of the fitness status of our nation's youths and adults evokes considerable concern (see Chapter 3 for a more thorough discussion). Recently completed national studies reveal that the fitness levels of the nation's young people has not improved in 10 years and, in some cases, has declined. Many children have less-than-satisfactory levels of cardiovascular endurance and upper body strength. Moreover, in comparison to youths 30 years ago, youths today have a higher percentage of body fat. There is considerable evidence that overweight children tend to become overweight adults. It is noteworthy that children who have a leaner body composition tend to be more physically active and watch less television; their parents tend to be physically active and exercise with their children.[6]

There is increased recognition that heart disease begins in childhood. A high percentage of body fat, a low level of cardiovascular endurance, and a pattern of inactivity are factors that contribute to cardiovascular disease. Children who possess these factors tend to retain them as they age, increasing their susceptibility to cardiovascular disease. Furthermore, only 36% of the nation's school children are enrolled in daily physical education. In 1990, Illinois was the only state that required daily physical education for all grades.[7]

Only 10 to 20 percent of adults in the United States exercise with sufficient intensity, duration, and frequency to develop and maintain adequate levels of health-related fitness.[2] While 40% of adults exercise sufficiently to realize some health-related benefits, another 40% are sedentary. The American Heart Association reports that 50% of all deaths each year in this country—nearly 1 million deaths—can be attributed to cardiovascular diseases. Approximately 60 million Americans suffer from hypertension and more than 60% of adults are overweight or obese. Low back pain is a serious health problem for over 75 million Americans, and it is estimated that over 80% of such pain can be attributed to improper muscle development.[8,9]

The hidden costs to industry resulting from the physical degeneration of employees are staggering. For example, loss of production in the United States because of premature death caused by chronic cardiovascular disease is $19.4 billion a year. Heart attacks alone cost the industry about 132 million work days yearly, which is approximately 4% of the gross national product. Low back pain is also costly; it is estimated that over $1 billion a year is lost in productivity and $250 million dollars a year in worker's compensation. These statistics do not take into consideration other important factors such as shortened workdays as a result of fatigue and of minor aches and pains or absenteeism caused by lowered physical resistance to disease.

The life-style of Americans has become increasingly sedentary. Modern technology has reduced the number of occupational and daily living tasks that require significant physical activity for their execution. Many of occupational tasks performed today require mental effort rather than physical labor. Daily tasks such as mowing the lawn have been made easier by power mowers. Driving has replaced much walking, and elevators have replaced much stair climbing. Many of our leisure activities are also sedentary in nature—most notably watching television. Consequently, Americans do not get sufficient vigorous physical activity to function at an optimum level.

Physical activity is important for healthful living. Many of the prominent health problems faced by Americans of all ages today can be attributed to lifestyle, particularly the lack of sufficient physical activity. Thus, there is a critical need for fitness education to help Americans understand the risks of inactivity, learn the skills and knowledge necessary to incorporate sufficient vigorous exercise into their life-style, and appreciate the contributions of physical activity to their health and quality of life.

Because many youths and adults do not fully understand and appreciate the importance of health and fitness, a heavy responsibility rests on the shoulders of educators. If a nation is to remain strong physically, mentally, spiritually, and socially, education for fitness must be undertaken. Furthermore, this education must take place largely through the formal processes of physical education, health education, recreation, and dance programs in schools and colleges. Knowledge about the human body must be imparted, desirable health attitudes inculcated, and proper health practices instilled. The responsibility for accomplishing this herculean task must be assumed mainly by physical educators, health educators, and dance and recreation educators. They must continually strive for sound school and community programs in their special fields.

It is also essential that an effort be made by professionals to reach adults no longer in the school setting. The fitness boom and knowledge of the health gains and related benefits to be derived from participation have motivated many adults, after years of inactivity, to get up from their armchairs and begin exercising. Corporate fitness programs, commercial health and fitness clubs, community sponsored programs, and continuing education programs can play an important role in educating all segments of the population about fitness and health. It is of critical importance that these programs be conducted under the direction of qualified professionals so that the desired outcomes can be achieved.

According to health experts, the way each human being lives will be a major determining factor for the health and fitness of that individual. Although heredity plays a part, to a large degree health and fitness are acquired characteristics. The food that is eaten, amount of rest obtained, physical activity engaged in, and other health practices that are followed play important roles in determining human welfare. In other words, it is important to follow a good health regimen if one is to be healthy and fit.

Education is essential to help people follow a healthful regimen. It is important to educate students about English so that they can communicate articulately with their fellow human beings, about mathematics so that they can add their grocery bills accurately, and about the fine arts so that they can appreciate and enjoy Chagall and Beethoven. It is also important to educate people about their physical selves so that they can function most efficiently as human beings and accomplish all they are capable of achieving. To attain this objective they need to know scientific facts essential to good health, possess desirable health attitudes, develop skills to make activity exciting and enjoyable, and be physically active. The end result will be productive, vigorous, and rewarding lives. As the philosopher Will Durant advised, health is mostly within each person's will. "In many cases, sickness is a crime," this philosopher stated. He continued, "We have done something physiologically foolish, and nature is being hard put to it to repair our mistakes. The pain we endure is the tuition we pay for our instruction in living."

Much of this education should take place early in life when the organic foundations are being laid, skills are more easily learned, and attitudes are formed. Unfortunately, too many people do not recognize the need for this education until cholesterol deposits have closed their arteries, ulcers have penetrated their duodenum, or cancer has started its insidious attack on their lungs. As one wise man has said, "We never appreciate health so much as when we lose it." Although it may be difficult to change the health habits of adults, schools and colleges *can* and *should* educate young people about their health and fitness. This is not only essential from the individual's point of view but also in view of this country's national posture. President Kennedy stated: "The strength of our democracy is no greater than the collective well-being of our people. The vigor of our country is no stronger than the vitality and will of our countrymen. The level of physical, mental, moral, and spiritual fitness of every American citizen must be our constant concern."

The fact that thousands of schoolchildren have undesirable health practices offers some evidence that educational programs are inadequate in this regard.

Sound school physical education programs are needed. To have outstanding programs, educators must have a clear understanding of the philosophy of physical education and its worth in education. The following definitions of terms and concepts will be helpful in setting the stage for fitness education of young and old persons alike be it in a school or a nonschool setting.

1. *Fitness implies more than physical fitness.* Fitness is the ability of a person to live a full and balanced existence. The totally fit person possesses not only physical well-being but also qualities such as good human relations, maturity, and high ethical standards. He or she also satisfies such basic needs as love, affection, security, and self-respect. Physical education programs are vitally concerned with physical fitness but also strive to contribute to total health and fitness.

2. *Physical fitness includes more than muscular strength.* The term *physical fitness* implies soundness of body organs such as the heart and lungs, a human mechanism that performs efficiently under exercise or work conditions (such as having sufficient stamina and strength to engage in vigorous physical activity), and a reasonable measure of skill in the performance of selected physical activities. Physical fitness is related to the tasks the person must perform, the potential for physical effort, and the relationship of physical fitness to the total self. The same degree of physical fitness is not necessary for everyone. It should be sufficient to meet the requirements of the job plus a little extra as a reserve for emergencies. The student who plays football needs a type of physical fitness different from the student who plays in the school orchestra. The question "fitness for what?" must always be asked.

Furthermore, determining the physical fitness of a person must be done in relation to that person's own human resources and not those of others. It depends on one's potentialities in the light of individual physical makeup. Finally, physical fitness cannot be considered by itself but, instead, as it is affected by mental, emotional, and social factors. A human being functions as a whole and not as segmented parts.

3. *Physical education is not the same as health education.* Although closely allied, health and physical education are separate fields of specialization. Whereas physical education is concerned primarily with education of and through the physical, the school health program is concerned with teaching for health (e.g., imparting facts about good nutrition), living healthfully at home (e.g., providing a healthful physical and emotional environment), and providing services for health improvement (e.g., instituting measures for communicable disease control).

4. *Physical education contributes to physical fitness.* The student needs to engage in regular physical activity but, in addition, needs to understand the impact this activity has on the body and mind. The student not only needs to have activities fitted to individual requirements but also to have these activities conducted in a safe and healthful environment. The student should develop skill in various sports as well as in first aid. These are only a few examples of how the physical education program helps to achieve the objective of physical fitness.

5. *Physical education must be an integral part of the educational program to achieve the goal of physical fitness most effectively.* This subject is not a frill or appendage of the school's curriculum or a means for entertaining students. It should be a vital part of every educational program in this country. Furthermore, such a concept must repeatedly be injected into programming, scheduling, and other practices that reflect the true educational philosophy of each school.

6. *Good leadership is the key to effective physical education.* The excellent physical education teacher is not someone who merely looks healthy, can produce a string of sports victories, or give a good speech before the Rotary Club. Leadership is basic to the physical education profession, and this means men and women who know their subject, the people they are teaching, and the best methods and techniques for teaching.

7. *Physical fitness is not synonymous with physical education.* Physical fitness is one objective of

physical education. It is important to have physically fit boys and girls. However, as long as the word *education* is a part of the term *physical education,* other responsibilities are implied. Developing physical skills, imparting knowledge about the human organism, and using the body as a vehicle for achieving desirable social traits also represent desirable goals. Any program or curriculum aimed merely at building strength and muscle is failing in its educational mission.

8. *Interscholastic athletics represent only one part of the total physical education program that contributes to physical fitness.* The school physical education program includes the class program for all students, the adapted program that fits the activities to handicapped or disabled individuals, the intramural and extramural program that provides a laboratory experience for skills and knowledge imparted in the class program, and the interscholastic athletic program for those students with exceptional physical skill. All four of these aspects of the physical education program must function in a manner that affords balance and harmony and allows for the achievement of physical fitness and other objectives for *all* students.

9. *The development of physical skills is a major contribution to long-term physical fitness of students.* Calisthenics and other forms of exercise yield organic benefit to the student, but one of the major contributions of any physical education program is to teach the student a wide variety of physical skills. All students should have the opportunity to develop proficiency in several lifetime sports such as tennis, golf, and swimming. Skills are the motivating agents that will encourage the student to engage in activities and to develop physical fitness, not only in the present but throughout life.

10. *Administrative support and understanding are needed to achieve physical fitness.* The quality of school physical education programs will be largely determined by the administrative leadership of the school and community. Boards of education, superintendents of schools, principals, business executives, and other administrative officials will decide the prestige these programs have in the eyes of the students, whether credit is given to the sub-

ject when calculating the requirements for graduation, how much money is provided in the budget for their development, the attention given to girls as well as to boys, the degree of emphasis on physically underdeveloped students compared with gifted athletes, and the answers to other administrative matters that affect the physical fitness of students.

11. *The American Medical Association (AMA) has outlined seven paths that lead to physical fitness.* The AMA list is as follows:

- *Proper medical care*—To be physically fit requires regular medical examinations, immunizations against communicable diseases, emergency care, and prompt treatment by qualified medical personnel when such care is warranted.
- *Nutrition*—"You are what you eat" is meaningful in regard to physical fitness. The right foods should be eaten in the right amounts.
- *Dental services*—Good oral hygiene is essential to physical fitness. This means regular visits to the dentist, treatment of dental caries, and proper mastication.
- *Exercise*—Exercise is important, but to have a salutary effect there must be a proper selection of activities adapted to the age, condition, and other needs of the individual, together with proper exposure to these activities in terms of time and intensity of the workout.
- *Satisfying work*—Work that is adapted to one's interests and abilities and performed in a satisfying working climate is essential to physical fitness. Good mental attitude, recognition, and a sense of achievement and belonging should be encouraged.
- *Healthy play and recreation*—To achieve physical fitness requires play and recreation in an atmosphere that has as its by-products fun, enjoyable companionship, and happy thoughts.
- *Rest and relaxation*—Adequate sleep, rest, and relaxation are essential to good health and physical fitness.

The physical educator should recognize the many-faceted approach to physical fitness and thereby understand that this quality cannot be achieved solely through physical activity.

Benefits of Exercise and Physical Activity

The positive contribution to health of regular exercise of appropriate frequency, intensity, and duration is well documented. Scientific evidence further substantiating the health benefits of physical activity continues to grow.

When viewed from a historical perspective, many of the serious health problems that faced people in earlier centuries were caused by infectious diseases such as typhoid, tuberculosis, and polio and poor living conditions such as poor sanitation, contaminated water supplies, and inadequate nutrition.[1] Advances in medical science, improved water treatment and sanitation, and better nutrition have reduced or virtually eliminated many infectious diseases in the United States.[1] Medical science also has provided much knowledge about the causes of disease and illness and what can be done to prevent them.

Many of the serious health problems confronting individuals are related, either wholly or in part, to the manner in which they lead their lives. It is now recognized that life-style can have a significant impact on one's health. Decisions an individual makes about eating, exercising, managing stress, engaging in unhealthy habits such as smoking, and practicing safe health practices such as visiting a physician regularly can have a profound influence on health and the quality of life.

One of the primary threats to the health and well-being of Americans is degenerative diseases, many of which can be categorized as hypokinetic diseases. Hypokinetic diseases are caused not by infection but by insufficient physical activity, often in conjunction with inappropriate dietary practices. Coronary artery disease, hypertension, osteoporosis, diabetes, chronic back pain, and obesity are examples of hypokinetic diseases. These diseases pose a serious threat to the health status of the nation; cardiovascular diseases are the leading cause of death in the United States.[2,8,9]

Regular, appropriate exercise leading to the achievement and maintenance of health fitness can help prevent and, in many circumstances, aid in the remediation of degenerative diseases. Therefore, incorporating exercise into one's lifestyle can have significant health benefits, both physical and mental.

Enhanced cardiovascular fitness is one health benefit of exercise. This helps reduce the risk of heart diseases. Benefits ascribed to cardiovascular fitness include a more efficient level of cardiovascular function, a stronger heart muscle, a lower heart rate, reduced blood pressure, increased oxygen carrying capacity of the blood, and improved coronary and peripheral circulation. Resistance to atherosclerosis is improved as desirable serum cholesterol levels are maintained; low-density lipids are reduced and protective high-density lipids are increased. The risk of a heart attack is lessened, while the chances of surviving a heart attack are increased. Physical activity can also help reduce other risk factors associated with cardiovascular disease such as obesity and hypertension.

Exercise can help maintain a desirable body composition. Excessive amounts of body fat is hazardous to one's health: Being overweight can shorten one's life. Elevated serum cholesterol levels, diabetes, hypertension, gall bladder disease, cardiovascular disease, osteoarthritis of the weight-bearing joints, and some types of cancer are all associated with being overweight. Research has shown that among persons whose weight exceeds normal by only 15% to 25%, death rates increase by approximately 30%.[2,8] Additionally, many adults and children who are obese experience psychological stress and self-concept problems. Exercising regularly helps maintain a healthy body weight by using excess calories and by preventing the addition of undesirable weight, thus reducing susceptibility to disease. Because overweight children often become overweight adults, and because the tendency to be overweight increases with age, it is important that proper exercise habits as well as balanced nutritional practices be acquired early in life. Exercise also can contribute to improved physical appearance and self-image.

Muscular strength, muscular endurance, and flexibility also are important components of health fitness. Millions of Americans suffer from problems with low-back pain. Many of these problems can be attributed to muscular weakness and imbalance, which in turn can be attributed to inactivity or participation in inappropriate activities. Achievement and maintenance of a desirable level of these components can decrease the risk of suffering from lower-back problems. Millions of elderly and disabled individuals may experience difficulty performing tasks of daily living because of insufficient development of these fitness components. Regular and appropriate physical activity can help these individuals achieve functional independence. Reduced risk of muscle and joint injury is also a positive outcome of regular and appropriate exercise.

The values of exercise are not limited only to the body; exercise also contributes to sound mental health. It may help alleviate mental illness and reduce susceptibility to depression and anxiety. Being fit can help individuals withstand and manage stress more effectively. Many people find exercising provides a release from tensions. Exercise makes a person feel better. Those who exercise often comment about this directly: "I feel more alive," "I have more energy," "I'm not as tired in the evening," "I can do a lot more with my life."

Regular participation in physical activity can contribute to the development of a positive self-concept and greater self-esteem. It enhances self-confidence, emotional stability, assertiveness, independence, and self-control. Individuals who are fit present a good appearance and maintain an appropriate body weight; individuals who are obese may suffer psychological problems, stress, and feelings of low self-worth.

Socialization is also provided by participation in exercise and physical activities. Sports, recreational activities, and exercise groups offer opportunities to fulfill the desire to belong to a group as well as for recognition. These are important psychosocial needs.

Achieving and maintaining health fitness can lead to improvements in many aspects of life. In addition to enhancing health, health fitness can contribute to increased work efficiency. Individuals who are fit have more energy, which contributes to greater productivity and efficiency of both physical and mental tasks. More energy is available for recreational activities and leisure time pursuits, fit individuals can also better withstand fatigue, and physical exercise can improve one's sleeping patterns.

Health fitness can improve overall general motor performance. Physical activities associated with daily living as well as sport skills can be performed more efficiently by individuals who are fit. Additionally, fit individuals recover more quickly from vigorous exercise and work than do unfit individuals. Physical activity enhances one's appearance and posture through the development of proper muscle tone, greater flexibility, and an enhanced sense of well-being.

Regular exercise can help mitigate the debilitating effects of old age. Generally, after age 30, physical qualities such as coordination and muscular endurance tend to diminish.[8,9] This degenerative process can be slowed by engaging in regular physical activity. To be most effective in mitigating the effects of aging, the integration of regular physical activity into one's life-style should begin early in life. Individuals who remain active and physically fit throughout their life will retain a more desirable level of cardiovascular health, muscular strength, muscular endurance, and body composition.

Individuals who exercise regularly are likely to engage in other positive forms of health-promoting behavior. Because they do not want to negate the benefits accrued from exercise, they may also strive to eat properly, get sufficient rest and relaxation, and manage the stress in their lives. Personal health and well-being becomes an important personal priority.

Regular and appropriate physical activity has numerous benefits. However, to realize these benefits, a person must be active all year. To function properly and at a high level, the human organism needs exercise as an essential ingredient on a regular basis, just as it demands nutritious food every day. Being active throughout one's life is essential for continued good health.

Principles of Fitness Training

Knowledge from the subdiscipline of exercise physiology offers guidelines for physical educators to use when planning and conducting programs to improve fitness. These principles should be fol-

An increasing number of adults are exercising with sufficient intensity, duration, and frequency to realize health benefits.

lowed whether the exercise program is being designed by an elementary physical educator to improve students' health fitness, by a coach to improve athletes' performance, by an exercise leader to enhance adults' fitness, or by an exercise specialist as part of a patient's cardiac rehabilitation program. Several physiological and behavioral factors must be taken into account if the sought-after benefits—improvement and maintenance of fitness—are to be realized.

1. **Principle of overload.** Overload is essential if fitness gains are to be realized. Simply, the principle of overload states that for improvements in fitness to occur, one must perform more than one's usual amount of exercise. For example, if improvement in muscular strength is desired, the muscles must be exercised with more intensity than normal. Once the desired level of fitness has been reached, individuals must continue to train at a level that will maintain the desired level.

2. **Principle of specificity.** The type of physiological changes that occur as a result of training are related to the type of training employed. Training programs should be designed with specific results in mind. For example, to realize the maximum gains in cardiorespiratory endurance, activities and programs should be designed specifically to achieve this aim.

3. **The individual's initial level of fitness must be considered.** An individual embarking on an exercise program should obtain approval from a physician. Then the individual's present level of fitness should be assessed. The individual's current fitness status should be taken into consideration in designing the exercise program. Individuals who have a relatively low level of fitness should start out their exercise program at a lower level of intensity than individuals who have a relatively high level of fitness. Exercise programs should be adjusted to the initial fitness level of the individual.

4. **Warm-up and cool-down activities are important.** Warm-up activities of at least 5 to 10 minutes in duration should proceed the vigorous part of the exercise session. Warm-up activities can help prevent injury and prepare the body for the strenuous activities that are part of the exercise program. Following the exercise program a cool-down period of 5 to 10 minutes is recommended to allow the body to begin to return to its normal state. Individuals with low levels of fitness or individuals who are middle-aged and older should take more time to warm up and cool down. Stretching exercises and low-level aerobic activity are suggested for warm-up.

5. **Progression should be followed in planning a program.** Progression is important in an exercise program. Progression depends on the individual. Using the individual's initial level of fitness as a starting point, as an individual becomes adjusted to the exercise program, the amount of exercise being performed should increase. This can be done by increasing the frequency, duration, or intensity of the exercise. Progression should be steady, and the individual's progress carefully monitored so that the individual is challenged by the exercise session but not overwhelmed.

6. **Individual differences must be taken into account.** The individual's needs and objectives must be taken into account when planning an exer-

cise program. Factors that may influence the individual's performance warrant attention as well. The nature of the individual's work, diet, and life-style should be considered when designing an exercise program. The amount of stress an individual is currently experiencing may significantly affect his or her performance as well.

7. **Safety is paramount.** Safety of the individual should be a primary concern. Prior to commencement of an exercise program, individuals should have a thorough medical screening. This is particularly critical when special conditions exist, such as beginning an exercise program after a long period of inactivity or as a means of rehabilitation after an illness (e.g., heart attack). Individuals engaged in physical activities involving body contact or other hazards should be strongly cautioned to use essential protective equipment, especially for the head, neck, eyes, and teeth (e.g., individuals playing racquetball should be required to use eyeguards). Individuals should be warned of proper precautions to take when exercising in special weather conditions such as high heat, high humidity, or extreme cold. Finally, individuals should learn how to monitor carefully their responses to exercise and to report any unusual occurrences (e.g., excessive breathlessness) to the professional conducting the program or to a physician.

In addition to outlining several physiological factors that must be taken into account in planning an exercise program, Pollock and Blair[10] stress that it is also important to consider behavioral factors that may influence an individual's fitness development. Consideration must be given to motivating individuals to adhere to their fitness programs and to incorporate their program into their daily living. Essentially, how can physical educators facilitate adherence by individuals to the exercise program that has been so carefully designed? How can individuals be motivated to work so that their optimal level of fitness can be realized?

First, Pollock and Blair[2] suggest that physical educators need to establish lines of communication with each participant. Communication can be enhanced by treating each person as an individual and by nonjudgmental acceptance of his or her exercise habits. Second, physical educators need to help each individual assume responsibility for his or her own behavior. The individual should be held accountable for following the exercise program. Next, the physical educator and the individual, working cooperatively, should set goals that are personally meaningful as well as realistic. Goals should be attainable. Both short-term and long-term goals should be set. For example, an individual may choose to embark on an exercise program because he or she wants to complete a 10 kilometer road race; this is a long-term goal. The short-term goal initially may be to go out and exercise three times a week for 30 minutes.

Physical educators can also facilitate adherence to the exercise program by having the participant maintain records of his or her performance. Record keeping helps the individual focus on the task at hand and provides a means for documenting progress toward goals. Positive reinforcement from the physical educator as well as friends may help the individual continue the exercise program. However, the best motivation is internal motivation, that which comes from within. Finally, physical educators can enhance individuals' adherence to exercise by being good role models. Physical educators should practice what they preach. They should exemplify a healthy, active life-style.

Physical educators must be cognizant of physiological principles when designing an exercise program. The principles of overload and specificity must be followed. Consideration must be made for individual differences as well. Behavioral strategies such as goal setting and positive reinforcement can facilitate exercise adherence. Physical educators should also realize the importance of being a good role model for a healthy life-style.

Planning an Exercise Program

To achieve and maintain fitness, individuals must exercise on a regular basis. When physical educators prescribe an exercise program for an individual, they must specify the intensity, duration, and frequency of exercise as well as the mode of exercise; these are the four prescriptive components of exercise. Individuals designing a personal exercise program must take these components of exercise into account.

Intensity is the degree of effort or exertion put forth by the individual during exercise. For example, the degree of effort put forth by a runner can be described as 80% of his or her maximum effort, and the amount of effort put forth during strength training can be described as the amount of weight lifted, for example, 80 pounds. Intensity is often viewed as the most important of the prescriptive components.

Duration is the length of the activity. Duration is typically expressed as time, such as 40 minutes of exercise.

Frequency refers to the number of exercise sessions per week, for example, three to five times per week. Achieving and maintaining health fitness requires that the individual exercise on a regular basis.

Mode is the type of exercise that is performed. Activities such as jogging, rowing, bicycling, stretching, and weight training are types of exercise that can be used to realize specific fitness gains. The selection of the type of exercise should be guided by the fitness goal to be achieved.

These exercise components are interrelated and can be manipulated to produce an exercise program appropriate to the individual and to the outcome desired. For example, cardiovascular improvement can be realized by jogging (mode) at 70% effort (intensity) for 40 minutes (duration) five times a week (frequency) or at 85% intensity for 20 minutes four times a week. Individuals who are just starting a program to improve their fitness may be more successful if they exercise at a lower intensity but for a longer session. Duration and frequency also can be manipulated to produce an exercise program designed to meet individual needs. For example, individuals who are obese may find it beneficial to exercise for shorter periods (duration) but more often during the week (frequency).

The interactive nature of the exercise components allows for the design of exercise programs to meet unique needs. Individualization is very important. Personal characteristics such as fitness status, medical status, and age must be considered when prescribing exercise. Individuals who have lower initial fitness levels require a lower level of intensity when beginning a program than individuals who are fit. Medical conditions, such as heart disease, diabetes, and asthma, must be taken into account when designing an exercise program. Appropriate modifications must be made so that the individual can safely participate while attaining desired fitness goals. Individuals beginning an exercise program at middle-age or older may require starting at a lower intensity. It is important to note that gender is not a limiting factor; men and women respond equally to training.

The participant's fitness needs and goals also must be considered when planning an exercise program. The program must be designed to provide opportunities for the development of the fitness quality the participant desires to improve. Selected activities should be specific to the goal. For example, if the participant's goal is to improve stamina or cardiovascular endurance, activities selected should stimulate the circulatory and respiratory system (e.g., running or cross country skiing) and the exercise components manipulated to allow the participant to achieve this goal.

Enjoyment is another critical factor in the selection of the mode of exercise. Adherence to the training program is enhanced when the participant enjoys the prescribed exercise. Activities should allow participants to achieve the desired fitness goals while maintaining interest and enjoyment. Individuals who find an activity enjoyable will be more likely to continue the exercise long enough to realize desired fitness improvements and to incorporate exercise into their life-style so as to maintain these improvements.

Equally important in planning an exercise program is the provision of experiences that will promote the development of the cognitive and affective outcomes so necessary for lifetime fitness. Achievement of a desirable level of fitness is a significant concern, but attention also must be directed to educating participants about the principles of designing a personal exercise program, assessing their own fitness, and resolving personal fitness problems. Development of a knowledgeable, independent fitness and health consumer—an individual who is capable of achieving and maintaining fitness for a lifetime—is an important priority. People need to take charge of their own lives and assume personal responsibility for their level of fitness.

HEALTH FITNESS COMPONENTS

The components of health fitness include cardiovascular endurance, body composition, muscular strength and endurance, and flexibility. In this section, each fitness component is defined, its relationship to health delineated, methods to improve the fitness component discussed, and techniques to measure the component identified.

Cardiovascular Endurance

Cardiovascular endurance is the ability of the body to deliver oxygen effectively to the working muscles so that an individual can perform physical activity. Efficient functioning of the cardiovascular system (i.e., heart and blood vessels) and the respiratory system (i.e., lungs) is essential for the distribution of oxygen and nutrients and removal of wastes from the body.

The performance of sustained vigorous physical activities is influenced by the efficiency of the cardiorespiratory system. The more efficient the system, the greater the amount of physical activity that an individual can perform before fatigue and exhaustion occur. Performance diminishes greatly when sufficient oxygen cannot be provided by the cardiorespiratory system to the working muscles.

Cardiovascular endurance is regarded as the most important component of health fitness. Because of the benefits that are derived from improved cardiorespiratory function—such as the potential for reducing the risk of cardiovascular disease, improving work capacity, and providing greater resistance to fatigue—this component, if properly developed, can make a major contribution to an individual's health.

Exercise can help prevent hypokinetic disease. Hypokinetic diseases are caused by insufficient physical activity. Persons who have hypokinetic disease frequently experience loss of flexibility, cardiovascular degeneration, bone and muscle

weakness, and bladder and bowel malfunction. One risk factor that contributes to premature susceptibility to heart disease and stroke is lack of physical activity. Moreover, it is believed that hypertension and obesity, which are also risk factors associated with heart disease, can be helped by participation in regular exercise.

Energy is necessary for performance. Two systems supply the energy necessary for performance: the anaerobic system and the aerobic system. The type of task performed determines which energy system will contribute the majority of the energy required.

The anaerobic system provides energy for tasks that demand a high rate of energy expenditure for a short period, for example, the 100-yard dash. This system releases a large amount of energy to supply the immediate demands of the body. Because body fuels are metabolized for energy without oxygen, the amount of work that can be performed anaerobically is limited. The anaerobic system can support high intensity exercise for only about 1 to 1½ minutes. One product of anaerobic energy production is lactic acid, which accumulates in the muscles and contributes to fatigue.

The aerobic system provides energy for tasks requiring a lower rate of energy expenditure over a longer period of time, such as jogging 5 miles. During the performance of aerobic tasks, a constant supply of oxygen is required by the muscles performing the work. The amount of oxygen taken in by the body must be sufficient to supply the energy required for the task.

The relative contribution of each of these energy systems will depend on the intensity of the exercise and its duration (see Table 6-2). For intense efforts lasting approximately 1½ minutes or less, the anaerobic system supplies the required energy. As the activity becomes less intense and the duration longer, the aerobic system predominates.

Cardiovascular endurance is concerned with the aerobic efficiency of the body. Aerobic efficiency is the ability of the body to supply fuel and oxygen to muscles. One of the major factors influencing aerobic efficiency is the capacity of the heart to pump blood. A well-conditioned heart is able to

TABLE 6-2 Energy Systems Used According to Length of Time and Type of Activity

Energy System	Length of Time	Type of Activity
Anaerobic	0-90 s	Any type of sprint (running, swimming, cycling) Short duration, explosive activities
Combined system	90 s-4 min	Medium distance activities (1/2- to 1-mile run) Intermittent sport activities
Aerobic	>4 min	Long distance events Long duration intermittent activities

exert greater force with each heart beat; consequently, a larger volume of blood is pumped through the arteries and throughout the body.

Another important factor of cardiorespiratory endurance is the efficiency of the lungs. The amount of oxygen that can be supplied to working muscles is a limiting factor in performance. To produce the energy needed for activity, oxygen is needed. Food is metabolized to provide needed fuel, and oxygen is needed for this process. Air is inhaled; oxygen from the air is transported to the heart and is then carried from the heart to the organs needing oxygen. From the organs the blood carrying carbon dioxide is returned to the heart and finally to the lungs, where it is exhaled.

When demands for oxygen increase, such as during strenuous exercise, the ability of the body to take in and provide oxygen to the working muscles is an important determinant of the amount of work that can be performed. The greater the ability of the body to take in and deliver oxygen, the longer a person can exercise before fatigue and exhaustion occur. Thus, individuals who have well-developed circulatory and respiratory systems can deliver more oxygen and, therefore, can exercise for a longer period.

Many benefits have been attributed to aerobic exercise. Aerobic exercise is activity that can be sustained for an extended period without building an oxygen debt in the muscles. Bicycling, jogging, skipping rope, rowing, walking, cross country skiing, and swimming are some examples of aerobic activities.

Some of the benefits of aerobic exercise include the ability to use more oxygen during strenuous exercise, a lower heart rate at work, the production of less lactic acid, and greater endurance. Aerobic exercise improves the efficiency of the heart and reduces blood pressure.

Cardiovascular endurance is important for the performance of many sport activities. In sport activities that require an individual to perform for an extended period, such as a 500-yard swim or a soccer game, cardiovascular endurance can have a profound impact on performance.

Individuals who have trained and developed a high level of cardiovascular endurance can work at a higher level of intensity without fatigue than individuals who are unfit. Additionally, fit individuals can perform more work before reaching exhaustion. Furthermore, following exercise, fit individuals recover faster than unfit individuals.

Cardiovascular fitness can be improved and maintained through a well-planned program of exercise. Physical activity of an appropriate intensity, duration, frequency, and mode can enhance cardiovascular fitness.

Intensity. To develop cardiovascular fitness, physical activities must be of sufficient intensity. During exercise, heart rate changes in proportion to the energy requirements of the task. As the energy requirements increase, there is a corresponding increase in heart rate. Thus, heart rate can be used to monitor the intensity of exercise. The box on p. 177 shows how to measure heart rate. Because heart rate slows within 1 minute following exercise, it is often recommended that the pulse be monitored for 10 seconds and then multiplied by 6 (or monitored for 6 seconds and multiplied by 10) to determine beats per minute. To obtain an accurate reading, the heart rate should be monitored within 15 seconds of the cessation of exercise.

Exercising at a proper intensity is essential for an effective and a safe workout. Intensity can be controlled by speeding or slowing the pace of the exercise. To realize training benefits, the intensity of the exercise must be regulated so that the heart rate is

A high level of physical fitness is required for wheelchair participants in the Annual Marine Corps Marathon.

MEASURING YOUR HEART RATE

Your heart rate can be determined by counting the frequency your heart contracts in a period of time and converting this to the standard measure in beats per minute. Make sure that you press just firmly enough to feel the pulse. If you press too hard it may interfere with the rhythm.

Your pulse can be detected by placing a finger or fingers on your lower arm near the base of the thumb.

Your pulse can also be easily detected over the carotid artery in the front of the neck.

DETERMINATION OF YOUR TARGET-ZONE HEART RATE

To determine target-zone heart rate, you must first determine maximal heart rate. This is not influenced by gender or level of fitness. It is almost entirely related to age.

For practical purposes your maximal heart rate can be estimated by subtracting your age (in years) from 220. This will usually be accurate within 10 beats per minute.

maximal heart rate   = **220 – age (years)**
(estimated)   = **220 – _____**
                           = **_____ beats/minute**

Calculate your target-zone heart rate
lower level   = **.70 × maximal heart rate**
[70% maximal heart rate] = **.70 × _____**
                           = **_____ beats/minute**

upper level   = **.85 × maximal heart rate**
[85% maximal heart rate] = **.85 × _____**
                           = **_____ beats/minute**

Target-zone heart rate _____ to _____

elevated to a predetermined level and maintained within a certain range. This level is called the target training heart rate and the range referred to as the target heart rate zone. Generally, the lower and upper limits of the target heart rate zone are between 70 to 85 percent of the maximum heart rate. However, individuals who are extremely unfit, excessively overweight, and/or have medical conditions that warrant special attention can begin working at a lower intensity, such as 60%, and still achieve beneficial results. Intensity can be progressively increased as conditions warrant. The box above shows how to calculate the target-zone heart rate.

Duration. To realize minimal improvement, it is generally accepted that a good workout requires at least 20 minutes of sustained activity of sufficient intensity to maintain the heart rate within its target zone. Generally, the greater the duration of the workout, the greater the benefit to the individual's cardiovascular system.

It is important to remember that the intensity and duration of the activity are critical to achieving and maintaining fitness. Generally, as the intensity of the activity increases, its duration decreases; conversely, as intensity decreases, the duration of the activity should increase. Typically, for development

of health-related cardiovascular endurance, lower intensities and longer durations are recommended. It is important to remember, however, that both the intensity and the duration of the activity must meet minimum requirements in order for fitness development to occur.

When determining the amount of time that should be allocated for an exercise session, it is important to include time for a warm-up and cool-down period. A 5 to 10 minute warm-up consisting of stretching and low-aerobic activity allows the body to gradually adjust to the stress of exercise. Stretching activities help reduce the chance of muscle injury and soreness. A 5 to 10 minute cool-down period after exercise is equally important as it allows the body to gradually recover from the exercise session. Figure 6-1 illustrates an appropriate structure for an exercise session.

Frequency. Three exercise sessions per week are necessary to realize minimal improvement in cardiovascular fitness. Many individuals choose to work out more often. It is important to remember, however, that the body must have time to recover from the effects of exercise. Many persons build this recovery time into their exercise program by exercising only every other day. Although daily

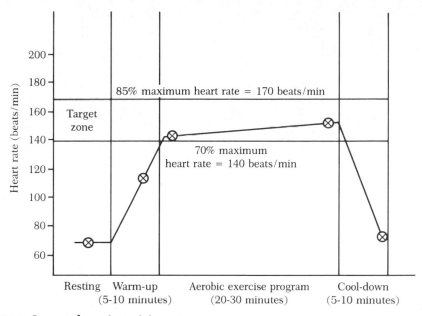

FIGURE 6-1 *Suggested exercise training pattern.*
(Modified from Zohman, LR: Exercise your way to fitness and heart health, 1974, American Heart Association.)

workouts are not required to develop health fitness, many other individuals choose to work out on a daily basis. In order to allow the body to recover, they often follow a hard, strenuous workout day with a less strenuous recovery day.

Mode. Aerobic activities should be used to develop cardiovascular endurance. Basically, aerobic activities are those in which a sufficient amount of oxygen is available to meet the body's demands. During the performance of these activities, the heart rate is maintained at an elevated level for an extended period. These activities typically involve vigorous and repetitive whole body or large muscle movements that are sustained for an extended period. Popular aerobic activities include jogging, running, walking, swimming, cycling, rowing, aerobic dance, and cross-country skiing. Because these activities are somewhat continuous in nature, the intensity of the workload can be easily regulated by controlling the pace. Intermittent activities such as racquetball, basketball, or tennis involve various intensities of effort during the course of the activity. Thus, it is more difficult to regulate the degree of effort expended during these activities. However,

these activities can contribute to the improvement of cardiovascular endurance if they are of sufficient intensity.

In summary, to develop and maintain cardiovascular fitness, it is recommended that the individual exercise three to five times a week, with an intensity sufficient to elevate and sustain the heart rate in the target zone for at least 20 minutes. Exercise should involve aerobic activities that are continuous, vigorous and, also importantly, enjoyable to the individual. Once a desirable level of cardiovascular fitness has been achieved, regular appropriate exercise is necessary to maintain it. Individuals who stop exercising tend to lose their fitness gains within 5 to 10 weeks. Achieving and maintaining a high level of this critical fitness component requires a long-term commitment and the incorporation of exercise into one's life-style.

Cardiovascular fitness can be measured. The best method to determine the level of cardiovascular functioning is to measure maximum oxygen consumption. The more oxygen the body is able to deliver and use, the more work the body is able to perform before becoming fatigued. Maximum oxy-

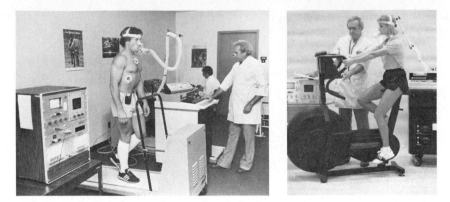

Use of a treadmill and a bicycle ergometer to determine maximum oxygen consumption.

gen consumption is the greatest rate at which the oxygen is processed and used by the body.

Measurement of maximum oxygen consumption requires a sophisticated laboratory setting and well-trained personnel to monitor carefully the performance of the individual during the test. This testing is usually done on an individual basis. Following prescribed test protocols, the individual exercises on a treadmill or bicycle ergometer and breathes through a specially designed mouthpiece. Various physiological and metabolic parameters are monitored, such as heart rate, respiration rate, and rate of oxygen consumption. The exercise task is made progressively more difficult until no further increase in oxygen consumption is noted; this point is considered to be the maximum oxygen intake for the task. Although this test yields highly accurate information, it is expensive, time consuming, and requires sophisticated equipment and highly trained personnel.

There are a variety of other methods that can be used to provide a good estimate of cardiovascular endurance. These tests measure the maximum amount of work that can be performed over a specified period. The most commonly used tests are the 12-minute or the 9-minute run-walk, the timed $1\frac{1}{2}$ or 1 mile run-walk, and the Harvard step test. These tests are most often used in school and community fitness programs. When properly conducted, results from these tests can be used to accurately estimate maximum oxygen consumption and provide an indicator of cardiovascular fitness.

Body Composition

Body composition is a description of the body in terms of muscle, bone, fat, and other elements. With respect to health fitness, it refers to the percentage of body weight that is composed of fat as compared with fat-free or lean tissue. Having a high percentage of body fat is a serious detriment to fitness and health.

Height and weight tables have been traditionally used to determine desirable body weight. Individuals whose body weight exceeds set standards for their sex, age, and physical stature by 10% to 20% are considered overweight.[8,9] Persons overweight by 20% of their optimum weight are obese, and those who are overweight by more than 50% of their optimum weight are considered morbidly obese or superobese.[11]

It should be noted that being overweight can be attributed to having an excess of either fatty tissue or lean tissue. For example, certain athletes such as football players could be classified as overweight. However, when their body composition is examined, the excess weight is attributable to muscular development and their overall percentage of body fat is quite low (e.g., a professional football player can

The run-walk test is often used in the school setting to assess cardiovascular endurance.

weigh 250 pounds or more, yet have only 12 percent body fat or less). The important consideration with respect to health fitness is not the weight of the individual but how much fat the individual has.

It is highly important that professionals and the public realize that a certain amount of adipose tissue or fat is essential for the body to function. Body fat also serves to protect internal organs. *The goal of fitness programs is not the elimination of body fat but helping individuals attain desirable levels of body fat.* The average percentage of body fat is 18% for men and 23% for women. With respect to health fitness, the desirable level of body fat for men is 12% or less and for women, 18% or less. The percentage of body fat should not be less than 3% in men and 12% in women (the higher percentage for women is necessary for the protection of the reproductive organs).[8,9] Extremely low percentages of body fat are hazardous to one's health.

A high percentage of body fat is associated with numerous health problems. Obesity contributes to an increased incidence of cardiovascular disease and is also associated with other cardiovascular risk factors, including hypertension. An increased incidence of diabetes, elevated serum blood cholesterol levels, respiratory problems, muscle and joint problems, low back pain, and certain psychological problems are also found among individuals with a high percentage of body fat. Mortality is higher at a younger age, and life expectancy is decreased for chronically obese individuals.

The problem of obesity is widespread. It is estimated that more than 50% of the adult population and about 40% of the school-age population in the United States is overweight. Moreover, overweight children typically grow up to be overweight adults.

Determination of the cause of obesity is important. In most cases obesity can be attributed to overeating and a lack of physical activity. In a few cases, however, obesity can be the result of disease. When dealing with obesity, particularly individuals who are superobese, it is important that a physician be consulted. A physical examination and careful monitoring of eating and exercise habits are helpful in determining the cause of the problem. A qualified physician can offer guidance in designing and implementing a sound fitness program to deal with the problem of obesity.

Body composition is primarily influenced by nutrition and physical activity. Although body composition is genetically related to body type, the nature and amount of food consumed and the extent of participation in physical activity exert a profound influence on body composition. Overeating and low levels of physical activity contribute to poor body composition. Individuals who are fat tend to eat more and are more sedentary.

Energy balance is the key to weight control. The relationship between food intake and energy expenditure is critical. This relationship is often referred to as energy or caloric balance:

Energy or caloric balance	=	Number of calories taken into the body as food	−	Number of calories expended

Energy is expended through three processes: (1) basal metabolism or maintenance of essential life functions; (2) work, which is any activity requiring more energy than sleeping and includes exercise; and (3) excretion of body wastes.

A neutral balance occurs when the caloric intake is equal to the caloric expenditure. Under these circumstances, body weight is maintained. When a positive balance exists, that is, when more calories are consumed than expended, the excess is stored as fat and body weight increases. A negative balance occurs when more calories are expended than consumed; this results in a weight loss. Weight control requires maintaining the appropriate energy or caloric balance. Individuals must be careful about food intake and conscious of energy expenditures. Caloric tables are useful in monitoring the number of calories consumed. Energy expenditure tables are helpful in monitoring energy expended. These tables provide information about the calories expended both during the performance of daily living tasks such as house cleaning and during participation in physical activities and exercise such as bicycling.

Body composition can be improved. Individuals who have an unhealthy percentage of body fat can reduce it by modifying their life-style. Weight loss can be accomplished by several means: (1) consuming fewer calories through dieting, (2) increasing caloric expenditures by increasing the amount of exercise, and (3) combining a moderate decrease in caloric consumption with a moderate increase in exercise or caloric expenditure.

It is recommended by experts that weight loss be accomplished through a combination of diet and exercise. For example, if caloric intake is reduced by 200 to 300 calories per day and caloric expenditures are increased by 200 to 300 calories a day, approximately 3500 calories—1 pound of fat—will be lost over the course of a week. Adoption of sound nutritional practices in conjunction with regular, appropriate exercise will help most individuals achieve a desirable body composition.

Exercise increasingly is being recognized as a critical component of weight loss. Often those desiring to lose weight focus on counting the number of calories consumed and neglect the exercise component. Exercise can help weight loss in several ways: (1) it can increase caloric expenditures (a 180-lb. person walking 4 miles in an hour will expend approximately 400 calories); (2) it can suppress one's appetite and thereby contribute to reduction in caloric intake; (3) it can increase the metabolic rate for some time after vigorous exercise, thereby permitting extra calories to be burned; and (4) it can contribute to the health fitness of the individual. Also, because sedentary living contributes to weight gain, incorporation of regular appropriate exercise into one's life-style helps to counteract weight gain and contributes to the ability to successfully manage one's weight.

It should be noted that those individuals who desire to gain weight should focus on increasing lean body mass (muscle) rather than body fat. This can be accomplished by following a sound muscle training program in conjunction with an appropriate increase in caloric intake to realize a gain of 1 to 2 pounds per week. Failure to incorporate a muscle training program as part of the total program will result in excessive calories being converted to fat. Thus, even though the weight gain is achieved, the percentage of body fat may be less than optimal. Therefore, a weight-gaining program should combine a reasonable increase in caloric intake and well-planned muscle training program to achieve an optimal body composition.

Sound practices should be followed in losing weight. Experts suggest the following guidelines regarding weight loss:

1. Prolonged fasting and diets that severely restrict calories are medically dangerous. These programs result in loss of large amounts of water, electrolytes, minerals, glycogen stores, and other fat-free tissue, with a minimal amount of fat loss.

2. Moderate caloric restriction is desirable such as consuming 500 calories less than the usual daily intake. It is important that the minimum caloric intake not go below 1200 calories per day for a woman and not below 1400 calories a day for a man and that sound nutritional practices are followed.

3. Appropriate regular exercise of the large muscles assists in the maintenance of fat-free tissue, including muscle mass and bone density, and results in the loss of weight, primarily in the form of fat.

4. A sound weight loss program should be comprehensive in nature. It should include a nutritionally sound diet with mild caloric

Hydrostatic or underwater weighing is one method to determine body composition.

restriction, regular and appropriate exercise to increase caloric expenditure, and behavior modification. Weight loss should not exceed 2 pounds per week.

5. Maintenance of proper weight and desirable body composition requires a lifetime commitment to proper eating habits and regular physical activity.

A word of caution: Some individuals become obsessed with weight loss, dieting, and exercise. This obsession can, in conjunction with a host of other factors, contribute to the development of an eating disorder. Two common eating disorders are anorexia nervosa and bulimia.

Anorexia nervosa is a disease in which a person develops a psychological aversion to food, resulting in a pathologic weight loss. Bulimia involves recurrent episodes of binge eating and subsequent purging by self-induced vomiting, use of laxatives, and/or excessive exercising. Both disorders have a higher prevalence among young women, although men do suffer from these conditions as well. These disorders pose a severe threat to health and require professional treatment.

Improper weight control programs and misconceptions about exercise abound. Americans spend billions of dollars a year in a quest to lose excess body fat and weight. Seeking to lose weight and inches quickly, countless people turn to specialized diet plans and pills or enroll in health clubs and fitness programs. Advertisements promote various gimmicks and gadgets to promote rapid weight loss. These include rubberized suits that purportedly sweat the weight off and mechanical devices that claim to vibrate and shake the fat off. While there are some approaches to weight loss that are based on sound scientific evidence, many approaches fall far short of the claims so fervently promised. Consumers must learn to discriminate between proper and improper weight loss approaches and realize that there is no quick and easy method to lose weight. The bottom line is that weight loss requires burning more calories than are consumed. Weight loss and weight maintenance require the integration of sound nutritional practices and regular exercise into one's life-style.

Despite the widespread public enthusiasm for fitness, many misconceptions about exercise and weight control still exist. Many people still believe that exercise burns relatively few calories, making its contribution to weight loss insignificant. In reality, exercise can significantly alter the energy or caloric balance, thus facilitating weight loss. It is also erroneously believed that exercise automatically increases appetite; the opposite has been shown to be true. Exercise tends to suppress the appetite and thus contributes to a reduction in caloric intake. Moreover, the increase in the metabolic rate from exercising continues after the workout, thereby burning additional calories.

Another common misconception is that exercise can be used for spot reducing, that is, it can reduce fat from a specific area of the body such as the thighs, upper arms, or abdomen. Research shows that fat loss occurs in proportion to the amount of fat in the body—fat loss is greater in those areas with large amounts of fat as compared with those areas where there is less fat. Exercise will, however, increase muscle development in a specific area and may produce a shift or change in body fluids. While this may enhance one's appearance, it does not significantly reduce the amount of fat in that specific area.

Steam baths and saunas are viewed by many people as an effective way to lose weight. Although weight is lost through sweating, such loss is only temporary. The lost fluid is quickly replaced, and the weight is regained. Another fallacy is that passive exercise machines can be used to reduce body weight. Vibrators, rollers, and whirlpools are commonly promoted as a means to reduce weight. Electrically powered exercise equipment, such as an exercycle that only requires the individual to turn it on and sit on it while it does all the work, are increasingly more common. None of these passive approaches to exercise can reduce body fat. Physical education professionals must educate the public about the facts pertaining to weight control and exercise.

Body composition can be measured. There are several methods that can be used to determine the percentage of body fat. One of the most accurate methods is hydrostatic weighing. This involves weighing an individual on land and then in an underwater tank. Body density is then determined, and this information is used to calculate the percentage of lean body weight and body fat. This technique is used most often in exercise physiology laboratories and hospitals. It requires expensive equipment and is time consuming, and thus is not practical for use with large groups of people.

Of the alternative approaches to measurement, the most common is the use of skinfold measurements. Skinfold measurements are taken from sev-

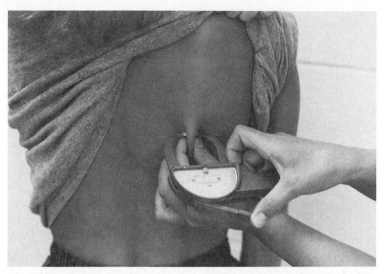

Skinfold measurements can be used to calculate the percentage of body fat.

eral selected sites such as the triceps, subscapular, or thigh with skinfold calipers. Different formulas are then used to calculate the percentage of body fat. This method is relatively inexpensive and can be used with large groups of people and produces accurate information when performed by well-trained individuals.

Muscular Strength and Endurance

Muscular strength is the ability of a muscle or muscle group to exert a force against a resistance. Specifically, it is the maximum amount of force that a muscle or muscle group can apply against a resistance in a single effort.

The ability of a muscle or muscle group to exert force repeatedly is known as muscular endurance. Muscular endurance also refers to the capacity of a muscle or muscle group to sustain a contractive state over a period of time.

Muscular strength and endurance are specific to each muscle or muscle group. That is, different muscles in the body can have different levels of strength and endurance. Moreover, muscles that are used more frequently are stronger and have greater endurance than those muscles that are used less frequently. Maintenance of strength and endurance requires that the muscles be used.

When muscles are not used, strength and endurance decrease.

Many people perceive muscular strength and endurance as important only for athletes or those engaged in occupations that require heavy work, for example, construction. While muscular strength and endurance are necessary for these people to perform their responsibilities effectively, these fitness components are also important for all people. Strength and endurance are necessary for performing everyday tasks, maintaining proper posture, and resisting fatigue. As individuals age, maintaining adequate levels of strength and endurance is particularly important as these fitness components play a critical role in the maintenance of functional independence. Additionally, the development of adequate strength and endurance is an important objective of many rehabilitation programs.

Muscular strength and endurance are important to good health. They contribute to the maintenance of proper posture and the improvement of personal appearance. Because strong muscles provide better protection for body joints, the risk of joint injuries is decreased. Millions of Americans suffer from low-back pain. Weak abdominal muscles and poor flexibility contribute to this problem. Strengthening the appropriate

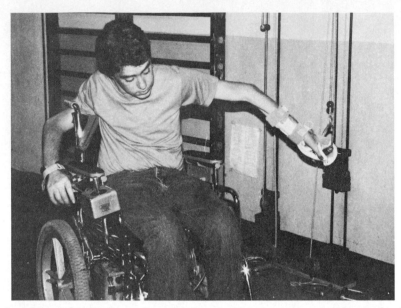

Maintaining adequate levels of muscular strength and endurance is important for people of all ages and abilities.

muscles and developing increased flexibility can help alleviate this condition.

For the average person, muscular endurance is probably more important than strength for fulfilling the responsibilities and tasks associated with everyday living. In terms of health fitness, the focus is on achieving and maintaining adequate muscular development so that all people, regardless of age, can fully enjoy life.

High levels of muscular strength and endurance are important for athletes. Many of the advances in athletic performance can be attributed to improvements in training techniques, especially the development of strength. Strength is a critical element of sport performance. Strength training for sport must be functionally specific in that it is specifically related to the particular characteristics required for performance of the sport. Thus, the strength training of a sprinter will differ markedly from that of a shot putter, which will be different from that of a gymnast. Each athlete requires the development of a high level of strength in specific muscles or muscle groups for effective performance.

Strength combines with other physical elements to enhance the quality of performance. For example, power, which is strength combined with speed, is an important motor-skill fitness component. Power is that quality that permits Michael Jordan to jump high and to snare rebounds off the backboard, Nancy Lopez to drive a golf ball 250 yards down the fairway, or Mary Lou Retton to execute a double-back somersault. Many movements in sport require an explosive effort during execution. When force is generated quickly, the movement is known as a *power movement.* Power is critical to successful performance in many sports today, and proper strength training can enhance this component.

Isometric, isotonic, and isokinetic exercises can be used to develop muscular strength and endurance. Body movements depend on the contraction of muscles. As a muscle contracts, tension is created within the muscle and the muscle shortens, lengthens, or remains the same.

Isometric exercises. A muscle contracts isometrically when it exerts force against an immovable resistance. Although tension develops within the muscle, the length of the muscle remains relatively

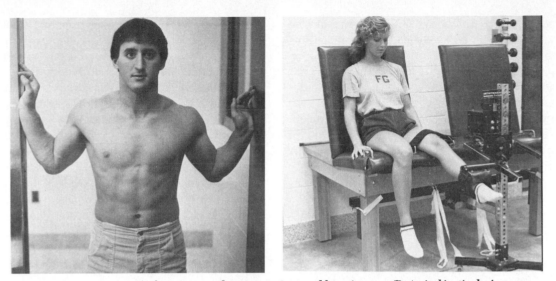

A, *An isometric exercise force is exerted against an immovable resistance.* **B,** *An isokinetic device, the Orthotron, provides resistance at a constant velocity.*

constant and there is little or no movement of the joint. This is also referred to as a *static contraction*.

When performing isometric exercises, the individual exerts maximum force against an immovable object and tension develops within the muscle. For example, stand in a doorway and place the palms of your hands at shoulder height against the frame. Push with all your might and feel the tension develop in your muscles. Even though you grunt and groan as you contract your muscles to their maximum, it is impossible for you to move the resistance, in this case the door frame. Another approach to performing isometric contractions is to contract one muscle against another muscle, applying an equal and opposite force; in this case, the opposing muscle serves as a resistance. For example, raise your arms to shoulder height and place your palms together. Push against your palms as you contract your muscles. There should be no movement as your muscles work against one another.

When performing isometric exercises, it is suggested that the muscle should generate a maximum force for 5 seconds, with the contraction repeated 5 to 10 times each day. Isometrics offer the advantage of not requiring any equipment; any immovable object, or your own body, serves as the resistance.

One frequently cited disadvantage of isometric exercises is that strength is developed at only a specific joint angle, not through the entire range of motion. Isometric exercises were most popular in the late 1960s to early 1970s. Isometric exercises now are most often used to develop strength at a specific joint angle to enhance a particular movement or for injury rehabilitation.

Isotonic exercises. Isotonic contractions occur when force is generated while the muscle is changing in length. Movement occurs at the joint and the muscles involved shorten and lengthen. For example, in order to lift a weight from its starting point when performing a biceps curl, the biceps muscle must contract and shorten in length. This is called a *concentric contraction*. In order to control the weight as it is lowered back to the starting position, the biceps muscle continues to contract while gradually lengthening. This is referred to as an *eccentric contraction*. When exercising isotonically, it is essential to use both concentric and eccentric contractions for the greatest improvement to occur and to exercise through the range of motion.

One problem associated with isotonic training is that the force applied to the weight varies throughout the range of motion. This is attributable to the effects of gravity and the system of levers within the body. Once the initial resistance is overcome, lifting the weight can be easy or difficult, depending on the position of the weight relative to the body. Thus the muscles are not working at or near their maximum effort throughout the range of motion.

Common forms of isotonic exercise equipment are free weights, barbells, dumbbells, and various machines such as the Universal gym. Some isotonic exercise machines, such as the Nautilus machine, have been designed specifically to vary the resistance throughout the range of motion. This permits the muscles to exert their maximum effort throughout the entire range of motion.

Isotonic exercises are probably the most popular means of developing strength and endurance. Millions of people use this approach to achieve and maintain desired levels of muscular development.

Isokinetic exercises. When performing isokinetic exercises, the length of the muscle changes while the contraction is performed at a constant velocity. Isokinetic devices such as Cybex, Orthotron, and Mini-gym are designed so that the resistance can be moved only at a certain speed, regardless of the amount of force applied. The speed at which the resistance can be moved is the key to this exercise approach. Because isokinetic machines can be expensive, they are most often used in the diagnosis and treatment of various injuries.

The advantages and disadvantages of each exercise approach have been debated in the scientific literature. Many researchers have examined the various types of exercise and training approaches in order to determine which are most effective and safest for producing a desired gain. Understanding how to design programs using each approach and their advantages and disadvantages probably will be included in your professional preparation coursework.

Muscular strength and endurance can be improved. There are many different methods of training that can be effectively used to develop these fitness components. Although weight training is not necessary to realize gains in muscular strength and endurance, this approach is popular with many people.

Although all principles of training should be incorporated into a weight training program, the principle of overload is of critical importance. Improvements in strength and endurance occur only when a muscle or muscle group is worked at a higher level than that to which it is accustomed—it must be overloaded. As muscle development increases, the body adapts to the level of resistance. To further improve, the workload must be progressively increased. Once the desired level of fitness is achieved, maintenance of this level requires continued training at the current resistance.

Before discussing the general guidelines for training, it may be helpful to define the following terms:

- *Resistance* is the workload or weight being moved.
- *Repetition maximum (RM)* is the maximum force that can be exerted or the weight of resistance lifted. One RM is the maximum weight that can be lifted in a single effort.
- *Repetition* is the performance of a designated movement or exercise pattern through the full range of motion.
- *Set* is the number of repetitions performed without a rest.

When planning a training program, consideration must be given to the amount of weight used per lift, the number of repetitions per set, the number of sets per workout, and the number of workouts per week. Because there are so many weight training programs available, only general guidelines with respect to the intensity, duration, and frequency will be presented.

Intensity. The intensity of the workout refers to the extent that the muscles are overloaded. Overload can be accomplished by any combination of the following: increasing the resistance or weight lifted, increasing the number of repetitions per set, increasing the number of sets per workout, increasing the speed at which the repetition is performed, and decreasing the time for rest between sets.

Programs can be designed to develop either strength, endurance, or both. The differences between these programs pertain to the number of repetitions and the amount of resistance. Generally,

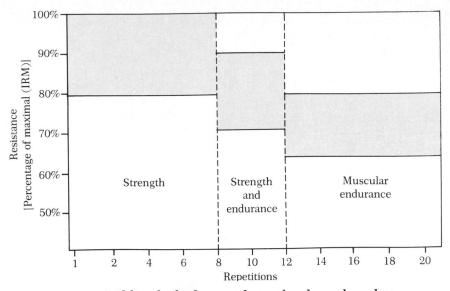

FIGURE 6-2 *Guidelines for development of strength and muscular endurance.*

a strength training program emphasizes a low number of repetitions (e.g., eight or less) with a heavy resistance whereas endurance training programs involve performing a high number of repetitions (e.g., 12 to 20) with a low resistance. For the development of both strength and endurance, a moderate number of repetitions (e.g., 8 to 12) and a moderate resistance are used. Guidelines for strength and endurance training are shown in Figure 6-2. The amount of weight that will create an adequate resistance varies according to each person and the goal of the program.

Duration. The duration of the training program varies depending on the person's level of fitness, fitness goals, equipment available, and time available to work out.

Frequency. The training program must include time for the muscles to rest and recover from the workout while adapting to a higher physiological level. The same muscle group should not be worked on successive days. It is recommended that exercises be performed 3 or 4 days per week or every other day.

Muscular strength and endurance can be measured. Because muscular strength and endurance are specific to each muscle or muscle group, the level of development can vary among the various muscles or muscle groups. Therefore, the strength and endurance of each muscle or muscle group must be measured.

Strength can be measured isometrically by using a dynamometer. As muscle contraction occurs, the force is transmitted to the instrument and can be recorded (e.g., the hand dynamometer can be used to determine grip strength). Strength can be measured isotonically by determining the maximum amount of weight that can be moved once through the designated range of motion (e.g., bench press); this is 1 repetition maximum or 1 RM.

Endurance can be measured by determining the number of repetitions of a particular movement that can be performed continuously (e.g., the number of repetitions of the bench press that can be performed with a designated resistance) or the number of repetitions performed within a specified period of time (e.g., the number of sit-ups that can be performed in 1 minute). Endurance also can be determined by measuring the amount of time a specific contraction can be sustained (e.g., how long a static push-up can be held).

Measurement of strength and endurance should be specific to the muscle or muscle group. In terms

Using a dynamometer to measure grip strength.

of health fitness, the AAHPERD Physical Best Fitness Program assesses abdominal muscular development and upper body muscular development with the use of modified sit-ups and pull-ups, respectively.

Flexibility

Flexibility can be defined as the maximum range of motion possible at a joint, that is, the extent of movement possible about a joint without undue strain. Although it is one of the most important fitness components, it is often overlooked and, consequently, its development is neglected.

Flexibility is not a general quality; it is specific to a particular joint, such as the knee, or to a series of joints, such as the spinal vertebral joints. This means that an individual can have a better range of motion in some joints than in others.

The extent of movement possible at a joint is influenced by the structure of the joint. For example, the elbow and the knee are hinge joints, allowing movement in one direction only; flexion (bending) and extension (straightening) are the only movements possible. In contrast, the shoulder and

hip are ball and socket joints; this joint structure allows movement in many directions, usually with a greater range than the hinge joint. Soft tissues such as muscles, tendons, and ligaments greatly influence the range of movement possible at a joint. Flexibility is affected by the length that a muscle can stretch (i.e., its elasticity). When muscles are not used, they tend to become shorter and tighter, thus reducing the joint's range of motion.

Flexibility is essential to performing everyday tasks and is also a critical component in the performance of many sport activities. Physical activities such as gymnastics, yoga, swimming, karate, and dance place a premium on flexibility. Limited flexibility decreases the efficiency with which everyday and sport activities can be performed. Thus, the development of flexibility should not be neglected in designing a fitness program.

Flexibility is important to good health. Flexibility is important for maintaining good posture. Poor postural alignment can cause pain as well as limit one's ability to move freely.

Flexibility can help prevent low back pain. Nearly

To be successful, athletes need to fully develop the specific fitness components required by their sport.

85 million Americans suffer from episodes of low back pain each year. This condition is caused by poor muscle development and poor flexibility. Improving muscle development and flexibility in conjunction with using proper care in sitting, standing, and lifting objects can help alleviate this condition.

Flexibility is also important for preventing muscle injuries. Poor flexibility can contribute to uncoordinated and awkward movements, thus increasing the potential for injury. Muscle soreness and body stiffness following vigorous physical activity can be allevi-ated by using a good stretching program to develop flexibility both before and after an activity session.

Flexibility is important for the performance of physical activities. Flexibility contributes to the efficient performance of all kinds of physical activities, including those associated with the performance of tasks of everyday living as well as those required for sport performance. Flexibility helps one perform these tasks to his or her fullest potential.

Flexibility is important to the performance of even the simplest everyday activities. Imagine how

Maintaining flexibility is important in helping the elderly retain their functional independence.

difficult it would be to get dressed without adequate flexibility. Developing and maintaining flexibility in the elderly are critical to helping them be functionally independent. Some physical conditions, such as arthritis or cerebral palsy, severely restrict flexibility. Improving flexibility to the greatest degree possible given the capabilities of each person can have a significant impact on the quality of life of the person— even to the extent of allowing a dependent individual to become functionally independent.

Athletes recognize the importance of flexibility in sport performance. Adequate flexibility can enhance performance capabilities by allowing the athlete to stretch and reach further, to generate more force when kicking or throwing an object, and to change positions more quickly and efficiently. Poor flexibility can adversely affect performance. For example, a sprinter may have a shorter stride length and less speed because tight hamstring muscles can adversely affect his or her ability to flex the hip joint. Because certain sports, by their very nature, require an extremely high degree of flexibility for successful performance, stretching exercises to enhance flexibility are typically included as part of an athlete's warm-up and cool-down activities. These activities enhance the elasticity of the mus-

cles and thus help reduce the likelihood of injury and muscle soreness.

Decreased flexibility can be caused by many factors. People who are active tend to have better flexibility than those who are sedentary. When muscles are not used, they tend to become shorter, tighter, and lose elasticity. Consequently, flexibility decreases. Age is another factor that influences the extent of flexibility. It is important to encourage people to remain active as they grow old so that the effects of aging on fitness will be minimized.

Excessive amounts of body fat impede movement and flexibility. Consider the difficulty of the severely obese when they are trying to tie their shoelaces—the fat deposits serve as a wedge between the parts of the body, thereby restricting movement.

Muscle tension can affect flexibility. Individuals who experience prolonged stress often respond by bracing or tensing the muscles in their neck, shoulders, and upper back. This tightens the muscles for long periods, thus reducing flexibility. Muscle imbalance also can restrict flexibility. When weight training, for example, if an individual strengthens one group of muscles around a joint while neglecting the development of the opposing group (e.g., the quadriceps muscle group in the front of the

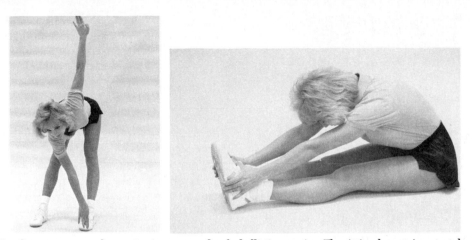

The alternate toe-touch exercise is an example of a ballistic exercise. The sitting hamstring stretch can be performed using the static stretching or the contract-relax techniques.

thigh is strengthened but the hamstring muscle group in the back of the thigh is not), flexibility will be decreased. Therefore, to ensure maximal flexibility when weight training, it is important to perform each exercise correctly, through the full range of motion, and develop opposing muscle groups.

Flexibility can be improved. There are several different approaches to developing flexibility. Participating in some physical activities can promote flexibility. Swimming, for example, can improve the flexibility of several joints. It should also be noted that because the activity is nonweightbearing, swimming in a warm pool is often recommended for people with arthritic conditions.

Flexibility also can be improved through a stretching program. Because flexibility is specific to each joint, improvement and maintenance of flexibility requires a program that incorporates specific exercises for the major joints of the body. Flexibility exercises can be performed using ballistic, static, or contract-relax stretching techniques.

Ballistic stretching. This dynamic method uses the momentum generated from repeated bouncing movements to stretch the muscle. Although effective, most experts do not recommend this technique because it may overstretch the muscle and cause muscle soreness or injury.

Static stretching. An extremely popular and effective technique, static stretching involves gently and slowly moving into the stretch position and holding it for a certain period of time. Movement should take place through the full range of motion until a little tension or tightness is felt in the muscle or muscle group. As the muscle relaxes, the stretch should be extended and held again. Stretching should not be painful. Care must be taken to not force the joint to move too far, which could cause an injury. Stretches should be held from 10 to 30 seconds and a minimum of five repetitions performed for each exercise. Flexibility exercises should be performed at least three to five times a week. If flexibility at a particular joint is extremely poor, a daily stretching program can be recommended. Flexibility exercises also should be performed at the start and at the end of a workout.

Contract-relax technique. When performing stretching exercises it is important that the muscles involved are relaxed. The contract-relax technique facilitates the relaxation of muscles. Muscles are arranged in pairs; when one contracts, the opposing muscle in the pair relaxes (e.g., when the quadriceps muscles contract, the hamstring muscles relax). To use this technique to develop flexibility, the muscle opposite the one to be stretched is con-

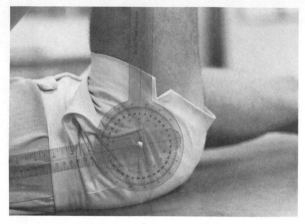

A goniometer is used to measure hip flexion.

tracted for at least 5 seconds. This results in the muscle to be stretched relaxing. Then the static stretch is performed on the desired muscle. To apply this technique to the development of hamstring flexibility, an individual would contract the quadriceps muscles, thus relaxing the hamstrings. Then a static hamstring stretch is employed. This technique allows the stretch to be performed through a greater range of motion.

Because flexibility is specific, a program for improvement and maintenance of flexibility must include exercises for each movement at the joint for which flexibility is being developed.

Flexibility can be measured. Because flexibility is joint specific, there is no one test that can be used to provide an overall measure of an individual's flexibility. The goniometer, a large protractor with moveable arms, provides a measurement of the range of movement in terms of degrees.

There also are a number of tests that have been developed to measure movement at certain joints and require little equipment to perform. The AAHPERD Physical Best Fitness Program, for example, uses the sit-and-reach test to assess the flexibility of the lower-back and hamstring muscles.

CONDUCTING FITNESS PROGRAMS

Physical educators must follow the principles of exercise when designing a fitness program. The principles of specificity, overload, and progression must be taken into account. Careful consideration must be given to providing for individual differences and for safety. When planning a fitness program to meet individual needs, practitioners must ensure that the participant exercises with sufficient intensity, duration, and frequency to attain desired fitness goals. Equally important to realizing long-term fitness benefits is the manner in which the program is conducted. Physical education programs in the schools; adult fitness programs in community, commercial, and corporate settings; and cardiac rehabilitation programs should be conducted in a manner that optimizes the chances for maintaining health fitness throughout life.

Fitness programs should include cognitive and affective educational goals as well as physical activity. For fitness to become an integral part of one's life, fitness knowledge and an appreciation for the benefits of fitness must be taught. Participants should know (1) why fitness is important, (2) the risks associated with being unfit, (3) guidelines for designing a personal exercise program, and (4) how to evaluate and solve their own fitness problems. Program experiences should be structured to develop a positive attitude and a long-term commitment to fitness. These goals can be accomplished by fostering an understanding of the contributions of fitness to one's quality of life. Program participants should have the opportunity to develop a proficiency in several physical activities that can be used throughout their lives.

Fitness should be fun. Boring and tedious exercises and calisthenics do little to develop enthusiasm for fitness. Fitness activities should meet the needs and interests of the program participants. Activities selected should be enjoyable to the individual while enabling the attainment of fitness objectives. Not everyone likes to jog; some prefer swimming, bicycling, tennis, or soccer. Practitioners should help each program participant to find an activity that is enjoyable yet sufficiently strenuous to contribute to the attainment of fitness goals. When participants engage in activities that are personally satisfying, they are more likely to incorporate those activities into their life-style.

Fitness goals should be established and a plan of action to attain them should be developed. Specific fitness goals based on individual needs should be established for program participants. Some individuals may wish to develop an optimal level of cardiovascular endurance, others hope to lose weight, and still others may strive to enhance their flexibility in order to perform daily living tasks more easily. Such individual objectives must be considered when conducting a program.

Goals provide a direction for participants and help to focus their energy and effort. Goals should be realistic and a reasonable amount of time allotted to attain them. Fitness does not happen overnight—it requires effort, determination, and discipline. Once long-term goals have been established, short-term, or weekly, goals should be set to help move toward the desired outcome. It is important for program participants to realize that the development of an acceptable level of fitness requires time. It is estimated that 60% or more of the adults who start an exercise program drop out within the first month. Participants should be informed that it will take time for the effects of their efforts to be noticed or felt. It may take as long as 8 weeks to experience many of the major benefits. However, by monitoring their weekly efforts, individuals will be able to see that they are making progress.

Fitness progress should be monitored. Progress should be monitored on a regular basis. This will help individuals to notice their improvement. Each participant should be encouraged to keep a personal fitness log of information such as the number, time, and intensity of exercise sessions; calories consumed and calories expended; weight changes; and personal feelings pertaining to exercise. Monitoring progress regularly is reinforcing and provides a means of assessing one's improvement.

Fitness requires a maintenance program. Once the desired fitness goals are achieved, a maintenance program is needed. When a person stops exercising, fitness gains are lost in a short time. Just as weight lost is quickly regained if a person reverts to his or her poor eating habits, fitness gains are

quickly lost if a person reverts to poor activity habits.

Participants in a fitness program often ask, "How long do I have to keep exercising?" or "Now that I have reached my goal, what do I need to do to keep it?" or "What will happen if I stop exercising?" Fitness gains are easily lost once training stops. Cardiovascular gains deteriorate most quickly and can disappear within a few weeks or months of inactivity (5 to 10 weeks).[8,9] Strength gains are longer lasting; some strength gains remain for 6 months to 1 year after cessation of training.[8,9]

Because fitness diminishes when exercising is stopped, an exercise program should be an integral part of one's life. Once the desired fitness goals are achieved, a maintenance program should be incorporated into one's life-style. Because it is easier to maintain fitness than to acquire it, modifications in the intensity, duration, or frequency of exercise can be made to the program. However, minimal standards for these components should be followed and exercise must be continued on a regular basis.

Fitness improvements and maintenance are a personal responsibility. Achievement and maintenance of an optimal level of fitness require a personal commitment. Individuals must take personal responsibility for their fitness. Fitness must be valued for the important contributions it makes to one's life. Each person must realize that the benefits accrued from participation in a fitness program are indeed worthy of the effort. All persons must be encouraged to incorporate fitness activities into their life-style.

Effects of Training

The results derived from regular periods of muscular work or exercise are many and varied. Individuals who participate regularly in exercise adapted to their needs and thereby attain a state of physical fitness may be called *trained*. Individuals who allow their muscles to get soft and flabby and are in a poor physical condition can be referred to as *untrained*.

A trained individual is in a better state of physical fitness than the person who follows a sedentary, inactive life. When two persons, one trained and

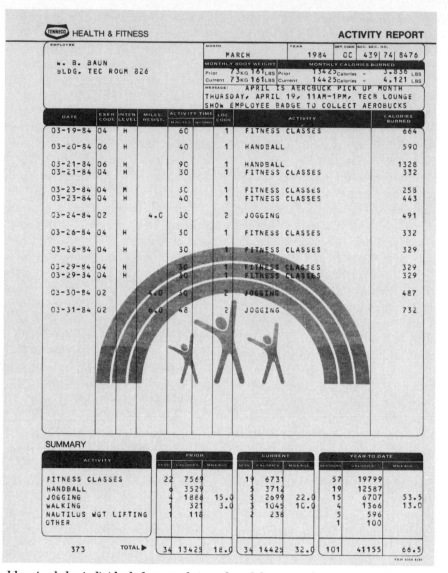

DATE	EXER CODE	INTEN LEVEL	MILES. RESIST.	ACTIVITY TIME MINUTES	ACTIVITY TIME SECONDS	LOC CODE	ACTIVITY	CALORIES BURNED
03-19-84	04	H		60		1	FITNESS CLASSES	664
03-20-84	06	H		40		1	HANDBALL	590
03-21-84	06	H		90		1	HANDBALL	1328
03-21-84	04	H		30		1	FITNESS CLASSES	332
03-23-84	04	M		30		1	FITNESS CLASSES	258
03-23-84	04	H		40		1	FITNESS CLASSES	443
03-24-84	02		4.0	30		2	JOGGING	491
03-26-84	04	H		30		1	FITNESS CLASSES	332
03-28-84	04	H		30		1	FITNESS CLASSES	329
03-29-84	04	H		30		1	FITNESS CLASSES	329
03-29-34	04	H		30		1	FITNESS CLASSES	329
03-30-84	02		4.0	30		2	JOGGING	487
03-31-84	02		6.0	48		2	JOGGING	732

TENNECO HEALTH & FITNESS — ACTIVITY REPORT

EMPLOYEE: W. B. BAUN, BLDG. TEC ROOM 826

MONTH MARCH   YEAR 1984   DEP CODE CC   SOC. SEC. NO. 439 74 8476

MONTHLY BODY WEIGHT: Prior 73 KG 161 LBS   Current 73 KG 161 LBS

MONTHLY CALORIES BURNED: Prior 13425 Calories = 3.836 LBS   Current 14425 Calories = 4.121 LBS

MESSAGE: APRIL IS AEROBUCK PICK UP MONTH THURSDAY, APRIL 19, 11AM-1PM, TEC8 LOUNGE SHOW EMPLOYEE BADGE TO COLLECT AEROBUCKS

SUMMARY

ACTIVITY	PRIOR SESS.	PRIOR CALORIES	PRIOR MILEAGE	CURRENT SESS.	CURRENT CALORIES	CURRENT MILEAGE	YEAR-TO-DATE SESSIONS	YEAR-TO-DATE CALORIES	YEAR-TO-DATE MILEAGE
FITNESS CLASSES	22	7569		19	6731		57	19799	
HANDBALL	6	3529		5	3712		19	12587	
JOGGING	4	1888	15.0	5	2699	22.0	15	6707	53.5
WALKING	1	321	3.0	3	1045	10.0	4	1366	13.0
NAUTILUS WGT LIFTING	1	118		2	238		5	596	
OTHER							1	100	
TOTAL 373	34	13425	18.0	34	14425	32.0	101	41155	66.5

TEN 5354 8/81

Record-keeping helps individuals focus on their goals and document their progress. Computer Activity Report used in Health and Fitness programs at Tenneco Inc., Houston, Tex.

one untrained, of approximately the same build are performing the same amount of moderate muscular work, evidence indicates that the trained individual has a lower oxygen consumption, lower pulse rate, larger stroke volume per heartbeat, less rise in blood pressure, greater red and white blood cell counts, slower rate of breathing, lower rate of lactic acid formation, and a faster return to normal of blood pressures and heart rate. The heart becomes more efficient and is able to circulate more blood while beating less frequently. Furthermore, in work of a strenuous nature that cannot be performed for any great period of time the trained individual has greater endurance, a capacity for higher oxygen consumption, and a faster return to normal of heart rate and blood pressure. Training results in a more efficient organism. Since a greater efficiency of heart action enables a larger flow of blood to reach the muscles and thus ensure an increased supply of fuel and oxygen, more work is performed at less cost; improvements in strength, power, neuromuscular coordination, and endurance occur; coordination and timing of movements is better; and an improved state of physical fitness results.

Contributors to Fitness

Proper nutrition, effective stress management, and recreational activities can all contribute to the attainment of a high level of health fitness. Nutrition is important for maintaining a desirable body composition. Physical activity can play an important role in stress management and in the use of one's leisure time.

Nutrition and Fitness

Nutrition has an important role in enhancing fitness. As a science, nutrition is concerned with the study of foods and their effect on the human body. Studying the food requirements necessary for production of energy for work, development and maintenance of the body, and regulation of body processes are central to the science of nutrition.

It is commonly acknowledged that what we eat can affect our health, growth and development, and ability to perform the various activities that fill our lives. In terms of health fitness, the foods that we consume can directly affect our body composition and weight as well as the energy we have available to engage in physical activity and exercise.

A nutrient is a basic substance that is used by the body to sustain vital processes such as repair and regulation of cellular functions and the production of energy. The six major categories of nutrients are carbohydrates, fats, proteins, vitamins, minerals, and water.

Carbohydrates, proteins, and fats—the three basic foodstuffs—provide the energy required for muscular work. They also have a critical role in the maintenance of body tissues and in the regulation

of their functions. Carbohydrates are the major source of energy for the body, and fats are a secondary source.

The energy derived from food is measured in kilocalories, though these are commonly referred to as calories. Regulating one's energy or caloric balance by carefully monitoring caloric consumption and expenditure is essential in attaining and maintaining a desirable body composition.

Vitamins and minerals have no caloric value. Although they are required only in small amounts, they are essential to body functioning. Vitamins are needed for normal growth and development. Vitamins do not provide energy directly, but play a critical role in releasing energy from the foods that are consumed. Minerals are essential to the regulation and performance of such body functions as the maintenance of water balance and skeletal muscle contraction.

Water is the most basic of all the nutrients—it is necessary to sustain life. The most abundant of all the nutrients in the body, water accounts for approximately 60% of the body's weight. Water is necessary for all of the chemical processes performed by the body. It is essential for such functions as energy production, digestion, temperature regulation, and elimination of the by-products of metabolism.

Maintaining a proper water balance is crucial. Insufficient water causes dehydration; severe dehydration can lead to death. People who are physically active should carefully monitor their water intake to ensure that an adequate fluid balance is maintained. This is particularly critical for individuals who exercise in a hot, humid environment. Exercising under these conditions typically causes excessive sweating and, subsequently, large losses of water. Sufficient water should be drunk to ensure that proper fluid balance is maintained.

If all of the nutrients required by the body are to be obtained, a well-balanced diet is necessary. To assist people in planning a good diet, the four-food-group plan is often used. This plan categorizes foods into four basic groups based on similarities in nutrient origin and content. The four basic food

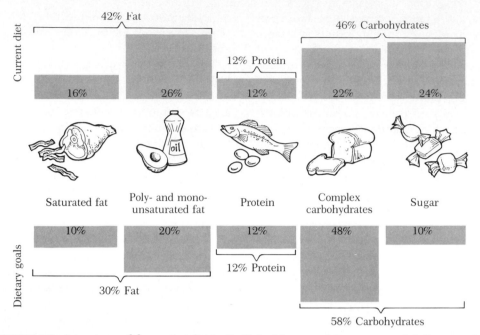

FIGURE 6-3 *A summary of the current diet in the United States and the recommended diet according to the US Senate Select Committee on Nutrition and Human Needs.*
(Modified from Payne WA and Hahn DB: Understanding your health, ed 2, St Louis, 1988, Times Mirror/Mosby College Publishing.)

groups and the recommended daily servings from each group are:

Breads, cereals, and grains	4 servings
Fruits and vegetables	4 servings
Meat and high proteins	2 servings
Milk and dairy products	2 servings

A well-balanced diet is achieved by eating a variety of foods from each food group and consuming the recommended number of servings. This is necessary if all the nutrients required by the body are to be obtained.

In planning a daily diet it is also important to carefully monitor caloric intake and the amount of carbohydrates, fat, and protein consumed. Current dietary practices and recommended dietary goals are shown in Figure 6-3. U.S. health officials have expressed a concern that the current American diet is too high in fat, cholesterol, sugar, and sodium and is lacking in carbohydrates and fiber. Dietary guidelines are shown in the box on p. 199.

Dietary planning requires the thoughtful application of nutritional knowledge to ensure that the diet is adequate and balanced. Individual conditions and factors such as age, sex, weight, medical conditions, environment, and level of physical activity must be considered in dietary planning. Because of the significant impact of nutritional practices on health, the production of energy for physical activity, and the regulation of body composition, attaining and maintaining desirable levels of health fitness requires careful attention to nutritional practices.

Stress Management and Fitness

Stress, according to Selye,[3] is essentially the rate of all the wear and tear caused by life. Each person experiences some degree of stress during each moment of existence. Stress can be a positive force, where it energizes the individual and improves performance. Stress also can be a negative force, where it is harmful to the individual and disrupts performance.

The term *stressor* is used to refer to a diversity of

DIETARY GUIDELINES FOR AMERICANS*

1. MAINTAIN IDEAL BODY WEIGHT. If you are overweight, chances of developing chronic disorders are greatly increased. To avoid being overweight consume only as much energy (calories) as is expended; if overweight, decrease energy intake and increase energy expenditure.
2. EAT A VARIETY OF FOODS. Include foods from each food group in your diet each day. Make sure to include proteins, which contain vitamins, minerals, and amino acids; essential fatty acids; and sources of energy.
3. AVOID TOO MUCH FAT, SATURATED FAT, AND CHOLESTEROL. A high blood cholesterol level is a major risk factor in heart attack. Fat is essential in the diet, but careful selection of foods can significantly reduce the intake of saturated fats.
4. EAT FOODS WITH ADEQUATE STARCH AND FIBER. Substitute starches for fats as an energy source. Foods high in fiber content reduce the likelihood of problems in the gastrointestinal tract.
5. AVOID TOO MUCH SUGAR. Sugar is the primary source of tooth decay. Sugar from fruit and vegetable sources is always more desirable than processed sugars.
6. AVOID TOO MUCH SODIUM. Excessive salt intake can lead to elevated blood pressure.
7. IF YOU DRINK ALCOHOL, DO SO IN MODERATION. Alcohol is generally high in calorie content and low in nutrient content. Excessive use of alcohol can cause cirrhosis of the liver and certain neurologic disorders.

*From US Department of Agriculture, Home and Garden Bulletin, no 232, 1985.

---

events or stimuli that elicit the stress response in the individual. The term *stress* refers to the physiological and psychological responses of the individual to the stressors he or she encounters.

Stress can have both positive and negative effects. A positive effect might result if an athlete is "psyched up" for a game and thus performs better. A negative effect might be the very high level of stress that results in depression.

A variety of stressors affect people today. Psychological stressors arouse emotions such as fear, anxiety, anger, and love. Physiological stressors are pollution, noise, heat, and cold, for example. Worrying about an examination is a stressor, and vigorous exercise and strenuous sports are stressors. All illnesses are stressors. Many stressors are of environmental origin, such as air pollution and crowding.

Stressors have different effects on different people. Also, people vary in the amount of stress that is part of their life-styles. For example, Type A people are always in a hurry, competitive, and aggressive. Type B people are relaxed and take more time to accomplish their tasks.

Signs of stress may include insomnia, backaches, headaches, inability to cope, anxiety, and irritability.

When a person encounters a stressor, the brain puts into action two interrelated physiological systems—the autonomic nervous system and the endocrine system. The result is an increased heart rate and blood pressure and elevated levels of oxygen and glucose in the blood. These responses prepare us for "fight" or "flight."

Evidence is mounting that many chronic ailments that affect persons, especially those in middle age, are directly related to stress. The hard driving, competitive corporation employee may be recognized as a likely candidate for a heart attack at an early age. Conditions such as ulcerative colitis, asthma, migraine headaches, and ulcers are directly related to stress, as are many psychosomatic disorders.

The important thing is that the body must be prepared to meet stress. The formula for enjoying life is learning how to make adjustments in a world that is constantly changing and in which events do not always run smoothly. These adjustments can more readily be made by the person who understands the body and ways of meeting stress. It is thought that to some extent disorders involving nervous disturbances, high blood pressure, and ulcers are caused by lack of understanding of adaptation.

Some methods that are used to control stress responses are exercise, relaxation, drugs, and biofeedback.

Physical activity has been found to be very helpful in controlling stress. It is believed that exercise burns up stress hormones. Exercise helps to release the tension that can accumulate when one is under stress. On the other hand, sitting and inactivity inhibit natural expression. As a result stress-induced tension is compounded by inactivity. Some psychiatrists have found that physical exercise performed on a regular basis produces psychological benefits such as relieving depression and anxiety.

A stress-regulated and controlled life-style is thought by some persons to provide a balance between work and play and rest and exercise.

Relaxation, Recreation, and Fitness

Relaxation contributes to health and may actually be in the form of physical activity. Relaxation is essentially a mental phenomenon concerned with the reduction of tensions that could originate from muscular activity but that are more likely to result from pressures of contemporary living.

A technique for achieving relaxation or nervous reeducation has been developed by Jacobson. It has two basic steps.

In the first step the individual learns to recognize muscle tension in subtle as well as in gross terms. Gross tension is easily identified. With fists tightly clenched, one holds the arms outstretched to the side at shoulder height for one minute. The individual observes the feeling of exertion and discomfort in the forearms and shoulders. The arms are dropped to the sides and the muscles of the arms and hand are relaxed completely. The effortless relaxation which Jacobson calls the "negative of exertion," can be noted. Subtle tension, involving less muscle effort than that just illustrated, is sometimes difficult to detect. It takes concentration and practice to learn to recognize minor tension in the trunk, neck, face, throat, and other body parts.

In the second step the individual learns to relax completely. First, the large muscle groups— arms, legs, trunk, and neck— are relaxed. Then the forehead, eyes, face, and even the throat have tension eased through a program of passive relaxation. Carried out in the proper fashion, the program teaches the subject to relax the whole body to the point of negative exertion. The result is a release of tension, an antidote to fatigue, and also an inducement to sleep.

Leisure-time activities such as games and sports, hobbies and avocations, and intellectual and artistic endeavors such as painting and sculpturing are considered to be excellent means for eliminating boredom and tension. These recreational activities provide a means of relaxation. Long abused as simply childish diversion or amusement, recreation is currently being suggested as an antidote for some of the tensions each person experiences in daily life.

Deterrents to Fitness

There are several deterrents to attaining a high state of fitness. Some of the more important of these are life-style, tobacco, alcohol, and drugs.

Life-style and Fitness

One of the greatest deterrents to physical fitness is the general life-style of our modern age. Many people are eating the wrong foods and drinking and smoking excessively. In many cases excessive affluence is detrimental to physical fitness in that affluence directly affects diet and promotes a sedentary life in which driving is favored over walking and watching television is given priority over physical exercise.

The results of our life-styles may be seen in increased coronary heart disease at younger ages. It is no longer unusual to see coronary patients in their midtwenties or younger! Obesity has become a great problem, and persons who are overweight tend to have a poor self-image, are disinterested in physical activity, and, most importantly, have a greater risk of heart disease and other malfunctions.

Positive changes in life-style can best occur through education. This education for fitness needs

Coeducational leisure time activities are offered in a variety of settings and are very popular.

to start with young children to make them aware of their bodies and the value of physical fitness to their emotional and physical well-being. In addition, public communication through literature, television, and radio should endeavor to educate adults so that they may take positive steps in improving their physical fitness.

Tobacco and Fitness

Smoking speeds the pulse rate, raises the blood pressure, constricts the blood vessels, and can cause other physical damage. Some evidence has shown that cigarette smoking interferes with the ability of red blood cells to release oxygen to body tissues. Although the evidence is not fully conclusive, it apparently indicates that blood from heavy smokers should be rejected for donation purposes because of this deficiency. Smoking has also been linked to many diseases. For example, the correlation between cancer and smoking has been established. Considerable evidence indicates that smoking is detrimental to the maintenance of physical fitness. No evidence indicates that it contributes to a higher level of physical performance.

Studies have been conducted in respect to smoking and physical performance. One study of 2,000 runners was conducted over several track seasons. It showed that the nonsmokers took more first places in competition than did those runners who smoked. Another study showed that students who did not smoke grew more in height, weight, and lung capacity than did those who smoked. The increase in the chest development among the nonsmokers was also greater. Tests of physical steadiness have shown that nonsmokers are steadier than smokers.

Coaches and physical educators are almost unanimous in thinking that athletic performance and muscular power are decreased by smoking. They believe that fatigue begins earlier among the smokers. Few coaches of high school and college teams knowingly permit their athletes to smoke.

In recent years the use of smokeless or chewing tobacco by young teens and adults has increased. As evidence mounts that its use could be hazardous to one's health, teachers and coaches must educate individuals about its dangers.

Alcohol and Fitness

Alcohol depresses the central nervous system. It acts on the higher brain centers that affect decisions, judgment, and memory. The control of the

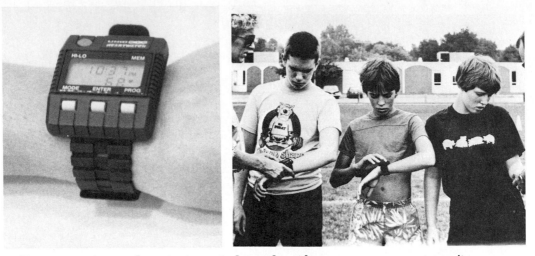

Heart rate monitors are becoming increasingly popular with consumers as a means to monitor heart rate during exercise. Students at Tilford Middle School, Vinton, Iowa use them to monitor their exercise efforts.

lower brain centers is lost, reaction time is slowed, and physical and emotional pain are reacted to more slowly.

Coaches almost universally will not permit their athletes to drink during the season of play or at any time during the school year. As in smoking, although considerable evidence shows that alcohol hinders physical performance, no evidence shows that it improves performance in any way. A great number of automobile accidents can be attributed to drinking.

Although drinking has become a popular custom in society, the young man or woman who is striving to achieve or maintain a high level of fitness should objectively examine the evidence that shows the results of such a habit.

Drugs and Fitness

Marijuana, heroin, LSD, cocaine, and similar drugs detach users from reality. They make them oblivious to danger, induce a sense of well-being by postponing feelings of fatigue, and start a habit of use that is difficult to stop.

The use of drugs such as amphetamine (found in pep pills), marijuana, cocaine, heroin, and LSD has become popular among some young people. Amphetamines have been found to produce toxic side effects and cause dependency. Research has indicated that amphetamines do not improve an individual's performance, but rather give an illusory feeling of an improved performance.

The use of drugs such as marijuana, heroin, cocaine, and LSD is illegal. The continued use of drugs brings about a permanent physical deterioration.

Some drugs have also been used in sports for which a high level of energy is required, such as in long-distance cycling races. Such a practice is denounced by physical educators, coaches, and sports medicine associations.

Many athletes (e.g., weight lifters) at the present time are utilizing drugs known as anabolic steroids to promote strength gains. They typically consume large or megadoses that can have serious short- and long-term side effects for the user.

Caffeine, which can be found in coffee, tea, and cola, is a stimulant. Moderate doses of caffeine can increase motor activity. Large doses, however, can increase the pulse rate, blood pressure, and respira-

GUIDELINES TO FOLLOW WHEN JOINING A HEALTH CLUB

1. Familiarize yourself with the many different types of facilities available, that is, spas, gyms, YMCAs, facilities at universities or high schools. Many times local schools or colleges will offer excellent facilities for public use at little or no cost. You can most often find a listing of facilities in the telephone book. It will be important to contact all the available sources to get the most detailed information.

2. Check the type of equipment available. Do they have weight equipment (free weights, Nautilus, Universal)? Is there a pool, whirlpool, sauna, steam room, running track, racquetball court, aerobic exercise room? Is there sufficient available locker space, with showers and changing areas? Do they have the type of equipment necessary for *your* fitness program?

3. Check the type and quality of programs offered such as individualized and supervised weight training, aerobic exercise classes, jogging classes, yoga, weight control programs, cardiac rehabilitation programs.

4. What are the hours of operation of the facility? Are they open 7 days per week? Is it a co-ed facility? What are the most crowded times?

5. What is the background of the personnel who will be supervising your program? You must be careful in checking the qualifications of the instructors. Many health and fitness clubs employ attractive, fit individuals whose primary function is to sell memberships to the club. Do they have a background in physical education, or athletic training? Are they certified by the American College of Sports Medicine as fitness instructors? Are they certified aerobics instructors? Do they have a background in applied physiology of exercise?

6. Before signing a contract, it is a good idea to spend several sessions working out there, talking with the instructors and with other club members. If there is some objection to doing this on the part of the management, then you should exercise extreme caution.

7. Health and fitness clubs tend to offer a wide range of membership contract options ranging from pay-by-the-visit to lifetime memberships. It is a good idea to avoid long-term contracts, especially in the beginning. Health clubs sell a lot of memberships because people tend to get caught up by the aesthetics of the facility and some very good salespeople. The firm commitment to consistently use the facility 3 to 4 times per week that you make in the sales office tends to become less important for most people over time. If all the people who bought memberships in a club were to show up at one time, chances are that you would not be able to get in the door. If you do decide to join, check on various payment options that best suit your budget. Also check on additional fees that you may have to pay for things like racquetball courts or aerobics classes.

8. It is probably best to avoid the clubs or organizations that advertise programs, classes, equipment, or techniques, that will result in "overnight" strength gains, weight loss, or improvements in appearance. You must realize that to reach the fitness goals you have set requires selecting an activity you enjoy, not overloading the system, progressing within your own individual limitations, being consistent in your training program, and accomplishing your goals safely by paying attention to the basic principles outlined within.

tory rate, and produce nervousness. Caffeine has also been found to interfere with carbohydrate and protein metabolism, which is necessary for the production of energy. Most researchers agree that large amounts of caffeine should not be part of the athlete's daily diet.

Fitness and the Consumer

The enthusiasm for health and fitness by many segments of American society has increased greatly during the past decade. Billions of dollars are spent each year by consumers on athletic shoes, workout apparel, exercise and sport equipment, diet foods and vitamins, and health club and diet center memberships. In an effort to reach the health and fitness consumer, advertising promoting these products and services is frequently seen.

Because many Americans aspire to look good and feel better, advertisers focus their messages on these desires. Vulnerable consumers are the target of unprecedented media attention, with advertisements using stereotypical images of healthy and fit individuals to promote their products. Although many advertisements are truthful in portraying their merchandise, much inaccurate information is disseminated in an effort to sell various health and fitness products to the public.

Thus, American consumers need to become educated about health and fitness products. Americans must learn to separate hype from fact. Consumers must educate themselves by critically appraising the product to be purchased. This process involves researching the product in reputable consumer magazines, speaking to such experts as physical education professionals, and buying from reputable sources. Consumers must take time to investigate the facts.

Millions of dollars are spent each year by Americans enrolling in health and fitness clubs. The pleasing aesthetics of a facility—the plush carpeting, profusion of wall mirrors, and abundance of high tech exercise equipment—and the unbelievable bargain prices for long-term memberships may entice consumers to join the club without taking time to carefully investigate the pro-

gram. Individuals contemplating joining a club should carefully consider the guidelines of Prentice and Bucher, which are shown in the box on p. 203.

There are many approaches to fitness in the marketplace. Individuals should carefully evaluate each to ensure that sound principles of fitness development and maintenance are an integral part of the approach they select to realize their fitness goals. Moreover, individuals must accept that the responsibility for getting fit and staying healthy is their own.

SUMMARY

Exercise physiology is one of the most rapidly growing areas in physical education today. Exercise physiology is the study of the effects of exercise on the body ranging from the system to the subcellular levels. Knowledge of the body's responses to exercise is needed by the practitioner to design meaningful exercise programs.

One concern of the exercise physiologist, albeit not the sole concern, is fitness. The American public is fitness-minded to an extent never before seen in its history. Professionals should take advantage of this interest to improve the fitness levels of all segments of the American population. In essence, physical educators should educate the nation about fitness.

Within the profession, interest in health-related fitness as opposed to performance-related fitness has increased. The components that comprise both health-related and performance-related fitness are largely the same. However, these components are developed to a greater extent in performance related fitness. The health fitness components are cardiovascular function, body composition, muscular strength and endurance, and flexibility. Lack of a desirable level of these components can lead to health problems. On the other hand, attainment of the desirable level of these components can enhance one's health and well-being.

Many benefits are derived from participation in exercise and physical activity. The belief that being active is essential for good health is strongly supported. Participants should follow medical guidelines and be sure that their programs follow sound training principles. Individuals should be cognizant that exercise performance can be affected by warmup and nutrition and that exercise can be beneficial in alleviating stress and fatigue. Several deterrents to fitness are life-style and tobacco, alcohol, and drug use.

SELF-ASSESSMENT TESTS

These tests are designed to assist students in determining if the material and competencies presented in this chapter have been mastered.

1. Define exercise physiology and discuss the importance of exercise physiology to the practitioner. Investigate one of the areas of study in exercise physiology and write a short paper on a selected topic of interest to you.

2. Prepare a position paper on the subject "Physical Activity is a Key Essential for Optimal Health."

3. Assess your own fitness level or that of your parents. Then, keeping in mind the guidelines for designing an exercise or a training program, construct a fitness program to achieve or maintain the desired level of fitness.

4. In a short paper discuss how an individual's life-style and habits may be a deterrent to a state of fitness and health.

5. What rationale would you use to convince a friend who was tired all the time, feeling overwhelmed by stress, and overweight to start a physical fitness program?

6. Prepare an essay in which you assess the physical fitness status of the nation's youth and adults. Conclude your paper with recommendations for improving the physical fitness status of each group.

REFERENCES

1. Siedentop D: Introduction to physical education, fitness, and sport, Mountain View, Calif, 1990, Mayfield.

2. Public Health Service, US Department of Health and Human Services: Promoting Health/Preventive Disease: Year 2000 Objectives for the Nation (draft), Washington, DC, 1989, US Government Printing Office.

3. Blair S, Kohl H, and Powell K: Physical activity, physical fitness, exercise, and the public's health, The Academy Papers 20:53-69, 1987.

4. Montoye H: How active are modern populations? The Academy Papers 21:34-45, 1988.

5. Ross JG and Gilbert GG: The national children and youth study: a summary of the findings, Journal of Physical Education, Recreation, and Dance 56(1):45-50, 1985.

6. Ross JG and Pate RR: The national children and youth fitness study II, Journal of Physical Education, Recreation, and Dance 58(9):51-56, 1987.

7. American Alliance for Health, Physical Education, Recreation and Dance, The shape of the nation: a survey of state physical education requirements, Reston, Va, 1987, AAHPERD.

8. Hockey RV: Physical fitness: the pathway to healthful living, St Louis, 1989, Times Mirror/Mosby College Publishing.

9. Prentice WE and Bucher CA: Fitness for college and life, St Louis, 1988, Times Mirror/Mosby College Publishing.

10. Pollock ML and Blair SN: Exercise prescription, Journal of Physical Education, Recreation, and Dance 52(1):30-35, 81, 1981.

11. Sherrill C: Adapted physical education and recreation, Dubuque, Ia, 1986.

SUGGESTED READINGS

American Alliance for Health, Physical Education, Recreation, and Dance: Physical best, Reston, Va, 1988, AAHPERD.

Explains the comprehensive fitness education and assessment program to motivate children and youth to participate in physical activity to develop their health fitness.

American Alliance for Health, Physical Education, Recreation, and Dance: Exercise physiology. Basic Stuff Series I, Reston, Va, 1987, AAHPERD.

Part of the Basic Stuff Series, this book summarizes selected knowledge in the area of exercise physiology and presents it in an easy-to-read format.

American Alliance for Health, Physical Education, Recreation, and Dance: The national children and youth fitness study, Journal of Physical Education, Recreation, and Dance 56(1):44-90, 1985.

These articles present the findings and discuss the results and the implications of the National Children and Youth Fitness Study completed in 1984.

Cooper KH and Collingwood TR: Physical fitness: programming issues for total well-being, Journal of Physical Education, Recreation, and Dance 55(3):35-36, 44, 1984.

This article focuses on program accountability, that is, "compliance to changing behavior and achieving goals," in fitness and health promotion programs. Participant compliance, program models, program elements, and organizational commitment are discussed.

Corbin CB: Physical fitness in the K-12 curriculum, Journal of Physical Education, Recreation, and Dance: 58(7):49-54, 1987.

Solutions to problems encountered in incorporating physical fitness into the school curriculum are discussed.

Flatten K, editor: Fitness evaluation and programming for older adults, Journal of Physical Education, Recreation, and Dance 60(3):63-78, 1989.

Five articles highlight fitness evaluation and programming for older adults, specific fitness tests for this population, the Senior Olympics, and programs for older adults.

Hockey RV: Physical fitness: the pathway to healthful living, St Louis, 1989, Times Mirror/Mosby College Publishing.

This text discusses the principles of fitness and the role of physical fitness in the attainment of health.

Katch FI and McArdle WD: Nutrition, weight control, and exercise, Philadelphia, 1988, Lea & Febiger.

This book provides an excellent overview of nutrition, weight control, and exercise.

Lamb DR: Physiology of exercise: responses and adaptations, New York, 1984, Macmillan Inc.

This text focuses on the mechanisms underlying the physiological responses of the body and its adaptations to exercise.

McSwegin P, editor: Assessing physical fitness, Journal of Physical Education, Recreation, and Dance 60(6):33-64, 1989.

Nine articles encompassing understanding fitness standards, fitness assessment procedures and results, and developing positive fitness behavior are presented.

Moore M: Are employee fitness programs for everyone? The Physician and Sportsmedicine 11(1):143-148, 1983.

This article discusses the benefits of corporate fitness programs, employee involvement, corporate responsibility, and types of programs.

Noble B: Physiology of exercise and sport, St Louis, 1986, Times Mirror/Mosby College Publishing.

This text provides a comprehensive, albeit practical introduction to exercise physiology. Emphasis is on helping the practitioner understand movement from the perspective of sport as well as health.

Pollock ML and Blair SN: Exercise prescription, Journal of Physical Education, Recreation, and Dance 52(1):30-35, 81, 1981.

The authors discuss the physiological components of an exercise prescription as well as behavioral factors that need to be considered. Guidelines for prescriptions to promote health-related fitness are presented.

Prentice WE Jr: Fitness for college and life, ed 3, St Louis, 1991, Times Mirror/Mosby College Publishing.

This text, specifically written for the college student, focuses on the nature and scope of physical fitness. The basic components of fitness and principles governing the development of fitness are presented.

Sharkley BJ: Physiology of fitness, ed 3, Champaign, Ill, 1990, Human Kinetics.

This text presents the principles underlying the development of aerobic and muscular fitness. Weight control and obesity as well as the role of fitness in one's life are discussed.

Shields SL: The physical education profession in the corporate sector, Journal of Physical Education, Recreation, and Dance 55(3):32-34, 1984.

The role of the physical educator in the promotion of wellness in corporate sector is discussed.

Wells CL: Women, sport, and performance: a physiological perspective, Champaign, Ill, 1985, Human Kinetics.

This text discusses the physiological aspects of women's sport performances.

Chapter 7

Psychological Foundations of Physical Education and Sport

INSTRUCTIONAL OBJECTIVES AND COMPETENCIES TO BE ACHIEVED

After reading this chapter the student should be able to—

- Identify and give illustrations of cognitive, affective, and psychomotor types of learning.
- Define motor learning and understand the influence of readiness, motor development, motivation, reinforcement, and individual differences in the learning of motor skills.
- Understand the information-processing model of motor learning and the stages of learning and be able to draw implications for the teaching of physical education.
- Apply to the teaching of physical education basic concepts of motor learning such as feedback, design of practice, and mental practice.
- Describe the psychological benefits from participation in sport and physical activities.
- Discuss the role of anxiety, arousal, and attention in the performance of motor skills and the application of intervention strategies to enhance performance.

The study of psychology has implications for physical educators in such areas as learning theory, motor development, motor control, motor learning, and psychology of sport. The word psychology comes from the Greek words *psyche,* meaning mind or soul, and *logos,* meaning science. Therefore from these Greek words it can be seen that psychology is the science of the mind and the soul. Psychologists study human nature scientifically, and rather than formulate conclusions from casual observations, they sort out and check and recheck human characteristics under reliable conditions. In this manner and through the use of acceptable scientific evaluation, it is possible for psychologists to determine the conditions under which certain human characteristics will operate or learning occur. These data should theoretically be objective and free from prejudice and bias and focus attention on impartial and realistic examination of all the evidence.

While the areas of motor development, motor control, motor learning, and sport psychology have their legacy in psychology, within the last 20 years these areas of study have grown tremendously as well as become increasingly specialized. Researchers in these areas, although they are highly interrelated, have developed their own methods of inquiry and focuses of study. In essence, these are subdisciplines within the realm of physical education and sport. However, because of the common psychological foundations inherent in these subdisciplines, these areas are all discussed within this chapter.

LEARNING

What is learning? Learning can be defined as a change in the internal state of the learner as a result of instruction, experiences, study, and/or practice. These internal changes are not readily discernible, thus learning must be inferred from behavior or performance. An observer, noting relatively permanent changes in an individual's performance, may assume that learning has taken place. Physical educators, whether they are working in a school or non-school setting, should be interested in helping the individuals with whom they work to realize their greatest learning potential. In accomplishing this task they will benefit from knowing the different kinds of learning, learning theories, key elements of the learning process, and the scientific basis for the learning and the control of motor skills.

Learning is typically divided into three areas of study or domains: (1) cognitive, (2) affective, and (3) psychomotor. The physical educator is concerned with facilitating learning in all three domains.

Cognitive Learning

In teaching for cognitive learning the physical educator is concerned with increasing the individual's knowledge, improving problem-solving abilities, clarifying understandings, and developing and identifying concepts. The development of cognitive learning makes use of the mental process as a primary form of activity. The degree to which time is spent teaching for cognitive development depends on factors such as the information to be imparted and the abilities of the individuals to understand the material being presented. Physical educators in the school setting may be concerned with teaching their students rules or strategies pertaining to specific sports or concepts such as those presented in Basic Stuff. Physical educators working in a community, commercial, or corporate fitness program may be concerned with teaching their students/clients the knowledge necessary to design their own exercise programs or the risk factors associated with coronary heart disease.

Affective Learning

In teaching for affective learning the teacher is concerned with attitudes, appreciations, and values. The primary goal of such teaching is that of developing proper and positive attitudes toward physical activity. Teachers may also be concerned about instilling such qualities as sportsmanship, leadership, followership, teamwork, and the need to play according to the rules that govern the game or activity. Fitness leaders may strive to help their clients appreciate the contribution of regular participation in physical activities to their lives.

Psychomotor Learning

In teaching for psychomotor learning the physical educator is concerned with the development and the improvement of motor skill. This type of learning is the heart of the physical education and sport experience. The focus of psychomotor learning is on the acquisition of motor skills; this includes both fundamental motor skills as well as selective skills in various physical education activities geared to the age, maturation level, and physical condition of each student/client. Since motor skill learning is such an important part of the psychological foundations of physical education and sport, it will be emphasized in this chapter.

Skill Learning

Motor learning is the study of the acquisition of movement skills as a consequence of practice. Learning of a movement skill is inferred from performance. For example, let us say the goal of instruction is to learn a tennis serve. To assess how well an individual learned the tennis serve, the instructor would observe the person performing this skill. As the student gains mastery of a skill through practice, his or her performance should improve and become more consistent, that is, less

Psychomotor learning involves teaching physical skills. Members of the Boys and Girls Clubs of Las Vegas receive tennis instruction from a racquet club professional.

variable. These changes in skill performance would lead the instructor to conclude that learning had occurred. Intimately related to motor learning is the area of motor control. Motor control is the study of the neural mechanisms and processes by which movements are learned and controlled. Understanding these principles is essential to teaching. By understanding the principles that govern motor skill acquisition and the control of movements the physical educator will be better able to design practices to promote learning.

Psychologists have attempted to explain the phenomenon of learning and to answer such questions as how it best takes place and what are the laws under which it operates. Over the years many theories have been advanced to explain the learning process. These theories are applicable to all three learning domains. Typically, professional preparation programs provide undergraduate students with information about these theories as part of psychology, education, and/or teaching methods courses. For the purpose of the brief discussion that follows,

the basic theories can be divided into three categories: connectionist theories, cognitive theories, and human machine theories.

Generally, the connectionist or behaviorist theories maintain that learning consists of the learner making a connection or an association between a stimulus and a response or responses. These theorists are concerned with how the bond between an event or stimulus and a behavior is formed. The development of laws and principles of how this bond is developed has been the work of noted researchers such as Pavlov, Thorndike, Guthrie, Hull, and Skinner.

The psychologists who support cognitive theories believe that a human being's various perceptions, beliefs, or attitudes (cognitions or mental images) that concern the environment determine behavior. The manner in which these cognitions are modified by the human being's experience indicates that learning has taken place. The basic principles underlying the cognitive theories were developed by Gestalt psychologists such as Koffa and Kohler.

Human-machine theories are based on the nature of the makeup of the nervous system. In formulating these theories an analogy was made between the human and a machine (computers). These theories hypothesized that the human nervous system is involved with elements such as input, transmission, processing, output, and feedback. These theorists maintain that learning such as motor learning is not a result of the strengthening of the stimulus-response process, as described in some of the learning theories already discussed. Instead, they believe that learning results from such things as the input, better processing of information that comes from input, and feedback. Through such a process the results will be identified more clearly, whether positively or negatively, errors will be more readily known and corrected, and more effective learning will take place. Human-machine theories include cybernetical theory, information theory, and feedback theory.

In recent years motor learning researchers have been interested in the process and mechanisms by which motor skills are controlled and learned. Increasingly the information-processing approach has been used to describe motor skill acquisition and performance.

Information-Processing Model

In its simplest form the information-processing model is comprised of four components or processes: input, decision-making, output, and feedback. This model is illustrated in Figure 7-1.

Input is the process of obtaining information from the environment. This information is transmitted to the central nervous system where the process of *decision-making* occurs. During this procedure the processing of the input takes place; that is, it is sifted, evaluated, and interpreted and in light of this information an appropriate response selected. The response and its execution is the *output. Feedback* is information about the performance of the movement and its quality, appropriateness, and/or outcome. This information can be utilized to provide *input* for the next skill attempt. The knowledge gained from feedback can be used to improve the decision-making process as well as the succeeding

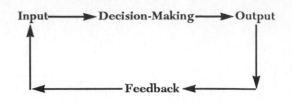

FIGURE 7-1   *Information-Processing Model.*

output. As an individual becomes more adept at performing the skill, often he or she also becomes more skilled at using the feedback to improve performance.

How the information-processing model works can be illustrated by this simple example. Suppose you are in a soccer game and are in possession of the ball within shooting range of the goal. Should you retain the ball and continue to dribble while maneuvering for a more favorable position? Or should you pass to a teammate? Or should you shoot for the goal?

To make this choice, you must first obtain information about your position on the field, the position of your teammates and the opposing players, and the distance between you and the goalie. This information serves as input. Next, as part of the decision-making process you must analyze and interpret this information with reference to your past experience in the game of soccer and specifically in situations similar to the present one. Within a fraction of a second, based on this analysis and evaluation you must choose the response to make. The decision is influenced by your own and your teammates' past successes in similar situations, the probable actions of the opposing team given their past reactions in similar situations, appropriateness of the various strategies available, and perhaps directions or guidelines from the teacher or the coach concerning the desirable course of action in situations of this nature. You may also consider your own ability as well as your feeling of confidence pertaining to your ability to execute the selected option, be it dribble, pass, or shoot.

Following these considerations and deliberations you select an option. Next, the movement selected is executed—you dribble, pass, or shoot. Last, both during and after the execution of the response you receive feedback about your performance. The feedback may focus on whether you executed the movement as intended and/or whether or not the outcome was successful (i.e., you scored a goal).

Physical educators should be familiar with the manner in which individuals learn skills as well as the factors that influence their performance. This understanding will help the physical educator design practices that facilitate an individual's opportunity to learn through appropriate structuring of the learning environment. The physical educator must provide learners with appropriate input through the careful selection of teaching methods, materials, and procedures. The physical educator must help the learner understand the goal of the movement and then distinguish between relevant and irrelevant information or cues with respect to that goal, drawing the learner's attention to cues essential for the decision-making process and teaching the learner to disregard the irrelevant ones.

The teacher next must help the learner to become a wise decision-maker. This can be accomplished by helping the learner evaluate his or her past experiences, by explaining the "why" underlying skills and strategies, by instructing the learner on how to use the available feedback, and by making sure that the learner is attending to the right cues and interpreting the information correctly. The teacher can facilitate the learner's development of the desired skill through the use of proper progressions and by providing the learner with appropriate and sufficient practice opportunities.

Finally, and importantly, the teacher can assist the learner by providing feedback about the learner's performance and communicating this information to the learner in an understandable manner. Additionally, the teacher must draw the learner's attention to the feedback available during the execution of the skill as well as the information regarding the outcome of the performance. This information can provide the basis for adjustments in the learner's movements.

An understanding of the manner in which individuals learn skills can help make the learning process more effective and more enjoyable, that is, less frustrating for the learner. The physical educator must also be cognizant that skill learning occurs in stages.

Stages of Learning

As an individual learns motor skills and makes the transition from unskilled to skilled performer, he or she progresses through several stages. Fitts and Posner [1] identified three stages of learning: the cognitive stage, the associative stage, and the autonomous stage. The physical educator must be cognizant of the characteristics of the learner at each stage to plan for instruction. Different instructional strategies and techniques are required at each stage to make practice more effective.

Cognitive Stage

The first stage of learning is the cognitive stage. During this stage the learner is endeavoring to understand the nature and/or goal of the activity to be learned. During this stage the learner might be concerned with such questions as "How do I stand?" "How do I hold the tennis racquet?" "How do you score in this game?" "What is the sequence of actions in this swimming stroke?" The learner also needs to pay close attention to the information provided by the instructor; this includes verbal directions as well as visual information perhaps from a demonstration of a skill or a videotape of a performer executing this skill. After analyzing this information the learner formulates a plan of action based on his or her understanding of the task and the specific directions provided by the instructor. The formulation of a plan of action is referred to as establishing a motor plan or an executive plan. A high level of concentration on the task is required as the learner tries to put the various parts of the skill together in the correct sequence.

As the learner makes his or her initial attempts at performing the skill, the performance is characterized by a large number of errors, usually gross in nature, and a great deal of variability. Although the learner may have an idea about what he or she is doing incorrectly, the learner may not know how to correct it. Specific feedback, communicated to the learner in understandable terms, is needed from the instructor to help the learner improve the skill. For example, someone just learning the tennis forehand must concentrate on moving to the correct position on the court, the grip of the racquet, the stance, turning the body, keeping an eye on the ball, making contact with the ball with the head of the racquet so that it goes over the net, shifting the body's weight, following through, and returning to ready position. The beginner at times will hit the ball so that it goes over the net; the next attempt may see the learner hit the ball into the net or out of the court or miss the ball entirely. The learner's actions, although performed in the correct sequence, may lack the smooth, polished look and the consistency of a highly skilled performer.

Associative Stage

The second stage is the associative stage. At this point the basics of the skill have been learned and the learner concentrates his or her efforts on refining the skill. During this stage the learner works on mastering the timing needed for the skill; the performance of the learner looks smoother. The number of errors committed are fewer and the same type of error tends to recur. The learner is also aware of some of the more obvious errors he or she is making in executing the task and can use this information to adjust the subsequent performance. The tennis player learning the forehand may notice more success in getting the ball over the net and inside the boundaries of the court, although he or she cannot place the ball with any assurance. The player may notice a frequent failure to follow through after contacting the ball, but he or she is not aware that the angle of the racquet face needs adjustment. The instructor can provide the learner with additional instruction focusing on specific actions and point out relevant cues to the learner.

Autonomous Stage

The third stage is the autonomous stage. This stage of learning is reached after much practice. The learner can perform the skill consistently with few errors. The skill is well-coordinated and may appear to be performed effortlessly. During this stage the skill has become almost automatic. The learner

Highly skilled performers exemplify the autonomous stage of learning.

does not have to pay attention to every aspect of the skill; he or she can perform the skill without consciously thinking about it at all. The tennis player no longer has to concentrate on the fundamentals of the skill; instead his or her focus can be directed to placing the ball in the court, varying the speed of the shot, placing spin on the ball, or game tactics. The learner also becomes more skilled at detecting errors and making adjustments, becoming his or her own teacher, so to speak.

Individuals do not proceed through these stages at the same rate. It may also be difficult at times to detect what stage an individual is in. However, to plan practices to promote effective learning, the physical educator needs to be cognizant of the characteristics and the needs of the learner in the various stages. The physical educator also needs to be aware of the forces that influence learning.

Forces Influencing Learning

Learning implies a change in person—a change in method of both practicing and performing a skill or a change in an attitude toward a particular thing. Learning implies a progressive change of behavior in an individual, although some changes are rapid, such as when insight into a problem is perceived. It implies a change that occurs as a result of experience or practice. It results in the modification of behavior as a result of training or environment. It involves such aspects as obtaining knowledge, improving skill in an activity, solving a problem, or making an adjustment to a new situation. It implies that knowledge or skill has been acquired as a result of instruction received in the school or some other setting or as a result of a person's own initiative in personal study. Learning continues throughout life.

To create an effective learning situation, physical educators must be cognizant of the forces influencing learning. Five of these forces—readiness, level of development, motivation, reinforcement, and individual differences—will be discussed.

Readiness and Motor Learning

Successful acquisition of new information or skills depends on the individual's level of readiness. *Readiness* can be defined in terms of physiological and psychological factors influencing an individual's ability and willingness to learn. Physiological readiness is the development of such qualities as the necessary strength, flexibility, and endurance as well as the development of the various organ systems of the body to such a degree that children can control their bodies in physical activities. Psychological readiness refers to the state of mind of the learner. The feeling or attitude a child or an adult has toward learning a particular skill, in other words the desire and willingness to learn, will affect the individual's acquisition of that particular skill. To create an effective learning environment the teacher must keep in mind the physiological and psychological readiness of the individual.

Learning experiences should be structured to be appropriate for the individual's abilitites.

Teachers planning learning activities must be cognizant of the individual's cognitive, affective, and physical characteristics as well as the individual's past experiences. This knowledge will help the teacher plan an atmosphere conducive to learning. The teacher should structure the learning experience so that the individual experiences success rather than the frustration that may come from trying to learn a task that is too difficult or beyond the ability of the individual at that time. The learning task may need to be modified to make it more challenging to the individual if it is too easy for his or her ability or be made easier if it is too difficult. For example, many Little League baseball teams have started letting the younger children hit the ball off a batting tee rather than hit a pitched ball. This adjustment was made because it was realized that the younger children were having difficulty tracking and successfully hitting a moving object. By allowing children to hit the ball while it was stationary—sitting atop a batting tee—the children were able to practice the skill of striking an object or batting and experience success in their endeavors. Certainly hitting the ball from the tee was more satisfying to the children than swinging at the pitched ball and missing. Adjusting the learning task to the individual's ability requires consideration of the individual's physiological readiness. Planning learning experiences that promote success enhances the individual's psychological readiness to learn.

Motor Development and Motor Learning

Noted psychologist Piaget stated that learning proceeds most rapidly when experiences that are presented to individuals are geared to their physical and intellectual abilities. For physical educators to correlate activities with the developmental levels of the individual they must have an understanding of intellectual, emotional, and motor development. An individual's intellectual and emotional development will probably be covered in psychology courses taken as part of the physical educator's professional preparation. Motor development may also be covered in psychology courses as well as methods or motor learning courses.

Motor development as an area of study in physical education goes back to the late 1940s. Some of the pioneers in this field were Anna Espenshade, Ruth Glassow, and G. Lawrence Rarick. Among other areas of study these pioneers attempted to better understand the relationship of such things as growth and development to human performance. In the beginning motor development was largely thought to be closely related to the human maturation process. In other words, motor development occurred in progressive stages as a person grew from childhood to adulthood. However, this concept has changed, and today motor development is recognized as being influenced greatly by the interaction of the individual and his or her environment. Furthermore, it is also recognized that motor development occurs not only in the early stages of life but also throughout life.

Current research in motor development is involved in such areas of study as longitudinal changes in human movement and genetic determi-

A person's motor development changes with time and age.

nants of movement. Several concepts that are relevant to motor development are the following: (1) a person's motor development changes with time and age, (2) physical education activities should correlate with the developmental level of the individual concerned, (3) nerve cell connections affect potential skill, (4) height and weight changes alter the mechanical nature of physical performance, and (5) the development of foundational skills is basic to success in the more complex skills.

Knowledge of the motor development and the ability to assess the individual's level of development is essential in planning appropriate experiences to promote motor skill learning for people of all ages. Another factor that has a powerful influence on learning is motivation.

Motivation and Motor Learning

Motivation is a basic factor in learning. The term *motivation* refers to a condition within an individual that initiates activity directed toward a goal. The study of motivation focuses on the causes of behavior, specifically those factors that influence the initiation, maintenance, and intensity of behavior.

Exercise specialists should understand an employee's motives for participating in a corporate fitness program. PepsiCo's employees use equipment at the multimillion dollar fitness facility in Purchase, NY.

Needs and drives form the basic framework for motivation. When individuals sense an unfulfilled need, they are moved to do something about it. This desire prompts people to seek a solution to the recognized need through an appropriate line of action. This line of action may require practice, effort, mastery of knowledge, or other behavior to be successful. For example, an individual who is hungry becomes motivated to seek food, whereas at the cognitive level the individual who wants to pass an examination to practice law desires acquiring the necessary knowledge.

Motivation refers to an individual's general arousal to action. It might be thought of as the desire or drive that a person has to have to achieve a goal to satisfy a particular need. The term *need* refers to an internalized deficiency of the organism. The need might be physiological or psychological. The term *drive* refers to the concept of the stimulus for action. Motivation, for example, might be asso-

ciated with the drive to exercise to satisfy the need to keep the body healthy. The motivating factor might be internal, resulting from the individual's own desire to be fit, or it might be the result of some outside force, such as peer pressure to be thin.

Although motives are internal in nature, they may be affected by external influences. The motives that cause an individual to participate in sport, for example, may be either internal or external. Motives such as the desire to develop one's body, to have fun, to test one's limits are examples of internal motives for learning. The desire to win awards, to appease parental pressures for participation, or to win money are examples of external motives for participation. An employee may decide to participate in an employee fitness program because of the desire to enhance his or her health status (internal motivation); on the other hand, the employee may participate because of the mandate by the boss to do so (external motivation). Internal motivation is more conducive to positive learning and performance and sustained particpation than external motivation. The worth of the activity should be the inducement for learning and participation rather than rewards, punishments, or grades. In physical education programs motives such as the desire to develop one's body, the desire to learn basic movement skills and eventually develop more advanced skills for specialized games, or the desire to do one's best are all valid and should be encouraged.

The physical educator should be aware of the motives for the individual's participation in physical education programs. Individuals' motives for learning and participation may differ considerably, thus consideration of individual differences is important. For example, as previously mentioned some participants in an employee fitness program may be internally motivated to join while others, whose presence was suggested by their employer, may be externally motivated and perhaps even reluctant to participate in the activities. However, during the course of the program the externally motivated participants may develop an internal motivation. The change could result because the physical educator made the program challenging, meaningful, and satisfying to the employee. As a consequence of the physical educator's efforts to make the program relevant to the individual, the once reluctant employee may become an enthusiastic participant in the program.

The actions of the physical educator can often have a positive affect on the individual's motivation. In a physical education program not all individuals will be motivated to the same extent to learn new skills; in fact, some individuals may not be motivated to learn at all. The teacher can enhance an individual's motivation for learning through goal setting, that is, establishing challenging, albeit attainable goals for the individual. Motivation can also be enhanced by structuring the learning environment for success and by making the learning experience a positive and enjoyable one. An individual's level of motivation may also be enhanced through reinforcement.

Reinforcement and Motor Learning

Physical educators should be alert to the need to reinforce the learning of skills and other behaviors of those under their supervision when the desired performance takes place. *Reinforcement* is using events, actions, and behaviors to increase the likelihood of a certain response (e.g., a skill or a behavior) recurring. Reinforcement may be positive or negative in nature. Reinforcement is considered positive when it is given following the desired response, and it is deemed negative when it is withheld following a desired response. Providing encouragement, praise, commendation, or a "pat on the back" following successful execution of a skill is an example of positive reinforcement. Such an acknowledgment of an individual's success will serve not only to reinforce correct skill performance but will also likely serve to motivate the individual to continue in his or her efforts to master the skill. If a physical educator continually belittles an individual's effort at performing a skill and discontinues this behavior when the individual finally successfully executes the skill, the physical educator is using negative reinforcement.

Two types of reinforcers are tangible and intangible. Tangible reinforcers are items such as an awards medal or money—material items. Intangible reinforcers include verbal praise, a "pat on the back," or a nod of approval.

Research suggests that reinforcement given immediately after a response is more effective than when it is delayed. Random reinforcement tends to be more effective than continual reinforcement. For reinforcement to be effective it must be meaningful to, important to, or desired by the recipient.

Reinforcement, motivation, readiness, and development are important forces in learning. One other important consideration in planning for learning is individual differences.

Individual Differences and Motor Learning

In any learning situation, be it with children or adults, the teacher must provide for individual differences among the learners. The importance of considering individual differences in motor development, readiness, motivation, and reinforcement

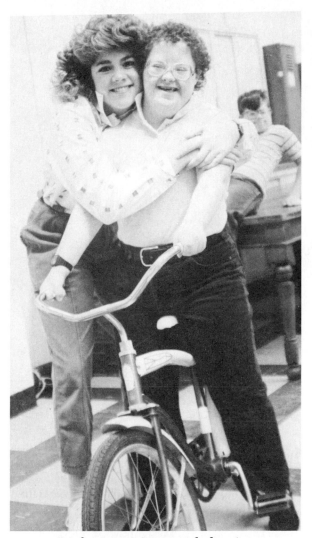

Reinforcement is important for learning.

has already been discussed. However, other factors should be taken into consideration by the teacher when planning for learning.

Differences in social and economic backgrounds should be considered—some individuals come from middle-class families while others are disadvantaged. These factors could greatly influence the prior experiences these individuals bring to the learning situation. Differences in physical abilities among individuals in the learning situation may be pronounced. Differences in intelligence and preferred learning styles hold implications for the manner in which the skills are to be taught. Personality differences must also be considered. Some individuals are outgoing, whereas others are shy and withdrawn. Some individuals are eager to try new skills, while others are reluctant or intimidated by the prospect of learning something new.

While consideration of individual differences is advocated, designing learning experiences to accommodate individual differences requires careful planning and commitment on the part of the physical educator. It is not an easy task to design learning experiences for a diversity of abilities, but it is not an impossible one. The physical educator should strive to help each individual to be the best he or she can be.

Motor Learning Concepts

In planning for motor learning the physical educator must take into consideration a learner's level of readiness, development, individual characteristics, motivation, and need for reinforcement. At this point it will be helpful to consider additional concepts, factors, and conditions that promote the learning of motor skills and improve performance.

1. *Practice sessions should be structured to promote optimal conditions for learning.* The manner in which practice sessions are organized can have a critical impact on the amount of learning that occurs. Practices should be organized so that distracting elements are eliminated from the setting. The teacher should ensure that the proper mental set has been established in the mind of the learner, the proper facilities and equipment are available, the learner has the proper background to understand and appreciate the material being presented, and conditions are such that a challenging teaching situation is present.

Much research has been done on the organization of practice with reference to the relationship between practice periods and rest periods. (In the literature this is referred to as massed versus distributed practice.) Schmidt,[2] after reviewing the research, stated that "we should recognize that a single, optimal distribution of practice and rest

Physical educators must provide for individual differences among learners. Elementary school students work with different shaped objects as part of a perceptual-motor program.

periods does not exist." The design of practice should consider the nature of the task to be learned, the characteristics of the learner, the energy costs of the tasks, and safety. Magill[3] stressed that practice sessions should be structured so that the number of opportunities the learner has to try the task is maximized. Siedentop[4] emphasizes the need to maximize the amount of time the learner is practicing a task (time-on-task) and the need for the task to be appropriate for the level of the learner.

2. *Learners must understand the task to be learned.* Helping the learner acquire a cognitive understanding of the nature of the task to be learned is one of the first steps in the learning process. As previously discussed in the stages of learning, the learner must establish an executive or motor plan for action; this involves understanding the nature of the task, analyzing the task demands, and devising techniques to achieve the task goal. This conception of the task or image serves as a guide for the learner's initial attempts.

Typically learners have been helped to establish an image of the task or skill through verbal instructions provided by the teacher. However, the teacher may overuse instructions when faced with the task of describing a complex movement. Too many instructions may overwhelm learners, and in an effort to cope with the avalanche of information about what to do and when to do it, they may disregard much of the information. Instructions should focus on key elements of the task.

Succinct, accurate instructions in conjunction with other techniques such as demonstrations may be more useful in helping the learner understand the task than instructions alone. Demonstrations of the skill allow the learner to form an image of the task. The teacher can use instructions to call the learner's attention to the critical components of the skill. During the learner's initial performances of the task the learner can model the performance exhibited. Children frequently learn skills on their own through imitating or modeling the performance of others. Teachers may also use films or videotapes of skilled performers to provide a model for performance.

3. *The nature of the skill or task to be learned should be considered when designing practice.* Skills can be classified in a variety of ways. To facilitate learning, practices should be appropriate to the type of skill to be learned.

Skills are generally classified on a continuum. One common classification is *open* versus *closed* skills. This classification is based on whether the environment is changing or not changing during the performance of a skill. An open skill is performed in an environment that is changing or variable during the performance of the skill. A closed skill is performed in a stable, unchanging environment. Shooting a goal during a soccer game, hitting a tennis forehand during a match, batting a pitched ball, and dribbling down the basketball court to execute a lay-up are examples of open skills. Driving a golf ball off the tee, executing a forward two-and-a-half somersault dive from the three-meter springboard, performing an uneven bars or parallel bars routine in gymnastics, and shooting a foul shot in basketball are examples of closed skills.

The teacher's design of practice should reflect the nature of the skill and the conditions under which the skill will eventually be performed. In practicing closed skills, since the environment remains relatively the same during the performance of the skill, the teacher should emphasize achieving consistency of movement. In performing open skills the changing environment requires that the performer make alterations in his or her performance to adjust to the changing conditions (e.g., movements of opponents and teammates, speed and direction of the ball, etc.). Thus practice should be variable with the student exposed to a variety of situations similar to those which he or she will encounter in the actual situation in which the skill will be performed.

During the initial stages of learning an open skill the teacher may structure the environment to be stable (closed) to make learning easier for the beginner. For instance, in learning to bat a pitched ball, the teacher may start the performer out hitting a ball off a batting tee; then the teacher may use a pitching machine set to pitch a ball at a certain speed and height. Finally the student is given the opportunity to hit balls thrown by a pitcher and must then learn how to adjust his or her swing to the varying speeds and heights of the ball. Thus while open skills may be practiced under closed conditions initially, once the performer is ready, open conditions should prevail. In teaching open skills the teacher has to help the performer identify relevant cues in the environment that signify the need to change his or her response. Unlike closed skills in which attainment of response consistency is emphasized, achieving response flexibility and diversity is stressed in open skills. Providing the performer with variable practice conditions is important in learning open skills.

Other motor skill classifications include fine versus gross motor skills, discrete versus continuous motor skills, and self-paced versus externally paced motor skills. Further information on these skills may be found in the suggested readings at the end of this chapter.

4. *The nature of the task and the background of the learner should be considered in deciding to teach the skill by the whole or the part method.* One decision that needs to be resolved by the instructor when teaching a skill is whether to teach the skill as a whole or whether to teach the skill by breaking it down into its component parts. Essentially, the question is do you teach the front crawl stroke as a whole or do you break the stroke down and teach it by parts—arm action, leg action, and breathing? What about teaching the jump shot in basketball? Or the tennis serve? If the learner is highly skilled and has had previous experience in the sport, is the whole or the part method best?

This area has been much researched, but the findings are somewhat confusing. At the risk of generalizing, the instructor should teach a highly complex task as parts. Tasks in which the skill components are highly interrelated such as in the jump shot in basketball should be taught as a whole. Parts should consist of individual, discrete skills. Highly skilled learners with previous experience in the sport will probably be able to learn effectively if the whole method is used. Low skilled learners or individuals with short attention spans such as young children may find it easier to learn if taught by the part method. It appears that learners, even if taught by the part method, would benefit from the experience of seeing a demonstration of the whole skill prior to learning the part; this would seem to enhance the organization of the information provided to the learner and the learner's understanding of the goal of the skill.

If the teacher were to teach the high jump by the part method the learners would be taught the approach (run to the bar); then they would be taught the jump; next, they would be taught the landing. After all components had been taught, the learners would practice the total skill.

Another option is to use the progressive part method, which consists of initially teaching the first two parts of the skill, combining these two parts into a whole, learning a third part, and then connecting this to the first two parts, and so on. For example, the first two sequences in a dance routine would be taught and practiced, then the next sequence taught, and then this third sequence would be added to the first two sequences and all three sequences practiced together. This process of progressively adding parts of a skill is continued until the entire skill is learned.

In summary, the structure of the task, both its complexity and organization, and the characteristics of the learner must be considered in selecting methods of instruction.

5. *Whether speed or accuracy should be emphasized in learning a skill depends on the requirements of the skill.* Physical educators are often required to make a judgment as to whether speed or accuracy should be emphasized in the initial stages of learning a skill. For example, a highly skilled tennis player endeavors to serve the ball with as much velocity as possible into the service court. When teaching the tennis serve, should the teacher emphasize speed, accuracy, or both speed and accuracy? When teaching pitching, should the teacher emphasize throwing the ball as fast as possible, get-

Teachers must decide whether speed or accuracy should be emphasized when learning a skill.

ting the ball into the strike zone all the time, or pitching the ball into the strike zone as fast and as often as possible? This dilemma—whether to emphasize speed or accuracy—is often referred to as a speed-accuracy trade-off. In essense, to perform the skill as accurately as possible means that the performer will have to sacrifice some speed and perform the skill more slowly. Attainment of maximum speed or velocity in performing a skill is at the expense of accuracy. When both speed and accuracy are desired, both qualities will decrease.

Different sport skills have different speed and accuracy requirements. Pitching a ball or performing a tennis serve requires both a high degree of speed and accuracy. In throwing the javelin, speed is more important than accuracy, whereas in the tennis drop shot accuracy in terms of court placement is more important than speed. The physical educator must understand the requirements of the task and design practices accordingly.

The research seems to suggest that the skills should be practiced as they are to be performed. This advice is relatively straight forward when the skill emphasizes either speed or accuracy. For example, based on the research findings, speed should be emphasized in teaching the javelin throw and accuracy emphasized in the tennis drop shot. However, what about skills that place a premium on being both fast and accurate, such as pitching a ball or executing a tennis serve? One approach would be to have the learner execute the skill as fast as possible and work on accuracy and control after speed has been attained. Another approach would be to have the learner focus on being as accurate as possible by reducing the speed of the movements; then, once accuracy was attained, increasing the speed of the movements would be stressed. Emphasizing both speed and accuracy would be another approach. The research suggests that when both speed and accuracy are of paramount concern, both variables should receive equal and simultaneous emphasis. The rationale is that mastery is sacrificed when an individual practices a motor skill at slower speed than is needed in the game situation, since the person has to readjust to the faster situation. The teacher should understand the speed and accuracy demands of a skill and structure practices so that the learner can practice the skill as it is to be ultimately performed.

6. *Transfer of learning can facilitate the learning of motor skills.* The influence of a previously learned skill on the learning or performance of a new skill is called transfer of learning. The influence exerted may be positive or negative. When a previous experience or skill aids in the learning of a new skill positive transfer occurs. For example, the student who knows how to play tennis readily learns how to play badminton because both skills require similar strokes and the use of the racquet. Most researchers agree that positive transfer most likely occurs when two tasks have similar part-whole relationships. Again, to use the example of racquet games, since many racquet games such as platform tennis, squash, tennis, racquet ball, and badminton have similar part-whole relationships, it is believed that some transfer takes place. Transfer, however, is

not automatic. The more meaningful and purposeful the experience, the greater is the likelihood of transfer. Transfer of training occurs to a greater degree in the following situations: with more intelligent participants, in situations that are similar, where an attitude exists and an effort is made by the learner to effect transfer, when the principles or procedures that are foundational to the initial task are understood, and in situations where one teaches for transfer.

Physical educators must also be aware of negative transfer. Negative transfer occurs when a previously learned skill interferes with the learning of a new skill. For example, an individual being introduced to the game of golf for the first time experiences difficulty in swinging the club because of his or her previous experience in another skill such as softball or baseball. In such cases the expression often heard is "You're swinging the golf club like a baseball bat."

Physical educators and coaches have become interested in transferring skills learned in practice sessions to actual game situations. To this end they strive to make their drills as much like a game as possible, or they make an effort in the practice environment to familiarize their team with situations they may encounter in the game. For example, during practice sessions before a basketball game coaches may have their substitutes imitate the actions of the opponents so that the varsity team is familiar with the opponents' style of play on the night of the game.

Transfer may either facilitate or hinder the acquisition of a skill. Physical educators need to be aware of the principles of transfer so that they can use positive transfer to promote skill learning and enhance performance and can readily counteract the effects of negative transfer.

7. *Feedback is essential for learning.* One of the most critical factors affecting learning is feedback. Feedback is information about an individual's performance. Feedback can serve several functions. It provides the learner with information about his or her performance. Using this information, the learner can make adjustments in the response prior to the next attempt. Second, feedback can serve to

Videotape feedback is a valuable learning tool. Omaha Public Schools use videotape equipment in physical education classes.

reinforce the learner's efforts, strengthening the correct response. Lastly, feedback may also serve to motivate the learner by providing information about his or her progress.

Feedback may be classified in many ways. Feedback for error correction may focus on the outcome of the movement or the movement itself. Knowledge of results (KR) provides information about the effects of the movement on the environment, information that tells the learner whether or not the goal of the movement was achieved. Knowledge of performance (KP) provides information about the movement itself. The learner's awareness and feelings about how correct the movement executed was in relation to the intended movement is knowledge of performance. For example, in shooting a foul shot in basketball the player can readily see if the goal of the movement—putting the ball in the basket—was attained. This is knowledge of results. However, the player may know even before the ball goes in the basket that the shot would be good because the movement "felt right." This is knowledge of performance. Knowledge of performance depends on the learner being sensitive to the "feelings" associated with correct and incorrect performance; in other words, the

learner becomes aware of what "feels right" and what "feels wrong." Changes in performance occur as the learner compares information about the outcome (KR) with the desired outcome and information about performance (KP) with his or her intended movement. The learner then adjusts his or her performance accordingly until the correct response is achieved.

Feedback may also be classified according to its source or according to when it is presented to the learner. Feedback may be described as intrinsic when the source of the information is the outcome of the task or skill itself.[5] Scoring an ace with a tennis serve, having the kick go slightly wide of the goal in soccer, and scoring on a foul shot in basketball are examples of intrinsic feedback. Information from external sources such as an instructor, friend, or a videotape is classified as extrinsic or augmented feedback.[5] When the learner receives information during the performance of the skill, this feedback is referred to as concurrent. Feedback given after the performance is completed is called terminal feedback. Oftentimes feedback may be a combination of information from various sources. For example, comments directed by the teacher during the learner's performance provide the learner with extrinsic concurrent feedback. A soccer player seeing the kicked ball go in the goal receives intrinsic terminal feedback.

The importance of feedback in the learning of skills is not doubted. Feedback is especially critical during the initial stages of learning a skill. It appears that knowledge of results is more helpful to the individual performing open skills and that knowledge of performance is more valuable to the individual executing a closed skill. However, with highly skilled performers, regardless of whether they are performing a closed or an open skill, knowledge of performance is the most helpful. Feedback should be communicated to the learner in a meaningful manner. The teacher should help the learner become aware of the feedback available and teach the learner how to utilize this information to improve his or her performance.

8. *Mental practice can enhance the learning of motor skills.* Mental practice is the symbolic rehearsal of a skill with the absence of gross muscular movements. The physical educator should be concerned with the role of mental practice in skill learning. Research seems to indicate that although physical practice is superior to mental practice, mental practice is better than no practice at all. Mental practice can enhance the learning of a new skill or the performance of previously learned skills. A combination of physical and mental practice appears to be best. For example, if due to equipment or space limitations all learners cannot physically practice a skill at the same time, those who are waiting their turn to perform can put the time to good use by engaging in mental practice. While one individual is performing a giant swing on the high bar, another student can mentally review the essential elements to be mastered. Another approach to mental practice encourages the learner, following a successful execution of the specific skill, to mentally view the performance over and over again, reinforcing the proper response.

Physical educators should encourage and provide time for students to engage in mental practice. Oftentimes participants in physical education programs spend a lot of their time waiting for a chance to practice a skill. This time, rather than being wast-

ed, can be used for mental practice. The teacher should guide learners' initial efforts at mental practice by giving them specific instructions for this task. It should also be mentioned that mental practice may not be very beneficial to younger children because of their mental development and short attention spans. Opportunities for younger children to physically practice skills should be emphasized.

9. *Learners may experience plateaus in performance.* The extent to which an individual has learned a skill may be inferred from his or her performance. When learning a new skill an individual may initially demonstrate a sharp improvement in performance. This may be followed by a plateau, or a period in which little or no progress is made. Finally, additional practice results in further improvements in performance.

The plateau may result from a variety of reasons, such as loss of interest and lack of motivation, failure to grasp a clear concept of the goal to be attained, lack of attention to the proper cues or attention to irrelevant cues, preparation for a transition from fundamental skills to more complex skills in the learning process, or poor learning conditions. Physical educators should be cognizant of the plateaus and the conditions causing little or no apparent progress in the activity. They should be especially careful not to introduce certain concepts or skills too rapidly, without allowing sufficient time for their mastery. They should also watch for certain physical deterrents to progress, such as fatigue or lack of strength. Some individuals cannot go beyond a given point because of physiological limits in respect to speed, endurance, or other physical characteristics. However, oftentimes the problem is not traceable to physiological limits but rather psychological limits that have to be overcome. By utilizing techniques to motivate the interest and enthusiasm of the learner, psychological limits can be overcome.

10. *Self-analysis should be developed.* During the early periods of instruction when the basic techniques of the skill are being learned, instruction and help from the teacher are needed frequently. However, as the skill is mastered the learner should rely less on the teacher's help and more on internal

resources. A good teacher will help the learner to be his or her own teacher. This involves providing the learner with opportunities for self-criticism and analysis. The learner should be taught how to detect errors and how to correct them. By assisting the student to become aware of his or her performance and techniques by which it can be improved, the teacher is promoting life-long learning.

11. *The leadership provided determines to a great degree how much learning will take place.* The amount of learning that occurs will depend to a great extent on the leadership provided by the physical educator. The physical educator should make sure that the learner has a clear idea of the objective to be accomplished. Practices should be designed to maximize the learner's opportunities to perform the skill and minimize unproductive activities such as waiting. The physical educator should be continually alert to detect correct and incorrect responses and encourage correct performance. The motivation of the learner can be enhanced through providing him or her with opportunities to experience success and through the presentation of activities that are meaningful to the individual. The physical educator should present material appropriate to the learner's level of understanding and be cognizant of individual differences. The physical educator should utilize his or her leadership to further the teaching situation.

• • •

This section was designed to provide the reader with a brief overview of some of the concepts and concerns within the realm of motor learning. An understanding of how individuals learn motor skills will help physical educators design experiences to promote effective learning. Promoting effective learning is a concern of physical educators working in both school and nonschool settings. In the school setting, for example, elementary school physical educators are concerned with helping children master fundamental motor skills, high school teachers focus their efforts on assisting students to acquire skills in a variety of lifetime sports, and coaches spend countless hours helping their athletes refine the skills necessary for high-level performance. In

the nonschool setting, athletic trainers may help injured athletes regain efficient motor patterns, while exercise leaders in a corporate or community program may help adults attain proficiency in such lifetime sports as golf or tennis. Thus, understanding how learning occurs and can be facilitated is important foundational knowledge for physical educators to possess. Additionally, the manner in which individuals control their movements (motor control) and the impact of development (motor development) on learning are also important considerations in the design of learning experiences.

PSYCHOLOGY OF SPORT

Psychology of sport means applying psychological theories and concepts to aspects of sport such as coaching and teaching. The sport psychologist uses psychological assessment techniques and intervention strategies in an effort to help individuals to achieve their optimal performance. While sport psychology is concerned with analyzing human behavior in various types of sport settings, it focuses on the mental aspects of performance.

The subjects of motor learning and sport psychology were closely associated at one time. However, in the last 20 years each has developed its own identity.

One of the first topics of concern to sport psychologists dealt with personality factors in sports. However, today the range of topics is more extensive. Sport psychologists are now concerned with a multitude of subjects such as violence and aggression, arousal, motivation, social reinforcement, and levels of aspiration. The effects of competition on various populations such as youths or elite athletes is also another area of study.

Within the last few years interest has increased in the field of cognitive sport psychology. Cognitive sport psychology focuses on the influence of mental factors on performance. Sport psychologists have acknowledged that an individual's thoughts and feelings can have a critical impact on his or her performance. Recognition has increased that mental skills, just as physical skills, can be taught. It appears now that both mental and physical skills are necessary for optimal performance. Areas of study include such topics as attentional focus, self-confidence and self-efficacy, self-talk, attributions, and sport intelligence. The effectiveness of various cognitive intervention strategies such as hypnosis, cognitive restructuring, thought stopping, mental rehearsal, and self-regulation is also addressed by cognitive sport psychologists. Although this emphasis on cognitive sport psychology is recent, Straub and Williams[6] believe that it will be the dominant approach for the next several years.

The field of sport psychology is broadening in other ways as well. Initially, much of its research efforts focused on elite men athletes. In recent years this has changed. Sport psychologists today are working with both men and women elite athletes and "average" athletes as well as individuals participating in noncompetitive activities. Sport psychologists are concerned with helping participants of all ages, from young children to older adults. Physical educators can use their knowledge of sport psychology in many settings, not only in the realm of competitive athletics. Exercise physiologists may use their understanding of sport psychology to help participants in cardiac rehabilitation programs overcome their fears regarding their ability to resume exercise. Teachers can draw on their knowledge of sport psychology to help individuals learn how to direct their attention to the relevant cues in the environment, improving their performance. Practitioners working with youth sports teams such as Little League baseball can use sport psychology to ensure that these young athletes have a positive experience. Coaches at all levels can use psychological techniques such as arousal regulation, imagery, goal setting, and thought stopping to help their athletes optimize their performance.

Recent years have seen the development of specialists who are interested in the practical and clinical aspects of sport psychology. Sport psychologists, for example, may work for professional teams in football, baseball, and basketball or help Olympic athletes from various sports prepare for competition. These practitioners focus on enhancing the performance of the athletes through the use of various psychological techniques.

People interested in the psychology of sport had no formal organization to belong to until 1965. At that time the North American Society for the Psychology of Sport and Physical Activity (NASPSPA) was formed. A second organization is the Sport Psychology Academy of the National Association of Sport and Physical Education (NASPE); NASPE is a substructure of AAHPERD. The Sport Psychology Academy was founded in 1975. These organizations hold annual meetings that provide a forum for discussion between researchers and practitioners. These meetings provide opportunities for interested professionals to share their needs and concerns as well as the latest developments and research findings.

The amount of research emanating from this field has grown tremendously over the past decade as sport psychologists have sought answers to a diversity of questions. Some of the questions addressed include the following:

- Is the personality profile of the outstanding or elite athlete different from that of the average athlete or of the nonathlete?
- How does participation in physical activities influence one's body image?
- What are the psychological benefits to be derived from participation in physical activities?
- Does one's personality change as a result of participation in sport?
- In what way does anxiety influence performance in various types of sports?
- How can an athlete most effectively deal with the stress of competition? What strategies are the most helpful for assisting an athelte to use stress to perform at an optimal level?
- What factors influence an individual's adherence to an exercise program or a rehabilitation program?
- Does an optimal attentional focus associated with a specific sport exist?
- How does an individual's self-confidence affect his or her performance? How can self-confidence be developed and then used to maximize performance?

The next section will provide a brief overview of some of the topics in sport psychology.

Selected Topics
Psychological Benefits from Physical Activity

An analysis of the professional literature indicates that certain psychological benefits accrue from engaging in physical activity and sport. These include generalizations such as the following:

- Individuals who participate regularly in physical activities indicate that they feel better. Many people indicate they simply feel better when they exercise than when they do not engage in physical activity. Perceptions of health and fitness help individuals to feel good.
- Vigorous activity is an effective means of reducing tension and depression. Various activities offer a means of getting rid of frustrations, aggressions, and "blowing off steam."
- Sport and other physical activities offer a means of affiliation with other human beings. This is a natural human desire. Sport and other physical activities serve as ways to achieve this need for affiliation.
- Physical activity and sport offer exhilarating experiences for some people. Sport and other activities are exciting, which is an attractive feature for many human beings. Participants have described the euphoria of being "lost" in the activity or experiencing the sensation of "flow."
- Some individuals look to dance and other forms of physical activity in search of aesthetic experiences.
- Some people desire to participate in sport in which aggression is controlled. Other individuals enjoy sport with a certain element of aggression.
- Physical activity provides relaxation and a change of pace from long hours of work, study, or stresses. Individuals return to their work or their daily routine refreshed.
- Physical activity and sport can provide a challenge and, when met successfully, provide a sense of achievement. Some marathon runners want to complete the course regardless of how much time it takes.
- People want to be healthy and fit—a common reason for participation.

- Some individuals believe that by mastering certain physical skills they improve their self-esteem. By gaining skill they experience a sense of accomplishment, which in turn raises confidence and satisfaction.
- Physical activities provide creative experiences. Activities such as dance enable individuals to express their emotions and feelings in a non-verbal manner.
- A positive addiction to exercise exists, in contrast to negative addiction to such things as drugs. A psychological dependence on physical activity is felt by some individuals who experience recognizable withdrawal symptoms when this need goes unmet for a period of time.

The psychological benefits to be gained from participation in physical activities and sport are many, and those realized depend on the individual. Individuals who participate in sport and physical activities may feel better, experience less anxiety, or feel refreshed. Participation offers the opportunity to experience excitement, affiliation, accomplishment, and satisfaction. The physical educator should be cognizant of the psychological benefits to be gained as well as the reasons for individual's participation in sport and physical activity.

Self-Attitudes and Body Image

Physical educators must be concerned with improving the self-attitudes of participants in their programs. Research indicates that physical education can be an important vehicle in the improvement of one's self-image. Physical fitness development may improve an individual's mental health, and motor skill learning may enhance an individual's inner feelings of self-worth.

Body image is important to individuals of all ages. At a time when society places a great importance on personal appearance, individuals should develop healthy attitudes toward their bodies. The attitudes and feelings of people toward their bodies affect personality development. For example, an individual who is obese and unfit may view his or her body as ugly, lack confidence in its performance, experience psychological problems such as low self-esteem as a result of being ridiculed or excluded from a group, and may, as a consequence, severely limit participation in physical activities. Being sedentary further contributes to being unfit and obese, and further exacerbates one's poor body image—a cycle that tends to be perpetuated. On the other hand, an individual may feel that his or her body is well-developed, have confidence that it can meet the challenges of many physical situations, and enjoy participation in physical activities. Feelings about one's body can affect relations with other people and also participation in physical activities.

Body image is particularly important during the adolescent period. For example, some research has shown that when a boy's physique is small, not well developed, and weak over an extended period of time, his behavior is affected. He will become overly shy or aggressive and will reflect internal discord. Individuals who mature late may find their relationships with their peers affected. Often they are excluded from games and sport activities because of the peers' desire to be successful in their game experience. These individuals, excluded from participation because of their lack of physical skills, may consequently develop an unfavorable attitude toward physical activity. This unfavorable attitude may persist to adulthood. The physical educator may find it difficult to get these individuals to join corporate fitness programs because of their unfavorable adolescent experiences. Individuals who mature early may encounter problems as well. These early maturers may find that although they were always the stars during early game experiences because of their superior physical characteristics in relation to their peers, this status was lost as their friends matured. The loss of star status proves a difficult adjustment for many individuals. Other personality problems have been found in boys with feminine characteristics, girls with masculine characteristics, individuals with narcissistic characteristics, and individuals who possess certain body types and postures.

Adults' attitudes toward physical activity and sport may have been significantly affected by their body image and associated positive and negative physical education experiences in their youth. With the increased emphasis on fitness and weight control in our society today, many adults are enrolling in physical activity and sport programs as a means to achieving these ends. Even adults turned off by physical education programs during their school years may decide to try once again to enjoy physical activity. It is important that the physical educator who is working with adult participants be cognizant of their previous experiences and put forth a concerted effort to make the present experience a positive and personally satisfying one.

Since many feelings toward participation are formulated in individuals' youth, it is important that teachers, family members, and other interested persons help each child "be at home in his or her own body." While it may not be possible for every boy or girl to develop the type of body they most admire, within the limitations of body structure each child should be helped to develop a fit and healthy body as well as a positive body image. Following are some suggestions:

- Understand the role of body image. In doing so one will be better able to appreciate why some boys and girls have certain attitudes and feelings toward sport and other forms of physical activity.

- Use empathy in relations with those youngsters who have a poor body image. Help them to live comfortably with their own body and physical features.

- Help young people to understand that it is possible in many instances to improve one's physical appearance. For example, boys and girls can improve their appearance by correcting postural faults and developing a better body build through exercises and activities.

- Help each child to achieve and be successful in physical activity experiences. Since success or failure influences self-concept and how one views new tasks and experiences, physical education programs should be planned and organized so that each child who engages in sport and physical activities achieves success. If a youngster believes he or she is a failure, then the program is also a failure. It should be noted that this refers to personal success

To perform to one's best ability, an optimal level of arousal is necessary.

rather than success based on a comparison of performance with other youngsters.

- Encourage participation in many different types of physical activities. If properly selected and meaningfully conducted, physical activities can improve self-image, since one will develop strength, endurance, and other desirable qualities.

As physical educators understand the role of body image, they will better be able to understand why various individuals have certain attitudes and feelings toward physical activity and the contributions physical education can make to these persons.

Personality

Physical education teachers and coaches have long been interested in the positive and negative effects of participation in sport on the development of an individual's personality. Although it has been shown that an individual's personality is formed early in life, it is thought by some experts that personality may be modified by later experiences. Some psy-

chologists theorize that participation in athletics can contribute to personality development. In some cases competitive athletics satisfy basic needs such as recognition, belonging, self-respect, and feelings of achievement, as well as provide a wholesome outlet for the drive for physical activity and creativity. These are desirable psychological effects that aid in molding socially accepted personalities. At the same time, however, competitive athletics can produce harmful effects. Two factors which may adversely affect an individual's personality are an overemphasis on winning by coaches, parents, and community members and placing individuals in situations not suited for their physical abilities.

Many sport psychologists have studied the relationship between personality and sport performance.[7] Researchers addressed questions such as "Do athletes differ from nonathletes?" "Can athletes in certain sports be distinguished from athletes in other sports on the basis of their personality?" "Do individuals participate in certain sports because of their personality characteristics?" "Do highly skilled athletes have different personality profiles than lesser skilled athletes in the same sport?" "Are there certain personality traits that can predict an athlete's success in a sport?"

Sport psychologists' findings have revealed contradictory answers to each of these questions. In many instances problems in research design have contributed to these contradictory results. Cox,[8] after an extensive review of the research on personality and sport, offered the following generalizations concerning men and women athletes relative to the questions posed above:

- Athletes and nonathletes differ with respect to personality characteristics. Various researchers have reported that athletes are more independent, objective, self-confident, competitive, outgoing or extroverted, and less anxious than nonathletes.
- Differences in personality traits between athletes and nonathletes are due to a "natural selection" process. This process occurs successfully in the mature individual. However, it has been shown that sport participation has a positive effect on the personality development of young athletes during their formative years. Thus the type of youth sport experience people are exposed to can positively or negatively affect the development of their personality.
- Athletes in one sport can be differentiated from athletes in another sport based on their personality characteristics. Perhaps the clearest example of this assertion occurs between individual sport athletes and team sport athletes. It has been shown that individual sport athletes are less extroverted, more independent, and less anxious than team sport participants.
- World-class athletes can be correctly differentiated from lesser skilled athletes by their psychological profile 70% of the time. Personality profiles that include situational measures of psychological states have been shown to be the most accurate in predicting level of athletic performance.

These statements hold several implications for the teacher and the coach. First, while Cox has advanced some generalizations based on an overview on research in the area, much of the research is still inconclusive. It is likely as the field of sport psychology grows advances in methodology will yield more definitive answers. Second, each athlete must be treated as an individual. One must recognize that a highly skilled athlete may differ from the "typical" personality; teachers and coaches must understand and respect individual differences in personality. This implies, for example, that different individuals may benefit from different motivational techniques. Third, practitioners who work with young children must be cognizant that participation in sport can have a positive or negative effect on an individual's personality. We can hope that sport psychologists in the future will be able to provide further insight into the relationship between personality and sport.

Anxiety and Arousal

Coaches, teachers, and sport psychologists have as their goal the optimizing of an individual's performance. To achieve this goal they must consider the effect of anxiety and arousal on performance. Anxiety, as defined by Levitt,[9] is a subjective feeling of apprehension accompanied by a heightened level of physiological arousal. Physiologic arousal is an autonomic response that results in the excitation of various organs of the body. Examples of this phenomena seen in athletes are sweaty hands, frequent urge to urinate, increased respiration rate, increased muscle tension, and elevated heart rate.

Anxiety is commonly classified in two ways. Trait anxiety is an integral part of an individual's personality. It refers to the individual's tendency to classify environmental events as either threatening or nonthreatening. State anxiety is an emotional response to a specific situation that results in feelings of fear, tension, or apprehension. The effects of both state and trait anxiety on motor performance have been studied by sport psychologists.

Coaches and teachers consistently attempt to find the optimal level of arousal that allows individuals to perform their best. An arousal level that is too low or too high can have a negative impact on performance. A low level of arousal in an individual is associated with such behaviors as low motivation, inattention, and inappropriate and slow movement choices. A high level of arousal in an individual can cause deterioration in coordination, inappropriate narrowing of attention, distractibility, and a lack of flexibility in movement responses. It is important for each individual to find his or her optimal level of arousal for a given activity. Physical educators can help the individual identify this optimal state. However, no one knows for sure exactly how to consistently reach this ideal state. A variety of approaches have been employed by physical educators in pursuit of this goal. These techniques include "pep talks," use of motivational slogans and bulletin boards, relaxation training, imagery, and, in some cases, the use of the professional services of a sport psychologist.

Sport psychologists and researchers have studied the relationships among anxiety, arousal, and sport performance. Cox,[8] after a review of the research in this area, offered the following ideas:

- Athletes who feel threatened by fear of failure will display a high level of anxiety. Physical educators should try to reduce an individual's fear of failure by defining success in individual terms and by keeping "winning" in perspective.
- Athletes who possess high levels of trait anxiety tend to experience high levels of state anxiety when confronted with competition. Physical educators should be cognizant of individuals' trait anxiety so that they may be aware of how individuals will be likely to respond in competitive situations. This knowledge will help them select strategies to adjust individuals' levels of state anxiety and arousal to the optimal level.
- Athletes' perceptions of a given situation influence their level of anxiety. Not all athletes will react to the competitive situation in the same manner. Each athlete perceives the same situation in a different way. Thus the physical educator must be aware that when placed in the same situation, each athlete may be experiencing different levels of anxiety. This is why "psych" talks may be an effective means of regulating the arousal level of some athletes and ineffective with other athletes.

- The relationship between athletic performance and arousal may be described as an inverted U. A too low or too high level of arousal will be detrimental to performance. It is important for physical educators to apply this theory when attempting to adjust the arousal levels of their athletes.
- An athlete's ability and the complexity of the skill to be performed is an important determinant of the optimal level of arousal. The necessary level of arousal varies with the task and its level of complexity. Simple tasks require a higher level of arousal than more complex tasks for best performance. The level of skill can also affect the level of arousal needed to perform a specific task.
- As the arousal level increases athletes tend to exhibit the dominant response. Under the stress of competition they tend to revert to skills they are most comfortable performing. Thus, if a volleyball player has been recently trained to pass the ball in a low trajectory to the setter, under the stress of competition the player may revert to the safer, easier-to-perform high trajectory underhand pass.

Research in the area of anxiety, arousal, and motor performance suggests several ways in which practitioners can achieve optimal performance from their athletes. Practitioners must accept the concept that individuals' perceptions of a situation influence their levels of anxiety and subsequently their levels of arousal. Optimal performance depends on individuals achieving their ideal level of arousal for the task. This ideal level will be influenced by the individuals' skills and the level of complexity of the task at hand. Understanding athletes' fear of failure will help the practitioner regulate their levels of anxiety. Anxiety can affect other factors that influence an individual's level of performance such as attention.

Attention

An individual's performance is greatly influenced by his or her attention to the task. As previously discussed, an individual must locate, select, and focus on relevant cues to be successful in performing the task (skill or game). Not only must the individual discriminate between relevant and irrelevant cues, but also he or she must maintain the necessary attentional focus for the task. If an individual focuses on the irrelevant cues or fails to maintain the appropriate attentional focus, the performance will be less than optimal.

Nideffer[10] defined attention as the ability to direct senses and thought processes to particular objects, thoughts, and feelings. Attention can be described in terms of two dimensions—width and direction. The width dimension varies from broad to narrow. The direction dimension may be described as external, that is, focusing on environmental cues, or as internal, that is focusing on thoughts, emotions, and sensations. In any particular situation an individual's attention may be described as broad external, broad internal, narrow external, and narrow internal. An individual who has a broad external focus is directing his or her attention to a wide range of environmental cues; an individual who has a broad internal focus is directing his or her feelings to a multitude of internal thoughts and sensations. In contrast, an individual who has a narrow external focus is concentrating on a few selected environmental cues; an individual who has a narrow internal focus is concerned with selected internal cues and thoughts.

To be successful an individual has to match his or her attentional focus to the task demands, which often change as the performance progresses. Thus to be successful, the individual must be able to switch rapidly back and forth between the various attentional styles at will. Let us use batting a pitched ball for an example. As the batter stands outside the batter's box waiting his or her chance to hit, attention may have a broad internal focus. As the batter waits, he or she is reviewing the coach's directions and the strategies previously favored by the pitcher. The batter internally constructs the current situation, identifying the number of outs and the position of the runners on base. The batter then prepares strategy. The focus is then narrowed to specific thoughts (narrow internal focus). As the batter stands in the box, he or she may adopt a broad external focus to predict the type of pitch by concentrating on cues from the pitcher. As the ball is released, attention shifts to a narrow external focus as the batter follows the path of the ball.

In an effort to assess individuals' attentional style Nideffer[10] developed the Test of Attentional and Interpersonal Style (TAIS). The TAIS is comprised of six scales designed to measure the width and direction dimensions of attention. The broad external scale, the broad internal scale, and the narrow scale (this scale includes both external and internal dimensions) represent effective attentional styles. Three scales reflect ineffective attentional styles. The overloaded external focus assesses the amount of confusion from trying to process too many environmental cues at the same time, while the overload internal focus represents the confusion from trying to think too much. Last, the underinclusive attentional focus reflects an excessive narrowing of attention, often referred to as "tunnel vision."

The TAIS measures attention in general situations. In recent years researchers measuring attention in sport situations have modified Nideffer's TAIS to reflect situations encountered in specific sport environments. Researchers have developed attention tests in the areas of tennis,[11] riflery,[12] volleyball,[13] diving,[13] soccer,[13] baseball,[13] and field hockey.[13] Physical educators need to be cognizant of the attentional requirements of various sports and sport skills as well as the ability of each individual to attain and sustain the appropriate attentional focus.

An individual's focus of attention may be affected by a variety of factors. One factor that has a critical impact on attention is anxiety. Anxiety tends to narrow and internalize an individual's attentional focus. The physical educator needs to be aware of the impact of various factors on an individual's level of attention. The physical educator must also be knowledgeable of the various intervention techniques that can be used to effectively deal with these factors.

Intervention Strategies

In recent years coaches, teachers, and sport psychologists have turned to a variety of intervention strategies to help performers achieve their optimal performance. As discussed earlier, anxiety and

Goal-setting can contribute to individual achievement.

arousal can have harmful effects on athletes' performance. Athletes' performance can also suffer due to lack of motivation, poor level of self-confidence, and, because of the intimate relationship between the mind and the body, negative thoughts and feelings about themselves and their capabilities. With the help of appropriate intervention techniques athletes learn skills and strategies to regulate their physiological state as well as their psychological state to achieve optimum performance.

Sometimes athletes experience excessive anxiety and arousal which causes a deterioration in their performance. Thus intervention strategies focusing on reducing this level would be beneficial to these athletes. One way to deal with elevated levels of arousal is through the use of a variety of relaxation techniques. These techniques teach the individual to scan the body for tension (arousal is manifested in increased muscular tension) and, after identifying a higher than optimum level of tension, to reduce the tension to the appropriate level by relaxing. Once specific relaxation techniques are learned, this process should take only a few minutes. Types of relaxation training include progressive relaxation,

autogenic training, transcendental meditation, and biofeedback. A note of caution is in order here, however. Athletes should be careful not to relax or reduce their level of arousal too much because this will have a harmful influence on their performance.

In recent years the use of cognitive strategies to facilitate optimum performance has gained increased acceptance. Cognitive strategies teach athletes psychological skills that they can employ in their mental preparation for competition. In addition to focusing on alleviating the harmful effects of anxiety and arousal, these cognitive strategies can also be used to enhance motivation and self-confidence and to improve performance consistency. These approaches include cognitive restructuring, thought stopping, self-talk, hypnosis and self-hypnosis, goal setting, and mental imagery.

Some cognitive intervention techniques focus on changing the thoughts and the perceptions of athletes. Sport psychologists have realized that athletes' negative thoughts about their abilities such as the "I can't" attitude can adversely affect performance. Athletes' internal dialogues, that is, the conversations that athletes in effect carry on with them-

Psychological skills can help athletes maximize their performance.

selves, have also been a focus of cognitive intervention strategies. This dialogue, both prior to and during performance, may reflect athletes' worries about succeeding, their fear of failure, or concerns that an undesirable past experience will repeat itself..."What if I choke like last time?"..."What if I strike out again?" Cognitive restructuring, self-talk, and thought stopping focus on eliminating negative thoughts and replacing them with positive ones such as "I can do it." Cognitive strategies can also be used to alter athletes' perceptions of events, thus reducing the athletes' anxiety. Affirmation of athletes' ability to succeed in an upcoming competition is another cognitive strategy frequently utilized to promote optimal performance.

Goal setting can assist athletes by giving them clear, specific objectives to strive to attain. Goal setting involves establishing long-term goals and then identifying specific short-term objectives that lead almost like steps to the achievement of the long-term goals. Goals should be stated in terms of observable behavior so that athletes can readily assess their progress toward their goals. For exam-

ple, a volleyball player may have as a goal the improvement of his or her performance. Stated as such this goal is difficult to measure and the player really has a hard time determining whether the stated goal has been achieved. This goal could also be stated as "making 90% of my serves and 40% of my spikes as kills." Presented in this manner, the player can chart progress toward the goal. Goals set should be challenging but reachable. Together the coach and the player devise strategies for obtaining the goal and frequently evaluate progress made toward achievement of the goal.

Imagery is the visualization of a situation. This technique has been used in a variety of ways to enhance performance. It can be used to mentally practice skills or to review outstanding previous performances. By remembering the kinesthetic sensations associated with the ideal performance, the athlete hopes to replicate or improve performance. Imagery has also been used as an anxiety reduction technique. Anxiety-producing situations are visualized and then the athlete "sees" himself or herself successfully coping with the experience, thus increasing confidence to perform successfully in similar situations.

Intervention strategies have proved useful in helping athletes maximize their performance. However, these strategies are not only for athletes but also have implications for all participants in physical education activities. For example, the beginning jogger may derive as much benefit from goal setting as the high-level performer. The practitioner in using these strategies must be knowledgeable of individual differences, otherwise performance could be affected adversely.

The growth of sport psychology has provided physical educators with a clearer understanding of various psychological factors that may affect an individual's performance. Sport psychologists have been able to enhance individual performance through the use of a diversity of intervention strategies. Although much of the work done in the area of sport psychology has been with athletes, many of the findings and techniques are applicable to participants in a variety of physical education settings such as school programs, community programs, and corporate fitness programs. As the field of sport psychology continues to expand, practitioners will gain further insight on how to enhance the performance of all individuals.

SUMMARY

Motor learning and sport psychology have their legacy in psychology. Both fields of study have expanded tremendously in the past decade. Although motor learning and sport psychology were once closely aligned, within the last 20 years they have taken on separate identities.

Motor learning is the acquisition of movement skills as a consequence of practice. One theory to describe the manner in which individuals learn motor skills is the information-processing theory. The physical educator needs to be aware that individuals pass through several stages when learning motor skills. Fitts and Posner[1] identified three stages of learning: cognitive, associative, and autonomic. Learning is influenced by several forces. Five of these forces are readiness, level of develop-

ment, motivation, reinforcement, and individual differences. The physical educator, to facilitate learning, should design practices based on sound motor learning concepts.

Sport psychology is concerned with the application of psychological theories and concepts to sport and physical activity. Psychological assessment techniques and intervention strategies are used by the sport psychologist to help individuals attain their optimal level of performance. The physical educator should be aware of the psychological benefits to be derived from participation in physical activity as well as the effect of physical activity on an individual's body image. An individual's personality, anxiety and arousal, and attention can influence his or her performance. Intervention strategies can be used to help individuals to prepare for athletic events. Sport psychology offers the promise of greater insight into the factors that influence performance.

SELF-ASSESSMENT TESTS

These tests are designed to assist students in determining if the materials and competencies presented in this chapter have been mastered.

1. Give examples in the field of physical education and sport of cognitive, affective, and psychomotor learning.

2. Define motor learning. You are a teacher in either a school setting, a community setting with students of all ages, or in a corporate fitness program with adults. Indicate in your teaching methods how you would provide for each of the following: readiness, motor development, reinforcement, motivation, and individual differences.

3. Select a skill that you are familiar with from your previous physical education experiences. Describe how you would teach this skill to a beginner. In your description include the information-processing model of learning as well as the stages of learning.

4. Identify five motor learning concepts and discuss their application to learning a motor skill.

5. Justify the claim that participation in sport and physical education activities can have positive psychological benefits.

6. In recent years the field of sport psychology has expanded tremendously. As a practitioner, be it as a teacher, coach, adapted physical educator, athletic trainer or exercise physiologist, you are concerned with optimizing individuals' performance. Discuss the role of anxiety, arousal, and attention in the performance of motor skills and the use of intervention strategies to enhance performance.

REFERENCES

1. Fitts PM and Posner MJ: Human performance, Belmont, Calif, 1967, Brooks/Cole.
2. Schmidt RA: Motor control and learning, Champaign, Ill, 1982, Human Kinetics.
3. Magill RA: Motor learning: concepts and applications, Dubuque, Iowa, 1985, Wm C Brown Co, Publishers.
4. Siedentop D: Developing teaching skills in physical education, Palo Alto, Calif, 1983, Mayfield.
5. Rink JE: Teaching physical education for learning, St Louis, 1985, Times Mirror/Mosby College Publishing.
6. Straub WF and Williams JM: Cognitive sport psychology, Lansing, NY, 1984, Sport Science Associates.
7. Vealey RS: Sport personology: A paradigmatic and methodological analysis, Journal of Sport and Exercise Psychology 11:216-235, 1989.
8. Cox RH: Sport psychology concepts and applications, Dubuque, Iowa, 1985, Wm C Brown Co, Publishers.
9. Levitt EE: The psychology of anxiety, Hillsdale, NJ, 1980, Earlbaum.
10. Nideffer RM: Test of attentional and interpersonal style, Journal of Personality and Social Psychology 34:394-400, 1976.
11. van Schoyck SR and Grasha AF: Attentional style variations and athletic ability: the advantage of a sport specific test, Journal of Sport Psychology 3:149-165, 1981.
12. Etzel EF: Validation of a conceptual model characterizing attention among international rifle shooters, Journal of Sport Psychology 1:281-290, 1979.
13. Fisher AC: Tests of attentional style for volleyball, diving, soccer, baseball, and field hockey (personal communication), Ithaca College, Ithaca, NY.

SUGGESTED READINGS

American Alliance for Health, Physical Education, Recreation, and Dance: Motor development. Basic Stuff Series I, Reston, VA, 1987, AAHPERD.
The influence of growth and development on motor performance is the focus of this book.

American Alliance for Health, Physical Education, Recreation, and Dance: Motor learning. Basic Stuff Series I, Reston, VA, 1987, AAHPERD.
The factors influencing motor learning and performance are discussed in this book.

American Alliance for Health, Physical Education, Recreation, and Dance: Psychosocial aspects of physical education. Basic Stuff Series I, Reston, VA, 1987, AAHPERD.
This book focuses on the psychological benefits to be derived from participation in physical activity as well as psychological factors that affect performance.

Bird AM and Cripe BK: Psychology and sport behavior, St Louis, 1985, Times Mirror/Mosby College Publishing.
This text provides a comprehensive overview of the realm of sport psychology, with attention devoted to traditional areas of study as well as timely topics such as applied sport psychology and cognitive sport psychology. One of the strongest assets of this text is its emphasis on practical application.

Cox RH: Sport psychology concepts and applications, Dubuque, Iowa, 1985, Wm C Brown Co, Publishers.
Divided into four parts—personality, attention and arousal, theories of motivation, and social psychology—this book provides a comprehensive overview of sport psychology. The many practical applications enhance the reader's comprehension of the principles presented.

Gallahue DL: Understanding motor development: Infants, children, adolescents, Indianapolis, 1989, Benchmark Press.
A comprehensive approach to motor development is presented, including an overview and models of human and motor development as well as biological, environmental, and physical factors influencing motor development. Implications for programming, education, and assessment are also presented.

Girdano DA, Everly GS Jr, and Dusek DE: Controlling stress and tension: a holistic approach, Englewood Cliffs, 1990, Prentice Hall.
This text provides an overview of the nature of stress, factors causing stress and influencing our responses to stress, and strategies that may be effectively used to manage stress.

Magill RA: Motor learning: concepts and applications, Dubuque, Iowa, 1985, Wm C Brown Co, Publishers.
This text provides a different approach to the study of motor learning. Specific concepts are presented, followed by practical applications of the concept, discussion, and then a summary.

Marburger DR: Peak experiences: helping students reach beyond themselves, Journal of Physical Education, Recreation, and Dance 59(1):72-73, 1988.
Offers suggestions to teachers to assist their students in achieving peak experiences during physical activities.

Martens R: Coaches guide to sport psychology, Champaign, Ill, 1987, Human Kinetics.
Part of the American Coaching Effectiveness Program, this book presents key concepts of sport psychology and how to develop psychological skills such as imagery, stress management, psychic energy management, attentional skills, goal-setting, and self-confidence.

Rink JE: Teaching physical education for learning, St Louis, 1985, Times Mirror/Mosby College Publishing.
This text focuses on the teaching process and the development of teaching skills to improve instruction.

Rudisill MR: Putting attribution theory to work-improving persistence and performance, Journal of Physical Education, Recreation, and Dance 60(7):43-46, 1989.

Offers practical strategies for teachers and coaches to help students and athletes view their performances more favorably, regardless of success or failure.

Schmidt RA: Motor control and learning: a behavioral emphasis, Champaign, Ill, 1988, Human Kinetics.

This text presents a comprehensive overview of motor behavior, integrating both neurophysiological and biomechanical research.

Siedentop D: Developing teaching skills in physical education, Palo Alto, Calif, 1983, Mayfield.

This text provides information about the various skills needed for effective teaching as well as strategies for their development.

Vealey RS: Sport personology: a paradigmatic and methodological analysis, Journal of Sport and Exercise Psychology 11:216-235, 1989.

This article examines trends and issues in the study of personality in sport.

Williams K, editor: What is motor development? Quest 41(3):179-234, 1989.

This entire issue of *Quest* is devoted to motor development, including defining motor development, reviewing the lifespan concept, and discussing the future of this field.

Ziegler SG: Negative thought stopping: a key to performance enhancement, Journal of Physical Education, Recreation, and Dance 58(4):66-69, 1987.

Offers specific strategies for helping individuals replace a negative internal dialogue (e.g., "I know I'll choke" or "I can't") with more positive and performance-enhancing talk.

Chapter 8

Sociological Foundations of Physical Education and Sport

INSTRUCTIONAL OBJECTIVES AND COMPETENCIES TO BE ACHIEVED

After reading this chapter the student should be able to—
- Show how sport is a socializing force in the American culture.
- Discuss the nature and scope of sport.
- Trace the growth of sport in educational institutions in the United States and the attitude of educators toward this growth.
- Discuss the sociological implications of educational sport.
- Know the dimensions of selected problems with which sport is confronted today such as those concerned with girls and women, children, minorities in sport, violence, and the Olympics.
- Formulate a philosophy of sport.

Sport is an important part of this nation's culture as well as of other cultures throughout the world. It captures newspaper headlines, holds television viewers' attention, produces millions of dollars a year in revenue for entrepreneurs, and has an impact on international affairs. Examples of how sport influences American life-style are many. Millions of Americans are "glued" to their chairs when featured baseball, football, basketball, and golf contests are scheduled to be televised. Advertisers target large percentages of their promotional budgets to buy air time during sporting events to sell their wares. For example, advertisements aired during football's Super Bowl XXIV (1990) sold for $750,000 for a 30-second commercial. Professional sports teams attract millions of spectators each year. Professional teams spend astronomical sums to obtain the best talent to sustain spectator support and interest and to ensure a profitable year for the management. Newspaper coverage devoted to sports consumes more space than all the arts combined, and sport symbols and jargon infiltrate American language, art, and politics.

The big business of sport has also influenced the nature of college and secondary school sport. Schools and colleges in an effort to field the best teams are often willing to compromise their academic standards. It is not uncommon for academically superior colleges to be more widely recognized for the feats of their athletic teams.

Within the last 10 years the number of sport par-

The emphasis on being number one is so strong in the U.S. that second place trophies are often perceived as reminders that someone else was better. Second place is often defined as a "loser's spot."

ticipants in our society has increased dramatically. Millions of people of all ages and abilities participate in a diversity of sport activities. Because of the social, political, legal, and educational influence of sport on cultures it is important to examine this phenomenon.

SOCIOLOGY OF SPORT

Sport pervades society to such an extent that it has been described by many experts as a microcosm of society. In other words, sport mirrors the values, structure, and dynamics of our society.[1] As such, sport reflects the characteristics of society. Eitzen and Sage[2] point out that among the characteristics that sport and our society have in common are a spirit of competitiveness, a large concern about materialistic things, the presence of a bureaucracy that dominates individuals, and an inequitable distribution of power. The pervasiveness of sport and

its institutional nature has led to the study of sport from a sociological perspective.

Sociology is concerned with the study of people, or groups or persons, and of human activities in terms of social behavior, groups, institutions, and social order within society. It is a science interested in such institutions of society as religion, family, government, education, and leisure. Sociologists are also concerned with the influence of social institutions on the individual, the social behavior and human relations that occur within a group or an institution and how they influence the behavior of the individual, and the interrelationships between the various institutions within a society, such as sport and education or religion and government.

As a medium that permeates nearly every important aspect of life, sport has led some physical educators and sociologists to believe that it should receive intensive study, particularly as it affects the behavior of human beings and institutions as they form the total social and cultural context of society. Sport sociology focuses on examining the relationship between sport and society. Coakley[3] lists the major goals of sport sociology as understanding the following:

- The relationship between sport and other aspects of society, such as family, education, politics, the economy, the media, and religion
- The social organization, group behavior, and social interaction patterns that occur within sport settings
- The cultural, structural, and situational factors that affect sport and sport experiences
- The social processes that occur in conjunction with sport, processes such as socialization, competition, cooperation, conflict, social stratification, and social change

As an area of study, the sociology of sport has grown considerably over the past 25 years. One important event that encouraged the development of sport sociology as a field of study was the initiative of a multinational panel of the International Council of Sport and Physical Education (ICSPE). This group was responsible for the creation of the International Committee of Sport Sociology (ICSS) in Geneva in 1964. In the late 1970s and early 1980s, the North American Society for the Sociology of Sport and the Sport Sociology Academy were established. The North American Society for Sport Sociology holds annual meetings and sponsors the *Sociology of Sport Journal*. The Sport Sociology Academy is one of the academies sponsored by the National Association for Sport and Physical Education (NASPE). It provides an opportunity for dissemination of research and a forum for discussion at the annual meetings of AAHPERD. The ICSS meetings are held in conjunction with those of the International Sociological Association; the ICSS cosponsors the *International Review for the Sociology of Sport* and the ICSS *Bulletin*.

Sport sociologists use sociological research strategies to study the behavior of individuals and groups within the sport milieu. They are concerned with understanding the influence of social relationships, past social experiences, and the social setting of sport activities on the behavior of individuals and groups within sport. Some questions sport sociologists might address are:

- Does participation in sport build character? Does it prepare individuals for life?
- Does sport help minorities, including women, become more fully integrated into society? How does participation in sport affect the social and economic status of minorities?
- How do the mass media affect sport?
- What are the effects of youth sport programs on the lives of participants? the participants' families?
- How are politics and sport related? religion and sport? the economic status of the community or the country and sport?
- How does interscholastic and intercollegiate sport influence the academic achievement of its participants?
- How do coaches influence the lives of their athletes?
- What will be the nature of the sport experience in the twenty-first century?

To address these and other questions, sport sociologists may examine historical circumstances, social conditions, economic factors, political climate, and relationships among the people involved.

As a field of study, sociology of sport will likely continue to grow, expanding both in depth and breadth. However, many challenges face the field. For example, Coakley[3] points out that there is a need for further research leading to the development of theories about sport and its relationship to society and social life. Furthermore, Coakley suggests that there is a need to focus additional attention on female participants in sport and on participation in sport throughout one's lifespan (currently only childhood and early adulthood participation are highlighted).

Sport can be viewed as a social institution and examined in relation to its impact on other social institutions such as the economy or the educational system. The effects of sport on its participants is also a vital area of study. Before discussing several areas of concern to sport sociologists, it may be helpful to define sport and discuss its nature and scope.

Definition of Sport

In order to study sport in a systematic manner, it is necessary to develop a specific definition of sport. Such a definition may, by its very nature, be limiting and restrictive. Yet such a definition is necessary to provide a focus and a shared perspective by which to understand the relationship of sport to society.

Coakley suggests that sport can be defined as follows:

Sport is an institutionalized competitive activity that involves vigorous physical exertion or the use of relatively complex physical skills by individuals whose participation is motivated by a combination of intrinsic and extrinsic factors.[3]

This definition refers to what is popularly known as organized sport activities. On the basis of this definition, three often asked questions can be addressed: (1) what kinds of activities can be classified as sport? (2) under what circumstances can participation in activities be considered sport? and (3) what characterizes the involvement of participants in sport?

Sport Activities

What physical activities can be considered sport? Is jogging a sport? chess? auto racing? weight lifting? Are children engaged in a pickup baseball game engaged in sport even though their activity is different in nature than the game professionals play?

Sport, as it is defined, requires that participants use relatively complex physical skills and physical prowess or vigorous physical exertion. Because these terms can be conceptualized as part of a continuum, at times it is difficult to make the distinction between physical and nonphysical skills, between complex and simple motor requirements, and between vigorous and nonvigorous activities. Because these terms are not quantified, determining what is complex physical activity and what is not can be a difficult task. Furthermore, not all physical activities involving complex physical skills or vigorous physical exertion are classified as sport. The circumstances and conditions under which these phys-

ical activities take place must be considered when classifying a physical activity as sport.

Conditions

The circumstances in which participation in physical activities can occur can be designated as ranging from informal and unstructured to formal and structured. For instance, compare the nature of a playground pickup game of basketball with a scheduled game between two professional teams. The individuals involved in both situations are playing basketball, but the nature and consequences of these games are different. Thus, the question—are both groups of individuals engaged in sport?

When sport sociologists discuss sport, they most often are referring to physical activity that involves competition conducted under formal and organized conditions. Given this perspective, friends engaged in an informal game of basketball are not participating in sport, whereas athletes participating on the professionals teams are participating in sport. From the sociological point of view, sport involves competitive physical activity that is institutionalized.

According to sociologists, institutionalization is a standardized pattern or set of behaviors sustained over a period of time and from one situation to another. Thus, competitive physical activity can be considered sport when it becomes institutionalized. Institutionalization occurs when there is standardization and enforcement of the rules governing the activity, emphasis on organization and the technical aspects of the activity (i.e., training, use of strategies, specialization and definition of the roles of players and coaches) and a formalized approach to skill development (e.g., use of experts to provide instruction). Through the process of institutionalization, unstructured and informal physical activities such as throwing a Frisbee become a sport known as *Ultimate Frisbee* where competition and organization are an integral part of the setting in which the activity takes place.

Participation Motives

Sport depends on maintaining a balance between intrinsic and extrinsic motivations. When the intrinsic satisfaction of being involved coexists with extrinsic concern for external rewards (e.g., money,

Sport is institutionalized when there is standardization and enforcement of the rules, emphasis on organization, and a formalized approach to skill development.

medals, approval from parents or a coach), sport occurs. The balance does not have to be 50:50 but when one source of motivation begins to greatly outweigh the other, changes in the nature of the activity and the experience of the participants occur. When participants' intrinsic motives prevail, the organization and structure of physical activity becomes one of play. When participants extrinsic motives such as medals or money prevail, physical activity changes from sport to what is often referred to as spectacle or work. It should be noted that during the course of a single sport event, participants may shift back and forth from intrinsic to extrinsic sources of motivation. At times participants may be absorbed in the flow of the action and revel in the satisfaction of being involved. Moments later the participants may be motivated by the desire to win a medal or receive the adulation of the crowd; the play spirit becomes replaced with the desire to reap external rewards.

In summary, according to Coakley's definition,

three criteria must be met for an activity to be defined as sport. The activity must involve physical skill, prowess, or exertion; it must be institutionalized and competitive in nature; and its participants must be motivated by a combination of intrinsic and extrinsic rewards. These criteria are useful in determining whether a physical activity can be classified as sport or not. Moreover, this definition serves as a focal point for sport sociologists to scientifically examine the role of sport in people's lives and in our society.

WHAT SPORT DOES FOR PEOPLE

Wilkerson and Dodder[4] have conducted research to determine what sport does for people. They found that sport has the following seven functions in society:

1. *Emotional release.* Sport is a way to express emotions and relieve tensions; it acts as a safety valve and a catharsis to relieve aggressive tendencies.
2. *Affirmation of identity.* Sport offers opportunities to be recognized and to express one's individual qualities.
3. *Social control.* Sport provides a means of control over people in a society where deviance is prevalent.
4. *Socialization.* Sport serves as a means of socializing those individuals who identify with it.
5. *Change agent.* Sport results in social change, new behavior patterns, and is a factor that changes the course of history. For example, it allows for interaction of all kinds of people and for upward mobility based on ability.
6. *Collective conscience.* Sport creates a communal spirit that brings people together in a cohesive manner in search of common goals.
7. *Success.* Sport provides a feeling of success both for the participant and the spectator when a player or a team with whom one identifies achieves. To win in sport is also to win in life.

It is evident that sport, especially in this age of increased participation, holds many meanings for its participants as well as having a significant impact on our society.

SPORT IN THE AMERICAN CULTURE

Sport has had an interesting history in the United States. From the colonial days, when sport for sport's sake was frowned on, until today, when sport has become big business, this phase of the American culture has grown steadily.

Colonial America was concerned with survival. The life-style of the early American settlers was concerned with work, not play. Play, in fact, was looked on as a sinful pursuit for adults, particularly in the New England colonies. Only on special occasions did the colonists permit themselves the luxury of engaging in hunts, contests of strength, and competition in wrestling, running, and jumping. However, as years went by and more settlers came to the United States, those activities that were popular in seventeenth-century Europe were introduced. These sports included horseracing, ninepins, hunting, fishing, marksmanship, and dice and card games. Also, the Dutch colonists introduced activities such as bowling, skating, and various types of ball games. With this influx of activities the opposition to sport as voiced by the Puritans gradually gave way to a more liberal and favorable attitude toward participation in games and related activities.

In the postrevolutionary period in the United States interest in sport increased, which continued through the remainder of the eighteenth century and into the nineteenth century. Activities such as rowing and sailing regattas, wrestling and shooting matches, and foot races became popular. In addition, this period saw the introduction of sports into some schools that were modeled after the English educational institutions. The first school to integrate games and sports into the curriculum was the Dummer Grammar School, Byfield, Massachusetts, in 1782. Soccer and batball were played at Exeter Academy early in the nineteenth century. In college sports started to be introduced in the middle 1800s, with tennis, baseball, football, rowing, handball, golf, roller skating, ice hockey, and lacrosse becoming popular.

During the last half of the nineteenth century the expansion of sport programs in colleges was slowed to some extent but still steadily increased in popularity. A significant development during this period was the formation of associations of various colleges and universities to have better control of their athletic programs.

In the early 1900s interest was renewed in sport throughout the nation as well as in educational institutions. For example, during the last quarter of the nineteenth century, for the first time in the United States there was a Kentucky Derby, a lawn tennis game, a National League baseball, an Amateur Athletic Union, a sports page in a newspaper, and a Madison Square Garden.

The 1920s saw one of the greatest explosions in sport in the United States. This period produced such outstanding sport figures as Babe Ruth, Bill Tilden, Jack Dempsey, and Ken Strong. The 1920s also saw the beginning of large crowds to witness sport spectaculars. For example, previous to this time boxing had only four $100,000 gates. However, in the 1920s it was common to exceed $1 million and even $2 million gates.

Since the 1920s a continual expansion of enterprises has occurred in all major areas of sport such as baseball, basketball, tennis, football, soccer, and golf. Sport has become big business with billions of dollars being spent on equipment, salaries, stadiums, and supporting supplies. The day of the million-dollar athlete also has arrived. Whereas superstars formerly signed for hundreds and thousands of dollars, some now sign contracts for millions of dollars. Indeed, the New York Yankees have so many high-salaried players that they have been referred to as the team of millionaires.

Sport is not just concerned with two teams meeting each other on the playing field. Sport activities are an important part of this nation's culture, and sport sociologists face a challenge in interpreting the role of sport in our way of life. Sport activities in the United States have been found by sociologists to be related to religion, economics, education, and government, to name a few.

Throughout the nation's history sport has been influenced by religious beliefs and economic conditions. During the nation's early developmental years sport activities, especially in New England, were severely hampered because of the religious attitude of the Puritan settlers. Religious attitudes have changed, and some religious institutions are now extremely active in sport. Throughout the nation organizations such as the Catholic Youth Organization and B'nai B'rith provide activities that give youth the opportunity to participate in sport. Schools and colleges under religious control sponsor sport programs.

Sport and the economic conditions of the nation are closely aligned. When the nation was developing, little opportunity was found to participate in sport. However, the rise in industrialization and the resultant increased leisure time have led to an increased awareness of sport. Sport activities have become an important part of the American way of life. Americans by the millions not only take part in sporting events through active participation, but they also spend millions of dollars on sport equipment. They also enjoy sporting events solely as spectators and fans.

In the area of education sport has become a part of schools and colleges in the nation. Physical education, intramural, club, and athletic programs have been created by educational institutions to give young people the opportunity to participate in these activities. Sport programs in schools in recent years have been associated with improving the fitness of our youth. The national government under the leadership of President Eisenhower and, later, Presidents Kennedy, Johnson, Nixon, Ford, Carter, Reagan, and Bush initiated and is supporting the President's Council on Physical Fitness and Sports, which has been concerned with improving the fitness of the nation's youth.

SPORT IN EDUCATIONAL INSTITUTIONS

The growth of sport in schools and colleges has been comparatively recent in the United States. The period from 1875 to 1900 saw for the first time a Harvard-Yale football game, a Big Ten Conference, and an All-American team. The advent of the radio and "lunar craters," as football coach Alonzo Stagg called the athletic arenas, resulted in an increase in "spectatoritis" and the exploitation of sport for its commercial value.

As sport programs grew, they were extended into the lower educational levels. Athletics started at the college level with a crew race between Harvard and Yale in 1852, followed by the introduction of other sports to the college campus. As higher educational athletic programs gained recognition and popularity, the high schools thought that sports should also be a part of their educational offerings. Next, the junior high schools initiated interschool athletic programs, many of which were carbon copies of those in the senior high schools, which previously had copied the colleges. Today some elementary schools are scheduling games as competitive sports are pushed further down the educational ladder.

From the beginning sport was of concern to educators because of its questionable educational worth and the way it can distort a school's or a nation's sense of values. For example, as reported in *Sports Illustrated,* in honor of Walter Camp Yale alumni helped raise $180,000 for the memorial gateway to the Yale Bowl, but other Yale admirers of Josiah Willard Gibbs, one of the greatest physicists the country had produced, were unable to muster $12,000 for a more modest tribute.

Another view of sport in institutions of higher education was advanced by J. Neils Thompson, past president of the National Collegiate Athletic Association (NCAA).[5] Thompson stated, "It seems clear that the image of the institution is clearly influenced by athletic performance. Halfbacks make better copy than philosophers—unfortunate perhaps, but true. Without question, the recruitment of students and the raising of financial support...can be favorably impacted by successful athletic programs."

Despite some educators' objections, athletics and sports in the nation's schools, colleges, and universities have continued to grow. In a single recent year (1988-89) the National Federation of State High School Associations[6] reported that 3,416,884 boys and 1,839,352 girls participated in interscholastic sports. In the same year the National Collegiate Athletic Association[7] reported that 156,765 men and 88,413 women participated in intercollegiate sports. (This figure includes only those sports in which the NCAA sponsors national championships; thus the overall participation figure is higher.) Title IX and the women's liberation movement have

Highly competitive sport opportunities for girls and women have increased in the past decade.

become factors in the participation of an increasing number of girls and women in sports in educational institutions. It is estimated that the number of girls and women participating will gradually approach a figure equal to that of boys and men.

Today school and college athletics are experiencing difficulties beyond those provided by their educational critics. The economy, austerity budgets, student criticism, academic performance of athletes, and concerns for minority and female athletes have caused some educational institutions to curtail, abolish, or reevaluate their sport programs. Since athletics play such an important role in American culture and in physical education programs, it is interesting to examine some of the sociological implications of sport.

Interscholastic Sports

Interscholastic sports are viewed by many people, including the National Federation of State High School Associations, as an integral part of the educational experience for high school students and, increasingly, junior high school students as well. The inclusion of interscholastic sports in the educational curriculum has typically been justified on the basis of sport contributing to educational goals.

While there is widespread support for interscholastic athletics, there has also been much criticism of these programs. Proponents of interscholastic athletics cite its valuable contributions to the educational mission of the schools. Critics take the position that sport interferes with the attainment of educational goals. Popular arguments for and against interscholastic athletics as presented by Coakley are shown in Table 8-1.

Participation in interscholastic sports can benefit students in several ways. Participation in sport can help students develop a high level of physical fitness and attain a high degree of proficiency in selected sport skills and knowledge of various aspects of the game. Other frequently cited benefits accrued through participation include the development of sportsmanship, cooperation, leadership, and loyalty. Sport can provide opportunities for personal growth, pave the way for the development of friendships, develop decision-making and thinking skills, teach self-discipline and commitment, enhance one's self-esteem and personal status, and promote the acceptance of others regardless of race or ethnic origins.

However, whether participation in sport enhances academic achievement is a very complex and debatable question. When viewed as a group, high school athletes generally have better grade point averages and express more interest in further education than their nonathlete peers.[3] It is important to note, however, that such differences are typically small. Moreover, academic achievement is linked to a number of factors, including academic goals, personal achievement values, and motivation.

TABLE 8-1   Popular Arguments for and against Interscholastic Sport

Arguments for	Arguments against
1. Involves students in school activities and increases interest in academic activities	1. Distracts the attention of students away from academic activities
2. Builds the responsibility, achievement orientation, and physical vigor required for adult participation in society	2. Perpetuates dependence and immaturity and focuses the attention of students on a set of values no longer appropriate in industrial society
3. Stimulates interest in physical activities among all students in the school	3. Relegates most students to the role of spectator rather than active participant
4. Generates the spirit and unity necessary to maintain the school as a viable organization	4. Creates a superficial, transitory spirit subverting the educational goals of the school
5. Promotes parental, alumni, and community support for all school programs	5. Deprives educational programs of resources, facilities, staff, and community support

It is also difficult to isolate the influence of sport participation from other factors known to influence academic achievement such as family background, economic status, support and encouragement from significant others, and individual characteristics.

Interscholastic sport can also heighten school spirit and engender parental support. In many locales across the country, interscholastic athletics provide a focal point for the community.

It appears that interscholastic programs do not use a disproportionate share of budgetary resources when they are maintained in a proper perspective. However, it should be noted that in times of austerity they are one of the first extracurricular programs to be threatened with cutbacks.

Whether or not interscholastic sport programs help participants attain desirable educational goals as well as provide a positive experience for those students involved depends a great deal on the manner in which the program is conducted. These desired outcomes do not occur automatically as a result of participation in the program. They can, however, be realized when school administrators and coaches make a concerted and thoughtful effort to structure sport programs to provide experiences that will lead to the attainment of educational goals and fulfillment of students' needs. Suggestions offered by Lumpkin[8] to help promote a positive interscholastic sport experience for participants and the realization of desirable goals are given in the box on p. 246.

Interscholastic sport programs are an integral part of the educational experience for millions of U.S. high school students and enjoy widespread support. Nevertheless, in many schools across the country interscholastic sport programs are in serious need of reform. Some programs have little relevancy to the education process. Critics of interscholastic sport also denounce the overemphasis on winning, restriction of opportunities for students, and eligibility requirements for participation. Concern has also been voiced pertaining to drug abuse, soaring costs, pressures from parents and community supporters, and coaches' behavior.

Overemphasis on winning is one of the most frequently voiced criticisms of interscholastic sport. This disproportionate emphasis is reflected in the increased specialization in one sport by athletes, the participation of injured athletes, the subversion of the educational process, and coaches' jobs depending on their win/loss records.

Compared with just 10 years ago, more high school athletes are foregoing multisport competition and specializing in one sport.[9] Whereas in the past athletes would compete in a fall, a winter, and a spring sport, there is a trend toward competing in only one sport a year. Increasingly, athletes engage in conditioning programs and informal practices for their chosen sport in the off-season and attend specialized sport camps and play in community leagues during the summer. Proponents of sport specialization stress that such an emphasis is needed to

THE INTERSCHOLASTIC PROGRAM

The Interscholastic Sports Program is an outgrowth of the basic instructional program and provides additional physical education experiences in a wide range of sports. The purposes of this program should be to help participants to:

Gain a better understanding of their physiological and psychological capabilities, and establish reasonable personal goals

View winning as a means to self-improvement and not as an end in itself

Assume leadership roles in planning and conducting intramural and interscholastic activities

Share in the decision-making process involved in those programs

Participate and/or compete fairly on the factors of age, ability, height, weight, physiological maturity and strength

Benefit from the expertise of coaches who are certified teachers possessing either a major or a minor in physical education and/or state coaching certification

Receive appropriate medical attention before, during and after intramural/interscholastic sports programs

1. Medical examinations should be required for all who participate in interscholastic activities.

2. A physician's statement indicating the student's fitness for resuming participation should be required following a serious illness or injury.

3. An athletic trainer or teacher/trainer should be present at all games and practices.

From an administrative standpoint, all secondary school interscholastic contests, including post-season games, should be conducted under the jurisdiction of state high school athletic associations, and the programs should be financed by local Boards of Education.

From AAHPERD.

---

develop proficiency in advanced skills and refine strategies, remain competitive with other teams, and increase an athlete's chances of receiving college grants-in-aid. Critics argue that specialization limits athletes' development, denying them opportunities to develop skills in other activities, participate with other athletes, and learn from other coaches. Athletes who specialize may be exploited by coaches seeking to win, are subjected to overuse injuries, and are at risk for athletic burnout (i.e., are tired and emotionally exhausted from participating) and may drop out of the sport, often near the point of reaching their fullest potential.

In an effort to win, coaches may resort to undesirable behaviors. They may pressure athletes to practice and play when injured. In an effort to maintain player eligibility, coaches may steer athletes toward easier courses, pressure teachers to pass athletes or, in some cases, alter athletes' grades.

Winning is overemphasized when teachers are hired or fired based on their coaching win-loss records rather than their abilities as teachers. Good teachers have been fired because of a poor coaching record, and poor teachers have been retained because of their outstanding coaching accomplishments.

If interscholastic sports are to realize their educational potential, it is important that winning be kept in perspective. The educational goals of learning and development should be emphasized, not the win-loss record.

The restricted number of opportunities for participation is another criticism of interscholastic sports. Interscholastic sports programs usually offer limited opportunities for participation. Schools typically have both a varsity team and a junior varsity team in a variety of sports, although larger schools also may have freshman teams and reserve teams. Thus, when a given school offers both a varsity and

Title IX has stimulated the growth of girls' and women's sport at all levels.

a junior varsity basketball team for boys and for girls, perhaps as few as 48 students will have the opportunity to participate. Many students who are less highly skilled are excluded, despite their love of the game, and often no other scholastic sport opportunities are provided for them. Furthermore, in addition to consuming a great deal of the time and energy of physical education teachers, interscholastic sport teams utilize monies, facilities, equipment, and other resources that could be used for general participation. In addition, even though federal legislation has mandated that boys and girls must have equal opportunities, often the informal support and commitment so necessary to develop and maintain quality programs for females is lacking (this is discussed elsewhere in this chapter).

Academic requirements for eligibility are also a controversial issue. Most high schools require that students meet certain academic standards to be eligible to participate in extracurricular activities, including sports. These standards often exceed the criteria required to stay in school. In recent years

many states have adopted "no-pass, no play" policies, setting forth even more stringent requirements for athletes to maintain their eligibility. These requirements vary but, typically, the policy bars from participation those individuals who do not pass all of their courses or fail to maintain a certain average during a marking period.

Advocates of this policy believe that establishing stringent standards for participation in sport programs will have a positive effect on athletes' academic performance. In order to maintain their eligibility, athletes will be motivated to pursue their studies. Critics of this policy point out that students who stayed in school mainly to play sports now find themselves ineligible and may drop out of school.

The central issue of the no pass, no play controversy is, according to Siedentop,[9] the educational importance of interscholastic sport. Eligibility standards may be appropriate if sport is an extracurricular activity and participation is a privilege to be earned. If, however, sport is an integral part of the educational experience—if it has educational value—then is it appropriate to deny this experience to any student? If participation in interscholastic athletics contributes to educational goals, if the experience can promote learning and foster personal development, why should any student be denied this opportunity? Siedentop[9] also relates this argument to the exclusionary nature of interscholastic sport discussed previously. If participation in sport is an important developmental experience for adolescents, it should be more widely available so that more students, both boys and girls, can benefit.

One of the most serious problems in the schools is drug abuse. Much media attention has been focused on the use of performance-enhancing drugs, such as anabolic steroids, in professional, international, and intercollegiate sports. However, such drug use is a problem in interscholastic sports as well. High school athletes seeking to improve their performance by increasing their strength may turn to anabolic steroids, which, when taken in amounts far exceeding the recommended dosage (megadoses) and coupled with intense physical workouts, can produce a significant increase in muscle growth. The side effects associated with such large dosages are serious and lead to irreparable damage. Coaches also must be prepared to address other serious problems such as the use of tobacco, alcohol, and illegal drugs such as marijuana, amphetamines, and cocaine.

Soaring costs are increasingly becoming a concern in interscholastic athletics. Rising costs for injury and liability insurance as well as costs associated with providing programs for girls and disabled students have caused some schools to reduce the scope of their athletic programs and/or require athletes to pay in order to participate. A "pay-to-play" policy requires that students who desire to participate in sports to pay for the opportunity. Critics have decried this policy because it discriminates against students who are unable to afford to pay. Some schools and communities, in response, have made provisions so that economically disadvantaged students can participate in the athletic program.

There are many pressures that exert an insidious influence on interscholastic sport programs. When pressures from school administrators, community members, and parents on coaches to win exist; when the expectations of parents exert too much pressure on their children to excel; and when coaches place undue pressure on their athletes to perform, the quality of the sport experience can deteriorate rapidly. Sport becomes unrewarding and less enjoyable than it should be and harmful to the participants. The educational experience becomes subverted and educational outcomes unrealized.

The quality and nature of the leadership provided is of critical importance in determining whether educational goals will be realized. If learning is to occur and personal development enhanced, then administrators and coaches must structure the program and provide experiences that will lead to the attainment of these goals.

When high school coaches exert undue pressure on athletes to perform, when they excessively control the lives of their athletes, and when they physically or verbally abuse their athletes to set an example for the rest of the team, then the educational goals of interscholastic sport will go unfulfilled. There are coaches who equate obedience with self-discipline, demand singleminded dedication to sport, and provide no opportunity for athlete involvement in decision-making (such as in setting team goals or planning game strategies). These coaches may win games but they are failing to further the aims of education. Coaches who foster personal development of their athletes by guiding them, by allowing them to make decisions and live with the consequences of those decisions, and by enhancing the worth and dignity of each athlete will help interscholastic sport fulfill its educational mission.

Intercollegiate Sports

The nature of intercollegiate sport in the United States varies greatly. Budgets for athletics may vary from $20,000 per year at small private colleges to over $15 million per year at some major universities.[3] The number of sports offered by a school can range from 1 to as many as 25 different activities for men and women.[3] In smaller institutions, the athletic program may be part of the physical education

The quality of leadership exhibited by coaches can strongly influence the experience of the participants.

department and be funded from its budget, the coaches have faculty teaching status, and one individual may serve as the coach for two or more teams. In contrast, at larger institutions, separate athletic departments exist, athletics has its own budget and generates substantial revenue from gate receipts and contributions, coaches have no teaching status, and one individual coaches only one sport. Program philosophies vary as well; in some institutions the educational nature of intercollegiate sport is emphasized while in other institutions sports are seen as big business. Financial assistance for athletes varies and may be directly influenced by the skill of the athlete. Some schools offer no athletic scholarships; financial assistance is based solely on financial need. Other schools offer athletes a full scholarship that covers all expenses for tuition, room, board, fees, and books. Still other schools may offer partial assistance to athletes, such as providing only a tuition waiver. Given the tremendous diversity of intercollegiate sport programs, it is reasonable to believe that the nature of the intercollegiate sport experience for participants varies widely throughout the United States.

Intercollegiate sport is regulated by three primary governing bodies: the National Collegiate Athletic Association (NCAA), the National Association of Intercollegiate Athletics (NAIA), and the National Junior College Athletic Association (NJCAA). These associations attempt to administer intercollegiate athletic programs in accordance with educational principles.

The NCAA is the largest governing body for 4-year colleges and universities. Its nearly 800 member institutions are divided into different divisions, based on the characteristics of their athletic program. Division I consists of about 280 institutions and includes those schools who conduct what is generally referred to as "big money" programs. Division II and III are composed of approximately 200 and 300 schools, respectively, and conduct programs that place less emphasis on gaining financially from their athletic teams.

Many intercollegiate sport programs, excluding the big Division I programs, operate in a manner similar to those found in larger high school programs. These intercollegiate sport programs include some Division I programs and those generally classified as Division II and III by the NCAA as well as those programs governed by the NAIA and the NJCAA. They offer participants similar experiences to those found in high-level interscholastic programs.

Athletes in big-time programs, particularly in revenue-producing sports, face tremendous pressures and demands to win.

However, unlike high school, college and university coaches need to recruit athletes for these teams. Athletes who choose to attend these schools may be offered some form of financial assistance. This can range from full athletic scholarships to need-based financial assistance.

In comparison to other intercollegiate programs, athletes who participate in the big Division I programs generally possess a higher level of athletic talent, face a greater time commitment to their sport, receive full athletic scholarships, experience a greater amount of travel, and benefit from greater media exposure. Pressures to have a winning program are often immense, and the consequences of winning and losing are usually much greater. Economic survival for these programs frequently depends on their ability to generate revenue through gate receipts, contributions, and, increasingly, television contracts. Winning teams generate interest among fans, which increases gate receipts, which provides more money to hire coaches with proven winning records to raise the athletic program to even greater heights. Commercialism and

entertainment dominate, educational goals are deemphasized and often subverted, and athletics is transformed into a business and entertainment venture.

Many of the positive educational outcomes ascribed to participation in interscholastic sport programs can be realized when intercollegiate programs emphasize the attainment of educational goals. Similarly, many of the problems associated with interscholastic programs are evident in intercollegiate programs throughout the country. The overemphasis on winning, concerns pertaining to the academic achievements of athletes and their eligibility for participation, and the use of drugs are some of the problems associated with intercollegiate sports.

As with interscholastic sport, overemphasis on winning can lead to the subordination of educational goals. Such goals as sportsmanship, character development, and social development may be abandoned when winning becomes the most important objective. Desire and pressure to win may lead to the subverting or the violating of rules in an effort to recruit the best athletes and maintain their eligibility.

The academic achievement of intercollegiate athletes is a major concern. There are many student-athletes that exemplify the true meaning of the word—they have combined sports and academics successfully. A prominent example is Senator Bill Bradley—he played basketball for Princeton University, was named a Rhodes scholar, and had an outstanding professional basketball career before becoming a U.S. Senator. There are, however, many instances where the term *student athlete* is truly a misnomer; in these cases athletics are given a much higher priority than academics.

In many colleges and universities, the academic achievements of athletes are comparable to those of their nonathlete peers. Studies have shown that the academic performance of athletes on women's teams, NCAA Division III teams, and other non–revenue-generating teams is similar to other college students.[10,11,12] However, studies of the academic achievements of athletes in big-time programs compared with their nonathlete counterparts have yielded confusing and conflicting results. Athletes in the big-time programs, particularly in revenue-generating sports such as football and basketball, face considerable demands on their time and energy that can interfere with their academic work.

There are athletes who can successfully balance the consuming demands of athletics with the rigorous demands of academics and excel in both areas. However, in many instances the pressures on coaches to win translates into pressure to keep athletes eligible. Focusing attention on eligibility rather than on learning can lead to many abuses. Coaches may recruit athletes who lack the academic preparation needed to successfully meet the academic challenges of college. They counsel athletes into taking easy courses, pressure professors to give them good grades, and encourage them to enroll in majors that require little academic effort. And, unfortunately, progress toward a degree is not monitored as carefully as is the maintenance of athletic eligibility.

Studies of the graduation rates of athletes in the big-time programs yield conflicting results because of the different methods that can be used to compute them. What is known is that in some schools and in some sports, the graduation rate of athletes is minimal.[3] The educational system is subverted and the athletes are exploited. Athletes are recruited and used during their years of eligibility by coaches who do little to ensure that they are making progress toward the completion of a degree. This tends to occur most frequently in revenue-producing sports such as football and basketball. Additionally, because many black athletes come from rural and inner-city high schools where quality education programs may be lacking, a higher proportion of black athletes than white athletes are affected. Special efforts by coaches, coupled with encouragement and financial support by program administrators, are needed to foster learning and to improve the graduation rates of athletes. Failure to do this compromises the academic integrity of the institution and imperils the educational relevance of sports.

In an effort to help remediate the academic abuses associated with big-time, revenue-producing sports and to restore academic integrity, the NCAA in 1983 adopted a rule establishing minimum standards for freshman athletes to be eligible to participate on varsity teams at Division I institutions. Commonly known as Proposition 48, this rule stipulates that in order to be eligible to participate in sports, a freshman athlete must enter college with a 2.0 grade point average (GPA) in 11 specified core high school courses and achieve a minimum score of 700 on the Scholastic Aptitude Test (SAT) or 15 on the American College Test (ACT). Implemented in 1986, this rule permitted students who met only one of the requirements to be accepted at a college and given athletic aid, but they were not permitted to practice with their teams during their freshman year and had to forfeit one year of eligibility.

The NCAA hoped that Proposition 48 would send a strong message to high schools and their athletes that academic achievement was a prerequisite for students participating in Division I athletics. It was further hoped that this rule would help colleges and universities break the habit of recruiting athletes who had neither the academic background nor the potential to graduate within a 4- or 5-year period. It also provided freshman athletes who needed it a year to strengthen their academic abilities without the added pressures and commitments associated with sports. In 1989, the NCAA adopted Proposition 42, which prohibits the awarding of athletic aid to freshman athletes who do not meet both standards.

These rulings are controversial. Critics charge that they discriminate against economically disadvantaged students who were not fortunate enough to have received a strong high school preparation for college or those who do not have the resources to retake the standardized tests or pay for commercial test preparation courses. Further concerns are voiced concerning the discriminatory nature of the standardized tests, in particular the SAT. When test scores are compared, 14% of whites score lower than 700 on SAT while 46% of blacks score lower than 700. Moreover, in the 3 years following the implementation of Proposition 48, nearly 90% of the athletes affected by the ruling were black.[3] Coaches who had set up academic programs to assist Proposition 48 athletes were particularly dismayed by the Proposition 42 ruling. They felt it interfered with their efforts to help young athletes who had the potential to succeed in college despite their poor academic preparation.

Supporters of these rulings suggest that it has had a favorable impact at the high school level.[13] Young athletes appear to recognize the need to take high school core courses and to regard standardized tests more seriously. Coaches appear to be more encouraging of academic efforts, and academic support services have been developed to help high school athletes strengthen their academic skills.

The long-term effectiveness of Propositions 48 and 42 remains to be seen. It is hoped that these rulings will lead to improved educational programs, to an increased emphasis on academic achievement for athletes at both the high school and the collegiate levels, and to restoring much-needed academic integrity to intercollegiate athletic programs.

There are several other problems that beset big-time intercollegiate sports. Big-time intercollegiate sports have become big business. This commercialism has led to financial concerns receiving a greater priority than the education and personal development of the athletes. Creating a winning program to generate increased fan support in order to achieve a greater profit is a vicious, spiraling cycle.

Many physical education and sport professionals are becoming increasingly concerned about the exploitation of athletes. Some intercollegiate athletes can generate millions of dollars for their institution but the only compensation permitted under NCAA rules is tuition, room, board, books, and fees. Even at the most expensive of institutions, when the total cost of the athletic scholarship is divided by the number of hours athletes are required to devote to their sport, the pay per hour is low.[9] Although critics say it is difficult to place a value on the benefits of a college education, oftentimes athletes are strongly encouraged to focus their energies and efforts on sports instead of academics. Moreover, these educational abuses cited detract from the nature of the educational experience. All too often athletic departments are concerned with athletes' academic status only until their 3 or 4 years of eligibility are used up; after this period, their concern about the academic progress of athletes is minimal. Most adversely affected by this practice are athletes from lower socio-economic backgrounds and those who have received poor preparation for college from their high schools. These athletes often do not have the financial resources to pay for the extra semesters needed to graduate. Furthermore, because much of their efforts had previously been devoted to sports rather than academics, they may find it difficult to cope with the academic demands without the extra assistance (e.g., tutors) previously available to members of sport teams.

There are several other issues in intercollegiate sport that must be addressed. The media has increased the public's awareness of violations of recruiting regulations. Illegal recruiting practices, such as cash payments to prospective athletes, must be stopped. Drug abuse also is a problem. Athletes, in an effort to enhance their performance, may abuse such drugs as amphetamines and anabolic steroids. Although drug testing policies and procedures have become more stringent, methods to mask the use of drugs have become more clever. The effect of win-loss records on the retention of coaches, the role of coaches within the institutions of higher education, and the role of alumni and other influential supporters in the hiring and firing of coaches must be carefully evaluated and monitored.

The 1980s have been marked by calls for the reform of intercollegiate athletics. Abuses have become so serious and so widespread that the academic integrity of educational institutions sponsoring these programs is challenged. Many suggestions have been offered to change intercollegiate athletics. These include elimination of freshman eligibility, limiting practice and game schedules, close monitoring of athletes' academic progress, tying athletes' graduation rates to the number of athletic scholarships that can be offered, and providing coaches with some form of job security to encourage them to strongly support athletes' academic endeavors and achievements.

Like interscholastic sports, intercollegiate sports have the potential to contribute to the educational goals of the institutions that sponsor them. Whether these educational goals are attained depends on the leadership. When winning is overemphasized, commercialism is rampant, and athletes are exploited, the educational relevance of these programs is called into question. When winning is placed in perspective, when academic achievement is strongly supported, and when athletes are encouraged and given opportunities to develop to their fullest potential, then the educational mission of intercollegiate athletics will be fulfilled.

TOWARD AN EDUCATIONAL PHILOSOPHY OF SPORT

It is interesting to note that the Greeks provided civilization with two disciplines. The first described how sport could be most helpful in the training of a strong and graceful performance and body. The second provided civilization with the basics of philosophical thinking. As the historian Isocrates said:

...Certain of our ancestors, long before our time, invented and bequeathed to us two disciplines: physical training for the body, of which gymnastics is a part, and for the mind, philosophy. These twin arts are parallel and complementary, by which their masters prepare the mind to become more intelligent and the body to become more serviceable, nor separating sharply the two kinds of education, but using similar methods of instruction, exercise, and discipline.

Every student of physical education and sport should develop a philosophy of that discipline. A philosophy will represent a guide to decision making, since it will clarify the worth of this field of endeavor in the human experience. Such a philosophy might include how sport should be conducted to make the greatest contribution to humankind. It should help to determine the parameters of educational sport as well as sport outside the formal domains of schools, colleges, and other educational institutions. It should provide an understanding of the history of sport and the contributions it has made over the years, as well as show how it has been misused and has been detrimental to humankind. A philosophy will also help point the way to achieving excellence of performance on the athletic field.

Sport is extremely popular and has a firm foothold in United States educational institutions and society. Therefore it is imperative to give direction to athletic programs in a way that will better contribute to the achievement of educational goals. The conduct of sport programs will be more worthwhile if the following four guidelines are used.

Guideline 1—Restructure Athletics to Achieve Cognitive, Psychomotor, and Affective Learnings

Cognitive, psychomotor, and affective learning outcomes are worthy goals for athletics in education. It has been demonstrated that cognitive learning, such as knowledge of rules, player assignments, and the game strategies associated with playing a sport, as well as the phenomena associated with the

There is a need for a greater number of qualified women coaches and athletic administrators.

economic, political, and other interrelationships that exist between sport and society, can be accomplished. It has also been demonstrated that psychomotor learnings in the form of physical skills that are acquired by the participant as a result of engaging in athletics can be achieved. However, affective learnings may not be accomplished in light of the research that questions the role of sport in bringing about behavioral changes. Therefore some restructuring may need to take place as a means of using sport as a medium for learning social behavior. Athletics, if properly structured, can provide the social environment whereby societal norms can be internalized by the participants and their social attitudes shaped in a positive manner through social situations.

Sport and athletics are the heart of physical education programs in schools and colleges in the United States and have great appeal to young people of all ages, races, colors, and creeds. At the same time society is faced with many social problems, including relations between blacks and whites, the need for cooperative endeavor in achieving goals in a democratic society, and the necessity for constructive rather than destructive competition as people attempt to achieve their personal goals. Therefore, if athletics through a restructuring process can help in bringing about more desirable social attitudes among the many young people who participate in them, in addition to achieving cognitive and psychomotor goals, they would obviously play a much more valuable role in educational programs.

Guideline 2—Provide an Athletic Program Where the Intensity of the Competition Is Developmental in Nature

Physical and motor growth follow a progressive sequence from the time of early childhood to maturity. In other words, they follow a developmental pattern (large muscles develop before fine muscles).

What is true of the physical is also true of the mental and emotional aspects—they are also developmental in nature. Therefore, since the intensity of athletic competition is related to a person's growth and development, it should also reflect a progressive sequence. It would then follow that athletic competition should be of a very low intensity during the early years of childhood and then gradually be increased as the child grows older and becomes more mature.

The intensity of athletic competition is increased when elements are introduced into the athletic experience that provide added motivation for and additional pressure on the participants to excel, and where more is at stake in the competition. For example, when spectators are in the stands, games are scheduled with schools in other communities, awards are offered, admission is charged, sports writers are in attendance, or playoff games for championships are sponsored, the intensity of the competition is increased.

Relating the elements that increase the intensity of the competition to the developmental levels of the student, it is proposed that four levels of intensity of competition for a developmental athletic program exist. These four levels of competition should be progressively scheduled during the school years in a way that best fits the student and also the administrative grade pattern in the school. The four levels of intensity of athletic competition are as follows:

1. *First developmental level.* Absence of any structured athletic competition.
2. *Second developmental level.* Intramurals with their low-key competitive involvement of classmates provide the first structured step-up in the intensity of competition.
3. *Third developmental level.* Extramurals, such as occasional play days, sports days, and invitational meets with schools in other communities, where the stress is on the social and fun aspects of the event rather than the winning, represent an intermediate athletic developmental competitive experience between intramurals and varsity interschool athletics.
4. *Fourth developmental level.* Varsity athletic competition represents a major step-up in the intensity of competition with elements such as spectators, publicity, leagues, and awards. This type of experience may be provided after each

of the previous developmental levels of competition has been utilized for a significant period of time and when the player can successfully cope physically, mentally, emotionally, and socially with such an experience.

Guideline 3—Provide More Athletic Opportunities for Girls, Women, and Disabled Athletes

Athletics are a part of the total school program and all students should have the opportunity to compete for a place on the team. Changing societal attitudes and federal legislation have promoted the growth of participation by girls, women, and disabled students. This growth should be encouraged through funding, proper coaching, and facilities; additional teams should be added when they are necessary to meet student needs. The benefits of athletic competition should be available to all students.

Guideline 4—Institute Changes in the Organization and Administration of Athletic Programs

School administrators play a key role in the development of a sound educational athletic program. They are the persons who are responsible for such programs and should provide the leadership necessary to bring about desirable change. Areas in which change is needed include the following:

1. Schedule and limit in length practice sessions and number of games played so as not to disrupt the educational process or take a disproportionate amount of the student's time.
2. Conduct sport contests only on school premises. The public arena, where educators are not in control and where gamblers and rabid spectators are present, is a questionable place to conduct athletic contests.
3. Appoint coaches on the basis of their educational qualifications. A knowledge of and an interest in participants, including their physical, mental, emotional, and social makeup, is one of the most important qualifications.
4. Administer athletics as an integral part of the total education program.

5. Sponsor a continuing research program to determine means by which sport can make its greatest contribution to human growth and development.

Sport reflects what the United States is—its people, its character, its values, and its philosophy of life. This country needs more sport and greater participation of more people. Furthermore, Americans need to recognize that regardless of individual ability, sex, race, or economic status, sport opportunities should be available to all people so that it may enrich their lives.

CONCERNS IN SPORT TODAY

Although sports are highly popular and are beneficial for the participants and for the nation, they are also beset by many problems. James A. Michener,[14] the noted novelist, points out the following problems in his book *Sports in America:*

1. Girls and women are discriminated against.
2. Adults who are in charge of children's programs place too much emphasis on winning.
3. Children are engaged in highly competitive sport at too early an age.
4. Money spent by universities to maintain big time sport teams is excessive.
5. The recruitment of high school athletes is often scandalous.
6. Television coverage of sporting events threatens to destroy many of the values that can accrue from sport.
7. Violence in sport is excessive.
8. City politicians use public monies to build large stadiums and then provide them to professional teams at minimal rental rates.

A few of the major problems facing sport today as we view them are discussed in this section. Problems in sport are also discussed in Chapter 15.

Girls and Women in Sport

Prior to the 1970s opportunities for girls and women to compete in sports were limited. Within the past 20 years there has been a dramatic increase in girls' and women's participation in sports. This increase is visible at all levels of competition—the Olympics, professional and amateur sports, inter-

collegiate and interscholastic sports, and youth sports.

The relatively recent increase in participation by girls and women in the United States can be attributed to several factors. These include federal legislation, the women's movement, the fitness movement, and an increased public awareness of female athletes.

Federal legislation, specifically Title IX of the Educational Amendment Act, was one of the most influential factors because it mandated equal treatment for women and men in programs receiving federal assistance. Passed in 1972, Title IX prohibits discrimination on the basis of sex in any educational program or activity receiving federal financial assistance. It states that "no person in the United States shall, on the basis of sex, be excluded from participation in, be denied the benefits of, or be subjected to discrimination under any educational program or activity receiving federal assistance."

Because Title IX is politically controversial and the guidelines complex, implementation and enforcement of this law is difficult. After its implementation, access to sport opportunities for women increased. However, it should be noted that in 1984, in *Grove City College v. Bell,* the U.S. Supreme Court ruled in favor of a narrow interpretation of Title IX, stating that it should be regarded as program specific. Thus, only programs directly receiving federal aid are required to comply with Title IX regulations, not the institution as a whole. Because athletic programs typically receive little if any direct federal funding, the threat of losing funding for noncompliance and nonsupport of women's athletics is not a substantial one. Subsequently, the 800 cases of alleged sex discrimination that were being investigated by the U.S. Department of Education's Office for Civil Rights were either narrowed in scope or withdrawn. Four years later, in 1988, the Civil Rights Restoration Act was passed. This law provided for a broad interpretation of Title IX by mandating equal opportunity for both sexes in all programs in any organization that received federal funds.

The impact of Title IX has resulted in noticeable increases in participation of girls and women at

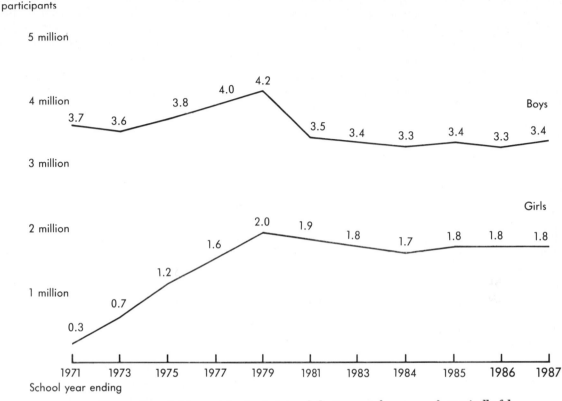

FIGURE 8-1 *The number of girls participating in interscholastic sports has grown dramatically following the passage of Title IX.*

both the interscholastic and intercollegiate level. The growth of participation by girls in interscholastic sports following the passage of Title IX can be seen in Figure 8-1. At the intercollegiate level, there was an increase in the number of intercollegiate teams for women, the hiring of qualified coaches, and the offering of athletic scholarships to outstanding high school women athletes. In 1972, 32,000 women competed in intercollegiate sports; in 1988 to 1989 the NCAA reported that nearly 90,000 women participated in its athletic programs. Spectator interest in women's sports has grown as well. This has resulted in increased attendance at games; for example, approximately 20,000 people attended the 1990 NCAA Women's Division I basketball championships. Television coverage of women's sports has increased; the NCAA championships in

swimming and diving, basketball, gymnastics, volleyball, and track and field have been televised in recent years. Even coverage of regular season events has expanded; during the 1988 to 1989 season, over 100 women's college basketball games were televised, although mostly on cable.

The women's movement has encouraged increased participation in athletics by women. It has helped redefine societal, occupational, and family roles for women and has given women more control over their lives. The idea that women are enhanced as human beings when they are given opportunities to develop competence has encouraged women of all ages to pursue an increasingly wide array of interests, including sport. Moreover, the changing cultural image of women athletes has contributed to the growth of women's sports. Where women athletes were once perceived by many as unfeminine or were stigmatized for engaging in high levels of competition, athletic participation by women is now regarded as acceptable. The extent of the change in attitudes is such that Leonard[15] suggests that athletics can be used by adolescent girls as a means of attaining status in much the same way as it is used for boys. Women athletes have been reported to have lower feminty scores than nonathletes; however, they also score higher on self-esteem, body image, and psychological well-being. Other research[16] suggests that women athletes may not experience role conflict to the extent previously thought. Women athletes, regardless of their age, sport, or level of experience, are found to experience relatively little dissonance between their roles as women and as athletes. Ideas about what is masculine and what is feminine are based on societal definitions and may be needlessly restrictive, creating barriers to participation.[3] In the future, as society's attitudes continue to change, more people may come to perceive sport not as a masculine activity but rather as a human activity.

Since the 1970s, the fitness movement has encouraged many women to participate in physical activities, including sport. Many women started engaging in jogging, walking, aerobics, and swimming to realize the associated benefits of fitness, particularly to feel good and look better. While there is still an emphasis on engaging in physical activities to look better and to preserve one's youthfulness, there is also a growing emphasis on the physical development of the body. Additionally, many women have moved from engaging in fitness activities to engaging in competitive athletes; joggers have gone on to participate in road races, marathons, and even triathlons. Interest in fitness has also led to an increase in the number of women participating in community sport programs in such sports as softball, volleyball, and basketball.

As participation by girls and women increase, there will be more women athlete role models. The increased coverage and publicity given to women athletes have allowed girls and women to read about the achievements and watch the performance of women athletes in a wider range of sports than

ever before. Noted athlete role models such as Nancy Lopez, Steffie Graf, and Mary Lou Retton have encouraged many girls to start athletic careers and pursue their athletic ambitions. Older sisters, mothers, and female friends who are athletes, while not famous, also serve as important role models for these future female athletes.

Legislation, the women's movement, the fitness movement, and increased visibility accorded female athletes have done much to expand opportunities for women in sport. However, while opportunities for girls and women in athletics have increased tremendously over the past two decades, whether participation rates will continue to grow for women depends to a great extent on the expanding of opportunities for involvement and the supporting and encouraging of female athletic endeavors. Some factors that may serve to limit participation are financial constraints, resistance both overtly and subtly to compliance with government policies and legislation, a decline in women's coaches, and the continued trivialization of women's sports.[3]

Financial considerations may serve to limit opportunities for participation by girls and women. When school, collegiate, and community athletic programs are threatened with cutbacks, programs for girls and women are most at risk for losing financial support. Because these programs are newer and not as established as similar programs for men and boys, they have had less time to engender administrative and community backing and may not be able to elicit sufficient support to survive cutbacks. Participation opportunities for females also may be adversely affected because the establishment and development of new programs generally requires greater financial support and resources than do established programs. Because many programs for females are new or in the process of development, successful growth of these programs requires financial commitment. Yet, despite the need, programs for females tend to be funded at lower levels than programs for males. This lack of funding hampers program growth and adversely affects opportunities for participation and quality competition.

In spite of the passage of Title IX and improve-

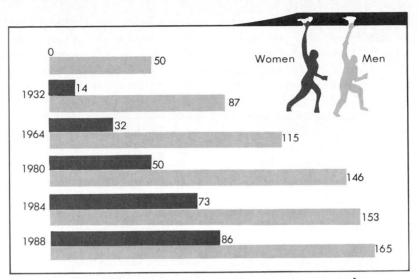

FIGURE 8-2 *Number of Summer Olympic events open to women and to men.*

ments in opportunities, sex discrimination is still a feature of many athletic programs. When new laws are passed, there is often resistance to them as well as questions as to how they will be implemented. Additionally, people tend to be reluctant to change the status quo. Individuals with a vested interest in maintaining the status quo may use their power and control of financial resources to thwart the progress of women's programs. Women across the nation at all levels of competition are still denied fair treatment. Such discrimination can be blatant and noticeable, such as the refusal to fund a program, but lack of equality often occurs in less noticeable forms, such as the provision of quality equipment, supplies, and uniforms; the assignment of games and practice time; the use of facilities and locker rooms; the allocation of equal funds for travel and the availability of travel opportunities; the access to quality coaches, size of coaching staff, and compensation of coaches; the opportunity to receive support services such as academic tutoring; the administration of medical and training services; and the publicity accorded to individual athletes and the team. Despite prohibitions by Title IX against discrimination, women still do not receive equitable treatment in sport. Furthermore, violations of Title IX are often not prosecuted vigorously.

Commitment, time, and effort are needed to ensure compliance with the law and that the spirit of the law becomes an integral part of athletic programs at all levels.

Discrimination is also noticeable in sports outside the school setting. At the international level, for example, where efforts to bring about changes have not been supported by legislation, women typically have fewer events in which to participate and are less likely to be rewarded for their efforts than men. Even though changes have occurred during the past two decades, women are still underrepresented in international sport. In the summer Olympic games (see Figure 8-2), women have fewer events than men and fewer participants (only 25.8% of the participants in the 1988 Seoul Olympics were women).[3] Moreover, the male-dominated International Olympic Committee (IOC) is slow to approve additional events for women. The IOC did not approve the 1500 meter run (the metric mile) until the 1972 Games in Munich and the marathon until the 1984 Games in Los Angeles, despite the fact that women have been running these events for years.

Today there are fewer female coaches for women's sports than in the years following the passage of Title IX. Despite the fact that women's sport programs have increased, the proportion of women in coaching and athletic administrative positions has declined. For example, at the intercollegiate level, Acosta and Carpenter[17] reported that the proportion of female coaches of women's sport programs decreased from 90% in 1970 to 58% in 1978 to 48% in 1988. Reasons for the underrepresentation of women in these positions have been debated widely and the results of the research is confusing. However, one reason that is frequently cited is the lack of well qualified women coaches and administrators. Recently, several programs have been implemented in the United States in an effort to recruit and train more women coaches. It is also important to note that the lack of visibility of women coaches and administrators within the sport structure provides few role models for females who aspire to careers in these areas.

Although women's participation in sport has increased dramatically during the last 20 years, the accomplishments of female athletes are often trivialized and ridiculed by both men and women. For example, women often have to suffer with team names and mascots that belittle physical competence and minimize the achievement of female athletes. To illustrate, at one university the men's teams are referred to as the Bears and the women's teams as the Teddy Bears; other examples are the Blue Hawks and Blue Chicks, the Rams and Rambelles, and the Tigers and the Tigerettes. Were the men's and women's teams at your high school or college referred to by different nicknames? If so, what messages do these names send to the public about the abilities of the athletes and the seriousness of their endeavors?

The media also tends to downplay the competence of female athletes and reinforces traditional, limiting definitions of gender. Male sport announcers often focus on women's physical attractiveness while directing less attention to their athletic accomplishments.[9] Analysis of the covers of *Sports Illustrated* (the most widely circulated sports magazine in the world) for the last 35 years reveals that only eight women, compared with 173 men, have been featured on three or more covers.[18] Three of these eight women "athletes" were models Cheryl Tiegs, Christie Brinkley, and Elle McPherson—frequently used as part of the magazine's annual swimsuit issue. The five women athletes that appeared were Chris Evert, Martina Navratilova, Mary Decker Slaney, Tracy Austin, and Florence Griffith-Joyner. While the media has increased its coverage of women's athletics at all levels, a greater effort is needed to highlight the accomplishments of women athletes.

Other factors that have contributed to the inequities experienced by women in sport are myths about the consequences of athletic participation and the physical, social, and psychological characteristics of women. Examples of these myths include the belief that strenuous participation in sport can lead to problems in childbearing (it has been shown that athletes who are in excellent physical condition have shorter and easier deliveries and experience fewer problems such as backache after the birth of a child) and the belief that the fragile bone structure of women makes them more likely to experience injuries than men (when both men and women athletes experience similar training regimens and care and practice under the leadership of qualified coaches, injury rates are similar for both sexes in any given sport). Other myths perpetuate the belief that participating in sports can threaten one's femininity (women athletes typically do not see their involvement as a threat to their image). Although research and education have done much to dispel these myths, they still persist and serve to needlessly limit participation by women.

Events of the past two decades have served to increase opportunities for participation by women in sport at all levels. Federal legislation, the women's movement, the fitness movement, and increased visibility and recognition of the achievements of women athletes have helped females of all ages to benefit from opportunities to participate in sports. However, while progress has been made, continued increases in participation by women will depend on eliminating barriers to involvement such as financial constraints, less than full compliance with Title IX, lack of women coaches and administrators, minimization of women's accomplishments,

As college football teams changed their offensive strategies so quarterbacks became more like running backs, more blacks were recruited for the position. In the University of Oklahoma's wishbone offense, the qualities of a good quarterback fit with the traditional stereotypes of the abilities of black athletes.

and unfounded beliefs or myths. Qualified and committed leadership is needed to change the structure of sport programs in order to reduce inequities and to further eliminate barriers to participation so that all individuals, regardless of sex, can enjoy the benefits of sport.

Minorities in Sport

Sport is often extolled as an avenue by which to transcend differences in race and cultural back-

grounds. It has been said, for example, that "sport is color blind"—that on the playing field a person is recognized for ability alone and rewards are given without regard to race and class. The widely televised performances of black and Hispanic male athletes in such sports as baseball, basketball, track and field, boxing and football suggest to millions of viewers that sport is relatively free of the prejudice and the discrimination often found in other areas of society. Despite a commonly held belief that sport allows individuals to accept one another on the basis of their physical competence, close scrutiny of the sport phenomena reveals that sport organizations are typically characterized by the same patterns of prejudice and discrimination found in the surrounding society.

Historically, sport in the United States has been characterized by racism and prejudice. While blacks and other minorities have a rich history of sport participation, prior to the 1950s minorities were rarely given access to mainstream sport competition in the professional leagues, colleges and universities, and schools. Members of minorities organized their own leagues and competed within them; for example, blacks had their own basketball and baseball leagues. The integration of professional sport did not occur until 1946 when Jackie Robinson "broke the color barrier" by playing for the then Brooklyn Dodgers. Integration of intercollegiate sports occurred later and was particularly slow to occur in the South. The U.S. Supreme Court's decision in *Brown v. Board of Education* in 1954 as well as the civil rights movement of the 1970s slowly led to the integration of schools and the opening of doors to sports for minorities.

In the 1990s, the participation of black athletes is concentrated in a few sports. Black athletes are overrepresented in certain sports such as football, basketball, and baseball. These sports typically require no expensive equipment or training, have coaches readily available through the public schools, and offer visible role models to aspiring athletes. Black athletes are underrepresented in such sports as volleyball, swimming, gymnastics, soccer, golf, and tennis. The expenses increasingly required for many of these sports, such as private lessons and elite coaching, expensive equipment, funds for travel, and club memberships, as well as the virtual lack of role models in these sports, discourages minority participation. Participation by black women has been very limited and accomplishments of black women athletes are typically accorded little attention. Furthermore, black men and women are seriously underrepresented in coaching and managerial positions in all sports.

These patterns of representation reflect forms of discrimination.

Discrimination is also reflected in the pattern of positions played by black athletes in certain team sports. In some sports, such as baseball, football, and women's volleyball, where teams are racially and ethnically mixed, players are stereotyped by position. Players from certain racial or ethnic groups are disproportionately represented at certain positions in a phenomenon known as *stacking*. For example, in professional baseball, black players are most heavily concentrated in the outfield positions, whereas white players are concentrated at the positions of pitcher, catcher, and the infield, although less so at first base (see Figure 8-3). Whites are disproportionately represented in positions requiring leadership, dependability and decision-making skills, while black players are overrepresented in positions requiring speed, agility, and quick reactions.[3] In women's intercollegiate volleyball, blacks are disproportionately represented at spiker while whites are overrepresented at setter and bumper.[3] Stacking patterns are widespread and occur in other sports and in countries throughout the world (for example, in British soccer, black West Indians and Africans are overrepresented in the wide forward position while white players are overrepresented at the goalie and midfielder position).[3] Stacking reflects stereotypical beliefs about different racial and ethnic groups, for example, that blacks are better jumpers while whites are better leaders. Although stacking is one of the most studied topics in sociology of sport, there are serious disagreements about why stacking patterns exist. But even though a consensus is lacking about the causes of stacking, it is important to recognize that stacking perpetuates patterns of prejudice and discrimination in sport.

Increasing recognition has been given to the problems confronting black and other minority athletes in collegiate sports. Among problems frequently cited are disparity in treatment by coaches, pressures to sacrifice educational goals for athletic goals, difficulty in overcoming an educational background that ill-prepared them for college, social iso-

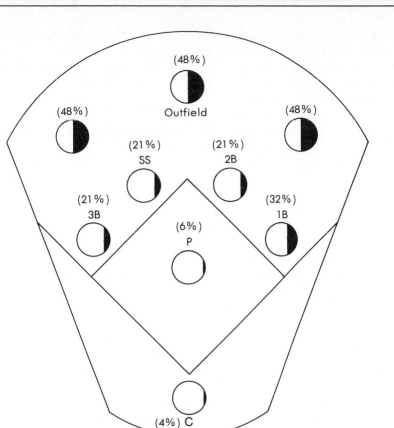

FIGURE 8-3 *This illustration portrays the phenomena of stacking. The percentage of black players in each baseball position during the 1988 major league baseball season is represented by the shaded areas. Blacks are concentrated at outfield positions and first base, positions defined as requiring speed and quick physical reactions. Whites are overrepresented at infield positions and at pitcher and catcher, positions defined as requiring quick reactions, dependability, and leadership.*

lation, and prejudicial attitudes held by coaches and teammates. Although desegregation has opened doors, it has not eliminated prejudice and discrimination.

Native Americans have long participated in sports, often uniting physical activities with cultural rituals and ceremonies.[19] Although many native Americans have achieved success in sports, little recognition has been given to their accomplishments. Public acclaim most often has focused on the few native Americans, such as Jim Thorpe, who were outstanding athletes on segregated government-sponsored reservation school football and baseball teams. On the whole, participation by native Americans in most sports has been and continues to be limited.

Poverty, poor health, lack of equipment, and a dearth of programs are factors that often serve to limit native American sport participation. Concern about loss of cultural identity, prejudice, lack of understanding, and insensitivity by others toward native Americans act in concert with the other factors previously mentioned to curb sport involvement.

One example of this lack of sensitivity is the use of school names and mascots that perpetuate the white stereotypes of native Americans. Team names such as "Indians" or "Redskins" or a team mascot dressed up as a savage running around waving a tomahawk threatening to behead an opponent reflect distorted beliefs of native Americans. Such inappropriate or distorted caricatures of native Americans who, as school mascots, are painted on gymnasium walls and floors, do little to increase student and public awareness of the richness and diversity of native American culture. It is even more ironic that this occurs in institutions that by definition exist to educate people about the different cultures within the world in which they live. These stereotypes are often accepted as valid depictions of native people and serve to demean the cultural heritage and history of native Americans.

Concerned American Indian Parents is a group committed to the elimination of native American stereotypes in advertising and sport. The poster in Figure 8-4 is one example of this group's efforts to heighten public awareness of the racism experienced by native Americans that has become an accepted aspect of sport in the United States. As Coakley[3] writes:

The use of the name Redskins cannot be justified under any conditions. To many native Americans, redskin is as derogatory as "nigger" is for black Americans. It is symbolic of such racism that the capitol city of the government that once put bounties on the lives of native peoples has a football team named the Redskins. It symbolizes a continuing lack of understanding of the complex and diverse cultures and the heritage of native peoples and is offensive to anyone aware of the history of native peoples in North America.

Attitudes change slowly. This is particularly true concerning prejudicial beliefs about different race and ethnic groups. Can sport be used to break down prejudices? Although sport can provide a means to break down prejudices, changes in attitudes do not occur automatically nor as often as is believed. Racial and ethnic prejudices are especially resistant to change. Dedicated and sensitive leadership on behalf of coaches and athletic administra-

tors and thoughtful efforts can help change people's prejudices. Minority athletes—regardless of sex, sport, or level of competition—should be treated fairly and equally.

Sport for Individuals with Disabilities

Disabled athletes, like girls and women, had limited opportunities for participation in athletics prior to the 1970s. Changing societal attitudes, the use of sport for rehabilitation, and federal legislation contributed to the growth of competitive sport opportunities for the disabled. Professional organizations such as AAHPERD advocated participation for all individuals including the disabled in physical education and athletics.

An estimated 28 million people 3 years of age or older have serious limitations affecting their performance of physical activities. About 3.5 million of these persons are school aged. Federal legislation has had a significant impact on the schooling of disabled individuals. P.L. 94-142, Education for All Handicapped Children Act, mandated a free and appropriate education in the least restrictive environment for disabled students. Provision for instruction in physical education was specifically mentioned in this law. The Rehabilitation Act, specifically Section 504 of P.L. 93-112, stated that disabled students must have equal opportunity and access to extracurricular activities including intramurals and athletics. The Amateur Sports Act of 1978, P.L. 95-606, called for the United States Olympic Committee (USOC) to assist amateur athletic programs for the disabled and, where feasible, expand the opportunities for meaningful participation by disabled athletes in competitions for able-bodied athletes.

In addition to federal legislation participation was encouraged by changing societal attitudes. A change was seen toward a more humanistic educational philosophy and a recognition by society of the rights of the disabled. Society's acceptance of individual differences and understanding of the capabilities of individuals with disabilities grew. These factors contributed to the mainstreaming of disabled individuals into society.

Changes occurred slowly. Orr[20] believes that the

FIGURE 8-4 *Poster developed by Concerned American Indian Parents to increase the public's awareness of racism toward Native Americans.*

reluctance of school personnel to provide sport opportunities for disabled persons results from myth, superstition, and sport control. In elaborating on the myth surrounding the handicapped athlete, Orr writes:

The imposed myth is that the handicapped person participating in sports is inferior and different from the so-called 'normal' athlete. The reality is that while the handicapped person usually does not have equal marks in performance of a quantitative nature, the qualitative performance may equal or surpass any other athlete. The effect of the myth has been to obstruct opportunity for the handicapped as time, energy, and funds have been funneled in other directions.

Participation on interscholastic and intercollegiate teams by the individuals with disabilities has been slow to increase. However, in recent years regional, national, and international competitions for individuals with disabilities have flourished. One of the most visible competitions has been the Special Olympics. The Special Olympics are sponsored by the Joseph P. Kennedy, Jr., Foundation. This foundation has focused more attention on sport for disabled persons than any other single organization or legislation.

The Special Olympics were organized in 1968. They were designed to provide mentally retarded youths 8 years of age and over with opportunities to participate in a variety of sport and games on local, state, regional, national, and international levels. Thousands of people volunteer to coach mentally retarded youngsters in Special Olympic events such as track and field, swimming, gymnastics, floor hockey, and volleyball. The volunteers include professional athletes in many areas of sport.

As a consequence of the Amateur Sports Act a Committee of Sports for the Disabled was established as part of the USOC.[21] Some of the committee's responsibilities included promoting sport for disabled individuals; conducting research and disseminating information on various aspects of competition such as sports medicine, equipment design, and performance analysis; and publicizing the accomplishments of disabled athletes. Seven major amateur sport organizations for the disabled were

In the past decade, sport opportunities for athletes with disabilities have increased. (Courtesy H. Armstrong Roberts)

recognized. One of the criteria for recognition as a major sport organization was that the organization had to offer national competition in two or more sports that are included in the program of the Olympic or the Pan American Games. These organizations are The National Association of Sports for Cerebral Palsy, American Athletic Association for the Deaf, National Handicapped Sports and Recreation Association, The National Wheelchair Athletic Association, United States Amputee Association, United States Association for Blind Athletes, and Special Olympics.

Although sport opportunities are being provided for many disabled youths the need is urgent to establish and conduct more sport programs if the sport needs of all individuals with disabilities are to be met. It is also necessary to encourage disabled athletes to participate with able-bodied athletes when feasible.

Sport for Children and Youth

For many Americans, participation in youth sport activities is an integral part of growing up. It is estimated that over 35 million boys and girls participate each year in youth sports, that is, organized sport activities that take place outside the school setting.[22] Furthermore, it is estimated that over 3 million volunteer coaches are involved with these programs. Youth sport ventures are organized around such sports as football, baseball, softball, tennis, ice hockey, golf, gymnastics, soccer, and swimming.[22] An increasing number of opportunities for girls to participate in these programs at all levels are being offered, and it appears that many children are beginning to compete in these programs at younger ages than ever before.

While participation in youth sports has grown tremendously over the past decade, there is widespread concern about the nature and outcomes associated with these programs. Even though these programs are extremely popular, considerable criticism is voiced about the manner in which they are conducted. As you read about the benefits, harmful effects, and criticisms of youth sport programs, it may be helpful to keep in mind your own experiences and those of your friends in youth sport. Consider the following questions:

- What did you like most and least about your experiences?
- What did you learn from participating in youth sports?
- How did your parents influence your participation and what was the extent of their involvement with the program?
- How would you characterize the nature and effectiveness of the coaching you received or observed?
- How did you, your teammates, parents, and coaches respond to your successes and failures?
- At what age did you discontinue your participation in youth sports and what were the reasons for stopping?
- What changes would you make in the organization of the program to make the experience a more positive one for all involved?

Like school sports, many benefits have been ascribed to participation in youth sport programs. Proponents of youth sports emphasize that they promote physical fitness, emotional development, social adjustment, a competitive attitude, and self-confidence. In addition, youth sport programs provide opportunities for the development of physical skills, encourage the achievement of a greater level of skill, give children additional opportunities to play, and offer a safer experience than participation in unsupervised programs.

Again, as with school sports, one of the greatest criticisms of youth sports is its overemphasis on winning. Critics also voice concerns that children's bodies may be underdeveloped for such vigorous activities, that there is too great an emotional strain and pressure on the participant, and that the players are too psychologically immature to compete in such a setting. Youth sport programs are cited as being too selective and excluding too many children who would like to participate and as promoting specialization at too early an age. Additional criticisms are directed toward overenthusiastic coaches and parents who take winning too seriously, who pressure children to achieve, and who place their needs before the needs of the child.

Overemphasis on winning has led to many of the abuses found within youth sport programs. The desire to win has led coaches to employ such behaviors as conniving to get the best players in the league on their team, holding lengthy practice sessions and endless drills to perfect skills, and berating children for their mistakes. Many physical education and sport professionals decry the overemphasis on winning. They believe that youth sport programs should be developmental in nature, that is, they should be organized and conducted in such a way as to enhance the physical, cognitive, and affective development of each child and youth participant. This development is particularly critical during the child's younger years. The fun of playing (rather than the beating of an opponent) should be stressed, participation opportunities for many children of all abilities should be provided (rather than limiting participation to the gifted few), and the development of skills within the sport and in other sports should be stressed (rather than specialization).

Specialization is another frequently voiced concern. During their early years, children should be given an opportunity to develop proficiency in fundamental motor skills and be exposed to a variety of sports. Some children are guided at an early age into a specific sport such as soccer or into a specific position within a sport such as a pitcher. This early specialization deprives children of an opportunity to develop an interest and skills in a variety of sports. Concern about specialization has further increased within the last decade. During this time there has been a growth of private sport leagues and clubs that emphasize the development of skills in a particular sport. This often leads to beginning high level sport instruction and competition at an early age; children may begin as early as 3 years of age in such sports as swimming, gymnastics, skating, and soccer.[9] Training is serious and often occurs on a year-round basis. Physically, children may be at risk for the development of overuse injuries because they are often involved in practicing on a daily basis for several hours at a time. Psychologically, these participants may experience burnout from doing the same thing year after year. They may drop out before reaching their optimal level of performance, even after many years of successful participation.

Some professionals in the field of physical education and sport take the position that competitive sport for youth is not inherently bad or good. Instead, they point out that sport is what one makes it. Under sound leadership, if the welfare of the child is the primary consideration, if the environment is warm and supportive, and if the sport is administered in light of the needs and characteristics of the participants, much good can be accomplished. However, if poor leadership is provided, harmful effects will accrue.

Many recommendations have been set forth by professionals to improve youth sports. Professionals suggest that programs be structured so that children can experience success and satisfaction while continuing to develop their abilities. This may mean modification of the rules, equipment, and playing area to promote success and participation rather than failure and elimination. For example, simplified and fewer rules, smaller balls, smaller fields, bigger goals, batting tees rather than pitchers, rule

changes to facilitate scoring, and a requirement of equal playing time for all participants are some of the ways that youth sports programs can be changed to make the experiences more positive for all participants.

Programs should be structured to include elements that children find enjoyable within their own informal games. Plenty of action, opportunity for involvement, close scores to keep the game exciting and interesting, and friendship are important to children; these elements should be infused into youth sport programming.[5] Children also should be given opportunities to be involved in decision making, such as deciding what strategies to use or planning a practice session. They can also be given the responsibility for self-enforcement of rules during the game.

As previously mentioned, the quality of leadership can exert a significant influence on the outcomes children derive from participating in youth sports. Coaches within the youth sport programs are typically volunteers, often parents, who have received little if any training on how to coach children. Recognizing this, there has been increased attention by professionals within the field directed toward the development of coaching education programs. These programs emphasize understanding the growth characteristics and developmental needs of children, modifying existing programs to meet these needs, incorporating proper training techniques into the design of the program, and supporting the efforts of children while providing developmentally appropriate opportunities to help them become better players. Enhancing children's self-esteem, recognizing their accomplishments, and praising their efforts are more appropriate than ridiculing, shaming, and belittling their achievements and attempts.

Under qualified leadership, many of the problems associated with youth sport programs can be rectified. Implementation of these recommendations can maximize the positive experiences and minimize the negative experiences of the youth sport participants. The key to successful youth sport programs is putting the needs of the child first. Programs should be designed to meet the children's

Too often our attention is focused on the action in the game when the important messages are coming from the bench or the dugout.

needs, not those of adults. Youth sport programs should be organized on a developmental model, not a professional model. Programs should focus on fostering children's physical as well as cognitive and affective development. The whole child as a moving, thinking, feeling human being should be considered when designing and conducting youth sport programs.

International Sport: the Olympics

Opportunities for elite nonprofessional athletes to compete in international events are numerous. International championships are contested annually in many sports and special competitions such as the Pan-American Games and the Asian Games that are held every 4 years. College and university students have the opportunity to compete in the World University Games that are conducted every 2 years. The opportunity to compete in these special international competitions is highly regarded, but the most prestigious of the international competitive events is the Olympic Games.

Since the rebirth of the Games in 1896 and the addition of the Winter Games in 1924, competitions for athletes from around the world have been held every 4 years under the direction of the International Olympic Committee (IOC). Many people still ascribe to the beliefs that the Olympics offer athletes an opportunity to extend their limits in a quest to achieve excellence by the accomplishment of personal athletic goals, to establish friendships with other competitors around the world, and to foster international understanding and peace by bringing together the nations of the world.

While these Olympic ideals are highly valued by many people throughout the world, there are many problems that prevent the attainment of these lofty goals. The Olympics have been used by many countries to further political goals. Examples of this include the use of the 1936 Olympic Games by Hitler and the Nazis to highlight Aryan supremacy, the terrorist shootings at the 1972 Munich Games to capture world attention, and the boycotts of the 1976, 1980, and 1984 Olympic Games to make political statements and to influence world opinion. The extent to which the Olympics have been used to promote vested national issues is so widely recog-

nized and accepted that Peter Ueberroth, president of the 1984 Los Angeles Olympic Organizing Committee, said that "we have to accept the reality that the Olympics constitute not only an athletic event but a political event."[5] Worldwide media coverage has intensified the politicization of the Olympics.

Nationalism also undermines the goal of international unity. Athletes march into the arena during the opening ceremonies under their nation's flag, compete as representatives of their nation, and stand proudly during award ceremonies as their national anthem is played. Team sports and national uniforms promote an "us versus them" attitude, judging biases occur in favor of political allies, and up-to-the-minute national medal counts by the media all serve to reinforce nationalism.

Governments recognize the political importance of the Olympics. As the United States traditional dominance of the Games became lessened and the successes of subsidized athletes from other nations such as East Germany and the U.S.S.R. grew, the U.S. government intervened and amateur sport was restructured. In 1978, Congress passed the Amateur Sports Act. Following its passage, the United States Olympic Committee (USOC) established the United States Olympic Training Center at Colorado Springs, Colorado. The national governing bodies for each Olympic sport were offered the use of training sites and resources to promote the development of athletes. Increasingly, funding is given to athletes by their sport governing bodies to assist them in defraying some of the expenses associated with training. For older athletes, receiving funds to help meet daily living expenses allows them to continue to train without the additional pressures and burdens of holding a full-time job to make ends meet.

The Olympic Games have become increasingly commercialized. In 1968, the Mexico Olympic Games cost $250 million to stage, while the 1980 Moscow Games cost $2.25 billion. Critics have questioned the high cost of the Games, especially in countries where planning and constructing facilities for the Olympic Games places a financial burden on its citizens and deprives them of resources that could be used to enhance their quality of life. The cost of securing television broadcasting rights has also escalated. In 1960 CBS paid $660,000 for broadcast rights; it cost NBC $401 million to secure television rights for the 1992 Games.

The Olympic Games were founded for amateur athletes, those individuals who compete for the love of sport. Defining amateurism and dealing with questions pertaining to participant eligibility have presented a significant problem for the IOC. As we move into the 1990s, the Olympics are becoming more of an open competition. Nonprofessional athletes are allowed, under certain conditions, to receive money, and professional athletes in such sports as tennis and basketball will be allowed to compete.

Many suggestions have been formulated to restructure the Olympics to attain the goals listed in the Olympic Charter.[5,8] Many people advocate the selection of a permanent neutral site in order to reduce the enormous costs associated with conducting the Games. Others believe that multiple sites should be used for each Olympics and events split between them to ease the economic costs associated with the games, permit more countries to host the Games, and allow participants and spectators to see more countries. Many advocate reducing nationalism and taking steps to promote internationalism. Some suggestions include abolishing national uniforms, revising opening ceremonies to allow athletes to march with athletes of other countries under the Olympic flag, replacing the national anthems and flags featured in award ceremonies with the Olympic anthem and flag, and either eliminating team sports or restructuring them so that players from different countries can play on the same team.

The Olympics offers participants from around the world the opportunity to attain athletic excellence and to develop international understanding. These goals can be accomplished when the Olympics are structured to achieve these noble goals.

Amateur Sport

An increasing number of individuals are finding challenging and personally satisfying sport experiences through participation in amateur sports. Each year millions of boys and girls participate in sport competitions organized under the auspices of such amateur sport organizations as the Amateur Athletic Union (AAU). For some AAU sport participants, one highlight is the opportunity to compete in the AAU/USA Junior Olympics where Olympic-style competitions are held in 22 sports. Youths who participate in these games have the opportunity to travel, make new friends, experience the excitement and thrill of competition, test their skills against a high level of competition, and be recognized for their achievements.

Many states, in response to an interest in amateur sport competition, are holding such Olympic-style state games. New York state's Empire State Games are the oldest, having started in 1977, and their $1.6 million budget is the largest. Other state games include the Badger State Games (Wisconsin), Cornhusker State Games (Nebraska), Garden State Games (New Jersey), and the Sunshine State Games (Florida). Texas, California, and Connecticut are anticipating starting state games in the near future. These state games attract amateur athletes of all ages and abilities. Some states have organized their games into divisions for youths up to college age, open divisions for college-age participants and adults up to age 35, and various masters divisions for those 35 and older, and divisions for disabled athletes. New York state added the Winter Games in 1981. A diversity of sports is offered. For example, 50 types of sports comprise the Garden State Games.

In many state games protocol similar to the Olympics is followed. During the opening ceremonies competitors may march in and participate in a torch lighting ceremony symbolizing the opening of the games. In a manner similar to the Olympic Village athletes from across the state are housed and fed together in college facilities. Medal ceremonies recognize the achievements of the games participants. Monetary support for the games may come from state funds or from commercial sponsors. The state game movement has drawn support from the United States Olympic Committee and the President's Council on Physical Fitness and Sports. These games offer athletes within the state the opportunity to compete against

The Junior Olympics provides amateur athletes with opportunities to compete with other athletes throughout the country.

each other and it broadens the base of amateur sport. It provides the opportunity to thousands of amateur athletes to experience the positive aspects of amateur sport competition.

Another example of the growth of amateur athletics is the National Sports Festival. The sport festival provides opportunities for amateur athletes from across the nation to compete against each other as well as develop friendships and wholesome rivalries. Several Olympic athletes have participated in both state games and the National Sports Festival. In 1986 the name was changed to the U.S. Olympic Festival.

The amateur athletic movement is not limited to the young, however. The Senior Games and master's competitions in various types of sport such as track and field and swimming promote participation in sport throughout one's lifetime.

Violence

Violence is one of the major problems facing sport today. The newspapers give glowing accounts, and movie and television shows depict it in vivid color. Incidences of violence are increasing among players as well as spectators. Violence is particularly noticeable in contact sports such as football and hockey. Fist fights occur periodically; whiskey bottles and beer cans are thrown out on the fields; fans are ejected from the stands; criminal charges have been brought against players. As Thomas Tutko, a psychologist at San Jose State University has said, "Too often athletics have become a direct substitute for war." A Harvard psychiatrist points out that in football "the coach must have his players feeling they not only can kill but they should kill."

Some experts suggest professionals in sport have become the model for such behavior and amateur athletes have followed their example. Then high school athletes in turn adopt similar attitudes. Other persons say that fighting and other examples of violence occur during the heat of the game and are a natural outlet when a player's adrenaline is flowing.

The question of how to deal with the problem of

violence in sport has no single solution. General agreement exists, however, that some type of control must be instituted and much of this control must start with persons who love sport and want to protect it from intrusions that will lower its value. They point out that violence is to be abhorred, particularly because it interferes with proper play, detracts from excellent player performance, and is barbaric in nature. Most spectators, it is suggested, do not want to see players hurt or crippled. They want to see clean, hard tackles and hard body checks. This is the essence of the game and sport itself.

Tutko suggests that to reduce violence the entire penalty structure of sport should be restructured. For example, if a quarterback in football is knocked out, the team responsible should also be forced to complete the game using a second string quarterback. In baseball, if a bean ball is thrown by a pitcher, the batter should be given as many as three bases as a penalty.

The real and best solution, however, to the problem of violence is a change in attitude on the part of all persons concerned. The ideals of playing within the spirit as well as the letter of the rules, defeating one's opponent when at one's best, and having respect for the other player will, if subscribed to by professional and amateur players, coaches, spectators, sport entrepreneurs, and the public in general, eradicate violence from the playing fields and sport arenas of the United States.

SUMMARY

Sport has become an important part of American culture. Sport pervades society to such an extent that it has been described as a microcosm of society. The pervasiveness of sport in our society has led to the study of it from a sociological perspective.

Sociology of sport focuses on the study of sport as an institution, the effects of sport on its participants, and the relationship of sport to other societal institutions. Sport may be described or studied from many levels of analysis: sport as a game occurrence, sport as an institutionalized game, sport as an institution, and sport as a social situation.

The growth of sport in schools and colleges in the United States has been comparatively recent. Since athletics play such an important role in educational institutions, it is interesting to examine their influence. Athletics can have positive or harmful effects on its participants.

Several problems are pressing in American sport today. The opportunities for girls, women, and disabled individuals in sport; the minority athlete; amateurism and the Olympics; and youth sport are some of the concerns of professionals.

It is important that every physical educator have a philosophy of sport. This will help give direction to the sport program and ensure that the desired goals are achieved.

SELF-ASSESSMENT TESTS

These tests are designed to assist students in determining if the materials and competencies presented in this chapter have been mastered.

1. Discuss how sport is a socializing force in American culture.

2. Define the nature and the scope of sport.

3. Trace the growth of sport in educational institutions in the United States. Then discuss this statement: "Sport in educational institutions was initiated at the college level and then expanded downward into the high school, junior high school, and elementary school levels."

4. Discuss the sociological implications of educational sport. What are the benefits and possible harms from participating in educational sport?

5. Discuss each of the following statements:

a. Title IX has resulted in an expansion in girls' and women's sport, but this expansion has created many problems.

b. Federal legislation has resulted in the growth of sporting opportunities for the disabled, but this growth has created many problems.

c. Elementary school children should not engage in highly competitive sport.

d. The Olympic Games should be abolished.

e. Violence is becoming a part of competition in sport.

6. Formulate a philosophy of sport that will clarify the worth of athletics and give direction for conducting it so that it will make the greatest contribution to humankind.

REFERENCES

1. Coakley J: Sport in society: issues and controversies, ed 3, St Louis, 1986, Times Mirror/Mosby.

2. Eitzen DS and Sage GH: Sociology of American sport, Dubuque, Iowa, 1982, William C Brown Co.

3. Coakley J: Sport in society: issues and controversies, ed 4, St Louis, 1990, Times Mirror/Mosby.

4. Wilkerson M and Dodder RA: What sport does for people, Journal of Physical Education, Recreation, and Dance 50(2):50-51, 1979.

5. Coakley J: Sport in society: issues and controversies, ed 2, St Louis, 1982, Times Mirror/Mosby.

6. National Federation of State High School Associations, January, 1990 (personal communication).

7. National Collegiate Athletic Association, January, 1990 personal communication.

8. Lumpkin A: Physical education and sport: A contemporary introduction, ed 2, St Louis, 1990, Times Mirror/Mosby.

9. Siedentop D: Introduction to physical education, fitness, and sport, Mountain View, Calif, 1990, Mayfield.

10. Eitzen DS: The educational experience of intercollegiate student-athletes, Journal of Sport and Social Issues 11(1,2):15-30, 1987.

11. Meyer BB: From idealism to actualization: the academic performance of female collegiate athletes, Sociology of Sport Journal 7(1):44-57, 1990.

12. Sack A: College sport and the student-athlete, Journal of Sport and Social Issues 11(1,2):31-48, 1987.

13. Lapchick R: The high school athlete as the future college student, Journal of Sport and Social Issues 11(1,2):104-124, 1987.

14. Michner JA: Sports in American society, New York, 1986, Random House.

15. Leonard WM: A sociological perspective of sport, Minneapolis, 1984, Burgess.

16. Allison MT and Butler B: Role conflict and the elite female athlete: empirical findings and conceptual dilemmas, International Review of Sociology of Sport 19(2):194-201, 1984.

17. Acosta RV and Carpenter LJ: Women in intercollegiate sport: a status report, Journal of Physical Education, Recreation, and Dance 56(6):30-37, 1985.

18. Short Shots, Women & Sport 3(2):2, 1990.

19. Oxedine JB: American Indian sports heritage, Champaign, Ill, 1988, Human Kinetics.

20. Orr RE: Sport, myth, and the handicapped athlete, Journal of Physical Education and Recreation 55(2):34-46, 1979.

21. DePauw KP: Commitment and challenges: sport opportunities for athletes with disabilities, Journal of Physical Education, Recreation, and Dance 55(20):34-46, 1984.

22. Martens R: Youth sport in the USA. In Weiss M and Gould D, editors: Sport for Children and Youth, Champaign, Ill, 1986, Human Kinetics.

SUGGESTED READINGS

Ashe AR Jr: A hard road to glory: a history of the African American athlete, New York, 1988, Warner Books.
> The involvement of African Americans in sports from 1619 to 1988 is chronicled.

Birrell S: Discourses on the gender/sport relationship: from women in sport to gender relations, Exercise and Sport Science Review, 16, 1988.
> Provides a comprehensive overview of recent literature on women and sport.

Coakley JJ: Sport in society: issues and controversies, St Louis, 1990, Times Mirror/Mosby.
> The text provides a critical analysis of many of the issues and controversies pertaining to sport.

Greendorfer SL: Psycho-social correlates of organized physical activity, Journal of Physical Education, Recreation, and Dance 58(7):59-64, 1987.
> Outcomes that accrue from participation in play, games, and sport activities are discussed.

Guttmann A: A whole new ball game: an interpretation of American sports, Chapel Hill, NC, 1988, University of North Carolina Press.
> This text provides insight as to the role of sport throughout American history.

Klatell DA and Marcus N: Sports for sale: television, money, and the fans, New York, 1988, Oxford University Press.
> Various issues pertaining to the relationship between sport and television are explored.

Orlick T: Winning through cooperation, Washington, DC, 1978, Acropolis Books, Ltd.
> Specific suggestions as to how cooperation may be incorporated into the sport experience are presented.

Oxedine JB: American Indian sports heritage, Champaign, Ill, 1988, Human Kinetics.
> Traces the role of sport in Indian society and the historical and current involvement of American Indians in sport.

Purdy D, editor: Sport and the student athlete, ARENA Review, 11(2), 1987.
> The 12 papers within this issue focus on the various experiences and issues pertaining to student athletes.

Segrave J and Chu D, editors: The Olympic Games in transition, Champaign, Ill, 1988, Human Kinetics.
> The 28 readings that comprise the text offer a critical examination of the philosophy, issues, and future of the Olympic Games.

Spears B and Swanson RA: History of sport and physical education in the United States, Dubuque, Iowa, 1988, William C Brown.
> The growth and development of physical education and sport in the United States is presented.

Todd T: Anabolic steroids: the gremlins of sport, Journal of Sport History, 14(1):87-107, 1987.
> The use of drugs in sport is analyzed from an historical perspective. Anabolic steroids and efforts to regulate their use are also discussed.

Chapter 9

Biomechanical Foundations of Physical Education and Sport

INSTRUCTIONAL OBJECTIVES AND COMPETENCIES TO BE ACHIEVED

After reading this chapter the student should be able to—
- Define the term biomechanics and indicate its relationship to kinesiology.
- Identify the value of biomechanics for the physical educator.
- Understand some of the terminology associated with the subdiscipline of biomechanics.
- Explain the meaning of mechanical principles and concepts that relate to stability, motion, leverage, and force. Illustrate the application of these principles to physical skills and sport techniques.
- Describe some of the techniques used to analyze motion.

Understanding the factors that govern human movement is essential for physical educators. Throughout history individuals have been interested in optimizing their physical performance. During prehistoric times, when survival depended on physical skills, individuals sought to improve their physical prowess to stay alive. Today physical abilities are not as essential to survival. However, the interest in physical fitness and physical activities is at an all-time high in our society, and individuals are interested in enhancing their physical skills.

Physical educators are concerned with helping individuals to learn how to move efficiently and effectively. In elementary physical education classes, the teacher is concerned with helping students learn fundamental motor skills such as throwing and running, which provide a foundation for the learning of more advanced sport skills. In competi-tive athletics, where the difference between winning and losing may be one hundredth of a second or a fraction of a centimeter, a coach may use scientific methods such as high-speed photography and computer simulation to fine-tune an athlete's form. The weekend golfer, seeking to break par, requests the assistance of the golf pro to eliminate a troublesome slice from his or her swing. The golf pro may then videotape the golfer's performance to determine the source of error and to illustrate to the golfer the needed changes. The athletic trainer rehabilitating an athlete recovering from shoulder surgery uses knowledge of the range of motion of this joint to help develop an effective rehabilitation program. The adapted physical educator analyzes the gait of a child with cerebral palsy in order to prescribe physical activities to improve it. The exercise instructor closely monitors a client working on a Nautilus machine to ensure the exercise is being performed properly through the range of motion. These examples show how physical education and sport professionals use the scientific knowledge of human motion from the realms of kinesiology and biomechanics to help individuals move efficiently and effectively.

BIOMECHANICS AND KINESIOLOGY

The study of human movement is the focus of both kinesiology and biomechanics. *Kinesiology* is the scientific study of human motion. The term kinesiology is derived from the Greek *kinesi,* meaning motion. The field of kinesiology is concerned with the anatomical and physiological elements that carry out movements—specifically bones, tissues, muscles, and nerves. To fully understand human motion, knowledge of how body movement occurs or kinesiology is needed.

It should be noted that the term kinesiology is often used in a broad sense to mean the study of human movement from the perspective of both an art and science. In 1989 the prestigious Academy of Physical Education voted to use the term kinesiology as a broad umbrella term to encompass the entire discipline of what has traditionally been called *physical education.* Many colleges and universities in the United States have renamed their physical education department the Department of Kinesiology.

Biomechanics, as a subdiscipline of physical education, focuses on the application of the scientific principles of mechanical physics to understand movements and actions of human bodies and sport implements (e.g., a tennis racquet). The term *biomechanics* can be better understood by examining the derivation of the word. *Bio* is from Greek and refers to life or living things and *mechanics* refers to the field of Newtonian physics and the forces that act on bodies in motion. Biomechanists study how various forces affect human motion and how movements can be improved.

Kinesiology and biomechanics are integrally related. An understanding of how the body moves, including the function and actions of the joints, muscles, and bony structure, is essential to the

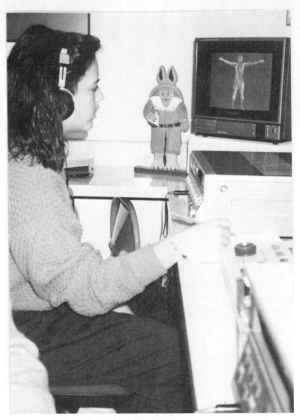

Kinesiology is concerned with the anatomical basis of movement. A student uses a self-paced instructional module to review anatomy.

understanding of biomechanics. In order to effectively study the influences of forces on motion —biomechanics—one must be knowledgeable about the actions of the joints and the muscles that cause these forces; this is the realm of kinesiology. Both kinesiology and biomechanics are fundamental to understanding human movement and to helping individuals attain their fullest potential.

Growth and Use of Biomechanics

The principles of biomechanics can be applied in many fields of study including biology, physiology, engineering, aerospace engineering, physical therapy, and medicine. Some physical education practitioners who would utilize this speciality include athletic trainers, coaches, teachers, and exercise physiologists. Until recently specialization in the study of biomechanics in the United States has been very limited, whereas in other countries this has long been a popular and accepted field of study. For example, Israel, England, Switzerland, East Germany, and Russia have had curriculums for physical education biomechanists for some time. Russia has many specialists in biomechanics and uses this field of study in a manner that has practical application to specific kinds of sport such as volleyball and track and field. In the United States until recently the emphasis has been on theory. In the last few years the emphasis has changed to reflect a more practical approach. For example, biomechanists worked as part of the United States Ski Team to prepare the athletes for competition in the 1984 Winter Olympics.[1] They investigated such things as whether dry land training developed the same muscles as used in actual skiing. Another contribution was an attempt to determine the most efficient body position for the downhill skiers. They used the wind tunnel to determine which position produced the least amount of drag, thus reducing wind resistance and increasing speed. The biomechanists employed high-speed photography to differentiate elite cross-country skiers from their less skilled peers. Through analysis they found that better skiers had longer stride lengths. With this knowledge the coaches were able to design practices to develop the longer stride length, thus improving the performance of the team members. The use of biomechanists to work with national calibre athletes and their coaches has become increasingly common, with the biomechanist becoming an integral part of the coaching staff. Biomechanists today work with various sport teams at the National Training Center in Colorado Springs.

In recent years several international conferences have been held on the subject of biomechanics, thus affording the opportunity for the mutual exchange of research findings and ideas. These meetings have been attended by a variety of specialists including physiologists, engineers, biomechanists, computer specialists, and rehabilitation experts. In the 1970s the International Society of Biomechanics and the American Society of

U.S. Olympic Sports Center / Facilities for 12 sports

Athletic Field at the U.S. Olympic Training Center

The U.S. Olympic Training Center.

Biomechanics were created, thus helping to ensure a further exchange of ideas in the future. The Kinesiology Academy of the National Association for Sport and Physical Education, a subdivision of AAHPERD, also provides a forum for the discussion of both biomechanics and kinesiology. The expansion of the knowledge and growth of interest in the field of sport biomechanics led to the formation of the International Society of Biomechanics in Sport in 1982.

Reasons for Studying Biomechanics

The emergence of biomechanics as a viable subdiscipline of physical education is now recognized. As a result of reading this chapter prospective physical educators will have a better understanding of the parameters of this field of study and will recognize the value it has to them in future careers. In some cases perhaps it will motivate further study and specialization in this field of endeavor.

Many professionals can profit from the study of biomechanics. Physical educators to be effective teachers and masters of their trade should have an understanding of the principles of biomechanics. The knowledge of biomechanics will provide the practitioner with a better understanding of the human body and the various internal and external forces that affect human movement as well as the forces that act on object motion. This in turn will enable physical educators to be better instructors of the many physical activities and skills involved in physical education and sport.

Coaches who want to be expert in their field need a sound foundation in the area of biomechanics. Biomechanics offers important scientific knowledge that can improve performance, and the best coaches are taking advantage of this knowledge. Coaches of athletes today who are involved in many areas of high school, college, and Olympic sport find competition very intense. Therefore, coaches of athletes who wish to excel must use all the knowledge and the best techniques available. Biomechanics can be used to improve sport techniques and equipment, thus enhancing athletes' performance while assuring their safety.

Some other professionals within the field of physical education and sport who use the principles of biomechanics to improve an individual's movements and skill performance are adapted physical educators, athletic trainers, and exercise leaders. Knowledge of kinesiology and biomechanics helps these professionals design and conduct programs to enhance individual movement skills.

Biomechanists are increasingly being employed by sport equipment, shoe, and clothing companies to design, test, and evaluate products. Many improvements in athletic equipment are attributable to the application of biomechanical principles to equipment design. Bigger tennis racquets help players better control the ball, runners' injuries are lessened and performance enhanced because of better designed running shoes, and improved helmets reduce the chances and severity of injury for football and ice hockey players.

Biomechanists have also been involved in the design of clothing, particularly aerodynamic clothing.[2] Aerodynamic clothing and equipment are of great importance to athletes in sports such as skiing, speed skating, bobsledding, and cycling. Because the speeds these athletes attain are so high, wind resistance can adversely affect performance. Wind resistance can be reduced by altering the position of the body (e.g., the egg-shaped form of downhill skiers reduces the effects of wind resistance) and by designing equipment to streamline the body (e.g., the elongated helmets worn by U.S. cyclists in the 1984 Olympic Games). Wearing smooth, tight clothing can also minimize wind resistance. Skiers, sprinters, cyclists, bobsledders, and speed skaters don sleek, skin-tight uniforms because of their potential to reduce drag, improve performance, and gain a competitive advantage.

The application of biomechanical principles is not limited to the realm of physical education and sport. Biomechanists working in industry use this information to ensure safe working conditions and efficient performance from the workers. In medicine, knowledge from biomechanics can be used by orthopedists to evaluate how pathological conditions affect movement or to assess the suitability of prosthetic devices for patients. As the field of biomechanics continues to expand, its contribution to our understanding of human movement will become even more significant.

Major Areas of Study

Biomechanics is concerned with two major areas of study. The first area is biological in nature as implied in the term biomechanics. Motion or movement involves biological aspects of the human body, including the skeletal and muscular systems. For example, movement occurs as a result of such things as force applied to bones, contraction of muscles, and bones acting as levers. Bones, muscles, and nerves work together in producing motion. It is not possible to understand motor skill development without first knowing about biological aspects underlying human movement such as joint action, anatomical structures, and muscular forces.

The second major area of study in biomechanics relates to mechanics. This area of study is important because it utilizes the laws and principles of Newtonian physics and applies them to human motion and movement. Biomechanics is also concerned with object motion. The study of mechanics includes *statics* or the study of factors relating to nonmoving systems or those characterized by steady motion (e.g., the center of gravity in positions of balance). It also includes *dynamics* or the study of mechanical factors that relate to systems in motion. In turn, dynamics can involve a *kinematic* or *kinetic* approach. Kinematics is concerned with the study of time and space factors in motion such as velocity and acceleration, whereas kinetics is involved with the forces that act on a system such as gravity and muscles.

Research in biomechanics is concerned with studying movement and factors that influence performance. The kinds of questions that may be studied are listed below:

- How do running motions change as children develop?
- How do forces summate to produce maximum power in the tennis serve?
- What are the movement patterns of world-class hurdlers?
- How can athletic shoes be designed to reduce injuries on artificial turf?
- What is the wrist action of elite wheelchair marathon athletes?
- What is the optimal design of the javelin?
- What are the critical performance elements of throwing? Of various fundamental motor skills? Of various sport skills? What are the common errors associated with the performance of these skills and how can they best be remediated?
- Which techniques are best for increasing the range of motion after reconstructive surgery of the shoulder?
- What is the best body position for swimming the butterfly stroke?
- Is a specific brand of rowing ergometer safe to use? Can individuals of all fitness levels effectively use this piece of fitness equipment? Are

the benefits claimed by the manufacturer for its use accurate?

These are only a few of many questions that can be addressed through the use of biomechanical research techniques. In answering these questions, researchers measure such factors as joint angles and muscle activity, force production, and linear and angular acceleration. The next section presents selected biomechanical terms.

SELECTED BIOMECHANICAL TERMS RELATING TO HUMAN MOTION

The field of biomechanics has a specialized scientific vocabulary that describes the relationship between force and motion. As previously defined, kinematics is concerned with understanding the spatial and temporal characteristics of human movement, that is, the direction of the motion and the time involved in executing the motion. Important terms related to kinematics include *velocity, acceleration, angular velocity, angular acceleration,* and *linear* and *angular motions.* Kinetics is concerned with the forces that cause, modify, or inhibit motion. Terms related to kinetics are *mass, force, pressure, gravity, friction, work, power, energy,* and *torque.*

Velocity refers to the speed and direction of a body and involves the change of position of a body per unit of time. Because bodies in motion are continually changing position, the degree to which the body's position changes within a definite time span is measured to determine their velocity. For example, the velocity of a baseball from the time it leaves the pitcher's hand to the time it arrives in the catcher's glove can be measured in this manner.

Acceleration refers to the change in velocity involving speed or direction of a moving body. An individual playing basketball, for example, can add positive acceleration when dribbling toward the basket on a fast break, or the player can change pace and slow down (decelerate) to permit another player to screen for him or her.

Angular velocity is the angle that is rotated in a given unit of time. *Angular acceleration* refers to the change of angular velocity for a unit of time. For example, when a bowling ball is rolled down a

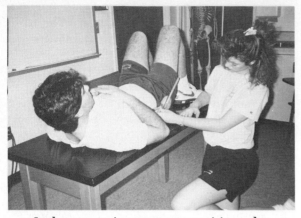

Students use goniometry to measure joint angles.

lane, its angular velocity can be computed mathematically in terms of revolutions per second. The angular acceleration, on the other hand, occurs after the bowling ball is released and the ball actually starts rolling, instead of sliding, which occurs immediately on release.

The relationship between linear and angular motions of body parts should be understood. Northrip, Logan, and McKinney[3] cite examples, such as that a throwing motion involves angular velocity of the wrist joint, which helps to determine throwing speed and that kicking a football, which involves the angular velocity of the kicker's ankle joint, and thus helps to determine kicking performance. The final linear velocity that results in both cases is achieved as the sum of many angular motions at the body joints. Because most body movements are rotational movements at the body's joints, to achieve the best results in skill performance it is necessary to integrate linear and angular motions.

Mass, the amount of matter in a body, is the ratio of a force acting on a body to the acceleration that is produced by that force. The larger the mass, the larger the force needed to produce acceleration. For example, a larger force would be needed in track and field to produce acceleration of a 16-pound shot than a 12-pound shot.

Force is any action that changes or tends to change the motion of an object. Forces have both a magnitude (i.e., size) and a direction. Forces on the body can occur internally, such as when a muscle contracts and exerts forces on the bone to which it is attached. External forces such as gravity also can act on the body.

Pressure refers to the ratio of force to the area over which the force is applied. For example, 16-ounce boxing gloves will distribute a given force over a larger surface area than 12-ounce boxing gloves, thus reducing pressure. In this case, distributing the pressure will ensure less chance of injury from blows when the 16-ounce gloves are used.

Gravity is a natural force that pulls all objects toward the center of the earth. An important feature of gravitational pull is that it always occurs through the center of weight or mass of an object. In the human body, the center of weight is known as the *center of gravity*. The center of gravity is the point at which all of the body's mass seems to be located and the point about which an object would balance. The center of gravity is constantly changing during movement. The center of gravity can be either within or outside the body, depending on the shape of the body. It always shifts in the direction of movement or the additional weight. When human beings stand erect with their hands at their sides, the center of gravity is located at the level of the hips. Athletes can use their knowledge about the center of gravity to better their skills. For example, the basketball player during a jump ball swings both arms forward and upward to assist in gaining height. Once in the air, the player allows one arm to drop to his or her side and strives to get maximum reach with the other arm. By dropping one arm to the side the player can reach farther beyond the center of gravity than with two arms overhead.

Friction is a force that occurs when surfaces come in contact and results from the sliding of one surface on the other. Friction can have negative or positive results. For example, it can lead to loss of motion and thus, under certain circumstances, produce negative results. On the other hand, it has positive results in the sport of baseball when pine tar or a glove is used to increase the friction between the hands and the bat and thus ensure better control of the bat.

Work refers to the force that is applied to a body through a distance and in the direction of the force. An individual who bench presses 240 pounds through 3 feet is doing work. The direction of the motion is the same as the direction of the force, and therefore the total amount of work is figured by multiplying 240 pounds by 3 feet, which equals 720 foot-pounds of work for each repetition.

Power is the amount of work accomplished in one unit of time. For example, a person performs a certain task, such as running, and exerts a certain amount of horsepower to perform the task in a given amount of time. In order to exert twice as much horsepower, the runner would have to perform the same task and accomplish the same amount of work (i.e., run the same distance) in half the amount of time.

Energy relates to the capacity of a body to perform work. Two types of energy used in biomechanics are (1) kinetic energy, the energy a body has because it is moving (such as a skier whose weight and velocity determine kinetic energy); and (2) potential energy, the energy that accrues as a result of the position that a body occupies relative to the earth's surface. The weight of the body and its height above the surface are used to determine potential energy. For example, a diver at the peak of the dive has the capacity to do work because of his or her position relative to the earth's surface. When he or she falls toward the water, the weight of the body does work equal to its magnitude times the distance the body moves in the direction of force.

Torque represents a twisting, turning, or rotary force related to the production of angular acceleration and is contrasted with the force necessary to produce linear acceleration. Torque can also be produced as a result of the rotation of a body or body part. For example, supination and pronation motions of the radioulnar joint can produce torque. The production of torque is essential in gymnastics,

with many movements required in routines using apparatus such as the high bar, parallel bars, uneven parallel bars, and rings.

MECHANICAL PRINCIPLES AND CONCEPTS RELATED TO MOVEMENT

Movements are governed by mechanical principles. Biomechanists use these principles in the analysis of movement. To illustrate some mechanical principles, selected principles and concepts relating to stability, motion, leverage, and force are presented in this section.

Stability

Stability is an important factor in all movement skills. The concept of stability is related to equilibrium. Equilibrium is a state of equalized forces on the body. Stability is the ability of the body to return to a position of equilibrium after it has been slightly displaced. In addition to regaining equilibrium, one may wish to maintain equilibrium or to displace equilibrium, depending on the action desired.

There may be both static equilibrium, in which the center of gravity is in a stable position (e.g., when one is standing or performing a headstand in gymnastics), and dynamic equilibrium, in which the center of gravity is in motion (e.g., when one is running or performing a cartwheel in gymnastics). In sport and movement terminology stability is referred to as balance. The ability of the body to maintain stability or balance is governed by three primary principles.

Principle

The lower the center of gravity is to the base of support, the greater will be the stability. In activities that require stability the directions should include bending the knees, thereby lowering the center of gravity. In running, for example, runners can stop more efficiently and quickly if they bend their knees (the weight drops closer to the base of support) and place their feet in a forward stride position. Other examples include the wrestler taking a semicrouched position and the football lineman assuming a three-point stance (center of gravity is lowered to increase stability).

Concept. To achieve greater stability, lower the body over the base of support.

Principle

The nearer the center of gravity is to the center of the base of support, the more stable the body. The line of gravity is the imaginary line that extends vertically through the center of gravity to the center of the earth. Directions utilizing this principle would include a suggestion to distribute the weight evenly. This puts the line of gravity over the base of support. In activities where the object is to move quickly in one direction, the weight is shifted in the direction of the movement. In starting a sprint race, for example, the runners will lean forward to get off the mark quickly.

Some activities such as walking on a balance beam require a small base of support. It is very easy to lose one's balance in these types of activities. When the balance is being lost while performing on the balance beam, the arm or leg on the opposite side from which the person is leaning is raised to shift the center of gravity back toward the base of support.

Concepts
1. For greater stability, maintain a body position with the center of gravity directly over the base of support.
2. When falling or leaning to one side, raise and lower the arms or legs or some other body part on the side opposite the direction of the fall or lean (distribute weight evenly).
3. When carrying or lifting a heavy object, keep the object close to the body while bending the knees and keeping the back straight.

Principle

The larger or wider the base of support, the more stable the body.

Concepts
1. Spread the feet to increase the base when standing. The feet should be spread in the direction of the movement for added stability.

2. For activities where a stance is required, using both hands and feet will create the widest base.
3. When receiving either a fast-moving object or a heavy force, widen the base of support in the direction from which the force is coming.
4. When applying a force, widen the base in the direction in which the force is to be applied.

Motion

Motion implies movement, which consists of destroying or upsetting the equilibrium of the body. A force is required to start a body in motion, to slow it down, to stop it, to change the direction of its motion, or to make it move faster. Everything that moves is governed by the laws of motion formulated by Sir Isaac Newton. These laws describe how things move and make it possible to predict the motion of an object.

Newton's First Law

The law of inertia states that a body at rest will remain at rest and a body in motion will remain in motion at the same speed and in the same direction unless acted on by some outside force.

For a movement to occur a force must act on a body sufficiently to overcome that object's inertia. If the applied force is less than the resistance offered by the object, motion will not occur.

Concepts
1. Once an object is in motion it will take less force to maintain its speed and direction (i.e., momentum). For example, it takes an individual more effort to start pedaling a bicycle to get it underway than it does to maintain speed once the bicycle is moving.
2. The heavier the object and the faster it is moving, the more the force that is required to overcome its moving inertia or to absorb its momentum. In football an opponent will have to exert more force to stop a massive, fast-moving lineman than he would to stop the lighter weight and slower moving quarterback.

Newton's Second Law

The law of acceleration states that a change in velocity (acceleration) of an object is directly proportional to the force producing it and inversely proportional to its mass.

If two unequal forces are applied to objects of equal mass, the object that has the greater force applied will move faster. Conversely, if two equal forces are applied to objects of different masses, the lighter mass will travel at the faster speed.

For example, in shot putting the athlete who is stronger and thus able to expend more force will toss the 12-pound shot further than an athlete who possesses less strength. Also, an athlete will find more force is needed to propel a 16-pound shot than a 12-pound shot.

Concepts

1. The heavier the object, the more force needed to speed it up (positive acceleration) or slow it down (negative acceleration).
2. An increase in speed is proportional to the amount of force that is applied; the greater the amount of force that is imparted to an object, the greater the speed with which that object will travel.
3. Momentum is a measure of both speed and mass. If the same amount of force is exerted for the same length of time on two bodies of different mass, greater acceleration will be produced in the lighter or less massive object. If the two objectives are propelled at the same speed, the heavier object will have greater momentum once inertia is overcome and will exert a greater force than the lighter object on something that it contacts.

Newton's Third Law

The law of action and reaction states that for every action there is an equal and opposite reaction.

Bouncing on a trampoline or springing from a diving board are examples of the law of action and reaction. The more force one exerts on the downward bounce, the higher the bounce or spring into the air. The thrust against the water in swimming is another example of an equal and opposite reaction—the water pushes the swimmer forward with a force equal to the force exerted by the swimmer on the backward thrust of the strokes.

Concept. Whenever one object moves, another object moves too and in the opposite direction. When you push something, it pushes back; when you pull on something, it pulls back.

Linear and Rotary Motion

Motion is linear or rotary. The human body usually employs a combination of both. The rotary action of the legs to propel the body in a linear direction is an example.

Linear Motion

Linear motion refers to movement in a straight line and from one point to another. In running, for example, the body should be kept on a straight line from start to finish. Also the feet and arm movements should be back and forth in straight lines rather than from side to side across the body.

Rotary Motion

Rotary motion consists of movement of a body about a center of rotation, called the *axis*. In most human movements rotary motion is converted into linear motion. Rotary motion is increased when the radius of rotation is shortened. Conversely, rotary motion is decreased when the radius of the moving body is increased. Examples include tucking the head when performing tumbling stunts to increase the rotation of the body and holding the arms out when executing a turn on the toes on ice to slow the body.

Leverage

Efficient body movement is made possible through a system of levers. A lever is a mechanical device used to produce a turning motion about a fixed point, called an *axis*. A lever consists of a fulcrum (the center or axis of rotation), a force arm (the distance from the fulcrum to the point of application of force), and a weight or resistance arm (the distance from the fulcrum to the weight on which the force is acting). The bones of the body act as levers, the joints act as the fulcrums, and the force to move the bone or lever about the joint or fulcrum is produced by the contraction of the muscles.

Three types of levers are determined by the relationship of the fulcrum (axis), the weight, and the point of application of force. In a *first class lever* the fulcrum is located between the weight and point of application of force. In a *second class lever* the weight is between the fulcrum and the force. In a *third class lever* the force is between the fulcrum and the weight.

Levers enable one to gain a mechanical advantage by producing either strength or speed. First class levers may produce both strength and speed, unless the fulcrum is in the middle of the force and weight, which produces a balanced condition. Second class levers produce force, and third class levers favor speed. The movements of the body are produced mostly through third class levers. An example of a third class lever operating in the body is the action of the hamstring muscles (the muscles in the back of the thigh) in flexing the lower leg. The quadriceps (muscles in front of the thigh) also act as a third class lever in straightening out the lower leg.

The length of the force arm is the key to producing either force or speed. If great force is desired, the force arm should be as long as possible. If great speed is desired, the force arm should be shortened. The internal levers of the body cannot be controlled in regard to the length of the force arm. However, when using implements such as bats and racquets long force arms would be created by holding the implement near the end, thereby producing greater force. If a person were interested in greater speed to swing a bat, he or she would "choke up" on the bat to reduce the force arm. When using an implement to produce greater force or speed, the size and the length of the implement must match the strength of the person who is handling the implement.

Concepts

1. Levers are used to gain a mechanical advantage by either producing speed or force.
2. Greater speed is produced by lengthening the resistance arm, and greater force is produced by lengthening the force arm.

Force

Force is the effect that one body has on another. It is invisible, but it is always present when motion occurs. It should be pointed out, however, that there can be force without motion. An example of a force in which no motion is evident is the push against a wall by a person. The wall does not move, although great force might be exerted. Another example occurs when two arm wrestlers are pushing against each other with equal force and their arms remain motionless.

Teachers should be aware of the principles relating to the production, application, and absorption of force when they teach movement activities.

Production of Force

Body force is produced by the actions of muscles. The stronger the muscles, the more force the body is capable of producing. However, the force of the muscle group or groups must be applied in the same direction and in proper sequence to realize the greatest force. In the high jump, for example, the body should be lowered on the last step before the jump. This lowering of the body will enable the jumper to contract the muscles of the thigh, which are the strongest of the body. The upward movement of the arms will give added force to the jump when coordinated with the upward push of the legs. It should be remembered that the principles of stability and the laws of motion must be observed in the performance of the high jump if the greatest height is to be attained.

Force must also be generated to propel objects. The same principles apply as mentioned above. In the swing of a softball bat the application of force is possible because of the production of force by different muscle groups in a coordinated manner. For maximum force the body should be rotated at the hips, shoulders, arms, and hands in a sequential order. The summation of these forces will produce the greatest momentum. A follow-through is necessary both to avoid jerky movements and to

A dynamometer is used to measure strength.

reduce the possibility of injury to the muscles or tendons.

Application of Force

The force of an object is most effective when it is applied in the direction that the object is to travel. Many activities in physical education involve the projection of the body or another type of object into the air. To project an object or the body forward most efficiently, the force should be applied through the center of the weight of the object and in a forward direction. To move the body upward, the body must be straight and all the force must be directed upward through the center of the body. The example of the high jump previously mentioned will illustrate this principle. Force from the

legs must be applied through the center of the body if the greatest force is to be applied to the jump. Some of the force will be dissipated if the jumper leans to one side when pushing off from the ground.

In throwing an object the following three main factors are of concern: (1) the speed of the throw, (2) the distance of the throw, and (3) the direction that the object will travel.

The *speed* of the throw depends on the speed of the hand at the moment of release of the object. The speed of the arm can be increased by lengthening it to its fullest, rotating the body, shifting the weight properly, and taking a step in the direction of the throw. These movements must be done in a continuous motion to maintain momentum. If an implement such as a bat or paddle is used, it becomes an extension of the arm. Therefore the same principle applies. The implement should be held as close to the handle end as possible to create a long movement arm. This will enable the person to apply more force.

The *distance* of the throw will be affected by the pull of gravity and air resistance. The distance that an object will travel, therefore, will depend on the angle of release in addition to the force imparted to the throw. The pull of gravity and air resistance will affect objects thrown less if they are released at an angle of approximately 45 degrees. This represents a compromise between releasing an object at a large angle and having it remain in the air but not go very far because of wind resistance and releasing the object at a smaller angle where the pull of gravity will keep it from traveling very far.

The *direction* or accuracy of the throw depends on the point of release of the object. The release must be a point in the arc of the arm at which the object is tangent to the target. To better achieve the desired angle of release, the throwing arm should be moved in a flatter arc at the time of release. In making the overhand throw in softball, for example, the hand should travel in the straightest line possible toward the target, both on the backswing and the follow-through.

In addition to gravity and air resistance, the flight

of thrown and batted objects is also affected by the spin of the object. The object will travel in the direction of the spin.

Absorption of Force

Many instances occur when persons must receive or absorb force. Examples include absorbing the force of a thrown object, as in catching a football or softball; landing after a jump; and heading a soccer ball. The impact of the force should be gradually reduced, and it should be spread over as large an area as possible. Therefore when catching a ball, the arms should be extended to meet the ball. On contact, the hand and arms should "give" with the catch. When landing from a jump, the person should bend the hips, knees, and ankles to gradually reduce the kinetic energy of the jump, thereby reducing the momentum. The feet must also be spread slightly to create a large area of impact (base).

Concepts

1. The more muscles that are used, the greater the force that is produced (provided, of course, that they are the same sized muscles).
2. The more elasticity or stretch a muscle is capable of, the more force it can supply. Each working muscle should be stretched fully to produce the greatest force.
3. When objects are moved, the weight of the objects should be pushed or pulled through the center and in the direction that they are to be moved.
4. When heavy objects are moved or thrown, the force of the muscles should be used in a sequential manner. For example, the order in throwing should be trunk rotation, shoulder, upper arm, lower arm, hand, and fingers.
5. When body parts (arms and legs) or implements such as bats and paddles are used, they should be extended completely when making contact with an object to be propelled. This creates a long movement arm, thereby creating the greatest force; the implements should be gripped at the end.
6. When receiving or absorbing the force of a thrown object (as in catching a ball), a fall, or

a kick, the largest possible area should be used to absorb the force. For example, the student should use two hands to catch a hard-thrown ball; more area will be available to absorb the force of the ball.
7. The absorption of force should be spread out as long as possible by recoiling or "giving" at the joints involved in the movement.

• • •

To analyze an individual's motor performance, physical educators need to be cognizant of the principles governing movement. Selected principles pertaining to stability, motion, leverage, and force were discussed in this section. Physical educators are also concerned about such concepts as friction, aerodynamics, hydrodynamics, and ball spin and rebound in the evaluation of performance. An understanding of both biomechanics and kinesiology provides the physical educator with a foundation for understanding and analyzing human movement.

BIOMECHANICAL ANALYSIS

Various instruments and techniques are used by biomechanists to study and analyze motion. During the past 15 years improvements in instrumentation coupled with advances in computers and microchip technology have greatly assisted biomechanists in their endeavors. Additionally, the development of better and more creative methods of using these instruments has greatly enhanced the understanding of human movement and the ability to improve performance.[4] These tools include computers, anthropometry, timing devices, cinematography, videography, electrogoniometry, electromyography, dynamography, and telemetry. These tools, as well as visual observation, can be used to perform quantitative and qualitative analysis of human movement.

Instruments

Computers have become increasingly important in biomechanical research. Biomechanical analysis requires dealing with prodigious amounts of data. The use of the computer in dealing with such data has become a necessity. Additionally, much of the

Computers are used to perform many functions in biomechanics. Here it is used to analyze film images of a performer that are projected onto the tablet.

instrumentation used in biomechanical research is linked to a computer. Much of the analysis of information can be performed on-line so that the results can be available almost instantly.

Computers can also be used to simulate movements. *Simulation* requires the use of mathematical formulas to develop models of a specific movement. Then, this computer model can be used to assist biomechanists in determining the effects of certain modifications in the movement or certain variables on performance. For example, simulation can address such questions as what is the effect of altering the take-off position of a dive on the subsequent performance? or how does air resistance affect a skier's performance? This approach assists researchers in determining how a performance can be improved. Comparisons between the optimal or ideal performance and an individual's actual performance is enhanced through the use of computer technology. The computer is used to generate graphic representations of the ideal performance and the actual performance. The drawing of the actual performance is compiled from the analysis of the films of the performer. These graphic representations of the ideal performance and an individual's actual performance can then be compared. This facilitates the detection of errors and the identification of strategies to improve performance.

Computers offer biomechanists tremendous assistance in understanding human movements.

Cinematography is one of the basic tools employed in biomechanical research. Sophisticated movie cameras are used to film an individual's performance. These cameras film at thousands of frames per second (home movie cameras operate at 16-24 frames per second). These high speed cameras capture details of movements that may escape the unaided eye of the physical educator observing the performer's movements. As a result of cinematography, it is possible to film movement and capture such things as the speed, angle, range, and sequence of moving segments. Cinematography provides a permanent record that can be studied after the movement action takes place. Slow-motion and stop-action techniques aid in the study of the performance. From the film, graphic representations of the movement can be developed, either through hand drawing or through computer analysis. Completion of mathematical calculations based on information provided from the films is an essential part of movement analysis. This process is greatly speeded and simplified through the use of computers.

Stroboscopy is a photographic technique that also is used for the study of movement. This technique allows filming to take place against a darkened background, with light being flashed onto the subject being filmed. The total movement is recorded on a single frame of film as a sequence of images. For example, with this technique it is possible to take a picture of the total forehand stroke in tennis, which shows the path of the various body segments in the total execution of the stroke. This facilitates the analysis of the individual's movements. Using this technique, a comparison can also be made of one person's execution of a movement skill (e.g., the forehand tennis stroke or the wrist action used) with that of another person or the ideal performance.

Videography is the use of video systems to record an individual's performance. Video systems consist of a video camera, recorder, and a playback unit. Unlike cinematography, video systems are relatively inexpensive, easy to use, and readily available to

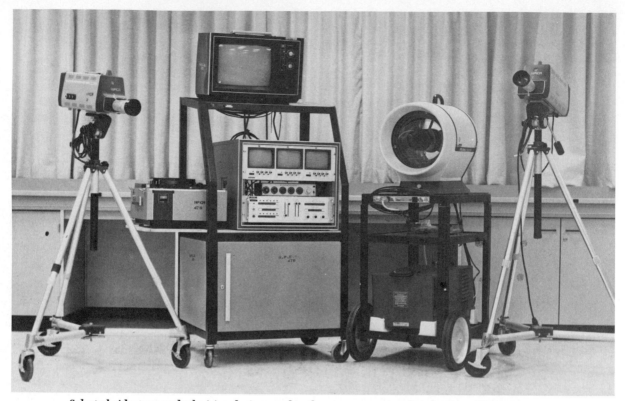

Selected videotape and television devices used in the measurement and evaluation of human movement.

practitioners. The ability to directly play back what has been recorded allows for immediate viewing by the analyst and prompt feedback to the performer. Videography systems can be interfaced with computers to provide movement analysis. This is one of the most inexpensive high technology systems for the analysis of movement. Advances in technology have led to better quality cameras as well as sophisticated playback capabilities that yield greater clarity of still and stop-action images.

Anthropometry is concerned with the measurement of the human body. The length, width, diameter, circumference (girth), and surface area of the body and its segments are measured. Correct identification of anatomical landmarks is crucial to obtaining accurate measurements. Information about the structure of the human body is used to calculate the forces acting on the joints of the body

and the forces produced by movement. Information about the structure of an individual's body is important in developing computer models of performance.

Timing devices or chronoscopes are used to record speeds of body movements and its parts. Some types of timing devices are stop watches, digital timers, counters, switch mats, photoelectric cells, and real-time computer clocks. The chronoscope is started at a preselected point in time, typically the initiation of a movement, and then stopped at a preselected time, such as the completion of a movement. The speed of movement is then calculated. Radar guns can also be used to provide instantaneous information about speed.

Electrogoniometry is a technique that can be used to provide information about the angles of the joint as part of a total motion pattern. Another term

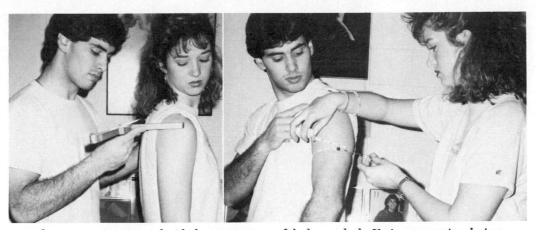

Anthropometry is concerned with the measurement of the human body. Various measuring devices are used to provide information about the body and its segments.

for an electrogoniometer is an elgon. A goniometer (see Chapter 6 for information about the use of goniometers to measure flexibility) is used in conjunction with an electrical device called a *potentiometer* to measure the degrees of movement at a joint. This information can be transferred directly to a computer, recording paper, or oscilloscope. For example, this instrument would permit the study of the knee–joint action when a particular skill, such as walking or running, is executed. It can also measure range of motion, angular velocity, and acceleration. Electrogoniometry may be particularly useful when combined with electromyography.

Electromyography (EMG) is used to measure the electrical activity produced by a muscle or muscle group. When properly processed, this measurement serves as an approximate indicator of the amount of force being developed by a muscle. This provides a means to observe the involvement of a particular muscle or muscle group in a movement. Surface electrodes are placed over the muscle or muscle group or fine wire electrodes are inserted into the muscle to be observed. Electrical impulses from muscle activity are then processed, recorded, and displayed on an oscilloscope, recording paper, or computer. EMG can be used to record the muscle activity associated with a particular performance; when done during various periods of time, a record of progress can be made. Certain rhythms of

muscle activity are associated with a performance. An athlete who is not performing well or is in a slump may display a different EMG rhythm than normal. This information can be used to assist the athlete correct errors and regain the desired form. EMG is often used in conjunction with electrogoniometry. Researchers may also make recordings of brain wave activity using the electroencephalograph (EEG) concurrently with EMG activity; this provides the researcher with information on how the brain influences motor activity (this is studied within the realm of motor control).

Dynamography is a technique used to measure the forces produced during a movement. When measuring strength, particularly static strength, spring devices and cable tensiometers are used. Strain gauges are devices that are also used to measure strength. They have been incorporated into equipment such as athletic footwear insoles, bicycle pedals, and uneven parallel bars to measure the force produced by the performers using this equipment. Another device that is used to measure force is the force platform. Force platforms can be built into the floor to measure the forces such as those associated with a foot striking the floor during walking. They can also be designed to measure force production by athletes during sprint starts, pole vaulting, and gymnastics.

Telemetry involves the wireless recording of vari-

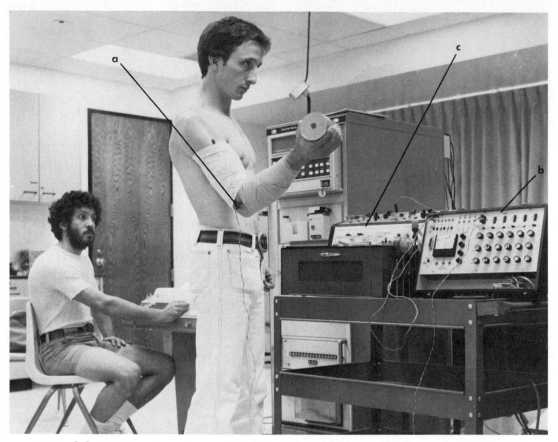

A typical electrogoniometry system consists of (a) an elgon, which is an electronic transducer for the measurement of angular position and movement of the body segments, (b) an amplifying module, and (c) a recorder. The recorder is interfaced with the computer for an on-line real-time analysis of angular motion.

ous aspects of movement. Telemetry systems consist of specialized electrodes that are attached to the individual and a transmitter that sends the information to the receiver that records it. Telemetry systems can be used to transmit information about heart rate or joint angles (electrogoniometry) during a performance. A distinct advantage of this technique is that it permits movement data to be recorded without encumbering the performer with wires and other equipment that can hinder performance.

Advances in computers and instrumentation as well as the manner in which they are used have contributed much to the understanding of human movement. These tools, in addition to visual evaluation, can be used to analyze human movement.

Analysis

Quantitative and qualitative methods can be used to analyze human movement. *Quantitative analysis* uses many of the techniques described above to provide specific numerical information about the movement being studied. Specific information, for example, about the joint angles during movement, the force generated, and the speed of movement, is provided. Quantitative analysis is used predominately in research efforts and is increasingly incorporated as part of the overall training program of

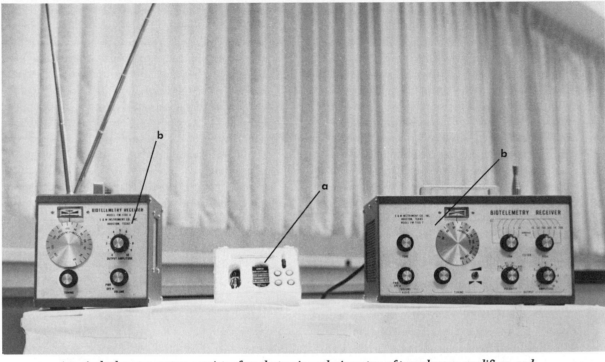

A typical telemetry system consists of an electronic analysis system of transducers, amplifiers, and recorders plus a radio transmitter and a radio receiver that can be interfaced with the system amplifiers. Shown here are the (a) Norco transmitter and (b) receivers.

elite athletes to help them optimize their performance (for example, biomechanists work with elite athletes at the U.S. Olympic Training Center at Colorado Springs, Colorado).

Qualitative analysis also provides important information about the movement being studied. Qualitative analysis relies most commonly on visual evaluation of the movement. The movement can be described in such terms as successful or unsuccessful or performed with difficulty or with ease. An individual's performance also can be compared with another individual's performance or against a standardized model. Videography, which can be used for quantitative analysis, can also be used effectively for qualitative analysis. Instead of using the videotape to calculate various kinematic and kinetic measures, the videotape of an individual's movement can be studied to identify performance errors and to determine effective corrections.

Qualitative analysis is most commonly used by practitioners. It offers practitioners who may not have access to sophisticated equipment nor have the background to employ advanced techniques a method to effectively analyze an individual's movements. Biomechanical analysis can be used by athletic trainers in designing a rehabilitation program, by physical educators for conducting an evaluation of fundamental motor skills, and by exercise leaders in ensuring that clients perform each exercise correctly.

Teachers and coaches can use biomechanical analysis to improve students' and athletes' performance of sport skills. Additionally, teachers and coaches are often faced with the task of evaluating several performers of diverse skill levels in a short period of time. The use of videotape and slow-motion/stop-action playback can be useful to the practitioner in assessing an individual's performance. Videotape equipment has become increasingly available in school and community settings.

If videotape equipment is not available, then the physical educator must rely directly on his or her observations of the individual's performance. Whether the physical educator is using videotape or directly observing the individual's performance, the physical educator should keep in mind relevant biomechanical principles, have a mental image of the ideal performance of the skill being observed, and thoroughly understand the nature of the skill being performed. As an observer, the physical educator should be objective and proceed in a systematic fashion.

Adrian and Cooper[5] and Brown[6] offer several suggestions to practitioners using visual evaluation techniques to assess skill performance. These suggestions, which can be incorporated into the practitioners' observation plan, are listed below:

- Observe the skill from a correct vantage point. Being in the correct position is essential to observe the critical components of the skill. When possible, view the skill from at least two perspectives.
- Observe the individual perform the skill several times before offering suggestions for improvement. This will permit the identification of consistent performance problems that may not be evident during a single performance attempt.
- Use the whole-part-whole method for the observation. After observing the total movement, focus on the movement of the body parts (i.e., legs, trunk). Observe the sequencing and timing of these parts. Observe the range of motion and look for unnecessary or extraneous movements. Then, again observe the whole body and focus on the coordination and sequencing of the movements of various body parts with respect to each other.
- If the performer is using an implement such as a racquet, or imparting force to another object such as throwing a discus or kicking a ball, it is also important to focus on the action of the implement.

- The overall effectiveness of the movement should be evaluated.
- A performance checklist can be used to guide the observation and to ensure that critical performance elements are viewed and not overlooked.

Once the observation is completed, practitioners should identify the errors in performance and give the performer accurate and relevant feedback about his or her performance (see Chapter 7 for a discussion of feedback).

The analysis of movement requires practice and an understanding of the biomechanical principles as well as kinesiology. Both kinesiology and biomechanics offer practitioners valuable information to help them understand human movement and improve the performance of the individuals with whom they work.

SUMMARY

Understanding the factors that govern human movement is essential for physical educators. Physical educators are concerned with helping individuals optimize their movements. To accomplish this task they need to thoroughly understand the mechanical principles that regulate movement. The analysis of human movement and sport object movement using the principles of physics and mechanics is called biomechanics. In recent years the study of biomechanics has grown tremendously in the United States and is commonly recognized as a subdiscipline of physical education. Additionally, in the United States a greater emphasis has been placed on practical applications in recent years as opposed to theoretical research.

Biomechanics is concerned with two major areas of study. The first area focuses on the anatomical aspects of movements while the second area concerns itself with the mechanical aspects of movement. Needless to say, these areas are closely related. Biomechanists have a specialized scientific vocabulary to describe their area of study. The terms power, acceleration, velocity, mass, pressure, friction, work, energy, angular velocity and acceleration, torque, and gravity were defined in this chapter. Selected biomechanical principles and concepts pertaining to stability, motion, leverage, and force were explained and illustrated.

Within the last 15 years improvements in instrumentation and its application have been numerous, which has greatly expanded the knowledge base. While the practitioner may not have access to much of the specialized equipment used by the biomechanist researcher, the practitioner can use available equipment such as videotape equipment or direct observation to analyze performance. Understanding of the principles of biomechanics is essential in improving individuals' performance.

SELF-ASSESSMENT TESTS

These tests are designed to assist students in determining if the materials and competencies presented in this chapter have been mastered.

1. Compare the study of biomechanics to the study of kinesiology. Discuss the relationship between these two subdisciplines.

2. Write an essay of 250 words on the worth of biomechanical knowledge to the practitioner in physical education. Write the essay from the perspective of a practitioner in a career that you are considering for the future, that is, teacher, coach, athletic trainer, exercise physiologist, or sports broadcaster.

3. Explain and illustrate the meaning of each of the following terms: power, acceleration, velocity, mass, pressure, friction, work, energy, torque, and center of gravity.

4. Using a sport with which you are familiar, illustrate principles and concepts relating to stability, motion, leverage, and force.

5. Describe some of the analytical techniques used by biomechanists in their research. Describe how a physical educator without access to sophisticated equipment can use biomechanical analysis in his or her work.

REFERENCES

1. Dillman CJ: Applied biomechanics research for the United States Ski Team, Journal of Physical Education, Recreation, and Dance 53(1):27-29, 1982.

2. Kyle CR: Athletic clothing, Scientific American 254(3):104-110, 1986.

3. Northrip JW, Logan GA, and McKinney W: Introduction to biomechanical analysis of sport, ed 2, Dubuque, Iowa, 1979, William C. Brown.

4. Atwater AE: Kinesiology/biomechanics: perspectives and trends, Research Quarterly for Exercise and Sport 51:193-218, 1980.

5. Adrian MJ and Cooper JM: The biomechanics of human movement, Indianapolis, 1989, Benchmark Press.

6. Brown EW: Visual evaluation techniques for skill analysis, Journal of Physical Education, Recreation, and Dance 53(1):21-26, 1982.

SUGGESTED READINGS

Adrian MJ and Cooper JM: The biomechanics of human movement, Indianapolis, 1989, Benchmark Press.

   A comprehensive presentation of biomechanical concepts and their application to understanding human movement and the performance of sport skills.

American Alliance for Health, Physical Education, Recreation, and Dance: Kinesiology. Basic Stuff Series I, Reston, Va, 1987, AAHPERD.

   This book provides an easy to understand overview of factors influencing human movement.

Bartels K: Performance analysis: applying mechanics to swimming, Strategies 3(1):17-19, 1989.

   In an article written for practitioners, the application of biomechanical principles to improve swimming techniques is discussed.

Cavanagh PR: Biomechanics of distance running, Champaign, Il, 1990, Human Kinetics.

   The book presents an historical analysis of the study of the mechanics of distance running that spans nearly 2500 years as well as current biomechanical research on distance running.

Dainty DA and Norman RW, editors: Standardizing biomechanical testing in running, Champaign, Il, 1987, Human Kinetics.

   This text provides information on standardization of testing of athletes including how to define and solve biomechanical problems as well as information on the use various instruments and procedures.

Enoka RM: Neuromechanical basis of kinesiology, Champaign, Il, 1988, Human Kinetics.

   This text integrates information on mechanics and neuromuscular physiology to help describe human movement.

Gowitzke BA and Milner M: Scientific bases of human movement, ed 3, Baltimore, 1988, Williams and Wilkins.

   This text presents an introduction to kinesiology as well as information on kinematics, kinetics, and application of mechanical principles to the body.

Kyle CR: Athletic clothing, Scientific American 254(3):104-110, 1986.

   The use of biomechanics to design athletic clothing and equipment and its contribution to sport records and safety are discussed in an easy-to-understand format.

International Journal of Sport Biomechanics 6(2), 1990, (entire issue).

   This issue presents biomechanical research studies that were conducted during the 1988 Seoul Olympic Games.

Minton S, editor: Dance dynamics: avoiding dance injuries, Journal of Physical Education, Recreation, and Dance 58(5):30-61, 1987.

This series of articles presents suggestions on how to avoid dance injuries and includes information on biomechanical considerations.

Widule CJ: Performance excellence: optimizing running performance, Strategies 2(5):17,27-28, 1989.

This practical article discusses how two basic mechanical components of running performance, stride length and step rate, relate to optimal running performance.

Wilkerson JD: Plyometrics: when and how does it work? Strategies 3(3):11-12, 26, 1990.

In an easy-to-understand format, plyometric exercises and relevant research are discussed.

Part

Careers and Professional Considerations in Physical Education and Sport

Three

Introduction

In Part Two the historical and scientific foundations of physical education were described. In recent years the expansion of the knowledge base has led to the development of subdisciplines in physical education. This expansion coupled with the tremendous growth of interest in sports and fitness in our society has resulted in the development of numerous career opportunities for qualified physical educators.

In Part Three various career opportunities for physical educators are described. Preparation for a career in physical education and sport is described in Chapter 10. Chapter 11 discusses traditional career opportunities such as teaching and coaching in the schools. However, the expansion of physical education programs to nonschool settings and to individuals of all ages has resulted in teaching and coaching opportunities outside of the school setting as well. The tremendous interest in physical fitness and health has stimulated the growth of fitness-, health-, and therapy-related careers. These careers are examined in Chapter 12. Chapter 13 describes career opportunities in media, management, performance, and other related areas. The pervasiveness of sport in our society coupled with the growth of the communications media has encouraged careers in sport communication, while the development of sport as big business has created a need for professionals trained in sport management. Opportunities for individuals interested in pursuing careers as performers have increased as well during the past decade.

It is critical at this time of growth that the profession be led by capable leaders. The development of leadership is discussed, the advantages of belonging to professional organizations described, and various professional organizations are listed in Chapter 14.

Chapter 10

Preparing for a Career in Physical Education and Sport

INSTRUCTIONAL OBJECTIVES AND COMPETENCIES TO BE ACHIEVED

After reading this chapter the student should be able to—
- Identify career opportunities in physical education and sport.
- Self-assess strengths, interests, goals, and career preferences.
- Understand his or her professional preparation curriculum.
- Discuss the role of practical experience in professional preparation.
- Describe strategies to enhance his or her marketability.

Traditionally careers in physical education and sport have focused on teaching and coaching in schools and colleges and universities. Lately teaching and coaching careers in nonschool settings such as community centers (e.g., YMCA or YWCA) and commercial clubs (e.g., gymnastics, tennis, or swimming clubs) have become increasingly available. In recent years interest in nonteaching careers has been great as well. These careers are often referred to as alternative or nontraditional careers because they differ from the traditional teaching-coaching career. While teaching and coaching are still popular career choices, many physical educators are pursuing careers in the fitness field working in health clubs or corporate fitness centers. Still other physical educators are employed in the areas of sport management, sports medicine, and sport media. The increased specialization within the field of physical education has created additional career opportuni-

ties. For example, biomechanists may work for sporting goods companies designing and testing sport equipment and apparel such as running shoes. Exercise physiologists may be employed in a corporate fitness center, hospital cardiac rehabilitation program, or in a sports medicine clinic. Career opportunities for a student who has studied physical education have never been greater. Professional preparation for a career in physical education and sport will be discussed in this chapter.

CAREERS IN PHYSICAL EDUCATION AND SPORT

Career opportunities in physical education and sport have expanded tremendously during the past 10 years. The widening career opportunities are a result of several factors. (See Chapter 3 for a further discussion.) First, the desire to be fit and awareness of the concomitant health benefits have

The fitness boom and wellness movement have led to a growth of career opportunities in corporate fitness programs. Kimberly-Clark employees work out in the company facility.

stimulated millions of Americans from all segments of our society to embark on fitness programs and engage in a variety of physical activities. This in turn has led to the need for fitness leaders and individuals trained in exercise science. Additionally, individuals seeking to use their increased leisure time in an enjoyable manner have sought out physical activities and sport. Specially trained individuals are needed to conduct recreational programs and to teach lifetime sport skills. The increased interest in competitive sports, again by all segments of the population, has served as the impetus for the growth of competitive sport programs, sport clubs, and leagues and the associated career opportunities in coaching, sport management, officiating, and athletic training. Finally, the increase of the depth and the breadth of knowledge in physical education has

led to the further development of subdisciplines and expanded career opportunities as bio-mechanists, sport psychologists, exercise physiologists, and adapted physical educators.

Career opportunities in physical education and sport are limited only by one's imagination. Lambert[1] points out that one's definition of physical education can serve to limit or expand one's horizons. Defining physical education only as "the teaching of sports, dance, and exercise in the public schools" can limit job opportunities to the traditional teaching-coaching career. However, if you define physical education as the "art and science of human movement," "sport education," "fitness education," or "preventive and rehabilitative medicine," many career possibilities become evident. Similarly, defining physical education as the "study of play," the "study of human energy," "perceptual-motor development," or as an "academic discipline that investigates the uses and meanings of physical activities to understand their effects and interrelationships with people and their culture" opens up other avenues of employment. Possible career opportunities are listed in Table 10-1; this list is by no means inclusive but will help readers realize the number and diversity of career opportunities in physical education and sport. These career options will be discussed further in other chapters. Careers involving the teaching and coaching of physical activity skills in a variety of settings are discussed in Chapter 11. Health- and fitness-related careers are described in Chapter 12. Career opportunities in sport management, sport media, and other areas are addressed in Chapter 13.

Your imagination also can be used to create new job opportunities suited specifically to your abilities and interests. The growth of the knowledge base combined with the expansion of our services to diverse populations has created many new and exciting career opportunities. By combining your abilities within a subdiscipline with your interest in working with a specific population and age group and within a particular setting you can create a career opportunity uniquely suited to you. Table 10-2 will assist you in exploring these various career options.

TABLE 10-1   Physical Education and Sport Career Opportunities

Teaching Opportunities	
School Setting	*Nonschool Setting*
Elementary School	Community Recreation/
Junior High School	Sport Programs
High School	Corporate Recreation
Junior/Community Colleges	Programs
College and University	Commercial Sport Clubs
Basic Instruction	Youth-serving Agencies
Programs	Preschools
Professional Preparation	Health Clubs
Programs	Military Personnel Programs
Adapted Physical Education	Resort Sport Programs
Overseas School Programs	Geriatric Programs
Military School Programs	Correctional Institution
	Programs

Coaching Opportunities	
Interscholastic Programs	Commercial Sport Clubs
Intercollegiate Programs	Community Sport Programs
Commercial Sport Camps	Military Sport Programs

Fitness and Health-Related Opportunities	
Cardiac Rehabilitation	Space Fitness Programs
Sports Medicine	Corporate Fitness Programs
Movement Therapy	Sports Nutrition
Health Clubs	Athletic Training
Community Fitness	Weight Control Spas
Programs	Military Personnel Programs

Sport Management Opportunities	
Athletic Administration	Sport Organization
Sport Facility Management	Administration
Commercial Sport Club	Health Club Management
Management	Sports Information
Community Recreation/	Sport Retailing
Sport Management	Corporate Recreation
Intramurals/Campus	Resort Sport Management
Recreation	

Sport Media Opportunities	
Sport Journalism	Sport Broadcasting
Sport Photography	Sport Art
Writing Sport-Oriented Books	

Sport-Related Opportunities	
Sport Law	Sport Officiating
Professional Athlete	Dancer
Entrepreneur	Sport Statistician
Research	Sport Consulting

The broadening of career opportunities in physical education and sport is an exciting development. Selecting a career from the many available options requires careful consideration of a number of factors.

Choosing a Career

How does one choose a career from the many available? Needless to say this is an important decision, involving a great deal of thought and deliberation. Perhaps you have already chosen a specific career in physical education and sport. You may have decided years ago that you wanted to be an athletic trainer or you may have recently decided during your last two years in high school to pursue a career in sport broadcasting. On the other hand, you may be like many other students, undecided about a specific career but know that physical education and sport is of interest to you and you have decided to explore the options within this area. Perhaps you can identify with other students who have not yet made a career choice and are spending their first year or two at college exploring different career options. Whether you are committed or undecided as to a career choice, college offers the opportunity to broaden your base of knowledge and explore various career opportunities.

Regardless of where you are in the career selection process you need to first be cognizant that you are choosing a career pathway as opposed to a specific job. A career pathway allows the pursuit of many different jobs within a specific area, such as sport management. Second, a career decision is not irreversible. Many students change their mind about the career they desire several times during the course of their college education. Third, a career is not a lifelong commitment. Changing careers has become increasingly common. You should evaluate your satisfaction with your chosen career periodically. Some people deliberately plan to pursue one career for a while to provide a foundation for a second career. For example, a student may choose to pursue a career as a teacher and a coach for several years before returning to school to receive training as a sport psychologist. The practical experience gained from coaching enhances the

TABLE 10-2   Creating Career Opportunities in Physical Education and Sport*

*Explore various career options within the field by combining an area of study with a population group, an age group, and a setting/environment to create a career that matches your individual interests. Add additional items to each column as you think of them. Match items from each column in *any* order. Create your own job title and define responsibilities. For example, combine exercise physiology with disabled youths in a home setting to create a job as a personal fitness trainer to an adolescent with a disability working in the individual's home.

Area of Study	Population	Age	Setting
Adapted physical education	Athletes	Adolescents	Athletic contests
Biomechanics	Cardiac risks	Adults	Clinic
Exercise physiology	Disabled	Children	College
Motor development	Inmates	Elderly	Commercial club
Motor learning	Military	Infants	Community
Sport history	Obese	Youths	Corporation
Sport management	Patients		Geriatric center
Sport medicine			Health/fitness club
Sport nutrition			Health spa/resort
Sport pedagogy			Home
Sport philosophy			Hospital
Sport psychology			Media setting
Sport sociology			Park
Measurement and evaluation			Prison
			Professional/sport organization
			Research laboratory
			Retail establishment
			School
			Space
			Sport facility

individual's new career as a practicing sport psychologist with a professional team.

Choosing a career is a decision-making process that involves gathering and then evaluating information about the alternatives available to you. The most important factors influencing your choice of a career are your strengths, interests, goals, and preferences. Having a realistic perception of your strengths and abilities is important in finding a satisfying career. In selecting a career you should draw on your current strengths and abilities as well as the ones that you have the potential and desire to develop further. Identifying your strengths and abilities involves the process of self-assessment. Self-assessment should be positive and on-going. Ask yourself the following questions:

- What are my strengths?
- What are my best personal characteristics?
- What personal abilities are reflected in my accomplishments?

- What abilities would I like to improve?
- What do I like to do?

Reflect on the compliments you have received from your parents, teachers, and peers to gather additional information about your abilities. Have you received frequent compliments on your leadership?…your organizational ability?…or your work with very young children?

You must also consider your academic abilities and interests.

- What are your academic strengths?…math? …science?…computers?…history?
- What areas of study do you enjoy?…music? …language?…math?…psychology?
- What special talents or skills do you possess? …Are you an accomplished photographer? …golfer?…painter?…basketball player?
- What talents and skills are you interested in developing?

Your decision to pursue a career in the area of

physical education and sport reflects your interest in this area. Pursual of a career in this area also reflects to a great extent an interest in working with people.

Consider your personal and professional goals while weighing your career options.

- What are your goals?
- What are you striving to accomplish at this point in your life? What do you wish to accomplish in 5 years, in 10 years, or 20 years?

Obviously your goals will have a great deal of impact on your selection of your career.

Finally, what are your preferences in terms of your life-style and your work?

- Do you want to work in a urban, suburban, or rural setting?
- What type of environment do you want to live in?
- What ages of people do you prefer to work with?
- Do you prefer to work with people in groups or on an individual basis?
- What type of facility do you want to work in? …school or college gymnasium?…hospital? …health spa?…community center?…corporation?
- What are your salary expectations?…would you be comfortable with a salary based on commissions?…merit?
- Is salary the most important consideration in the selection of a career or do you value other rewards associated with the job more? For example, is the personal satisfaction gained from helping a cardiac patient resume a normal activity level more important than your salary?
- What hours and days of the week do you prefer to work?
- How much vacation time would you like each year? Would you be satisfied having two or three weeks off a year or does two months off appeal to you more?
- How important is job security?…career advancement?…fringe benefits?

As a result of this self-assessment process you will become more cognizant of your strengths, interests,

goals, and life-style and work preferences. If you had difficulty in determining your personal characteristics you may want to take advantage of services offered by the career planning office or the counseling center at your college or university. Trained personnel can help you recognize your assets and articulate your goals. A variety of paper-and-pencil inventories can be taken to help identify your abilities and preferences for different types of careers. One test commonly used is the Strong-Campbell Interest Inventory. Talking and soliciting advice from others may also be helpful in the process. Discuss your self-assessment findings with your parents, professors, and your friends. Listen to the advice they have to offer, but remember that, although they may suggest that you pursue a certain career, ultimately the career decision is yours alone to make. You are the one who has to find the career satisfying and rewarding.

Information about yourself—your abilities, interests, goals, and preferences—should be matched to the characteristics of your prospective career. For example, you can combine your organizational ability with your mathematical ability to pursue a career in sport management. However, before you can accurately match your own assets with a career you need to find out further information about your possible vocation.

Matching assets with careers requires an understanding of the nature of the career you are considering. This information is available from a variety of sources. Career planning or counseling center personnel are excellent resources. They can provide you with information about careers and job characteristics as well as prospects for employment in your selected career. College and university libraries are also a good source of information. Ask the reference librarian for assistance if necessary. Two publications that might be helpful are the *Occupational Outlook Handbook*[2] and the *College Placement Annual*.[3] The *Occupational Outlook Handbook* is published annually and provides information about the job market in numerous areas. The *College Placement Annual* provides information on potential employers in your specific interest area. Another source is the *Encyclopedia of Associations*[4];

this reference lists professional organizations active in your career area. For example, under fitness the encyclopedia lists the American Running and Fitness Association, American Medical Joggers Association, National Athletic Health Institute, Aerobics International Research Society, Association for Fitness in Business, and the National Fitness Association, just to name a few. If you want further information about wellness you could write to the Wellness and Health Activation Networks or the National Wellness Association. Browsing through the athletic section of the encyclopedia will reveal career opportunities that perhaps you never even realized existed.

Another excellent way to find out about potential careers is to talk to practitioners. Most people would be happy to talk with you about their career and their perceptions. Consider asking the individual these questions:

- What is a typical workday like?
- What are the specific responsibilities of the job?
- What do you like or dislike about your work?
- What are the rewards associated with this career?
- What are the negative aspects of this line of work?
- What motivated you to seek employment in this area?
- How did you prepare yourself professionally for this position?
- What is the typical beginning salary associated with this position? What are the fringe benefits available?
- What opportunities are there for advancement in this field? What are the qualifications for advancement?
- To what professional organizations do you belong? What conferences or workshops do you typically attend?
- What advice would you give someone seeking to enter this field?

Try to talk to several people in the same career area because individuals' perceptions will vary as will their experiences.

Still another way to find information about vari-

ous careers is through your own practical experience. This will be discussed later in the chapter.

Your professional preparation courses will also provide you with information about various career opportunities and their requirements. It is hoped that reading this text and participating in this class will assist you in making a career choice or in solidifying one made previously.

After gathering information about yourself and the characteristics of the career you are choosing, try to make a match between your assets and the requirements and characteristics of your potential career. While you may have a career in mind, as you embark on your professional preparation program be open minded, flexible, and ready to explore other career opportunities that interest you.

Maximizing Professional Preparation

The process of preparing for a career is referred to as professional preparation. Professional preparation is the attainment of knowledge necessary to be an educated person as well as knowledge essential to understanding the discipline of physical education. Professional preparation also includes maximizing strengths and developing abilities with reference to one's chosen career. In addition to gaining the knowledge and skills necessary to be a successful practitioner, professional preparation may be thought of as the process of increasing personal marketability. When viewed from this perspective professional preparation includes not only your coursework and academics but related career experiences as well.

Education

Typically professional preparation curriculums have been oriented toward preparing individuals for careers in teaching and coaching. This has changed as a result of the widening job opportunities. The changing job market has stimulated the development of curriculums to prepare individuals for these expanded opportunities in physical education and sport. While professional preparation curriculums at different institutions may vary, these curriculums do have some commonalties.

Professional preparation curriculums typically

include liberal arts courses. Liberal arts courses provide the individual with the opportunity to obtain a broad base of knowledge. Examples of liberal arts courses include sciences, math, languages, English, art, and music. Certain liberal arts courses may be required of all students at the college or university; this can be referred to as the core curriculum. For example, all freshmen may be required to take a writing course or two and a speech course. Additional liberal arts courses are often mandated, with the number of courses and specific courses required differing according to the major area of study. Some courses of study and state accreditation may mandate specific courses while others may allow students to elect the liberal arts courses they wish to take; sometimes a certain num-

ber of courses may be required and a certain number deemed elective.

Building on this liberal arts foundation are the professional physical education courses. Professional theory courses focus on conveying the knowledge within the discipline of physical education. Professional theory courses required for physical education and sport majors pursuing the same career paths may vary among institutions. If your institution offers more than one major in physical education and sport, certain professional theory courses may be required of all majors, irrespective of their career pathway, that is, teaching-coaching, fitness, or athletic training. These courses provide students with a common framework for understanding the discipline of physical education and serve to acquaint students with the vocabulary and areas of study within the discipline. For example, all majors may have to take the introductory course or certain science courses. Many institutions require that all physical education majors take a certain number of professional activity courses.

The professional theory courses provide students with knowledge relative to the discipline and are designed to prepare majors for their chosen career. Courses outside of the realm of physical education are required as well. Usually courses and the sequence in which they are to be taken are specified. Thus students preparing for a career in teaching-coaching may take courses in physical education that include curriculum design, teaching methods, activity courses, performance analysis courses, and coaching courses; courses taken outside the area include education courses and psychology courses. Students preparing for a career in exercise science may take professional science courses and outside courses focusing on science (e.g., chemistry and physiology), psychology, and nutrition. In addition to the required professional courses students may take electives in this area.

Most curriculums have electives although the number of electives vary from program to program and from institution to institution. Requirements may be associated with the electives, such as a certain number must be from the liberal arts and a cer-

Traditionally professional preparation curriculums have focused on preparing students for careers in teaching and coaching.

tain number from the professional area. Some electives may be unrestricted and students can choose from any area. Electives may be used to pursue a special interest, broaden your liberal arts background, and/or to enhance your marketability by complementing and strengthening your career preparation. Electives should be used wisely.

An increasing number of students are taking advantage of their electives to pursue minors and/or concentrations or areas of specialization. (Different institutions define these terms differently so you should be familiar with how these terms are used at your own institution.) By doing so they broaden their career options and increase their marketability. These directed areas of study may be offered within the department or the school of physical education (depending on the size of the department or school) or in other academic areas across campus. Some physical education major curriculums require a minor or a concentration. Sport management majors frequently are required to have a minor in business or if not a minor to take a substantial number of business, economic, accounting,

and management courses. Sport communication majors may have a minor in journalism, photography, or speech. Exercise science majors may minor in science or perhaps nutrition and health. Teaching-coaching majors may minor in health, communication, or psychology. In some states if physical education teaching majors take enough credits in a second specific academic area, they can become certified to teach in that area as well. Often the number of credits required for certification is only a few more than the number required to complete a minor at your institution. Thus, physical education teacher majors can become certified to teach math, science, or health. Using credits judiciously can pay big dividends for all students regardless of their course of study.

Provision for practical experiences has become a common feature of many physical education curriculums regardless of the career being pursued. In the teaching-coaching area this practical experience has long been a tradition and is referred to as student teaching. Student teaching typically takes place in the latter part of the student's junior year

Computer skills are becoming a necessity for an ever-increasing number of careers in physical education and sport.

Physical educators may find opportunities in management. Here the sales manager of a health and fitness club completes the required daily reports.

dent teaching experience. These courses focus on placing students in a practical setting on or off campus. Exercise science majors enrolled in fieldwork may work with clients in a commercial fitness center or health club. As interns exercise science majors may work in a hospital cardiac rehabilitation program or in a corporate fitness center. Sport management majors may intern with a professional athletic team while sport media majors may gain practical experience with a radio or television station. Athletic trainers usually gain practical experience on campus, putting in hundreds of hours working in the training room and serving as the trainer for various athletic teams. Many professionals view the practical experience gained through fieldwork, internships, and student teaching as vital in career preparation.

You can also enhance your professional credentials by taking advantage of various certification programs offered through the college or university and by outside agencies. For example, many students take first aid courses offered by the American Red Cross as part of their curriculum. However, you can also become certified as an instructor in first aid by taking one additional Red Cross course, First Aid Instructor. This certification will allow you to teach first aid and certify your students as meeting the standards of the American Red Cross. The Red Cross offers instructor certification in cardiopulmonary resuscitation (CPR), permitting you to teach and certify people in this important skill. Certification in this area is also offered by the American Heart Association. If you are planning a career in exercise science such as in a corporate fitness center instructor, certification in CPR and first aid would allow you to train employees in these lifesaving areas. These certifications are also helpful if you are pursuing a teaching-coaching career. Even if your institution does not offer these courses, your local American Red Cross can provide you with the necessary training in a short period of time.

If you are interested in a career in athletic training or in exercise science you may want to consider becoming certified as an Emergency Medical Technician (EMT). The American College of Sports Medicine (ACSM) offers a certification program

or during the senior year; this experience may last for a quarter or for a semester. In recent years a concerted effort has been made by professionals to provide their prospective teachers with practical or field-based experiences prior to their student teaching. This allows students to practice the teaching skills learned in their courses and can assist them in solidifying their career decision.

Practical experiences associated with nonteaching physical education programs are commonly referred to as fieldwork or internships. Fieldwork is typically shorter in duration than an internship; an internship may be similar in length to the stu-

Certifications such as those offered in swimming by the American Red Cross and practical experience can be assets in preparing for a career.

for individuals interested in fitness and exercise science.

ACSM certification is offered for individuals involved in preventive and rehabilitative exercise programs. Certifications include Program Director, Exercise Specialist, Exercise Test Technologist, Health/ Fitness Director, Health/Fitness Instructor, and Exercise Leader/Aerobics. Certification as an athletic trainer is given through the National Athletic Training Association (NATA).

Certifications can also be obtained in specific sport areas. For example, you can work toward becoming certified as a golf professional or a scuba instructor. Certification by the American Red Cross as a Water Safety Instructor will enable you to teach all levels of swimming. Officiating ratings in various sport areas can also be obtained. If your institution does not offer some of these certification opportunities or you are unable to fit them into your course schedule, you may be able to attain these certifica-

tions on your own through appropriate agencies and professional organizations.

One of the factors that will determine your career opportunities and professional success is your academic performance. Potential employers view academic performance as a strong reflection of a prospective employee's abilities and often as a reliable indicator of one's potential to succeed. You should make a commitment to your academic performance at the start of your college years. Your academic performance may affect your ability to enroll in graduate school.

More students are entering graduate school immediately after completing their undergraduate degree. The increased specialization within the profession has made graduate school a necessity for many students and an attractive option for those seeking to increase their knowledge in their area of interest. Attending graduate school for further work in exercise physiology, biomechanics, sport management, sport psychology, sports medicine, adapted physical education, and pedagogy is the choice of many undergraduates. However, this option may not be open to someone who has a poor academic record. Most graduate schools require a minimum grade point average (GPA) of 3.0 on a 4.0 scale. An even higher GPA may be required to get into the graduate school of your choice. Your undergraduate academic average may influence whether or not you are awarded a graduate assistantship to defray the expenses of graduate study. Graduate assistantships are also highly prized because of the practical experience they afford the recipient.

As a student it is important that you become familiar with your curriculum so you can plan your education and strengthen your qualifications for your chosen career. Most institutions assign professors to serve as academic advisors. Work closely with your advisor in planning your program of study. Take advantage of all your education has to offer to become an educated individual and a professional. Create career options along the career pathway you have chosen through judicious selection of courses and commitment to your academics. Your activities and related experiences can also contribute to your professional development.

Related Experiences

Your activities and related experiences can significantly enhance your career preparation. Your extracurricular activities can help you develop skills that are applicable to your chosen career. Perhaps it would help to view them as an unofficial fieldwork or internship of sorts. Certainly participation on an intercollegiate athletic team as an athlete, manager, or statistician can enhance your expertise in that sport. Your experience as a sport photographer, sport writer, or editor of the campus newspaper provides you with excellent training for your career in sport media. Being active in the physical education majors club, if your institution has one, contributes to your professional growth. Serving as a member of the student government may develop leadership as well as speaking, planning, and organizational skills applicable to a diversity of careers.

Your work experience can contribute to your pro-

fessional development as well. Work experience gained through part-time and summer employment can give you valuable on-the-job experience. Although employment opportunities may be difficult to secure, try to find work that relates to your career goals. In the summer gain experience teaching and organizing activities for people of all ages by working in a community recreational program. Perhaps you can get a job working in a fitness or health club, teaching clients how to use the various pieces of exercise equipment and supervising their workouts. To gain practical experience you may want to consider sacrificing a higher paying job or working the career-related job and getting a second job to make ends meet.

Another source of practical experience is on-campus jobs. If you have financial need you may qualify for a work-study job. As a freshman you may not be able to get the job you want and have to settle for working in the cafeteria, but as an upperclassman you will have a better chance to secure the job you desire. Work-study jobs may be available as an intramural assistant, researcher, tutor, lab assistant, computer assistant, or you may be assigned to do general work in the athletic director's office, for example. Of course, you need to have the necessary skills to perform the job or the willingness to learn if afforded the opportunity to do so. Another campus employment opportunity open to qualified students is being a resident assistant in the dormitories (that is, if your institution is a residential college or university). As a resident assistant you will learn how to work closely with people and develop counseling and programming skills.

Volunteering is another means to gain practical experience. Although volunteering does not pay you any money, try to view volunteering as an investment in your future. Perhaps you would like to work for the summer at the corporate fitness center, but found that they were unable to hire you due to budgetary constraints. Ask if they would be willing to accept your services as a volunteer. This means that if you need money for tuition and related costs you may have to work nights and weekends to secure the necessary funds for school. However, volunteering may pay big dividends when it comes

Participation on an athletic team can enhance one's expertise in the sport and prove valuable in securing employment as a coach.

to your career. One word of advice. Even if you are a volunteer, devote as much time and energy to the job as if you were a paid employee. You are being viewed by the management as a potential employee. Perhaps if you do a good job this summer you may be hired on a regular basis for the next summer. Volunteering is a good way to gain entry into your career field. Considering a career in sport broadcasting? Volunteer to be a "go-fer" at a local television station to gain exposure to life behind the scenes. Perhaps this will place you in the right place at the right time to take advantage of any opportunities that may come your way. Volunteering will also allow you to make professional contacts for the future.

As mentioned previously, fieldwork and internships are a good way to gain practical experience. If they are not mandated by your program, find out if you could do one for credit or on a volunteer basis. Many professional organizations would be delighted to provide internship experiences for volunteers. AAHPERD, for example, offers internships to interested students. Contact professional organizations within your field of study to see if they would be willing to accept an intern.

Consider volunteering to work with one of your professors on a research project he or she is conducting in your area of interest. If you are attending an institution with a masters or doctorate program in physical education, volunteer to help one of the graduate students collect data for a research project. This research experience will prove enlightening and be of help when you are involved in your own graduate education. Again, a reminder. Make a commitment to the research project and let the researcher know you can be counted on to fulfill your responsibilities.

Extracurricular activities, work experiences, and volunteer activities can contribute to your professional development. These practical experiences provide you with the opportunity to work in your chosen career, learn necessary skills, and develop professional contacts. Even though you are just starting your professional preparation for your career, it is not too early to start thinking about being a professional and planning for the future.

Professional Involvement

Start early to become a professional. Professional activities are a source of knowledge and growth. One way to start is by becoming active in your physical education majors club at your institution. If there is not a professional club, try to start one with the help of fellow students and interested faculty. Join the national association affiliated with your career choice. Join AAHPERD, ACSM or NATA, for example. Many professional organizations offer student memberships at reduced rates. Attend the national conventions where you will have the opportunity to meet professionals, make personal contacts, and attend meetings and workshops on research findings and new techniques. If it is not possible to attend the national meetings, many organizations have state or regional associations which hold their own conventions. These may be more convenient to attend and allow you to meet professionals within the same area. Association members, as part of their membership fee, receive professional periodicals. For example, AAHPERD members can select the *Journal of Physical Education, Recreation, and Dance* as one of their publications.

Start to build a professional library. In addition to the professional periodicals to which you subscribe, organize and retain your class notes, handouts, and texts. Many a professional who threw out notes for a particular class or sold textbooks found it meant a lot of additional work and money later on when the materials were needed for a job. These materials serve as resources when you are starting out in your career. Undergraduate notes and materials also prove helpful in completing course work in graduate school.

Attaining a Professional Position

Whether you are seeking full-time employment following graduation, part-time or summer employment, an internship, a graduate assistantship, or a position as a volunteer within an organization, obtaining the desired position requires a well planned, concerted effort. Highly desirable positions may attract numerous applicants and competition may be strong. Therefore, it is important to market yourself effectively and prepare thoroughly for this effort.

Early in your educational career you should begin the process of developing a resume. A resume is a summary of your qualifications and experiences. To facilitate the writing of your resume, keep a record of all your activities on an on-going basis throughout your career. People who fail to do so often inadvertently exclude important activities or honors from the resume because they have been forgotten. Some examples of activities that would be important to include are honors, athletic participation, employment, professional memberships, and volunteer activities.

One way to keep track of your activities is to use an index card system. Label a file folder "Resume," and each time you participate in a professional activity, engage in an extracurricular activity, or are awarded an honor, make note of it on an index card and put it in the folder. Some students, instead of using index cards, use a computer to effectively keep track of their accomplishments and activities.

Make sure the information you record, be it on an index card or a computer, is accurate and complete. For student teaching, internships, work, and related experiences, be sure that you have the correct position, title, the correct spelling of the organization, the address, and the name and the title of the person who supervised you. Make sure responsibilities that you performed are accurately portrayed, and the relevant dates given. For example, let us say that you just completed an internship at Xerox Corporation in their corporate fitness program. You would write down on the index card:

Internship at Xerox Corporation. Industrial Drive, Rochester, NY, 14859. Supervisor: Dr. Richard Smith, Director of Corporate Fitness. Responsibilities: Assisted with the administration of stress tests; designed individual exercise prescriptions, supervised individual exercise programs, counseled participants in the areas of nutrition, smoking cessation, and stress management. Dates: January–May 1990.

Have you ever been awarded any honors, such as being named to the Dean's List? Make note of it: Dean's List, Fall 1989. Write down extracurricular activities on a yearly basis as well—intramurals, intercollegiate athletics, Physical Education Majors' Club member, representative to student government, attendance at the state Association for Health, Physical Education, Recreation, and Dance convention, volunteer for Special Olympics, and so on. Make note of the dates that you attained certifications as well, for example: 1990—certified by the American Red Cross as a Community CPR Instructor. It is also helpful to make a note of your special skills, such as speaking a foreign language or a high level of competency with computers. Record each item separately so as to facilitate the sorting and appropriate organization of these various activities into appropriate categories when constructing your resume.

There are many different formats for writing resumes, depending on the purpose for which it is being used. For example, resumes can be used to obtain an interview, as a follow-up to an interview, as a means of highlighting your qualifications for the position, and as a complement to a letter of application. Career planning and counseling centers offer students guidelines for its construction. A sample resume is shown in Figure 10-1. There are also several computer programs available to assist in the writing of a resume.

Customize your resume for the particular position that you are pursuing. This may lead to having several different resumes, tailoring your background, strengths, and experience to fit the position being sought. Your index cards or computer records serve as a master list from which to select information and activities to present the best picture of you to the potential employer and enables you to include all relevant information on the resume. Preparing your resume on a computer will allow you to easily edit it and to prepare different versions.

Resumes should be meticulously prepared and proofread several times to ensure that there are no errors. The resume serves as a writing sample and reflects how well you can communicate. It also reflects your neatness and attention to detail. The resume should be organized in a manner such that the reader's attention is easily drawn to the most important information. It should be printed on high quality, standard-size bond paper using a high quality photocopier, laser printer, or typesetter.

As a senior, you should open up a placement file at your institution's placement office. Placement files generally contain demographic information, a resume, and letters of recommendation. Letters of recommendation should be solicited from people who are well acquainted with your abilities. Professors familiar with your work, student teaching or internship supervisors, and individuals for whom you worked may be able to accurately assess your abilities and qualifications for employment or further study.

There are many sources that will assist you in locating job openings. College/university placement offices maintain job listings and update these on a continuing basis. Some professional organizations offer placement services to their members and periodically disseminate information about job openings. AAHPERD, the National Athletic Trainers Association (NATA), and the American College of Sports Medicine (ACSM) offer placement services and job listings to their members. Newspapers, state employment offices, and some state education departments have lists of job openings. Personal contacts are very helpful in the job search. Let faculty members, friends, relatives, and former employers know that you are seeking employment.

ROBYN LEE WEST

School Address   Permanent Address
221 Eastview Road, Apt.1   132 Cherry Lane
Ithaca, NY 14856   Floral Estates, NY 11003
Phone: 607-276-5555   Phone: 516-776-5476

CAREER OBJECTIVE	To teach physical education in an elementary school, work with children with disabilities to improve their motor performance, and coach soccer and track

EDUCATION	Ithaca College, Ithaca, NY, May 1991
	  Bachelor of Science in Physical Education
	    Provisional certification K-12
	    Minor in Health
	    Concentration in Adapted Physical Education

PROFESSIONAL EXPERIENCES	Student teacher, Pine Elementary School (1/3-3/7 1991) Student teacher, Cayuga High School (3/10-5/14 1991) Fieldwork in adapted physical education, United Children's Center (1/4-5/2 1990) Youth Bureau volunteer soccer coach (Fall 1989-1991) Counselor for children with special needs, Floral Estates Youth Summer Camp (Summers 1987-1991)
HONORS AND AWARDS	Dean's List (Fall 1988, 1990, 1991; Spring 1988, 1990) Who's Who in American Colleges and Universities Ithaca College HPER Professional Achievement Award
COLLEGE ACTIVITIES	Physical Education Majors' Club (1987-1991; Vice-President 1990) Intercollegiate Soccer Team (1987-1990; Captain 1990) Intercollegiate Track and Field Team (1988-1991) Intramural volleyball and basketball official (1988-1990) Peer counselor, Health Center (1989-1991) President's Host Committee for Admissions (1989-1991)
CERTIFICATIONS	American Red Cross CPR Instructor American Red Cross Water Safety Instructor American Red Cross Adapted Aquatics Instructor Rated official in volleyball and basketball
PROFESSIONAL AFFILIATIONS	American Alliance for Health, Physical Education, Recreation, and Dance New York State Association for Health, Physical Education, Recreation, and Dance Finger Lakes Board of Officials
REFERENCES	Available from the Placement Office, School of Health Sciences and Human Performance, Ithaca College

FIGURE 10-1 *Sample resume*

Follow up on all leads in a timely fashion.

Once aware of possible vacancies, send a copy of your resume along with a cover letter requesting an interview and/or application. The cover letter is to interest an employer in hiring you. When possible, the letter should be addressed to a specific person by name. It should set forth the purpose of the letter, refer the reader to the resume to note certain qualifications particularly relevant to the position, and relate why you are interested in the position, emphasizing your career goals and potential contributions to the organization. The letter should close with a request for action, either an interview or an application, and thank the reader for his or her time.

If you are invited for an interview, prepare carefully—in other words, do your homework. Find out as much as possible about the organization, the job responsibilities, and other relevant information. Before the interview, take some time to formulate answers to commonly asked interview questions. The following list contains some common questions.

- What are your career plans and goals?
- When and why did you select your college major?
- How has your education prepared you for this job?
- Which of your experiences and skills are particularly relevant to this job?
- What are your greatest strengths? What are your major weaknesses?
- What is your philosophy of physical education? Can you give an example of how your philosophy has guided your actions?
- What jobs have you held? How were they obtained and why did you leave? What would your former supervisors tell us about your job performance?
- What can you tell me about yourself?
- What accomplishments have given you the greatest satisfaction?
- What have you done that shows leadership, initiative, and a willingness to work?
- What salary do you expect to receive? How many hours per week do you expect to work?
- Why should I select you above all other candidates for this position?
- What questions do you have about our organization?

As part of the preparation process, you also should prepare a list of questions to ask the interviewer.

- What are the opportunities for personal growth?
- What are the training programs or education opportunities offered to employees?
- What are the challenging aspects of this position?
- What are the organization's plans for the future?
- What qualities are you looking for in new employees?
- What characteristics distinguish successful personnel in your company?
- How would you describe the organization's management style?
- How would you best use my skills within the organization?

Develop additional questions appropriate to the specific job for which you are interviewing.

First impressions are critical, so create a positive one by your professional appearance, attitude, and personality. Dress appropriately for the interview. So you'll be sure to be on time, plan on arriving ahead of the scheduled appointment time. Greet the interviewer with a firm handshake and be courteous, poised, interested, responsive, and enthusiastic. Be prepared to discuss your accomplishments, skills, interests, personal qualities, and work values in an honest, self-confident manner. Be self-assured, not arrogant or aggressive. Listen to each question carefully and take some time to formulate a thoughtful, concise answer. Remember that you are being evaluated not only on your achievements, but on your ability to think and communicate. At the close of the interview, thank the interviewer for his or her time.

Follow each interview with a thank-you letter. The letter should stress your interest in the position and highlight important topics that you believe went particularly well in the interview. Be sure to thank the interviewer for his or her time and consideration. If you decide after the interview that the position is not for you, thank the interviewer for his or her time and let them know that you are not interested in the position.

When offered a position, again carefully weigh the characteristics of the job with the results of your self-assessment pertaining to your skills, interests, personal and work values, and career goals. If you accept the position, your letter should confirm previously agreed-upon terms of employment and reflect your excitement at meeting the challenges of the position. Should you decide to decline the offer of employment, the letter of rejection should express your regrets as well as thanking the employer for his or her time, effort, and consideration.

Attaining a desired position requires a commitment to marketing yourself effectively. Actively seeking information about position vacancies and diligently pursuing all leads is important for conducting a successful job search. Your resume should truthfully portray your abilities and accomplishments and be tailored to fit the position. Prepare thoroughly for each interview and present yourself as a young professional. Make your final decision thoughtfully and communicate this decision to your potential employer in a professional, timely manner.

Professional preparation for a career includes your academic studies, related experiences, and professional activities. Preparation and planning for a career requires an understanding of the requirements of the work to be performed. As you embark on your career preparation be flexible, open minded, and willing to explore career opportunities presented to you.

SUMMARY

Traditionally careers in physical education and sport have focused on teaching and coaching in schools and colleges or universities. Lately, teaching and coaching careers have expanded to nonschool settings and all segments of the population. Within the last decade nonteaching careers have become increasingly popular.

Selecting a career pathway from the many available options requires careful consideration of many factors. Choosing a career involves the process of decision making. To make an informed decision, information must be gathered from the appropriate sources and evaluated. Your personal strengths, interests, goals, and preferences are the most important considerations in choosing a career. Discerning this information requires a process of self assessment. In selecting a career you must also consider information about the career itself. This information may be gathered through research and by talking to practitioners in your prospective career.

Professional preparation for a career involves academic studies, related experiences, and professional activities. Planning for a career demands understanding of the nature of the work to be performed and the requirements of the job. As you read about different career opportunities in physical education and sport, be flexible and open minded and explore career opportunities that interest you.

SELF-ASSESSMENT TESTS

These tests are to assist students in determining if the materials and competencies presented in this chapter have been mastered.

1. Identify 10 career opportunities in physical education and sport that interest you. List briefly the potential employers and population served. Identify the skills needed by someone pursuing a career in these areas.

2. Using the questions provided in the text as guidelines, self-assess your strengths, interests, goals, and preferences. Based on this information, what potential careers might you choose? If you want, share this information with a fellow student and solicit each other's input regarding possible careers.

3. Obtain a copy of your professional preparation curriculum. Copies are usually available in the college or university catalogue. Identify the number and type of liberal art courses required, professional theory courses and professional activity courses specified, and the number of electives available. Identify possible minors or specialized areas of study that would enhance your preparation for your career. Again, the college or university catalogue probably carries a listing of all minors offered.

4. Discuss the role of practical experience in professional preparation. What practical experiences have you already had that could contribute to your professional preparation?

5. Describe strategies to enhance your marketability.

REFERENCES

1. Lambert CL: What is physical education? Journal of Physical Education, Recreation, and Dance 51(5):26-27, 1980.

2. US Department of Labor: Occupational outlook handbook, current edition, Washington, DC, The Department.

3. College Placement Council: CPC annual, current edition, Bethlehem, Pa, College Placement Council.

4. Akey DS, editor: Encyclopedia of associations, Detroit, Gale Research Co, current edition.

SUGGESTED READINGS

Bolles RN: What color is your parachute? a practical manual for job-hunters and career changers, Berkeley, Calif, 1989, Ten Speed Press.

This book provides practical guidelines for obtaining a job and/or changing careers. The resource section of the book is comprehensive and a valuable guide for obtaining career information.

Clayton RD and Clayton JA: Careers and professional preparation, Journal of Physical Education, Recreation, and Dance 55(5):44-45, 1984.

Desirable features of professional preparation programs are discussed as well as career opportunities in health, physical education, and recreation.

College Placement Council: CPC annual, current edition, Bethlehem, Pa, College Placement Council.

Available through the career planning office, this annual periodical offers advice on career planning, the job search, and graduate school.

Lambert C: What can I do besides teach? Journal of Physical Education, Recreation, and Dance 51(9):74-76, 1980.

Career opportunities other than public school teaching are described.

Lambert C: What is physical education? Journal of Physical Education, Recreation, and Dance 51(5):26-27, 1980.

The author emphasizes that broadening one's definition of physical education from the traditional "teaching of sports, dance, and exercise in the public schools" can open many career options. Resources for finding available jobs, developing professional contacts, and obtaining practical experience are discussed.

Lambert C: Career directions, Journal of Physical Education, Recreation, and Dance 55(5):40-43, 53, 1984.

This article mentions growing career fields and discusses factors that influence career decisions.

Miller DM: Preparing physical educators: some new ways are needed, Journal of Physical Education, Recreation, and Dance 59(5):68-72, 1988.

Professionals are encouraged to reexamine our professional preparation programs, and suggestions are offered for the future.

Scahill JL: New PE career options—time for assessment, Journal of Physical Education, Recreation, and Dance 59(5):65-67, 1988.

It is suggested that it is time for physical education departments to assess curricula used to prepare students for nontraditional career options.

VanderZwaag HJ: Coming out of the maze: sport management, dance management and exercise science—programs with a future, Quest 35:66-73, 1983.

The author contends that physical education today lacks a clear focus and proposes a reorganization of the field into the areas of sport management, dance management, and exercise science.

Chapter 11

Teaching and Coaching Careers in Physical Education and Sport

INSTRUCTIONAL OBJECTIVES AND COMPETENCIES TO BE ACHIEVED

After reading this chapter the student should be able to—
- Describe the qualities of an effective teacher and his or her responsibilities.
- Describe the advantages and disadvantages of pursuing a teaching career in a school or a nonschool setting.
- Describe the similarities and differences between teaching and coaching.
- Discuss the problem of burnout and its effects on teachers and coaches.
- Discuss strategies to maximize opportunities for employment in a teaching or coaching position.

Teaching and coaching opportunities for physical educators have expanded from the school to the nonschool setting and from school-aged populations (i.e., 5 to 18 years) to people of all ages, ranging from preschoolers to senior citizens. Although traditional opportunities in the public school are available, professionals are seeking other avenues of teaching and coaching careers. The national interest in fitness and sport has contributed to the opening of these alternative areas of employment. Moreover, the continued emphasis on fitness, physical activities, and sport opportunities for all age groups presents an encouraging employment picture to potential physical education teachers and coaches. Professionals interested in pursuing a career in these areas will find that attaining a position is possible for those physical educators who possess the appropriate credentials and exhibit perseverance.

The challenge to those who wish to enter the teaching or coaching professions is reflected in the words of Aristotle. He said that those who educate children well are to be honored more than those who produce them, for those who produce children give them only life, but those who educate them give them the art of living well.[1] A physical education teacher or a coach has the responsibility to inspire students or athletes with the desire to learn, to have them recognize the need to develop physical skills and be physically active, to see that each one develops to his or her capacity, and to ensure that each one has a successful experience.

THE TEACHING PROFESSION
Choosing a Teaching Career

Teaching offers many rewards, regardless of whether it takes place in the traditional school or an alternative nonschool setting. Probably most important is that it offers an opportunity to help shape people's lives and promote a healthy life-style. Students select teaching as a career for many reasons. Each prospective teacher should take the time to list the reasons he or she has for choosing this career.

Many physical educators want to teach because of their love of children and their desire to help others. The conviction that involvement in a sound physical education program can have a significant impact on the quality of life of its participants motivates some individuals to enter the teaching profession. Prospective teachers who have been fortunate to reap the benefits of participation in a sound physical education program often express the desire to share with others the same benefits that they themselves have realized. Other individuals who had poor experiences while students in physical education enter the teaching profession because of the desire to improve the quality of physical education programs so that the benefits known to be associated with quality programs can be attained.

Certainly personal interests, likes, and dislikes influence one's decision to enter the teaching profession. Many choose to teach physical education because of their love for sport and perhaps the desire to transmit this love to others. The opportunity to be outdoors, to work out and stay physically fit, and to have fun are often given as reasons for entering the teaching profession.

The nature of the job attracts many individuals. In the school setting the long vacations, the informality of teaching in the gymnasium as compared to the classroom, and the security offered by tenure are some of the positive benefits that prompt some people to seek a teaching career. Others may enter teaching because they desire to coach and teaching in many schools is a prerequisite to coaching. Teaching may also be used as a stepping stone to other careers such as administration.

Many of the above reasons for entering the teaching profession are valid for those seeking to work in nonschool settings. The opportunity to capitalize on one's proficiency in a sport, the desire to share the benefits of participation with others, and the love of working with people may motivate physical educators to prepare for a teaching career in an alternative setting.

The reasons that individuals pursue teaching careers are varied, ranging from a desire and commitment to improve society and the quality of life to a desire to bask in the sun for several months during the vacations. The rewards that accrue from teaching depend to a large degree on the individual and what each person makes of his or her opportunities. The inner rewards, plus the financial and other benefits, can be great for the person who applies himself or herself diligently and sincerely to teaching.

What Are the Benefits and Drawbacks Associated with Teaching?

The teaching profession is considered to be a service-oriented profession. Those who enter it must often be satisfied with intrinsic rather than with extrinsic rewards. Several benefits are associated with teaching physical education in the school setting. First, one benefit is the salary. Although teachers' salaries appear to be very low in contrast with those offered in other careers, in actuality a beginning salary of $18,000 to $21,000 for nine months or approximately 180 days is equivalent to a salary of approximately $21,000 to $25,000 for a typical 12 month job with two weeks of vacation. Nationally, the average pay of a teacher exceeds $30,000 a year. The long vacation periods provide the opportunity to earn additional monies, to travel, or to continue one's education. While teaching is not a lucrative profession, the financial picture in many cases is not as bleak as one is led to believe.

Second, teaching in an educational setting offers job security in the form of tenure. Tenure is typically granted in the public schools after three years of satisfactory service to the school district and at the college and university level after six years. Other benefits include the opportunity to serve as a role model, opportunity to teach a diversity of activities and skills, the opportunity to have a significant impact on the lives of others, or the opportunity to help someone become a better person.

The physical education teacher and coach need to be well-prepared for their field of endeavor. Here a student receives feedback from the instructor regarding her micropeer teaching.

On the other hand, one should be cognizant that there are several disadvantages to pursuing a teaching career in a school setting. The public support and recognition of educators as performing a valuable service is at an all-time low. Although the public's confidence in teachers appears to be improving, the lack of whole-hearted commitment has resulted in problems of morale, lack of financial support, and pressure to do more with less money and to get by with often inadequate facilities. The teacher is often beset with discipline problems, confronted with overpopulated classes that contain unmotivated students, and are required to absorb teaching loads that are too heavy. Teachers often do numerous tasks not related to teaching such as lunchroom and study hall supervision, hall duty, and playground or bus patrol.

Several benefits are associated with teaching in the nonschool setting. Examples of teaching opportunities in the nonschool setting include working as a tennis or golf professional and teaching in a community recreation program, YMCA/YWCA, or commercial sport club such as a gymnastics club, swim club, or racquetball club. First, since participation in these programs is voluntary, the teacher generally works with individuals and students who are highly motivated and eager to be involved in the activity. In contrast, the teacher in the school setting may have to deal with disinterested students who are mandated to take "gym class." The opportunity to teach physical education without having to deal with problems associated with the schools or other duties required of teachers in the school setting (study hall, etc.) is appealing. Second, many physical educators elect to teach in the nonschool setting because of the opportunity to specialize; many physical educators like the idea of just teaching golf, tennis, or swimming. However, many nonschool settings such as YMCA/YWCA and community recreation programs require the ability to teach a diversity of activities.

There are some drawbacks to teaching in the nonschool setting. Unlike teaching in the schools, a lack of job security is typical. The number of participants enrolled in a program may determine whether it continues to be offered and may also determine the teacher's salary. Salaries may vary widely as well. In contrast to school, where the working hours are confined to the weekdays (unless one is coaching), working hours at a nonschool setting may be later afternoons and evenings and often the weekends. Working hours need to be responsive to the hours the clients have available for leisure time pursuits. Work may also be seasonal in nature, but this depends on the nature of the activity and the location. Golf pros in the Northeast may find work only from May to September, but those pursuing this profession in the South may find work to be year round.

Prospective teachers should identify their reasons for entering the teaching profession as well as evaluate the benefits associated with this career in terms of their personal priorities. Advantages and disadvantages are associated with teaching in both the school and nonschool setting. These must be considered in making a career choice.

What Is Effective Teaching?

Teaching can be defined as those interactions of the teacher and the learner that make learning more successful.[2] Although it is possible for learning to occur without a teacher's involvement, it is generally accepted that teachers facilitate the acquisition of knowledge, skills, and attitudes. Teachers who are effective use a variety of pedagogical skills and strategies to ensure that their students are appropriately engaged in relevant activities a high percentage of time, hold positive expectations for their students, and create and maintain a classroom climate that is warm and nurturing.[1]

Salient teacher behaviors can be divided into several broad areas: organization, communication, instruction, motivation, and human relations. These characteristics are common to effective teachers, regardless of the skill to be learned, the age of the students, or the setting in which the teaching occurs.

Organizational skills are very important in establishing the learning environment and facilitating student involvement in activities. The manner in which the teacher structures instruction is of major importance. To be effective the teacher must ensure that the lesson to be presented relates to the stated objectives, meets the needs of the individual

learners, and is presented in a logical, systematic manner. Effective teachers minimize transition time, that is, the time to move from place to place, and management time, that is, time used for managerial tasks such as taking attendance, through efficient and thorough planning. Lessons are planned to ensure that students receive maximum opportunities to practice relevant skills and experience success. Actively supervising and monitoring student performance and providing students with appropriate feedback are characteristics of successful teachers. Effective teachers make a concerted effort to closely observe and monitor students' performance. Skilled teachers bring each lesson to an end by summarizing what has been accomplished and by providing students with an assessment of progress toward the stated objectives.

Communication skills needed by the teacher include verbal and nonverbal expressive skills, written competencies, and the ability to use the various media. Effective verbal communication skills are essential in the teaching process. The ability to speak clearly and project one's voice in a pleasing manner is essential. Another attribute of a successful teacher is the ability to give clear, precise directions and explanations and use terminology and vocabulary that is appropriate to the activity and the level of the learners. The ability of the teacher to use questions to elicit student input, to promote student involvement, and to clarify student understanding of the material being presented enhances the effectiveness of the learning process. Effective teachers are also aware of the influence of their nonverbal behavior on the students and learning process. Use of eye contact, smiles, and pats on the back are some of the methods of communicating with students in a nonverbal manner. Through their verbal and nonverbal behaviors effective teachers model the kinds of behaviors they wish their students to exhibit, such as interest in and enjoyment of the activity and respect for other persons' opinions and needs. Effective teachers communicate enthusiasm, both through their verbal and nonverbal behavior.

Written communication skills are essential especially in the planning and evaluation phase of teach-

Effective communication skills are essential for successful teaching.

ing. Those teachers who possess effective written communication skills are able to express themselves clearly. The ability to communicate with supervisors, participants, and interested others will help to establish a more successful program.

Expertise in the use of various instructional media techniques is a quality of effective teachers. Use of transparencies, slides, movie projectors, and videotape equipment are skills that should be mastered early in one's career. Appropriate use of media can enhance and accelerate student learning.

Competency in a variety of instructional skills is essential for effective teaching. When planning experiences for students, effective teachers use their knowledge of the content to be taught, in conjunction with instructional objectives and students' needs, to provide appropriate experiences leading to the attainment of stated goals. Effective teaching requires the ability to sequence movement tasks by adding difficulty and complexity as students progress, and by providing opportunities for students not only to develop skills but to apply them.

Good teachers must not only be able to implement planned experiences effectively but they also must be flexible so that they can appropriately modify planned experiences to suit the needs of the students and the situations that arise within the learning environment.

Effective teachers are able to maintain an orderly, productive learning environment, handling discipline problems appropriately while encouraging and providing opportunities for students to learn responsibility and to be accountable for their actions. A wide variety of teaching methods and instructional strategies are judiciously employed to maximize students' active and successful engagement in relevant tasks. The ability to present clear explanations and offer accurate demonstrations contributes to learning. Effective teachers actively monitor their students' performance and are concerned about the quality of their efforts. Teachers are aware of, and capably respond to, the myriad events that occur within the instructional environment; this quality, "with-it-ness," is often described as "having eyes in the back of one's head." Evaluation skills are also important. Teachers must be able to observe and analyze student performance, focusing on the critical elements in relationship to the goal, with feedback reinforcing or modifying responses as necessary.

The communication of high expectations for each student is also important. High expectations should be held by teachers for both student learning and behavior. Positive expectations, including the belief that all students are capable of learning, are important in establishing a warm, nurturing classroom climate and a productive learning environment.[2]

The ability to motivate students to perform to their potential is the goal of every teacher. Skillful teachers will use a variety of teaching techniques to stimulate interest in participation and will seek creative techniques to involve students in the learning process. They also use appropriate reinforcement techniques to maintain student involvement and promote a high level of student effort. These may include checklists, contracts, award systems, and verbal and nonverbal feedback. Praise is used thoughtfully; it is contingent on the correct performance, is specific in its nature and intent, and is sincere. Successful teachers continually update their lessons in an effort to meet students' needs and to make the material presented relevant and challenging to the students.

Effective teachers possess superior human relations skills. They listen to students and accept students as individuals, treating them as such. They strive to instill in each student a sense of self-worth. Effective teachers show concern for the well-being of each student in their classes and endeavor to provide students with opportunities that will enhance their self-confidence. The ability to establish and maintain rapport with students and staff and readiness to acknowledge one's own mistakes are also characteristics that many successful teachers possess. A sense of humor is a welcome attribute as well.

In summary, effective teachers are able to successfully utilize a variety of skills pertaining to organization, communication, instruction, motivation, and human relations. However, effective teaching requires more than the ability to use these skills; it requires the ability to assess accurately the needs of the moment and to tailor these skills to the specific context and situation. Although many of these skills appear to be innate to certain individuals, all of them can be developed or improved by individuals who desire to become effective teachers.

TEACHING RESPONSIBILITIES

Teachers, both in the school and nonschool settings, perform a myriad of tasks everyday. Prospective teachers need to be cognizant of their responsibilities. In addition to actually teaching, teachers perform many administrative and professionally related tasks. Gensemer[3] groups the activities of teachers into three areas: instructional tasks, managerial tasks, and institutional tasks. Instructional acts are those responsibilities and activities that relate directly to teaching. These acts encompass such tasks as explaining and/or demonstrating how to perform a skill; describing how to execute a particular strategy in a game; evaluating students' performance; motivating students through the use of various techniques; and using questions to check students' comprehension of the material being presented to determine the clarity of the presentation and to elicit student input.

Managerial acts are those activities related to the administration of the class. In the school setting these activities may include taking attendance, dealing with discipline problems, and patrolling the locker room. In the nonschool setting such as in a commercial health club or sports center managerial responsibilities may include setting up and dismantling equipment, equipment repair, handing out towels, distributing workout record sheets, and recording individuals' progress.

Institutional acts are those activities related to the institution in which teaching occurs; institution refers to the school or organization for which the teachers work such as the YMCA/YWCA. In the school setting teachers may find themselves assigned to hall duty or lunchroom supervision, expected to attend curriculum or departmental meetings, and conducting parent-teacher conferences. Many

Locker room supervision is a managerial responsibility of teachers.

physical educators note that counseling students about matters that affect the development of their physical selves and advising students on personal problems occupies a great amount of their time, but the opportunity to be of service to students in this manner is a rewarding one. In the nonschool setting teachers may also perform institutional duties such as checking membership cards at the front desk, mailing promotional brochures to attract new members, and filling out a variety of reports. In some situations managerial and institutional responsibilities will occupy more of a teacher's time than actual teaching.

Teachers have numerous professional responsibilities in addition to the responsibilities previously described. Teachers may conduct research in an effort to push back the frontiers of knowledge. Another professional responsibility is to interpret the worth of physical education and sport to the public. This requires that physical educators be well versed in the scientific foundations of the discipline so that they may accurately interpret the worth of

physical education and sport to others. Physical educators need to be cognizant that the programs they conduct reflect the aims and the worth of the field. Physical educators symbolize their commitment to the profession by being a role model for what they preach; they should exemplify a healthy, active life-style. Professionals need to take advantage of opportunities to speak to educators, the community, and civic and other groups about their field of endeavor.

Many physical educators may also have community responsibilities. These are usually engaged in voluntarily. However, the special qualifications and skills of physical educators make them a likely target for requests from community groups to assist with youth and other sport programs such as Little League or adult recreational programs. Physical educators should be interested in providing leadership for community programs involving sport, athletics, and recreational activities. By exercising a leadership role they can help ensure that such programs are organized and administered in the best interests of youths and adults. By their participation physical educators are afforded an opportunity to interpret physical education and sport to the public in general. In doing so physical educators become respected and important leaders in the community and gain greater support for their program.

Teachers' responsibilities are not limited to teaching. They perform a wide variety of activities during the course of their workday. Managerial, administrative, institutional, and professional responsibilities are associated with teaching. The exact nature of these tasks may vary from setting to setting. Teaching opportunities in school and non-school settings and with people of all ages will be discussed in the following section of the text.

TEACHING CAREERS

If teaching seems to be your career goal you must begin to identify the setting and the population with whom you wish to work. Basically, the setting for your work can be divided into school and nonschool settings, while the age group can range from preschoolers through school- and college-aged students to adults and even senior citizens. Physical education teaching opportunities are diverse and the potential teacher can usually find an area that meets his or her interests.

The next section of this text will discuss teaching opportunities available in school and nonschool settings so that prospective physical educators can narrow their scope of interest while also learning about the variety of teaching options available.

Teaching in the School Setting

Teaching positions in the school setting are available in public and private school systems, higher education, and special schools. Public and private schools are organized according to various administrative patterns. The traditional grade configuration is elementary school, which is composed of kindergarten and the first through eighth grades, and high school, which is composed of grades 9 through 12. Another pattern that is used is the elementary, junior high, and high school configuration (i.e., grades K to 6, 7 to 9, and 10 to 12). An increasingly

common pattern incorporates the middle school; thus, the grade configuration becomes K to 5, 6 to 8, and 9 to 12.

In higher education, professional opportunities include teaching in 2-year junior colleges or community colleges and 4-year colleges or universities. There are also teaching positions for those professionals who want to work with the disabled and for those who aspire to instruction in a professional preparation program. Teaching opportunities also exist in special schools, such as vocational and technical schools, as well as in developmental centers.

Teaching in the Elementary School

Physical education in the elementary school is emerging as the art and science of human movement. Quality elementary school programs and teachers seek to instill in children the why of movement, the how of movement, and the outcomes or the physiological, psychological, and sociological results of movement. One of the primary objectives of these programs is the sound development of movement skills and motor patterns that comprise the movement repertoire of human beings.

The provision of a quality physical education program for young children is critical. Participation in a quality program during these formative years will likely instill in the child a love for physical activity that may last a lifetime as well as a favorable attitude regarding the importance of physical education. If the experience is less than positive, the youngster may come to hate physical education as well as physical activity, a feeling that could remain with the individual for life. Because of the close relationship between physical activity and health, this could have a significant impact on the quality of the child's life.

Movement experiences are recognized as educationally desirable in the early life of the child. This is the time when a solid movement foundation can be developed, providing children with a base for future physical development and achievement in various forms of physical activity. Furthermore, it is through movement that children express themselves, are creative, develop self-image, and gain a better understanding of their physical selves. It is

Kindergarten class using barrels with bottoms cut out at Oak View Elementary School, Fairfax, Va.

through such movement experiences that young children explore, develop, and grow in a meaningful manner.

In the primary grades K to 3, a great emphasis is placed on learning fundamental motor skills such as running, jumping, climbing, throwing, catching, kicking, and striking (see Chapter 4). Children participate in guided discovery and problem-solving activities focused on movement concepts, including body awareness, spatial awareness, qualities of movement, and relationships. Conceptually based programs, such as Basic Stuff, further enhance the child's understanding of movement. Perceptual motor activities help children to further develop such necessary skills as eye-hand and eye-foot coordination, laterality and directionality, and tracking of an object. The primary grade curriculum is concerned with developing within each child a positive self-image as a mover. Attention also should be given to developing desirable social skills, such as working with others. Individualized learning, in which students learn at their own pace, is compatible with problem solving, guided discovery, and a

creative approach to learning for primary school children.

In the upper elementary school grades, the physical education curriculum focuses on refining fundamental motor skills and applying these skills to the development of sport-related skills. During this time all children should be given the opportunity to participate in a wide range of sport and physical activities rather than be encouraged to specialize in a few selected sports. A school curriculum that offers soccer and football in the fall, basketball and volleyball in the winter, and softball and track in the spring is not providing the diversity of activities necessary to ensure optimum skill acquisition at these grade levels. In addition to being exposed to traditional team sports, students at this level should receive instruction in dance, gymnastics, individual activities (i.e., track and, whenever possible, aquatics). Acquisition of knowledge relative to physical education and the development of qualities of good sportsmanship, leadership, and fellowship should be encouraged.

Specific state requirements should be considered

in structuring the elementary school physical education program. Although there is no national curriculum, elementary school physical educators may find the guidelines developed by the Council on Physical Education for Children (COPEC), a substructure of NASPE of AAHPERD, helpful in designing and implementing their programs. COPEC recommends that a quality instructional program provide opportunities for each child to develop motor skills and efficient movement patterns, attain a high level of fitness, learn to communicate through movement, acquire self-understanding, interact socially, and realize desired psychomotor, cognitive, and affective outcomes. COPEC guidelines also suggest that elementary school children participate in a quality physical education program for a minimum of 150 minutes per week.

Many reasons are given by physical educators for preferring teaching in the elementary schools. At this level students are typically motivated, eager, enthusiastic, and take pride in their progress. Children at this age enjoy being active and usually appear to have boundless energy. Many physical educators enjoy the challenge of working with children during their most impressionable and formative years. The rapid, visible skill improvement typical of elementary school students is rewarding and motivating to the teacher.

Teaching in Middle School or Junior High School

Teaching students enrolled in the middle school or junior high school presents a unique series of challenges to physical educators. Students are in a period of their development that is fraught with many physical, social, and emotional changes. Because of the anatomical and physiological characteristics of this age group, activities must be selected with care. Students at this level are in a period of rapid growth that causes them difficulty in coordinating their actions and often results in awkwardness and excessive fatigue. Students are faced with the task of coping with the myriad changes associated with puberty, including the development of secondary sex characteristics. Social and emotional changes are also experienced. The desire to be independent and

Students practice outdoor survival skills in physical education class at Lyons Township High School, LaGrange, Ill.

the influence of peers is particularly strong. Physical educators need to be cognizant of and sensitive to the many changes students are experiencing. Students may often seek out the physical education teacher for guidance and support during this time of transition.

At this level physical education programs should include a balance between individual and dual sport activities such as aquatics and tennis and team sport activities such as soccer and basketball. Dance, gymnastics, and fitness activities also should be an integral part of the curriculum. It is important to build upon the skills and positive experiences of the elementary school level. Those students who have

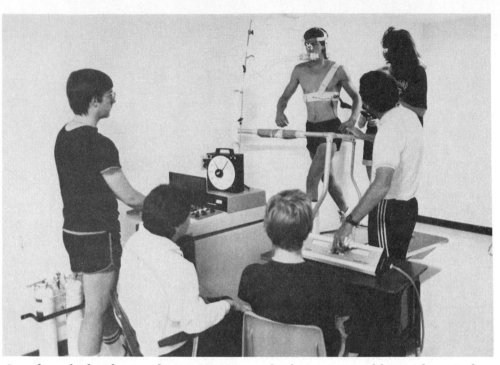

Secondary school students conduct an exercise test under the supervision of their teacher at Rock Springs High School, Rock Springs, Wy.

not progressed as rapidly as their peers in motor development should receive special attention to help them improve their skills. Students' knowledge of physical education should be further expanded and opportunities to apply this knowledge provided. During these school years, students begin to specialize in certain physical activities and actively pursue those interests.

NASPE's Committee on Middle School Physical Education advocates that middle school physical education programs provide opportunities for each student to engage in activities that promote motor skill and fitness development throughout life. Programs at this level should advance knowledge of physical education while enhancing social and emotional development through increased self-responsibility and self-direction. Within the physical education program students should be grouped by interest and ability, and careful attention be given to avoiding sex-role discrimination and stereotyping. A

minimum of 250 minutes of physical education per week, distributed over at least three days, is recommended. Additional opportunities for students to participate in physical activity experiences should be provided through intramural programs, club activities, and, when appropriate, interscholastic sports.

Teaching in the High School

At the high school level, students exhibit increased physical, mental, social, and emotional maturity. This is the time of transition from adolescence to adulthood.

One of the primary goals for physical educators teaching at the secondary school level is to socialize students into the role of participants in physical activities suited to their needs and interests. Pangrazi and Darst[4] state that "the most important goals of a secondary physical education program should be to help youngsters incorporate some

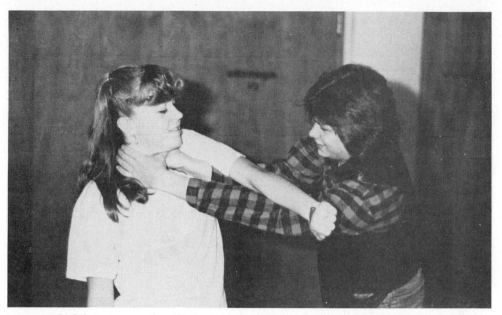

Self-defense is a popular offering in secondary school physical education programs.

form of physical activity into their life-style." This means that teachers must design and implement physical education programs in such a manner that the students' attitudes, knowledge, and skills are developed with a view to realizing this objective. Pangrazi and Darst[4] contend that the ultimate measure of successful high school physical education program is the "number of students who incorporate physical activities such as exercise, sport, dance, and outdoor adventure activities into their life-styles."

The curriculum is generally oriented toward lifetime sports, although team sports also may be popular. It is critical that the physical educator take into consideration the interests and needs of the students in planning the curriculum. During this time students should have the opportunity to develop sufficient skills so that when they leave school they will have the desire and the knowledge to participate in physical activities and sport successfully and enjoyably. Because many students do not continue on to college, it is essential that they acquire the competencies and interest before they leave high school.

NASPE's Secondary School Physical Education Council recommends that programs at the high school level focus on refining skills in a wide range of activities and on the development of advanced skills in lifetime activities personally selected by the student. Students should learn how to develop personal programs to gain and maintain optimal levels of fitness throughout their lifetime. Knowledge of the scientific principles related to physical education, self-direction in the conduct of individual physical activity programs, and an appreciation of the role of physical activity and sport in society are also outcomes of a quality secondary school physical education program. It is recommended that daily physical education be provided for all students. The length of the class period, the size of the class, and the quality standards used for credit should be comparable with those used for other subject areas within the curriculum.

Many high school physical education programs, while required of the students, offer students the opportunity to select units in which they want to participate. An increasing number of schools have expanded their course offerings by using off-

Physical education instructor directs students in an exercise class at Ithaca College.

campus community facilities such as a golf course, ice rink, aquatics center, or ski slope. The trend is toward providing students with increased knowledge and understanding of physical education concepts. This is often accomplished by offering mini-courses to students on topics of interest such as fitness or weight management or by the integration of concepts, such as those presented in Basic Stuff, into regular activity classes. Intramurals, inter-scholastic sports, and sport clubs offer students additional opportunities to participate in sport, develop expertise, and realize other desirable outcomes.

Teaching Physical Education in Higher Education

Prospective physical education teachers may also take advantage of opportunities to teach in higher education. Often a master's degree in an area of physical education is a prerequisite to obtaining a job at this level. In some institutions coaching responsibilities may be associated with teaching

positions while in other institutions coaches carry no teaching responsibilities.

Opportunities may be found to teach at two-year community colleges or at four-year colleges or universities. While typical college students are 18 to 22 years of age, there is a trend toward older individuals returning to college. Physical educators like to teach at this level for several reasons. The students are more mature and working on a college campus is enjoyable. Freedom to structure classes is greater and some individuals believe that more prestige is associated with teaching at the college level. Some physical educators end up teaching at the college level because it is a requirement associated with a coaching position.

The status of general or basic instruction physical education programs* in colleges and universities in

---

*These programs are designed to serve all students on campus and are not to be confused with programs designed to educate prospective physical education majors; those programs are referred to as professional preparation programs.

the United States has changed in recent years. At one time many colleges and universities required all students to take a physical education course each semester, for example, one course a semester for two years. Today physical education at this level is usually voluntary, thus placing responsibility on the physical education department to offer courses that are appealing to the students. Because of this need, curriculums at this level tend to be more flexible and to change more often in response to students' interests and needs.

Lifetime sports and recreational activities are stressed at this level, including such activities as tennis; self-defense; aerobic dance and exercise; outdoor pursuits such as canoeing, camping, rock climbing; and aquatic activities. Some colleges and universities offer students the opportunity to enroll in theory courses in which students study the *why* of physical education. Such courses may explore such topics as health concepts, cardiovascular fitness, principles of exercise, training techniques, biomechanical principles, and development of personalized fitness programs. Sport clubs provide interested participants an opportunity for social group experiences and enjoyment of a particular sport activity. Intramurals and intercollegiate sports play an important part in college and university physical education programs. They offer students additional opportunities for participation according to their abilities, needs, and interests.

Teaching Physical Education in Professional Preparation Programs

Physical educators who aspire to teach at the college and university level and are interested in shaping the direction of their field by preparing future leaders have many opportunities to render this valuable service in the more than 600 institutions that have such a program.

The qualifications for teaching in professional preparation programs include advanced degrees, an acceptable academic record, an interest in and understanding of college students, a broad view of educational problems, and, many times, previous experience at elementary or secondary school levels. The college teacher must be particularly well versed and competent in the field and have desirable personality and nonacademic traits such as good character.

A professor in a professional preparation program may teach theory courses in the subdisciplines and other areas such as history and philosophy of physical education, tests and measurements, motor control, motor learning, motor development, biomechanics, exercise physiology, curriculum and methods, organization and administration, sociology of sport, sport psychology, and adapted physical education. These individuals typically possess doctorate degrees in their areas of expertise. Individuals who aspire to teach in professional preparation programs may also teach professional activity and skills courses as well as courses in coaching methods. These individuals usually possess a high degree of skill in their areas of expertise. Professionals teaching activity and skills courses possess master's degrees although some individuals may have earned doctorate degrees.

In addition to their teaching responsibilities, teachers are expected to conduct research, participate on department and college or university committees, and advise and counsel students. These teachers are expected to write for professional publications, perform community service, consult, and participate in the work of professional organizations.

The services rendered by physical educators in professional preparation programs can be rewarding. By providing experiences that will help develop desirable qualities, competencies, and attributes in students preparing to become leaders in the field and by doing an outstanding job in this training experience, a teacher's work will live on forever in the lives of students and other leaders of future generations.

Teaching Adapted Physical Education

Opportunities for teaching individuals who are physically handicapped, sensorially impaired, developmentally disabled, mentally ill, or socially deviant also exist. With the advent of Public Law 94-142 and other legislation, many of these individuals have been mainstreamed into regular school classes.

Physical education activity for individuals with disabilities.

However, some individuals find that they cannot safely or successfully participate in regular classes and therefore pursue physical education with people who have similar abilities. School, college, and university programs have been established in which individuals with disabilities are taught with their peers. Physical education often is part of the curriculum.

Physical educators may render many different services to individuals with disabilities. Some schools or school systems have an adapted physical education specialist who provides direct services to individuals with disabilities. In other settings the adapted physical educator serves as a consultant to help other teachers provide needed services. Physical educators working with disabled individuals should participate in the development of individualized educational plans (IEPs). These plans may help students to correct physical conditions

that can be improved through exercise, assist each student to achieve the highest level of physical fitness within his or her capabilities, help the student identify physical activities and sports suited to his or her abilities and interests, and provide each student with positive experiences conducive to the development of a healthy self-concept.

Prospective physical education teachers interested in working with disabled individuals should prepare for this opportunity by taking additional course work in the area of adapted physical education. It is recommended that practical experience with individuals with disabling conditions be gained as part of the preparation for a physical education career.

Teaching Physical Education in Special Schools

In addition to the students enrolled in public and private schools that serve many children and youth in the United States, other students are enrolled in special schools. These include trade and vocational schools, preschools, and schools for men and women who are primarily interested in adult education.

Many schools exist to prepare for careers in certain trades, crafts, and other vocations. These schools may be affiliated with school districts or may be privately owned and operated. They prepare students for careers in technical fields such as computer repairs or health-service fields such as dental assisting. Some of these schools offer some type of physical education program for their students that is usually similar to those discussed under secondary schools.

In recent years the number of preschools has grown rapidly. Many of these preschools offer physical education programs focusing on perceptual-motor development and movement experiences.

Adult education is also thriving throughout the country. Programs are being established in most communities that provide experiences for men and women who desire to enrich their lives. These experiences cover the gamut of educational activities including English, Spanish, music, art, and word processing. Courses are also offered in sport skills such as golf and tennis, and recreational sport opportunities are provided. Interest is shown not only in developing fitness but also in learning about the components of fitness and the role of fitness in the attainment of optimal well-being.

• • •

A diversity of opportunities exist for individuals interested in teaching in the school setting. These opportunities encompass individuals of all ages. Many opportunities also can be found for the physical educator who is interested in working overseas. Teacher exchange programs and the Peace Corps offer the opportunity to teach in elementary and secondary schools as well as colleges and universities in other countries. The United States Armed Forces also operates elementary and secondary schools on overseas bases for students of personnel; it is not necessary to be a member of the military to teach in these schools. Job possibilities are numerous for the prospective physical education teacher who actively seeks a position teaching in the schools.

Teaching in Nonschool Settings

Several options are available for physical educators who desire to teach, but not in the school setting. The growth of interest in sport by people of all ages has stimulated the growth of these other teaching avenues. Teaching opportunities may be found today in commercial sport clubs, community recreational and sport programs, resorts, the Armed Forces, senior citizen and retirement centers, and correctional institutions.

The requirements for employment in these positions, working conditions, salaries and other benefits vary widely. Some of these teaching positions require a high level of expertise in a particular sport, while others require individuals able to teach a diversity of activities. Working hours vary a great deal as well. For these positions hours are often dictated by the time the clients or students are available. If one is working with youths, hours are likely to be after school and on the weekends. If one is working with adults, hours tend to be on the weekends and in the evenings. Daytime work is also available, however. These positions may pay on the per hour basis, have a set salary (which can vary from $10,000 to $25,000 a year or more), or may depend on the number of students taught. Benefits may vary from none to complete medical, dental, and life insurance plans.

Some teaching positions require that individuals assume other responsibilities as well. These may include public relations work, soliciting memberships, record keeping, and equipment and facility maintenance. Some type of work may be seasonal in nature, depending on the climate and/or type of facility. For example, if you were a teacher and/or director of aquatics at an outdoor facility in the northeastern United States, your employment would probably last from June to September; working at an indoor facility in the Northeast would likely result in a year-round position. In the Southwest,

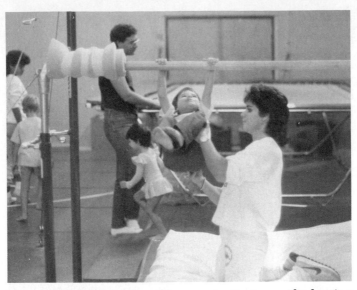

Physical educators may find teaching and coaching opportunities in nonschool settings. The instructor assists a child in a preschool gymnastics program.

the same job might be year-round, regardless of the type of facility.

Because these jobs require, in essence, teaching skills, many physical educators who desire to teach in the nonschool setting also complete the requirements for teaching certification. By doing so, they increase the range of job opportunities from which they can select. Other physical educators, having prepared for teaching in the schools, look to these other avenues of employment when they are unable to find a teaching position suited to their needs and interests or as a means of part-time and summer employment. Many employers hiring physical educators to fill these positions also view favorably the credentials of those applicants able to list a teaching certificate on their resume. For some positions special certificates may be required, such as as certification by the Professional Golfers' Association (PGA) or Ladies Professional Golfers' Association (LPGA) as a golf professional.

The physical educator should also be cognizant of the reasons of adults and youths for seeking instruction. Adults seek instruction at these organizations for many reasons. First, they may not have had instruction in the activity or activities during

their youth in their physical education classes. Second, they may seek instructions for their own personal growth and pleasure. Instruction may be sought for social reasons, such as the desire to be able to participate in specific activities with friends and family. Some adults may seek instruction, for example, in golf to be able to successfully participate with business associates in this accepted social activity. The desire to improve and refine one's performance by seeking instruction from a professional is often cited as the reason for enrolling in instructional classes.

Youths enroll in these organizational programs and classes for many of the same reasons as adults. Additionally, youths may enroll in certain activity classes because instruction in that activity or interscholastic competition in that activity is not offered in their school. Youths desiring to develop more advanced skills such as in gymnastics or to compete in certain sport activities such as swimming may find these organizations offer experiences that meet their needs. Youths and their parents may seek expert instruction because of aspirations to be a professional player such as in golf and tennis or because of the desire to successfully compete for a college scholarship in certain sport areas; they may find nonschool instructional opportunities essential to the realization of these goals.

Teaching in Commercial Sport Clubs

In recent years the number of commercial sport clubs and facilities has grown tremendously. Tennis and racquetball clubs, gymnastics clubs, swimming clubs, country clubs offering golf and tennis, karate and judo schools, and bowling establishments are examples of commercial sport enterprises.

Since commercial sport clubs usually focus around a particular sport, physical educators who desire to teach in such an organization should possess a high level of expertise in a particular sport. In many instances this expertise can be gained through participation in intercollegiate athletics. Many physical educators also have gained expertise by participating in private clubs such as gymnastic clubs during their youth and continuing their participation throughout their college years. Teaching responsibilities may include private lessons as well as group lessons. There may be the opportunity to coach high-level performers as well. Additional responsibilities may include setting up tournaments such as in a tennis and racquetball club, selling sport equipment and apparel such as in a golf pro shop at a country club, or transporting individuals to competitions such as in a swimming club or a gymnastics club. Many commercial clubs expect the teachers to assume managerial responsibilities at times as well.

Employers, in addition to requiring a high level of expertise as a condition of employment, may also require certification. In the aquatics area certification as a Water Safety Instructor, Lifeguard Instructor, and in pool management may be required. Certification as a golf professional such as through the PGA and LPGA may be necessary. While not required, certifications may enhance one's opportunities to gain employment.

Teaching in Youth and Community Organizations

The Young Men's Hebrew Association (YMHA), the Young Women's Hebrew Association (YWHA), the YMCA, and the YWCA and similar organizations such as Boy's Clubs, Girl's Clubs, and the 4-H Clubs serve both the youth and the adult populations in the community. Religious training was originally the main purpose of many of these organizations. However, sport and fitness are now an important part of their programs. Classes in various physical activities; athletic leagues for industry employees, youth, and adults; and young people's groups are all a part of the program. The cost of financing such organizations is usually met through membership dues, community and business contributions, and private contributions.

These organizations are designed to improve participants socially, physically, morally, mentally, and spiritually through their programs of physical activity. Usually these organizations employ physical educators and recreation specialists to teach a wide diversity of activities. In many communities events are scheduled from early morning to late at night—early bird swim at 6 AM for business and professional people before work and late hour racquetball games. Besides instructing clients in sport activities, the physical educator may have the opportunity to serve as a coach of a team. Many youth clubs offer young people and adults the opportunity to compete on athletic teams at the local, state, regional, and national level. Additional responsibilities include developing health and fitness programs, facility and budget management, and supervising personnel. Many centers, in addition to physical activities, offer programs in exercise and fitness evaluation, cardiac rehabilitation, and health counseling. A background in these areas as well as in teaching would be helpful in seeking employment. Although salaries vary, they are comparable to public school teaching positions.

While the YMCA, YWCA, YMHA, and YWHA certainly constitute a widespread organization, it is not the only community organization offering employment opportunities to the physical educator. Other opportunities include working for town and city recreation departments, community centers, youth centers similar in nature to the YMCA/YWCA and playgrounds. Some of these opportunities may be seasonal, generally available in the summer, but the trend is for more and more programs to operate

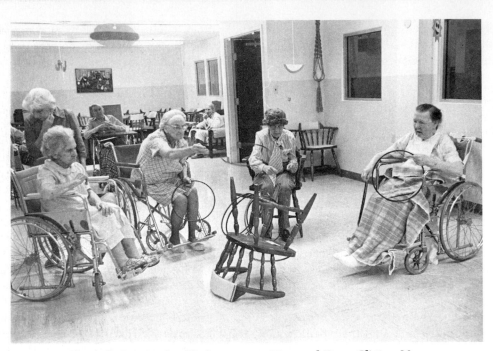

Physical education for elderly persons at Westwood Home, Clinton, Mo.

year round. These programs provide instruction in physical activities for people of all ages, recreational sport leagues, and recreational activities. In addition to teaching and coaching for these organizations, other job possibilities include the supervision of personnel and program development.

Teaching in Centers for the Elderly

In recent years elderly persons have received considerable attention from the United States government and other agencies. The number of elderly in the population is about 11%, and this percentage is increasing yearly. There is also concern for the physical fitness of elderly persons and their need to be physically active to maintain a state of optimum health. In recent years programs for elderly persons by recreational agencies, retirement centers, and health care facilities have expanded in the number and types of offerings.

Many of these programs offer instruction in physical activities suited to the abilities and interests of the participants. Exercise is frequently included in these programs. In addition to the physical benefits, physical education programs provide the opportunity for socialization. Physical educators interested in working in such programs may benefit from classes in adapted physical education, sociology, psychology, and gerontology.

Teaching in Resorts

The increase in leisure time has stimulated an increase in the travel and tourism industry. The number of resorts has grown, and many resorts offer instruction in various physical activities as part of their programs. Activities offered may include sailing, scuba, tennis, golf, swimming, water skiing, and snow skiing. Expertise in specific sport areas is required for employment in these resorts. Instruction is usually done in small groups or in private lessons. Additionally, responsibilities may include managerial activities and directing social activities. Pay varies and depending on the location of the resort work may be seasonal, although many resorts operate year round. Working in a resort offers many desirable side benefits, such as working in an attractive location and usually lush surroundings, and the opportunity to work with changing clientele.

Teaching in the Armed Forces

The Army, Navy, Marines, Coast Guard, National Guard, and the Air Force have extensive physical activity programs that aid in keeping service personnel in good physical and mental condition. In addition to personnel used to direct the fitness and physical training programs of these organizations, physical educators are needed to instruct service personnel in physical activities and sport for their use in their leisure time. The military sponsors extensive recreational programs on its bases, and qualified personnel are needed to direct these programs. Coaches are also needed to assist military athletes in their training for competitions throughout the world. For many of these positions physical educators do not have to be a member of the military. The military also sponsors schools for children of military personnel. Physical educators who desire to teach overseas may wish to consider employment in these schools. Physical educators interested in further information about these opportunities should talk to their local military recruiter.

Teaching in Correctional Institutions

The method of treating criminals, delinquents, and individuals who have displayed antisocial conduct has changed greatly during recent years. Formerly it was thought inmates of penal institutions should be regimented, disciplined, and forced to pay for their crimes or misdoings by suffering the rigid routines of prison life. Today, however, prison, reform school, and juvenile home authorities realize that activities may help in the rehabilitation of these individuals. In many of these institutions instruction in physical activities is offered. Inmates also have the opportunity to work out with weights and other equipment to improve their physical condition. Intramurals and competitive athletic teams may also offer inmates the opportunity to participate in physical activity and derive satisfaction from these opportunities. Responsibilities of the physical edu-

cator in these institutions vary widely, depending on the type of facility and the population.

American Red Cross

The American Red Cross in its various program offerings provides a setting for physical education activities along institutional lines. These activities are mainly concerned with some phase of aquatics, water safety, first aid, and hospital recreation. Instructional programs in this area are offered to school groups, community organizations, and local businesses. Employment by the American Red Cross in this area involves not only teaching these courses, but probably coordinating the activities of volunteer instructors and perhaps volunteers concerned with blood drives and disaster services as well.

• • •

In recent years the number of nonschool or alternative teaching opportunities has increased. The population served, setting, conditions of employment, and benefits vary widely. However, the continued interest by society in physical activity, fitness, and sport make these teaching opportunities viable alternatives for physical educators desiring to teach in the nonschool setting.

CERTIFICATION FOR TEACHING IN THE SCHOOLS

Each state has established minimum requirements that must be met by prospective teachers before they become legally certified to teach. The certification of teachers protects schoolchildren by ensuring a high level of teaching competency and by permitting employment of qualified personnel.

In recent years several changes in approaches to teacher certification have occurred. These include a competency-based program, a freer movement of qualified teachers across state lines, a simplification of the types of certificates issued, an approved program approach where the college or university has its teacher preparation program endorsed and then accepts responsibility for training and certifying teachers who graduate from that program, and certification based on the teacher's demonstrated abilities rather than on the completion of courses in a collegiate program.

Certification procedures and requirements vary from state to state. The prospective teacher should therefore inquire either from the appropriate person at his or her college or university or directly to the state education department (division of teacher certification) for the exact requirements. Because of variations in state requirements, a certificate to teach in one state is not necessarily valid in another state. However, reciprocity among states in the same region is a trend, particularly for graduates of an accredited teacher preparation program. Furthermore, prospective teachers often become certified in another state merely by taking a few additional required courses.

Localities within a state sometimes have specific regulations governing the selection of teachers. These are often more rigid than the standards established within the state itself. Detroit and New York City, for example, have their own set of qualifications that must be met by their teachers.

Some states have begun to require that candidates for teaching positions within the state take the National Teachers Exam (NTE). State officials hope that such a requirement will improve teaching by making sure that all teachers meet minimum standards of competence.

The NTE is a standardized test consisting of two parts. The first, the core battery tests, evaluate a candidate's communication skills, general knowledge, and professional teaching skills. The second, the specialty area test, evaluates knowledge within the discipline.

The core battery is comprised of three tests:

1. Communication Skills Test, which is designed to measure listening, reading, and writing
2. Test of General Knowledge, which focuses on general knowledge pertaining to the arts, literature, math, science, and social studies
3. Test of Professional Knowledge, which assesses the knowledge and cognitive processes the teacher uses and the understanding of the teaching process

The specialty examination is broad-based in scope, designed for individuals who plan to teach physical education at any grade level. It encompasses six content areas:

1. History and philosophy of physical education as well as its aims, objectives, and trends
2. Scientific foundations, encompassing the psychological, sociological, and biological foundations as well as growth and development
3. Curriculum development and planning, including characteristics of students, behavioral and performance objectives, activity selection and sequencing, program and facility considerations, instructional strategies, and knowledge of various activities
4. Organization and administration of the total program as well as health, safety, public relations, legal concerns, sports medicine, and working with individuals with disabilities
5. Professional responsibilities such as knowledge of professional organizations, critical issues, ethics, and research
6. Evaluation, focusing on such areas as selection and use of instruments, assessment of individual achievement, and determination of program effectiveness

Each state established its own passing scores for each of the three core battery tests and the specialty test. Thus a candidate can be deemed to pass in one state and not in another. Candidates who perform poorly on a specific test may retake that specific test without having to retake the entire exam.

The types and values of certificates issued by states vary nearly as much as their regulations. In some states, for example, there are merely two categories of certification, probationary and permanent, while another state may have as many as 22 different varieties of certification. The length of time the teaching certificate is valid varies as well, ranging from 1 year for a probationary certificate to life for a permanent certificate. Generally, a certificate enables the teacher to teach in any public school system within the state and many private schools within the state, except those where local standards require further qualifications. It may also qualify teachers to practice in neighboring states, depending on reciprocity agreements.

Individuals desiring to attain certification to

teach in the public schools in a specific state should contact the state education department or the appropriate authority at their college or university to determine the requirements for certification.

Teaching certification also may be an asset to teachers seeking to instruct in the nonschool setting. Prospective employers may be impressed by candidates who have fulfilled the necessary requirements for certification.

COACHING CAREERS

Many prospective physical educators aspire to a career as a coach. Because a teaching certificate is required by many states to coach, many aspiring coaches enroll in a study leading to a teaching certificate in physical education. Some of these prospective coaches seek a dual career as a teacher and a coach, while others desire solely to coach and view a teaching career as a means to attain their ultimate ambition of being a coach.

Within the last decade coaching opportunities have increased tremendously. The passage of Title IX legislation promoted the growth of interscholastic and intercollegiate competition for women. The increased interest in sport by people of all ages also served as a stimulus to increase opportunities in competitive athletics.

Similar to teaching, opportunities to coach today exist in both the school and nonschool setting. At the interscholastic level, opportunities are available to coach at both the junior high and senior high school levels. Intercollegiate coaching opportunities are found in 2-year community colleges as well as 4-year colleges and universities. In nonschool settings coaching opportunities are available with professional teams, commercial sport clubs, and community recreation and sport programs. The line of demarcation between coaching and teaching is fine at some commercial clubs and community centers. Teaching or coaching elite gymnasts or working with age-group swimmers are examples of opportunities in these fields.

Teaching responsibilities may be associated with coaching. At the interscholastic level it is expected that coaches will teach classes in the school; often coaches teach physical education. At the collegiate

Many individuals seek to enter the coaching profession because they aspire to work with highly skilled and motivated individuals.

level some coaches are hired solely to coach and have no teaching responsibilities associated with their position. At other higher education institutions coaches may have teaching responsibilities in the general physical education program or, if there is one, in the professional preparation program. Administrative responsibilities may be associated with coaching.

Choosing a Coaching Career

Individuals aspire to a coaching career for many reasons. Often individuals seek coaching careers because of their love for the sport, their own previous involvement on athletic teams, and the enjoyment they derived from participation. The desire to continue this involvement and association with athletics, perhaps to share some of what one has learned through athletics, is a strong motivating factor in selecting a coaching career. Individuals may choose to coach because of the profound influence one of their coaches had on their lives. Having a coach who was a positive role model and a desire to emulate this individual can influence one's decision to pursue a coaching career.

Many choose to coach because of their love of children. The opportunity to work with highly skilled and motivated individuals is often cited as a reason for coaching. Many coaches enter the profession because of their belief that participation in athletics can be a positive experience; they are committed to providing their athletes with the opportunities by which they can develop to their fullest potential, both as an athlete and as a person.

Coaching is a highly visible occupation. Coaches may have a great deal of influence and power within both the institution and the community. The excitement, attention, influence, and recognition associated with coaching make it an attractive career choice.

What Are the Benefits and Drawbacks of Coaching?

Like teaching, a coaching career has several advantages and disadvantages. Many intrinsic rewards are associated with coaching. The opportunity to work with athletes and strive side by side with them to achieve their fullest potential, the excitement of winning and the satisfaction associated with giving the best of oneself, and the respect accorded to a coach are some of the intrinsic benefits of coaching.

There are several drawbacks associated with coaching. The hours are long and arduous. The practice hours and hours spent coaching during the competition are the most visible indications of the amount of time involved in coaching. Untold hours may be spent in preparing practices, reviewing the results of games and planning for the next encounter, counseling athletes, performing public relations work, and at the collegiate level, recruiting.

Salaries vary greatly, depending on the level coached, the sport coached, and the coach's position as head or assistant coach. Salaries at the high school level can range from a small stipend to a few thousand dollars, while the coaches at the collegiate and professional levels may have contracts worth hundreds of thousands of dollars.

A high turnover rate is associated with coaching. Unlike teaching, coaches are often placed under tremendous pressure to achieve—to have a winning season. Many coaches are fired because of a lackluster win-loss record or for having a poor working relationship with the administration or alumni. Other coaches choose to leave the profession voluntarily, overwhelmed by the pressures and exhausted by the demands, suffering from burnout, disenchanted with the profession, or desirous of a career change.

Teaching and Coaching

Since coaching is in essence teaching, the qualities that exemplify good teachers—organizational, communication, human relations, instructional, and motivational skills—may also be characteristics of effective coaches. Coaches must be able to organize their practices to allow for maximum opportunities for all players to learn the skills and strategies essential for play. They must be actively engaged in monitoring the efforts of their athletes. They must be able to communicate what is to be learned in a clear manner and provide athletes with appropriate feedback to improve their performances. Coaches must instill in each athlete a feeling of self-worth and self-confidence, and be able to motivate all players to put forth their utmost effort to achieve their goals.

There are many qualities that characterize the outstanding coach. First, this person has the ability to teach the fundamentals and strategies of the sport: he or she must be a good teacher. An effective coach possesses skills common to an effective teacher: skills in organization, communication, instruction, motivation, and human relations. Second, the coach understands the player: how a person functions at a particular level of development, with a full appreciation for skeletal growth, muscular development, and physical and emotional limitations. Third, he or she understands the game coached. Thorough knowledge of techniques, rules, and similar information is basic. Fourth, the coach is a model for the players, a person of strong character. Patience, understanding, kindness, honesty, sportsmanship, sense of right and wrong, courage, cheerfulness, affection, humor, energy, and enthusiasm are imperative.

Although coaching is similar in nature to teach-

Coaches spend countless hours preparing for practices and games.

ing, there are some dissimilarities. Both teachers and coaches are engaged in instructional activities and both must provide opportunities for the learners—students and athletes—to attain the skills and knowledge presented. However, coaches must have the expertise to teach their athletes more advanced skills and are held much more accountable for their athletes' learning than teachers for their students. The calibre of a coach's instruction is scrutinized by both the administration and the public. If the coach is deemed inadequate in the preparation of the athletes or their learning by the often used standard of the win-loss record, then the coach may be dismissed. Teachers, on the other hand, have less pressure and less accountability for their students' learning and even if the success rate is not high, will most likely be allowed to retain their position. The coach must work in a pressure-filled arena while the teacher works in a less stressful environment.

Teachers must work with a diversity of skill levels and interests within their classes. Students may be mandated to take "gym" class and may be difficult

to motivate. In contrast, coaches work with highly skilled athletes who often possess a high level of commitment to their sport. Their decision to participate is voluntary, and they may be united in their effort toward a common goal. Thus, although there are some similarities between teaching and coaching, there are some striking differences.

Coaching Responsibilities

Many responsibilities are associated with coaching. As in teaching, these responsibilities may be classified as instructional, managerial, and institutional in nature.

The coach's instructional responsibilities include conducting practice and coaching during the game. Although the coach is working with highly skilled athletes, the coach must be a good teacher to instruct the athletes on the more advanced skills and strategies necessary to perform at this level. During practices and games the coach must motivate the athletes to put forth their best effort so that their optimal level of performance can be achieved.

In many cases the instructional responsibilities may be the least time consuming of all the coach's responsibilities.

Many coaches spend untold hours in evaluating practices and the results of competitions, and then using this information to plan for forthcoming practices and competitions. For those coaches fortunate enough to have assistant coaches, time must be spent with them reviewing this information and delegating responsibilities for future practices and games. Team managers may relieve the coach of many of the necessary but time-consuming managerial tasks such as dealing with equipment or recording statistics. Additionally, the coach must take care of the necessary public relations functions such as calling in contest results, giving interviews, and speaking in front of groups. Where allowed, recruiting occupies a tremendous amount of time. Phoning prospective athletes, arranging for campus meetings, talking with parents, and scouting contests for potential athletes adds many hours to the day.

The institutional responsibilities are many as well. Interscholastic coaches are expected to take part in many school activities in addition to their teaching responsibilities. Intercollegiate coaches may be expected to attend athletic department meetings or represent the institution on a community committee.

Many other responsibilities and expectations are associated with coaching. Coaches occupy highly visible positions in their institution. In institutions of higher education it is not uncommon for more students to recognize the face of the football or basketball coach than the face of the college president. The coach is expected to reflect a positive image and exemplify the values associated with sport. The actions of the coach as the team wins or loses will influence the public's opinion of the sport program. Establishing and maintaining positive relationships with the community, alumni, and parents is often seen as vital to a coach's success in generating support for the athletic program. Because of their influence and visibility, coaches may be sought after to take an active part in community and civic affairs. They may be called on to train volunteer coaches

for community recreational and sport programs or to spearhead a fund raising drive for United Way.

Many other duties are incumbent on the coach by virtue of his or her position. The coach, because of the close relationship that develops from the many hours of working together with his or her athletes toward a common goal, often undertakes the role of the counselor with athletes or assumes the role of a surrogate parent. Athletes turn to their coach for advice about a myriad of problems. Athletes may have problems associated with their athletic performance or financial, academic, and/or personal concerns. Because of their position as a leader, coaches are viewed as role models. They are expected to exemplify the highest standards of conduct and are under pressure to live up to these expectations.

Coaches must fulfill many professional responsibilities. Coaches must attend sport and rules clinics so that they are aware of the current trends and latest rule changes in the sport. They are often active in professional organizations related to the sport they coach as well as professional organizations such as AAHPERD. They may be called on to serve as a clinician at some of these meetings or asked to write an article for a professional journal.

The responsibilities and expectations associated with coaching are many. Instructional, managerial, institutional, community, and professional responsibilities comprise the work of the coach.

Securing a Coaching Position

Depending on the level you wish to coach, several steps can be taken to enhance your chances of securing the coaching position that you desire. First, coaching requires a great deal of expertise. Playing experience in the sport you wish to coach may be helpful in this respect. Attending clinics and workshops on advanced techniques and rules may add to your knowledge. Consider becoming a rated official in your sport. Take advantage of coaching certification and licensing programs also, such as the one offered for soccer by the United States Soccer Federation. Second, particularly for coaching at the interscholastic level, a teaching certificate may be required. However, this depends on the

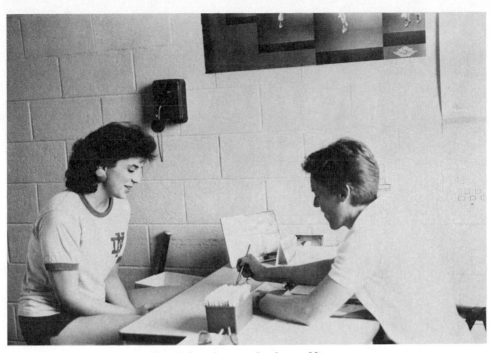

Coaches and teachers need to be good listeners.

state in which you wish to coach. Coaching at the intercollegiate level often requires a master's degree.

Prospective coaches should consider developing expertise in a second sport, preferably one that is not in season at the same time as your major sport. For example, if one aspires to coach soccer, a fall sport, one should develop expertise in a spring sport such as lacrosse, baseball, or softball. In many institutions, both at the interscholastic and intercollegiate level, coaches may be required to coach two sport activities or sometimes be the head coach in one sport and serve as an assistant coach in a second sport. At other institutions, a coach may be involved in one sport throughout the year because of the length of the season.

Practical experience is helpful as well. Volunteering to serve as an assistant coach or working with a youth sport program as a coach during your undergraduate preparation is a step in the right direction and is an invaluable experience. It is important that prospective coaches realize that oftentimes one must be willing to work in other positions in the coaching organization before achieving the head coaching position desired. Serving as a junior varsity coach, working as a graduate assistant coach, or accepting a position as an assistant coach can be helpful in attaining a head coaching position at the desired level.

Certification of Coaches

Criteria for certification of coaches at the interscholastic level vary from state to state, as does certification for teaching. Only about half of the states require interscholastic coaches to possess a teaching certificate, though not necessarily in physical education. Furthermore, the increased need for coaches and the lack of teachers available to fulfill these needs has led to the hiring of many nonteacher coaches. Subsequently, there are many individuals holding coaching positions who lack the professional preparation and competencies so necessary to conduct educationally sound and safe programs.

Excessive demands can often lead to burnout among teacher-coaches.

Discrepancies in the requirements necessary to coach and concern about the safety and welfare of the participants were two of the reasons for the establishment of the AAHPERD Task Force on the Certification of High School Coaches. The task force recommended that for certification, coaches should have knowledge of the medical aspects of coaching, an understanding of the psychological and sociological foundations of coaching, familiarity with the kinesiological foundations of coaching, understanding of the physiological aspects of coaching, and knowledge of coaching theory and techniques.

Young professionals aspiring to coach should prepare carefully for assumption of this important responsibility. This may be accomplished by enrolling in relevant courses and by attending workshops and clinics. Athletic participation and gaining practical experience by working as an assistant coach or a volunteer youth coach in a community program may enhance the professional qualifications of prospective coaches. There are also several

coaching certification programs sponsored by private and professional organizations. Among these programs are the American Coaching Effectiveness Program (ACEP), The North American Youth Sport Institute (NAYSI), and the National Youth Sports Coaches Association (NYSCA). Prospective coaches can use these programs to enhance their effectiveness in this critical area.

BURNOUT

Burnout is becoming increasingly prevalent among teachers and coaches. Burnout is defined as physical, emotional, and attitudinal exhaustion. Because burnout can have a devastating effect on dedicated individuals, young professionals need to be aware of the causes and consequences of burnout and strategies that they can use to prevent its occurrence.

There are many causes of teacher burnout. Lack of administrative support, lack of input into the curriculum process, and public criticism and the accompanying lack of community support are all factors contributing to burnout. Inadequate salaries, discipline problems, too little time to do the ever-growing amount of work, large classes, and heavier teaching loads may also contribute to this problem. The lack of challenge, inadequate supervisory feedback, and the absence of opportunities for personal and professional growth also may lead to burnout.

In the coaching realm burnout may be caused by seasons that seem to go on without end, administrative and community pressures, and time pressures. Teacher-coach role conflict may also lead to burnout. This role conflict occurs when a disparity exists between the expectations associated with being a teacher and a coach; this results in a multitude of simultaneous, somewhat diverse demands. The teacher-coach, unable to satisfy these demands, experiences role conflict.

In both the teaching and coaching realms personal problems may interact with professional problems to exacerbate burnout. Personal problems such as conflicts within one's family, money difficulties, or perhaps even divorce or problems with relationships may cause additional stress for the individual. These stresses coupled with professional problems may hasten the onset of burnout.

The consequences of burnout are many and are often quite severe, affecting teachers as well as their students. Farber and Miller[5] asserted that the most critical impact of burnout may be on instruction. Burned out teachers may cope with the demands of teaching by sitting on the sidelines, going through the motions of teaching by "throwing out the ball." Infrequent and careless planning of classes, complacency, and behavioral inflexibility may occur as well. Teachers' interactions with their students may also suffer. Burned out teachers may treat their students in a depersonalized manner, providing them with little encouragement, feedback, and reinforcement of their efforts. Lower expectations for student performance may also be held by teachers experiencing burnout. Teachers who are burned out may feel dissatisfied with their accomplishments and believe they are wasting the best years of their lives. Burnout can result in deterioration of their health. Insomnia, hypertension, ulcers, and other stress-related diseases may manifest themselves in burned out teachers. Coaches and athletes may experience similar consequences relative to burnout.

What can be done to cope with burnout? The varied causes and consequences of burnout require a diversity of solutions. Supervisors such as principals and athletic directors can play a crucial role in the prevention and remediation of burnout. Supervisors can provide teachers and coaches with meaningful in-service programs, focusing on developing a variety of teaching and coaching techniques, learning efficient time management, and acquiring effective communication skills. They can also provide teachers and coaches with more feedback about their performance; this would serve as a stimulus for growth. Teachers and coaches could seek out new ideas, professional contacts, and opportunities through participation in professional organizations and conferences. Taking some time off to revitalize oneself during the summer is also a successful strategy. Developing and participating in hobbies or nonwork-related activities are also helpful ways to deal with burnout. Establishing and maintaining an appropriate level of fitness, practicing proper nutrition, and getting enough sleep are also positive approaches to dealing with burnout.

Some teachers and coaches seek to cope with the consequences of burnout by adopting inappropriate solutions such as alcohol or drugs. The pervasiveness of burnout and the serious consequences for the teachers, coaches, students, and athletes should make dealing with burnout an important professional priority.

INCREASING YOUR PROFESSIONAL MARKETABILITY

If you are interested in a teaching career in the public schools or in nonschool settings, you can often enhance both your marketability and your ability to teach by building on your assets and interests. Through careful planning of your program and wise use of your electives and practicum experiences you can easily improve your chances of gaining the professional position you desire. Many of the same strategies are applicable to coaching as well.

You should enhance your opportunities to teach in the public schools in several ways. One way is to build on talents or skills that you already possess. For example, the need is great for bilingual educators. Perhaps you have gained proficiency in a second language because of your family background, the location in which you grew up, or foreign language courses you studied in secondary school. These language skills can be built on with further course work at the college or university level.

Second, additional course work can be beneficial in broadening the abilities of the prospective teacher. Courses in the area of adapted physical education are an asset regardless if one is interested in working only with special needs children or not. Since adapted physical education places an emphasis on individualized instruction, the knowledge gained from its study can be applied to normal children as well as those children with special needs mainstreamed into regular physical education classes. Additional courses in health may be helpful because physical educators are often expected to teach one or two health classes. The close relationship between wellness and fitness makes knowledge of health important to the practitioner.

Another possibility, depending on the state in which you plan to teach, is to gain certification to teach in an additional academic area. If you enjoy other areas such as math, science, or health, dual certification would enable you to qualify for additional jobs such as a teaching position that had a teaching load of one-third math and two-thirds physical education or one-third health and two-thirds physical education. Certification in driver education is also a popular choice that enhances one's credentials. To gain dual certification several courses in your alternate area of study are required. Often, the number of courses required for certification may not be many more than required by your college or university for a minor. The education department in the state in which you plan to teach can provide you with additional information about the requirement for certification.

Individuals interested in teaching in a nonschool setting can enhance their marketability in just the same way as individuals preparing for a teaching position in the public schools. Depending on where one seeks employment, having a bilingual background would be an asset. Experience in adapted physical education could be useful in working with individuals of different abilities and ages. Courses in math and business may be helpful if one is employed by a commercial sport club or fitness center, or community sport program, where often managerial duties in addition to teaching are part of the responsibilities. Because many of these organizations offer some type of health counseling and the interest of many of the clientele in health, courses in health would be an asset as well. Many employers may view possession of a teaching certificate by someone seeking to teach in these nonschool settings as an asset. Expertise in one or several sport areas may also be a plus as would possession of specialized certifications.

In the coaching realm one's previous experience as an athlete in the sport is an asset. Many former athletes have capitalized on their experience to secure coaching positions. Previous work as an assistant or head coach certainly is in one's favor. Professional contacts, officials ratings in a sport, and membership in a professional organization are helpful in getting hired or advancing. Many states require that coaches hold teaching certification; holding such certification gives one more flexibility in selecting from job opportunities.

Finally, one can enhance one's credentials by gaining as much practical experience as possible working with people of all ages and abilities. This holds true whether you are seeking work in a school or nonschool setting or in coaching. This experience can be gained through volunteer work, part-time employment, summer employment, or through supervised field-experiences sponsored by your college or university. Being able to cite such practical experiences on your resume may prove invaluable when you are seeking to gain employment. Membership in professional organizations and professional contacts may also be helpful in securing employment.

Prospective teachers and coaches can enhance

their marketability. Building on one's skills, taking additional courses, and gaining as much practical experience as possible will increase your options and enhance your opportunities for employment.

SUMMARY

Teaching and coaching opportunities have broadened from the traditional school setting to the nonschool setting and from school-aged populations to people of all ages, ranging from preschoolers to senior citizens. Teaching opportunities in the school setting are available at the elementary level, secondary level, and in higher education. Prospective teachers may also teach physical education in adapted physical education programs and in professional preparation programs. In the nonschool setting opportunities exist in commercial sport clubs, community and youth agencies, resorts, the Armed Forces, correctional agencies, and in service organizations such as the American Red Cross. Many individuals choose a teaching career because of their strong desire to work with people, because of personal interests, and because of the nature of the job. Individuals desiring to pursue a teaching career, regardless of setting, should be cognizant of the numerous advantages and disadvantages of such a career.

Many prospective physical educators aspire to a career as a coach. Some of these prospective physical educators seek a dual career as a teacher and a coach, while others desire solely to coach and view a teaching career as a means to attain their ultimate ambition. The prospective coach should be knowledgeable of the benefits and drawbacks of this career.

In an effort to improve teaching researchers have sought to identify characteristics of effective teachers. They determined that effective teachers possess organizational, communication, human relations, instructional, and motivational skills. Teachers have a myriad of responsibilities; their responsibilities may be classified as instructional, managerial, and institutional in nature. Coaching is similar in many respects to teaching. Effective coaches possess many of the characteristics of effective teachers

and must assume many of the same responsibilities as well.

One problem that has become increasingly prevalent among teachers and coaches is burnout. Burnout is physical, mental, and attitudinal exhaustion. The causes of burnout are many, and personal problems may interact with professional problems to exacerbate burnout. There are also a variety of solutions to this problem.

Many strategies can be used by prospective teachers and coaches to enhance their marketability. They can build on their talents and interests, take additional course work in a supporting area, and gain as much practical experience as possible.

SELF-ASSESSMENT TESTS

These tests are designed to assist students in determining if the materials and the competencies presented in this chapter have been mastered.

1. In light of the qualities for effective teachers and their responsibilities assess your own qualifications for this field of endeavor.

2. Discuss the advantages and disadvantages of pursuing a teaching career in a school and a nonschool setting. If possible, try to interview a physical educator presently working in each setting.

3. Interview a teacher and a coach and describe their perceptions of the similarities and differences between teaching and coaching.

4. List the causes of burnout and describe specific solutions for each of the causes listed.

5. What are some strategies a prospective teacher or coach could use to maximize opportunities for employment in these careers?

REFERENCES

1. Bucher CA and Koenig CR: Methods and materials for secondary school physical education, St Louis, 1983, Times Mirror/Mosby College Publishing.

2. Siedentop D: Developing teaching skills in physical education, ed 2, Palo Alto, Calif, 1983, Mayfield.

3. Gensemer RE: Physical education: perspectives, inquiry, and applications, Philadelphia, 1985, Saunders College Publishing.

4. Pangrazi RP and Darst PW: Dynamic physical education curriculum and instruction for secondary school students, Minneapolis, 1985, Burgess Publishing Co.

5. Farber BA and Miller J: Teacher burnout: a psycho-educational perspective, Teachers' College Record 83(2):235-243, 1981.

SUGGESTED READINGS

American Alliance for Health, Physical Education, Recreation, and Dance: Justifying physical education, Journal of Physical Education, Recreation, and Dance 58(7), 1987.

This feature addresses the current status of physical education in the schools and means by which it can be improved.

American Alliance for Health, Physcial Education, Recreation, and Dance, Graham G. editor: profiles in excellence, Journal of Physical Education, Recreation, and Dance 53(7), 1982.

George Graham edited this series of 11 articles, which profile excellence in teaching at the elementary school level. These teachers provide insight into the nature of their work; their commitment to quality education for their students is evident.

American Alliance for Health, Physical Education, Recreation, and Dance, O'Brien DH, editor: The teaching/coaching challenge, Journal of Physical Education, Recreation, and Dance 52(9), 1981.

Problems confronting the teacher-coach are examined in this feature edited by DH O'Brien. Prevention of the problems and innovative solutions for dealing with stress, burnout, and role conflict are presented as well.

American Alliance for Health, Physical Education, Recreation, and Dance, Templin TJ, editor: Profiles in excellence, Journal of Physical Education, Recreation, and Dance 54(7), 1983.

Profiles of 12 outstanding secondary physical education teachers are presented in this series by TJ Templin. The teachers' enthusiasm and professional commitment are reflected in these portrayals.

Auxter D and Pyfer J: Adapted physical education and recreation, St Louis, 1985, Times Mirror/Mosby College Publishing.

This text provides an introduction to adapted physical education and recreation. Various handicapping conditions are covered and suggested activities to maximize individuals' involvement are presented.

Conn J and Razor J: Certification of coaches: a legal and moral responsibility, Physical Educator 46, 161-65, 1989.

The need for coaching certification is reviewed and means for attaining certification presented.

Harrison JM: A review of research on teacher effectiveness and its implications for current practice, Quest 39, 36-55, 1987.

Teacher effectiveness research is reviewed with respect to teacher expectations, classroom management and organization, learning environment, direct instruction, curriculum pacing, student opportunity to learn, and grade level differences.

Lombardo BJ: The humanistic coach: from theory to practice, Springfield, Ill, 1987, Charles C Thomas.

This book explains humanism and its application to coaching and provides numerous practical examples.

Siedentop D: Developing teaching skills in physical education, ed 2, Palo Alto, Calif, 1983, Mayfield.

This text focuses on providing the reader with information about effective teaching, strategies to improve teaching, and means by which to assess teaching.

Sisley BL, Capel SA, and Desertrain GS: Preventing burnout in teacher/coaches: Journal of Physical Education, Recreation, and Dance 58(8):71-75, 1987.

Factors associated with burnout are described and practical strategies to alleviate this problem are presented.

Vendien CL and Nixon JE: Physical education teacher education, New York, 1985, John Wiley & Sons, Inc.

Five topical areas are covered in this text: preparation of teachers and coaches, research in teaching and coaching, student teaching, the transition from being a student to being a teacher and/or coach, and illustrations of physical education teacher preparation programs.

Chapter 12

Fitness- and Health-Related Careers in Physical Education and Sport

INSTRUCTIONAL OBJECTIVES AND COMPETENCIES TO BE ACHIEVED

After reading this chapter the student should be able to—
- Discuss the responsibilities of a fitness or an exercise specialist.
- Describe the various employment opportunities for a fitness or an exercise specialist.
- Discuss the responsibilities of an athletic trainer and physical educators working in a health-related career.
- Describe the opportunities available to an individual desiring to pursue a therapy-related career.
- Discuss the various strategies that can be used to enhance one's professional marketability in fitness-, health-, and therapy-related careers.

Within the past decade a dramatic increase in interest in preventive medicine and a greater public awareness of the values of exercise and physical activity has occurred. Research has substantiated the benefits of exercise and appropriate physical activity in reducing the incidence of cardiovascular disease and in enhancing the rehabilitation of those experiencing this common malady. The increased public awareness of the role of exercise in health promotion and disease prevention, coupled with the interest in fitness by many segments of society, has stimulated the growth of community, commercial, and corporate fitness programs. Subsequently, employment opportunities for professionals with preparation as exercise and fitness specialists have grown tremendously. The number of physical educators who have found employment opportunities working in preventive and rehabilitative exercise programs has risen sharply, and it appears that this trend will continue in the years ahead.

Another field that has experienced growth is athletic training. While professional and college athletic teams have typically employed athletic trainers, their employment at the secondary school level is rising. Furthermore, the public's increased participation in a variety of sport activities and the medical profession's interest in sport has led to increased employment opportunities for qualified athletic trainers in commercial sports medicine clinics, physical therapy clinics, and hospitals.

Employment opportunities also have become more available for qualified individuals in weight control and health spas and clubs. Qualified individuals may be employed as dance exercise specialists,

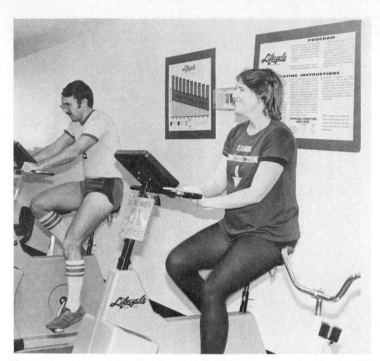

Today the public is more aware of the role of exercise in the attainment of optimal well-being. Fitness clubs and health spas offer a variety of activities, including stationary bicycling.

exercise leaders, exercise test technologists, and weight management counselors.

An increase has been seen in the recognition of the physical as well as the psychological and therapeutic values of movement in helping individuals attain an optimal state of well-being as well as in the rehabilitation of illness. Careers in movement therapy, recreation therapy, and dance therapy are available to physical educators who desire to work in a therapeutic setting.

FITNESS- AND EXERCISE-RELATED CAREERS

The last decade has seen a tremendous increase in the number of physical educators pursuing fitness- and exercise-related careers in preventive and rehabilitative exercise programs. The growth of these exercise programs is attributable in great part to the growing awareness of the role of exercise and physical activity in the promotion of health and the prevention of disease as well as in the rehabilitation of diseased individuals. This awareness by the public, corporate sector, and by the medical profession of the benefits of exercise has stimulated the growth of preventive and rehabilitative exercise programs.

Preventive and rehabilitative exercise programs differ in their focus and in the nature of the participants; the setting in which these programs are conducted often is different as well. Preventive exercise program specialists work with healthy adults to increase their level of fitness and realize concomitant gains in health. Rehabilitative exercise program specialists work primarily with individuals who exhibit the effects of coronary heart disease and focus on helping these individuals attain a functional state of living and an enhanced quality of life. Preventive exercise programs are commonly found in corporate fitness centers, commercial fitness centers, and community agencies such as the YMCA/YWCA. Rehabilitative exercise programs are most often found in hospitals, although some may

The trained exercise professional must be able to evaluate participant's level of fitness. A PepsiCo, Inc., staff person administers the sit-and-reach test to a program participant.

be found in medical clinics or community agencies or be affiliated with corporate fitness centers.

Preventive and rehabilitative programs often vary in their scope and comprehensiveness. However, some commonalities may be discerned. Typically, while these programs focus on improvement of fitness, they may include other program components such as educational programs, health promotion programs, and life-style modification. The fitness component of these programs most likely includes some assessment of the individual's current level of fitness, prescription of a program of exercise and activity, opportunities to engage in exercise and activities, and periodic reevaluation of the individual's level of fitness. Educational efforts may focus on instructing individuals on the principles underlying the performance of exercises and physical activity so that they may learn to properly plan their own exercise and activity programs. Health promotion

efforts may include health education, such as providing participants with nutritional information, as well as measures focusing on the early detection of disease, such as hypertension screening and cancer detection. Life-style modification may include counseling individuals regarding stress management, weight control, smoking cessation, and alcohol and drug abuse. In addition to these program components, recreational sport opportunities may be offered.

Cooper and Collingwood[2] noted that fitness and wellness programs vary in their structure and offerings. In an effort to maximize the benefits to be realized from participation and to promote adherence to these programs, the Institute for Aerobics Research identified several elements as "generic" services for such programs. Programs should make provisions for medical screening of their participants to ensure that they are safe exercise risks.

Program personnel should also evaluate participants' level of fitness and their life-style. Exercise programs should focus on individual goal setting; thus exercise and nutritional prescriptions should be developed for each individual. To motivate participants to get started on their programs, supervised group exercise and activity programs should be offered. To sustain changes in fitness and life-style, educational classes should be held and provisions should be made for motivation and reinforcement of participants' efforts. Feedback should be ongoing in nature. These generic elements are critical to the success of preventive exercise programs and seem appropriate for rehabilitative programs as well.

The trained exercise and fitness professional working in preventive and rehabilitative exercise programs must be able to perform a wide variety of tasks and be capable of assuming responsibility for numerous aspects of the exercise program. Sol[3] identified the responsibilities of an exercise program specialist as follows:

- Direct the exercise program, which may be oriented to prevention and/or rehabilitation
- Train and supervise staff
- Develop and manage the program budget
- Design and manage the exercise facility and laboratories
- Market the exercise program
- Evaluate—in conjunction with a physician —each participant's medical and activity history, a graded exercise test, the pulmonary function tests, and assorted fitness tests
- Develop individual exercise prescriptions for participants
- Evaluate and/or counsel participants, on request, about nutrition, smoking, weight control, and stress
- Accumulate program data for statistical analysis and research
- Maintain professional affiliations
- Perform other program-specific duties

The responsibilities that each professional in the program will be asked to assume depend on several factors. These factors include the scope and comprehensiveness of the program, the number of participants, the size of the staff, and qualifications of other staff members. In programs that have a broad range of services, a large number of participants, and several staff members, responsibilities tend to be more specialized. One staff member may direct the program, administer the budget, market the program, and conduct in-service training for other program staff. Some staff members may have as their sole responsibility the conducting of graded exercise tests and the writing of exercise prescriptions. Still other staff members lead the fitness classes and may provide instruction in activities. Providing participants with counseling for life-style modification or educating participants about exercise may be the responsibility of other staff members. Finally, another professional may be assigned to accumulate data and conduct statistical analyses. In programs that are narrower in scope or are conducted for fewer participants, the staff tends to be smaller in number and one professional will perform many more functions.

Since the mid-1970s, the use of exercise as an integral part of preventive and rehabilitative health programs has become well-accepted. Qualified personnel are needed to appraise fitness levels, conduct graded exercise tests, execute exercise prescriptions, lead exercise classes, and administer safe and effective programs. In response to the growing demand for qualified professionals in this field, the American College of Sports Medicine (ACSM) instituted a certification program in 1972. The certification program assesses the competencies of professionals involved in conducting various aspects of exercise programs and protects the consumer against individuals who are not qualified to administer exercise programs.

Currently, the ACSM certification program encompasses both preventive and rehabilitative exercise programs, providing three levels of certification within each program. For preventive programs, the three levels of certification are (1) Exercise Leader/Aerobics, (2) Health/Fitness Instructor, and (3) Health/Fitness Director. For rehabilitative programs, the three levels of certification are (1) Exercise Test Technologist, (2) Exercise Specialist, and (3) Program Director. Certifications

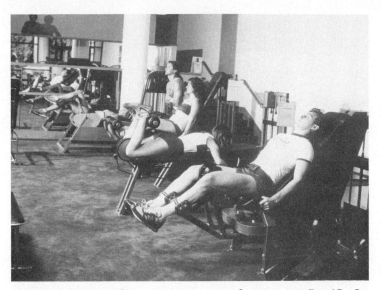

Many corporations view corporate fitness programs as sound investments. PepsiCo, Inc., employees work out at the corporation's multimillion-dollar fitness center in Purchase, NY.

within both programs reflect a progressive level of knowledge, skills, and competencies.

Certification requires satisfactory performance on both a written and a practical examination. Optional workshops and seminars are usually offered relative to the skills required for each level of certification prior to the examination. Information about certification can be obtained from the American College of Sports Medicine, PO Box 1440, Indianapolis, IN 46206-1440.

In addition to gaining ACSM certification, physical educators aspiring to work in various fitness and exercise programs should, because of the strong emphasis on health promotion, take courses in health. Nutrition, drug education, pharmacology, and stress management courses would be particularly helpful. From the discipline of psychology, courses in motivation, behavior modification, and counseling would be useful. Computer science courses, statistics, and research methodology would be helpful in the administrative and evaluative responsibilities associated with these positions. Finally, business courses would be helpful in dealing with the myriad managerial responsibilities associated with exercise programs such as budgeting, marketing, and personnel supervision.

Membership in professional organizations and the establishment of professional affiliations are important for the young professional. Physical educators interested in a career in this area should belong to AAHPERD, ACSM, or the Association for Fitness in Business (AFB). Not only will membership in a professional organization lead to the development of professional contacts, it also will provide the opportunity to update one's skills and knowledge through continuing education programs, workshops, and conventions.

Corporate Fitness Programs

An estimated 50,000 business concerns in the United States spend approximately $5 billion annually on their employee fitness, worksite wellness, and recreational programs. Corporations are willing to commit their funds to these programs for several reasons. One payoff from these programs is increased employee productivity and better work performance. Healthy employees can work harder and more effectively. Companies are also investing in fitness programs in an effort to reduce their spiraling health care costs. Businesses lose an estimated $15 billion annually due to health problems and close to $20 million a year from premature em-

Aerobic dance is a popular offering at health spas, fitness clubs, and corporate fitness centers.

ployee death.[5] The cost of health care insurance premiums continues to rise astronomically. The short- and long-term health benefits to be accrued from employee fitness programs make good sense economically; if employee illnesses can be curtailed and premature deaths reduced, businesses stand to reap substantial savings in health care and insurance costs. Companies may also invest in fitness programs because of the benefits in terms of human relations and enhancement of morale. As the number of fitness programs continues to grow, fitness programs may become an important fringe benefit to employees.

The business firms endorsing and providing fitness programs range from major corporations to small businesses. Government agencies are investing in fitness programs as well. The United States Army has instituted a "corporate fitness" program for its 6000 civilian and military personnel at the Pentagon. This effort was undertaken to improve employee health, increase productivity, and reduce medical costs for illness.

The type and comprehensiveness of employee fitness programs vary widely. Some companies

invest in multimillion dollar facilities—gymnasium, pool, racquetball courts—while other companies may subsidize employee membership in commercial and community fitness clubs and programs. In some programs the cost is borne entirely by the company, in other companies the cost is divided in various proportions between the company and the employees, and in other companies employees must pay fees to use the company's facilities. The services provided vary as well. Services may run the gamut from full-fledged, comprehensive fitness and health promotion programs to fitness-only programs, in which the employer provides the facilities and little else. Some corporations sponsor cardiac rehabilitation programs for their personnel. It should be noted that, unfortunately, not every program contributes to employee fitness. Some are nothing more than a sauna and a massage table, where executives of the firm can unwind after a tough day. Still other companies only pay lip service to the idea of fitness rather than promote actual participation.

Many businesses offer recreational sport programs as well. These recreational programs may include softball and bowling leagues as well as competitive teams. Instruction in physical activities may be offered to employees.

Opportunities for employment in corporate fitness programs are increasing for qualified professionals. In addition to opportunities to work as a fitness and exercise specialist, opportunities are available for individuals to conduct recreational programs and to provide instruction in physical activities and sport skills.

Commercial and Community Fitness Programs

The number of adult fitness programs offered by commercial fitness clubs and community agencies such as the YMCA/YWCA are also increasing. These programs offer many of the same services as comprehensive employee fitness programs. These programs may offer graded exercise tests, individualized fitness programs based on the exercise prescription developed from the results of the graded exercise test, educational programs, health promotion programs, and life-style modification. Other programs may be less comprehensive in nature; these may focus primarily on the promotion of fitness.

Fitness programs tailored to meet the needs of different age groups are becoming more common. Toddler and preschool programs as well as programs for the aged are being offered by both community and commercial agencies and, increasingly, by schools. Professionals working within these programs must be particularly attuned to the developmental characteristics of the age group and adapt programs accordingly.

An increased number of fitness programs are available to address the special needs of individuals with disabilities. There are approximately 36 million Americans with some form of physical disability. Access to gymnasiums, sophisticated equipment sensitive enough to accommodate a wide range of individual needs, and professionals willing to adapt workouts for the disabled have enabled many persons with disabilities, some for the first time, to realize the benefits of fitness. For example, specific exercise programs have been developed for individuals who use wheelchairs, have multiple sclerosis, or are deaf and blind. The *Fitness is for Everyone* program, directed by the association for National Handicapped Sports (NHS), helps professionals learn to adapt workouts for individuals with disabilities. The NHS also offers a series of videotaped workouts for specific disabilities, such as spinal cord injuries and cerebral palsy. Professionals are also taking steps to help integrate or mainstream individuals with disabilities into community fitness programs.

Professional responsibilities within commercial enterprises and community programs are similar to those found within the corporate sector. Employment opportunities within these areas have grown dramatically within the past few years.

One factor that may counter the growth of employment opportunities is the tremendous increase in the sales of home exercise equipment. Many adults who in the past would have paid a membership fee to participate in these programs have chosen to invest the money in home exercise equipment, such as weight machines, bicycle ergometers, cross country ski machines, and rowing machines. These individuals prefer the convenience of being able to exercise at home. Some physical educators have capitalized on this trend by offering one-on-one fitness instruction in the home.

A number of physical educators have pursued careers as personal fitness trainers. They meet with clients individually in their homes on a regular basis, sometimes as often as five or six days per week. For each client, the personal trainer conducts a fitness assessment, develops specific goals and designs a program leading to their attainment, coaches the individual through the workout, and monitors progress. Additional services often include nutritional counseling. Some fitness programs and health clubs are also offering the services of a personal trainer to its membership at an additional cost. Members like the one-to-one attention offered by a personal trainer, believing it enhances their motivation and their effort in performing their program.

Many individuals prefer to exercise at home rather than at a club or community program.

Rehabilitation Programs

As the role of exercise in the rehabilitation of individuals with illness, particularly cardiovascular diseases, has become increasingly well documented, the number of these programs has grown. Typically, rehabilitation programs are offered at hospitals and clinics, although some programs may be offered through community agencies such as YMCA/YWCAs. Besides the development of fitness, health promotion and life-style modification are integral parts of these programs.

Opportunities for employment are similar to those in corporate fitness and adult fitness programs. However, professionals working in these programs tend to work more closely with physicians in monitoring the performance and progress of the programs' participants. To plan rehabilitators' programs, the professional needs to be familiar with the medical aspects of the participants' illness, cognizant of the limitations imposed by the illness, and aware of drugs commonly used by the participants and their effects. Professionals working in rehabilitative programs require training to help individuals deal with the psychological aspects of their illness. Professionals must also be ready to deal with partic-

ipants' fears concerning exercise, such as the often expressed fear that exercise will lead to another heart attack.

In the past decade, employment opportunities for physical educators interested in a career as a fitness or exercise specialist have grown. Qualified professionals may find employment in preventive and rehabilitative exercise programs conducted by corporations, commercial organizations, community agencies, and hospitals. Salaries range from $18,000 to over $40,000 a year, depending on the number of hours worked and the responsibilities assigned. Opportunities for individuals interested in working in health-related careers such as athletic training have also grown in the past decade.

HEALTH-RELATED CAREERS

Health-related careers in the realm of physical education have grown. Careers in athletic training have become increasingly available. Career opportunities also exist for physical educators in health and weight control clubs and spas.

In recent years, employment opportunities have increased for physical educators with expertise in athletic training. Traditional employment opportunities can be found at the college and professional levels. Employment opportunities at the secondary school level also exist, although fewer than 10% of the nation's high schools currently employ certified athletic trainers. It is likely that employment opportunities at this level will increase in the near future as states and school systems, concerned about the safety of their athletes and their legal liability, mandate the hiring of certified athletic trainers for interscholastic sports.

Another avenue of employment that is available to athletic trainers is in sports medicine clinics. These clinics can be commercial enterprises, affiliated with hospitals, or associated with physical therapy practices. The increase in sport participation by all segments of society has resulted in the need for qualified individuals to evaluate, treat, and rehabilitate injuries.

An athletic trainer's responsibilities are numerous and varied in nature, focusing primarily on the prevention of injury and the rehabilitation of injured athletes. In terms of injury prevention and safety, the athletic trainer performs such preventive measures as the taping of ankles and knees of athletes prior to practices and competitions. The athletic trainer works closely with coaches in designing and supervising conditioning programs. Advising coaches and athletes regarding the prevention of injuries is an important responsibility of the athletic trainer. Athletic trainers may also assist in preseason physicals. Checking equipment and facilities for safety are tasks often performed by the athletic trainer.

The athletic trainer is often the first person to reach an injured athlete. Thus the athletic trainer must be prepared to deal with a variety of emergencies. The athletic trainer diagnoses injuries and refers athletes to the appropriate medical personnel for treatment. Working closely with the physician, the athletic trainer implements the prescribed rehabilitation program and administers the appropriate therapeutic treatments. The athletic trainer closely monitors the athlete's efforts and progress during the rehabilitation program. Rehabilitation may be a long and arduous process, and the athletic trainer may need to motivate and encourage the athlete during this trying period of time to put forth the

Both men and women trainers have work opportunities at the college or university level.

necessary effort to attain complete recovery. Keeping accurate records of athletes' injuries, the treatment program prescribed, and the athletes' progress during the rehabilitation program is part of the job of the athletic trainer.

An athletic trainer must possess, in addition to competencies pertaining to training, excellent interpersonal skills. The athletic trainer must work closely with the coaches and the team physician. Establishing and maintaining good rapport with these individuals contributes to a harmonious working relationship. Often the athletic trainer is placed in a position of telling a coach that an athlete cannot practice, play in an upcoming game, or return to the competition after an injury. Professional competency and a good rapport help make these difficult tasks a bit easier. The athletic trainer often finds himself or herself serving as a counselor to the athletes. Athletes may talk to the athletic trainer about problems relating to their own performance or that of their teammates or about problems on the team. The athletic trainer must be able to deal with the concerns of injured athletes; injured ath-

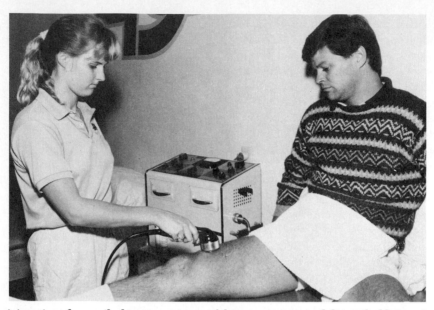

Administration of prescribed treatment is one of the primary responsibilities of athletic trainers.

letes may be fearful that they may not be able to return to 100% of their ability, that the injury will limit their performance in some way. The athletic trainer must be able to deal with these concerns in a sensitive, but truthful manner. The athletic trainer may also be sought out by athletes for advice about their personal and academic problems. The athletic trainer must be able to deal with these numerous problems and concerns in an appropriate and professional manner.

The hours worked by trainers are long. In addition to being in the training room before practice and on the sidelines during practice and competition, the trainer must often spend several hours in the training room at the conclusion of practices and competitions, dealing with any injuries that may have occurred and giving treatments. Trainers may have to come in on weekends for practice or contests and to give athletes treatments. During the season the athletic trainer travels with the team and this travel can be quite extensive. Since athletic trainers frequently work several sport activities during the year, the season can go on without end. Less visible responsibilities also consume quite a bit of

the athletic trainer's time. Cleaning up the training room, rerolling bandages, sterilizing the whirlpool, and ordering supplies are some of the other responsibilities of the athletic trainer. The long and demanding hours and lack of days off have resulted in some athletic trainers experiencing burnout, a condition similar to teacher and coach burnout. (See Chapter 11 for a further discussion of burnout and its solutions.) Despite the long hours and other demands, many individuals pursue careers in athletic training because of the opportunity to help athletes attain their fullest potential and their desire to be closely associated with athletics. The intrinsic rewards, such as the satisfaction in helping an injured athlete return to competition quickly and at full potential, are many.

At the professional level, the athletic trainer's responsibilities include injury prevention and the care and rehabilitation of injured athletes. At the collegiate level, the athletic trainer's responsibilities may be expanded to include teaching courses in the physical education or health program. In an institution that offers an approved athletic training curriculum, athletic trainers can teach courses within the curriculum as well as supervise student athletic trainers.

At the secondary level, an athletic trainer may be employed in several different capacities. A school may employ a full-time athletic trainer, or the district may employ a full-time athletic trainer to serve all of the schools within the district. An individual may also be hired as a teacher/athletic trainer. Therefore, athletic trainers may find it advantageous to possess a teaching certificate in physical education or another academic area. Some schools may contract with a sports medicine center for an athletic trainer and for related services.

Athletic trainers affiliated with clinics generally work fewer hours than individuals in a school or professional setting, and their work schedule is often more regular. Trainers who work in these settings typically work on a one-on-one basis with the athlete. However, an increasing number of schools and community sports programs are contracting with these clinics for services. Therefore, hours worked and working schedules may be similar to those trainers employed in a school setting.

Salaries for athletic trainers vary from $18,000 to over $35,000 per year. The work setting, responsibilities, and amount of experience possessed by the individual influence the salary.

NATA offers a certification program in athletic training; this certification is becoming required increasingly often to obtain a position. Certification can be attained by two routes. An individual can complete an approved athletic training program or can work under the direction of an athletic trainer as an intern or apprentice, so to speak. An approved athletic training curriculum includes courses in biological and physical sciences, psychology, first aid, and specific courses relative to training. Certification requires membership in NATA and passing a written and a practical exam. Information regarding certification procedures can be obtained from an athletic trainer or by writing to NATA, PO Drawer 1865, Greenville, NC 27834.

Some athletic trainers choose to continue their education and attain a master's degree in physical therapy to add to their skills. Prospective athletic trainers interested in pursuing work in physical therapy should check early in their undergraduate career with institutions offering master's degrees in physical therapy as to requirements for admission, including course prerequisites. Often courses in physics, chemistry, and math are required for admission to these schools. By knowing the prerequisites early, students can possibly use these courses as electives in their undergraduate professional preparation program. Other athletic trainers choose to continue their education by enrolling in a program leading to a master's degree in athletic training. Being active in professional organizations provides the opportunity to continue one's education through attendance at professional meetings and workshops.

Health and Weight Control Clubs and Spas

The number of health and weight control clubs and spas has increased greatly during the last decade. Many commercial enterprises have been established to capitalize on the individual's desire to be physically fit, to have a slim figure, and to look one's best. Some of these businesses may be privately owned while others are franchises. It is a multibillion dollar industry. As a result some health and weight control clubs and spas are only seeking the public's dollar rather than trying to be of service. However, at the same time many spas are reputable, are hiring trained personnel, and have excellent programs. Physical educators not only will find a setting for employment in health and weight control clubs and spas, but also they can contribute to upgrading the standards of these businesses.

The activities and services offered by health clubs and spas vary widely. Fitness activities are an integral part of spas. Some spas may even offer graded exercise tests as part of their program. Many spas provide their clientele with instruction and the opportunities to practice a variety of sport activities such as tennis, racquetball, volleyball, and swimming. Aerobic dance, swimnastics, weight training and a diversity of exercise classes are common. Facilities may include pools; racquetball, handball, squash, and tennis courts; and such amenities as whirlpools, saunas, steam rooms, tanning booths, and massages. Health-promotion activities such as

Women engage in a fitness program at a spa.

diet and nutritional counseling are often offered to the clientele.

The cost of membership in these commercial health clubs and spas varies widely, ranging from a few hundred dollars to over a thousand dollars a year. In recent years the number of resort-type spas has grown; individuals desiring to shape up and lose weight check into the spa and stay from one to several weeks.

Another pronounced trend is the growth of commercial diet centers and weight-control spas and clubs. Similar to the health clubs and spas, these may be privately owned or franchises. The focus of these businesses is on weight reduction. Exercise classes and fitness activities, similar to those offered in health clubs and spas, may be part of the weight reduction programs at these commercial enterprises.

The growth of these health and weight-control clubs and spas has led to a diversity of employment opportunities for physical educators interested in working in these health-related careers. Responsibilities associated with these positions vary widely. Physical educators may gain employment in these commercial enterprises as activity instructors or as exercise leaders. They may be responsible for leading an aerobic dance class or for setting up a weight training program for clients and monitoring their performance. In large clubs physical educators may be responsible for training the club's instructors in various exercise techniques and supervising their work with the club's clientele. Where weight control and nutritional counseling is a prime concern, physical educators may evaluate the clients' dietary habits, design a diet to help them reach their goal, plan individual exercise programs to be followed in conjunction with the diet, and offer nutritional counseling. In many cases the physical educator will be required to attend in-service workshops on the specific diet approach espoused by the business and will also receive training in nutritional counseling and psychological techniques such as behavior modification.

Physical educators may also be employed to manage these facilities. Even if physical educators are employed as fitness instructors they have many other responsibilities that are managerial in nature. These responsibilities may include record keeping, training and supervising employees, developing and implementing social programs, and membership solicitation. The varied responsibilities associated with these jobs suggest that in addition to courses in fitness, physical educators should take courses in health, business, psychology, and recreation.

Salaries can range from $18,000 to $35,000. Hours and days worked vary. As the interest in being fit and healthy in our society grows, opportunities for employment in these settings appear to be excellent.

THERAPY-RELATED CAREERS

Increasingly movement in its many forms has been used as a means of therapy. Dance therapy, recreational therapy, and movement therapy are recognized as means to improving the physical, mental, emotional, and social well-being of individuals of all ages.

Dance Therapy

The use of dance has proved very helpful in alleviating physical, emotional, and social problems. It has received wide acceptance as a psychotherapeutic means of physical and emotional expression. Through dance the patient or client has freedom of movement and gains a sense of identity. Dance encourages individuals to recognize their emotions and express them. Through dance, by varying movement qualities, individuals can convey their feelings and ideas to others and perhaps portray emotions that they cannot verbally express. Dance provides a means not only to express one's feelings and emotions to others but also a means of gaining insight into oneself. Dance, by its very nature, can promote sensitivity and awareness.

Dance therapy is one of the fastest-growing professions. It is used in such places as rehabilitation centers, psychiatric centers, geriatric programs, hospitals, and in programs for disabled individuals. Dance therapy is used with all segments of the population from very young to very old persons. Certification standards for dance therapists have been established by the American Dance Therapy Association (ADTA).

Recreational Therapy

Therapeutic recreation is concerned with problems of physically, emotionally, and socially disabled persons and with elderly persons. Recreational therapists work in community and institutional settings where these individuals are located. Therapists use

the role of play and other recreational activities in achieving appropriate goals in physical, emotional, mental, and social development. Games, sports, arts and crafts, and social activities are modified to meet the needs of the patients or clients so that the goals of the program can be realized. Job opportunities for recreational therapists exist in such places as nursing homes, senior citizen centers, child and day care centers, recreational programs, YMCA/YWCAs, hospitals, clinics, and private agencies.

Degree programs in therapeutic recreation are available. However, there are employment opportunities for physical educators who have the background and desire to work in this area. Physical educators working in a community recreation agency may direct therapeutic recreation programs in addition to their responsibilities in teaching physical skills and leading activities.

Movement Therapy

Movement therapists use movement as a means to provide an opportunity for expression for individuals as well as to develop movement skills. Movement therapists work with individuals of all ages. In a preschool program a movement therapist may work with children to develop perceptual-motor skills. Another avenue for employment is the hospital setting or clinic where individuals who have suffered impairments can be helped to learn essential movement skills. Developmental centers or special schools for the disabled may also employ movement therapists.

• • •

Individuals interested in pursuing careers in dance, recreational, and movement therapy may benefit from courses in adapted physical education, psychology, health, recreation, and counseling. Many physical educators build on their background in physical education at the undergraduate level to pursue master's degrees in physical, occupational, and corrective therapy. Physical educators aspiring to continue and pursue careers in physical, occupational, and corrective therapy should early in their professional preparation identify courses that are needed as prerequisites for entry into master's

Homes for elderly persons represent a setting for recreation and leisure services. Students from a local middle school, under the supervision of a leader, assist residents in making "popcorn" with several balls on the parachute at Westwood Home, Clinton, Mo.

degree programs in these areas. Physical educators may then use these prerequisite courses as part of their electives in their undergraduate curriculum.

As recognition of the therapeutic, recreational, and social benefits of movement increases, employment opportunities for physical educators in these areas will expand.

INCREASING YOUR PROFESSIONAL MARKETABILITY

Physical educators who are interested in fitness-, health-, or therapy-related careers can do much to increase their professional marketability. Taking additional course work, pursuing certification, building on one's talents and interests, and gaining practical experience will enhance the credentials of physical educators seeking a position in these areas.

Additional courses in health will increase one's marketability. Conducting health-promotion programs—nutritional counseling, weight management, substance abuse, smoking cessation, and stress management—is often a responsibility associated with positions in this career area. Thus courses in nutrition, stress management, pharmacology, and

drug education would be helpful to the physical educators preparing for careers in these areas. Courses in counseling, psychology, and sociology would be helpful as well. Physical educators need to develop the skills necessary to help individuals change their fitness and health habits. Understanding various decision-making approaches, motivational techniques, and behavior-modification strategies will assist physical educators in helping their clients achieve their goals, whether these goals are increased fitness, weight loss, or learning to manage stress. Since many fitness- and health-related careers include responsibilities such as budgeting, program promotion, membership solicitation, and bookkeeping, courses in business and computer science would help physical educators perform these aspects of the job.

Attaining certification may also increase one's marketability. In many of the exercise specialist and fitness-related jobs, ACSM certification is becoming an increasingly common requirement. Even if such certification is not required for employment, certification as a Health/Fitness Instructor, for example, may be viewed positively by a prospective employer.

While American Red Cross certification in CPR and first aid may be required, it may be helpful to pursue additional certification as a CPR or First Aid Instructor. These instructor certifications would enable one to teach CPR or first aid in a corporate fitness center. Physical educators interested in working as an exercise specialist or as an athletic trainer may wish to become certified as an EMT. This will provide additional expertise in the area of emergency care. Belonging to professional organizations such as AAHPERD, ACSM, AFB, NATA, or the National Therapeutic Recreation Society (NTRS) will also allow one to take advantage of workshops and clinics in one's area of interest.

Building on one's interests and strengths through extracurricular and outside experiences can contribute to one's professional expertise. If you are interested in weight training, for example, and work out frequently, take the time to learn about the different approaches to weight training. Expertise in dance is necessary to those seeking a career as a dance therapist, but can also enhance the skills of physical educators seeking to work in corporate and community fitness centers and preschool programs. Aerobic dance has become a very popular approach to fitness and is often used in fitness centers. A background in dance is very helpful to physical educators working with preschool children in designing movement experiences and helping children express themselves through movement.

Gaining practical experience through internships, fieldwork, volunteering, or part-time and/or summer employment can enhance one's marketability. There is no substitute for experience. Take advantage of the opportunities to work in potential places of employment to gain insight into the day-to-day work. Working as an assistant to a recreational therapist or physical therapist in a hospital, volunteering as a movement therapist in a preschool, assisting in a sports medicine clinic, supervising clients working out in a health spa, and interning in a corporate fitness center will provide practical experience and the opportunity to put theoretical knowledge gained in your undergraduate preparation into practice as well as learn the skills necessary for employment in these positions. Through various practical experiences, professional contacts can be developed as well.

Physical educators can increase their opportunities for employment in fitness-, health- and therapy-related careers by several means. Taking additional course work, building on one's interests and strengths, attaining relevant certifications, and gaining practical experience are strategies that will enhance physical educators' marketability.

SUMMARY

Within the past decade opportunities for physical educators desiring to pursue a career as a fitness or exercise specialist have increased tremendously. Career opportunities exist in preventive and rehabilitative exercise programs. Preventive exercise programs are conducted by corporations, community agencies, and commercial fitness clubs. Rehabilitative exercise programs are typically conducted in a hospital setting, but may be affiliated with corporate fitness programs and community agency programs.

Opportunities for physical educators to pursue health-related careers have also grown rapidly. Professionals possessing qualifications in athletic training may find employment working with athletic programs at the professional, collegiate, and increasingly at the secondary level. Employment opportunities also are available in sports medicine clinics, physical therapy clinics, and hospitals. Physical educators have also been successful in securing employment in health and weight control spas and clubs.

The recognition that participation in movement and physical activities has therapeutic and psychological benefits as well as physical benefits has stimulated the growth of therapy-related careers. These include careers as dance therapists, movement therapists, and recreational therapists.

Physical educators seeking employment in fitness- and health-related careers can increase their marketability by taking additional course work in health, business, and psychology. Gaining as much practical experience as possible will also be an asset in securing employment.

It appears that opportunities for qualified physical educators in fitness- and health-related careers will continue to increase in the future.

SELF-ASSESSMENT TESTS

These tests are designed to assist students in determining if materials and competencies presented in this chapter have been mastered.

1. Describe the responsibilities of a fitness or an exercise specialist. If possible, interview a professional in this career regarding his or her responsibilities and qualifications.

2. Describe the various employment opportunities for a fitness or exercise professional. Review the want ads in several large city papers for three weeks for employment opportunities in this area; describe the positions that you found available.

3. Based on information from the text as well as information gained from talking to professionals in these careers, describe the typical day of an athletic trainer or an individual working in a health or weight club or spa.

4. Discuss the therapeutic and psychosocial values of movement and physical activity. Further investigate one of the therapy-related career opportunities.

5. Describe how a prospective physical educator seeking employment in a fitness- or health-related career can increase his or her marketability.

REFERENCES

1. Wilson PK and Hall LK: Industrial fitness, adult fitness, and cardiac rehabilitation: graduate programs specific to training exercise specialists, Journal of Physical Education, Recreation, and Dance 55(3):40-43, 1984.

2. Cooper KH and Collingwood TR: Physical fitness: programming issues for total well being, Journal of Physical Education, Recreation, and Dance 55(3), 35-36, 44, 1984.

3. Sol N: Graduate preparation for exercise program professionals, Journal of Physical Education, Recreation, and Dance 52(7):76-77, 1981.

4. American College of Sports Medicine: Guidelines for graded exercise testing and exercise prescription, ed 3, Philadelphia, 1986, Lea & Febiger.

5. Forouzesh MR and Ratzker LE: Health promotion and wellness programs: insight into the Fortune 500, Health Education 15(6):18-22, 1984-85.

SUGGESTED READINGS

American College of Sports Medicine: Guidelines for graded exercise testing and exercise prescription, ed 3, Philadelphia, 1986, Lea & Febiger.

    Information on program standards and guidelines for personnel are included in this text.

American College of Sports Medicine: Resource manual for guidelines for exercise testing and prescription, Philadelphia, 1988, Lea & Febiger.

    Current information on topics related to exercise testing and programming for preventive and rehabilitative programs is presented.

Arnheim DD: Modern principles of athletic training, St Louis, 1989, Times Mirror/Mosby Publishing Co.

    This text provides a comprehensive source for information about the field of athletic training.

Cooper KH and Collingwood TR: Physical fitness; programming issues for total well being, Journal of Physical Education, Recreation, and Dance 55(3):35-36, 44, 1984.

    Human factors, program models, program elements, and organizational commitments are discussed relative to program accountability, defined as the extent of compliance to changing behaviors and reaching set goals.

Fain GS, editor: Employee recreation, Journal of Physical Education, Recreation, and Dance 54(8), 32-62, 1983.

    This series of articles provides an overview of various employee recreation programs, including the benefits of recreation programs, programming issues, and assessing the effectiveness of such programs.

Flatten K: Fitness evaluation and programming for older adults, Journal of Physical Education, Recreation, and Dance 60(3):63-78, 1989.

    A series of articles that discusses fitness evaluation, programming, and sport opportunities for the aging population and suggests the development of professional standards for their conduct.

Forouzesh MR and Ratzker LE: Health promotion and wellness programs: insight into the Fortune 500, Health Education 15(6):18-22, 1984-85.

    The results of a survey describing the nature and the extent of health promotion and wellness programs in Fortune 500 companies are presented.

Rankin J: Athletic trainer education: new directions, Journal of Physical Education, Recreation, and Dance 60(6):68-71, 1989.

    A curriculum that provides prospective athletic trainers with a background in human performance as opposed to the traditional background in teaching is presented.

Shields SL: The physical education profession in the corporate sector: its role and influence, Journal of Physical Education, Recreation, and Dance 55(3):32-34, 1984.

    The past role of physical education in the promotion of wellness is discussed as are the directions that colleges and universities should take to establish physical educators as leaders in the wellness movement.

Stopka C and Kaiser D: Certified athletic trainers in our secondary schools: the need and the solution, Athletic Training 23(4):322-324, 1988.

This document was prepared to help professionals and interested individuals substantiate the need for certified athletic trainers within the secondary schools and offer various employment options.

Vertinnsky P: Risk benefit analysis of health promotion: opportunities and threats for physical education, Quest 37:71-83, 1985.

The potential threats to individuals from health promotion programs are described, and caution in health promotion advocated. Opportunities for physical education in health promotion and fitness are presented.

Chapter 13

Sport Careers in Media, Management, Performance, and Other Related Areas

INSTRUCTIONAL OBJECTIVES AND COMPETENCIES TO BE ACHIEVED

After reading this chapter the student should be able to—

- Describe career opportunities in sports media and how preparation in physical education can assist individuals in these careers.
- Identify opportunities for physical educators in sport management and entry level positions in these careers.
- Describe career opportunities in performance and other sport-related careers.
- Discuss how physical educators can increase their professional marketability.

The growing interest and influence of sport in our society and the technological advances and growth in the communications media has led to numerous opportunities for individuals interested in careers in sports media. The growth of sport and sport-related businesses has resulted in the need for individuals trained in sport management. Subsequently, individuals interested in this area can find employment in a diversity of settings. Talented individuals may also find careers as performers, specifically as professional athletes or as dancers.

CAREERS IN SPORTS MEDIA

The pervasiveness of interest in sport in our society coupled with the growth of the communication media—television, radio, newspapers, and magazines—has contributed to the growth of career opportunities in sport communication. Not only has the communication industry grown, but the last

decade has also seen an increase in sport coverage by the media. The growth of media specifically dealing with sport has been phenomenal. For example, the number of sport periodicals has grown, including the number of periodicals dealing with specific sport areas such as running, body building, skiing, swimming, and bowling. Now there are even cable television channels such as ESPN that provide round-the-clock coverage of sport. This growth has led to a number of career opportunities in sports media.

An individual interested in sports media can pursue one of several careers. These careers include sport broadcasting, sportswriting, sports journalism, sport photography, and sports information.[1]

Sport Broadcasting

Sport broadcasting is one career opportunity that has become increasingly popular. Sport broadcasting opportunities may be found with radio and television stations, including cable television, at local, regional, and national levels. Sport broadcasting requires not only knowledge of the game but also the ability to communicate in a clear, articulate fashion.

Preparation in physical education will be helpful to the sportscaster. Sportscasters need to be knowledgeable of the skills, strategies, tactics, and rules used in sport, including the techniques of officiating. A background in physical education will enable the sportscaster to be cognizant of the sport skills used in the competition and be readily able to detect errors in the athletes' performance. Studying physical education will provide the sportscaster with an understanding of the manner in which athletes train for competition, the physiological effects of performance, and psychological insight into the athlete's actions. Sportscasters must be able to relate this information to the public in easily understood terms, providing the public with insight into the nature of the competition and the essence of the athletes' efforts. Familiarity with the sport enables the sportscaster to fluidly describe the play-by-play or moment-to-moment action accurately and to present to the listening and watching public a vibrant portrayal of the athletes' actions.

Sportscasters need to be familiar with a wide range of sport; in the eyes of the public the sportscaster is regarded as an expert on the sport that he or she is covering. Therefore it is important that the sportscaster have an extensive preparation in sport. In a physical education preparation program the potential broadcaster may be exposed to the more common sports areas such as football, basketball, baseball and softball, aquatics, golf, track and field, tennis, and gymnastics. The sportscaster also needs to be familiar with other sports such as auto racing, horse racing, skiing, surfing, boxing, ice hockey, and figure skating.[1] Because instruction in many of these sports areas is typically not provided in professional preparation programs, the sportscaster must seek out experts in these sport areas for instruction, learn through on-the-job experience, or by research.

Sportscasters' days are often long. Hours spent in

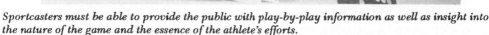

Sportcasters must be able to provide the public with play-by-play information as well as insight into the nature of the game and the essence of the athlete's efforts.

front of the camera or the microphone are most visible. In preparing for a broadcast the sportscaster may put in numerous hours researching the upcoming competition, compiling statistics on athletes' performances, writing scripts, rehearsing certain aspects of his or her performance, arranging and preparing for on-the-air interviews, gathering background information on the athletes, and preparing in numerous other ways. While many of the top broadcasters have help with these aspects of the job, individuals just starting their career may have to do all this preparation on their own. In fact, many individuals start out their broadcasting careers by performing just such tasks for the established broadcasters.

Individuals desiring to pursue a career in broadcasting need to be knowledgeable about the various sport areas. Additionally, they need to be able to speak well and not be inhibited by speaking into the microphone or in front of the camera. The ability to think on one's feet is important because the action must be described as it unfolds. Courses or a minor in communication, particularly courses in speaking and interviewing, are critical. Courses or a minor in radio and television, if offered by the college or university, are valuable as well.

Practical experience can greatly contribute to one's success in attaining an entry level position in this career field. If your college or university has its own television or radio station, become involved in some aspect of its work. Understand that in many situations to gain a foothold it may be necessary to work on behind-the-scenes chores, such as researching material for the upcoming competition, before being afforded the opportunity to work in front of the microphone. If your college or university does not have a station or you are unable to attain a position at the station, perhaps you can gain experience by volunteering to announce and provide live commentary at college or university sporting events or events at the local high school. Try to gain employment or even serve as a volunteer at a local television or radio station for the summer or on a part-time basis throughout the year. Take advantage of opportunities provided by your college or university for fieldwork or internship at radio and television stations. The prospective sportscaster should also collect samples of his or her work to share with future employers. Audiotapes and videotapes of one's performance as a broadcaster and copies of any reviews received can be an asset in gaining employment in this field.

The hours worked by a sport broadcaster may be varied; they are usually at night and on the weekends. Depending on the position, a lot of travel may be associated with the job. Rewards are great; there are opportunities to meet athletes, watch numerous contests, share one's love of sport with the listening or viewing public, and become intimately involved with the sport. Salaries vary according to one's location, for example, working for a local station as compared to a national network; one's reputation as a broadcaster (well known or just beginning and without a reputation); and the sport covered. Individuals interested in this career may wish to join professional organizations such as the National Sportscasters and Sportswriters Association (NSSA), PO Drawer 559, Salisburg, NC 28144.

Sportswriting/Journalism

Physical educators with a talent for writing may decide to pursue a career as a sport journalist or a sportswriter. The sport journalist may find opportunities for work with newspapers and in numerous sport magazines, the number of which seems to be increasing all the time. Sport magazines may provide coverage of several areas such as *Sports Illustrated* or provide coverage of one specific sport such as *Runner's World.*

Sportswriters and journalists may cover events live or write in-depth or feature articles about athletes or various topics in the sport world. As in sport broadcasting, covering the athletic event and reporting it is the most visible part of this occupation. Researching stories, compiling statistics, and interviewing athletes and coaches are all functions of the sportswriter and journalist. The ability to meet deadlines and to write stories under time pressure are required. The work hours, opportunities to travel, and the rewards associated with this profession are similar to those associated with sport broadcasting.

A background in physical education and sport will be helpful to the sportswriter and journalist. A physical education background provides the writer and journalist with a broader understanding of the demands and nature of sport. For example, a sport journalist with course work in sport psychology may be better able to explain to the public why some athletes fail to perform under pressure or "choke," while other athletes appear to rise to the occasion. A sportswriter with an understanding of exercise physiology may be better able to explain what happens physiologically to athletes as they endeavor to complete the rigorous marathon. Sportswriters can call on their background in sport philosophy to describe the transcendental experience of an athlete winning an Olympic gold medal.

Prospective sportswriters and journalists can benefit from course work or a minor in writing and journalism. Practical experience, as in all careers, is an asset in gaining employment. Many sportswriters and journalists have gotten their starts covering sports for their high school papers and continued this work for their collegiate newspaper. Experience working as an editor of the high school or college paper is an asset as well. These experiences can help prospective sportswriters and journalists gain internships or employment with local newspapers and sport publications. To assist in gaining employment in this field, individuals should keep a well-organized scrapbook of their work. Individuals interested in pursuing a career in this area should consider joining NSSA.

Some physical educators engage in sportswriting as a part-time career. For example, physical educators may use their expertise to write textbooks and sport skills books. Another career opportunity in this area is working for a publishing company, editing physical education and sport texts.

Sport Photography

A career as a sport photographer may be attractive to physical educators with a strong interest in photography and the desire to communicate to others the essence and meaning of sport through photographs. Talent as a photographer is a prerequisite to such a career. Opportunities for sport photographers exist with newspapers and sport publications; many sport photographers pursue their careers independently as free-lance photographers.

One's background and preparation as a physical educator can enhance one's career as a sport photographer.[2] Having a knowledge of the essentials of the skills from work completed in biomechanics can help the photographer in knowing the critical aspects of the skill performance and where to position himself or herself to get the right angle for the best photograph. Knowledge of the stress endured by athletes working at their utmost level of effort gained from exercise physiology, understanding of the significance of sport in our society gained from the sociology of sport, and appreciation of the personal meaning that sport holds for its participants gained from sport philosophy can help the sport photographer better capture the true nature and meaning of sport in pictures.

Courses in photography, graphics, and art would be of assistance to the potential sport photographer. Take advantage of opportunities to gain practical experience. Covering sporting events for the campus or local newspapers, taking sport photographs for the yearbook, and contributing photographs to the sport information office to be used in promotional brochures are several ways to gain practical experience and exposure. Sport photographers should maintain a portfolio of their work so that potential employers may readily discern their talent.

Sports Information Director

The sports information director's primary function is to promote athletic events through the various media. Opportunities for employment as a sports information director are found mainly at colleges and universities. At the professional level many of the same responsibilities performed by the sports information director are handled by the director of public relations.

The sports information director has many responsibilities. The sports information director must maintain records and compile statistical information on all teams. He or she must design and prepare promotional brochures; this involves writing the

Qualified managers are needed to direct the growing number of health and fitness clubs.

copy for the text, obtaining photographs of the athletes, preparing the layout, and making arrangements for printing. Preparation of programs for various contests, including obtaining advertisements for the programs, is another responsibility of the sports information director. The sports information director provides assistance to the media covering home contests, phones in contest results to various media, writes press and television releases, writes commercials, and arranges for press conferences and interviews for the media with coaches and athletes. Organization of special promotional events is also the responsibility of the sports information director. In a small school the sports information director may handle all these responsibilities personally, while in a larger school the sports information director may have several assistants. The hours are long as the sports information director may be expected to personally cover many of the athletic events, and quite a bit of travel may be required.

Being a sports information director requires the ability to work closely with the members of the college and university administration as well as the athletic administration, coaches and athletes, and members of the various media. Excellent communication skills—writing, speaking, and interpersonal skills—are essential to this profession. In addition to a background in sport, courses in public relations, advertising, writing, and speech would be helpful. Experience working as a sportswriter or journalist and/or as a sport broadcaster gained in covering high school or college sport is valuable. Faced with numerous responsibilities and demands, many college sports information directors would welcome volunteers interested in working in this career field. Volunteers may be assigned to work on promotional brochures, travel with teams to cover the competition, or to work with the media covering home events. Volunteers should keep a file of their work. Prospective sports information directors may wish to obtain additional information from the College Sports Information Directors of America (COSIDA). (See Chapter 14 for further information.)

CAREERS IN SPORT MANAGEMENT

The increased growth of competitive athletics, sport participation by all segments of society, and sport-related businesses has created a need for individu-

Job opportunities in sport retailing may include direct sales and serving as a manufacturer's representative.

als trained in sport management. Many career opportunities exist for qualified individuals in this field.

In recent years there has been a trend by professionals to expand the realm of sport management to include a diversity of opportunities in a variety of settings. Employment opportunities encompass sport administration, management of sport clubs and facilities, sport and leisure social services, and sport marketing and promotion.

An increasing number of colleges and universities are offering undergraduate and graduate programs in sport management in response to the growing need. Typically, students in these programs complete core requirements in physical education in addition to courses pertaining directly to the sport management area. These courses cover the principles of sport management, sport policy, sport promotion, and sport facility management. Courses in business, law, health promotion, computer science, and communications are included within the program, depending on the focus of study. As much practical experience as possible should be gained before graduation. This can be accomplished by

taking advantage of opportunities for fieldwork and internships offered by the college or university, by volunteering one's time, or by working in a sport management position during the summer or on a part-time basis during the school year. Practical experience is also a good means to investigate different career opportunities within this broad field.

Individuals interested in pursuing a career within this area should understand that they will likely begin their career with employment in an entry level position, often with limited responsibilities. From this position, competent individuals can work their way through middle management and top management positions to assume increased and more broad-ranging responsibilities. Salaries in this field vary widely, ranging from $20,000 to $30,000 per year, although some salaries may be greater than $50,000 per year.

Director of Athletics

The director of athletics is responsible for the administration of competitive athletic programs. These positions may be found at high schools as well as at colleges and universities. Typically, at the high school level the athletic director may be employed as a teacher and in smaller schools as a coach as well. At the collegiate level athletic directors may have teaching and coaching responsibilities in addition to their responsibilities as athletic director. However, in many schools, particularly those with large competitive programs, the athletic director may have as his or her sole responsibility the conduct of the competitive program. In many instances athletic directors will have assistant athletic directors to help them in the performance of their work.

The athletic director is responsible for performing a myriad of tasks. The athletic director may delegate these tasks to assistants or perform them himself or herself. The athletic director is responsible for the administration of men's and women's athletics. This includes both the hiring and ongoing supervision of coaches and assistant coaches. The athletic director must be knowledgeable regarding the rules and regulations governing athletic competition, including rules pertaining to the recruitment and the eligibility of athletes. Scheduling of athletic contests; arranging for officials, and, for competitions involving travel, planning for transportation, lodging, and meals are tasks performed by athletic directors.

The athletic director is also responsible for the safety of the coaches, athletes, and spectators at home contests. This involves working closely with security personnel and making careful provisions for crowd control. At home contests the athletic director supervises the ticket office and concessions. The athletic director must work closely with other personnel involved in athletics such as the athletic trainers and sport information directors. Establishing a good working relationship with the facilities manager and maintenance staff is important as well.

Development and management of the athletic budget is an important function of the athletic director. The athletic director is often expected to work as a fund raiser. Establishing and maintaining good relationships with the community, local support groups such as Booster Clubs, and alumni are seen as vital to the success of the athletic program. The athletic director must also attend professional meetings so as to be aware of current changes in rules and governance.

The hours worked are long; the athletic director may have to teach or work in the office during the day and attend competitions during the afternoon and evenings as well as on the weekends. Salaries vary widely, depending on the extent of the responsibilities and the size of the program. For individuals who enjoy working with athletics, a job as an athletic director can be very rewarding.

Director of Intramurals and/or Campus Recreation

College and university intramural programs and campus recreation programs have expanded in recent years. Traditional intramural programs have grown to include a variety of recreational opportunities. These programs have also expanded to include not only students but faculty, staff, and other campus personnel.

Many titles have been used to describe the individual charged with the administration of these programs. These titles include Director of Intramurals, Director of Recreational Sports, and Director of Campus Recreation. Depending on the institution, the intramural and campus recreation programs may be administered through student services, the physical education department, or the athletic department. In schools with large athletic programs the director may have an assistant or several staff members to help conduct the program.

Responsibilities associated with this position are wide ranging. One of the primary responsibilities is to promote participation. This requires scheduling activities and tournaments that are of interest to the students, publicizing programs, and working closely with campus groups such as residential life and student government to promote these programs. Training and supervision of officials is essential if programs are to run smoothly and safely. The director may also be responsible for instructional programs and the supervision of sport and recreation clubs. Often the director is assigned to supervise physical education and athletic facilities and open recreation programs such as recreational swimming. This may entail the training and supervision of numerous students to serve as lifeguards, gymnasium supervisors, or building security guards.

The intramural director may or may not have teaching responsibilities, depending on the size of the program. Programs are usually offered from late afternoon to late at night; frequently in schools with limited facilities intramurals cannot start until the athletic teams have finished their practices. Programs may be also offered on the weekends. Professionals who are interested in promoting educational values through activities and in providing opportunities for others to experience the satisfaction derived from participation will find working in intramural and campus recreation programs an enjoyable career.

Director of Industrial Recreation

More and more companies are providing recreational and sport opportunities for their employees.

As the number of programs have increased, so has the need for qualified professionals to direct these activities. The responsibilities associated with this position are similar to those associated with the director of intramurals and/or campus recreation. These responsibilities include establishing a program of activities, setting up athletic teams, scheduling contests, providing for instruction, and supervising personnel. As industrial recreation programs continue to grow so will opportunities for qualified professionals.

Sport Facility Management

Positions as a facility manager can be found in a diversity of settings.[2] Facilities managers are traditionally employed by colleges and universities. Facilities managers are needed to direct community, municipal, and commercial facilities such as aquatic centers, ice arenas, domed stadiums, sports complexes, and golf courses. The growing number of fitness centers and health clubs has also increased opportunities for individuals interested in facility management.

Depending on the size of the facility, nature of programs, and number of individuals using the sport facility, the sport facility manager may perform all the responsibilities by himself or herself or may have an assistant or several staff persons under his or her direction. In some situations the facility manager may have additional responsibilities; for instance, in a fitness club the facilities manager may also teach exercise classes or monitor individuals' workouts.

One of the prime concerns of the sport facilities manager is the safety of individuals using the facility. This involves making sure that the facility and equipment are maintained according to accepted standards. Knowledge of building codes, health and sanitation requirements, and law is necessary in this position. In facilities that are used for competitions such as stadiums the facilities manager needs to make provisions to ensure the safety and well-being of spectators as well as participants. The manager must be concerned with crowd control and is responsible for the security personnel. The facility manager is concerned about the business aspects of managing the facility as well. The facility manager can have an impact on the financial success of the facility. The facility must be scheduled to ensure maximum use so as to ensure a profitable financial status. The manager may also supervise other financial aspects of the facility such as ticket sales, concessions, and parking. As the number of facilities continue to grow, opportunities in this area for qualified personnel will expand.

Sport Retailing

Sales of sporting goods—equipment, apparel, and shoes—have grown rapidly in recent years. Sports equipment sales totaled $9.6 billion in 1988 and continue to rise.[3] The growing interest by the public in sport, fitness, and physical activities has stimulated sales and the traditional markets such as schools, colleges and universities, and professional teams have remained strong. Consequently, job opportunities in sport retailing, both in management and sales, have increased.

The area of sport retailing has several opportunities. Jobs are available as salespersons selling directly to the consumer in sporting goods stores. Job opportunities also are available as manufacturer's representatives. An individual employed in this capacity, perhaps as a representative for Nike Shoes, may sell to buyers for sporting goods stores and to athletic teams in a certain region. Manufacturer's representatives are committed to increasing their company's share of the market. This position entails a great deal of travel. Hours may be spent on the phone setting up appointments with potential buyers and following up on sales calls. Whether a manufacturer's representative is successful depends to a great extent on the quality and reputation of the product he or she is selling and the establishment of personal contacts with buyers for these stores and institutions. Manufacturer's representatives may often submit bids for equipment and goods wanted by stores and institutions. Successful bidding requires that the salesperson be able to meet the buyer's specifications for the equipment and goods at the lowest cost. Manufacturer's repre-

Louisiana's Superdome, constructed on the fringe of New Orleans' central business district, is a spectacular sight on the city skyline. The mammoth, multipurpose structure seats more than 80,000 people and is the world's first complete stadium-auditorium-convention-entertainment complex.

sentatives may also represent their companies by setting up a sales booth at conventions such as the AAHPERD National Convention. Other opportunities in sport sales include positions as a manager or owner of a company.

Salaries for sales positions vary widely. Salespersons may receive a set salary. However, often salespersons receive a salary based on commissions and bonuses for the sales they have completed; thus one's salary from month to month may vary widely. Salespersons who travel may receive a company car or an allowance for the use of their personal car as well as an expense account. Salespersons may receive free equipment and goods or be able to purchase them at substantial discounts.

Being a salesperson requires that an individual be extremely knowledgeable about the products that he or she is selling. The consumer in a sporting goods store often expects the salesperson to be an expert on all types of equipment. Buyers for institutions and stores expect manufacturers' representatives to know all the specifications for the equipment and goods they are selling. One's background in physical education is helpful in understanding the demands and nature of various sport areas and the requirements for equipment and goods for these kinds of sport. Courses in business management and accounting are helpful for salespersons. Being a salesperson requires strong interpersonal skills and ability to identify individuals' needs and to sell them a product that meets their needs. As the interest in sport, physical activities, and fitness continues to grow, opportunities for salespersons will expand as well.

Career Opportunities in Professional Organizations

Qualified physical educators may find employment in one of the many professional or specific sport organizations as AAHPERD, NCAA, National Federation of State High School Associations (NFSHSA), LPGA, or United States Tennis Association (USTA), to cite a few examples. The jobs available within professional organizations vary, depending on the nature of the organization and its size. Entry level managerial positions may be available dealing with the day-to-day operations of the organization. Other positions may entail fund raising, handling public relations, conducting membership drives, and directing special projects. If the organization sponsors a national convention, professionals are needed to assist in this endeavor; providing support and guidance to members preparing for local and regional conventions and coordinating meetings of the organization may also be part of one's responsibilities. Writing for the organization's newsletter and editing its periodicals are also jobs performed by individuals working for professional organizations. Professionals are also needed to serve as liaisons with the various committees of the organization. Still other positions within the organization may involve conducting special research projects, gathering data, and performing statistical analyses.

Individuals interested in this type of career can find out further information by directly contacting professional organizations in their area of interest. A few professional organizations are described in Chapter 14. A complete listing of professional organizations may be found in the *Encyclopedia of Associations;* this book will likely be located at the reference desk of most libraries. Some organizations, AAHPERD for example, may offer internships to students. Students interested in internships should write directly to the organization requesting information on these opportunities.

PERFORMANCE AND OTHER SPORT CAREERS
Dance Careers

Individuals talented in the various forms of dance may aspire to careers as professional dancers. While college and university programs offer a major or a minor in dance performance, more than likely college-age dancers have developed their talents through many years of private lessons, often commencing these lessons at an early age. Opportunities for professional dancers may be found with dance companies, theater companies, and television shows. Resorts and clubs, where nightly entertainment is offered to guests, are also other settings for employment.

Individuals who enjoy dance but do not aspire to careers as professional dancers may decide to transmit their love for dance to others through teaching. Opportunities for dance teachers may be found at schools, colleges, and universities. Many individuals choose to teach dance at private studios; some start their own studios as well. A career as a dance therapist (Chapter 12) is also a viable career choice.

Expanding opportunities for individuals interested in a dance-related career can be found in dance administration. Dance administration may be an attractive choice for young dancers as well as dancers who are ready to retire from their performing careers. Lee[4] states that "dancers should capitalize on their professional strengths of fund raising, promotion, management, and administrative skills while integrating their knowledge of dance in such careers in dance company management as artistic director, managing director, development officer, public relations officer, and booking agent." Further information on dance careers may be obtained from the National Dance Association (NDA) (see AAHPERD, Chapter 14 for further information).

Dance is a career that requires a great deal of preparation and a high level of skill. Dance class at Florida A & M University, Tallahassee, Fla.

Professional Athletics

Highly skilled athletes may desire to pursue a career in professional athletics. While many aspire to a career as a professional athlete, few individuals are actually successful in the attainment of this goal. The expansion of men's teams and greater opportunities for women desiring to compete at this level have contributed to increased opportunities for skilled athletes of both sexes to pursue a professional career. However, even though the opportunities are greater than in previous years, the number of positions for individuals in professional sports is very limited.

The salaries paid to top professional athletes are astronomical and range from hundreds of thousands to millions of dollars. Well-known athletes earn thousands or even millions of dollars more in commercial endorsements. Other professionals may not fare as well. Baseball players may spend years in the minor leagues before being sent up to the majors, while golfers may spend years on the tour,

struggling to make ends meet before attracting a sponsor or winning enough money to break even.[5]

Because of the limited opportunities within professional sports, and because many professional careers can be short-lived, individuals who desire to pursue this career should make every effort to complete their college degree. All aspiring professional athletes should take it upon themselves to ensure that they have the skills to earn a living should they fail to attain the professional ranks or have to leave the professional arena after a few years.

Officiating Careers

Sports officiating usually starts out as a part-time job, but some individuals elect to pursue it on a full-time basis. The growth of competitive athletics at the high school and collegiate levels has created a need for qualified officials for all sports. Opportunities are also available at the professional level.

Part-time officials can increase their chances for

The growth of athletics at all levels has created a need for qualified officials.

work year round by becoming certified or rated in two or more sports, each with a different season. Attaining a rating typically requires passing a written exam as well as a practical exam. In some sports, beginning officials must spend a certain period of time working with experienced officials before being able to officiate alone. Individuals interested in information about becoming a rated official should ask an official in the sport, contact the local officials association or board of officials, or write the National Association for Girls and Women in Sports (NAGWS) at AAHPERD.

Individuals interested in officiating should take advantage of opportunities to practice. Officials are needed for high school and college intramurals, summer adult recreational leagues, and youth sport leagues. Volunteering to work at home contests at your college or university as a scorekeeper or in some other capacity is another way to gain experience in this area. In officiating, not only is the knowledge of the rules important but one must possess good officiating mechanics. For example, being able to position oneself in the right position at the right time requires an understanding of the flow of the game. Practice will enhance one's officiating skills.

Officials usually work on afternoons, nights, and the weekends because this is when most athletic contests are conducted. Some travel is involved. Salaries have improved considerably during the last few years, and officials may be reimbursed for their travel costs. In addition to being knowledgeable about the rules of the sport and skilled at the mechanics of officiating, officials need to be able to work under pressure. Officiating also requires good interpersonal skills and communication skills to work with coaches and athletes in highly competitive and stressful situations. Officiating can be a challenging career on a part-time or full-time basis.

Sport Law

One career opportunity that has attracted the interest of some physical educators is a career in sport law.[6] In litigation involving sport a physical educator's background and practical experience as a teacher and a coach can be an asset.

A career in sport law is not a career that can be prepared for directly through one's undergraduate academic experiences. The practice of sport law requires the completion of law school, which typically involves a three-year program of study. Admission to law school is very competitive. Admission requires an excellent academic average, and many law schools also have prerequisites or preferences regarding candidate's areas of undergraduate study. However, for practitioners with experience seeking to change their career focus, sport law may be an attractive area of study. The growth of sport management curriculums has also created a need for individuals with preparation in sport law to teach courses in sport law and liability. Another career opportunity for individuals with expertise in sport law is in working with professional athletes, serving as their agents in contract negotiations.

Entrepreneur

An increasing number of professionals are using their skills and competencies to become entrepreneurs. These individuals develop services and products to meet the public's needs and interests. The broad area of physical education offers many entrepreneurial opportunities to motivated professionals. You may choose to pursue these opportunities on a full- or part-time basis.

Perhaps the most visible of all entrepreneurs within the profession are physical fitness instructors. As discussed in Chapter 12, these professionals work one-on-one with the client, designing and implementing fitness programs tailored specifically to the client's needs. Personal fitness trainers typically visit the client's home to monitor the workout.

Programming in the area of fitness and health promotion offers many entrepreneurial opportunities.[7] Today many individuals are interested in improving their fitness and health. They are willing to pay professionals for the opportunity to learn the skills necessary to achieve a high level of wellness. Entrepreneurs can design and offer health enhancement programs to meet these needs. Programs could focus on fitness assessment and improvement, nutrition, stress management, or weight reduction. These programs could be presented to interested individuals during the afternoon or evening. These programs also could be marketed to corporations desiring to offer these services to their employees but do not have the expertise to conduct such programs. Creative individuals also could produce and market instructional books and videos focusing on fitness and health.

Some professionals with a strong background in exercise science and administration use their skills to serve as a consultant. They visit various fitness sites, such as a health club, assess the current program, make recommendations for improvement, train employees, and organize a system for ongoing program and employee evaluation.

Another opportunity for enterprising individuals with competency in exercise science is the establishment of a mobile fitness and health appraisal business.[8] Using a van filled with appropriate equipment, the professional can travel to different worksites to offer fitness appraisal and health enhancement programs to employees.

Personal coaching is a viable opportunity for individuals with expertise in a specific sport and the ability to coach individuals to achieve a high level of performance.[8] Parents may be interested in obtaining private coaching to help their children further develop sport skills. Many amateur and professional athletes use the services of a personal coach on a regular basis. Opportunities for personal coaching are most commonly found in individual sports such as swimming, diving, golf, tennis, track and field, and ice skating, although participants in team sports (e.g., basketball) may use a personal coach on an intermittent basis to refine selected aspects of their performance.

Professionals with expertise in biomechanics can offer computerized skill analysis services to athletes

Sports camps have grown in number and popularity. Here campers practice their soccer skills.

sport, although the most popular sports tend to be soccer, baseball, softball, tennis, golf, and volleyball. Programs are also offered to develop fitness and reduce weight. Directing camps offer many fine entrepreneurial opportunities.[8] Because many of these programs are offered during the summer months or school vacations, professionals in such areas as teaching and coaching can use these programs to supplement their salary.

There are numerous entrepreneurial opportunities for motivated physical education and sport professionals. Individuals aspiring to such a career must ask themselves two critical questions: (1) Do I have a viable, marketable service or product? and (2) Is there a consumer desire for the service or product? Furthermore, professionals must make sure they have the dedication, enthusiasm, initiative, and self-confidence to pursue this career successfully. The amount of financial resources necessary varies; some services, such as personal fitness instructor, require very little monetary investment, whereas other services, such as a mobilized health and fitness business, may require considerable capital to purchase the necessary equipment. Young professionals who are innovative and aspire to be their own bosses will find a host of entrepreneurial opportunities available to them in the 1990s.

INCREASING YOUR PROFESSIONAL MARKETABILITY

Physical educators interested in working in sport communication and sport management careers can increase their professional marketability in several ways. Taking course work and minors in appropriate areas can enhance one's marketability. For individuals interested in sport media careers, courses or a minor in speech, photography, journalism, and broadcasting will be an asset. Physical educators interested in sport management careers can benefit from courses in business, management, law, and communication. Physical educators also need to take courses specifically applying knowledge from other disciplines to sport communication and sport management as well, for example, courses in sport journalism or sport law.

as well as to coaches interested in furthering their team's performance.[8] The athlete is videotaped and the performance is computer analyzed. The analysis is reviewed with the athlete and suggestions for improvement are given. Instructional videotapes can be offered to complement this service. Sites for this service typically include golf courses, tennis clubs, sporting goods stores, and various other sport facilities. The professional can also contract for this service with interested individuals, such as a coach desiring an analysis of individual team members' skills or a parent wishing a more detailed assessment of his or her child's skill performance.

Throughout the United States, sport and fitness camps for individuals of all ages are proliferating. Instructional camps are available for virtually every

Individuals interested in pursuing sport media, sport management, performance, and other sport-related careers need to be cognizant that the positions described in this section are often top level positions. Attaining them requires a willingness to work one's way "up the ladder," so to speak, to the top. Professionals should gain access to these positions through entry level positions. For example, if you aspire to a career as an athletic director, you may have to work as an assistant athletic director for a period of time to gain the necessary experience and skills.

Practical experience is necessary to move up the career ladder. Practical experience can be gained from volunteering one's services, summer employment, and collegiate fieldwork and internship opportunities. Practical experience not only allows one to gain and refine the necessary skills but allows one to develop professional contacts and exposure. These skills and professional contacts will contribute to gaining employment and advancing up the career ladder.

SUMMARY

The pervasiveness of interest in sport in our society coupled with the growth of the communication media has resulted in the expansion of career opportunities in the field of sport media. Individuals interested in this area can pursue careers in sport broadcasting, sportswriting, sports journalism, sport photography, and sports information.

Sport has developed into a big business. Subsequently, individuals trained in sport management are needed. Qualified professionals interested in sport management may pursue careers as athletic directors, directors of intramurals and campus recreation, directors of industrial recreation, and sport facilities managers. Individuals interested in retailing may choose a career in sport business management and sport sales. Managerial opportunities may also be found working for professional organizations.

Talented individuals may elect to pursue a career as a performer. Other sport-related careers that

may be attractive to qualified individuals are sport officiating and sport law.

Physical educators can use many strategies to enhance their professional marketability. Taking course work in supporting areas and gaining practical experience will help individuals in attaining the position that they desire after graduation.

SELF-ASSESSMENT TESTS

These tests are designed to assist students in determining if the materials and competencies presented in this chapter have been mastered.

1. Discuss how education in physical education can be an asset to individuals pursuing a diversity of sport media careers.

2. If possible, interview individuals working in a sport management position. Ask each person to define his or her responsibilities and the skills that are the most helpful in the performance of their job. Determine the entry level positions in this area. Ask each individual for suggestions about advancing to top level managerial positions in the field.

3. Discuss the positive and negative aspects of pursuing a performance career. Since performance careers may be of short duration, how can individuals prepare for another career after the culmination of their performance career?

4. Select two careers from those discussed in this chapter or in Chapters 11 and 12 that interest you. How can you improve your professional marketability for these careers?

REFERENCES

1. Lambert C: Sports communications. In Considine WJ, editor: Alternative professional preparation in physical education, Washington, DC, 1979, National Association for Sport and Physical Education, an Association of AAHPERD, pp. 85-92.

2. Clary J: Careers in sports, Chicago, 1982, Contemporary Books.

3. Samuelson RJ: The American sports mania, Newsweek, September 4, 1989.

4. Lee S: Dance administrative opportunities, Journal of Physical Education, Recreation, and Dance 55(5):74-75, 81, 1984.

5. Heitzmann WR: Opportunities in sports and athletics, Lincolnwood, Ill, 1984, National Textbook Co.

6. Hoch D: What is sports law? Some introductory remarks and suggested parameters for a growing phenomena, Quest 37:60-70, 1985.

7. Westerfield RC: Entrepreneurial opportunities in health education, Journal of Physical Education, Recreation, and Dance 58(2):67-70, 1987.

8. Pestolesi RA: Opportunities in physical education: what the entrepreneur can do, Journal of Physical Education, Recreation, and Dance 58(2):68-70, 1987.

SUGGESTED READINGS

AAHPERD: Entrepreneurial opportunities in health, physical education, recreation, and dance, Journal of Physical Education, Recreation, and Dance 58(2):64-77, 1987.

A series of six articles that provide the reader with an overview of entrepreneurship and opportunities in health, physical education, recreation, and dance.

Desensi JT and Koehler LS: Sport and fitness management: opportunities for women, Journal of Physical Education, Recreation, and Dance 60(3):55-57, 1989.

Current trends, career opportunities, and future directions are discussed relative to women in sport and fitness management.

Goldberger AS: Sport officiating: a legal guide, Champaign, Ill, 1984, Human Kinetics.

An overview of legal issues pertaining to officiating is provided.

Hoch D: What is sports law? Some introductory remarks and suggested parameters for a growing phenomenon, Quest 37:60-70, 1985.

The various facets of sport law are discussed through descriptive case studies. The four aspects of sport law discussed are traditional negligence liability claims, professional athletic contracts, violence, and social issues in sport.

Labrecque B: Art in sport and dance photography, Journal of Physical Education, Recreation, and Dance 53(2):33-34, 84, 1982.

The art of photographing sport and dance activities and discussion of various photographic techniques are presented.

Leith LM: The underlying processes of athletic administration, Physical Educator 40:211-217, 1983.

Leith describes three essential skills for administration—technical skills, human skills, and conceptual skills—and discusses how they may be developed. Additionally, four elements of administration are discussed: planning, organizing, leading, and controlling.

Parkhouse BL: Sport management, Journal of Physical Education, Recreation, and Dance 55(7):12-22, 1984.

The series of articles focuses on professional preparation for a career in sport management, guidelines for selection of programs of study, advice on how to pursue a sport management career, and information regarding sport management and fund raising.

Parks J and Zanger B: Sport management: career strategies and professional content, Champaign, Ill, 1990, Human Kinetics.

A conceptual overview of the realm of sport management is presented, and various career opportunities are discussed.

Sutton WA: The role of internships in sport management, Journal of Physical Education, Recreation, and Dance 60(7):20-24, 1989.

Strategies to develop an effective internship program are presented.

VanderZwaag HJ: Coming out of the maze: sport management, dance management and exercise science—programs with a future, Quest 35:66-73, 1983.

VanderZwaag proposes a major reorganization of the field of physical education to provide a clear focus. As an alternative program of physical education he proposes the development of sport management, dance management, and exercise science programs.

Weeks S, editor: Dance careers in the 80s, Journal of Physical Education, Recreation, and Dance 55(5):73-81, 1984.

This series of articles focuses on exploring selected dance careers in the 1980s. Administrative opportunities in dance, dance careers, and performing opportunities are described.

Chapter 14

Leadership and Professional Organizations in Physical Education and Sport

INSTRUCTIONAL OBJECTIVES AND COMPETENCIES TO BE ACHIEVED

After reading this chapter the student should be able to—
- Understand some of the reasons why excellent leadership is needed in the profession.
- Define the term *leadership* and indicate the personal qualities needed to achieve such a position.
- Describe three professional qualities leaders in physical education and sport should possess.
- Appreciate why professional organizations exist and why it is important for physical educators to be active members of organizations.
- Identify the major professional organizations associated with the field of physical education and sport, including their purpose, nature of their membership, and publications.

Physical education and sport as a profession is passing through one of the most exciting, yet critical periods in its history. At this time interest in fitness continues to grow among young and old alike, sport activities are being played by more people of both sexes, and concern about health and wellness is great. People are interested in pursuing life-styles that will further their well-being and their quality of life. On the other hand, the economy is in turmoil, school and college budgets are being trimmed, needed personnel are not being hired, abuses and problems within physical education and sport have gained increased notoriety, and personnel burnout is a trend of the times.

The years ahead are filled with many uncertainties and problems and, yet, great promise. Professional leadership is needed in physical education and sport to cope with these uncertainties and problems. On the shoulders of the students who are in professional preparation programs in colleges and universities today rests the responsibility for providing this leadership in the future to enable us to realize our fullest potential. Although many outstanding professionals in the field today are giving fine leadership, new leaders are urgently needed to continually emerge so that there will be no interruption. The physical education and sport profession desperately needs an influx of new, scholarly, energetic, and well-trained future leaders. If today's students fulfill the requirements for leadership, the dividends will be great not only for the profession but also for the students themselves.

Young people represent the future of the profession of physical education and sport. If leadership potential exists among the students now preparing for this profession in the nation's colleges and universities, the profession will prosper. If the leadership potential does not exist among these students, the profession will deteriorate.

DEFINITION OF LEADERSHIP

The term *leadership* represents the art of influencing people to work together harmoniously in the achievement of professional goals that they endorse. Leadership influences a person's feelings, beliefs, and behavior. In a sense, a leader is a person who can help a group to achieve goals with as little friction as possible, have a sense of unity, and provide an opportunity for self-realization. Leadership involves motivating and vitalizing the members of the profession to contribute a maximum effort. It taps vital resources and encourages higher levels of achievement. It eliminates inertia, apathy, and indifference and replaces them with inspiration, enthusiasm, and conviction. It provides for self-fulfillment and satisfying endeavor. It results in power *with* the members, not power *of* the leader.

The leader should be very conscious of the need for self-realization on the part of each member of an organization or profession. Each individual needs to believe that he or she counts for something, is recognized, is somebody, and has a sense of worth. At the same time the leader should recognize that each individual has different interests, urges, abilities, attitudes, talents, capacities, and creative powers to contribute. These traits must be taken into consideration by the leader who must show how not only the profession, but each individual in the profession profits as a result of such an association. In addition, the practitioners should be involved in determining what the profession is trying to accomplish. In the final analysis the test of leadership is determined by the number of people's

lives it enriches. It is a process of helping people to discover themselves; it is not a process of exploitation.

Some personality characteristics of leaders include scholarship, intelligence, dependability, sociability, initiative, persistence, self-confidence, adaptability, insight, emotional stability, communication skills, cooperation, and knowing how to get things done. A general conclusion from an analysis of these characteristics is that leaders are made, not born, since the only inherited or partially inherited trait is intelligence, and the relationship of this quality to leadership is low. Therefore it is within the power of most students to develop the essential qualities for strong leadership.

McIntyre,[1] in a discussion of leadership skills for administrators in physical education, suggests that leadership skills can be taught through developmental programs. These skills are also appropriate for an individual seeking to become a leader in the profession. Among these skills are peer skills, leadership skills, conflict resolution skills, information-processing skills, decision-making skills, and introspective skills.[2]

Peer skills relate to establishing and fostering effective group and individual peer relationships. Leadership skills include developing a variety of leadership styles, performance evaluation skills, planning skills, and skills to foster positive morale. Conflict resolution skills refer to the ability to deal with group conflict in a positive manner. Information processing skills are skills dealing with the gathering of information, evaluation of information, formulation of action plans based on the information, and dissemination of information to the others. Decision-making skills typically follow the model of problem identification, generation of alternative solutions, evaluation of the outcomes of possible solutions, and selecting a solution from among the alternatives. Finally, introspection skills include sensitivity to one's own behavior and its effects on others. Development of these skills will enhance one's ability to be a leader within the profession.

It should be noted that while certain traits appear characteristic of leaders, leadership is also situation-

Leaders must have enthusiasm, a strong belief in the value of their endeavors, and the ability to convey these values to others. Physical educators run with their class at Tilford Middle School, Vinton, Iowa.

al. Much of the current research on leadership seems to suggest that successful leadership depends on the interaction of both the situation and the individual's traits. Thus an individual possessing certain traits may be successful as a leader in one situation but not as successful in another situation.

PERSONAL QUALITIES NEEDED FOR LEADERSHIP

Some qualities that students should develop if they wish to be leaders were set forth many years ago by Ordway Tead in his classic book, *The Art of Leadership*.[3] In this case they have been adapted to relate to leaders in the field of physical education and sport.

Energy

Leaders need energy to cope with the many demanding hours of work required and the effort that is expended in the process. In addition, as Tead stresses, an effective demonstration of energy on the part of leaders begets energy on the part of followers. Energy is contagious. Leaders set the pace and are examples for others to follow.

Sense of Purpose and Direction

Leaders must have conviction regarding what they espouse, what has to be done, and where they want to go professionally. The leader's goals are clear and definite, and the road ahead is clearly delineated. This conviction, sense of purpose, and direction requires knowledge and understanding of one's profession and the objectives that need to be achieved.

Enthusiasm

The word *enthusiasm* comes from the Greek words that mean "possessed" and "inspired by some divinity." It refers to the quality of having vitality for one's purpose. Leaders not only have a strong belief in professional goals, but also a strong desire to further them. Leaders are excited about these goals and the profession that is trying to accomplish them. This feeling is so intense that it also results in exciting others.

Integrity

People must have trust in their leaders. They must know that their leaders are honest and reliable. They want their leaders to keep promises, be honest in their dealings, speak the truth, and say exactly what they mean. Leaders who have integrity act in accordance with the high expectations of their constituency.

Friendliness and Affection

Leaders have a passion for people that is exemplified not by words but by action. Leaders are concerned about the well-being and happiness of other people and are aware of their desires and goals. The leader's affection for people is so great that it influences others. Affection begets affection.

Technical Mastery

Just as exercise physiologists must possess technical mastery of the knowledge and skills needed to evaluate an individual's level of fitness or just as a teacher must possess technical mastery of the skills involved in teaching, so must leaders have a technical mastery of the organization or profession of which they are striving to be leaders. This means that leaders must know the process by which goals are achieved and must understand how each person's task fits into the total enterprise.

Decisiveness

Leaders must get results. The goals of the organization or profession must be achieved. Therefore decisions must be made, courses of action selected, and action taken. This requires courage as well as soundness of judgment. In fulfilling this responsibility, leaders must follow a sound procedure in arriving at decisions that will enhance the profession.

Intelligence

The term *intelligence* is used here, not in the sense of an intelligence quotient, but in a way that relates to how the goals of the profession are accomplished. It refers to the ability to appraise situations and then be able to conceptualize the course of action that should be taken. Leaders who have this type of intelligence are able to sense relationships among various aspects of the enterprise, utilize past experiences when pertinent to solve present problems, and see a line of wise action that needs to be taken. Leaders who have this type of intelligence have imagination as well as sound reasoning powers.

Teaching Skill

Good leaders are also good teachers in the sense that they set goals, pose problems, guide activities, and create interest. Leaders, like teachers, develop a feeling that the activity being accomplished is important and worthwhile. Leaders, like teachers, start where the member is, with what he or she knows and feels, and proceed from that point.

Faith

Leaders have faith that the effort they expend in professional goal accomplishment is worthwhile and that their faith will inspire others. Leaders must have an inner conviction that they are involved in something that will make the world a better place in which to live and that the quality of life of people that it touches will be enhanced. As Tead states:

> The greatest leaders have been sustained by the belief that they were in some way instruments of destiny, that they tapped hidden resources of power, that they truly lived as they tried to live, in harmony with some greater, more universal purpose or intention in the world.

PROFESSIONAL QUALITIES NEEDED

Three professional qualities that physical education and sport leaders need to find the answers to the many perplexing problems that their profession faces are creativity, interest in research, and accountability.

Creativity

Of all the challenges facing physical education today, the need for creativity is extremely important. Creativity, as used here, refers to the discovery of something in physical education and sport that is truly new and that will be an achievement in its own right. Examples of creativity in the history of the world were the development of the theory of relativity and the invention of the telephone. In education it was such things as the nongraded school and computer assisted instruction. An example in physical education might be the development of the game of basketball by Naismith. Each of these examples of creativity resulted in a novel work that was accepted as useful and satisfying to society.

Physical education has had few exciting and dynamic creative ideas in its history. Leaders are needed to help it to play a more dynamic role in education. More creative ideas are needed like Wood's *new physical education,* Laban's *movement education,* and Hetherington's *fundamental education.*

A review of the literature reveals some characteristics of the creative person. The creative individual possesses imagination, inner maturity, the ability to think and to analyze, a rich background of knowledge in his or her field, and flexibility in approaching problems. This person will be skeptical of accepted ideas and less suspicious of new ones, persistent, sensitive to the environment, fluent in the production of ideas, and self-confident.

Physical educators need to think more about the present status of their field of endeavor, including the problems they face and the goals they wish to achieve, and then come up with some creative ideas that will help to solve these problems and achieve these goals.

Interest in Research

Basically, closing the gap between research and practice in physical education constitutes a threefold challenge to all professionals.

The first phase of this challenge is that physical education has available valid research findings that are not being applied in programs across the country. For example, much is known about learning theory in general and about motor learning in particular—but it is not applied. Some excellent articles in the professional literature and several books have summarized the pertinent research findings in motor learning. However, some of the skill teaching that goes on today is a hit-and-miss procedure based on traditional ways of doing things or on an individual teacher's own unscientific opinion. In addition to learning theory much is known but not applied in human behavior, physical fitness, activity and weight control, body image, and other important areas in physical education. This gap between what is known to be right and what is practiced must be closed. This is indeed a major challenge, which requires the proper dissemination of research information and the desire and interest on the part of physical educators to see that it becomes part of their programs.

The second phase of the problem is that more scholarly research is needed on many of the problems with which physical educators are faced today. For example, the professional needs to know such things as the value of selected physical education activities and programs on disabled individuals of all ages; the relationship of coaching styles to the development of certain character traits in youth; the most desirable length, frequency, and intensity of exercise for postheart attack patients; and the structure of practice periods to ensure optimal learning of various physical skills.

These represent only a few examples of problems that, if the answers were known and applied, would produce physical education and sport programs more scientifically based, as well as contribute significantly more to the consumers of their services.

The third phase of the problem is that of interpreting the research findings. Many physical educators do not understand research terminology and how to interpret research findings. It is a language far beyond their grasp. As a result, research fails to be used in many cases. One answer to this problem is to have significant research studies interpreted in language that is meaningful to the physical educator on the job. It might be helpful for physical educators to read reports of technical subjects in magazines such as *Reader's Digest* and *Time.* Even the

Professionals discuss research presented at a poster session at an AAHPERD national convention.

most technical details are spelled out so that the material is intelligible to a person with only a grade-school education. Consequently, the material is read by great numbers of people, and the circulation of these magazines runs into millions of copies. Similarly, the physical education and sport profession must also make an effort to ensure that research findings are communicated to practitioners in an understandable fashion. One example of the effort to bridge the gap between research and practice is a feature included in the *Journal of Physical Education, Recreation, and Dance* called "Research Works." The purpose of this feature is to promote widespread dissemination of research findings and to communicate these findings in an easily understood manner to a diverse audience of professionals. Further efforts similar to this endeavor are

needed and, if forthcoming, will help upgrade practitioners' efforts considerably.

The challenge of closing the gap between research and practice represents one that must be met if physical education and sport is to become a respected, established profession.

Accountability

Accountability is needed in the physical education and sport profession if it is to grow and reach its destiny. There must be accountability to the consumer (i.e., students, clients), society, and oneself. Most important, there must be accountability to the profession. Only through accountability can physical and sport educators render a unique and worthwhile service to society in general and to their profession in particular.

Accountability as a member of the physical education and sport profession is most important. First, to be accountable one must have a sound foundation of knowledge regarding the worth of his or her field of endeavor. In other words, the goals the profession is stating it is attempting to achieve must have a scientific basis. This scientific basis and theory are found in such areas as exercise physiology; motor control; motor development; motor learning; biomechanics; and the philosophy, sociology, and psychology of physical education and sport. Therefore each potential leader should possess a mastery of this information. In this era of specialization it is important that each leader be familiar with the breadth as well as the depth of the discipline of physical education. Specialized areas of study and the subdisciplines should not be studied in isolation but in relation to the discipline as a whole.

Second, in addition to the scientific theory foundation, goals must be clearly stated in terms of performance and behavioral objectives for the consumer. In other words, physical and sport educators must be able to prescribe and conduct the activities and other experiences that will achieve stated goals for the consumer.

Third, a system of scientific evaluation and assessment must prove the goals set forth by the profession and the outcomes predicted for the consumer are actually accomplished in practice by physical and sport educators.

Through professional accountability such as that which involves these three components, the profession will take on a new respectability in the academic world as well as among the public in general. It will be recognized that physical and sport educators have the proper credentials since they can prove scientifically that the services they render to society can enhance the quality of life for human beings.

FORMULA FOR ACHIEVING LEADERSHIP STATUS

There are six qualities that each student should possess and that collectively will help to ensure becoming a leader in the field of physical education and sport regardless of which career opportunities are being pursued. These six qualities are health and personality, applied intelligence, articulation, dedication and hard work, respect for other people, and desire.

Health and Personality

A person desiring to become a leader in the profession will find that good health and a pleasing personality represent assets in achieving this goal. Good health is important for many reasons, but especially since many long hours of work will be involved. Unless a person has good health, it will be very difficult to be professionally productive. Further, most physical and sport educators should exhibit the ingredients that epitomize good health. This is important since physical and sport educators serve as role models for many children and youth.

One's personality is also important. Leaders should have positive attitudes; reflect energy, drive, and ambition; have composure, possess poise, a diplomatic approach, and a sense of humor; inspire trust; and be likable. Various physical characteristics also need attention. Obesity is a negative quality, particularly for the leader in physical education and sport. Dress and manners are important since they have to do with making an impression. Good posture and an image of self-confidence connote leadership qualities.

Physical education and sport professionals, by

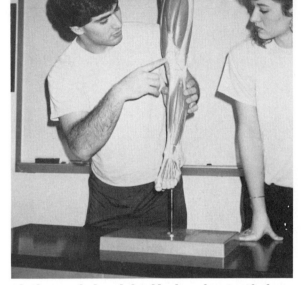

A leader must be knowledgeable about the scientific foundations of the field.

virtue of the nature of their work, are highly visible. Because of this visibility it is important that professionals be role models, that they indeed "practice what they preach." Professionals should exemplify a healthy, fit, active life-style.

Applied Intelligence

Students who are admitted to colleges and universities should have the intelligence necessary to acquire the scientific knowledge and skills pertinent to their field of expertise.

A leader must have an excellent background in physical education and sport. This means possessing the competencies that professors are trying to provide in the various courses that comprise the program. A superficial preparation will not do. Leadership requires a mastery of the knowledge, skills, and attitudes that are related to the biological, sociological, biomechanical, and psychological scientific foundations associated with this area of expertise.

A prospective leader should become a specialist in some area of physical education and sport such as elementary or secondary school physical education, college physical education, exercise physiology, biomechanics, motor learning, intramurals, or athletic administration. It is important to acquire all the information one can concerning the chosen area of specialization. A prospective leader's objective should be to try and know more about his or her area of specialization than any other person. The goal should be to become recognized as a person who possesses the "knowhow" in regard to the specialty.

However, it must be emphasized that while it is important for physical educators to be knowledgeable in their specialized areas, they should have an understanding of the discipline as a whole and the relationship of their specialized area to this whole.

Various opportunities present themselves for gaining such recognition, including teaching, research, writing articles and books, and serving on professional committees. Other opportunities include serving as a clinician at a workshop, making presentations at conferences, and becoming active in professional organizations.

Articulation

Articulation is very important. One must know how to communicate effectively. Leaders must be able to write and speak coherently. They are constantly in front of the public, making speeches, and communicating the goals of their profession. As such, they cannot afford to be weak in their written or oral language.

Although specialization is important, one's learning should not stop there. A leader should also be cultured and well-rounded. This means it is important to know something about such fields as art, architecture, politics, travel, languages, economics, literature, and music. Since all of this knowledge cannot be gained in college, much of the work will

need to be done on one's own. Among other benefits, such learning will help a person converse intelligently with other people. It is important for the student to recognize that as a leader he or she will not be limited to associating only with people in his or her specialty. Instead, there will be meetings with doctors, lawyers, business persons, politicians, and many other people in various occupations. Persons who are intelligent and cultured will make an impression on those with whom they come in contact.

Dedication and Hard Work

A dedication to the field is a necessity. This does not mean a casual interest that has developed because a student was a star athlete in high school or college. Instead, it means a strong desire and conviction that this profession is important because it represents a way of providing a useful and desirable service to society.

Hard work is also essential to success. The best things in life are not free—one has to work for them. The people who have leadership positions did not arrive in such positions by chance—they worked hard to achieve such status.

Respect for Other People

Respect for other people is an essential quality that begins with respect for oneself. Self-respect requires self-awareness, an understanding and acceptance of your personal characteristics and abilities, and your goals and your commitment to realize them. It involves acceptance of yourself as an individual of worth and dignity. Respect for others is an extension of respect for yourself.

As a leader, it is important to have respect for the worth and dignity of each individual. This encompasses an appreciation for diversity in cultures, values, and opinions. Leadership involves working with others in such a manner as to bring out the best in each person. An effective leader uses each person's capabilities to the fullest and at the same time helps individuals grow toward realization of their potential. Respecting and caring about the people with whom you work is essential to becoming a leader.

Desire

Students have seen persons who possessed a strong desire and accomplished great things although many obstacles were thrown in their paths. The important thing was that these people kept their goals clearly in mind, were not sidetracked, and kept striving for what they wanted out of life.

Most young people have a strong desire to be successful. They dream beyond the actual and think beyond their fingertips. They commit themselves to being a professional and strive toward the attainment of their goals. They are active and role models for what they preach. By doing so, they are becoming all that they are capable of being.

Professionals must realize their responsibility to continue their education through their lifetime. Professionals seeking to become leaders in the profession must also find ways to become involved in the profession, to have a significant role in its conduct, and to shape its future. One way to fulfill these responsibilities is to become actively involved in professional organizations.

PROFESSIONAL ORGANIZATIONS IN PHYSICAL EDUCATION AND SPORT

Professional organizations are the heartbeat of the profession. The greatest changes in the profession have their beginnings in organizational meetings and conferences. Scholarly research, curriculum development, certification requirements, and hundreds of other topics are discussed in detail at conferences. The physical education and sport profession, both in the United States and in other countries of the world, has an imposing list of associations concerned with every aspect of the field.

All physical educators should belong to their national and state associations and to others, as far as it is possible. The fact that many physical educators do not belong to their national association, AAHPERD, is indicated by statistics showing more than 200,000 persons in the field today and only approximately 40,000 AAHPERD members. Yet the thousands who are not members accept, experience, and participate in the advances, better working conditions, and benefits that the association has accomplished. This should not be the case. If all physical educators belonged to and worked for their professional organizations, the concerted effort of such a large professional group would result in greater benefits and more prestige for the profession.

Why Belong to a Professional Association?

Belonging to a professional organization has many advantages. Factors that every physical educator should recognize about such membership include the following:

1. *They provide opportunity for service.* With the many offices, committee responsibilities, and program functions that professional associations provide, the individual has an opportunity to render a service for the betterment of this field of work.

2. *They provide an opportunity to shape the future of the profession.* Members can work actively to influence the direction of the field in the future. This can be accomplished through involvement in committees, task forces, and goverance. Members can also be active in influencing legislation that will be of benefit to the profession. For example, NASPE, an association of AAHPERD, is actively crusading for daily physical education for all school children and is using their congressional lobby as one means to achieve this objective.

3. *They provide a channel of communication.* Communication in a profession is essential so that members may know about what is going on, the latest developments in teaching techniques, new emphases in program content, and many other trends that are happening continuously in a growing profession. Through associations, an effective channel of communications exists by way of publications, meetings, and announcements that are periodically made.

4. *They provide a means for interpreting the profession.* The physical education profession must be interpreted to the public on national, state, and local levels. This interpretation is essential if public support is to be achieved for the services rendered by the professional practitioner. The professional association provides an opportunity for the best thinking and ideas to be articulately interpreted far and wide. As a result of such endeavors, recogni-

Conventions offer the opportunity for professional communication and fellowship.

tion, respect, prestige, and cooperation with other areas of education, professions, and the public in general can be achieved.

5. *They provide a source of help in solving one's professional and personal problems.* Each physical educator has problems, both professional and personal. Through their officers, members, conferences, and other media, professional associations can play an important role in solving these problems. If a person is a member of an association, he or she does not "go it alone" but, instead, is surrounded by professional help on all sides. Associations are interested in helping and rendering a service. The associations can be of assistance, for example, in solving a professional problem involving the administration of an adapted program or a personal problem of life insurance.

6. *They provide an opportunity for fellowship.* Through association conferences and meetings the physical educator gets to know others doing similar work, and this common denominator results in friendships and many enjoyable professional and social occasions. A person gets a "shot in the arm" by associating with other persons dedicated to the same field of endeavor.

7. *They provide a forum for research.* Professions must continually conduct research to determine how effective their programs are, how many contributions they are rendering to human beings, how valid their techniques are, and the answers to many other questions that must be known if the profession is to move ahead and render an increasingly larger service.

8. *They yield a feeling of belonging.* A basic psychological need is to have a feeling of being part of a group and accomplishing work that is recognized and important. A professional association can contribute much in meeting this human need.

9. *They provide a means for distributing costs.* The work accomplished by a professional association is designed to help the members who belong to the association. The work accomplished requires financial means. By joining a professional association, physical educators help to share the expenses that they rightfully have the responsibility to share. If one participates in the benefits, one should also share in the costs of achieving these benefits.

10. *They are valuable in gaining employment.* Through organizations physical educators can develop professional contacts that may prove useful

in gaining employment. Through such professional contacts physical educators can learn of prospective employment opportunities or obtain a letter of recommendation for a desired position. Many professional organizations offer placement services for their members. AAHPERD, AFB, and NATA, for example, send their members updates of job openings and have placement services at their national conventions. This is helpful not only in gaining one's first job but in changing jobs as well. Employers often view membership in professional organizations as a hallmark of a professional; this can influence whether or not one gets hired.

Numerous professional organizations exist within the realm of physical education and sport to meet the diverse interests and needs of professionals within the field. Young professionals should become active members in the professional organizations to which they belong. From the many organizations available, you should select carefully the organizations that best meet your needs and interests. Become involved—be a committed, active professional willing to work hard to shape the direction and future of this dynamic field.

Professional Organizations

It would be difficult to discuss all the organizations that pertain to the physical education and sport profession. The growth of physical education and sport has led to the formation of numerous organizations; it seems that for every specialized area of study as well as for each sport there is a professional organization for interested professionals. Thus only some of the organizations with which the physical educator should be familiar are discussed. Physical educators can find out about organizations in their areas of interest in several ways. First, talk to other professionals such as faculty at your undergraduate institution that may share the same interests. Talk to practitioners in your prospective field of employment and find out the organizations in which they hold membership. Second, another source of information is AAHPERD. Third, a comprehensive listing of all organizations in the United States is given in the *Encyclopedia of Associations*. The listing for each organization in the encyclopedia includes the

purpose of the organization; name, address, and phone number of the person to contact for further information; size of the membership and the association staff; and publications of the association. The encyclopedia is probably available at the reference desk or in the reference section of most college and university libraries.

AAHPERD and professional organizations in the area of sports medicine, corporate fitness, sport information, athletic training, intramurals, and recreation are discussed. Associations for professionals interested in sport psychology, sport sociology, sport history, and sport philosophy are also mentioned. Finally, examples of organizations for professionals interested in specific sport areas are provided.

American Alliance for Health, Physical Education, Recreation, and Dance

The AAHPERD was established in 1885 under the title of American Association for Advancement of Physical Education. The leaders in this initial organization were 35 physicians, educators, and other individuals. They were called together by Dr. William G. Anderson, then on the staff of Adelphi Academy. Other physical education leaders who were prominent in the early history of the association were Dr. Hitchcock of Amherst, Dr. Sargent of Harvard, Dr. Gulick of the YMCA, Dr. Arnold of Arnold College, and Dr. Savage of Oberlin College. In 1903 the name of the association was changed to American Physical Education Association. In 1937 the Departments of School Health and Physical Education of the National Education Association were combined to form the American Association for Health and Physical Education, a department of the National Education Association. In 1938 the term *recreation* (AAHPER) was added to the title.

In 1974 the AAHPER was officially reorganized to give more visibility and autonomy to the various specialities and fields of endeavour of which the organization is composed. Each of the major areas of endeavor became an assosciation with its own offices (i.e., budget), and the AAHPER in its totality became an alliance and the term *dance* was added to its title.

Under the reorganization plan the AAHPER became the AAHPERD. The six associations that comprise this alliance and their focus are described below:

- The American Association for Leisure and Recreation (AALR) is concerned with the promotion of leisure services at the community and national levels and recreation education within the school.
- The Association for the Advancement of Health Education (AAHE) is involved with the conduct of health education programs in schools, colleges, and communities as well as being concerned with addressing societal health issues, such as drinking and driving, and promotion of health-oriented legislation.
- The Association for Research, Administration, Professional Councils, and Societies (ARAPCS) consists of various special interest groups, such as the Council on Outdoor Education and the Council of Aging and Adult Development, and administrative groups, such as the College and University Administrators Council.
- The National Association for Girls and Women in Sport (NAGWAS) focuses on improvement of leadership sport opportunities for girls and women at all levels of competition.
- The National Association for Sport and Physical Education (NASPE) is concerned with the promotion of physical education and sport at all levels.
- The National Dance Association (NDA) seeks to promote dance both within the educational setting and on the community and national level.

Each of the six associations of AAHPERD has various substructures and activities that focus on specific needs, interests, and concerns of professionals. For example, NASPE, the largest association, has several substructures. There are nine academies: Curriculum and Instruction, Exercise Physiology, Sport History, Kinesiology, Motor Development, Philosophy, Sport Psychology, Sport Sociology, and Sport Art. These academies provide a forum for interested professionals to exchange information and to work on projects furthering these areas of study. There are also several councils within NASPE. These councils include the Council on Physical Education for Children, the Middle and Secondary School Physical Education Council, the College and University Physical Education Council, the College and University Physical Education Department Administrators Council, the National Council of Secondary School Athletic Directors, the Coaches Council, and the Youth Sports Coalition. These councils sponsor various activities, such as workshops for professional development, recognition of outstanding accomplishments by professionals, and preparation and dissemination of position papers and guidelines on various issues.

The national office of AAHPERD is located at 1900 Association Drive, Reston, VA 22091.

The publications of the alliance are many and varied. Beginning in 1896 the *American Physical Education Review* was the official publication. This was discontinued in 1929 when it was combined with the *Pentathlon,* the publication of the Middle West Society of Physical Education. Then the new publication of the association became known as the *Journal of Health and Physical Education.* This periodical is known at the present time as the *Journal of Physical Education, Recreation, and Dance* (JOPERD). The AAHPERD also publishes the *Research Quarterly for Exercise and Sport, Strategies, Update,* and *Health Education.* In addition, the AAHPERD publishes many other pamphlets, books, and materials pertinent to the work of the alliance.

Members of AAHPERD are designed as professional members, associate members, fellows, life members, life fellows, student members, honorary members, emeritus members, and contributing members.

Nationally AAHPERD is divided into six district organizations. The Eastern, Southern, Central, Midwestern, Southwestern, and Northwestern districts have a similar purpose as AAHPERD, elect officers, and hold district conventions. These district organizations provide leadership opportunities for professionals and allow AAHPERD, through the district organizations, to present programs pertinent to area needs and address issues relevant to regional

The American Alliance for Health, Physical Education, Recreation, and Dance, the largest professional organization, has provided leadership for over 100 years.

concerns. Membership in AAHPERD covers membership in one's district organization.

State associations provide services to professionals within each state. These organizations have purposes similar to AAHPERD. Membership in the state organization requires a membership fee; membership in the national organization is optional. State associations provide wonderful opportunities for young practitioners to become involved in their profession.

The services performed by the alliance include the following:

1. Holding state, district, and national conventions periodically.
2. Acting as a clearinghouse for information concerning positions in health, physical education, recreation, and dance.
3. Publishing pamphlets, brochures, and other pertinent information.
4. Influencing public opinion.
5. Providing consultant services in related areas.

6. Acting as a consultant to the President's Council on Physical Fitness and Sports.
7. Working with legislatures concerning education and research programs.

AAHPERD also offers placement services to its members. Internship opportunities at AAHPERD headquarters in Reston, Virginia are available. Interested students should contact AAHPERD headquarters directly.

The AAHPERD Student Action Council (SAC) is an organization of students that works for the benefits of its members through student involvement. The group's objectives include (1) greater student involvement in AAHPERD, (2) promotion of professionalism among majors, and (3) the promotion of professional interest groups. The alliance in cooperation with SAC has made available special membership plans for students.

American College of Sports Medicine

On April 23, 1954, a few outstanding leaders in the fields of medicine, physiology, and physical education met in New York City and founded the ACSM. The purposes this group set forth for the association include the following:

1. To promote and advance scientific studies concerning sport and other motor activities.
2. To cooperate with other organizations concerning sports medicine and related areas.
3. To encourage research and postgraduate work in related areas.
4. To publish a journal and maintain a library concerned with sports medicine and related areas.

There are approximately 12,000 members in the ACSM and there are 13 regional groups such as the Mid-Atlantic Chapter of the ACSM. Of the three membership categories (medicine, physiology, and physical education), the largest membership is in physical education.

The college is affiliated with the International Federation of Sports Medicine (IFSM), an organization that has played an important role for many years in Europe and South America. The official publication of the IFSM is the *Journal of Sport and Physical Fitness*.

ACSM publishes several periodicals. These include *Medicine and Science in Sports and Exercise, Sports Medicine Bulletin,* and the *Encyclopedia of Sport Sciences and Medicine.*

The activities of the college and the research papers cover topics such as the treatment and prevention of athletic injuries, the effects of physical activity on health, and the scientific aspects of training. It reports recent developments in the field of sports medicine on a worldwide basis.

ACSM sponsors certification programs for professionals interested in working preventive and rehabilitative exercise programs (see Chapter 12). For further information about the organization write ACSM, PO Box 1440, Indianapolis, IN 46206-1440.

Association for Fitness in Business

The AFB was founded in 1974 as the American Association for Fitness Directors in Business and Industry (AAFDBI). There are over 5000 members. The membership is composed of professionals working in corporate and organizational employee fitness programs. Membership is also open to students who are interested in pursuing a career in this field.

This organization has several purposes. One purpose is to provide professional support and assistance in the development and promotion of quality health and fitness programs in business and to create an awareness of the benefits of maintaining a high level of fitness and health among employees. AFB strives to cooperate with other organizations concerned about the fitness level of Americans such as the President's Council on Physical Fitness and Sports. The organization recommends certification standards for fitness personnel such as adherence to the ACSM qualifications and standards. AFB sponsors seminars and other programs for professionals and annual conventions and regional meetings. Promotion of research, dissemination of research findings, and serving as a clearinghouse for information on fitness are among the AFB's activities. AFB also offers its members information about job opportunities.

Publications include *Action,* which is a newsletter, and Fitprints, a research bulletin. For further information contact Executive Director, AFB, 1312 Washington Rd, Stamford, CT 06902.

College Sports Information Directors of America

The COSIDA was formed in 1957 after separating from the American College Public Relations Association. The primary objectives of the organization include standardizing sport statistics, press box procedures and routines, and score books. The organization is made up of individuals in college and university sports information departments, public relations departments, and news bureaus. The association has active, associate, and student memberships.

Some of the activities sponsored by COSIDA include the sponsorship of university and college division and academic all-American football, basketball, and baseball teams. COSIDA gives the Jake Ward Award annually to a person associated with the communication media for outstanding work in covering college athletics and the Arch Ward Memorial Award for contribution to the profession. COSIDA also supports the Helms Hall Foundation and Hall of Fame and annually makes awards to individuals named to the Helms Hall of Fame by COSIDA. The organization also publishes *News-Digest* on a monthly basis.

For more information write in care of Campus Box 114, Texas Agricultural and Industrial University, Kingsville, TX 78363.

National Athletic Trainers Association

The NATA was founded in Kansas City, Missouri, in 1950. The purpose of this organization was to establish professional standards and to have a medium for disbursing to the membership information and materials pertinent to this profession. Since its beginning professional standards have been raised and a code of ethics established. The Association permits to membership those persons who are qualified and subscribe to the code of ethics and standards that have been developed. The NATA publishes a quarterly journal, *Athletic Training: The Journal of the National Athletic Trainers Association.* It also convenes a conference of associ-

Conventions provide professionals with an opportunity to find out about various products and services.

ation members each year where new developments are discussed and other events are part of the agenda.

The *Trainer's Code of Ethics* of the NATA stresses honesty; integrity; and loyalty to oneself, others, and to the profession.

National Intramural-Recreational Sports Association

In the school year 1948–1949 William Wasson, an instructor at Dillard University in New Orleans, received a Carnegie grant-in-aid to study intramural programs in 25 colleges and universities. It was from this study that he conceived the idea of having the intramural directors meet annually and of developing a medium through which an exchange of information and ideas could take place.

The first meeting was held at Dillard University on February 22 and 23, 1950. At this meeting the National Intramural Association was formed.

In 1973 the name of this association was changed to the National Intramural-Recreational Sports Association or NIRSA.

NIRSA is an affiliate member of AAHPERD. Its objectives are as follows:

1. To provide a common meeting ground for intramural directors and members of their staff to discuss current problems and policies.
2. To provide an opportunity to exchange ideas and thoughts for improvement in the operation of the intramural program.
3. To determine policy, principles, and procedures to guide intramural directors in performance of their duties.
4. To promote and encourage intramural and recreational programs.
5. To serve as a medium for the publication of research papers on intramurals of both members and nonmembers.
6. To work in close cooperation with the AAHPERD, the National Recreation and Park Association (NRPA), and the educational policy committee of our respective institutions.

The official publication of NIRSA is the *NIRSA Journal.*

Membership in the association, in addition to providing a subscription for a copy of the annual conference proceedings, offers other advantages, including information service and an opportunity to help in promoting higher standards for the profession.

For further information write to the Dixon

Recreation Center, Oregon State University, Corvalis, OR 97331.

National Recreation and Park Association

The National Recreation and Park Association (NRPA) is an organization dedicated to the conservation and beautification of the environment and the development, improvement, and expansion of park and recreation programs, facilities, leadership, and services. It is an independent, nonprofit organization whose primary goal is to continue the advance of environmental quality and an improved quality of life.

The NRPA had at least part of its beginnings in 1906 when the Playground Association of America was organized. At the time of the founding of this association only 41 cities reportedly had playgrounds with qualified leadership. One of the association's main objectives was to achieve the goal of having adequately trained men and women conducting play and recreation programs on a community basis. The association also furthered the cause of spending leisure in a wholesome, profitable manner.

In 1965 the American Association of Zoological Parks and Aquariums, the American Institute of Park Executives, the American Recreation Society, the National Conference on State Parks, and the National Recreation Association united and became the NRPA. (In 1971 the American Association of Zoological Parks and Aquariums again became an independent organization.)

The objectives of the NRPA are public policy formation, education, community service, citizen development service, and professional development services.

NRPA publishes several periodicals: *Parks and Recreation Magazine, Journal of Leisure Research,* and *Therapeutic Recreation Journal.* An annual guide to books on parks and recreation is also published.

The national headquarters of the NRPA is at 3101 Park Center Dr., Alexandria, VA 22302, where a professional staff of specialists in parks, recreation, and conservation, and associated fields is carrying on the work of the association.

• • •

Many of the subdisciplines of physical education also have professional organizations or associations. Examples of four of these organizations are listed.

North American Society for the Psychology of Sport and Physical Activity

The North American Society for the Psychology of Sport and Physical Activity (NASPSPA) was founded in 1965 and became incorporated as a nonprofit corporation in 1967. NASPSPA is affiliated with the International Society for the Psychology of Sports (ISPS).

The society is composed of professional people (psychologists, psychiatrists, and physical educators) whose primary purpose is to promote scientific research and relations within the framework of sport psychology and physical activity by means of meetings, investigations, publications, and other activities. Membership in NASPSPA is open to all people interested in the psychology of sport and physical activity.

The society publishes the *Sport Psychology Bulletin,* a quarterly bulletin, which keeps its members informed about affairs of the society, as well as the field of sport psychology in general. The society also publishes newsletters detailing the activities of the annual convention, which is usually held in the spring. For further information concerning the NASPSPA write to the society in care of Craig Weisberg, School of HPER, University of Tennessee, Knoxville, TN 37996.

The Philosophic Society for the Study of Sport

The Philosophic Society for the Study of Sport (PSSS) is a new organization founded in 1972 at the annual meeting of the American Philosophical Association, Eastern Division. The membership includes persons with varied backgrounds and skills, all having a widespread interest in the philosophy of sport. The central thrust of the organization is the scholarly investigation of sport, including implications for practical pursuit. There are four types of membership: sustaining, active, constituent, and student.

The PSSS publishes newsletters and the *Journal of the Philosophy of Sport*. For further information contact Professor James E. Genasci, Dept. of Physical Education, Springfield College, Springfield, MA 01109.

North American Society for Sport History

The North American Society for Sport History (NASSH) was founded in 1972. The membership is comprised of individuals interested in sport history, social history, and physical education. The purpose of NASSH is to promote the study, research, and writing of sport history. Another objective is to cooperate with other organizations with similar aims. NASSH publishes the *Journal of Sport History*. Additional information may be obtained from Prof. Ronald A. Smith, NASSH, 101 White Building, Pennsylvania State University, University Park, PA 16802.

North American Society for the Sociology of Sport

Founded in 1980, the North American Society for the Sociology of Sport (NASSS) is concerned with the promotion of the study of the sociology of sport. Dissemination of research on this topical area is another objective of NASSS. NASSS publishes the *Sociology of Sport Journal*. Further information may be obtained from Dr. Susan Greendorfer, Department of Physical Education, University of Illinois, Champaign, IL 61820.

• • •

Numerous organizations are affiliated with specific sport areas. Professionals in the sport are a good source of information about these sport associations. Another source is the *Encyclopedia of Associations*. For example, a professional interested in the sport of swimming, consulting the *Encyclopedia of Associations* would find the following professional organizations listed:

American Swimming Coaches Association
College Swimming Coaches Association of America
Council for National Cooperation in Aquatics
International Amateur Swimming Federation

United States Swimming, Inc.
United States Diving, Inc.
United States Synchronized Swimming, Inc.

A professional interested in the sport of tennis may find membership in one or more of these organizations helpful:

Intercollegiate Tennis Coaches Association
Professional Tennis Registry
United States Professional Tennis Association
United States Recreational Tennis Association
United States Tennis Association
United States Tennis Writers Association
Women's Tennis Association

Some professional organizations may require the meeting of certain qualifications for membership while others may be open to interested individuals.

SUMMARY

Physical education and sport is going through one of the most dynamic times in its history. Professional leadership is needed to ensure the continued growth and vitality of the profession. It is critical that leaders emerge from among students now preparing for this profession. If leaders emerge, the profession will prosper; if not, the profession will deteriorate.

Leadership represents the art of influencing people to work together harmoniously in the achievement of professional as well as personal goals. Several personal qualities have been identified as needed for leadership. These qualities include energy, sense of purpose and direction, enthusiasm, integrity, friendliness and affection, technical mastery, decisiveness, intelligence, teaching skill, and faith.

To find the answers to many problems confronting the profession, physical education and sport leaders need creativity, interest in research, and accountability. To achieve leadership status professionals must possess the qualities of health and personality, applied intelligence, articulation, dedication and hard work, respect for other people, and desire. Leaders need to become actively involved in their profession and one means to do this is to belong to professional organizations.

There are many advantages to belonging to a professional organization. Professional organizations provide opportunities for service, facilitate communication among professionals, and provide a means to disseminate research findings and other information to professionals. Membership in a professional organization provides opportunities for fellowship, a resource for resolution of personal and professional problems, and may enhance one's employment opportunities.

Numerous professional organizations exist. To find out about professional organizations in one's specific area of interest, a student can consult a professor or practitioner in the field, AAHPERD, or the *Encyclopedia of Associations*. Several professional organizations—their purposes, nature, and membership—are discussed in this chapter. Information on how to obtain further information about each professional organization is provided as well.

SELF-ASSESSMENT TESTS

These tests are designed to assist students in determining if the materials and competencies presented in this chapter have been mastered.

1. Without consulting your text discuss some of the reasons why outstanding leadership is critical to the profession of physical education and sport in the future.

2. Through self-examination determine what personal qualities you have at the present time that are needed for leadership in the profession. What qualities should you develop that you do not possess at this time?

3. Outline a plan by which you can develop the three professional qualities leaders of physical education and sport should possess (creativity, interest in research, and accountability).

4. Write a short essay discussing the reasons every physical educator should belong to professional organizations.

5. Identify each of the following professional organizations in a brief paragraph. Assume that you are preparing the report for individuals unfamiliar with these organizations: AAHPERD, ACSM, AFB, COSIDA, NATA, NIRSA, NRPA, NASPSPA, PSSS, NASSH, and NASSS.

REFERENCES

1. McIntyre M: Leadership development, Quest 33(1):33-41, 1981.
2. McIntyre M: In Mintzberg H, editor: The nature of managerial work, New York, 1973, Harper & Row, Publishers.
3. Tead O: The art of leadership, New York, 1935, Whittlesey House.

SUGGESTED READINGS

AAHPERD: How fit are physical educators? Journal of Physical Education, Recreation, and Dance 59(7):73-87, 95, 1988.

These four articles address the physical fitness of physical educators and the problem of being a role model.

Crase D: Current periodicals in physical education and the sport sciences, Journal of Physical Education, Recreation, and Dance 56(8):76-80, 1986.

A listing of current periodicals in physical education such as this one is helpful to professionals and students. Crase lists close to 50 periodicals and includes such information as the editor/publisher, cost per year, and scope of the periodical.

Maggard NJ: Upgrading our image, Journal of Physical Education, Recreation, and Dance 55(1):17, 82, 1984.

Maggard discusses the negative image of physical educators and the profession and provides practical suggestions on how "our" image can be upgraded.

McIntyre M: Leadership development, Quest 33(1):33-41, 1981.

Problems associated with leadership, guidelines for leadership development skills, and eight essential leadership skills are among the topics discussed.

Part

Issues, Challenges, and the Future of Physical Education and Sport

Four

Introduction

As professionals, physical educators need to be aware of the issues and challenges facing the profession today. If physical educators hope to influence the future direction of physical education and sport in our society, they must take an active leadership role.

Following an overview of issues in physical education and sport today, Chapter 15 examines five of the issues confronting professionals. Four of the challenges to physical educators are addressed as well. Chapter 16 discusses trends and the future of physical education and sport.

Chapter 15

Issues and Challenges in Physical Education and Sport

INSTRUCTIONAL OBJECTIVES AND COMPETENCIES TO BE ACHIEVED

After reading this chapter the student should be able to—

- Discuss the role of the physical educator in the consumer education movement relative to physical activity and fitness.
- Discuss how the physical educator can promote the development of values in physical education and sport.
- Interpret the role and contribution of the physical educator in the conduct of youth sport programs.
- Identify suggested names for the discipline currently entitled physical education and discuss the implications of the growth of the field.
- Discuss the gap that exists between research and practice, and describe how this gap can be lessened.
- Identify and describe strategies physical educators could use to promote quality daily physical education throughout the country.
- Explain the importance of quality public relations programs in a variety of physical education and sport settings.
- Define the role of the physical educator and the profession in attaining the specific fitness and exercise goals delineated in the report *Objectives for the Nation* and *Year 2000 Objectives*.
- Describe specific strategies that could be used to help promote lifespan involvement in physical activity and sport.

Many issues and challenges confront the physical education and sport profession today. As professionals we need to be cognizant of the issues concerning the profession at all levels. As a physical educator you may be perceived by the public as an expert in matters involving physical education and sport. As such you need up-to-date information on current issues so that you may give accurate and knowledgeable answers to the public's queries in an easily understood manner. This requires that you keep abreast of events and developments through daily reading of newspapers and watching of the television news, by reading professional journals, and by attending professional meetings and conferences.

The profession is also facing a great number of challenges. As professionals we must take an active role in meeting these challenges. This requires commitment and professional leadership at all levels. The continued growth of the profession, its vitality and its future, depends on practitioners' commitment and leadership.

This chapter focuses on some issues and challenges confronting the profession. To address all of these issues and challenges would require a separate text. The purpose of this chapter is to introduce some of the issues facing the profession today and then to discuss five of the issues at greater length. This chapter then concludes with a discussion of four of the challenges to the physical education and sport profession and its members.

ISSUES IN PHYSICAL EDUCATION AND SPORT TODAY

Numerous issues are confronting professionals in physical education and sport today. The media have brought many of these issues to the forefront, increasing their visibility. Newspapers, periodicals, and television programs are rife with stories of corruption in professional sport. Gambling and drug abuse within the professional ranks has commanded a great deal of attention. Strikes on the part of players and game officials, astronomical player salaries, and players staging contract holdouts have been topics of often heated discussion. Increased fan violence has led some professional teams to limit the sale of alcohol at events. Player violence has escalated as well. In the professional tennis world concern about competitors "burning out" at an early age has led to attempts to curtail the playing schedules of younger athletes and has led to a minimum age requirement for players to join the tour. Some professional coaches have also acknowledged burnout as a factor in their retirement from the game.

The increased politicization of the Olympics has led to voicing of concern about their survival. The 1980 Summer Olympics in Moscow were boycotted by the United States and several of its allies, while the 1984 Summer Olympics in Los Angeles were boycotted by the Soviet Union and nations friendly to its cause. Feelings of nationalism appear to be as strong as ever. The debate about professionalism

Violence is a problem in sport today.

continues within the International Olympic Committee. Meanwhile, athletes continue to participate while receiving considerable amounts of money for product endorsements or, in the case of certain countries, while enrolled in the armed forces and assigned to practice their sport as part of their service responsibilities. The Olympics have become increasingly commercialized. To televise the 1988 Calgary Winter Games ABC television paid $309 million, and NBC television paid $300 million in addition to adopting a revenue-sharing plan to gain the rights to televise the 1988 Seoul Summer Games.

Collegiate sport has attracted attention as well. The increasing professionalization of collegiate sport has been decried by many. Collegiate sports in many institutions have become big business. Additionally, many believe that sport is overemphasized at the expense of academics. Scandals involving the recruitment of athletes, tampering of grades on transcripts to ensure the admission of athletes to schools or their continued eligibility, illegal drug use, and gambling abuses have attracted national attention.

At the high school level questions have been

raised about the academic qualifications of athletes as well. The practice of passing students because they are athletes has resulted in some cases in the graduation of athletes who were illiterate. Many of these illiterate athletes have been accepted into colleges on the basis of their athletic talents. The adoption of the "no-pass–no-play" rule whereby students must maintain a certain academic average to participate in extracurricular activities has raised furor as well. In some schools athletes are deliberately held back a year so that their skills and talents have a further chance to develop. The question arises, "What is the educational value of sport?"

Issues today are by no means limited to sport and athletics. Concern is expressed for the status and nature of physical education programs in the schools today, both at the elementary and secondary levels. The public has increased awareness of the concomitant health benefits to be gained from participation in fitness and physical activities. Students must be educated about the benefits of fitness and receive instruction in physical activities in their school years. During this time they must gain the skills and knowledge necessary to participate in physical activities throughout their lifetime. However, the growing educational reform movement and its increased emphasis on academics threatens physical education school programs. Physical educators need to use public relations techniques to educate the public about the positive and lifelong outcomes of a sound and well-planned physical education program; they need to fight for time for physical education programs in the school curriculum.

The possible changes in the manner in which children are educated threaten the status of school physical education programs as well; children in the future may attend schools only three days a week and work the remainder of the time at home using interactive computers and cable television.

One of the most critical problems confronting education today is that of teacher burnout. Teacher burnout has had a significant effect on the quality of instruction provided to students and has resulted in many teachers leaving the profession.

The growth of nonschool physical education opportunities are of concern as well. Many of these nonschool programs are being conducted by individuals without training in physical education. The growth of commercial sport clubs, fitness centers, and health clubs in response to the public's demand for instruction in physical education and fitness has led to the employment of many individuals without professional preparation. Physical educators need to establish leadership in these areas.

The growth of interest in competitive sport has led to the development of recreational and competitive sport teams for individuals of all ages. The growth of youth sport programs has raised serious concerns regarding the conduct of these programs and the emphasis placed on winning at these early ages.

This section of the chapter provided a brief overview of some of the issues confronting the profession today. The remainder to the chapter will examine in more detail five of the issues facing physical education and sport and four of the challenges that need to be met by physical educators.

The American Academy of Physical Education[1,2] is composed of individuals who have made significant contributions to the profession. In 1981 the Academy was asked to identify contemporary social problems of importance to physical education. Twenty-six issues were identified initially, and a poll of Academy members revealed the three most urgent issues. They were (1) the need for physical educators to become active in educating consumers about physical activities, (2) the need for increased emphasis on affective behavior in school physical education programs, and (3) the need for physical educators to assume a more active role in conducting youth sport programs. These three issues will be discussed briefly in the following section. Additionally, two other issues will be examined—the growing discipline of physical education and closing the gap between research and practice.

Many challenges also confront physical educators today. Four of these challenges will be addressed in the last section of the chapter. Physical educators must become more active in working to make daily quality physical education programs in the nation's schools become a reality. They also must become more active in public relations efforts to promote physical education programs. Physical educators are challenged to attain the health objectives for the year 2000 and to promote lifelong involvement in physical activity and sport for all people.

Leadership in Consumer Education Movement

Physical educators must become active in the consumer education movement relative to physical activities and exercise.[1] The past decade has witnessed dramatic increases in participation in fitness and physical activities by people of all ages. As individuals have sought to become involved in physical activities and fitness, an unprecedented proliferation of products and programs designed to capitalize on these interests has occurred. While many of these programs are sound in nature and conducted by professionals, others are not as reputable. The profession is concerned about the validity of claims made for some programs and products.

All types of diets, diet pills, and diet and health foods have been advertised as aids to weight reduction, weight management, and healthy living. The marketplace offers the consumer a wide choice of exercise equipment and sport apparel. Books and periodicals concerned with various aspects of fitness and sport occupy conspicuous spaces on the newsstands and bookstore racks. Videotapes of movie stars leading specially designed fitness programs are bestsellers. Commercial sport clubs, fitness centers, and health spas often advertise their services and programs as leading to quick and dramatic results.

Consequently the wide range of products and programs available relative to physical activities and fitness makes it important that members of the public make an educated choice from among the services and goods available; participation in programs that are unsound or the use of products that are of questionable value can have harmful results. Bearing this in mind, the Academy urges physical education professionals to take a more active role in the education of consumers relative to physical activities and fitness. Physical educators must edu-

cate both their students and the adult public about physical activities and fitness. This requires that physical educators not only be knowledgeable about the various facets of physical activities and fitness, but also that they make the public aware that they are the experts and a resource to which the public can come to seek answers to their questions. Physical educators must also provide the public and their students with the necessary skills and knowledge to evaluate their own fitness and physical activity needs and problems. This involves educating the consumer about the "hows" and "whys" of exercising properly. Professionals must also help their students and the public to gain the skills necessary to be lifelong learners and self-educating with regard to physical activity and fitness. The Academy also urged professionals to take increased responsibility to conduct research of a practical and applied nature with respect to fitness and the psychological aspects of physical activity. Professionals need to translate appropriate research findings into practical applications easily understood by the layperson.

Professionals should be leading the fitness movement and exerting a significant influence on its direction. Corbin,[3] in a *Journal of Physical Education, Recreation, and Dance* editorial, asks, "Is the fitness bandwagon passing us by?" Corbin points out that physicians, self-appointed experts, and movie stars are at the vanguard of the fitness movement. Many of these people lack the qualifications, training, and expertise to be directing this movement. Corbin asks, "What is the problem?" He states:

> While many physical educators are experts, many are not. Some have no desire to be! I *am not* arguing that we should devote all our efforts to physical fitness or exclude other important educational objectives. I *am* arguing that one of the most important social services we can provide is to teach about fitness and exercise. Like no other profession, we should be knowledgeable in this area.

Corbin suggests that professionals can do several things to "lead the parade!" Physical educators should actively seek leadership roles in the fitness movement. First, physical educators should as

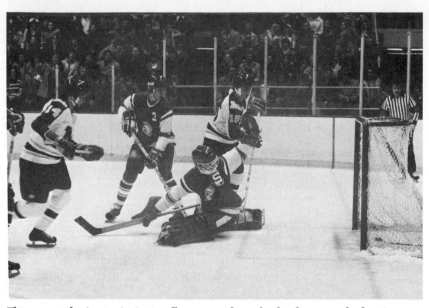

The overemphasis on winning at all costs can deter the development of values in sport.

experts be cognizant of current findings in the field. Second, the consumer needs to be made aware that physical educators are experts in this field and are a resource for answers as well as advice. Physical educators should educate their students and the public to be wise consumers of exercise programs and products. Additionally, physical educators should provide their clientele with the knowledge and the skills to solve their own exercise and physical activity problems and to evaluate their own fitness needs.

Physical educators must take an active role in the fitness movement. As professionals we must provide leadership for this movement because it falls within our domain. We must take advantage of this interest in fitness and physical activity to educate people of all ages about fitness and physical activities and to teach them skills necessary for lifetime participation.

Teaching Values in Sport

Ethical and moral abuses associated with sport have gained increased notoriety in recent years. Sport has long been extolled as a vehicle for building character and teaching such values as sportsman-

ship, fair play, honesty and integrity, and citizenship. Athletes were often viewed as role models for traditional American values. The disparity between the educational outcomes claimed and the behaviors all too often and lately too visibly exhibited by those associated with sport—athletes and coaches—has often been attributed to the overemphasis on winning at all costs.

The Academy,[1,2] concerned about the moral and ethical abuses in sport, encouraged professionals to take action to remedy these abuses. First, although physical education and sport programs offer the opportunity to teach values, for these desired outcomes to be realized winning must be placed in perspective. Second, an increased effort to provide opportunities for moral and ethical judgments by participants as a basis for the development of values must be made. Situations that promote the development of the desired values must be carefully planned for and professionals should take advantage of teachable moments to promote desired behavior. Positive reinforcement of appropriate behavior should be given by professionals. Professional preparation programs should stress ethical and moral values as well as the importance of professionals serving as role models for their students and athletes.

Finally, the Academy urged that the profession establish criteria by which to select appropriate moral and ethical values to be developed. Formal plans of instruction to promote these values should be designed. Two of the *Basic Stuff Series* booklets, *Psychosocial Aspects of Physical Education* and *The Humanities in Physical Education*, are examples of such endeavors. Additionally, the profession should develop additional methods and means to assess the results of such endeavors.

Whether sport and physical education activities can develop moral and ethical values depends on the quality of leadership. The leaders must be role models for the values they espouse. Leaders must also include the development of values as part of their objectives and, as such, plan for their attainment. This holds true regardless of the setting for physical education and sport programs.

Leadership in Youth Sport

Participation in youth sport programs has grown dramatically in the past decade. Most communities now offer youth sport programs, often in several sport areas. It is estimated that close to 30 million boys and girls participate in these programs. Adult volunteers, without which these programs could not function, number approximately 3 million.

The explicit purposes of these youth sport programs are to promote the healthy physical, psychological, and social development of participants. Although these goals are worthy ones, youth sport programs have been severely criticized by educators, physical educators, physicians, parents, and the media for the manner in which the attainment of these goals has been approached and for the failure in many cases to achieve them. "Untrained adult volunteers are often the focus of this criticism. The lack of volunteers' knowledge about growth and development factors, psychological processes, training principles, nutrition, equipment use, safety, and injury prevention and treatment has precipitated the criticism."[4]

Adult volunteers are essential for the conducting of youth programs. An adult volunteer hugs a child finishing a Special Olympics race.

Because of the controversy surrounding youth sport programs and criticism directed at these endeavors, the American Academy of Physical Education urges that professionals assume a greater role in the conduct of these programs.[1,2] Physical educators have the knowledge and expertise to ensure that all participants have a satisfying and beneficial experience in youth sport. There are several ways in which professionals can assist in the conduct of youth sports programs. Professionals can work collaboratively with youth sport program administrators and volunteers to develop sound program guidelines. Professional organizations can be contacted for assistance. AAHPERD publications such as *Youth Sports Guide for Parents and Coaches* and *Guidelines for Children's Sports* will be helpful in this endeavor. Another resource is the Institute for the Study of Youth Sports at Michigan State University.

Professionals can serve as a resource for program personnel. Professionals can share their knowledge with adult volunteers through in-service workshops. Information about scientific findings and knowledge pertaining to skill development, psychological development, officiating, and safety and first aid are essential to the conduct of sound programs. Professionals can also assist in the establishment of minimal competencies in skill and knowledge and possibly the establishment of certification programs for volunteers. The training of volunteers to attain these standards is also a way that professionals can contribute to the development of sound programs. The *American Coaching Effectiveness Program,* published by Human Kinetics Publishers, Inc., may be of assistance to professionals in this endeavor. This program provides a comprehensive, progressive sequence of objectives and knowledge to be used by program directors and professionals in the training of youth sport volunteers.

The Academy also urges that professional preparation programs provide prospective teachers and coaches with more information about teaching the young child. The developmental approach to skill acquisition, practical opportunities for students to work with young learners of all skill levels, and remediation techniques for gross motor skills should receive more emphasis in undergraduate professional preparation.

Vern Seefeldt,[4] director of the Institute for the Study of Youth Sports, in a 1985 *Journal of Physical Education, Recreation, and Dance* editorial, addresses the controversial nature of youth sport. While many adults applaud the benefits of participation in youth sport programs, opponents of youth sport allege that the detrimental effects far outweigh the benefits. Seefeldt suggests that youth sport programs are "neither inherently good nor bad. Like other educational endeavors, their value depends on the quality of adult leadership and the supporting environment."[4]

Much dissatisfaction with youth sport programs may be attributed to the disparity between their outcomes and the interests and expectations of the program participants. The overemphasis on winning and competition makes it difficult to realize the objectives of motor, psychological, and social development of the children. The Bill of Rights for

young athletes, developed by AAHPERD, offers coaches and parents guidance in structuring the sport experience to achieve more positive outcomes (Figure 15-1).

Seefeldt encourages program volunteers to focus on promoting the continued sport involvement of children rather than emphasizing winning. Coaches must be cognizant of the reasons children participate in these activities. "Children become involved in sports to have fun, learn specific motor skills, socialize with their friends, and experience the excitement of competition on their own terms. These objectives are so wholesome and compelling that coaches should strive to incorporate them into every practice and contest."[4]

If youth sport is to achieve the desired outcomes, three interdependent changes are necessary according to Seefeldt. First, youth sport program directors must "resist the temptation to maintain the status quo."[4] Changes must be made in youth sport programs to accommodate children of all abilities and interests, not only those children who are highly skilled and competitive. Second, more research must be undertaken. Research is essential if programs are to be based on sound principles. Numerous questions require answers. Areas that need to be addressed include the nature and extent of injuries, optimal ages for learning specific skills, length of practices and duration of playing season, influence of different coaching methods on children's behavior and psychological development, and team selection for greatest equality. Third, sound training programs for youth sport coaches and personnel need to be developed and implemented. These programs should focus on the acquisition of basic competencies in skills, teaching, knowledge, first aid, and psychology that are prerequisites for coaching. In-service workshops are needed to help the millions of adult volunteers acquire these competencies.

Youth sport programs have grown dramatically and this growth will likely continue. If children are to benefit from participation in these programs, professionals need to take a more active role in their direction. Sound training programs for the millions of volunteers need to be developed and implemented so that the sought-after physical, psychological, and social benefits are realized.

The Growing Discipline

Since the early 1960s the body of knowledge about physical education has expanded tremendously. Because of the proliferation of research and scholarship, the theoretical base of physical education is becoming increasingly sophisticated and complex.

The expansion of the depth and breadth of knowledge has led to the development of subdisciplines within the field of physical education that have emerged as areas of study in their own right. These distinct subdisciplines, which once were joined under the umbrella of physical education, have become separate, specialized areas with their own research traditions, professional organizations and publications, and specialized occupations. This specialization is currently increasing. Specialized areas of study are emerging within the subdisciplines, for example, cardiac rehabilitation is becoming a specialized area within the subdiscipline of exercise physiology.

Many professionals have voiced concern about the increasing fragmentation and specialization of the discipline.[5,6] Lack of communication and coop-

eration between the increasingly specialized areas is a major concern. Moreover, the increasing splintering of physical education into narrow specialties may be harmful to one of the central missions of the physical educator: helping individuals learn the skills, knowledge, and understanding necessary to move effectively and to enhance health and well-being.

It must be remembered that physical educators are concerned with the development of the whole person through the medium of human movement, not just with the development of children's motor skills, physical fitness in adults, or psychological skills enabling elite athletes to perform at an optimum level. It is important not to forget that these specialized areas are actually parts of the greater whole. It is equally important that we not lose sight of our purpose.

Despite the calls for integration by many professionals, it is likely that the specialized areas of study will continue to further develop and become increasingly separate. However, there is a growing realization of the need to help professionals integrate the growing knowledge base to respond better to the needs of the individuals with whom they work.[6] This integration of knowledge would take into account the population being served, the population's needs, and the setting in which the services are provided. Calls also abound for closing the gap between research and practice, with a greater effort being made to integrate theory and practice.

As the discipline of physical education continues to grow, many professionals are becoming dissatisfied with the term being used to represent the discipline: *physical education.* Within the past 25 years, physical education's professional emphasis on teacher preparation has changed. Whereas teacher preparation was once the primary focus, it is now only one of many professional programs within the discipline. Professional preparation programs in physical education have become increasingly diversified. The emergence of the exercise and sport sciences has led to many new professional programs such as cardiac rehabilitation, adult fitness, sport management, sports medicine, and sport communication. Many professionals feel that the term physi-

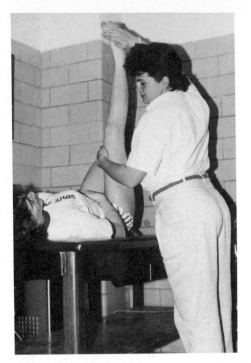

Practitioners have adopted titles to more accurately reflect what they do. Here, an athletic trainer administers treatment.

cal education does not accurately describe the current nature of the field. They believe a new term is needed to represent this discipline more accurately and to describe what professionals in the field do.

Today, practitioners in the schools continue to refer to themselves as physical educators. However, professionals working with other populations and in other settings have adopted different terms to represent the specialized nature of their work. These professionals may refer to themselves as athletic trainers, sports medicine specialists, adapted physical educators, exercise physiologists, sport psychologists, sport sociologists, fitness instructors, sport specialists, recreation leaders, and so on.

Many terms have been suggested to replace physical education. In this book the term *physical education and sport* has been used to encompass the traditional field of physical education and the growing field of sport sciences. It is likely, however, that by the year 2000 physical education, rather

than being the umbrella term for the discipline, will refer to a specialized area under another title for the field. As such, the term physical education would then embrace professionals teaching physical education in the schools at all levels.[7]

In 1989 the American Academy of Physical Education endorsed *kinesiology* as the new umbrella term for the field. Kinesiology, defined as the art and science of human movement, was believed to reflect the true focus of study. Other terms that frequently have been suggested as a name for the discipline are *sport sciences* and *exercise and sport sciences*. Across the country, many college and university departments of physical education have changed their names to reflect the changing nature of physical education.

Regardless of which term is selected as a name for the discipline or the area of specialization, it is important that all professionals realize their responsibility to contribute to the field. Professionals must help physical education establish its identity, its jurisdiction, and its leadership. Whether the discipline will continue to grow and to realize its potential to enhance the health and well-being of individuals of all ages will depend a great deal on the commitment of professionals to this goal.

The Gap between Research and Practice

One of the major problems facing the profession is the need to close the gap between research and practice.[8] Often a disparity exists between research findings and their application. A significant time lag is seen between the conducted physical education research and the utilization of relevant findings. If our programs, regardless of their setting, are to be based on sound principles, then this gap must be narrowed.

Factors responsible for the gap between research and practice are many. Some of these factors may be attributed to the practitioner, while others are associated with the researcher. One factor contributing to this gap is inadequate knowledge of research by the practitioner.[9] Practitioners, in both their undergraduate and graduate preparation, may have not been adequately instructed in research methods and the technical and conceptual skills

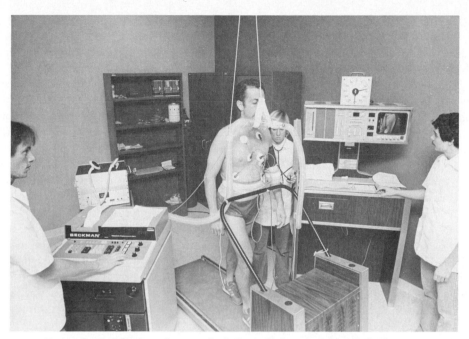

Research contributes to the growth of physical education's knowledge base.

necessary to conduct and interpret research. Locke[10] writes, "The ordinary teacher, unfamiliar with basic terms and subtle distinctions in the vocabulary of research, is likely to find the usual research report nearly incomprehensible." The lack of preparation hinders communication between researchers and practitioners and the consumption of research reports by practitioners. Practitioners who receive a sound background in research and statistics will be better equipped to communicate with the researcher who conducted the study and to interpret the findings.

Another factor that contributes to the gap is a negative attitude toward research held by practitioners. This negative attitude may deter them from using information revealed through research. Several reasons have been suggested to account for this negative attitude, including the view that research is irrelevant and impractical to the concerns of practitioners,[9,11] an inadequate understanding of research,[10] and failure to answer specific questions practitioners want answered[12] such as those about the teaching-learning process.

Whatever the reason for this negative attitude, it militates against the effective use of research findings that may optimize learning.

The lack of time and resources to apply research findings to practical situations contributes to the gap between research and practice.[13] For example, it is often heard that teachers are too busy to deal with theoretical matters; they must concentrate on daily tasks. In addition to teaching, teachers often are assigned homeroom duty, bus duty, locker room duty, hall duty, study hall supervision, and may have coaching responsibilities as well. These extra, but required, responsibilities fill up the teacher's day and inhibit the implementation and utilization of research by the teacher. The lack of facilities and equipment with which to implement many of the research findings exacerbates the problem.

Application of research findings to practical settings is also hindered by the limited availability of the results of research findings. Researchers most often attempt to publish the results of their studies in prestigious professional journals.[10] Many of these journals are not readily available to practitioners.

Another source of research information is theses and dissertations. While theses and dissertations (or their abstracts) are available in college libraries, these unpublished sources of research are not available to practitioners at a distance from these sites, practitioners may be denied access to the libraries, or practitioners may not have the inclination to spend the time looking up the materials. Researchers need to be cognizant that practitioners often spend their time reading journals with a more practical orientation, such as *Journal of Physical Education, Recreation, and Dance* or the *Physical Educator.*[13]

The relatively poor quality of research and relatively few conclusive research findings contribute to the gap between research and practice. Many research studies suffer from inadequacies, especially with regard to methodological concerns. Locke[10] notes: "... research that is poorly designed, inadequately reported, and seriously misleading constitutes a major impediment to the intelligent guidance of physical education." The fact that different researchers reach disparate conclusions regarding the same research topic makes it difficult for practitioners to apply these findings in a practical setting. The conflicting results of studies present problems for practitioners who wish to use the findings to guide and support their endeavors.

Finally, the unwillingness of researchers to be concerned with the application of their findings contributes to the gap between research and practice. Much of the significant research affecting educational practice in the last 50 years is the result of basic research, that is, research that is concerned with the development of theories or broad generalizations. The failure of investigators engaged in basic research to be concerned with the application of their findings might be a cause of a lag in some cases. Complicated theoretical propositions that are sometimes advanced by researchers engaged in pure or basic research without some explanation of their practical uses are of little value to practitioners. It appears that if significant information provided by basic researchers is to be useful, investigators engaged in basic research should devote a portion of their time to development and dissemination functions.

How can we close the gap between research and practice? We have taken the initial steps in this endeavor by recognizing that the gap does exist. There are several means by which this gap can be reduced. Professional preparation programs can do a better job in preparing physical educators to read and interpret research. A thorough background in research and statistics will enable the physical educator to develop a knowledge of research theory and statistics, locate research reports, and evaluate research studies and interpret their findings. Another approach is for practitioners and researchers to work cooperatively on joint research projects. Researchers also must make a concerted effort to bridge this gap as well. Researchers should endeavor to address the practical implications of their work when reporting their investigations in journals.

Last, individuals to serve as "translators" of research are needed to be charged with the task of developing and disseminating research findings for use by practitioners. This job needs to be done on a large scale if research findings are to be put to use without the normal "research lag." One step in this direction is the effort by the editorial board of the *Journal of Physical Education, Recreation, and Dance.* In January 1985 the editors instituted a new feature, "Research Works." This feature is designed to provide an opportunity for researchers to share their findings with interested colleagues. The focus is on presenting research findings in an applied format, specifically discussing the importance of these findings to the practitioner.

While it is difficult to delineate the size of the chasm between research and practice, it is important that both researchers and practitioners work to narrow this gap. Over the last 10 years the profession has experienced a tremendous growth in knowledge. If this knowledge is to influence the manner in which professionals conduct their programs, a concerted effort to narrow the gap between research and practice must be undertaken by all professionals.

CHALLENGES

High-Quality Daily Physical Education

The provision of high-quality daily physical education programs in the nation's schools is a challenge to all physical educators. There is evidence that many of the nation's children and youth are inactive and unfit.[14,15] Inactive life-styles, sedentary leisure pursuits, and the lack of quality and regular physical education programs in the schools contribute to the poor level of fitness of American children and youth.

There is increasingly strong support that regular and appropriate physical activity can contribute to good health and enhance the quality of life for individuals of all ages.[16] There is also increased recognition that to achieve the maximum benefits of exercise an individual must begin to exercise early in life and continue to exercise throughout the lifespan. Daily physical education in school is one of the best means to help individuals learn the skills, knowledge, and values necessary to incorporate physical activity into their life-style.

Many benefits are ascribed to participation in regular and appropriate physical activity. Whether students can attain these benefits through participation in school physical education programs depends on the time alloted to the program and the quality of the program. Additionally, the physical education program must be specifically designed to attain these objectives. The benefits of participation in a program of regular and appropriate physical activity are as follows[17]:

- Reduced risk of heart disease; physical activity counteracts the major coronary risk factors—obesity, inactivity, and hypertension
- Improved health
- Stronger bones
- Weight regulation and improved body composition
- Skill development, which allows for enjoyable participation in physical activities and leisure pursuits
- Self-discipline and responsibility for one's own actions, fitness, and health
- Improved judgment, self-esteem, self-confidence, and peer relationships
- Promotion of mental health and reduction of depression
- Stress reduction; physical activity provides an outlet for tension and anxiety
- Health promotion through the prevention of the onset of some diseases and the postponing of the debilitating effects of the aging process
- Promotion of a more active life-style and a more positive attitude toward physical activity

These benefits can be accomplished through a properly planned and conducted physical education program. High-quality physical education programs provide students with an effective means of enhancing their health and well-being throughout their lives. Attainment of these benefits, however, requires commitment; physical education programs must be sequentially designed to realize these outcomes.

Despite the evidence supporting the value of daily, high-quality physical education, the status of physical education in our nation's schools is disheartening. The National Association for Sport and Physical Education (NASPE) recommends that elementary school children receive 30 minutes of physical education every day and that secondary school students receive 45 to 55 minutes of physical education every day.[17] Many schools across the country are not meeting these guidelines. A survey of state physical education requirements conducted by AAHPERD in 1987 entitled *The Shape of the Nation*[18] (Figure 15-2) revealed the following:

- Only one state, Illinois, requires all students in grades K to 12 to participate in physical education every day.
- Only 10% of the states require elementary school students to participate in physical education for 30 minutes per day as recommended by NASPE.
- Only 8% of the states require middle or junior high school students to participate in physical education 50 minutes a day as recommended by NASPE.

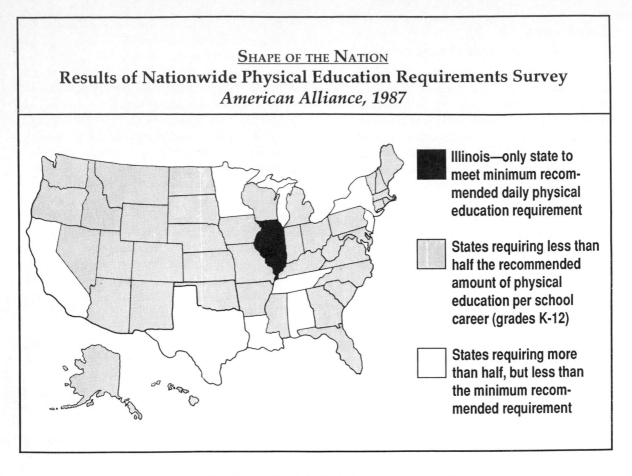

SHAPE OF THE NATION
Results of Nationwide Physical Education Requirements Survey
American Alliance, 1987

Illinois—only state to meet minimum recommended daily physical education requirement

States requiring less than half the recommended amount of physical education per school career (grades K-12)

States requiring more than half, but less than the minimum recommended requirement

FIGURE 15-2 *Results of national physical education requirement survey.*

• Only 12% of the states require high school students to participate in physical education for all 4 years; 44% of the states require physical education to be taken only for 1 year.

Inadequate time for physical education in the schools is a serious problem. In an effort to address this problem, the United States Congress in 1987 passed the National Physical Education Resolution or House Concurrent Resolution 97. This resolution encourages state governments and local educational agencies to provide high-quality daily physical education programs for all children in grades K through 12. Because the federal government usually recommends educational actions rather than mandating them, this resolution has no force of law. However, it is being used nationally by concerned teachers and parents as a lobbying tool to convince state and local educational policymakers to require daily physical education in all schools.

In addition to concerns about inadequate time for physical education in the schools, there is concern about the quality of the programs offered. Although there are many examples of exemplary programs throughout the United States, many programs are of low quality.

According to NASPE,[17] a quality physical education program should be sequential and educational in nature. The program should focus on teaching students to:

• Understand and participate in vigorous physi-

School physical education programs should include an aerobic component to develop cardiovascular fitness.

cal activities that can assist in developing and maintaining physical fitness throughout the lifespan

- Understand and improve their sports and motor skills
- Enjoy using their skills and knowledge as an advantage in establishing a healthy life-style
- Understand how their bodies work

A variety of activities should comprise the physical education program.[17] Activities should include:

- Aerobic exercises to improve cardiovascular endurance
- Exercises to improve flexibility, strength, and muscular endurance
- Sport, games, dance, and other activities to develop motor skills
- Instruction in how physical activity can contribute to personal health and well-being

NASPE further identifies the components of a quality physical education program.[17] A quality physical education program:

- Provides evidence of its effectiveness through the assessment of outcomes that have been achieved
- Provides daily opportunities for the development of movement skills and physical fitness

- Fosters an understanding of why, when, and how physical activity can be incorporated into a life-style
- Focuses on the health-related benefits of physical activity and how these benefits can be acquired and maintained
- Promotes the development of movement skills for participation beyond grades K through 12
- Accommodates the needs and developmental levels of all students regardless of physical and mental ability levels
- Teaches students how to apply the concepts of proper exercise in their daily lives

The incorporation of all these activities, the inclusion of these program components, and the realization of the maximum benefits from participation in a high-quality physical education program depend on the program's being offered on a daily basis for a sufficient amount of time throughout all the school years. Equally important, physical education should be taught by certified physical education instructors. Just as noncertified and unqualified teachers are not tolerated in other academic areas, they should not be tolerated in physical education. Qualified and dedicated leadership is needed if the benefits associated with daily high-quality physical education programs are to be achieved.

In an effort to educate the public about the potential benefits of daily high-quality physical education, AAHPERD designed the *Fit to Achieve through Quality Daily Physical Education* program.[17]* A public relations initiative, the *Fit to Achieve* program focuses on educating and motivating parents, educational policymakers, and community members to improve the status of physical education programs in their schools and states.

Through AAHPERD, physical educators may obtain *Fit to Achieve* promotional materials to help educate the public about what physical education is and the need for daily high-quality programs. These promotional materials include a videotape, various brochures, and a Grass Roots Action Kit. This action kit contains materials that can be used by professionals to increase public awareness of the need for daily high-quality physical education. These materials include sample news releases, feature stories, editorials, public service announcements, and special event ideas. Strategies that can be effectively used to create change are also presented as part of this program.

Each physical education teacher must be willing to take responsibility for promoting the crusade for daily high-quality physical education. Evidence supporting the value of regular and appropriate physical activity continues to mount. Furthermore, there is recognition that health behaviors are formed at an early age and that it is easier to shape positive health behaviors in children than to change unhealthy ones in adults. Moreover, while the current societal interest in wellness and fitness remains strong, now is the time to engender support for daily high-quality physical education programs. Improving the status of physical education in the schools and helping make the dream of daily high-quality physical education a reality for all children and youth is an important professional priority.

---

*Information about the *Fit to Achieve* program can be obtained from AAHPERD, 1900 Association Drive, Reston, VA 22091.

Public Relations

Physical educators in all careers must take an active role in the promotion of their physical education programs. Now is the time to capitalize on the widespread public interest in sport, physical fitness, and health. Physical educators teaching in the school setting; instructing in community and recreational sport programs; working in commercial sport clubs, fitness centers, and health spas; and directing corporate and community fitness programs must use public relations techniques to market their programs. Professionals must inform the public and prospective clientele of the values of physical activity and exercise that accrue from participation in a sound program.

In the school settings where physical education is often regarded as an extra or is cut to make more time for academic subjects, where budgetary cutbacks are becoming increasingly common, and where class sizes are expanding, teachers must be willing to promote their programs to gain the personal and budgetary support of school administrators, politicians, and parents. This requires a commitment to offer an outstanding instructional program and to promote the values of participation in such a program to the public in an understandable manner. Physical education has changed considerably in the 25 years or so since the adult public participated in these programs during their school years. Physical educators must be willing to demonstrate how physical education programs have changed by allowing the adults to observe their programs, conducting demonstrations and other promotional activities, and talking to parents and community groups.

In other settings promotion and marketing of programs is essential as well. Prospective clientele for community and commercial programs must be aware of the nature of the programs offered and the benefits to be derived from participation in such programs. In the corporate fitness setting physical educators must promote the values and benefits to be derived from participation not only to the employees but to the management as well. Corporate management personnel will be reluctant to invest corporate resources, particularly money, to

Physical educators should play an effective role in the community. Physical education major volunteers lead and participate with children in warm-up activities prior to the community's Special Olympics Race for the Gold track meet.

support these programs if they are not aware of their value and/or if the stated benefits are not realized.

Adults may not have had the opportunity to participate in sound instructional programs during their school years and may not be aware of how physical education programs have changed today. Perhaps they remember physical education classes as a time to perform calisthenics, march, and play the same game over and over again. They may have memories of their lack of success in performing activities in gym class and the ridicule they experienced because they were not skilled athletes. Consequently, some adults may be reluctant to experience failure again and will not enroll in adult fitness programs. Physical educators may have to educate men and women about the nature of the program and its benefits. Physical educators in all settings must be actively involved in the promotion of their athletic programs, assisting in encouraging and recruiting new participants.

Physical educators must make a concerted effort to actively promote and interpret their programs to their clientele and the public. To assist physical educators in this endeavor the *Physical Education Public Information* (PEPI) project was developed by NASPE, an association of the AAHPERD.* Promotional materials have been developed to help the public become aware of the basic values of physical education. Among the values emphasized are the following:

- Physical education is health insurance.
- Physical education contributes to academic achievement.
- Physical education provides skills and experiences that can last a lifetime.
- Physical education helps in developing a positive self-image and the ability to compete and cooperate with others.

*Information about the PEPI program can be obtained from AAHPERD, 1900 Association Drive, Reston, VA 22091.

PEPI has focused its efforts on getting these messages across to the public, particularly taxpayers, students, teachers, administrators, school boards, parents, and funding agencies. Throughout the nation over 600 PEPI coordinators have been identified. The coordinators organize and interpret physical education in their own geographical areas through such means as radio, television, newspapers, and other media. Coordinators have been carefully selected on the basis of their interest in the profession and in public relations, their reputation for working with people, and their ability to get the job done. Currently PEPI is stressing the "new" physical education—emphasizing that physical education has changed and is more relevant to the times.

As part of its public relations effort PEPI promotes National Physical Education and Sport Week, May 1 to 7. Each year a theme is selected for this week as a basis for demonstrating the importance of physical education. For example, the theme for 1990 was "Fit to Achieve through Quality Daily Physical Education." Other previous themes include "Physical Education: Essential for Excellence" and "Physical Education is for Every Body." Physical educators in school settings as well as in community and corporate settings should take advantage of National Physical Education and Sport Week to highlight their program, particularly its contribution to the enhancement of the quality of life for all people.

Another visible effort is the project *Jump Rope for Heart (JRFH).** JRFH is an educational program sponsored by the AAHPERD to benefit the American Heart Association (AHA). JRFH promotes the value of rope jumping as aerobic exercise through demonstrations and fund-raising events. The goal of JRFH is to give all students a chance to participate in the events while raising money through pledges for the AHA. Millions of students have participated in JRFH since its inauguration in 1978 and its recognition as a national project in 1980. The JRFH program has

*Information about the Jump Rope for Heart Program can be obtained from AAHPERD, 1900 Association Drive, Reston, VA 22091.

Poster used in public relations effort to promote National Physical Education and Sport Week and quality daily physical education.

served to inform millions of youths and adults of the importance of maintaining a physically active and healthy life-style. The use of rope jumping as a lifelong aerobic activity is promoted through the JRFH program. The JRFH program provides opportunities for physical educators to present a positive image as a professional involved in community service as well as academic affairs. The JRFH program benefits research and education programs of the AHA. Since its inception over $40 million has been raised for the AHA to be used in research and educational programs aimed at fighting cardiovascular diseases such as high blood pressure, arteriosclerosis, heart attack, and stroke. AAHPERD and state AAHPERD associations have received a small percentage of the monies raised for the AHA. This funding has been used to help promote the role of physical activity in the enhancement of qualify of life.

Public relations efforts are critical to the success of physical education programs in all settings. Professionals need to become directly involved in public relations programs designed to educate the public about the values and benefits of physical activity and exercise and the contribution of physical education to the enhancement of the quality of life of people of all ages.

Objectives for the Nation

Another challenge confronting professionals is the attainment of the goals delineated in the Surgeon General's reports *Objectives for the Nation*[19] and *Year 2000 Objectives.*[20] These objectives were developed to reach the health goals outlined in the previous Surgeon General's report, *Healthy People,* released in 1979. *Healthy People*[21] chronicled the gains in the health of the American people during the past century. Additionally, the report reviewed the current preventable threats to health and identified 15 priority areas. If these priority areas are properly addressed, gains in health by American people could be realized in the next decade. Physical fitness and exercise was one of the 15 priority areas.

The 1980 report *Objectives for the Nation* and the forthcoming report *Year 2000 Objectives* delineated specific goals for each priority area. For each priority area the reports describe the current status and trends, identify prevention and promotion measures, delineate specific national objectives, present the assumptions underlying the objectives, and specify the data needed to assess progress toward the attainment of the objectives.

The current fitness status of the American people, the trends set forth by these reports, and the specific objectives are described in Chapters 2 and 3. These objectives for 1990 and 2000 were based on the assumption that increases in appropriate physical activity by people of all ages will result in concomitant health gains. The reports also assumed that the primary motive for participation in physical activity will be a personal commitment to improve one's health and enhance the quality of one's life.

The objectives for 1990 and 2000 focus on improvement of the health status of all Americans, regardless of age; reduction of risk factors through increased participation in appropriate physical activity; increase in the knowledge of the public and professionals relative to the role of exercise in the promotion of health; improvement and expansion of services; and development of improved evaluation systems to assess the public's progress toward these goals.

The specific objectives for the Year 2000 relative to physical activity and fitness were outlined in Chapter 3. Briefly, in terms of risk reduction, the objectives focus on increasing the proportion of people age 6 and older who participate in regular and appropriate physical activity to enhance health fitness. Priority is also given to reducing the number of people who are overweight. The objectives pertaining to public awareness focus on increasing the proportion of people age 6 and older who are knowledgeable about the benefits associated with regular exercise and who can correctly identify the frequency, intensity, and type of exercises that will contribute to health fitness.

Improving professional education and awareness is another objective. Specifically, the focus is on increasing the number of primary care providers who assess and counsel their patients about physical activity habits as part of a thorough evaluation.

Improved services and protection are also important to the promotion of health. One objective is to increase the proportion of children and youth who receive daily physical education to 45% from a baseline of 36% in 1984 to 1986. Increasing the amount of time physical education teachers spend on skills and activities that promote lifetime sport participation is another objective. Expanding the number of employer-sponsored fitness programs and the services offered is yet another objective. Community physical activity programs can also play an important role in developing and maintaining health fitness. Promoting participation in these programs and expanding the recreational facilities offered are two objectives that need to be achieved.

As you can see, our profession can make an important contribution to the improvement of the

Increasing the amount of time physical educators spend on teaching lifetime sports is one of the Year 2000 Objectives.

Each of us in the profession must make a personal commitment to achieve or maintain a good level of physical fitness. How can we be effective in promoting health and fitness if our bodies are not living testimonies of our commitment? What we are communicates so much more than what we say!

As professionals we must practice what we preach. We must work together to educate the American public in a variety of physical activities in which they can participate throughout their lives.

Lifespan Involvement for All People

One of the most heartening changes in the profession within the last 20 years has been the expansion of physical education services and sport programs to people of all ages and to a diversity of settings. Traditionally, physical education and sport programs have focused on children and youth and have been conducted in the school and community-recreation settings. However, within the last two decades, the scope of physical education and sport programs has expanded tremendously.

The expanded focus of physical education and sport has led to the provision of physical education services to new populations. Services have expanded to encompass individuals of all ages. Programs have been developed for infants and toddlers as well as for adults and senior citizens. There has been an increased effort to meet the needs of all people, whether they are skilled or unskilled, whether they are fit or unfit, and regardless of their abilities or disabilities.

There is an increased recognition that regular and appropriate physical activity can make a vital contribution to the health and lives of all people. It can enhance the quality of one's life as well as its quantity or longevity. Additionally, it has become increasingly apparent that our efforts should focus on early childhood education and intervention. Individuals gain the maximum benefits from exercise and physical activity when they begin at an early age and continue their participation throughout the lifespan.

During childhood, fitness and leisure habits are developed; once developed, they become difficult to change. Moreover, it has been shown that such

health status of the American public. Professionals should take an active role in working with other health professionals to attain these objectives. Moreover, our involvement in the attaining of these objectives will contribute to increased public recognition of the worth and value of our profession. Additionally, one benefit that will accrue from our participation in this endeavor is the development of increased employment opportunities.

Employment opportunities for qualified professionals will increase, and new career opportunities will develop. The objective promoting daily physical education will result in a demand for more teachers. Instructors also will be needed to teach physical activities to adults and the elderly and educate them about the benefits of such activities. The growth of corporate fitness programs will create a need for more professionals qualified in this area.

Can we attain the objectives for 2000? Although professional organizations such as AAHPERD will provide leadership, whether we can meet the challenge depends on each practitioner's willingness to make a commitment to work toward the attainment of these goals and to being a role model for a healthy, active life-style. Wilmore[22] states:

We must capitalize on the children's enjoyment of moving to foster active participation throughout one's lifespan.

insidious diseases as obesity and coronary heart disease can begin in childhood. Therefore it is important that efforts be made to assist children in acquiring the skills, knowledge, and positive attitudes conducive to good health. Children must be educated to form good health and physical activity habits early in life. Physical educators, parents, and other health professionals should focus their efforts on helping children adopt an active rather than a sedentary life-style and on providing them with the skills and knowledge to effectively manage their life-styles as adults.

It is important to note that the number of programs being provided for preschoolers is growing: it is likely that the number of these programs will increase in the next decade. Motor development

programs are being offered to infants and toddlers in hospital and clinical settings. Preschools and day care centers are incorporating physical education programs into their curricula.

In the past decade the fitness and the wellness movements have encouraged an increasing number of adults to begin to incorporate regular physical activity into their life-styles. Many adults are now engaging in physical activities and exercise of sufficient intensity, duration, and frequency to realize health benefits. Unfortunately, many more adults are not. The majority of adults exercise only moderately or lead sedentary lives. The incidence of physical inactivity increases with age and is influenced by such factors as sex, race, socioeconomic status, educational level, occupation, and geographic location (see Chapter 3 for further information). As a profession, we need to help these people change their physical activity and health habits and adopt health-enhancing life-styles. Creative and educational programs are needed to accomplish this objective.

As we approach the next century, the proportion of elderly in the population will continue to increase. In the 1980s people over the age of 65 comprised approximately 11% of the population. It is estimated that by the year 2000 the elderly will comprise 13% of the population and this percentage will rise to nearly 22% in the year 2050.[23] Furthermore, the elderly will be increasingly healthy and vigorous. Professionals must make provisions to meet the physical activity and leisure needs of this population group. Regular and appropriate physical activity will affect not only the health of this age group, but also the quality of their lives, particularly in terms of maintaining functional independence.

The last decade has also seen an increase in physical education opportunities available to individuals with disabilities. Physical activity can contribute as much to the health, well-being, and self-esteem of individuals who are differently able and who have special needs as it can for individuals who are able-bodied.

Sport involvement among people of all ages continues to increase as well. Millions of children

Dance is an enjoyable activity for people of all abilities. **A,** *Senior citizens particpate in square dancing at the State University of New York at Potsdam.* **B,** *Participants respond to the square dance call "Take your arms out to the side, like you can hold the ocean tide."*

throughout the country participate in youth and interscholastic sports. Intercollegiate sport participation continues to rise. Communities are developing more sport opportunities for adults of all ages. Competitive and recreational leagues offer adults the opportunity to continue their participation in organized sports at a desirable level of intensity. Masters' competitions and competitions for seniors in a variety of sports and at a number of levels—local, state, national, and international—allow many adults and senior citizens across the country to continue their sport involvement. Sport organizations for individuals with disabilities also provide a diversity of opportunities for competition in a wide range of individual and team sports.

As we continue to expand our focus to meet the needs of new populations, we must also continue to broaden our programs. Because the populations that are served are becoming increasingly heterogeneous, a greater diversity of programs is needed to meet their needs. New program models must be developed to fit individual needs. Changes in program content and the manner in which programs are conducted will be necessary to accommodate a wide range of individual differences.

Programs have and will continue to expand from the school setting to the community, from the public sector to the private sector. The school setting will be used increasingly as a site for community programs for individuals of all ages. Programs in day care centers, preschools, hospitals, developmental centers, senior centers, nursing homes, community settings, and corporations will continue to expand. Commercial programs in the private sector also will continue to increase. Health clubs, fitness centers, private clubs offering sport instruction, and private sport leagues will develop more programs to meet the needs of paying clients. As programs expand to meet the needs of various populations, it is important that provisions be made to ensure that all individuals have access to these programs. Fitness and health opportunities should not be available only to those who have the means to pay. Fitness and health opportunities should be

available to all individuals regardless of socioeconomic background.

As the scope of physical education and sport increases and as the focus of the programs offered expands, it is important that professional programs prepare students to capably assume responsibilities within these growing areas. Professional preparation programs have traditionally focused on preparing students to work with children and youth within the school setting. Professional preparation programs must provide students with the skills and knowledge necessary to work with different population groups and conduct effective programs to meet their needs.

Promoting lifespan involvement in physical activity and sport is a challenge to all professionals. Lifespan involvement can enrich the lives of all people, the young and old, male and female, able-bodied and disabled, rich and poor, fit and unfit, and skilled and unskilled. Making lifespan involvement a reality for many people requires qualified and dedicated professionals willing to work toward attaining this goal.

SUMMARY

Many issues and challenges confront professionals in physical education and sport today. The widespread interest in sport by people in our society and the media has made many of these issues very visible.

Following an overview of the issues in physical education and sport today, three issues identified by the American Academy of Physical Education as being of great importance to the profession were discussed. First, the Academy stressed that professionals need to become more active in the physical activity and fitness consumer movement. Second, physical educators must place more emphasis on teaching ethical and moral values through physical education and sport programs. Third, the Academy perceived a need for physical educators to become more active in the conducting of youth sport programs. Two additional issues were also discussed. As the discipline of physical education continues to grow, professionals are concerned about the fragmentation of the field and the title of the discipline. The final issue examined was closing the gap between research and practice.

Many challenges face physical educators. Four particularly important challenges were discussed. First, physical educators are faced with the challenge of promoting daily high-quality physical education in the schools. The second challenge is to become more actively involved in public relations. Professionals in all settings must market their programs. The third challenge is to attain the goals set forth in the reports *Objectives for the Nation* and *Year 2000 Objectives*. These specific fitness and exercise objectives focus on improving the health status of all Americans. If these objectives are to be achieved, each physical educator must make a personal commitment to work with professional organizations to accomplish this task and to be a role model exemplifying a healthy, active life-style. Lastly, promoting lifespan involvement in physical activity requires physical educators to provide a diversity of services to individuals of all ages. Physical education and sport has the potential to enhance the health and quality of life of people of all ages. Helping individuals to realize this potential is one of our biggest challenges.

The issues and challenges confronting professionals are many. If we are to deal with them, physical educators must be knowledgeable about the discipline of physical education and be willing to assume leadership positions. The manner in which the profession deals with these issues and meets the challenges confronting it will influence the future of physical education and sport.

SELF-ASSESSMENT TESTS

These tests are designed to assist students in determining if the materials and competencies presented in this chapter have been mastered.

1. For the three-month time period selected by your instructor, select one periodical and review the coverage of physical education and sport. Take notes regarding the issues that are covered, and make a short presentation about your findings to the class.

2. Discuss the role of the physical educator in the consumer education movement relative to physical activities and fitness.

3. Explain how physical educators can promote the development of values in their programs, regardless of the setting.

4. Discuss how physical educators can help adult volunteers conduct sound youth sport programs. Discuss the need for physical educators to help in the conduct of youth sport programs in light of your own youth sport experiences.

5. How can the growing disciplinary knowledge be integrated to help practitioners effectively accomplish their responsibilities?

6. Identify strategies to reduce the gap between research and practice.

7. What specific strategies could be employed to encourage the state legislature and the local school boards to mandate daily physical education?

8. Describe the importance of public relations programs in the physical education setting of your choice.

9. Describe how physical educators through various programming efforts can help individuals attain the fitness and exercise goals set forth in the *Year 2000 Objectives* .

10. Describe various strategies that could be utilized to promote lifespan involvement for people of all ages, abilities, and socioeconomic backgrounds.

REFERENCES

1. Park RJ: Three major issues: The Academy takes a stand, Journal of Physical Education, Recreation, and Dance 54(1):52-53, 1983.

2. The American Academy of Physical Education: The Academy papers: reunification, no 15, Reston, Va, 1981, AAHPERD.

3. Corbin CB: Is the fitness bandwagon passing us by? Journal of Physical Education, Recreation, and Dance 55(9):17, 1984.

4. Seefeldt V: Why are children's sports programs controversial? Journal of Physical Education, Recreation, and Dance 56(3):16, 1985.

5. Sage GH: The future and the profession. In Massengale JD, editor: Trends toward the future in physical education, Champaign, Ill, 1987, Human Kinetics.

6. Siedentop D: Introduction to physical education, fitness, and sport, Mountain View, Calif, 1990, Mayfield.

7. Lumpkin A: Physical education and sport: a contemporary introduction, St Louis, 1990, Times Mirror/Mosby.

8. Bucher CA and Thaxton NA: Physical education and sport: change and challenge, St Louis, 1981, Times Mirror/Mosby.

9. Rothstein AL: Practitioners and the scholarly enterprise, Quest 20:59-60, 1973.

10. Locke LF: Research in physical education, New York, 1969, Teachers College Press.

11. Stadulis RE: Bridging the gap: a lifetime of waiting and doing, Quest 20:48-52, 1973.

12. Barnes FP: Research for the practitioner in education, Washington, DC, 1963, Department of Elementary School Principles, National Education Association.

13. Broderick FP: Research as viewed by the teacher, Paper presented at the AAHPER National Convention, Detroit, 1971.

14. Ross JG and Gilbert GG: The National Children and Youth Study: a summary of the findings, Journal of Physical Education, Recreation, and Dance 56(1):45-50, 1985.

15. Ross JG and Pate RR: The National Children and Youth Fitness Study II, Journal of Physical Education, Recreation, and Dance, 58(9):51-56, 1987.

16. Seefeldt V, editor: Physical activity and well-being, Reston, Va, 1986, AAHPERD.

17. The National Association for Sport and Physical Education: Fit to Achieve educational information, Reston, Va, 1989, AAHPERD.

18. AAHPERD: Shape of the Nation: a survey of state physical education requirements, Washington, DC, 1987, AAHPERD.

19. US Department of Health and Human Services: Promoting health/preventing disease: objectives for the nation, Washington, DC, 1980, US Government Printing Office.

20. Public Health Service, US Department of Health and Human Services: Promoting health/preventive disease: year 2000 objectives for the nation, Washington, DC, 1989, US Government Printing Office (draft).

21. US Department of Health, Education, and Welfare: Healthy people: the surgeon general's report on health promotion and disease prevention, Washington, DC, 1979, US Government Printing Office.

22. Wilmore JH: Objectives for the nation: physical fitness and exercise, Journal of Physical Education, Recreation, and Dance 53:(3), 41-43.

23. Dychtwall K and Flower J: Age wave: the challenge and opportunities of an aging America, Los Angeles, 1989, Jeremy P Tarcher, Inc.

SUGGESTED READINGS

American Alliance for Health, Physical Education, Recreation, and Dance: Shaping the body politic, Reston, Va, 1983, AAHPERD.

This book provides elementary and secondary school physical educators with a variety of ideas and strategies to help promote their programs to the public, parents, and legislators.

American Coaching Effectiveness Program, Champaign, Ill, Human Kinetics Publishers.

This multilevel program is designed to help coaches gain a basic understanding of the knowledge necessary to coach athletes at various levels and in a diversity of sports. Further information about this extensive coaching program can be obtained from Human Kinetics, Box 5076, Champaign, IL 61820.

Berg K: A national curriculum in physical education, Journal of Physical Education, Recreation, and Dance 59(8):70-75, 1988.

The rationale for a national curriculum is presented, steps for implementation are listed, and the content of the curriculum is identified (sport mastery, fitness, and academic).

Crase D and Walker H Jr: The black physical educator: an endangered species, Journal of Physical Education, Recreation, and Dance 59(8):65-69, 1988.

The present status of black faculty and students in physical education is discussed, and suggestions to recruit individuals into the profession are presented.

Dychtwall K and Flower J: Age wave: the challenge and opportunities of an aging America, Los Angeles, 1989, Jeremy P Tarcher, Inc.

The authors discuss the many challenges the increase in the number of elderly persons presents to the nation and also highlight the opportunities presented.

Seefeldt V: Handbook for youth sport coaches, Reston, Va, 1987, AAHPERD.

Designed for volunteer coaches, this book provides information about the benefits of youth sports, the role of the coach, the foundations of coaching, the fundamental skills of coaching, and special considerations.

Wandzilak T, Carroll T, and Ansorge CJ: Values development through physical activity: promoting sportsmanlike behaviors, perceptions, and moral reasoning, Journal of Teaching in Physical Education 8(1):13-22, 1988.

The results of a study designed to assess the efficacy of a values model in producing changes in behavior of male interscholastic basketball players are presented.

Renson R: From physical education to kinanthropology: A quest for academic and professional identity, Quest 41:235-256, 1989.

The dissatisfaction with the term physical education is examined and overview of conceptual trends with respect to the term kinanthropology is presented.

Sage GH, editor: Sport, culture and society, Journal of Physical Education, Recreation, and Dance 59(6):34-63, 1988.

This seven-article feature examines such issues as the role of sport in culture including human movement, sport film, restructuring of school sports, sport and social change, equity, and female coaches.

Tannehill D, Konoczak J, and Zakrajsek D: Physical education research and the practitioner, Physical Educator 45(1):34-38.

Factors that tend to deter the application of research findings to professional practice are identified, and suggestions to remediate this problem are presented.

Chapter 16

Future of Physical Education and Sport

INSTRUCTIONAL OBJECTIVES AND COMPETENCIES TO BE ACHIEVED

After reading this chapter the student should be able to—
- Indicate how physical educators can capitalize on the increased public interest in health and fitness.
- Discuss how the changing nature of education and technological advances will influence physical education and sport in the future.
- Show how physical educators can establish jurisdiction over their own domain.
- Describe how physical education and sport can improve its delivery system.

What will our world be like in the future?[1] What will physical education and sport be like in the twenty-first century? What do we want the future to be? To make the most of the future means planning and knowing to some extent what the future will be like. The future of physical education and sport is *coming*—but only physical educators can decide where it is *going*.

Human beings have always been interested in the future. Today numerous "think tanks" such as the Rand Corporation and the Hudson Institute, and futurists, individuals who study the future, endeavor to unravel the mysteries of the years ahead.

Futurists attempt, using a variety of techniques, to describe the future. They try to predict the course of past and current trends and identify the consequences of selected courses of action. Futurists attempt to define priorities that will lead to a future of our choice. Future studies imply the identification of both desirable and undesirable outcomes. The futurist must assume the responsibility for seeking the alternative that creates a future as close as possible to the desired outcomes.

Some individuals using methods such as expert advice, trend extrapolation, technological forecasting, and scenarios have been very accurate in forecasting the future.

Dateline 1932: Aldous Huxley[2] wrote in his book *Brave New World*, "The Director [of the school] described the technique for preserving the excised ovary alive...showed them how the eggs were inspected...immersed in a warm bouillon containing free-swimming spermatozoa...."

Dateline July 25, 1978: Forty-six years later Louise Brown, the first "test-tube baby" (the first child in history to be conceived outside of the womb), was born in England.

Of course, all prognosticators have not been as accurate in their predictions:

Dateline 1957: George Romney, former Governor of Michigan and President of American Motors, predicted that in 1980 the Nash Ram-

Airshelters. The city of the future.

bler would be the most popular automobile in America.

Although errors are made in forecasting, it is still imperative to try to predict what will happen in the years ahead. Why? Because all of us are going to spend our lives in the future. Why? Because the future to some extent is known and to some extent can be controlled. Why? Because it affects our beliefs and assumptions. We can anticipate problems. We can plan. Why? Because people shape the future. The space program of the 1960s resulted in man walking on the surface of the moon, and NASA has the goal of placing a space station in space sometime in the 1990s. One scientist has stated that "An important reason for studying the future is not so we can learn what may happen, but rather to help us decide about what kind of future we want and develop ways to achieve it."

Although forecasting the future of physical education and sport is difficult, it is important that it be undertaken before we are overtaken by future events. One means to plan for the future is to accept the premise of futurist Daniel Bell. Bell indicates that time is not an "overarching leap" from the present to the future. Instead, it has its origins in the past, incorporates the present, and extends into the future. By using imagination and insight combined with a knowledge of the facts concerning the past, present, and what futurists, scientists, and experts predict for the future, it is possible to forecast what will happen in society as well as physical education and sport in the years ahead.

Planning for the future recognizes that rapid change is a characteristic of our way of life. With each day that passes we live in a different world. Human beings who are age 50 or older have witnessed in their lifetime the start of the atomic age, the space age, and the computer age. They have seen more than 80 new nations appear, the world population double, and the gross world product double and then redouble. As C.P. Snow, the noted British scientist, said, "The rate of change has increased so much that our imagination can't keep up."

Next, recognizing that change is ever present, certain trends and developments can be identified that lend themselves to a better understanding of the future of physical education and sport. These trends and developments include the wellness movement, the fitness movement, the educational reform movement and the changing nature of education, the expanding frontiers of the habitable universe, and technological advances.

SOCIETAL TRENDS AND CURRENT DEVELOPMENTS

The Wellness Movement

The wellness movement represents one of the most opportune moments in our history. The wellness movement stresses self-help and emphasizes that one's life-style—the way in which one lives—influences greatly the attainment and maintenance of personal health. This movement supports efforts directed toward health promotion and disease prevention rather than focusing on the treatment of illness. The wellness doctrine is based on the premise that it is the responsibility of the individual to work toward achievement of a healthy life-style to realize an optimal sense of well-being. A healthy life-style should reflect the integration of three components—proper nutrition, regular and appropriate physical activity and exercise, and stress management—and the elimination of controllable risk factors (e.g., smoking, excessive alcohol consumption).

Strong support for health promotion and disease prevention efforts was given by three national health reports: *Healthy People*,[3] *Objectives for the Nation*,[4] and *Year 2000 Objectives*.[5] *Healthy People* identified exercise and fitness as 1 of 15 priority areas that could have a significant impact on the health status of the individual as well as that of the nation. Specific fitness and exercise goals for all segments of the population to be achieved by 1990 were set forth in the *Objectives for the Nation*. Goals for the twenty-first century were delineated in the *Year 2000 Objectives*. Whether or not these goals are achieved depends to a great extent on physical educators' willingness to make a commitment to meeting these goals and to work cooperatively with various other professionals and professional organizations to attain them.

The corporate sector has also become interested in the wellness movement. This has led to the development of corporate fitness and wellness programs for the employees. Corporations are willing to invest in these programs because they have found that they result in increased employee productivity, decreased absenteeism, better employee health, and lower insurance costs.

Physical education can make a significant contribution to the wellness movement in many ways. Physical education can provide individuals with the skills and knowledge to exercise properly; help individuals develop abilities in a variety of sport activities that are meaningful and satisfying, thus promoting lifetime participation; and teach individuals a variety of stress management techniques.

Fitness Movement

Enthusiasm for exercise and fitness is at an all-time high in the United States today and will continue to increase in the future. Sales of sport equipment, apparel, and home exercise equipment have reached astronomical levels. The number of individuals participating in exercise and sport activities continues to rise, and it appears that exercise and fitness have become an ingrained way of American life. This enthusiasm is reaching many segments of the population. The positive effects of remaining active throughout one's life have motivated many adults to embark on a fitness program and millions of others to continue their participation past the typical stopping point, the end of the school years.

However, when the information about adult participation in physical activity is examined more closely, only approximately 10% to 20% of adults exercise with sufficient intensity, duration, and frequency to develop and maintain adequate levels of health-related fitness.[5] It is estimated that approximately 40% of the adult population engages in physical activity of moderate intensity often enough to realize some, but not all, health-related benefits.[5] Given this information, it appears that a large segment of the adult population, nearly 40%, are lead-

Many adults who ceased exercising after their school years are now turning to commercial health clubs to develop fitness. It is important that these clubs hire qualified physical educators to conduct sound physical programs for their members.

ing rather sedentary lives.[5] Increasing the number of people who are physically active is one objective stated in the *Year 2000 Objectives*.

Moreover, while more adults than ever before appear to be actively engaged in physical activity, there is some concern that the fitness movement is not reaching the children and youth of the country. The recently completed National Children and Youth Fitness Study I[6] and II[7] substantiated this concern. These studies revealed that children and youths have become fatter since 1960. Only about one third of students participate in daily physical education programs. Secondary school physical education programs tend to focus largely on competitive and team sports rather than on the development of individual and lifetime sport skills that can

be used by adults throughout their lives. The reports also indicate that the majority of physical activity of the students is performed outside of the school setting, primarily in community settings.

Physical educators need to assume a more active role in the leadership of the fitness movement. At the vanguard of the movement are physicians, self-appointed experts, and even movie stars.[8] Many of these individuals lack the proper training and qualifications to direct this activity. Professionals must actively strive to assume a leadership role in this movement. Physical educators also need to make a concerted effort to help the fitness movement reach the youth of this country. Physical educators working in the school setting should provide students with the skills and knowledge necessary to assume the responsibility for their own fitness throughout their lifespan.

Finally, physical educators must become more involved in physical education–oriented programs in nonschool settings that are designed to meet the needs of all persons. More physical education and sport programs must be established to meet the needs of the elderly, the very young, and the disabled. Also, programs need to be developed to reach individuals who are economically disadvantaged; they lack the financial resources to join health clubs or pay for private sport instruction. Fitness equity is an important professional concern.

Education

Cries for educational reform have pervaded the United States within the past few years. Advocates of reform have called for a greater emphasis on the basics such as English, math, social studies, computer science, and science. The status of physical education in the school curriculum has been subjected to much debate. Some educators perceive physical education as an extra or a frill and would eliminate physical education from the curriculum. Other educators view physical education as an integral part of the educational process. To solidify the place of physical education in the educational curriculum in the coming decade, physical educators must clearly and articulately set forth why physical education is an integral part of the educational program of every educational institution. Physical educators must generate support for physical education in the curriculum by conducting sound, exemplary programs and by informing the public, legislators, and other decision makers about the contribution of physical education to the educational process. Physical educators must also stress that physical education teaches individuals skills that contribute to well-being throughout the student's lifetime.

High-quality daily physical education for all students is an important professional priority. Physical education programs in the schools have received support from several different sources. In 1987 the US Congress passed House Congressional Resolution No. 97, which encourages state and local

Physical educators must accept the challenge to help young athletes and students to become responsible for their own health and fitness.

governments to provide high-quality daily physical education programs for all students in grades K through 12. In addition to AAHPERD, other professional organizations have spoken in favor of high-quality daily physical education; these include the National Education Association, the American Heart Association, and the National Association for Elementary School Principals. The American Medical Association and the American Academy of Pediatrics also support physical education programs in the schools. As professionals, we must capitalize on this support to make high-quality daily physical education in our nation's schools a reality.

For years education was considered preparation for life. Now it is looked on as a lifelong experience. More than 2 million persons 35 years of age or older are returning to school or beginning their higher education. Alvin Toffler[9] in his book, *The Third Wave,* stresses that the aging or "graying" population implies a need for much greater public attention to the needs of the elderly.

Lewis[10] stated that the rapid acceleration and growth of technology, the information era, and demographic shifts will have a tremendous impact on the nature of education and our society. He writes that it is of paramount importance that all students acquire the basic skills of reading, writing, and computing. Students must be able to access information, analyze it, synthesize it, and apply information in a meaningful manner. Educators must also teach students how to be lifelong learners and to assume responsibility for their own learning.

Changes in the nature of the school structure will occur as we enter the 1990s. Futurist Marvin Cetron,[11] president of Forecasting International Inc., stated that students may spend only three days a week in school. Students would spend the other days at home being educated through interactive cable television. Textbooks will be supplanted by computers; this will provide students with information that is current and is regularly updated. Cable television will be used more widely. The use of cable television will allow students at several schools to receive instruction from a central source. This will help equalize the quality of education provided to all students. Adults will regularly return to school to keep abreast of rapidly growing advances in knowledge and technology in their fields.

What are the implications of the educational reform movement and the changing nature of the structure of the school for physical education? First, to retain physical education as an integral part of the educational curriculum in the future, physical educators must clearly set forth the contribution of physical education to the educational process. To solidify the place of physical education in the educational curriculum in the next decade, physical educators must educate the public and decision makers about the values to be derived from participation in physical education, both in terms of the education and the health of the individual. Physical educators can generate support for physical education in the schools by conducting sound, exemplary programs. Second, as more adults return to school to update their skills, physical educators need to be ready to conduct instructional programs to meet adult needs. Third, just as education must teach students to be lifelong learners, so must physical

education. Students in physical education class need to learn knowledge as well as skills so that they may be self-educative. Finally, as more and more education takes place out of the classroom in the home, physical educators need to establish instructional programs in the community. These programs should be designed to meet the needs of individuals of all ages. More services need to be provided for the elderly, particularly as recognition of the ability of physical activity and exercise to enhance the quality of an individual's life increases.

Expanding Frontiers

The frontiers of the habitable universe are expanding. People in the future may be living as part of a space station colony or on a moon base. The work of the astronauts and the NASA programs has laid the basis for the future in respect to space travel. Space travel may become become commonplace in the future. Citizens will be able to purchase a ticket for space travel in the space shuttle much in the same way they purchase a ticket for airline travel.

The July 1976 issue of *National Geographic*[12] visualizes the outcome of a serious proposal that was developed by a group of 30 engineers and social and physical scientists. They describe what a typical colony in space will be like. Ten thousand people, their mission to build more colonies, will live under artificial gravity in an encircling tube called a *torus*. The torus is divided into six separate sections each of which has supermarket, farming and residential areas and such facilities as theaters, sport arenas, schools, and libraries. Sunlight is filtered and dispersed by means of mirrors that can be tilted to produce an 8-hour night every 24 hours. Farming is very productive as a result of controlled sunlight, an unfailing water supply, ample fertilizer, equable temperature, and a somewhat higher carbon dioxide content in the air than on Earth. The crop yields are many times of those on Earth.

A second area of the habitable universe that will be an especially exciting place to live in the future is underwater. Since more than two-thirds of the planet is covered with ocean, there will be sufficient room to construct many underwater communities.

Futurist Rosen reports on the work of scientist William Backley who has developed a submerged capsule equipped with observation ports that is a model for future underwater communities. A superstructure to the capsule has a helicopter landing pad and docking facilities for surface craft. The capsule is held in place by anchors and is made stable by a concrete mat suspended beneath the unit. An airlock and elevator offer easy access either to the ocean floor or to the surface. Backley's work represents a model for the construction of a future underwater colony that will have residential areas, farming, and other facilities comparable to those that will exist in space.

Physical educators need to prepare themselves to assist individuals to attain their optimal level of fitness while living in these space and underwater environments. Space travelers to distant planets need help in keeping fit while living for long periods of time under conditions of zero gravity. Physical educators must conduct research concerning the effects of weightlessness on the body and artificial gravity. Designing exercise programs to deal with differences in the environment falls within the realm of the physical educator.

Technology

This decade is one of rapid technological advances. Many of these technological advances hold implications for the future of physical education and sport. We have entered the computer era. Developments in computer technology combined with increasingly sophisticated research techniques have enabled us to widen the base of knowledge in physical education and will contribute to further growth in the future. Computer technology has facilitated biomechanical analysis of performance. Computer-generated graphical representations of protypical sport performance will enhance the development of motor skills. Computers have also enabled researchers to better understand brain activity during learning, and subsequently design more effective instructional strategies; perhaps in the future physical educators will be able to predict with a great deal of certainty learning outcomes. The increased availability of personal computers will allow the practitioner to analyze individuals' performances such as on fitness tests and to keep up-to-date records easier than ever before.

Developments in the field of communication hold promise for the future of physical education and sport. Cable television is growing rapidly. The number of special interest programs presented on cable television is increasing as well. Sports programs are offered 24 hours a day. Naisbitt[13] writes in regards to the future of cable television: "Cable television will be like special interest magazines: You will be able to tune into *Runner's World....*" Videotape equipment has become easier to use, and provides a valuable instructional tool for physical educators in all settings. Video cassette recorders are experiencing phenomenal growth; many individuals are investing in exercise videotapes so that they can work out in the privacy of their own home and at their convenience. In the future instructional tapes for different sport skills will help individuals learn at home at their own pace.

Developments in biotechnology hold implications for the future of physical education and sport. Today muscle fiber typing allows researchers to identify whether an individual has a greater potential to succeed in athletic events requiring strength or endurance. Perhaps in the near future genetic engineering will be used to program an individual's genes for success in certain sport activities.

Advances in technology have led to improvements in sport equipment, facilitating better performances by both skilled and unskilled persons. Graphite-composite tennis rackets have begun to replace metal and metal-composite tennis rackets, which replaced wooden rackets years ago. Pole vaulters using fiberglass poles have attained heights previously only dreamed about by vaulters using wooden poles. Technology applied to the manufacturing of running shoes has led to increased comfort and fewer injuries for runners of all abilities. Grass fields are being replaced by artificial surfaces, cinder tracks by all-weather tracks, and open stadiums by domed arenas. There are numerous examples of how technology has affected physical education and sport, and the influence of technology on physical education and sport will continue in the future.

New instructional technologies can be used to provide for more individualized learning.

PREPARING FOR THE FUTURE

It is tempting to look back at the 1970s and bask in the glow of such achievements as the birth of AAHPERD; the professional stature gained for exercise physiology, biomechanics, and motor learning; the recognition of the value of movement education; and the passage of Title IX and PL 94-142 as laws of the land. However, if physical educators are interested in the future of their profession, they must also look at areas in which they can improve.

Oberle,[14] in a discussion about the future directions for health, physical education, recreation and leisure, and dance, stressed the importance of exerting quality control within these professions. He suggested each of the disciplines consider the following actions to enhance their effectiveness:

- Establish minimum standards of competency.
- Develop programs and services that are flexible to meet changing needs while accomplishing avowed disciplinary objectives.
- Provide meaningful programs that will meet needs today as well as tomorrow.

- Reduce ineffective programs.
- Establish minimum standards for entry into professional preparation programs.
- Provide high-quality experiences for professionals within the discipline, such as inservice education and graduate education.
- Develop a system for relicensure for all professionals, not only public school personnel.
- Establish professional accreditating agencies, as the American Medical Association has done, to ensure quality control.
- Develop high-quality model programs and build facilities that can serve as the standard for the profession.

As we move into the future, we must establish our professional stature.

A review of the past decade shows two areas—jurisdiction over the physical education domain and the delivery system of physical educators—that need the attention of professionals. First, some of the shortcomings of each of the two areas will be described and then a scenario will be painted for each area in the 1990s.

PHYSICAL EDUCATORS' ESTABLISHMENT OF JURISDICTION OVER THEIR DOMAIN

Physical education's future could lie in physical educators becoming the publicly recognized leaders in their field of physical activity. Many of the services with which physical educators are presently associated are within the public domain. Unfortunately, physical educators are not directing these services. Muscle builders, entrepreneurs, and movie stars associated with health spas, exercise salons, and weight-reducing clinics have invaded the physical educator's domain, often without proper credentials. Additionally, the public is often not aware of the nature of physical education and the tremendous worth and substance of this field of endeavor. For example, in 1982 Bucher divided the students in his classes into three groups and told them to go out on the street and ask people at random to answer the following three questions:

1. Who would you ask to help your sport-minded son learn to throw a baseball correctly?

2. Where can you get help for a child who is uncoordinated and lacks body awareness?

3. To whom would you go for advice if you are soft and overweight and want to become more physically fit?

The answers to these questions shocked the class: Jack LaLanne, Reggie Jackson, Erma Bombeck, Dr. Joyce Brothers, Billy Martin, the coach of our Little League team, Ann Landers; but most discouraging was the fact that only seven individuals in over 200 surveyed said they would consult a physical educator to find answers to these questions.

If physical educators are to become the publicly recognized leaders in their field, it will be because they have provided themselves with the proper credentials. The credentials necessary to achieve this leadership position are described below:

- *Credential 1.* A systematic knowledge base will exist that describes the unique social service rendered by our practitioners. This knowledge base will (1) support the art and science of human movement as it relates to sport, dance, play, and exercise; (2) document the fact that physical education and sport foster human growth and development; and (3) convincingly show that a better human being will result by developing the proper relationship of body, senses, mind, and spirit.

- *Credential 2.* Physical education will have two program priorities (although there are others) that provide consumers with self-direction in light of the emphasis on self-help medicine and the rising cost of health care. The first priority will be *knowledge*—knowledge that is (1) concerned with the science of movement and the healthful impact that proper physical activity has on the functioning of the human organism and (2) based on scientific findings that are constantly updated and provided to practitioners via retrieval systems in language that can be understood and used.

    The second priority will be *skills*—skills taught scientifically, utilizing not only the basic concepts of motor learning, but also advanced technology such as linking the computer with closed circuit television, enabling persons to be taught and to progress as evaluated against learning models.

- *Credential 3.* Physical education teaching will become a science as well as an art; it will be governed by rigorous laws enabling physical educators to predict with a high degree of certainty the outcome of learning.

As professionals, we must assume the challenge of leadership for the domain of physical education and sport. We must be accountable for our programs. High-quality programs are essential. We must promote our programs and take steps to ensure that the people who participate in them accrue the stated and personally desired benefits. Physical education and sport programs in the future will become more diverse as we expand our focus to include more populations. Professionals must be sensitive to individual needs when designing programs. Additionally, we must improve our delivery systems to more effectively serve individuals of all ages.

PHYSICAL EDUCATORS' DELIVERY SYSTEMS

In the future physical education and sport will need to change the manner in which it provides services as well as the populations served. In other words, physical education needs to change its delivery system.

Some remarks heard from various groups during the past few years suggest that our delivery systems need attention. Here are a few of the comments:

1. Junior high school students at a science fair where models depicting space and underwater living were on display: "How do we get our physical bodies in shape for this existence that we are very likely to experience in the years ahead?"

2. Group of physicians: "You physical and sport educators do a good job making healthy people healthier and skilled people better skilled but a terrible job making unhealthy people healthy and poorly skilled people skilled."

3. Rotary Club: "I look at school physical education and community recreation programs and can't tell the difference between the two.

Physical education and sport are a means to foster human growth and development. Physical education and sport programs can help individuals learn how to help others.

They overlap in the activities they offer and the people they serve. There's also a duplication of facilities and personnel. Why all this waste?"

4. Senior citizen club: "The elderly represent 11% of the population in this country. Is your profession devoting 11% of its total effort to this group?"

5. Student group: "Why don't we have a record system listing information about each person's personal physical education and sport history? We have records pertaining to people's health history. Why not a physical education and sport history record?"

Physical education's delivery system requires an overhaul, and new developments in the field of technology and communication as well as the changing nature of education will greatly affect the system in the future.

The following examples illustrate how trends and developments may shape the future of physical education.

1. The delivery system will render services to the new frontiers of space colonies and underwater communities. Meetings will be held with futurists and scientists. Conditions that simulate space and underwater living will be established in college and university laboratories. Physical educators and their students will pursue studies in these areas.

2. The delivery system will provide closer articulation between school physical education and sport programs and community programs. These programs will be combined and centrally administered. This program structure will (1) ensure efficient use of facilities, equipment, and personnel; (2) eliminate overlapping; and (3) provide for progression throughout life in the program of activities. It will meet the needs of all individuals in the community, including those in their later years who want to become involved in physical education, sport, and recreational activities.

Also, a computerized record system will follow each person throughout life wherever he or she goes or lives.

3. The delivery system will make extensive use of television, particularly cable television. Programs will be packaged and syndicated. There will be such features as demonstrations of the step-by-step approach to developing skill in dance, sport, and other activities; lectures relating to such areas as exercise physiology; and demonstrations of methods by which one's physical fitness can be assessed and maintained.

Videotape feedback of one's performance will become increasingly common, and generation of computerized models of ideal performances and actual performances will help individuals learn and improve their motor skills more easily.

4. Computers will play an increasingly important role in our delivery system. Computer information databases and services will be used to disseminate research findings, allowing practitioners to more easily keep abreast of current research developments within the fields. Collaborative research endeavors with colleagues at other institutions and with practitioners at various sites throughout the country will be facilitated through telecommunication networking. Additionally, practitioners can network with one another to share ideas and programs and to jointly resolve problems confronting them. Computerized resource databases will allow practitioners to more easily individualize programs to meet individual participant's needs. Computer record-keeping will make it easier for practitioners to identify individual's needs and to monitor as individual's progress toward the attainment of his or her goals.

As we move into the 1990s, we must change our delivery systems to use new technologies to more effectively provide services to an ever increasing clientele. Our delivery systems should encourage participation and maintain involvement in our programs.

THE FUTURE

As they prepare for the future, physical educators must do the following:

1. Provide themselves with the proper credentials to establish jurisdiction over their domain.
2. Utilize technological advances to improve the delivery system.
3. Prepare for space and underwater living as well as for changes in our society.
4. Become a positive role model for a fit and healthy life-style, so that others will be favorably influenced to emulate this life-style.
5. Help persons to become increasingly responsible for their own health and fitness.
6. Recognize that individuals will live longer and become more fit and active in the years to come.
7. Provide for all persons, regardless of age, skill, disabling condition, and socioeconomic background, throughout their lifespan.
8. Remember that we are involved with the development of the whole person as a thinking, feeling, moving human being.
9. Make a commitment to conduct high-quality programs that are sensitive to individual needs so that physical education and sport's potential to enhance the health and quality of life for all people can be achieved.

Whether or not physical educators meet these challenges depends on the members of the physical education profession. Remember, the future of physical education is coming, but physical educators can determine where it is going. This requires dedicated leadership and the commitment on the part of each professional to be involved in working toward our future. We must take charge of our professional destiny and create a future that allows the full potential of physical education and sport to be fulfilled.

It is likely that all of us, at some time in our lives, will have a significant experience that as years pass will come to embody the personal meaning of physical education and sport. Noted physical education leader and author of previous editions of this text,

Charles Bucher, related an experience that helped him personally and perhaps will help you to realize anew the tremendous potential physical education and sport have in our society. Bucher wrote about the New York City marathon, one of the largest marathons in the world, the following passage:

I was particularly enthralled as I watched the runners, some of whom took as many as five, six, and seven hours to cross the finish lines. Most runners gritted their teeth, gasped for breath, and put on an extra burst of speed as they pounded across. Some runners had given so much of themselves that they were helped onto a stretcher or were carried across.

A runner from Italy, in fourth place, whipped off his sweatband and waved it to the crowd. A runner from California, in second place among the women, clenched her teeth and went the last few strides on sheer will before collapsing across the line. When a long-haired Polish woman, sweat streaming down her face, stumbled slowly toward the line, the crowd cheered and chanted, "Finish it! Finish it!" And *she did.*

A few runners completed the race hand-in-hand. Some went barefoot and some carried their shoes. Each person got a tremendous cheer, but perhaps the loudest cheers of all were for two men who crossed the finish line in wheelchairs.

The runners had done their best—not for acclaim, for a loving cup symbolic of supremacy, or to be a champion—but to prove to themselves that they could do it.

No one could watch the sight without realizing that he or she was witnessing a great moment in America and the world.

No one in physical education and sport could be a part of that experience without feeling the power and potential for our field of endeavor—the power and potential for improving the quality of life for all our citizens.

The marathon perhaps in many ways is symbolic of our society, of America, of physical education and sport, and of the qualities that make our society great, and that we in our field try to develop. It recognizes that the training of the physical is important; but perhaps more important, it shows how the physical *can* and *should* be used as a vehicle that brings into play such desirable qualities as courage, a belief in oneself, a feeling of accomplishment, and, most important, a blending of the mind, body, and spirit in the accomplishment of worthy goals.

Physical education and sport is a dynamic, growing field of endeavor. Its future is very promising. In 1988, an editorial by the executive directors of AAHPERD published in the *Journal of Physical Education, Recreation, and Dance* expressed a sense of optimism for the 1990s. They stated:[15]

At no time in the history of American Alliance for Health, Physical Education, Recreation, and Dance have we, as executive directors of the national associations, seen more opportunities for professional growth and service within the entire profession. We are highly encouraged by the signs we see for new impact on society, stimulation of teaching and leadership personnel, development of significant projects, and potential for growth in membership.... Society wants and needs us. Now is the opportune time!

Physical education and sport is a dynamic and growing field of study. After reading this text, it is hoped that you, as the reader, have an appreciation for the tremendous substance and worth of this field that you have chosen to study. Physical education and sport has a tremendous potential to enrich and enhance the health and quality of life of all people. Whether this potential is realized depends on each professional's willingness to make a personal commitment to the achievement of this goal. At the beginning of this text, you were encouraged to take advantage of your educational opportunities and challenged to make a commitment to excellence. At the conclusion of this text, I challenge you, as a young professional, to go forth and be the best you can be.

SUMMARY

Planning and knowing what the future will be like is essential if physical educators are to take an active part in the direction and shaping of the future. Professionals must start planning for the future now. Such planning requires that professionals recognize that rapid change is characteristic of our way of life.

Several societal trends will influence the future of physical education and sport. The wellness movement and the fitness movement present excellent opportunities for physical educators to involve individuals of all ages in appropriate physical activity. The educational reform movement and the changing nature of education indicates that physical educators, more than ever before, need to inform the public and decision makers about the contribution of physical education to the educational process. Expanding frontiers of the habitable universe, developments in communications, and other technological developments will influence the future of physical education and sport as well.

Physical educators can prepare for the future in several ways. First, physical educators need to establish jurisdiction over their domain by obtaining the proper credentials and actively seeking leadership positions. Second, physical educators need to improve the delivery systems. We must provide for people of all ages and utilize technological advances to facilitate learning. We must take an active role in helping individuals prepare for space and underwater living. The future of physical education and sport is *coming,* but only physical educators can determine where it is *going.*

SELF-ASSESSMENT TESTS

These tests are designed to assist students in determining if the materials and competencies presented in this chapter have been mastered.

1. Prepare a plan that lists several ways by which physical education can capitalize on the increased interest in wellness and fitness that exists in the United States today.

2. Discuss the implications of the changing nature of education and the impact of technological developments on physical education and sport in the future.

3. Your professor has requested that you supply information to show how physical education can establish jurisdiction over its own domain. Prepare a report on this topic and present it to the class.

4. Develop a plan for the late 1990s that provides specific suggestions for improving physical education's delivery system.

REFERENCES

1. Bucher CA and Thaxton NA: Physical education and sport: change and challenge, St Louis, 1981, Times Mirror/Mosby.

2. Huxley A: Brave new world, New York, 1932, Modern Library.

3. US Department of Health, Education, and Welfare: Healthy people: the surgeon general's report on health promotion and disease prevention, Washington, DC, 1979, US Government Printing Office.

4. US Department of Health and Human Services: Promoting health/preventing disease: objectives for the nation, Washington, DC, 1980, US Government Printing Office.

5. Public Health Service, US Department of Health and Human Services: Promoting Health/Preventive Disease: Year 2000 Objectives for the Nation, US Government Printing Office, Washington, DC, 1989 (draft).

6. Ross JG and Gilbert GG: The National Children and Youth Study: a summary of the findings, Journal of Physical Education, Recreation, and Dance 56(1):45-50, 1985.

7. Ross JC and Pate RR: The National Children and Youth Fitness Study II, Journal of Physical Education, Recreation, and Dance 58(9):51-56, 1987.

8. Corbin CB: Is the fitness bandwagon passing us by?, Journal of Physical Education, Recreation, and Dance 55(9):17, 1984.

9. Toffler A: The third wave, New York, 1981, Bantam Books.

10. Lewis AJ: Education for the 21st century, Educational Leadership 41(1):9-10, 1983.

11. Cetron M: Schools of the future. Presented at Convention of the American Association of School Administrators, Dallas, August 1985.

12. First colony in space, National Geographic 150(1):76-89, 1976.

13. Naisbitt J: Megatrends: ten new directions transforming our lives, New York, 1982, Warner Books.

14. Oberle GH: A future direction plan for our profession, Journal of Physical Education, Recreation, and Dance 59(1):76-77, 1988.

15. AAHPERD Executive Directors: In our view, Journal of Physical Education, Recreation, and Dance 59(8):14, 1988.

SUGGESTED READINGS

Bain LL: Beginning the journey: agenda for 2001, Quest 40:96-106, 1988.

An analysis of societal trends and their implications for physical education programs in higher education is presented.

Brandt R: On education and the future: a conversation with Harold Shane, Educational Leadership 41(1):11-13, 1983.

Futurist Shane discusses educational trends, curriculum, role of the parents, and preparation for the future.

Cetron MJ, Soriano B, and Gayle M: Schools of the future: education approaches the twenty-first century, Futurist 23(4):18-23, 1985.

Factors affecting the future of schools, characteristics of the students of the future, and changes in the status of teachers and the manner of instruction are described.

Daniel C, editor: Moving into the Third Age, Journal of Physical Education, Recreation, and Dance 57(1):30-61, 1986.

This series of articles focuses on physical activity and the age, including the benefit of physical activity on the aging process, lifelong fitness, and dance and recreation for the aged.

Ellis MJ: The business of physical education: the future of the profession, Champaign, Ill, 1988, Human Kinetics.

A thought-provoking examination of the future of physical education, this book examines major societal trends and their implications for physical education, the activity and leisure industry, the changing nature of the profession, status of physical education in the school setting, and challenges to be faced.

Lawson HA: Looking back from the year 2082, Journal of Physical Education, Recreation, and Dance 53(1):15-17, 1982.

Three catalysts to change in the nature of physical education as practiced in 2082 are discussed. These are the growth of sport instruction and participation in the community, the self-help movement, and the development of the disciplinary foundation that helped stimulate the growth of alternative careers.

Lewis AJ: Education for the 21st century, Educational Leadership 41(1):9-10, 1983.

Three trends are discussed in relation to the future—development of technology, growth of information, and demographic shifts. The development of basic skills and teaching individuals to become self-directed learners are viewed as critical in the preparation for the future.

Massengale JD: The unprepared discipline: selection of alternative futures, Quest 40:107-114, 1988.

This article provides information on futurism, future research, and consideration of alternative futures in physical education.

Massengale JD, editor: Trends toward the future in physical education. Champaign, Ill, 1987, Human Kinetics.

Current societal and professional trends and their implications for the future of physical education are examined. The eleven articles discuss the future of the profession, university women, school physical education, the business of physical education, wellness, and sport management.

Naisbitt J and Aburdene P: Megatrends 2000: ten new directions for the 1990s, New York, 1990, William Morrow and Company.

Ten trends that will shape the future including the global economy, the rise of women in leadership, the increased privatization of the welfare state, the increased emphasis on religion, and the growth of the individual are presented, as well as implications for the future.

Oberle GH: A future direction plan for our profession, Journal of Physical Education, Recreation, and Dance 59(1):76-77, 1988.

The author presents several specific suggestions to help professionals prepare for the future and to master the new technologies.

Sanoff A, Witkin G, and Hawkins S: Training our Olympians high tech style, US News and World Report, pp 62-63, March 19, 1984.

The use of high technology to train Olympic athletes is described.

Toffler A: Future shock, New York, Random House, 1970.

The future and the changes that it will bring are discussed in this classical book.

Weinstein R: Jobs for the 21st century, New York, Collier Books, 1983.

The nature of the 21st century, including jobs, is described in this book. Weinstein foresees the continuation of the fitness movement and wellness movement, resulting in increased career opportunities in these areas.

Credits

Introduction   P. 2, Scott Watson; p. 3, President's Council on Physical Fitness and Sports

Chapter 1   P. 7, The Forbes Magazine and Fitness Center, New York. From Bucher CA: Administration of physical education and athletic programs, ed 8, St Louis, 1983, Times Mirror/Mosby College Publishing; p. 8, A from Bucher CA: Management of physical education and athletic programs, ed 9, St Louis, 1987, Times Mirror/Mosby College Publishing; B, Matthew Castiglione; p. 10, A, Matthew Castiglione; B from Bucher CA: Management of physical education and athletic programs, ed 9, St Louis, 1987, Times Mirror/Mosby College Publishing; p. 11, Sarah Rich; p. 12, University of Nevada, Las Vegas; p. 13, A, Ithaca College Sports Information; B, Ithaca College Sports Information; p. 14, Matthew Castiglione; p. 15, Linda Buettner; p. 16, Figure 1-1 from American Association for Health, Physical Education, and Recreation: Tones of theory, Washington, DC, 1972, AAHPER; p. 20, University of Nevada, Las Vegas; p. 21, From Lumpkin A: Physical education and sport: a contemporary introduction, ed 2, St Louis, 1990, Times Mirror/Mosby College Publishing; p. 23, Barbara M. Armstrong; p. 27, From Bucher CA: Management of physical education and athletic programs, ed 9, St Louis, 1987, Times Mirror/Mosby College Publishing; p. 30, From Nichols B: Moving and learning: the elementary school physical education experience, ed 2, St Louis, 1990, Times Mirror/Mosby College Publishing.

Chapter 2   P. 36, Office of Public Relations, Smith College, Northhampton, MA; p. 37, From Nichols B: Moving and learning: the elementary school physical education experience, ed 2, St Louis, 1990, Times Mirror/Mosby College Publishing; p. 38, A, B, and C from Nichols B: Moving and learning: the elementary school physical education experience, ed 2, St Louis, 1990, Times Mirror/Mosby College Publishing; p. 40, A, Linda Buettner; B, Sarah Rich; p. 41, A, Hope College, Holland, MI; B, George Mowbray; p. 42, Ithaca College Sports Information; p. 44, Sarah Rich; p. 45, Beth Kirkpatrick, Tilford Middle School, Vinton, IA; p. 47, Health Education and Exercise Programs, Health Management Program, Kimberly-Clark Corp, Neenah, WI; p. 52, Hope College, Holland, MI; p. 53, From Auxter D and Pyfer J: Principles and methods of adapted physical education and recreation, ed 6, St Louis, 1989, Times Mirror/Mosby College Publishing; p. 54, From Bucher CA: Management of physical education and athletic programs, ed 9, St Louis, 1987, Times Mirror/Mosby College Publishing; p. 55, From Bucher CA: Management of physical education and athletic programs, ed 9, St Louis, 1987, Times Mirror/Mosby College Publishing; p. 56, From Bucher CA: Management of physical education and athletic programs, ed 9, St Louis, 1987, Times Mirror/Mosby College Publishing; p. 57, Figure 2-1, Fitnessgram, Institute for Aerobic Research, Dallas, TX.

Chapter 3   P. 65, Figure 3-1 from Tanner D: Using behavioral objectives in the classroom, New York, 1972, Macmillian, Inc; p. 66, A from Nichols B: Moving and learning: the elementary school physical education experience, ed 2, St Louis, 1990, Times Mirror/Mosby College Publishing; B, Fred Estabrook; p. 67, A, Paul Grube, Rock Springs High School, Rock Springs, WY; B, Ithaca College Sports Information; p. 69, University of North Carolina at Greensboro; p. 70, Ithaca College Sports Information; p. 71, St Louis Cardinals, from Arnheim DD: Modern principles of athletic training, ed 6, St Louis, 1985, Times Mirror/Mosby College Publishing; p. 72, Suzi D'Annalfo; p. 76, From Nichols B: Moving and learning: the elementary school physical education experience, ed 2, St Louis, 1990, Times Mirror/Mosby College Publishing; p. 77, from Auxter D and Pyfer J: Principles and methods of adapted physical education and recreation, ed 6, St Louis, 1989, Times Mirror/Mosby College Publishing; p. 78, Dept of Intramurals, Club Sports, and Recreation at Colgate University, Hamilton, NY; p. 80, From Bucher CA: Management of physical education and athletic programs, ed 9, St Louis, 1987, Times Mirror/Mosby College Publishing; p. 81, Scott Watson; p. 82, Deborah A. Wuest; p. 83, A and B, Deborah A Wuest; p. 84, Suzi D'Annalfo; p. 85, Linda Castiglione.

Chapter 4   P. 90, Oak View Elementary School, Fairfax, VA; p. 91, From Nichols B: Moving and learning: the elementary school physical education experience, ed 2, St Louis, 1990, Times Mirror/Mosby College Publishing; p. 94, From Nichols B: Moving and learning: the elementary school physical education experience, ed 2, St Louis, 1990, Times Mirror/Mosby College Publishing; p. 95, Barbara Stonikinis, Longwood College, Farmville, VA; p. 96, University of Nevada, Las Vegas; p. 97, Deborah A Wuest; p. 98, University of Nevada, Las Vegas; p. 99, Figure 4-1 from Nichols B: Moving and learning: the elementary school physical education experience, ed 2, St Louis, 1990, Times Mirror/Mosby College Publishing; p. 100, Linda Castiglione; p. 102, Suzi D'Annalfo; p. 103, Suzi D'Annalfo; p. 104, From Nichols B: Moving and learning: the elementary school physical education experience, ed 2, St Louis, 1990, Times Mirror/Mosby College Publishing; p. 105, Cathy Haight; p. 106, Matthew Castiglione; p. 109, Omaha Public Schools, Omaha, NE; p. 111, Matthew Castiglione; p. 113, Cathy Haight.

Chapter 5   P. 119, Smith College Archives, Northhampton, MA; p. 121, University of Nevada, Las Vegas; p. 123, Harold L Ray, Western Michigan University, Kalamazoo, MI; p. 131, A and B, Deborah A Wuest; p. 132, From Lumpkin A: Physical education and sport: a contemporary introduction, ed 2, St Louis, 1990, Times Mirror/Mosby College Publishing; p. 135, Harold L Ray, Western Michigan University, Kalamazoo, MI; p. 136, Harold L Ray, Western Michigan University, Kalamazoo, MI; p. 137, J Clarence Davies Collection, Museum of the City of New York; p. 138, Library of Congress Photographic Collection; p. 139, Harold L Ray, Western Michigan University, Kalamazoo, MI; p. 140, Smith College Archives, Northhampton, MA; p. 142, Aldrich and Aldrich; p. 143, Smith College Archives, Northhampton, MA; p. 144, From Journal of Health, Physical Education and Recreation, 40: left, March 1969, right, February 1969; p. 149, From Auxter D and Pyfer J: Principles and methods of adapted physical education and recreation, ed 6, St Louis, 1989, Times Mirror/Mosby College Publishing; p. 151, Ron Adams, Children's Rehabilitation Center, University of Virginia Medical Center, Charlottesville, VA; p. 153, American Alliance for Health, Physical Education, Recreation and Dance; p. 155, Barbara M Armstrong.

Chapter 6 P. 161, University of Nevada, Las Vegas; p. 165, Health Education and Exercise Programs, Health Management Program, Kimberly-Clark Corp, Neenah, WI; p. 172, Deborah A Wuest; p. 176, From Prentice WE and Bucher CA: Fitness for college and life, ed 2, St Louis, Times Mirror/Mosby College Publishing; p. 177, A from Bucher CA: Management of physical education and athletic programs, ed 9, St Louis, 1987, Times Mirror/Mosby College Publishing. Box, from Hockey R: The pathway to healthful living, ed 6, St Louis, 1989, Times Mirror/Mosby College Publishing; p. 178, From Hockey R: The pathway to healthful living, ed 6, St Louis, 1989, Times Mirror/Mosby College Publishing; p. 179, From Hockey R: The pathway to healthful living, ed 6, St Louis, 1989, Times Mirror/Mosby College Publishing; p. 180, From Hockey R: The pathway to healthful living, ed 6, St Louis, 1989, Times Mirror/Mosby College Publishing; p. 181, From Nichols B: Moving and learning: the elementary school physical education experience, ed 2, St Louis, 1990, Times Mirror/Mosby College Publishing; p. 183, Smith College, Northhampton, MA. From Bucher CA: Administration of physical education and athletic programs, ed 8, St Louis, 1983, Times Mirror/Mosby College Publishing; p. 185, From Prentice WE and Bucher CA: Fitness for college and life, ed 2, St Louis, 1988, Times Mirror/Mosby College Publishing; p. 186, From Lumpkin A: Physical education and sport: a contemporary introduction, ed 2, St Louis, 1990, Times Mirror/Mosby College Publishing; p. 187, A and B from Prentice WE and Bucher CA: Fitness for college and life, ed 2, St Louis, 1988, Times Mirror/Mosby College Publishing; p. 189, From Hockey R: The pathway to healthful living, ed 6, St Louis, 1989, Times Mirror/Mosby College Publishing; p. 190, From Hockey R: The pathway to healthful living, ed 6, St Louis, 1989, Times Mirror/Mosby College Publishing; p. 191, From Arnheim DD: Modern principles of athletic training, ed 6, St Louis, 1985, Times Mirror/Mosby College Publishing; p. 192, From Lumpkin A: Physical education and sport: a contemporary introduction, ed 2, St Louis, 1990, Times Mirror/Mosby College Publishing; p. 193, A and B from Hockey R: The pathway to healthful living, ed 6, St Louis, 1989, Times Mirror/Mosby College Publishing; p. 194, From Prentice WE and Bucher CA: Fitness for college and life, ed 2, St Louis, Times Mirror/Mosby College Publishing; p. 196, From Bucher CA: Management of physical education and athletic programs, ed 9, St Louis, 1987, Times Mirror/Mosby College Publishing; p. 198, From Hockey R: The pathway to healthful living, ed 6, St Louis, 1989, Times Mirror/Mosby College Publishing; p. 199, From Hockey R: The pathway to healthful living, ed 6, St Louis, 1989, Times Mirror/Mosby College Publishing; p. 201, From Lumpkin A: Physical education and sport: a contemporary introduction, ed 2, St Louis, 1990, Times Mirror/Mosby College Publishing; p. 202, A from Hockey R: The pathway to healthful living, ed 6, St Louis, 1989, Times Mirror/Mosby College Publishing; B, Beth Kirkpatrick, Tilford

Middle School, Vinton, IA; p. 204, From Prentice WE and Bucher CA: Fitness for college and life, ed 2, St Louis, 1988, Times Mirror/Mosby College Publishing.

Chapter 7 P. 209, Boys and Girls Clubs of Las Vegas, NV; p. 212, Barbara M Armstrong; p. 213, From Arnheim DD and Pestolesi RA: Elementary physical education: a developmental approach, ed 2, St Louis, 1978, the CV Mosby Company; p. 214, Matthew Castiglione; p. 215, From Bucher CA: Management of physical education and athletic programs, ed 9, St Louis, 1987, Times Mirror/Mosby College Publishing; p. 217, From Auxter D and Pyfer J: Principles and methods of adapted physical education and recreation, ed 6, St Louis, 1989, Times Mirror/Mosby College Publishing; p. 218, Cathy Haight; p. 220, From Mood D, Musker FF, and Rink JE: Sports and recreational activities for men and women, ed 9, St Louis, 1987, Times Mirror/Mosby College Publishing; p. 222, From Bucher CA: Administration of physical education and athletic programs, ed 8, St Louis, 1983, Times Mirror/Mosby College Publishing; p. 228, Ithaca College Sports Information; p. 232, From Nichols B: Moving and learning: the elementary school physical education experience, ed 2, St Louis, 1990, Times Mirror/Mosby College Publishing; p. 233, From Mood D, Musker FF, and Rink JE: Sports and recreational activities for men and women, ed 9, St Louis, 1987, Times Mirror/Mosby College Publishing.

Chapter 8 P. 238, From Coakley J: Sport in society: issues and controversies, ed 4, St Louis, 1990, Times Mirror/Mosby College Publishing; p. 241, From Coakley J: Sport in society: issues and controversies, ed 4, St Louis, 1990, Times Mirror/Mosby College Publishing; p. 244, George Mowbray; p. 245, Table 8-1 from Coakley J: Sport in society: issues and controversies, ed 4, St Louis, 1990, Times Mirror/Mosby College Publishing; p. 246, From Lumpkin A: Physical education and sport: a contemporary introduction, ed 2, St Louis, 1990, Times Mirror/Mosby College Publishing; p. 247, From Coakley J: Sport in society: issues and controversies, ed 4, St Louis, 1990, Times Mirror/Mosby College Publishing; p. 249, From Coakley J: Sport in society: issues and controversies, ed 4, St Louis, 1990, Times Mirror/Mosby College Publishing; p. 251, From Coakley J: Sport in society: issues and controversies, ed 4, St Louis, 1990, Times Mirror/Mosby College Publishing; p. 254, From Coakley J: Sport in society: issues and controversies, ed 4, St Louis, 1990, Times Mirror/Mosby College Publishing; p. 257, Figure 8-1 from Coakley J: Sport in society: issues and controversies, ed 4, St Louis, 1990, Times Mirror/Mosby College Publishing; p. 259, Figure 8-2 from Coakley J: Sport in society: issues and controversies, ed 4, St Louis, 1990, Times Mirror/Mosby College Publishing; p. 261, From Coakley J: Sport in society: issues and controversies, ed 4, St Louis, 1990, Times Mirror/Mosby College Publishing; p. 263, Figure 8-3 from Coakley J: Sport in society: issues and controversies, ed 4, St Louis, 1990, Times Mirror/Mosby College Publishing; p. 265, Figure 8-4 from Coakley J: Sport in society: issues and controversies, ed 4, St Louis, 1990, Times Mirror/Mosby College Publishing; p. 266, From Auxter D and Pyfer J: Principles and methods of adapted physical education and recreation, ed 6, St Louis, 1989, Times Mirror/Mosby College Publishing; p. 269, From Coakley JJ: Sport in society: issues and controversies, ed 2, St Louis, 1982, Times Mirror/Mosby College Publishing; p. 271, Christine Pritchard.

Index